The Letters of F. Scott Fitzgerald

" . . . brilliant . . . fascinating. . . ." —The Christian Science Monitor

"There are no dull pages in this rich collection. . . ."
—Cleveland Plain Dealer

ANDREW TURNBULL, author of the recent best-selling biography of Fitzgerald, has grouped the letters around the people who were closest and most important to Fitzgerald (although there is also a specially compiled chronological listing for those who prefer to follow the letters in sequence). There is a section of letters to Scottie, his daughter, which are extraordinarily self-revealing and touching. There are letters to his wife Zelda, his editor Maxwell Perkins, his agent Harold Ober, to Ernest Hemingway, Edmund Wilson, and many others. Through all the letters shines Scott Fitzgerald's unique mark: grace, candor, and generosity of spirit.

*Edited and with an
Introduction by
Andrew Turnbull*

The Letters of
F. Scott Fitzgerald

A LAUREL EDITION

Published by
Dell Publishing Co., Inc.
750 Third Avenue
New York, N.Y. 10017

Reprinted by arrangement with Charles Scribner's Sons
New York

First Laurel Edition—July, 1966

Printed in the U.S.A.

Contents

A Chronology of the Main Events in Fitzgerald's Life

1896	Sept.	Born in St. Paul
1898	April	Family moves to Buffalo
1901	Jan.	Family moves to Syracuse
	July	Birth of his sister, Annabel
1903	Sept.	Family moves back to Buffalo
1908	July	Family moves to St. Paul
	Sept.	Enters St. Paul Academy
1911	Sept.	Enters Newman
1913	Sept.	Enters Princeton
1915	Jan.	Meets Ginevra King
	Dec.	Drops out of Princeton for the rest of the academic year
1917	Sept.	First sale—a poem to *Poet Lore*
	Nov.	Commissioned a Second Lieutenant in the regular army. Reports to Fort Leavenworth, Kansas, for officer's training.
1918	March	Finishes first draft of *The Romantic Egotist*
	July	Meets Zelda Sayre
1919	Feb.	Discharged from the army and goes to New York
	March	Takes job with the Barron Collier Advertising Agency
	June	Zelda breaks their engagement
	July	Returns to St. Paul to rewrite novel
	Sept.	*This Side of Paradise* accepted by Scribners
	Oct.	Sells first story to the *Post* ("Head and Shoulders")
	Nov.	Re-engaged to Zelda
1920	March	*This Side of Paradise* published
	April	Marries Zelda
	May	Moves to Westport
	Aug.	*Flappers and Philosophers* published
	Oct.	Moves to apartment near Plaza
1921	May	First trip to Europe
	Aug.	Moves to St. Paul
	Oct.	Scottie born

1922	April	*The Beautiful and Damned* published
	Sept.	*Tales of the Jazz Age* published
	Oct.	Moves to Great Neck
1923	Nov.	Failure of *The Vegetable*
1924	May	Moves abroad. Meets Gerald Murphy
1925	April	*The Great Gatsby* published
	May	Meets Ernest Hemingway
1926	Feb.	*All the Sad Young Men* published
	Dec.	Returns to America
1927	Jan.	First trip to Hollywood
	March	Moves to Ellerslie outside Wilmington
1928	April	Goes to Paris for summer
	Sept.	Returns to Ellerslie
1929	May	Moves abroad
1930	April	Zelda breaks down
	June	Zelda enters Prangins
1931	Jan.	Visits America to attend his father's funeral
	Sept.	Returns to Montgomery following Zelda's release from Prangins
	Nov.	Second trip to Hollywood
1932	Jan.	Zelda's second breakdown—Phipps
	May	Moves to Baltimore and rents La Paix
1933	Dec.	Moves to 1307 Park Avenue in Baltimore
1934	Jan.	Zelda's third breakdown—Sheppard-Pratt
	April	*Tender Is the Night* published
1935	Feb.	First visit to Tryon
	April	*Taps at Reveille* published
	May	Moves to Asheville
	Sept.	Moves to Cambridge Arms in Baltimore
1936	July	Moves to Asheville
	Sept.	His mother dies
1937	June	Six months' contract with M-G-M
	July	Moves to the Garden of Allah Hotel in Hollywood
		Meets Sheilah Graham
	Dec.	Year's renewal of contract with M-G-M
1938	April	Moves to Malibu Beach
	Oct.	Moves to Encino
	Dec.	M-G-M contract not renewed
1939	Feb.	Trip to Dartmouth
	Oct.	Writing first chapter of *The Last Tycoon*
1940	May	Moves to Hollywood, 1403 N. Laurel Ave.
	Nov.	First heart attack
	Dec.	Dies

INTRODUCTION

FITZGERALD'S gift for intimacy was a large part of his charm, and the hallmark of the letters in this volume is a graceful candor, an insinuating warmth. Admittedly a few of them are harsh and even bitter, yet on the whole they transcend vituperation and testify to a generosity of spirit. "I have honestly never gone in for hating," Fitzgerald wrote Hemingway in 1934.

Scattered through the letters is some of Fitzgerald's finest prose, though seldom, as in his fiction, does he pause to paint a picture or elaborate a scene. Décor gives way to gossip, introspection, and analysis seasoned with humor. Here is Fitzgerald the literary critic, shrewdly discriminating for all his impressionism of mind. And here is Fitzgerald the moralist, who, as he tells his daughter, might have gone the way of Cole Porter and Rodgers and Hart had he not wanted to preach to people in some acceptable form.

More than anything he wrote, Fitzgerald's letters admit us to the tension and drama of his private life, where every day was a tournament with victory in sight if only this or that obstacle could be overcome. His dreams and expectations go bounding ahead of his performance. The gay, histrionic near-extrovert who reached fame at twenty-three becomes toward the end a lonely violin, a victim of black sweats and desperate melancholies, but with a last-ditch fight and pluck that wins our esteem.

The letters to his daughter which begin the book are uniquely self-revealing and touching in their concern. As though reliving his life through her, Fitzgerald advises her from the depths of his conscience, and no American author of his stature has put so much of himself on paper for the sake of one of his offspring. His sternness, amounting almost to tyranny at times, sprang from an excess of love—

an anxiety lest Scottie repeat his mistakes and fall short of
her potential. "I want you to be among the best of your
race," he tells her, "and not waste yourself on trivial aims.
To be useful and proud—is that too much to ask?" Compared with these letters, those to his wife, Zelda, seem
meager and perfunctory, for they date from his last two
years (few earlier ones exist) when she was a hopeless invalid living far away, and his once overwhelming love for
her had dwindled to a sense of duty and responsibility and
partnership in their child. Still, there are retrospective
glimmers of happier days, and at the end we watch Fitzgerald racing death to complete his novel, *The Last Tycoon*.

Next comes a panorama of Fitzgerald's career, the letters
to editor Maxwell Perkins—the first one written July 26,
1919, to announce a rough draft of *This Side of Paradise*,
the last one written December 13, 1940, eight days before
his death. In between, despite the difficulties and disappointments which he confides in Perkins, we see him
steadily growing in authority and knowledge of his craft,
while his interest in other authors and his zeal in promoting their work, coupled with his grasp of the literary scene,
bear out Perkins' observation that he would have made a
good publisher if he hadn't written.

Of the letters to Ernest Hemingway, all but two have
come to light within the past year, and what an insight they
give us into that fierce friendship! They point up Fitzgerald's
generosity, but also his self-contempt in the face of one who
seemed a more dedicated artist. They show Fitzgerald's
fascination with the Hemingway legend, his amused defer-
ence to the other's more commanding personality, and
finally his dignity and magnanimity after Hemingway
turned on him.

Already familiar are the letters to Edmund Wilson and
John Peale Bishop, a number of which appeared in Fitzgerald's posthumous volume, *The Crack-Up*, though eight
to Wilson and four to Bishop are published here for the first
time, and some of the deletions in *The Crack-Up* letters
have been restored. Wilson and Bishop had been Fitzgerald's friends and mentors since Princeton days, when
Bishop had infected him with a love of poetry, and Wilson,
forever after The Critic in Fitzgerald's universe, had blue-
pencilled his first stories for the *Nassau Lit*. Christian
Gauss, Professor of Romance Languages and later Dean

of the College, was then the Socrates of this aspiring trio, and Fitzgerald's letters to Gauss constitute another group. In addition, there are groups of letters to Shane Leslie, a young Irish author visiting America who took Fitzgerald under his wing while he was groping his way toward *This Side of Paradise;* to Mrs. Richard Taylor, Fitzgerald's favorite relative, a first cousin on his father's side; to Gerald and Sara Murphy, admired friends to whom *Tender Is the Night* was appropriately dedicated; to Mrs. Bayard Turnbull, a friend and neighbor of the Baltimore years; and to Harold Ober, Fitzgerald's literary agent and executor.

A word must be said about Fitzgerald's relations with Ober. It is axiomatic that when an author's agent becomes his banker as well, their association is jeopardized, for if, as usually happens, the agent is obliged to stop lending money, the author feels he has been let down. Between 1934 and 1937 Ober lent Fitzgerald, at great sacrifice to himself, some $12,500 in an effort to get him back on his feet after the failure of *Tender Is the Night.* By 1937, however, the high-priced magazines, Fitzgerald's chief source of income, were no longer buying his stuff, and he had to go to Hollywood as a script-writer to pay off his debts. Then in 1939, disillusioned with the studios and they with him after his fiasco at the Dartmouth Winter Carnival, he thought of reestablishing himself with the magazines and turned to Ober for financial support. Ober reluctantly refused. His expenses had been growing, his margin of profit was small, and he foresaw another imbroglio of hopeless debt. Fitzgerald's letters to Ober at this time, and his remarks in letters to others, do his agent less than justice. Kind, selfless, and loyal, Ober was deeply attached to Fitzgerald, and he and Mrs. Ober treated Scottie almost as their own child during her boarding school and college years. Ober, moreover, had shown considerable forebearance in backing Fitzgerald as long as he did. In retrospect, Ober, like Perkins whom he resembled in character, was one of the benign influences on Fitzgerald's destiny.

A miscellaneous section, composed of single letters and correspondences less rich or sustained than those in the letter-groups, completes the volume. There are a few regrettable gaps. All Fitzgerald's letters to Ring Lardner have vanished; likewise those to Sigourney Webster Fay, the cultivated Monsignor to whom *This Side of Paradise* was dedicated. The three existing letters from Fitzgerald to his father—that courtly, pale, defeated man whom he loved—were too slight to merit inclusion. But on the whole the people who meant the most to him are duly represented.

The letters here printed are a selection from perhaps twice this number that were available. They have been chosen for readability, literary quality, and with an eye to displaying the variousness of their author's complex nature. Priority has been given to those that illuminate his work, and hence, of the individual correspondences, the one with Perkins is considerably the longest. Letters from the Thirties predominate not only because Fitzgerald, in his decade of eclipse, took more pains with them and saved carbons of many, but because he himself was wiser, mellower, and, all things considered, more interesting than in the hey-day Twenties. It being the essence of a letter that we should have the whole of each, no cuts have been made save in passages that might offend the living, and in most cases it has been sufficient to substitute blanks for names.

All omissions of words and sentences have been indicated by four dots since Fitzgerald sometimes used three dots as punctuation. In general his punctuation has been observed, except where it confuses the sense. The use of italics and quotation marks have been standardized, however (titles of books, plays, movies, magazines and newspapers in italics, titles of poems and short stories in quotes). Fitzgerald was a lamentable speller. Following his ear, he habitually made such slips as "def*in*ate" and "crit*is*ism," and proper names were his downfall. He always reversed the "ei" in "Dreiser," "Stein," and "Hergesheimer," and, despite the hundreds of times he had seen "Hemingway" in print, he wrote it either "Hemmingway" or "Hemminway" and was capable of "Earnest" for "Ernest." Those who are interested will find copious examples of his boners in previous books about him; here it has seemed advisable to correct them. Sometimes his memory of a book title was a little off (*Good-bye to Wisconsin* for *Good-bye, Wisconsin*, *The Lost Lady* for *A Lost Lady*), but as the titles are easily recognizable, they have been left as he wrote them.

Inscribing *Tender Is the Night* to a friend he hadn't seen in years, Fitzgerald wrote, "Dear Katharine/ Please read this/ Love, Scott/ & not just formal. For me the past is forever." Fitzgerald's attachment to those who had shared his time and experience here on earth, his sense of identity with them, his caring—that is perhaps the final burden and beauty of these letters.

ANDREW TURNBULL

PART ONE

Letters to
Frances Scott Fitzgerald

La Paix, Rodgers' Forge
Towson, Maryland

August 8, 1933

Dear Pie:

I feel very strongly about you doing [your] duty. Would you give me a little more documentation about your reading in French? I am glad you are happy—but I never believe much in happiness. I never believe in misery either. Those are things you see on the stage or the screen or the printed page, they never really happen to you in life.

All I believe in in life is the rewards for virtue (according to your talents) and the *punishments* for not fulfilling your duties, which are doubly costly. If there is such a volume in the camp library, will you ask Mrs. Tyson to let you look up a sonnet of Shakespeare's in which the line occurs *"Lilies that fester smell far worse than weeds."*

Have had no thoughts today, life seems composed of getting up a *Saturday Evening Post* story. I think of you, and always pleasantly; but if you call me "Pappy" again I am going to take the White Cat out and beat his bottom *hard, six times for every time you are impertinent.* Do you react to that?

I will arrange the camp bill.

Halfwit, I will conclude.

Things to worry about:
  Worry about courage
  Worry about cleanliness
  Worry about efficiency
  Worry about horsemanship
  Worry about. . .
Things not to worry about:

Don't worry about popular opinion
Don't worry about dolls
Don't worry about the past
Don't worry about the future
Don't worry about growing up
Don't worry about anybody getting ahead of you
Don't worry about triumph
Don't worry about failure unless it comes through your
     own fault
Don't worry about mosquitoes
Don't worry about flies
Don't worry about insects in general
Don't worry about parents
Don't worry about boys
Don't worry about disappointments
Don't worry about pleasures
Don't worry about satisfactions
Things to think about:
   What am I really aiming at?
   How good am I really in comparison to my contempo-
raries in regard to
   (a) Scholarship
   (b) Do I really understand about people and am I able
       to get along with them?
   (c) Am I trying to make my body a useful instrument
       or am I neglecting it?

                              With dearest love,

                              [Daddy]

P.S. My come-back to your calling me Pappy is christening
you by the word Egg, which implies that you belong to a
very rudimentary state of life and that I could break you
up and crack you open at my will and I think it would be
a word that would hang on if I ever told it to your contemporaries. "Egg Fitzgerald." How would you like that
to go through life with—"Eggie Fitzgerald" or "Bad Egg
Fitzgerald" or any form that might occur to fertile minds?
Try it once more and I swear to God I will hang it on you
and it will be up to you to shake it off. Why borrow
trouble?

                              Love anyhow

Grove Park Inn
Asheville, North Carolina
[Summer, 1935]

Scottina:

It was fine seeing you, and I liked you a lot (this is aside from loving you which I always do). You are nicer to adults—you are emerging from that rather difficult time in girls, 12–15 usually, but you are emerging I think rather early—probably at 14 or so. You have one good crack coming but—well:

"Daddy the prophet!" I can hear you say in scorn. I wish to God I wasn't so right usually about you. When I wrote that "news-sheet" with events left out, you know—the letter that puzzled you—and headed it "Scottie Loses Head," it was because I saw it coming. I knew that your popularity with two or three dazed adolescent boys would convince you that you were at least the Queen of Sheba, and that you would "lose your head." What shape this hay-wire excursion would take I didn't know—I couldn't have guessed it would be writing a series of indiscreet letters to a gossipy and indiscreet boy who would show them to the persons for whom they were not meant (Understand: I don't blame Andrew[1] too much—the fault was yours—he didn't, will you notice, put into writing an analysis of his best friends of his own sex!).

However, that's of no seriousness. But I think that the next kick will be a bad one—but you will survive, and after that you will manage your affairs better. To avoid such blows you almost *have* to have them yourself so you can begin to think of others as valuing themselves, possibly, quite as much as you do yourself. So I'm not afraid of it for you. I don't want it to be so bad that it will break your self-confidence, which is attractive and is fine [if] founded on positive virtues, work, courage, etc., but if you are selfish it had better be broken early. If you are unsel-

[1] Andrew Turnbull.

fish you can keep it always—and it is a nice thing to have. I didn't know till 15 that there was anyone in the world except me, and it cost me *plenty*.

Signs and portents of your persistent conceit: Mrs. Owens[1] said to me (and Mrs. Owens loves you), "For the first time in a long while Scottie was *nice,* and not a burden as I expected. It was really nice to be with her."

Because, I guess, for the first time you entered into their lives, humble lives of struggling people, instead of insisting that they enter into yours—a chance they never had, of belonging to "high society." Before, you had let them be aware of what *you* were doing (not in any snobbish sense, because heaven knows I'd have checked you on that)—but because you never considered or pretended to consider their lives, their world at all—your own activities seemed of so much more overwhelming importance to you! *You did not use one bit of your mind, one little spot!* to think what *they* were thinking, or help *them!*

You went to Norfolk and gave out the information (*via* the Taylors, *via* Annabel, *via* mother) that you were going to Dobbs. That doesn't matter save as indicative of a show-off frame of mind. You know it was highly tentative. It was a case, again, of boasting, of "promoting yourself." But those signs of one big catastrophe (it'll come—I want to minimize it for you, but it can't be prevented because only experience can teach) are less important than your failure to realize that you are *a young member of the human race,* who has not proved itself in any but the most superficial manner. (I have seen "popular girls" of 15 become utterly *déclassé* in six months because they were essentially selfish.) You and Peaches[2] (who isn't selfish, I think) had a superficial head-start with prettiness, but you will find more and more that less pretty girls will be attaching the solider, more substantial boys as the next two years will show. Both you and Peaches are intelligent but both of you will be warped by this early attention, *and something tells me she won't lose her head;* she hasn't the "gift of gab" as you have—her laughter and her silence takes the place of much. That's why I wish to God you would write some-

---

[1] Mrs. Allein Owens had been Fitzgerald's secretary since May, 1932.
[2] Peaches Finney, a close friend of Scottie's.

thing when you have time—if only a one act play about how girls act in the bath house, in a tent, on a train going to camp.

I grow weary, but I probably won't write again for a month. Don't answer this, justifying yourself—of *course* I know you're doing the best you "can."

The points of the letter are:

1st   You did spill over, rashly!

2nd   You are getting over the self period—thank God!

3d   But it'll take one more big kick, and I want it to be mild, so your backside won't suffer too much.

4th   I wish you'd get your mind off your precious self enough to write me a one act play about other people—what they say and how they behave.

> With *dearest* love,
> Your simply so-perfect too-too
>
> Daddy

Please, turn back and read this letter over! It is too packed with considered thought to digest the first time. Like Milton —oh yeah!

> [*New York City*]
> [*July, 1935*]

Darlin':

Am on a flying visit to New York. Spent yesterday afternoon with, of all people, Elissa Landi. She sailed for Europe last night. She is very nice.

I am not going to write you much this summer but you know my heart is with you always. Remember the one thing about riding—that you can't be as reckless at it as you can about swimming, because there's another factor besides yourself involved, the *horse*. So that no matter *how* good you were if the horse was bad there might be trouble. Different from diving, for example, where you have only yourself to blame. The point is, don't do anything or try anything that the riding master doesn't approve of. He knows just the point you've reached at handling the mount.

Good-by double durling. Aunt Rosalind,[1] Mr. Ober[2] and
Mr. Perkins[3] all invite you to spend a few days with them
in N.Y. when camp is over. We shall see. I leave for the
South Monday.

Your utterly irresistible

Daddy

[Grove Park Inn]
[Asheville, North Carolina]
August 4, 1935

Darling:

I always thought the first book of that series was one of
the most exciting books I ever read.[4] Ernest Hemingway
thought so too. Please read it with a view to a possible
dramatization of it and tell me your opinion. I never went
any further in that series than the first one on account of no
English versions being available.

I am glad you fell off your horse. Here in Carolina the
only conveyance is by zebra. I have one zebra named
Clarence.

My correspondence is now limited to five people: Elissa
Landi, Mrs. Roosevelt, Aquilla,[5] and a fourth whom I
need scarcely mention, because I hardly know his name.

Darling, I am working hard and getting very well.

Please unleash yourself in your letters to your mother
without mentioning riding catastrophies which might make
her nervous.

Give my affectionate regards to Virginia, Helen [and]
Betty and tell your counselor what a really obnoxious person you might turn out to be unless carefully watched.

Your stoogie—

Daddy

---

[1] Zelda's sister, Mrs. Newman Smith.
[2] Harold Ober, Fitzgerald's literary agent.
[3] Maxwell Perkins, Fitzgerald's editor.
[4] An Alexander Dumas series, which one uncertain.
[5] At one time Fitzgerald's chauffeur.

[*Grove Park Inn*]
[*Asheville, North Carolina*]
[*July, 1936*]

Darling:

O.K. about the tutoring. Let it slide. But I hate to let one season slip by at your age without one difficult advance.

Do something for me! I'm proud of the swimming but summer's only summer. Give me a time maybe, and know always I'm thinking of you and for you, and my plans will come to you as soon as crystallized, sometime in August. Slim chance of my getting up to Pennsylvania. All Europe ideas definitely out. Spain was what I wanted to see and Spain is in what the newsmen call the "throes of revolution."

Your mother likes your letters so much. Hope you have nice tent mates. I don't agree with Mrs. Tappan on that subject, but that's a whole story and I know whatever the situation is you'll make the best of it in your own courageous way.

Oh darling Scottie—I don't want to force you but it does please me when you can make a connection between the Louisiana Purchase and why Fred Astaire lifts up his left hind foot for the world's pleasure. I want you to be among the best of your race and not waste yourself on trivial aims. To be useful and proud—is that too much to ask?

I enclose you the jacket of my latest book. I have decided to write in Scandinavian from now on!

Your devoted

Daddy

Grove Park Inn
Asheville, North Carolina
July 31, 1936

Darling:

I am enclosing in this some pictures that tell a sad story. I had a terrific accident and broke my shoulder. I thought I would be very smart and do some diving and after a year and a half of inactivity I stretched my muscles too much in the air and broke my shoulder. It has all been very troublesome and expensive but I have tried to be as cheerful as possible about it and everyone has been very kind; the people here have rigged up a curious writing board for me so that I work with my hand over my head rather like this.[1]

I enclose money for your present small needs. It may be that the expenses of this injury will preclude your going to an expensive school this fall but life sometimes does those things to you and I know you are brave and able to adjust yourself to changing conditions and to know that all the effort that I have will be thrown into your education and the care of your mother. If I had not had this operation on my shoulder the doctor tells me I would never have been able to raise my arm above my shoulder again. It is still an open bet as to whether or not I will ever be able to raise it above my shoulder.

I am proud of you and I am only a little angered by the fact that you have not managed to read more than one of the French books.

Sunday night I leave for Baltimore and you can write me either there care of Mrs. Owens or here where I am returning. Isn't it lucky I did not go to Spain after all! Or maybe it would have been rather fun.

Your loving

Daddy

Grove Park Inn
Asheville, North Carolina
October 20, 1936

Dearest Scottina:

I had already decided to go up Thanksgiving which I will do, God willing, and so on your own suggestion I have killed the idea of going up on your birthday. You seem

---

[1] Fitzgerald had drawn a picture of himself seated at his writing board.

to understand the fact that I cannot afford at the moment to make two trips within the same month; so I know you won't be unduly disappointed.

To finish up news of me, the arm is really definitely out of danger and I am going to be able to use it again, which I doubted for three or four weeks. Went out to [a] football game with the Flynns last Saturday, the same sort of game exactly that we went to last fall at very much the same time. Lefty was his usual handsome self and Nora was charming as always. They asked about you repeatedly, and not because they thought they ought to but because they have a real affection for you, and I mean both of them. They were so happy to know that you are getting along so well at your school.

Confirming my Christmas plans, they are, briefly: that we shall have a party for you in Baltimore at the Belvedere or the Stafford, if we can afford it! Then the actual Christmas Day will be spent either here with your mother (it won't be like that awful Christmas in Switzerland), or else you and your mother and the trained nurse will go to Montgomery and spend Christmas with your grandmother; perhaps with a little time afterwards in Baltimore before you go back to school.

Don't be a bit discouraged about your story not being tops. At the same time, I am not going to encourage you about it, because, after all, if you want to get into the big time, you have to have your own fences to jump and learn from experience. Nobody ever became a writer just by wanting to be one. If you have anything to say, anything you feel nobody has ever said before, you have got to feel it so desperately that you will find some way to say it that nobody has ever found before, so that the thing you have to say and the way of saying it blend as one matter—as indissolubly as if they were conceived together.

Let me preach again for a moment: I mean that what you have felt and thought will, by itself, invent a new style, so that when people talk about style they are always a little astonished at the newness of it, because they think that it is only *style* that they are talking about, when what they are talking about is the attempt to express a new idea with such force that it will have the originality of the thought. It is an awfully lonesome business, and, as you know, I never wanted you to go into it, but if you are going into it at all I want you to go into it knowing the sort of things that took me years to learn.

Why are you whining about such matters as study hall, etc., when you deliberately picked this school [1] as the place you wanted to go above all places? Of course it is hard. Nothing any good isn't hard, and you know you have never been brought up soft, or are you quitting on me suddenly? Darling, you know I love you, and I expect you to live up absolutely to what I laid out for you in the beginning.

                                                        Scott

Grove Park Inn
Asheville, North Carolina
November 17, 1936

Dearest Pie:

I got a School Letter saying that Thanksgiving Day is best, and it is better for me that way. There is no particular advantage in going out two or three times rather than one, without particular objectives; the idea is to go out once and have a good time. I'll be delighted to meet whoever you want, and our engagement is on Thanksgiving Day.

(This is a parenthesis: I got the little charms that you sent me for my birthday, the bells dangling and the mule, and appreciated your thought of me—you little donkey!)

Park Avenue girls are hard, aren't they? Usually the daughters of "up-and-coming" men and, in a way, the inevitable offspring of that type. It's the "Yankee push" to its last degree, a sublimation of the sort of Jay Gould who began by peddling bad buttons to a county and ended, with the same system of peddler's morals, by peddling five dollar railroads to a nation.

Don't mistake me. I think of myself always as a northerner—and I think of you the same way. Nevertheless, we are all of one nation and you will find all the lassitude

[1] Ethel Walker's.

and laziness there that you despise, enough to fill Savannah and Charleston, just as down here you will find the same "go getter" principle in the Carolinas.

I don't know whether you will stay there another year— it all depends on your marks and your work, and I can't give you the particular view of life that I have (which as you know is a tragic one), without dulling your enthusiasm. A whole lot of people have found life a whole lot of fun. I have not found it so. But, I had a hell of a lot of fun when I was in my twenties and thirties; and I feel that it is your duty to accept the sadness, the tragedy of the world we live in, with a certain *esprit*.

Now, insofar as your course is concerned, there is no question of your dropping mathematics and taking the easiest way to go into Vassar, and being one of the girls fitted for nothing except to reflect other people without having any particular character of your own. I want you to take mathematics up to the limit of what the school offers. I want you to take physics and I want you to take chemistry. I don't care about your English courses or your French courses at present. If you don't know two languages and the ways that men chose to express their thoughts in those languages by this time, then you don't sound like my daughter. You are an only child, but that doesn't give you any right to impose on that fact.

I want you to know certain basic scientific principles, and I feel that it is impossible to learn them unless you have gone as far into mathematics as coordinate geometry. *I don't want you to give up mathematics next year.* I learned about writing from doing something that I didn't have any taste for. If you don't carry your mathematics such as coordinate geometry (conic sections), you will have strayed far afield from what I had planned for you. I don't insist on the calculus, but it is certainly nothing to be decided by what is easiest. You are going into Vassar with mathematical credits and a certain side of your life there is going to be scientific.

Honey, I wish I could see you. It would be so much easier to go over these important matters without friction, but at a distance it seems rather tough that you are inclined to slide into the subjects that are easy for you, like modern languages.

No more until I see you Thanksgiving.

With dearest love,

F. Scott Fitz

P.S. Sorry you are on bounds—feel as if I had been the same for six months. However I have bought an ancient Packard roadster and get out more now. I always allow for your exuberance but I hope this doesn't come from a feud with any special teacher, or from any indiscretion of speech, a fault you should be beginning to control.

Grove Park Inn
Asheville, North Carolina
December 12, 1936

Dear Scottie:

As I wired you, there is no question of having ninety people. The most you can possibly ask is about sixty people; and even that is counting on ten or twelve refusals. If I had thought that the Ethel Walker School was going to give you a peculiar idea of what your financial resources are, it would have been far, far better to send you to a modest school here in the Carolina mountains. You are a poor girl, and if you don't like to think about it, just ask me. If you don't make up your mind to being that, you become one of those terrible girls that don't know whether they are millionairesses or paupers. You are neither one nor the other. The dance for you in Baltimore is a very modest one. It will have dignity because it pretends to nothing that it isn't. It will give you a certain amount of whoopee and it will probably lack a certain amount of things that you would expect. For instance, I am determined to have a hurdy-gurdy for the orchestra—you know, an Italian with a monkey, and I think the children will be very content with that. They don't want much, children of sixteen or seventeen, and they will be amused by the antics of the monkey. Your idea of a swing orchestra seems zero to me.

However, in the next room I will have some of the older

people with a swing orchestra that I have engaged, and from time to time you may bring some of your choice friends in there to dance.

—But remember that I expect you and your crowd to dance by the hurdy-gurdy during the whole afternoon, quietly and slowly and without swing music, just doing simple waltz dancing.

You can stay all night all you want with people up to the night of December 24th, when you and I are going to make a hop South.

With dearest love,

Daddy

P.S. You ask what to put on the cards. It should be about like this

Miss Frances Scott Fitzgerald
F. Scott Fitzgerald
December 22nd
Four to six
Hotel Belvedere   Dancing

[*Oak Hall Hotel*]
[*Tryon, North Carolina*]
[*Spring, 1937*]

Darling Scottina:

I loved having you here (except in the early morning) and I think we didn't get along *so* badly, did we? Glad you had a gay time in Baltimore and New York and have a friend at Groton. They are very democratic there—they have to sleep in gold cubicles and wash at old platinum pumps. This toughens them up so they can pay the poor starvation wages without weakening. (By the way, the older boys *only* can smoke at Andover and in a special place—you wretched liar you!)

The horse show is Wednesday. Everyone asks about you and really means it, some of them. La Sprague said her mother forgot to invite you to some party she gave and

was in tears. She has two Williams boys who are here at
the hotel on her trail. Caroline Kelly sends her love. I
see your mother tomorrow. Finally finished my story (very
good) and am starting another and a play on the side.
Hollywood postponed but may come through.

What did you do in Baltimore? How were Peaches and
Meredith? *Answer*.

> With dearest love to my slew-footed angel,

> Daddy

P.S. What about the toil? Are you sweating gall and
vinegar?

> [*Enroute to Hollywood*]
> *Postmarked July 5, 1937*

Dearest Pie:

What an exit! Horrors of life in the sticks—nothing could
have turned around there except a model T Ford. Sorry
to leave you and Grandma in such a mess.

The air trip was fine—very thrilling as always. I'm sending this to the Obers where I hope you are by now. Also
by the time you get this I'll have heard from the Mac-
Arthurs though I know it's all right. It will be great to
have you with me in Hollywood. I know Freddie Bartho-
lomew will love taking you around to birthday parties in
the afternoons, and you'll find Shirley Temple as good a
pal as Peaches and more loyal.

Where on earth did you get that preconception that I
think of you as a scarlet woman? Hell, you're a romantic
but that's not in your disfavor. It's all right to like affection, but not when you drive, in the immortal words of
Mitzi Green. I simply don't want you in danger and I
don't want you to do anything inappropriate to your age.
For premature adventure one pays an atrocious price. As
I told you once, every boy I know who drank at eighteen
or nineteen is now safe in his grave. The girls who were
what we called "speeds" (in our stone-age slang) at sixteen were reduced to anything they could get at the marry-

ing time. It's in the logic of life that no young person ever "gets away with anything." They fool their parents but not their contemporaries. It was in the cards that Ginevra King should get fired from Westover—also that your mother should wear out young. I think that despite a tendency to self indulgence you and I have some essential seriousness that will manage to preserve us. Whatever your sins are I hope you never get to justify them to yourself.

> With dearest love,
>
> Daddy

> [*En route to Hollywood*]
>
> [*July, 1937*]

Dearest Pie:

This may be the last letter for a time, though I won't forget the check when I get at my check book.

I feel a certain excitement. The third Hollywood venture. Two failures behind me though one no fault of mine. The first one was just ten years ago. At that time I had been generally acknowledged for several years as the top American writer both seriously and, as far as prices went, popularly. I had been loafing for six months for the first time in my life and was confident to the point of conceit. Hollywood made a big fuss over us and the ladies all looked very beautiful to a man of thirty. I honestly believed that with *no effort on my part* I was a sort of magician with words—an odd delusion on my part when I had worked so desperately hard to develop a hard, colorful prose style.

Total result—a great time and no work. I was to be paid only a small amount unless they made my picture—they didn't.

The second time I went was five years ago. Life had gotten in some hard socks and while all was serene on top, with your mother apparently recovered in Montgomery, I was jittery underneath and beginning to drink more than I ought to. Far from approaching it too confidently I was far too humble. I ran afoul of a bastard named de Sano, since a suicide, and let myself be gypped out of command. I wrote the picture and he changed as I wrote. I tried to get at Thalberg but was erroneously warned against it as "bad taste." Result—a bad script. I left with the money, for this was a contract for weekly payments, but disillusioned and disgusted, vowing never to go back, tho they said it wasn't my fault and asked me to stay. I wanted to get East when the contract expired to see how your mother was. This was later interpreted as "running out on them" and held against me.

(The train has left El Paso since I began this letter— hence the writing—Rocky Mountain writing.)

I want to profit by these two experiences—I must be very tactful but keep my hand on the wheel from the start —find out the key man among the bosses and the most malleable among the collaborators—then fight the rest tooth and nail until, in fact or in effect, I'm alone on the picture. That's the only way I can do my best work. Given a break I can make them double this contract in less [than] two years. You can help us all best by keeping out of trouble—it will make a great difference to your important years. Take care of yourself mentally (study when you're fresh), physically (don't pluck your eyebrows), morally (don't get where you have to lie) and I'll give you more scope than Peaches.

Daddy

[*The Garden of Allah Hotel*]
[*Hollywood, California*]
October 8, 1937

Darling Pie:

I'm awfully sorry about that telegram. I got a letter from Bill Warren, saying that it was all around Baltimore that I was making twenty-five hundred a week out here, and it disturbed and upset me. I suppose it was one of Rita Swann's ideas. I don't know why I suspected you—I should have known you would be more discreet and would at least name some believable figure. You see what a reputation you've made with your romantic tales!

As to the missing three days, I really don't blame you for that either. The trouble was that Harold Ober didn't know where you were either. If you had wired him instead of Aunt Rosalind, it would have been all right. However, it gave me only one bad hour, as I really don't fret about you as much as I used to. I did worry about your smoking this summer, but you gave me your word that you wouldn't smoke at Peaches' so that was all right; and I don't care much who you go out with so long as you are in at a decent hour and don't get the practice on your mind. From next summer on, you can find you'll have more privileges, but I don't want them to become habits that will turn and devour you. You have got to devote the best and freshest part of your energies to things that will give you a happy and profitable life. There is no other time but now.

No special news—things have been quiet. Had the questionable honor [of] meeting _____ _____, a shifty-eyed fellow surrounded by huge bodyguards. Norma Shearer invited me to dinner three times but I couldn't go —unfortunately, as I like her. Maybe she will ask me again. Also have seen something of Buff Cobb, Irving Cobb's daughter, who is an old friend; and Sheilah[1] who, by the way, has broken her engagement to the Marquess Donnegal. (The poor man was about to get on a boat, but it was a sort of foolish marriage in many ways.) Also have been to much tennis and saw Helen Wills come back in company with Von Cramm to defeat Budge and his partner. Took Beatrice Lillie, Charlie MacArthur and Sheilah to the Tennis Club the other night, and Errol Flynn joined us—he seemed very nice though rather silly and fatuous. Don't see why Peaches is so fascinated. Frank Morgan came over and talked to me, telling me that we had a fight in the cloak room at Gloria Swanson's seventeen years ago, but I had no recollection of the incident except that I had a scuffle with somebody. But in those days there [were] so many scraps that this one doesn't stand out in my memory.

I hope you thought over my analysis as to how to deal with the neatness habit, and if for one week you put each thing away individually *from the moment of touching it to the moment of its final disposal*—instead of putting away three things at a time—I think that you would lick it in a

[1] Hollywood columnist Sheilah Graham.

month and life would be easier for you in one more way. *Please tell me about this when you write.*

Looking over your letters and answering them in turn— it was nice of Peaches to give a party for you, and I'm glad Stanley is divine-looking; sorry Andrew is repulsive. I'm glad that you went out with that great heart-throb, Bob-the-Baker. Was Bob Haas nice? Your next letter comes from Exeter. Sorry you can't go to Annapolis—you'll be invited there again. Here I have a postcard and, by God, I'm awfully sore at you about that tutoring. I don't understand how on earth the letter could have been mislaid. I posted it from the airport in Spartanburg that night. So you are still dwelling on the Fisher's Island party in retrospect!

Another letter tells of visiting Mary Earle on Long Island. It sounds fine, but you are right that romantic things really happened in roachy kitchens and back yards. Moonlight is vastly over-estimated. It was all right what you borrowed from Harold. He will put it on my account. So Meredith called from Baltimore! Aren't you afraid of stirring up those old embers? Your disloyalty to Princeton breaks my heart. I sent Andrew football tickets. Your dress sounds fine, Scottie, my bonnie lass.

Lastly, the letter with the Yale postmark—I bet you bought that stationery. It reminds me of something that happened yesterday. On such paper, but with the Princeton seal, I used to write endless letters throughout sophomore and junior years to Ginevra King of Chicago and Westover, who later figured in *This Side of Paradise*. Then I didn't see her for twenty-one years, though I telephoned her in 1933 to entertain your mother at the World's Fair which she did. Yesterday I get a wire that she is in Santa Barbara and will I come down there immediately. She was the first girl I ever loved and I have faithfully avoided seeing her up to this moment to keep that illusion perfect, because she ended up by throwing me over with the most supreme boredom and indifference. I don't know whether I should go or not. It would be very, very strange. These great beauties are often something else at thirty-eight, but Ginevra had a great deal besides beauty.

I was hoping that they'd get up a "Higher French" course for you. Was nothing done about that? Miss Walker mentioned it in her letter. Your learning German seems to me rather pointless but don't construe this into any tendency to loaf on it. Knowing just a little bit would be a foundation especially if we go abroad for a few weeks next summer.

I sent the thirteen dollars to Rosalind.

What do you want for your birthday? You might make a suggestion.

I think of you a lot. I was very proud of you all summer and I do think that we had a good time together. Your life seemed gaited with much more moderation and I'm not sorry that you had rather a taste of misfortune during my long sickness, but now we can do more things together—when we can't find anybody better. There—that will take you down! I do adore you and will see you Christmas.

Your loving

[Daddy]

[*Metro-Goldwyn-Mayer Corporation*]
[*Culver City, California*]
November 4, 1937

Dearest Pie:

I admit I'm a terrible correspondent but I hope it isn't the pot calling the kettle black—i.e., do you write your mother regularly once a week? As I assured you before, it is of the greatest importance, even if Bob-the-Butcher or Bill-the-Baker doesn't get the weekly hook in his gills.

News about the picture: The cast is tentatively settled. Joan Crawford had her teeth in the lead for a while but was convinced that it was a man's picture; and Loretta Young not being available, the decision rests at present on Margaret Sullivan. Certainly she will be much better than Joan Crawford in the role. Tracy and Taylor will be reinforced by Franchot Tone at present writing, and the cameras will presumably roll sometime in December. An old friend, Ted Paramore, has joined me on the picture in fixing up much of the movie construction, at which I am still a semi-amateur, though I won't be that much longer.

Plans about Christmas depend on whether I will be held here for changes through the shooting. I don't think that's

probable, and if it weren't my first picture that I'm anxious
to get as perfect as can be, I wouldn't let it be possible,
because I can always have a vacation on three weeks' notice
—but I want to mention it as a very faint chance. However,
let us suppose I come East, as I will nine chances out of
ten—I will expect to spend the time with you and your
mother, perhaps a little in Baltimore, some in Asheville.
Maybe I can take your mother to Montgomery, though
that is very faint indeed and should not be mentioned to
her. Also I want to spend a couple of days in New York
and I have no doubt that you will want to be with me
then.

Have you any plans of what you'd like to do? Would
you like another party in Baltimore? I mean just an afternoon affair like the last. It might become a sort of an institu-
tion, a yearly round-up of your Baltimore friends. Write me
immediately what you thought you wanted to do—of course
you also will go to see your mother sometime during the
holidays.

By ill chance the Harvard game tickets for Andrew went
astray and were sent me here. I'm sorry. He must have
been disappointed—save that he missed the worst drubbing
Princeton has had in many years.

My social life is in definite slow motion. I refused a
good many parties and am now in the comfortable position of not being invited much any more. I had dinner at
Gladys Swarthout's last week with John McCormick and
some of the musical crowd. I have taken in some football
games with Sheilah Graham, and met the love of my youth,
Ginevra King (Mitchell), after an interval of twenty-one
years. She is still a charming woman and I'm sorry I didn't
see more of her.

How much do the ads cost for your year book? Please
let me know.

I have a small apartment now at the Garden of Allah,
but have done nothing about the house situation, as there
seems no chance of your mother coming out here at the
present.

I am anxiously awaiting your first report and will be
more inclined to go. . . .[1]

---

[1] The rest of the letter is missing, except for the postscript.

Congratulations on Cheerleader, etc. Can you turn a cart-wheel?

[*The Garden of Allah Hotel*]
[*Hollywood, California*]

[*February, 1938*]

Dearest Scottina:

So much has happened out here, and in the East, that a letter can't tell it.

Beginning at the end—*Three Comrades* went into pro-duction today and I started on the new Joan Crawford picture—as yet unnamed. I am half sick with work, over-whelmed with it and yet vaguely happier that I've been in months. The last part of a job is always sad and very diffi-cult but I'm proud of the year's output and haven't much to complain of.

Your mother was better than ever I expected and our trip would have been fun except that I was tired. We went to Miami and Palm Beach, flew to Montgomery, all of which sounds very gay and glamorous but wasn't particu-larly. I flew back to New York intending to take you out with your friends Saturday but I discovered you were on bounds. My zero hour was Monday morning in California so there was nothing to do except fly back on Sunday afternoon. I didn't think you and I could cover much ground with the horses flying around the tan bark and steaming in Rosa Bonheur's steel engraving on the wall.[1]

One time in sophomore year at Princeton, Dean West got up and rolled out the great lines of Horace:

> "Integer Vitae, scelerisque pueris
> Non eget mauris, facule nec arcu—"[2]

—And I knew in my heart that I had missed something by being a poor Latin scholar, like a blessed evening with a

---

[1] Refers to the reception room at Ethel Walker's.
[2] Horace actually wrote:
> "Integer vitae, scelerisque purus
> Non eget mauris iaculis neque arcu"

lovely girl. It was a great human experience I had rejected through laziness, through having sown no painful seed.

But when anything, Latin or pig latin, was ever put up to me so immediately as your chance of entering Vassar next fall I could always rise to meet that. It is either Vassar or else the University of California here under my eye and the choice is so plain that I have no sympathy for your loafing. We are not even out of debt yet, you are still [a] scholarship student and you might give them a break by making a graceful exit. They practically took you on your passport picture.

Baby, you're going on blind faith, as vain as Kitsy's belief that she wouldn't grow a whisker, when you assume that a small gift for people will get you through the world. It all begins with keeping faith with something that grows and changes as you go on. You have got to make all the right changes at the main corners—the price for losing your way once is years of unhappiness. You have not yet entirely missed a turning, but failing to get somewhere with the Latin will be just that. If you break faith with me I cannot feel the same towards you.

The Murphys, Nora, etc., asked after you. We will without fail go somewhere at Easter—your mother's going to make a stay in Montgomery with a companion and she'll meet us. Some New York gallery has taken some very expensive pictures of you—do you want any? I like them but my God they cost.

With dearest love always,

Daddy

[*Metro-Goldwyn-Mayer Corporation*]
[*Culver City, California*]
February 22, 1938

Dearest Pie:

I never hear from you any more. Please drop me a line and tell me if all goes well.

I started my new picture which is after all a piece called *Infidelity* and will star Joan Crawford and I don't know who else. I will finish the first draft Easter and will come East to take you somewhere.

Three Comrades is halfway through. I have seen some of the shooting and some of the "rushes" (where they run off what they've shot that day) but you can't tell much from either. To my mind, the producer seriously hurt the script in rewriting it. It may be I am wrong.

People ask after you, but I am the most curious of all. May I be permitted to ask after you? I'd like a line about your health, your work, your morale, success or failure of the play and such affairs. If you will let me know when the play is, I will send you a message of congratulation or flowery tokens if you prefer.

I think of you always, darling, and will try to invent something very nice for Easter.

Just heard from Mrs. Turnbull who said you had three especial qualities—loyalty and ambition were two, the third I'll tell you later. She felt that would protect you from harm. I make no comment. She seemed very fond of you.

Also the Finneys have sent me the work of a musician to do something about, and I am taking the matter in hand.

> With dearest love,
>
> Daddy

> [*The Garden of Allah Hotel*]
> [*Hollywood, California*]
> *March 11, 1938*

Dearest Pie:

I'm glad you got 74. If you had gotten that the first term, we'd have something to start on now. A letter came at the same time from Miss Walker, in which she referred to your "low position in the class." Of course this is not at all what you implied to me when I saw you in January, and I do wish you would be more accurate. To suggest a state of affairs which doesn't exist merely stalls off the final reckoning. The most important thing in your life now is to get good marks at school and pass the examinations for Vassar in June. It is so important that if you don't, I am unable, off-hand, to think of any satisfactory alternative. You will be exactly in the position of a man who has done a bad job and been fired, which will be a nice black mark against you at sixteen. You can't and mustn't let this happen. I am not going to spend Easter lecturing you and this is to forestall any attitude on your part that I am unreasonable not to be appeased by your success in other lines.

On the other hand, I am of course pleased that you did well as Mrs. Bennett (Harold Ober wrote me that your acting stood out). Also, I am glad that the musical comedy you wrote was so successful at school. Why don't you get a volume of Gilbert and Sullivan and read the extraordinary and amazing lyrics of *Iolanthe* and *Patience*. I used to study them like mad when I was writing the Triangle shows at Princeton. (I see, by the way, that a boy named James W. Huntley has been elected to the Cottage Club at Princeton. Did you know him in Baltimore?) I wish I could say as nice things about the poem after Ogden Nash (I dined with him and Bill Leonard night before last). It was a long way after. Ogden Nash's poems are not careless, they all have an extraordinary inner rhythm. They could not possibly be written by someone who in his mind had not calculated the feet and meters to the last iambus or trochee. His method is simply to glide a certain number of feet and come up smack against his rhyming line. Read over a poem of his and you will see what I mean. Your poem has every line in a different meter. One changes from a two-four rhyme to a gallop, to a waltz, and so forth, and the total effect is nil. I know you didn't think much of it but you did send it to me, so I am telling you the truth.

I am glad you have gotten around to liking Dorothy Parker and that you had the good taste to pick out her "Diary of a New York Lady." It is one of her best pieces. As to knowing her, you do know her, but that was in the days when you were a little weary of my literary friends. I knew Elizabeth Firestone's father very well and liked him very much. What are you going to do for the Firestone Tire Hour? Thank God you got a credit for posture. That's really good news. I think you can have the suit you want for spring. Shall I send you the money or what? Write me immediately.

I think your Pinehurst suggestion is rather good for Easter. Jim Boyd lives at Southern Pines next door; in fact, he owns most of it. We might do a few days there and a few days at Virginia Beach. However, the geographical part of our plans will depend on what the doctor will let your mother do.

Dearest love always.

Daddy

I liked the lyrics you told me last January—very well turned. I suppose they were in the show. Ordered none of those photos—they were so tight-lip one imagined that they concealed gold teeth. I heard there was a flood here but didn't look out the window as I was busy.

[*The Garden of Allah Hotel*]
[*Hollywood, California*]

[*March, 1938*]

Dearest Pie:

Your letter was welcome but I'm sorry you waited to write me until you had nothing pleasant to say—all about hating people, and where you were going to college and how you were about to replace DeMille and Berlin next year. Together with some impertinent cracks about my absurd unreasonableness. I simply conclude that you were in a bad humor because none of it makes much sense.

As to Bryn Mawr, I am entering you at St. Timothy's next year so if you miss at Vassar you will be able to be near Baltimore, which I gather you want. If you thought you were going to spend next year weekending in Baltimore you must have suddenly come to one of those decisions of yours that I am a sucker. I have no such plans for you. Either you accept responsibilities and let me graduate from this unwelcome role of stern father or you stay another year in jail with the children. Your whole liberty turns on the question of your work and nothing else—the kind of talent in demand out here doesn't walk out on a job.

In any case I'm coming East this month and we'll go somewhere and we'll find out your objections to this dog's life you lead and if they're valid we'll change them.

Love,

Daddy

[*The Garden of Allah Hotel*]
[*Hollywood, California*]
April 18, 1938

Dearest Pie:

Got your postcard. A couple of days ago got a wire from my old friend, Alice Lee Myers. You remember, the woman who took Honoria and some other girls abroad last summer. She is taking a party this year which will include Fanny, and I think it sounds very good. Traveling is always fun; you always meet young people on the boat and in hotels during the summer, and the trip itself would include a station wagon tour of France, Belgium, Holland, and perhaps a taste of England. I won't mention that it would help your French, because that sounds too much like work, but I will say that if it works out you will be a very lucky girl, for quite possibly these are the last few years in which you will be able to see Europe as it was. Though I may add that if you get caught in a war this summer, I will simply deny knowing you and you will have to get out of it the best way you can; *but please don't start one*.

God, how I'd like to go myself. Everything is work here, just as I expected, and of course I came back without any rest and it was two or three days before I was really able to get going again. I like the work part, but seem to have to do it in big, heartbreaking doses, which is bad for the constitution. Sorry we didn't have as many talks as I had hoped for. You had no special plans for the summer, I gathered, except what general invitations might be available, and I really don't want you out here for the whole summer because there is no Helen Hayes and really nothing much to do that would interest you except a repetition of last summer—only less interesting, as I am out of touch with Norma, Joan, etc. However, if you come for a week in June with Peaches, I will open up relations again and try to make an impression on her. I am writing the Finneys today. I wouldn't talk around school about summer plans until they are more definite. I will have to bargain with Alice Lee Myers about the European trip, and for the Hollywood trip see if Pete will trust his precious into my hands. Your mother, Obers, etc., are to know nothing yet— the teachers nothing.

Now the European trip would be due to start either June 22 or July 2nd. I imagine that I could have the dates changed a little, or rather that, as you are one-fourth of the party, the time of your examinations would have to be a determining point in the itinerary. When will they be over? What are the actual dates? What would you say, if the European trip is decided on, to the idea of leaving school after graduation, coming out here and taking your boards here in Hollywood and then, if time is short, flying back to New York? I don't mind your flying now as I did last summer. It is as nearly safe in June as such things can ever be. *Also, I want a truthful answer as to whether the school would rather you stayed there.* Please don't make me take this up with Miss Walker. If they would rather, by a margin of 60-40, that you stayed, I want to know, and I want to know *now, by airmail.* The marks were really so very mediocre that, if I was Vassar, I wouldn't take you unless the school swore that you were a serious character —and the school is not going to swear you are a serious character if you let a prep school dance stand even faintly in the way of your success. Besides, if they don't want you to stay, and the trip abroad works out, I would like to catch a glimpse of you during that time. *I don't want to come East in June if it can possibly be avoided.* After all, you are going to college, so this is not your real graduation. Nobody came to mine, and I don't remember being hurt. Nevertheless, if it were not for the hazards involved, such as bringing your mother there or else hurting her feelings by not bringing her, and the fact that it may come right at the crucial point of this picture (due to roll in June, but perhaps not starting till the fifteenth), I would love to go and see you standing flowerlike among the other fashionable peonies. Moreover, if it means an overwhelming lot to you, I will try to arrange it, but you can well understand how I dread any repetition of this Easter trip.

I got a vague word from Harold that you were going to "study hard" but I have no word from anybody about whether you took the Latin and how many lessons you took. The report is the same in detail from all your teachers and it is too dispiriting to go into. If you will trust my scheme of making a mental habit of doing the hard thing first, when you are absolutely fresh, and I mean doing the *hardest* thing *first* at the *exact moment that you feel yourself fit for doing anything* in any particular period, morning, afternoon or evening, you will go a long way toward mastering the principle of concentration. It has been so ironic to me in after life to buy books to master subjects in which I took courses at college and which made no impression on me whatsoever. I once flunked a course on the Napoleonic era, and I now have over 300 books in my library on the subject and the other A scholars wouldn't even remember it now. That was because I had made the mental tie-up that work equals something unpleasant, something to be avoided, something to be postponed. These scholars you speak of as being bright are no brighter than you, the great majority not nearly as quick nor, probably, as well endowed with memory and perception, but they have made that tie-up, so that something does not stiffen in their minds at the mention that it is a set task. I am so sure that this is your trouble because you are so much like me and because, after a long time milling over the matter, I have concluded that it was mine. What an idiot I was to be disqualified for play by poor work when men of infinitely inferior capacity got high marks without any great effort.

Write me what you think about the summer plans. The alternative is not sitting around in some attractive suburb with a bunch of Gilman School boys chewing on your ear, pleasant as the prospect might appear. I am afraid you would be somewhat second-hand by autumn, and I prefer you as you are for a little longer.

Dearest love.

Your Progenitor in
the Direct Line

Will you kindly touch on *every point* in this letter when

you answer it? I am keeping a carbon, hoping you will. This is a time when we ought to be able to communicate— we are unconflicting on 90% of things—all except your lazy belly which my thin gut shrinks from. Please work— work with your best hours.

[*Metro-Goldwyn-Mayer Corporation*]
[*Culver City, California*]

[*Spring, 1938*]

Dearest:

I hope Mary Earle won't find the trip too expensive. It *is* if you are not going to Vassar, but if you are I think it will be such a worthwhile thing and I wish to God I could go over with you.

We have reached a censorship barrier in *Infidelity* to our infinite disappointment. It *won't* be Joan's next picture and we are setting it aside awhile till we think of a way of halfwitting halfwit Hayes and his Legion of Decency. Pictures needed cleaning up in 1932-33 (remember I didn't like you to see them?) but because they were suggestive and salacious. Of course the moralists now want to apply that to *all* strong themes—so the crop of the last two years is feeble and false, unless it deals with children. Anyhow we're starting a new story and a safe one.

About *adjectives:* all fine prose is based on the verbs carrying the sentences. They make sentences move. Probably the finest technical poem in English is Keats' "Eve of Saint Agnes." A line like "The hare limped trembling through the frozen grass," is so alive that you race through it, scarcely noticing it, yet it has colored the whole poem with its movement—the limping, trembling and freezing is going on before your own eyes. Would you read that poem for me, and report?

I'm having a controversy with the Highland Hospital. They want to keep your mother there with only six weeks out a year and a few trips with Dr. and Mrs. Carroll. I can't see it—I think she should be out from one-fourth to one-half the time, using the hospital only as a base. If I insist, they threaten to release her altogether to me which would be simply a catastrophe—I can't work and look after her. And she wouldn't obey any companion unless the hospital has authority back of the companion. Mrs. Sayre wants her to come and sit beside what will soon be a death-bed and I can't see that as promising any future (I don't mean Mrs. Sayre is sick but she is almost so). She (your mother) wants to come to your commencement with Newman and Rosalind—O.K. if it can be arranged for a nurse to take her to and from N.Y.

I don't dare at the moment to tell your mother about the Alice Lee Myers trip or the fact that I've taken a shack at the beach here (address Garden of Allah still). She would feel as if we were happy and she was in prison. If only old Carroll was less obstinate—however it should be solved within a few weeks—I *may* have to go East but God forbid.

A letter from Miss Walker. Never has my intuition so surely informed me of a thing than now—that you are walking on a most delicate line there. No matter how you feel I should play a "straight" role for five weeks, lest they mistake any action for a frivolous attitude. All through life there are such games to play—mine for instance, when I first came here, to keep away from any bars, even though I wasn't tempted to drink. The connection of "bar-drunk" was too easy to establish in people's minds after my past performances. But don't tell your best friend that you are playing a sober role—such things travel fast and far. You will be smart in playing nun for the time being—five weeks will win you many months.

                              Dearest love always.

                              Daddy

                              [*Metro-Goldwyn-Mayer Corporation*]
                              [*Culver City, California*]

                              [*May, 1938*]

Dearest Pie:

I'm glad you acted decently in the end about that in-firmary affair. We'll consider it closed.

About the college courses, in case you get in—for freshman year at least I want them to be subject to discussion
between us—I don't think, for example, that you are ready
for philosophy. I made some bad mistakes in choosing my
own curriculum on silly careless premises, because courses
came at the right time, were rumored easy, etc. I thought
I'd read Italian to read Dante and didn't get to first base.
I should have known from my wretched French that I had
no gift for languages. Similarly you went into physics instead of taking more French and you must have been a
considerable drag on the rest of the class. So we will discuss your curriculum when we meet. The enclosed is merely
to indicate to you that a course in economics might be interesting in these troubled times. I am not insistent about
science but at least one line you follow must be useful
rather than cultural.

It's been a bad year for you. I hope you'll save the remnants by getting into college and I do wish you wouldn't
blame others ever for what happens to you. A famous
gunman who was lately electric-shocked from among us
said he only shot the policeman because he wasn't let alone.
Right up to the chair he thought he was being put upon.
You were never anti-social in youth—it is one regard in
which this year your reasoning is more like your mother's
than mine. Never in her whole life did she have a sense
of guilt, even when she put other lives in danger—it was
always people and circumstances that oppressed her. I
think, though, that you are walking toward some awful
sock in the next few months that will have a sobering effect
on you and I will be glad when it's over and you are your
old modest and charming self again.

Do try to make your mother happy for two days—excuse
her enthusiasm. In her youth, she didn't know such schools
existed. Tell her you may go abroad if your exams are
good.

If you do, and I am very anxious you should, I can't
bring you and Peaches out here this June—September
would be better. I have no facilities for chaperonage at the
moment but if there is cooperation in your heart this summer I will arrange it for next September. I gather Mary
Earle's mother wasn't interested in the European trip.

The censors have stopped *Infidelity* as we were about to
go into production. I am doing the screenplay of *The*

Women for Norma Shearer. My God—what characters! What gossip! Let me remind you never to discuss my affairs with a living soul.

> With dearest love,
>
> Daddy

> [*Metro-Goldwyn-Mayer Corporation*]
> [*Culver City, California*]
> *July 7, 1938*

Dearest Scottie:

I don't think I will be writing letters many more years and I wish you would read this letter twice—bitter as it may seem.[1] You will reject it now, but at a later period some of it may come back to you as truth. When I'm talking to you, you think of me as an older person, an "authority," and when I speak of my own youth what I say becomes unreal to you—for the young can't believe in the youth of their fathers. But perhaps this little bit will be understandable if I put it in writing.

When I was your age I lived with a great dream. The dream grew and I learned how to speak of it and make people listen. Then the dream divided one day when I decided to marry your mother after all, even though I knew she was spoiled and meant no good to me. I was sorry immediately I had married her but, being patient in those days, made the best of it and got to love her in another way. You came along and for a long time we made quite a lot of happiness out of our lives. But I was a man divided—she wanted me to work too much for *her* and not enough for my dream. She realized too late that work was dignity, and the only dignity, and tried to atone for it by working herself, but it was too late and she broke and is broken forever.

It was too late also for me to recoup the damage—I had

---

[1] After graduation, while studying for college boards at Ethel Walker's, Scottie had broken bounds and been asked to leave the school. Fitzgerald's fear that it might prevent her from getting into Vassar occasioned this letter.

spent most of my resources, spiritual and material, on her, but I struggled on for five years till my health collapsed, and all I cared about was drink and forgetting.

The mistake I made was in marrying her. We belonged to different worlds—she might have been happy with a kind simple man in a southern garden. She didn't have the strength for the big stage—sometimes she pretended, and pretended beautifully, but she didn't have it. She was soft when she should have been hard, and hard when she should have been yielding. She never knew how to use her energy —she's passed that failing on to you.

For a long time I hated *her* mother for giving her nothing in the line of good habit—nothing but "getting by" and conceit. I never wanted to see again in this world women who were brought up as idlers. And one of my chief desires in life was to keep you from being that kind of person, one who brings ruin to themselves and others. When you began to show disturbing signs at about fourteen, I comforted myself with the idea that you were too precocious socially and a strict school would fix things. But sometimes I think that idlers seem to be a special class for whom nothing can be planned, plead as one will with them—their only contribution to the human family is to warm a seat at the common table.

My reforming days are over, and if you are that way I don't want to change you. But I don't want to be upset by idlers inside my family or out. I want my energies and my earnings for people who talk my language.

I have begun to fear that you don't. You don't realize that what I am doing here is the last tired effort of a man who once did something finer and better. There is not enough energy, or call it money, to carry anyone who is dead weight and I am angry and resentful in my soul when I feel that I am doing this. People like ____ ____ and your mother must be carried because their illness makes them useless. But it is a different story that *you* have spent two years doing no useful work at all, improving neither your body nor your mind, but only writing reams and reams of dreary letters to dreary people, with no possible object except obtaining invitations which you could not accept. Those letters go on, even in your sleep, so that I know your whole trip now is one long waiting for the post. It is like an old gossip who cannot still her tongue.

You have reached the age when one is of interest to an adult only insofar as one seems to have a future. The mind of a little child is fascinating, for it looks on old things with new eyes—but at about twelve this changes. The adolescent offers nothing, can do nothing, say nothing that the adult cannot do better. Living with you in Baltimore (and you have told Harold that I alternated between strictness and neglect, by which I suppose you mean the times I was so inconsiderate as to have T.B., or to retire into myself to write, for I had little social life apart from you) represented a rather too domestic duty forced on me by your mother's illness. But I endured your Top Hats and Telephones until the day you snubbed me at dancing school, less willingly after that. . . .

To sum up: What you have done to please me or make me proud is practically negligible since the time you made yourself a good diver at camp (and now you are softer than you have ever been). In your career as a "wild society girl," vintage of 1925, I'm not interested. I don't want any of it—it would bore me, like dining with the Ritz Brothers. When I do not feel you are "going somewhere," your company tends to depress me for the silly waste and triviality involved. On the other hand, when occasionally I see signs of life and intention in you, there is no company in the world I prefer. For there is no doubt that you have something in your belly, some real gusto for life—a real dream of your own—and my idea was to wed it to something solid before it was too late—as it was too late for your mother to learn anything when she got around to it. Once when you spoke French as a child it was enchanting with your odd bits of knowledge—now your conversation is as commonplace as if you'd spent the last two years in the Corn Hollow High School—what you saw in *Life* and read in *Sexy Romances*.

I shall come East in September to meet your boat—but this letter is a declaration that I am no longer interested in your promissory notes but only in what I see. I love you always but I am only interested by people who think and work as I do and it isn't likely that *I* shall change at my age. Whether you will—or want to—remains to be seen.

Daddy

P.S. if you keep the diary, please don't let it be the dry stuff I could buy in a ten-franc guide book. I'm not interested in dates and places, even the Battle of New Orleans, unless you have some unusual reaction to them. Don't try to be witty in the writing, unless it's natural—just true and real.

P.P.S. Will you please read this letter a second time? I wrote it over twice.

> [*Metro-Goldwyn-Mayer Corporation*]
> [*Culver City, California*]
> [*July, 1938*]

Dearest Pie:

When I wrote down those architectural terms hoping to encourage a "Gothic Quest" I overlooked what was right under my eye. Rotterdam, oddly enough, is the center of modern architecture. J. P. P. Oud, who was invited to give the Kalin lectures at Princeton some years ago, is the greatest living architect in all probability, and his workers' dwellings, designed when he was city architect of Rotterdam, are a model for the world. See them if you come back that way and compare them with New York slums. Also, if this reaches you in Paris, you might find Caffin's easy book on architecture at Brentano's. Please buy it.

Also if you're in Paris when this reaches you, a *pneumatique* might reach Nanny at 23 rue Pascal-Lecointre. I think it would be nice if you took her to lunch. If you do, make her feel happy and important—she did a great deal for you. Give her my love.

I have been trying to get your actual college board ratings. Do you realize now that all that bother about French has saved you one whole year of education? I mean that French was the deciding factor in your skipping a grade. So that if you should marry at 19 you will have had one more year of education than if you had let it slip. I hadn't intended to bring up the college matters definitely in this letter, but, since I've said this, [I] might as well add that you should approach Vassar as if you were going to do the four years. A girl's life is so different from a boy's in

America that the odds are incalculable as to whether or not you will take a degree—but who knows? Your mother had a broken engagement on her hands a few days before her nineteenth birthday—what could have been better than to have had something to go on with? It is very exceptional for a grown person to jump straight from one serious love affair into another.

Aside from that—and you know I'd be happy if you didn't marry before twenty at the earliest—I think it would have an effect on your own morale and the feelings of other students towards you if you signed up "for the duration of the war." To half of the girls there, Vassar will be their whole world as Princeton was mine and, though they might enjoy a little butterflying, their resentment against the self-confessed butterfly who is only killing time with them will be very deep in their hearts, and will deepen as the years increase. So I should soft-pedal my social ambitions and ride with the times. After all the president of last year's Vassar senior class just married a Rockefeller and the Clark girl of Boston made her debut as a singer instead of on Beacon Hill. The Bachelors' Cotillion simply doesn't mean what it did twenty years ago—or even ten. I suppose it means a lot to _____ _____ because she's not likely to have anything any better.

All that is snobbish talk but the part about going in whole-heartedly, and publicly so, is very important and real. I want college to be good—I was pretty discouraged there for a while—I felt myself losing interest, and illness has made me pretty selfish and self-protective. I could see you stranded with a lot of childhood memories—and two thousand trivial letters. I even had a talk with a man who owns a canning factory in San Diego with the idea of giving you the works from the bottom. It would have made you or broken you (i.e., made you run away). But it was pretty drastic medicine and I'm glad I didn't have to resort to it. In an odd way you are an old-fashioned girl, living half in the world of Mrs. Finney and Mrs. Turnbull (you should have seen the latter's face the day the banks closed in '33 and I had the only money on the place— $1800 in gold). Often I have encouraged that because my generation of the radicals and breakers-down never found anything to take the place of the old virtues of work and courage and the old graces of courtesy and politeness. But

I don't want you to live in an unreal world or to believe that the system that produced Barbara Hutton can survive more than ten years, any more than the French monarchy could survive 1789. Every girl your age in America will have the experience of working for her living. To shut your eyes to that is like living in a dream—to say "I will do valuable and indispensable work" is the part of wisdom and courage.

                                    With dearest love,

                                    Daddy

P.S. At the *Saturday Evening Post* rate this letter is worth $4000. Since it is for you only and there are so many points, won't you read it twice?

                [*Metro-Goldwyn-Mayer Corporation*]
                [*Culver City, California*]
                September 19, 1938

Dearest Pie:

Here are a few ideas that I didn't discuss with you and I'm sending this to reach you on your first day.

For heaven's sake don't make yourself conspicuous by rushing around[1] inquiring which are the Farmington Girls, which are the Dobbs Girls, etc. You'll make an enemy of everyone who *isn't*. Thank heaven you're on an equal footing of brains at last—most of the eventual leaders will be high school girls and I'd hate to see you branded among them first week as a snob—it's not worth a moment's thought. What *is* important is to go to the library and crack your first book—to be among the 5% who will do this and get that much start and freshness.

A chalk line is absolutely specified for you at present because. . . . besides the "cleverness" which you are vaguely supposed to have "inherited," people will be quick to deck you out with my sins. If I hear of you taking a drink before you're twenty, I shall feel entitled to begin my last and greatest non-stop binge, and the world also will have

[1] At Vassar.

an interest in the matter of your behavior. It would like to be able to say, and would say on the slightest provcation: "There she goes—just like her papa and mama." Need I say that you can take this fact as a curse—or you can make of it a great advantage?

Remember that you're there for four years. It is a residential college and the butterfly will be resented. You should never boast to a soul that you're going to the Bachelors' Cotillion. I can't tell you how important this is. For one hour of vainglory you will create a different attitude about yourself. Nothing is as obnoxious as other people's luck. And while I'm on this: You will notice that there is a strongly organized left-wing movement there. I do not particularly want you to think about politics, but I do *not* want you to set yourself against this movement. I am known as a left-wing sympathizer and would be proud if you were. In any case, I should feel outraged if you identified yourself with Nazism or Red-baiting in any form. Some of those radical girls may not look like much now but in your lifetime they are liable to be high in the councils of the nation.

I think it would be wise to put on somewhat of an act in reference to your attitude to the upper classmen. In every college the class just ahead of you is of great importance. They approach you very critically, size you up and are in a position to help or hinder you in anything you try. I mean the class *just* ahead of you. A sophomore class is usually conceited. They feel that they have been through the mill and have learned something. While this is very doubtful, it is part of wisdom to humor that vanity in them. It would pay dividends many times to treat them with an outward respect which you might not feel and I want you to be able to do such things at will, as it happens that all through life you may be in a position in which you will constantly have to assume a lowly rank in a very strict organization. If anybody had told me my last year at Princeton that I would stand up and take orders from an ex-policeman, I would have laughed. But such was the case because, as an army officer, he was several grades above me in rank and competence—and that is not the last time it has happened.

Here is something you can watch happen during your college course. Always at the beginning of the first term about half a dozen leaders arise. Of these at least two get so intoxicated with themselves that they don't last the first year, two survive as leaders and two are phonies who are found out within a year—and therefore discredited and rated even lower than before, with the resentment people feel for anyone who has fooled them.

Everything you are and do from fifteen to eighteen is what you are and will do through life. Two years are *gone* and half the indicators *already point down*—two years are left and you've got to pursue desperately the ones that point up!

I wish I were going to be with you the first day, and I hope the work has already started.

                                    With dearest love,

                                    [Daddy]

                    [*Metro-Goldwyn-Mayer Corporation*]
                    [*Culver City, California*]
                    [*Fall, 1938*]

Dearest Scottie:

I am intensely busy. On the next two weeks, during which I finish the first part of *Madame Curie,* depends whether or not my contract will be renewed. So naturally I am working like hell—though I wouldn't expect you to understand that—and getting rather bored with explaining the obvious over and over to a wrong-headed daughter.

If you had listened when Peaches read that paper aloud last September this letter and several others would have been unnecessary. You and I have two very different ideas —yours is to be immediately and overwhelmingly attractive to as many boys as you can possibly meet, including Cro-Magnons, natural-born stevedores, future members of the Shriners and plain bums. My idea is that presently, not quite yet, you should be extremely attractive to a very limited amount of boys who will be very much heard of in the nation or who will at least know what it is all about.

The two ideas are *irreconcilable,* completely and utterly inverse, obverse and *contradictory!* You have *never* understood that!

I told you last September that I would give you enough to go to Vassar, live moderately, leave college two or three times during the fall term—a terrific advantage in freedom over your contemporaries in boarding school.

After four weeks I encountered you on a weekend. Here is how it was spent—God help the Monday recitations:

> Friday—on the train to Baltimore
>   Dance
> Saturday—to New York (accidentally) with me
> Sunday—to Simsbury to a reunion

The whole expedition must have cost you *much more* than your full week's allowance. I warned you then, as I had warned you in the document Peaches read, that you would have to pay for your Thanksgiving vacation. However, in spite of all other developments—the Navy game, the Dean's information, the smoking, the debut plans—I did not interfere with your allowance until you gave me the absolute insult of neglecting a telegram. Then I blew up and docked you ten dollars—that is exactly what it cost to call you the day of the Yale-Harvard game because I could not believe a word you said.

Save for that ten dollars you have received $13.85 every week. If you doubt this I will send you a record of the cancelled checks.

There is no use telegraphing any more—if you have been under exceptional expenses that I do not know of I will of course help you. But otherwise you must stay within that sum. What do you do it for? You wouldn't even give up smoking—and by now you couldn't if you wanted to. To take Andrew and Peaches—who, I think you will agree, come definitely under the head of well-brought-up children—if either of them said to their fathers: "I'm going to do no favors for you but simply get away with everything I can"—well, in two minutes they'd lose the $25 a month they probably get!

But I have never been strict with you, except on a few essentials, probably because in spite of everything I had till recently a sense of partnership with you that sprang

out of your mother's illness. But you effectively broke that
up last summer and I don't quite know where we stand.
Controlling you like this is so repugnant to me that most
of the time I no longer care whether you get an education
or not. But as for making life soft for you after all this
opposition—it simply isn't human nature. I'd rather have
a new car.

If you want to get presents for your mother, Peaches,
Mary Law, Grandmother, etc., why not send me a list and
let me handle it here? Beyond which I hope to God you
are doing a lot about the Plato—and I love you very much
when given a chance.

Daddy

P.S. Do you remember going to a party of Rosemary
Warburton's in Philadelphia when you were seven? Her
aunt and her father used to come a lot to Ellerslie.

[Metro-Goldwyn-Mayer Corporation]
[Culver City, California]
November 15, 1938

Dearest Scottie:

I haven't heard from you yet but I'm assuming that
your common sense has asserted itself and I'll get a fair
answer to my letter. How you could possibly have missed
the answer to my first question I don't know, unless you
skipped pages 160 to 170 in *Farewell to Arms*. Try again!
There's nothing vague in these questions of mine but they
require attention. I hope you've sent me the answer to the
second question. The third question is based on the book
Ecclesiastes in the Bible. It is fifteen pages long and since
you have it in your room you ought to get through it carefully in four or five days. As far as I am concerned you
can skip the wise-cracks in italics on pages 766, 767 and
768. They were written by somebody else and just stuck
in there. But read carefully the little introduction on 754
and note also that I do not mean "Ecclesiasticus" which is
something entirely different. Remember when you're read-

ing it that it is one of the top pieces of writing in the world. Notice that Ernest Hemingway got a title from the third paragraph. As a matter of fact the thing is full of titles. The paragraph on page 756 sounds like the confession of a movie producer, even to the swimming pools.

Am glad you were reading about Twentieth Century Sophists. You meet them every day. They see their world falling to pieces and know all the answers, and are not going to do anything about it.

Did the quilts come? The Baltimore stuff and also the one from New York, which, of course, was a duplication as it turned out. Isn't it common courtesy to acknowledge such matters? Also, Harold said he sent you that old *Redbook* story of mine. Did you read it?

Dearest love.

Daddy

P.S. Your failure to send me that slip on the second page gummed up the list of Elizabethan lyrics I'd made, so that there was some repetition in the second list. Your teachers must love you for that splendid casual quality but I don't think you'd hold a job five minutes.

[*Metro-Goldwyn-Mayer Corporation*]
[*Culver City, California*]
November 18, 1938

Dearest Scottie:

I'm certainly glad to catch a glimmer of wisdom in your attitude—even though you unveiled the story of the blow-away pink slip *after* the telegraph company had checked on you. And even though in one page of your letter you had intended to go to Baltimore from Thursday to Saturday, while in another part you hadn't intended to go at all.

I'm sorry about _____'s tea. I've nothing against her except that she rather stuck her neck out about Vassar, which I suppose she is attending for the social prestige involved. She seemed very nice, quite transparent—a type that turned up all too frequently in the Cottage Club at Princeton. I do wish you would find some more interesting friends. To take the curse off your not going to her party I wrote a nice letter to her mother explaining my apparent tyranny in forbidding it. Same to the mother of ____ ____.

In answering my questions you asked some yourself. The one about Baltimore can be answered from *Ecclesiastes*, "There is a time for weeping, a time for laughing," etc. Fourteen was simply not the time for you to run around on evening dates—at least Pete Finney and I thought not in our erroneous ways. The parents of ____ ____ and ____ ____ thought differently. Who is interested in a girl with her bloom worn off at sixteen? The one thing you still reproach me for is letting you go, against my better judgment, to the dance at St. Andrew's School.

It is now perfectly sensible for you to go with college boys. (I didn't want you to stay in Baltimore this fall because I felt it would shoot you into Vassar with your mind full of gayety or love, which it apparently did, for your first month there was a flat bust. Also, I did not want you to start with a string of football games this fall.) If you are invited to the Yale or Princeton proms this winter or next spring by a reputable boy—and I'm entitled to the name, please—I'd have absolutely no objection to your going.* *The whole damn thing about going to the college is to keep it in proportion.* Did you ever hear of a college boy, unless he were an idiot, racing from Smith to Vassar to Wellesley? There are certain small sacrifices for a college education or there wouldn't be any honor in having gone to college.

But the New York thing is as wrong now as the auto date was at fourteen. I will quote you from a letter I wrote Harold Ober: "Those debutante parties in New York are the rendezvous of a gang of professional idlers, parasites, pansies, failures, the silliest type of sophomores, young customers' men from Wall Street and hangers-on—the very riff-raff of social New York who would exploit a child like Scottie with flattery and squeeze her out until she is a limp colorless rag. In one more year she can cope with them. In three more years it will be behind her. This year she is still puppy enough to be dazzled. She will be infinitely better off here with me than mixed up with that sort of people.

_____

* If it doesn't come in an examination week.

I'd rather have an angry little girl on my hands for a few months than a broken neurotic for the rest of my life." But I don't have to tell you this—you probably read the *Life* article on the dim-witted _____ girl and the razz on her in *The New Yorker*.

As to the money. Your full allowance for next Monday, $13.85, will reach you almost as soon as this does. I'm sorry you were inconvenienced at the loss of the $10.00, but it is a trifle compared to the inconvenience you have caused at this end. I will also send an additional $5.00, which will make $18.85 for the Baltimore trip, but that $5.00 will come off the following week's allowance. I want you to stay in Baltimore until Sunday, and I mean specifically in Baltimore, not at Vassar, not at Scarsdale. This money must absolutely take care of the Baltimore trip!

Yes, it *is* too bad you have to be checked up on like a girl of ten. I'd hoped you'd be rather different this year. If Peaches hadn't been with you that first day in Hollywood I would have squelched the idea of rooming with a debutante as I had meant to. I let it go because I didn't want to open her visit that way. I'm as sick of this bloody matter as you are. I can just see people pointing at you at New York dances and saying, "That's Scott Fitzgerald's daughter. She likes her champagne young. Why doesn't he do something about it?"

Even if your aims are the most worldly, the road that I am pointing out is the right one. A great social success is a pretty girl who plays her cards as carefully as if she were plain.

> With dearest love,
>
> Daddy

P.S. Please address all future correspondence to my new address, 5221 Amestoy Ave., Encino, Los Angeles, California.

[*Metro-Goldwyn-Mayer Corporation*]
[*Culver City, California*]
November 25, 1938

Dearest Scottie:

I'm concerned about the history test though I know the classroom work *may* have been better. However, at Walkers your tests ran almost equal to your classroom work, usually ahead of it, and finishing early rather indicates that you were out of material, doesn't it? But I feel that if you like that work you can pass it. I never blame failure—there are too many complicated situations in life—but I am absolutely merciless toward lack of effort. That's why I finally lost interest in _____ _____. I'm sending you a book that seems to have helped some people at Princeton. You might glance over it. You must admit that my prophecy has proven true. I said that to get decent grades you would have to study at least as hard as you did between leaving Walkers and taking the board examinations. I don't mean that it will be tough sledding indefinitely but there will have to be a period of tough sledding before you come to Easy Street. Why don't you let it be now? You can still pull out of this hole before Christmas—and put me in a most generous mood.

Knowing your character, here's about the way things will go in the next month. You have four weeks before Christmas and probably you intend to try hard but at the moment you have gotten into some entanglement in Baltimore that you either want to go deeper into or get out of, or put on ice—in any case, that will require two or three days of letter writing and absorption. Then you will do well for three days—until the reply to your letter sets you off again. By now your impetus will be exhausted and you will have a good three-day low—the movies and New York, forget to hand in a theme, or something like that. Two weeks gone. Then, alas, one of those things will happen against which only the wisest will guard—a two-day cold, an unexpected change of Christmas plans, some personal trouble or upset. Then there's only a week left and despite frantic hours you will have another failure on your hands. Don't you see that this is just how it happens? Where's that "common sense" that you boast about?

I begin to wonder about the postal service there. I wrote

you some weeks ago that the second question was:

During the retreat from Caporetto, Lieutenant Henry was haunted by one of the poems in the second list, which came into his memory in distorted form. What poem was it?

That should take you only a minute. Also, did you ever get my letter in which I included a letter you wrote me from Walkers last June?

The address given you before is incorrect. The right address is: 5521 Amestoy Ave., Encino, Los Angeles, California.

> With dearest love,
>
> Daddy

P.S. $5.00 of the $10.00 advanced you is deducted from this week's check, which please find enclosed.

> *[5521 Amestoy Avenue]*
> *[Encino, California]*
> *[December, 1938]*

Dearest Scottie:

A letter from Miss Barber tells me you may very possibly be on probation. I am disappointed but not broken-hearted as it was on the cards from September. In one way you are like me—that when things seemed to be going oh so smoothly they were really slipping from underneath subtly and surely. But on the other hand remember that when you are struggling and fighting and perhaps feeling you are getting nowhere, maybe even despairing—those are the times when you may be making slow, sure progress. I hope December has been one of those times—I hope it is the beginning of an effort that, if the probation *is* imposed, will see it lifted very soon.

I thought the letter from Miss Barber had a somewhat impertinent tone. This is doubtless because you seem to have told her you were *eighteen* which of course would throw an entirely different light on my wishes about New York and make me rather silly. This rather detracted from the sympathy that I first felt for you, which prompted my wire.

Presuming you are hard up I am sending a small advance on your Dec. 19th allowance to keep the wolf from the door.

My plans are all uncertain. Is that Princeton pamphlet any good?

With dearest love,

Daddy

P.S. Your letter came. Touched that you wish I wouldn't worry about the marks and enlightened to know why freshmen are marked hard. "I don't see why you're so furious because I'm not brilliant" is a sentence that touches my heart. I don't know whether it's the thought or the style that impresses me most. Which was your philosophical poem? "Be my little little little, little wife?"

Which reminds me. I sent you the librettos of W. S. Gilbert. What I want you to read is *Patience* which was written as a counterblast to Wilde's asceticism. Did you like the Dowson poem? What notorious modern novel takes its title from a line of it?

About your masterwork—the diary. (Seriously it has some nice writing in it, sharp observation, flashes of wit, etc. I cut pages 1 and 2 from a typed version and sent it to your grandmother.)

The editing I did was slight—names changed (Myers, Murphys, etc.); reference to your mother's not getting well. . . . There is not a word or a line changed—nor even a correction of spelling. Excuse my map—I never did know how you got from Switzerland to Paris.

Who are you going to visit in Baltimore if you go there? I have no time to dig you up stuff about Ernest but his first book *In Our Time* tells a lot about himself. I have not taken a week from your allowance. I wish in your letter now—the last I'll get before vacation—you would tell me *in bulk* just *how much you owe!*

Daddy

[*5521 Amestoy Avenue*]
[*Encino, California*]

[*January, 1939*]

Dearest Pie:

I believe you have to deposit this by the third of February. Anyhow as soon as you know you are going on give it to them. I have added the music charges from the catalogue—of course you get no scholastic credit for preliminary music.

I suppose you have finished the essay. If you are still writing it don't forget that the age of marriage is largely a biological question. Girls in India mature at thirteen, in the American tropics at about fifteen or sixteen, and in Scandinavia as late as twenty-one. Most questions in life have an economic basis (at least according to us Marxians), but this is one where biology undermines economics. Hence the Spanish duenna and the French chaperone, because these races realize that while economically it's better to wait, nature in southern lands has quite contrary intentions.

I will take care of the Turnbull matter.

By this time you will have heard from exams. I hope it goes well. You are the first woman on either side of your family to try for a higher education—though many of them have been well-read. If you get to know a little bit you will combine a great deal of latent power in yourself, and be able to live more fully and richly than the majority of pretty girls whose lives in America are lop-sided, backward-looking and wistful.

How about "Cynara," etc.? I feel a slowly mounting exasperation.

My address is simply

Encino,
California.

Your letter was a masterpiece of polite evasion.

Love,

Daddy

[*5521 Amestoy Avenue*]
[*Encino, California*]

[*Winter, 1939*]

Dearest Scottie:

I know you looked first at the check, but it does *not* represent a business transaction. I am too tired at the moment to argue but your figures are wrong. However, I'm having it all checked up by my secretary. I think there is a gift somewhere.

Sorry you got the impression that I'm quitting the movies —they are always there—I'm doing a two-weeks rewrite for Paramount at the moment, after finishing a short story. But I'm convinced that maybe they're not going to make me Czar of the Industry right away, as I thought 10 months ago. It's all right, baby—life has humbled me— Czar or not, we'll survive. I am even willing to compromise for Assistant Czar!

Seriously, I expect to dip in and out of the pictures for the rest of my natural life, but it is not very soul-satisfying because it is a business of telling stories fit for children and this is only interesting up to a point. It is the greatest of all human mediums of communication and it is a pity that the censorship had to come along and do this, but there we are. *Only*—I will never again sign a contract which binds me to tell none other than children's stories for a year and a half!

Anyhow, I'm on the new Madeleine Carroll picture (go to see *Café Society*—it's pretty damn good, I think. This one is the same producer-director-stars combination) and anyhow the movies are a dull life and one hopes one will be able to transcend it.

You've let me down about the reading. I'm sorry you did because I'll have to bargain with you. Read *Moll Flanders*, for any favors asked. I mean this: skip *Tono Bungay* but if you don't care enough about my advice to do some fractional exploring in literature instead of skimming *Life* and *The New Yorker*, I'm going to get into one of those unsympathetic moods—if I'm not sorry for people's efforts there seems to be an icy and inhuman reaction. So please report on *Moll Flanders* immediately . . . meanwhile air-mail me another travel folder on Mrs. Draper and her girls. Who is she and they? And who is Moll Flanders?

I hope you enjoy the Princeton prom—please don't be overwhelmingly—but no, I am done with prophecies—make your own mistakes. Let me only say "Please don't be overwhelmingly anything!" and, if you are, don't give my name as the responsible parent! (And by the way never give out any interview to any newspaperman, formal or informal—this is a most definite and most advised plea. My name and you, bearing parts of it, is (are) still news in some quarters—and my current policy, for reasons too numerous to explain, is *silence*. Please do me this courtesy!)

I should like to meet you somewhere early in April—the third or fourth.

Your mother *is* in Florida—it seems to have been delayed.

Of course I'm glad and it warms me all over to know that even ungrammatically "both your French English and history teachers" etc. Though you are pretty completely hatched and I can be little more than your most dependable friend, your actions still have a most decided effect on me and at long range I can only observe you thru the eyes of Vassar. I have been amazed that you do not grasp a certain advantage that is within your hand—as definite as the two-headed Russian eagle—a girl who didn't *have* to have an education because she had the other women's gifts by accident—and who *took one anyhow*. Like Tommy Hitchcock who came back from England in 1919 already a newspaper hero in his escapes from Germany and the greatest polo player in the world—and went up to Harvard in the same year to become a *freshman*—because he had the humility to ask himself "Do I know anything?" That combination is what forever will put him in my pantheon of heroes.

Go thou and do likewise.

Love,

Daddy

[*5521 Amestoy Avenue*]
[*Encino, California*]
[*Winter, 1939*]

Dearest Pie:

Day of rest! After a wild all-night working on *Gone with the Wind* and more to come tomorrow. I read it—I mean really read it—it is a good novel—not very original, in fact leaning heavily on *The Old Wives' Tale*, *Vanity Fair*, and all that has been written on the Civil War. There are no new characters, new techniques, new observations— none of the elements that make literature—especially no new examination into human emotions. But on the other hand it is interesting, surprisingly honest, consistent and workmanlike throughout, and I felt no contempt for it but only a certain pity for those who considered it the supreme achievement of the human mind. So much for that—I may be on it two weeks—or two months. I disagreed with every- body about how to do *Madame Curie* and they're trying it another way.

Your cold stirred certain gloomy reflections in me. Like me, you were subject to colds when young, deep chest colds near to pneumonia. I didn't begin to be a heavy smoker until I was a sophomore but it took just one year to send me into tuberculosis and cast a shadow that has been extremely long. I wish there was something that would make you cut it out—the only pay-off is that if you're run down by June to spend a summer in the open air, which is a pity with so much to do and learn. I don't want to bury you in your debut dress.

My own plans are uncertain. I am pretty disgusted with pictures after all that censorship trouble and want to break off for a while when I have another good credit (I won't get one on *The Women*)—but *when*, I don't know.

Haven't read *De Monarchia*. Read several pieces by Cornelia Skinner and found them thin and unamusing. Since you've undertaken the *Dorian Gray* I hope you make a success of it but I hope the professor knows what you're doing. She might not consider the rearrangement of some- one else's words a literary composition, which would leave you out on a limb. Are you taking swimming?

Dearest love.

Daddy

P.S. Of course I do not care if you postpone "Cynara," etc., though it's such a detail, and you must be in the library every day. Your college work comes first—but I can't help wondering how, if time is reduced to such minuscules, you would ever have thought of trying out for a play. That of course is entirely out at present—last year should have taught you *that* lesson.

> 5521 Amestoy Avenue
> Encino, California
> *March 11, 1939*

Dear Scottie:

Thanks for your long letter about your course of subjects.

Generally, I think that your election of French as a major is a wise decision. I imagine that there will be some competition for the Sorbonne but it might be something to aim at. Also, if you want to take one English course I think you have chosen wisely. Once again I concur about the History of Music if it pleases you. But I wish you would thoroughly reconsider the chemistry question. It is an extremely laborious subject—it requires the most meticulous care and accuracy during long laboratory hours. Moreover, unless your mathematics are at your fingertips —and you were never very good at mathematics—you will be continually re-doing experiments because of one small slip, and I just can't see it fitting in with hours of music practice and some regular exercise.

One suggestion is to take *preliminary* physics. I don't know whether, if you have already offered that as an entrance, they would allow it, but they might and it would be a fairly easy running over of it as a very essential and interesting subject. I do not mean that I advise a second-year physics course because that would run into as much mathematics as chemistry. But if, God help us, they insist on a science I should advise you to consider them in the following order: botany, physiology, or child study. Think of the enormous pleasure amounting, almost, to the consolation for the tragedy of life that flowers have been to your mother and your grandmother. Mabe you could be a landscape architect like LeNotre but the personal element is equally important. I felt all my life the absence of hobbies except such, for me as abstract and academic ones, as military tactics and football. Botany is such a definite thing. It has its feet on the ground. And after reading Thoreau I felt how much I have lost by leaving nature out of my life.

I am sorry about the philosophy. I should think that if anything your test questions will deal with the big key figures, and a certain concentration of work upon Plato, Aquinas, and Descartes would pay more dividends than trying to study over entirely the course from the beginning. Please don't give it up as a bad job. Are you sure that you entirely understand the great usages thru the ages of such terms as *nominalists* and *realists?* I want you to keep your interest at least as far as Hegel from whose stem all Marxian thinking flows; certainly you will agree that Marxism does not concern itself with vague sophistries but weds itself to the most practical mechanics of material revolution.

I should suggest that you go to Sea Island with the party and return by yourself, passing at least a full day with your mother in Asheville, and a day, if you like, in Baltimore; that is, I think the Finneys would be a little offended if you did not pay at least a courtesy visit. I shall try my best to be East by the second, and at least cross your path—perhaps in Asheville—but I have let myself be inveigled into another picture and it may possibly run on to the tenth of April; on the other hand it may blow up tomorrow. (It is the new Carroll-MacMurray picture.)

With dearest love,

Daddy

P.S. Can you give me some sort of budget for your trip to Sea Island?
2nd P.S. You are not entirely right about the translations (poetry, of course, cannot be translated, but even there we have exceptions such as *The Rubaiyat*). Constance Garnett's Russian translations are excellent, while Scott-Moncrieff's *Proust* is a masterpiece in itself. And please do not leave good books half-finished, you spoil them for yourself. You shouldn't have started *War and Peace,* which

is a man's book and may interest you later. But you should finish both the Defoe and the Samuel Butler. Don't be so lavish as to ruin masterpieces for yourself. There are not enough of them!

[5521 Amestoy Avenue]
[Encino, California]
[March, 1939]

Dearest Scottie:

I was incredibly happy when I heard that the cloud had lifted. *Don't* let it come down again! I was so happy when it lifted for me at Princeton and let me in for everything I'd wanted that I forgot. And the second time I never did manage to get out of a scholastic mess all the time I was in college. If you don't get *too* happy this spring, don't lose the ground you've gained—it's going to be all right.

Congratulations—I know what it means to you, something you did for and by yourself. A sort of justification. The only excuse for the damper up above is that we have to continue to justify ourselves each week of our lives and it would seem there would be rest sometimes. Did you ever read Christina Rosetti's

"And does the road wind uphill all the way?
   Yes—to the very end—"

I want you to get Peaches a present—rather a useful one. This seems somewhat lavish but this is a world of give and take. I am allowing you twenty-five dollars for it. As it is a lavish gesture it should be a simple present—something she should find practical and useful—on the other angle from a ring-watch. Something that if you hadn't bought it, Peter would have had to buy it. You know her well enough to give her familiar things. Ponder this carefully—if you buy her a "bauble" the idea will defeat its purpose.

Also take your mother something for $15. So I'm sending:

6 days at Sea Island at $13.00	$ 78.00
2 presents	$ 40.00
Railroad fare	$100.00
Clothes	$ 50.00
Expenses	~~$310.00~~ $50.00

$310.00 *(sic)*

And to cover the airplane I'm making it $350.00. You have no leeway on your incidentals. I know the instinct to delight everybody with a big tip but in the end we too generous people die of heart trouble, trying to make it good, and have rewarded the wrong people, so be a little penurious and calculating with your small change.

I'm just as glad Cottage lost out. They've been dominant for five years—it's time it should be someone else. The only healthy thing about the God-awful system is that no one of the four is triumphant for long. In my time it was Tiger Inn—since then they've all taken turns. Did you run into a man named Ralph Wyer at the prom? He's a Minnesotan and seems to me an altogether admirable fellow. I saw him lose a tooth with great grace at the Dartmouth Winter Carnival in the hockey game.

Your comment on the satirical quality in English fiction is very apt. If you want a counter-irritant read *Bleak House* (Dickens' best book)—or if you want to explore the emotional world—not now, but in a few more years—read Dostoevski's *Brothers Karamazov*. And you'll see what the novel can do. Glad you like Butler—I liked the place where Ernest's father "turned away to conceal his lack of emotion." My God—what precision of hatred is in those lines. I'd like to be able to destroy my few detestations—
————, for example—with such markmanship as that.

Again thanks for wiring me. I must love you a lot for you have quite a power to lift me up and cast me down.

> Jove,
>
> (Sometimes known as Jupiter or "Papa Angelicus")

[*5521 Amestoy Avenue*]
[*Encino, California*]

April 5, 1939

Dearest:

Thanks for your letter.

When you get time give me a sort of budget of what you did with the money I sent you. I mean, estimate roughly what became of it. Also, did you take any planes to and from Sea Island or Asheville? As I wrote you, most of those eastern lines are safe after the first of February. In spite of the storm you ran into on the way back East last fall, I think it's rather old-fashioned not to get used to airplane travel and use it as a convenience.

You made a great impression on your mother. How different from a year ago at Virginia Beach when you seemed as far apart as the poles, during those dreary tennis games and golf lessons! Of course, the fact that she is so much better accounts for a good deal of it, but I believe that was the time you had first discovered love, in the person of _____ _____, and were in a sort of drugged coma until you could get back to Baltimore.

Spring was always an awful time for me about work. I always felt that in the long boredom of winter there was nothing else to do but study. But I lost the feeling in the long, dreamy spring days and managed to be in scholastic hot water by June. I can't tell you what to do about it—all my suggestions seem to be very remote and academic. But if I were with you and we could talk again like we used to, I might lift you out of your trouble about concentration. It really isn't so hard, even with dreamy people like you and me—it's just that we feel so damned secure at times as long as there's enough in the bank to buy the next meal, and enough moral stuff in reserve to take us through the next ordeal. Our danger is imagining that we have resources—material and moral—which we haven't got. One of the reasons I find myself so consistently in valleys of depression is that every few years I seem to be climbing uphill to recover from some bankruptcy. Do you know what bankruptcy exactly means? It means drawing on resources which one does not possess. I thought I was so strong that I never would be ill and suddenly I was ill for three years, and faced with a long, slow uphill climb.

Wiser people seem to manage to pile up a reserve—so that if on a night you had set aside to study for a philosophy test you learned that your best friend was in trouble and needed your help, you could skip that night and find you had a reserve of one or two days preparation to draw on. But I think that, like me, you will be something of a fool in that regard all your life, so I am wasting my words.

Query: Are you taking up the swimming during the spring term? I hope tremendously you will, but I suppose that's been decided already. If not, what are you doing for spring athletics?

Query No. 2: Is there any way—and don't kid me—in which you can take driving lessons? Also, if you get time —and this is not important—give me a slight picture of what the life is at Sea Island. Also, when you get time, write your mother, because I've been putting off a visit to her and may possibly have to be here three weeks longer on this damned picture and she probably feels that I'm never coming.

Dearest love always.

Daddy

P.S. Got a nice thank-you letter from Frances Turnbull for the check I sent her.

[5521 Amestoy Avenue]
[Encino, California]
May 6, 1939

Dearest:

I am sending you four weeks' allowance and hope you can make it go. Found your very sweet letter when I got back. *Please* pay up your debts in full. You know if things get really out of hand you can always call on me, but I am in for a little siege of illness and I will have to count pennies for a few months until this time is over, so don't splurge on any new big spring wardrobe.

Plans for June all depend on factors that I am absolutely unable to regulate now. Literally, I do not know what we are liable to do. In spite of the fact that I have this house and may possibly bring your mother out here for a month or so (now this must absolutely not be mentioned in any letter to her because everything is ready by the hospital and I haven't yet divulged any plans to Dr. Carroll) I still don't see you out here. You see, it would inevitably force us into that old relationship which was unsuccessful five years ago in Baltimore of my being more or less in the unpleasant position of a spy on your private affairs.

I am turning over several possibilities in my mind. One of them is would you like to go to Russia with a group of girls on an economically organized tour? I am sure such things must be going on at Vassar and you need only make inquiries about it and give me the data. I mean something for three or four weeks. I agree that I don't want you to go back to France this summer. But it might just be an experience to go to Russia on some non-deluxe affair. Form your own opinion about how the experience might work out. I have several more strings to my bow, but I am not telling you all of them at once. But Hollywood—why?

What do you want to do out here? I can no more see you as a reader in a studio wading through bad novels and worse magazine stories all summer and being so dog-tired at the end of the day that you would probably be ready for anything, even these empty-headed California boys. The question of getting you a test has occurred to me too, but I have got at least three or four reasons against it. First, I believe you ought to wait another year,—second, I want you to have one more year at Vassar and then make your debut in Baltimore. Suppose you were good? Then it would completely upset the applecart which we have elaborately set up back East. And what else can you do out here? Do you want to come out and be my secretary? *Let us laugh quietly and mirthlessly with a Boris Karloff ring.* As for some of the ideas you had before, it skips my mind whether we discussed them, but I remember one of them was whether you should go to summer stock in one of those New England towns. Honey, I may as well hand you over to the white slavers and make a thorough job of it. For girls like you, it is nothing but a complete playtime job and strong competition between the girls to see who gets the honor of being seduced by the leading man.

Doubtless all sorts of ideas have occurred to you and, if so, why not list them and send them to me—maybe we will find out of them one that fits both our ideas.

I think I have answered almost everything in your letter and I have another idea about the driving which I am going to leave for another month because it seems to me almost dangerous for a girl your age not to know how to drive.

Dearest love.

Daddy

[*5521 Amestoy Avenue*]
[*Encino, California*]

[*July, 1939*] [1]

My plan would be to start you out here the last day of the month—that is ten days from the time of writing this letter. The only thing that would prevent this would be some unexpected turn of illness. This is unlikely, but possible. I don't know how this trip is going to work out and feel a certain trepidation. I am of course not drinking and haven't been for a long time, but any illness is liable to have a certain toxic effect on the system and you may find me depressing, over-nervous about small things, and dogmatic—all these qualities more intensified than you have previously experienced them in me. Beyond this I am working very hard and the last thing I want at the end of day is a problem while, as it is natural at your age, what you want at the end of the day is excitement. I tell you all this because lately we had planned so many meetings with anticipation and they turned out to be flops. Perhaps forewarned will be forearmed.

If the experiment proves upsetting I will have no further choice than to pack you off East somewhere again, but there are several friends here whom you could visit for a time if we failed to make a satisfactory household. So the trip will be worthwhile. Also I am more of a solitary than I have ever been but I don't think that will worry you because you had your dosages of motion picture stars on two other trips. To describe how humorless I feel about life at this point you have simply to read the Tarkington story called "Sinful Dadda Little" in the *Post* issue of July 22 (still current, I believe) and remember that I read it

[1] The first part of this letter is missing.

without a particle of amusement but with a complete disgust at "Dadda" for not drowning the two debutantes at the end.

Probably I am underestimating you, as everyone seems to be pleased with your good manners and your "attitude" (I know you hate that word) this summer—notably Mrs. Owens and your mother. But you left a most unpleasant impression behind last autumn with many people, and I would rather not see you at all than see you without loving you. Your home is Vassar. Anything else to be supplied at present is a mockery of a home. It is too bad it should be this way but the only thing is to treat it as a visit and for us both to remember the rules of common courtesy toward each other. I take my sleeping pills regularly between eleven and twelve so we won't have any of those midnight wrangles that disfigured your June and September visits. Can't the party wait till you get here to discuss? Beneath all this, you understand, I have so much to talk to *you* about. (Incidentally, your memory has played you false about the philosophy. If the taking of it was a mistake it was mine not yours. I chose it one day when we were sitting on my bed with the catalogue at the beach a year ago. And I had some correspondence with Vassar trying to get you into the course at all. The history and French are as much a mystery to me as you say they are to you.)

Please give your mother this enclosed letter when you are alone with her as I don't want it to go through the sanitarium. (Changed. Am writing her [Zelda] separately. Enclosed is for yours and her expenses at boarding house.)

With dearest love,

Daddy

P.S. I am pretty definitely breaking with Ober but he doesn't know it yet.

[5521 Amestoy Avenue]
[Encino, California]
[July, 1939] [1]

---

[1] The first part of this letter is missing.

I am certainly glad that you're up and around and sorry that your selection of post-Flaubertan realism depressed you. I certainly wouldn't begin Henry James with *The Portrait of a Lady* which is in his "late second manner" and full of mannerisms. Why don't you read *Roderick Hudson* or *Daisy Miller* first? *Lord Jim* is a great book— the first third at least and the conception, though it got lost a little bit in the lawcourts of Calcutta or wherever it was. I wonder if you know why it is good? *Sister Carrie,* almost the first piece of American realism, is damn good and is as easy reading as a *True Confession.*

I wish I could say the same about a recent article in *Mademoiselle.* I grant you the grace of having been merely a dupe as I warned you you would be—for I cannot believe that you would announce that you pursued your education yourself while I went around to the speakeasies. There's nothing to do about it now, but in future please call yourself by any name that doesn't sound like mine in your writings. You must have wanted fifty dollars awfully bad to let them print such a trite and perverted version of your youth, unless you mean that it was the Fred Astaire pictures that taught you that gallant stance upon "your own two feet." This isn't in the nature of quarreling but you certainly owe me an explanation because I see no earmarks of the "dutiful daughter" about any of it.

By the time you get this it will be the eleventh. Your plan was to leave for California the fourteenth—your mother's has varied between a trip to Virginia Beach and a quiet time at Saluda. Both of you have something on me because I can't quite decide what *is* best. I am waiting to hear from Montgomery about the exact state of your grandmother's health and also to make up my mind how much work I can undertake in the studios and under what conditions—a matter which depends on X rays, the willingness of the studio to let me work at home, and other such factors.

I want to have you out here for part of the summer. I have a nice cottage in the country, but very *far* out in the country, and utterly inaccessible if one doesn't drive well. Whether a piano here would be practical or not I don't know (remember how I felt about radio) but all that might be arranged if the personal equation were not doubtful (a situation for which for the moment I take full blame). Since I stopped picture work three months ago, I have been through not only a T.B. flare-up but also a nervous breakdown of such severity that for a time it threatened to paralyze both arms—or to quote the doctor: "The good Lord tapped you on the shoulder." While I am running no fever above 99, I don't know what this return to picture work is going to do and when and if my health blows up you know what a poor family man I am. It seems best—and I am merely feeling my way as I write this letter—for you to spend at least another week in the East and you might as well spend it in or near Asheville, especially as it gives your mother such a great pleasure. A long pilgrimage with her would almost certainly require a nurse and run into expense as all trips that your mother and I make have a way of doing.

However, if things seem more stabilized out here toward the end of this month I may change my mind and bring you out here and let your mother go to Montgomery. For the moment, there is nothing for you to do but wait and get along as well as possible with your music and writing and what money I can send you. I have a bill from Dr. Hamman for $25.00. Either he was very dilatory or you didn't go to see him till the end of your visit in Baltimore for his diagnosis arrived the day of the operation and it was money thrown away. He seemed to agree, however, that four times out of five you would have had eventual trouble with the appendix.

I have sent for your marks. If you get them, airmail them to me. If they average around "B" I should think you've done well in pulling yourself out of a very difficult hole.

You can read as much or as little of this letter to your mother as you want. I don't mean it to be disagreeable, but I was naturally surprised when instead of carrying out your announced intention of writing about the difference between northern and southern girls you chose to ride on my shoulder and beat me on the head with a wooden spoon.

Your bank statements came through. I noticed there were half a dozen slips marked "insufficient funds." Marshall Neilan, once an ace director out here, went to jail for that little failing last week. These are days when if you haven't got it you better do without. Sorry about Meredith too—I always liked him. The Ober mix-up accounts for his recent coolness. I'm sorry—we got along pretty well for twenty years. _____ isn't smug or even stuffy—he's a nice adolescent who married a smooth-faced _____ person.

Love,

Daddy

P.S. Sent Peaches a nice present. Was going to do the same for the _____ girl but John gave me a "subtle" talk about some dim-witted brother who was reformed by a year in a drink sanitarium, and almost got his bottom kicked on 33rd Street.

Encino, California
5521 Amestoy Avenue
October 31, 1939

Scottina:

(Do you know that isn't a nickname I invented but one that Gerald Murphy concocted on the Riviera years ago?) Look! I have begun to write something that is maybe great, and I'm going to be absorbed in it four or six months. It may not *make* us a cent but it will pay expenses and it is the first labor of love I've undertaken since the first part of *Infidelity*. (Do you remember that half-finished script the censor stopped that I showed you in Norfolk two years ago last Easter? You read it in the cabin of one of those Baltimore-Norfolk liners.)

Anyhow I am alive again—getting by that October did something—with all its strains and necessities and humiliations and struggles. I don't drink. I am not a great man, but sometimes I think the impersonal and objective quality of my talent and the sacrifices of it, in pieces, to preserve its essential value has some sort of epic grandeur. Anyhow after hours I nurse myself with delusions of that sort.

And I think when you read this book, which will encompass the time when you knew me as an adult, you will understand how intensively I knew your world—not *ex*tensively because I was so ill and unable to get about. If I live long enough I'll hear your side of things but I think your own instincts about your limitations as an artist are possibly best: you might experiment back and forth among the arts and find your niche as I found mine—but I do not believe that so far you are a "natural."

So what? These are such valuable years. Let me watch over the development a little longer. What are the courses you are taking? Please list them. Please cater to me. Please do not ask me to rise to heights of nervous energy—in which I can usually discern the name of the dye on your instructor's hair at long distance or reconstruct the murder of March, 1938, from a rag and a bone and a hank of hair. But give me some outlines.

a. What do Obers say about me? So sad?
b. What is this about my telling Mrs. Owens you were a heel?
c. What play are you in?
d. What proms and games? Let me at least renew my youth!
e. As a papa—not the mad child of a mad genius—what do you do? and how?
f. What furniture? Do you still want etchings?
g. What did Rosalind write?
h. Do you want a test here?
i. Did you ever think of calling on the Murphys to make *them* happy—not to deprecate _____?

I'm glad you read Malraux. Did you get the driver's license? Is Mary Earle nice? I got an instant impression in Connecticut of a brave, lovely, impish person. . . .

With dearest love,

Daddy

5521 Amestoy Avenue
Encino, Califorina
November 4, 1939

Dearest Scottie:

Sorry my letter crossed yours—I mean the letter where

I said you were not "a natural." If you brought or helped to bring off the show there, I am more than pleased. Without sentimentality, I think it would be nice to give Vassar something back of what it has given to you.

The only important questions in my letter were about your relations in Baltimore, naturally, I will have to send appropriate gifts, etc.

Answer me that question, and also I would like to know how big a part you played in the show.

I have been trying to think of a name that is better for you than "Paint and Powder Club." What do you think of calling it the "Song and Story?" Not so good—or is it?

I am sorry I wrote you that letter. Again let me repeat that if you start any kind of a career following the footsteps of Cole Porter and Rodgers and Hart, it might be an excellent try. Sometimes I wish I had gone along with that gang, but I guess I am too much a moralist at heart and really want to preach at people in some acceptable form rather than to entertain them.

Will send you a small check herewith.

Dearest love.

Daddy

5521 Amestoy Avenue
Encino, California
January 25, 1940

Dearest Scottie:

Communication having apparently ceased from your end, I conclude that you are in love. Remember—there's an awful disease that overtakes popular girls at 19 or 20 called emotional bankruptcy. Hope you are not preparing the way for it. Also I have a bill from a doctor which includes an X ray. Have you had a cough? Please give me a little information, no matter how skimpy.

You have earned some money for me this week because I sold "Babylon Revisited," in which you are a character, to the pictures (the sum received wasn't worthy of the magnificent story—neither of you nor of me—however, I am accepting it).

> Dearest love always.
>
> Daddy

> 5521 Amestoy Avenue
> Encino, California
> February 19, 1940

Dearest Scottie:

Delighted that you're working on a play. In answer to a query in one of your past letters I do like Thomas Mann—in fact I had put his *Death in Venice* on that list I gave you last summer. Have sent your treasurer his check.

I was very interested to hear about Kilduff. Let me know what becomes of Andrew in the club elections. Things are still very vague here.

> With dearest love,
>
> F. S. Fitz

Have paid Peck & Peck & Peck & Peck & Peck

> [5521 Amestoy Avenue]
> [Encino, California]
> March 15, 1940

Dearest Scottie:

No word from you for some time but I suppose a letter will cross this. I think it was you who misunderstood my meaning about the *Comrades*. The important thing is this: they had best be treated not as people holding a certain set of liberal or conservative opinions but rather as you might treat a set of intensely fanatical Roman Catholics among whom you might find yourself. It is not that you should not disagree with them—the important thing is that you should not argue with them. The point is that Communism has become an intensely dogmatic and almost mystical religion and whatever you say they have ways of twisting it into shapes which put you in some lower category of mankind ("Fascist," "Liberal," "Trotskyist") and disparage you both intellectually and personally in the process. They are amazingly well-organized. The pith of my advice is: think what you want, the less said the better.

I am sorry about the physiology. There is no answer except the advice that I used to give you constantly in your less receptive days: that sometimes you can lick an especially hard problem by facing it always the very first thing in the morning with the very freshest part of your mind. This has so often worked with me that I have an uncanny faith in it.

No particular news. The Sayres are of course delighted that your mother is coming out. Your mother said something in her letter about spending vacations with you. As you know, I will not have this, except in the most limited fashion. I think the pull of an afflicted person upon a normal one is at all times downward, depressing and eventually somewhat paralyzing, and it should be left to those who have chosen such duties as a life work. So if there are any inquiries from that source about your summer plans I think it would be wise to answer them in the most general terms, even hinting that you had work mapped out in the North.

With dearest love,

Daddy

P.S. When does your Easter vacation begin? This is very important. Don't forget to tell me about the fate of Turnbull and other Baltimorians—and about the play.

[5521 Amestoy Avenue]
[Encino, California]
March 18, 1940

Dear Scottie:

Thanks for your very full letter. Of course I am terribly

curious to hear about the show and how big a business it was—for I don't doubt that it was a success, and I think your idea to found a sort of Triangle was most ingenious and energetic and exactly the sort of thing that gives me great pride in you. The satiric theatre is perhaps a better method of expression for you than journalism and perhaps it is just as well that you did not get on the *Miscellany* board. Naturally I would give anything to see the play but will await your description of it when I see you.

Am enclosing $75.00, which I hope will cover your vacation. Negotiations on the screenplay of "Babylon" are still in course. If they should go through and you should be in Baltimore a week from now I would like you to go to Asheville and spend a night with your mother. As things are now I can't afford it but we will see.

Thanks for the news about the Princeton boys. Colonial is a good club, older than Cap and Gown, in fact. At one time people used to refer to the "Big Five," but in my day Colonial got an unfortunate drinking reputation. Now I believe it specializes in boys out of the social register who don't quite make the grade in the big time. I hope Andrew is happy there, though I don't doubt that he is a little disappointed. If I were you I should not discuss the matter with him at all. I still think it is a lousy cruel system.

We'll discuss the summer later. It so much depends on how much money I have. I think that doubtless some movie job could be found for you out here. Competent people with a little pull have no trouble finding places in the small income brackets. It is when your price is $1000 and up a week that it is another story. However I'm not exactly sure it's the best thing.

I will attend to those New York bills when the first money comes in. I wish you would write me immediately *where* you will be during vacation. I mean the approximately exact dates so that I can reach you by wire in case it is feasible for you to go to North Carolina.

Dearest love.

Daddy

P.S. I wish very much you would call on the Murphys during your spring vacation. If there is any way in which

you could help Honoria[1]—to a date, for instance—I think
it would be mutually very advantageous. Of course, it
shouldn't look as if the suggestion came from me. I know
it is difficult to pick up an old thread after an interval but it
would please me immensely if you could at least pay a
call there.

> 5521 Amestoy Avenue
> Encino, California
> March 27, 1940

Dear Scottie:

I am going to work on "Babylon" at a lousy salary—a
week from Monday. Anyhow it's something.

A letter from Baltimore disturbed me this morning—
what have you done to your hair? Three different people
have seen fit to correspond with me about it. Can't you
tone down the effect a little? You heightened it so gradually
that I don't think you realize yourself now just what it
looks like. Nobody minds if a woman over thirty wants to
touch hers up but why imitate a type that is passé even in
pictures? It was a cute trick when you had one blond
strand that looked as if the sun might have hit it, but going completely overboard defeats any aesthetic purpose.

Best luck for the spring term. I know it's always the
hardest and I have that almost uncanny fear for you at
the moment that comes sometimes. Perhaps it's the touch
of overconfidence and self-justification in your leters (i.e.,
the Daisy Chain) that I haven't seen for over a year.
Please give yourself a margin for hard luck.

> Love,
>
> Daddy

P.S. I can *understand* the overconfidence—God haven't I
had it? But it's hard as hell to recognize it in oneself—
especially when time's so short and there's so *much* we
want to do.

[1] The Murphys' daughter.

[*5521 Amestoy Avenue*]
[*Encino, California*]
April 11, 1940

Dearest Pie:

Thanks for your letter. I'm writing this on a Sunday
night, *sans Francoise*[1] and I hope you can read it. I go to
cinema work tomorrow on a sort of half-pay, half-"spec"
(speculation) business on my own story "Babylon Revisited." Which is to say Columbia advances me living
money while I work and if it goes over in installments with
the producer, the company, the releasing people, I get an
increasing sum. At bottom we eat—at the top the deal is
very promising.

Why I'm writing tonight is because I foresee three
months of intensive toil. (I feel like a criminal who has
been in a hideout, been caught, and has to go back to the
Big House. I've been visited by my crooked doctor and my
moll and Frances the Fence has protected me. Now the
Big House—oh Jees them guards!)

To put you in a good humor for the ensuing gratuitous
though friendly advice, let me say I got a letter from
Andrew today, out of two years' silence, in which he
"judges you objectively" as a very fine girl. I was pleased
naturally and wish they hadn't counteracted the work I
did on him by sending him to a school with a professional
Holy-Joe for headmaster. His letter would make you very
conceited—shall I send it? You seem to be a big shot down
there.

The advice consists of this— _____ _____'s name bobs
up in so many of your letters that I assume he plays a big
part in your life, no matter how seldom you see him. I've
naturally formed a picture of him—vaguely I associate it
with my relation with Marie Hersey at about your time of
life. I think she told herself that I was hers for the *special*
effort. But they had become matter-of-fact to me—lesser
girls would have rivalled them for new excitement and
anyone who summed them up, or seemed to [me] like your
mother, would simply have washed them out of my mind.

Supposing _____ to be self-absorbed, charming, success-

[1] Frances Kroll, Fitzgerald's secretary for the past year.

ful, and full of the same psychology I had—how definitely handicapped you might be in counting on him! By the very fact of old familiarity, old experience in common, it would be difficult, for men, if they're alive, are continually looking for the new. I mean that he might, so to speak, meet the Queen of Abyssinia in his travels. And how can you rival her?

I'm not driving at the obvious answer of having many strings to your bow. I suppose you have. But haven't you taken _____ as the only *type?* Women are capable of loving three or four types of masculine excellence like the women in *Candida* and *Strange Interlude.* You ought to have, for example: as a cold intellectual, someone who's made the *Harvard Law Review*—you can find him with a little effort. He'll probably be taken already but it can be done. The point is that you have not exhausted any other type at its best except _____; you have only examined the second-rate unproved man of other species (_____, _____, etc.). You should know the young predatory business type, hard as hell. He will lick you maybe but you should know him. A lead at Princeton would be one of the Ivy boys—not Harvey, but he might be a wedge—a boy inheriting a big business.

All the above is probably very obvious so forget it. Are any of the enclosed friends of yours?

Dearest love.

Daddy

P.S. Have paid the Wallace Co. $35.00 and Altmans $40.00 on account. The printed enclosure reminded me that if you have occasion to drive, I forgot to tell you that in the rain *don't depress the clutch*—use the brake *only.* And on hills—go down in the gear in which you'd have come up. I am moving in town to be near my work, so will you address me care of my new agent, Phil Berg, 9484 Wilshire Boulevard, Beverly Hills, or General Delivery, Encino, as they will forward it? Will write you as soon as I have a permanent address.

[*5521 Amestoy Avenue*]
Encino, California

April 12, 1940

Dearest Scottie:

I'm sorry about the tone of the telegram I sent you this morning, but it represents a most terrific worry. You are doing exactly what I did at Princeton. I wore myself out on a musical comedy there for which I wrote book and lyrics, organized and mostly directed while the president played football. Result: I slipped way back in my work, got T.B., lost a year in college—and, irony of ironies, because of scholastic slip I wasn't allowed to take the presidency of the Triangle.

From your letter I guess that you are doing exactly the same thing and it just makes my stomach fall out to think of it. Amateur work is fun but the price for it is just simply tremendous. In the end you get "Thank you" and that's all. You give three performances which everybody promptly forgets and somebody has a breakdown—that somebody being the enthusiast.

Please, please, please delegate every bit of the work you can and keep your scholastic head above water. To see a mistake repeated twice in two generations would be just too much to bear. This is the most completely experienced advice I've ever given you. What about that science and the philosophy? You've got to find hours to do them even if you have to find a secret room where you can go and study.

Dearest love always.

Daddy

[*5521 Amestoy Avenue*]
[*Encino, California*]

April 27, 1940

Dearest Scottina:

I am of course delighted about the play. Now that it is over I can admit that I thought it was quite a conception from the beginning and quite an achievement—I just had a moment when I was afraid that you were wearing yourself out over it. Musical comedy is fun—I suppose more "fun" than anything else a literary person can put their talents to and it always has an air of glamor around it.

I was particularly interested in your line about "feeling that you had lost your favorite child." God, haven't I felt that so many times. Often I think writing is a sheer paring away of oneself leaving always something thinner, barer, more meager. However, there's not anything to worry about in your case for another twenty years.

I am glad you are going to Princeton with whom you are going. I feel you have now somehow jumped a class. Boys like Kilduff and Lanahan are on a guess more "full of direction" than most of the happy-go-luckies in Cap and Gown. I don't mean more "ambition," which is a sort of general attribute of youth and is five parts hope to five parts good will, but I mean some calculated path stemming from a talent or money or a careful directive or all of these things, to find your way through the bourgeois maze—if you feel it is worth finding. Remember this, though, among those on both sides of the fence there are a lot of slow developers, people of quality and distinction whom you should not overlook. Particularly you will find them among those of difficult exteriors like Eleanor Turnbull or of a great pervading shyness or personal ugliness, etc. I certainly had to dig under a bushel of spoiled blackberries to find _____ _____ at Princeton and often the same in later life. Needless to say I've made bad mistakes—one of them was _____ _____.

I was going to speak to you about the summer plans—without anything special to contribute. Could you let me know more specifically about the New England idea? Who would you be with? What girls? I know you could make up a lot of names but please tell me pretty specifically what would be the housekeeping set-up? I think I could manage to back something like that. I rather hate to think of you out here unless you were going right out for money by displaying your person in celluloid. It is a half-tropical and listless atmosphere.

I am working on this "Babylon Revisited" picture at a rotten salary but it is rather fun and may amount to some-

thing. Your mother seems happy to be home. I don't expect the trouble to begin for at least two months.

                    With dearest love,

                    Daddy

                    [*5521 Amestoy Avenue*]
                    [*Encino, California*]
                    May 4, 1940

Dearest Scottina:

Glad you got a break in the New York papers. Bet you
were thrilled. Notice you got the [?] picture into the background to show you were a glamor girl at heart. No kidding, it was a good job. All I hope is you don't flunk out.
You are always welcome in California though. We are
even opening our arms to Chamberlain in case the British
oust him. We need him for Governor because we are afraid
the Asiatics are going to land from Chinese parasols. Never
mind—Santa Barbara will be our Narvik and we'll defend
it to our last producer. And remember, even England still
has Noel Coward.

I actually have a formulating plan for part of your summer—if it pleases you—and I think I'll have the money
to make it good. I'm working hard, guiding by the fever
which now hovers quietly around the 99.2 level, which is
fairly harmless. Tell Frances Kilpatrick that though I
never met her father he is still one of my heroes in spite of
the fact that he robbed Princeton of a football champion-
ship singlehanded—he was probably the greatest end who
ever played football. In the future please send me clippings
even though you do crack at me in the course of your in-
terviews. I'd rather get them than have you send me accounts of what literary sour bellies write about me in their
books. I've been criticized by experts including myself.

I think I've about finished a swell flicker piece. Did you
read me in the current *Esquire* about Orson Welles? Is it
funny? Tell me. You haven't answered a question for six
letters. Better do so or I'll dock five dollars next week to
show you I'm the same old meany.

Honestly, Pie-crust, I'm tickled about the play. I hope to God your health is good.

Love,

Daddy

P.S. Enclosed 50¢ in stamps to buy the *Esquire* with the Orson Welles piece.

[*5521 Amestoy Avenue*]
[*Encino, California*]
May 7, 1940

Dearest Scottie:

We write to each other without ever answering the other's questions. For once I'll answer one of yours. You asked me whether I thought that in the Arts it was greater to originate a new form or to perfect it. The best answer is the one that Picasso made rather bitterly to Gertrude Stein:

"You do something first and then somebody else comes along and does it pretty."

In the opinion of any real artist the inventor, which is to say Giotto or Leonardo, is infinitely superior to the finished Tintoretto, and the original D. H. Lawrence is infinitely greater than the Steinbecks.

Last thought about your review. You will be interviewed again and once more I ask you please do not discuss your mother or myself even faintly with them. You once made the astounding statement that you were immediately going to write our biographies. I'll always agree with myself that I would never write anything about my own father and mother till they had been at least ten years dead, and since I am forty-three and may still have a lot to say for myself I think you'd be somewhat premature. I realize that you are now fully mature and would realize the unwisdom of talking about family affairs consciously—but sometimes these newspaper people twist things out of you.

My movie progresses and I think it's going to be damn good. If your summer plans mature in any way keep me in the know. I send you a bonus of five dollars, not for any reason but simply because a letter without a check will probably seem to you half-filled. If you have no need for it just add it to your bank account.

> Dearest love.
>
> Mad Fitz (once the Scourge of the San Fernando)
>
> (Daddy)

> [5521 Amestoy Avenue]
> [Encino, California]
> May 11, 1940

Dearest Scottina:

Unfortunately the stub of the money order was just *the one* of many that Frances happened to have misplaced (she has all the others). I've threatened her and great tears are oozing out of her eyes as she takes this dictation. However, even if it hadn't been lost it would have been impossible to do much about a signed money order, especially from this end. I hope you went into the Vassar post office branches and identified yourself and put the clerks on watch. So don't let it worry you. I lose ten dollars which is all in a day's work and you lose the five which I was giving you as a bonus. A little later I'm going to ask you to send me a summary of your bills—not that I'll be able to pay them all immediately but I'd like to know how you stand at the term's end. Please try to address me c/o Phil Berg Agency, Wilshire Boulevard, Beverly Hills. This isn't so hard to remember.

You confused me rather about your summer plans. If you were rooming with Mary Earle does that mean Cape Cod or does it mean at Vassar under Miss Hallie Flannigan? If it means Cape Cod I know some particularly interesting people up there—not at all the kind that are called "old friends" whom you automatically are prejudiced against but some people who might open many rather camouflaged gates to you—some that your contemporaries don't know about. I'm signing up for an apartment in the middle of Hollywood where there is a spare room for any

wandering daughter, though if you come out here it should
be for a reason as it is a dreary town for anyone with
nothing to do.

I'm glad you didn't start going to Princeton at sixteen
or you'd be pretty jaded by this time. Yale is a good year
ahead of Princeton in sophistication, though, it should be
good for another year. Though I loved Princeton I often
felt that it was a by-water, that its snobby institutions were
easy to beat and to despise and unless I was a natural
steeplechaser or a society groom I'd have to find my own
private intellectual and emotional life. Given that premise
it is a lovely quiet place, gentle and dignified, and it will
let you alone. Of course, it is at its absolute worst in the
Jane Hall atmosphere you described. Sometime go down
with a boy on one of those weekends when there's almost
nothing to do.

You've had a good year, haven't you—the fruition of a
great deal that went before. I'd love to see you and just
talk a blue streak with you for about two days about plans if
we could afford it financially which we can't. But who can
tell, maybe by late June or July we can. Please arrange to see
your mother at the earliest possible time because I think
those are going to be restless days for her. You don't
necessarily have to meet her in Montgomery. Perhaps you
could meet somewhere else halfway. If there could be
some arrangement where she wouldn't be entirely left out
and you wouldn't be away with some boy at all hours.

Dearest love.

Daddy

[5521 Amestoy Avenue]
[Encino, California]
May 18, 1940

Dearest Scottie:

No word from you this week. I do want to hear all about
your plans. Can you see your mother before you go to
Baltimore? You say you want eight days. If you're planning a sylvan idyll or doing anything rash like throwing

away your honeymoon in advance—well, I can't do anything about it except advise you that women from Aphrodite to Kitty Foyle have tried it impulsively and found that they threw away their lifetime with their honeymoon. I know it's none of my business any more and I hope to God that I'm speaking out of turn. But you seemed so particularly fervent about it.

Isn't it funny how different things are after only six months. For example, wasn't your suggestion to the *Miscellany* board people about changing their paper rather like suggesting to the local church that it would be more fun if it were a burlesque house? And didn't they take it about the same way, only more drily? I mean, you seem much wiser month by month and I don't think you would have gone about it quite that way now. You would have made the paper first, posing as being in complete agreement and *then* throwing your bomb. Did you see in *Time* that the editor of the *Yale News* and nine other boys threw Bones this spring and aren't you glad now that Vassar hasn't a formal social system? . . . .[1]

> 1403 Laurel Avenue
> Hollywood, California
> (new address)
> June 7, 1940

Dearest Scottie:

Thank you for your letter. Planning from week to week, I am not quite sure yet about anything, but go ahead about the summer school, make reservations and so forth. I think it can be managed all right. I went to San Francisco with some friends for one day, and found it much too long to see that singularly second-rate and uninspired Fair— though they had some good Cranachs and El Grecos in the art exhibition.

Vassar's only fault to the outer world is the "Vassar manner"—which of course is founded on the sense of intellectual intensity that you memtion. I found it particularly

[1] The rest of the letter is missing.

annoying in _____ _____'s daughter in Tryon some years
ago. She told me all about American literature in the first
half hour I met her—I believe she had been editor-in-chief
of the *Miscellany* the year before. Of course it does not
usually show itself like that, but, like the Harvard manner
of 1900 which gave Harvard a country-wide unpopularity,
makes itself known in a series of smug silences. Southern
manners *are* better—especially the rather punctilious defer-
ence to older people. The chances are that some toothless
old codger who doesn't open his mouth may turn out to be
the greatest authority in the world on some recondite subject, and you feel rather a fool when you have judged him
and settled his hash with the glossy learning of a year or
so. So be careful of it, especially this summer when you
will meet many idiots, some in hysterical panic about the
war and others too dumb to know what is going on.

You credit me with a gift of prophecy I don't have. I *did*
feel the war was coming in '39 and said so to a lot of
people, but it was calculated by the time when Germany
would have several new replacement classes to make up for
the decreased birth-rate from 1915 to 1918. We all knew
the German army wasn't beaten and Woodrow Wilson
didn't want it to be beaten, not appreciating the utter helpless decadence of the English—something that has been
apparent to even English intellectuals for twenty years.
The intellectuals, those few who ever dabbled in military
affairs, knew that the war was lost at Munich and that the
Germans would tear the Allies to pieces, in Europe at least.
And the American rich will try to betray America in exactly
the same way as the British conservatives. A pogrom could
be organized overnight against all the "subversive elements"
(whose power is tremendously overestimated at the moment) but the rich will have to have the pants scared off
them before they stop skulking in their tents and begin to
get their boys safe jobs in the quarter-master department.

The Comrades out here are in a gloomy spot; _____
_____ goes around groaning how "the Revolution will have
to come the hard way," in other words the party line is to
let National Socialism (Nazism) conquer us and then somehow milk Marxism out of Hitler's sterile teats! Stalin has
pulled another boner just as he did in Finland. He had no
intention of letting Hitler go this far.

With the situation changing as fast as it does now, it is

difficult for Liberals to have a policy. The war may lead
to anything from utter chaos to a non-Comintern American Revolution, but the world that I knew and that you
have had eighteen years of will never exist again in our
time. On the other hand I do not think it possible for the
Germans to win the South American war against us. The
native Yankee is still the most savage and intelligent
fighter in the world. He plays the toughest, hardest games
with a cooler head and it is simply unthinkable that an oppressed stock could be whooped up in one decade to conquer him. Still I think many of your friends will probably
draw their last breaths in Paraguay or the forests of the
Chaco. Did you see that Lehman has called for anti-aircraft
defense for New York? What a cowardly panic! Next we
will have Louis B. Mayer calling for anti-aircraft guns to
defend Metro.

This letter has turned into gossip, and I have much to
do. I finished the picture and am doing a short story. Had
intended to rest for a week, but there wasn't a chance. Dear,
I have had a very depressed letter from your mother and
another from your grandmother—the second told me in
cautious language that your mother had had a "toxic
attack." I know what this means, only I expected her to
hold out at least two months. She seems to be recovered
from that, but her own letter shows a great deal of despair,
and your grandmother's has a defeatism that I have never
seen before. I don't know what is going to happen, but as
this may be the last time you have a chance to see your
mother in a sane period, *I want you to find ten days to
spend with her this June.* This may bust hell out of your
plans, but remember that for ten months you have lived for
yourself and you owe this to me. I don't care when you go,
except it is to be before summer school opens, and not just
three or four days.

The *Harper's* business is all right for me if you can fit it
in with everything else. Will you tell me what you are going to take at summer school? I think I wrote you that I
thought your next year's Vassar course is fine, except for
the Greek Civilization and Literature, which seems to me
a profound waste of time. Your other three courses are so
completely cultural that I wish that the fourth could be as
practical a one as Vassar offers—I wish they had business
school—or else a supplementary French course or another

language. Greek Civilization and Literature is something you cannot learn in nine months, and it seems to me a rather dilettantish way of wasting time.

I expect to hear in a day or so whether I am going back to work on my picture story—I told you once it was an old *Saturday Evening Post* story called "Babylon Revisited" that I wrote in 1931. You were one of the principal characters.

With dearest love,

Daddy

*1403 North Laurel Avenue
Hollywood, California*

June 12, 1940

Dearest Scottina:

Thanks for your nice full letter—it made me happy, and I don't doubt your sincerity about work. I think now you will always be a worker, and I'm glad. Your mother's utterly endless mulling and brooding over insolubles paved the way to her ruin. She had no education—not from lack of opportunity because she could have learned with me— but from some inner stubbornness. She was a great original in her way, with perhaps a more intense flame at its highest than I ever had, but she tried and is still trying to solve all ethical and moral problems on her own, without benefit of the thousands dead. Also she had nothing "kinetic," which, in physics, means internal driving force—she had to be led or driven. That was the tired element that all Judge Sayre's children inherited. And the old mother is still, at times, a ball of fire!

I could agree with you as opposed to Dean Thompson if you were getting "B's." Then I would say: As you're not going to be a teacher or a professional scholar, don't try for "A's"—don't take the things in which you can get "A," for you can learn them yourself. Try something hard and new, and try it hard, and take what marks you get. But you have no such margin of respectability, and this borderline business is a fret to you. Doubt and worry—you are as crippled by them as I am by my inability to handle money or my self-indulgences of the past. It is your Achilles' heel —and no Achilles' heel ever toughened by itself. It just gets more and more vulnerable. What little I've accomplished has been by the most laborious and uphill work, and I wish now I'd *never* relaxed or looked back—but said at the end of *The Great Gatsby:* "I've found my line—from now on this comes first. This is my immediate duty—without this I am nothing." . . . .

Please wire me what days you have chosen to go South so I can make financial arrangements.

Can't you tell some story down there that it's urgently necessary to go to summer school because you've been on the edge of flunking out? Otherwise they'll wonder why the money couldn't be spent for a seaside vacation for you all. I'm living in the smallest apartment here that will permit me not to *look poor,* which I can't afford to do in Hollywood. If the picture goes through, I will give your mother a trip in August. At the moment I am keeping her on a slender allowance, as for ten years she has absorbed the major proportion of the family income.

I *did* listen to the radio all through my trip. Jesus! What a battle!

Please at least *go in to see Gerald Murphy at Mark Cross for five minutes in passing thru N.Y. this summer!*

Send me the details about Harvard Summer School. Can I pay in installments?

Even as a construction man, Pinero was inferior to both Shaw and Ibsen. What purpose is served in teaching that second-rate Noel Coward at Vassar?

The *New Yorker* story might hamper you if you attach too much importance to it. The play *was* an accomplishment—I admit it with pride and pleasure. I'd like to see the story. *Can't you send me a copy?*

Reading over *your* letter, you don't sound like an introvert at all. You sound a litle flushed and overconfident, but I'm not worried.

With dearest love,

Daddy

P.S. You want to go to summer school. I will have to do extra work for that, and I'll do it gladly. But I want you to spend ten days with your mother first. And *please* give me a *full* complete report on your mother's condition. Your request for $15.00 just came as I was putting this in an envelope. To get it to you (Frances is away) cost me my morning. You must not ask me to wire you money—it is much harder to get than last summer. I owe *thousands*. I couldn't have had this trip except that the Rogers were going and invited me. Sorry to close the letter this way but you must count your pennies.

> 1403 North Laurel Avenue
> Hollywood, California
> June 15, 1940

Dearest Scottie:

Here is your round trip fare to Montgomery. I'm sorry it can't be more but, while my picture *is* going to be done, the producer is going to *first* do one that has been made for the brave _____ _____ who will defend his country in Hollywood (though summoned back by the British government). This affects the patriotic and unselfish Scott Fitzgerald to the extent that I receive no more money from that source until the company gets around to it; so will return to my old standby *Esquire*.

Meanwhile I have another plan which may yield a bonanza but will take a week to develop, so there's nothing to do for a week except try to cheer up your mother and derive what consolation you can in explaining the Spenglerian hypotheses to Miss _____ and her fellow feebs of the Confederacy. Maybe you can write something down there. It is a grotesquely pictorial country as I found out long ago, and as Mr. Faulkner has since abundantly demonstrated.

Anyhow they need you. I will dig you out in time for the summer school.

> Love,
>
> Daddy

P.S. As I said, I am trying to give you $30.00 a week this

summer, and when there is a lot of traveling to be done will increase this somewhat. For instance, I gave you $20.00 extra to get out of Vassar and there is $10.00 extra in this check which makes $30.00 and which will cover a good deal of transportation to date (including the round trip fare to Montgomery). Will send the next check there.

1403 North Laurel Avenue
Hollywood, California
June 20, 1940

Dearest Zelda and Scottie:

I wish I were with you this afternoon. At the moment I am sitting rather dismally contemplating the loss of a three-year-old Ford and a thirty-three-year-old tooth. The Ford (heavily mortgaged) I shall probably get back according to the police because it is just a childish prank of the California boys to steal them and then abandon them. But the tooth I had grown to love.

In recompense I found in *Colliers* a story by myself. I started it just before I broke my shoulder in 1936 and wrote it in intervals over the next couple of years. It seemed terrible to me. That I will ever be able to recover the art of the popular short story is doubtful. At present I'm doing a masterpiece for *Esquire* and waiting to see if my producer can sell the "Babylon Revisited" screenplay to Shirley Temple. If this happens, everything will look very much brighter.

Scottie, I got the marks and was naturally pleased you were off probation at last. It brought back memories of phoning you from Los Angeles to see if you were at the Harvard game, of the dean's gloomy picture a year ago last October, of years of distress about your work with threats and prayers and urgings and rewards and apologies and promises and then suddenly the first change about a year ago when you found that Vassar didn't care whether you studied or not—or whether you stayed in or not. It is a story of hair-breadth escapes, and extraordinary devices going back to the French schedule that we had at "La

Paix." All sorts of people have been drawn into it. Hours, days and weeks have been consumed. Stories, scripts, trips have been put aside—all to achieve what might have been prevented if I had carried out my first plan—never to let you go near an American school, or else I should have let you become a doll. I couldn't leave you hanging—

The police have just called up telling me they've recovered my car. The thief ran out of gas and abandoned it in the middle of Hollywood Boulevard. The poor lad was evidently afraid to call anybody to help him push it to the curb. I hope next time he gets a nice, big, producer's car with plenty of gas in it and a loaded revolver in each side pocket and he can embark on a career of crime in earnest. I don't like to see any education left hanging in the air.

Enclosed find four checks, two of which (including one of yours, Scottie) should go to Mrs. Sayre for provisions, etc. By Monday I should be able to make some plans for you, Scottie. Meanwhile you will have written whether you would like to go to Harvard alone which I do not think should frighten you. You have those two Vassar credits to make up if you are going to get an A.B. degree and I presume this would do it.

From the larger attitude one doesn't know from day to day what the situation will be. We may be at war one week after the extinction of the British, an event which at present writing seems scarcely a fortnight away. It will probably mean our almost immediate embroilment both in Northern Canada and Brazil and at least a partial conscription. Scottie, you've been as lucky as anybody could be in your generation to have had a two months' look at Europe just before the end and to have gotten in two years of college in times of peace before such matters are drowned in the roar of the Stuka bombers. And you have seen the men's colleges as they may not be again in our time, with the games and proms. Maybe I'm speaking too quickly— if the British hold out two months until we can get aid to them—but it looks to me as if our task will be to survive.

Even so I would rather you didn't get tied up in any war work except of a temporary nature for the present. I want you to finish your education. If you have any plan for this summer that displaces summer school and is actually constructive please tell me immediately but I know you want to do something.

My thoughts are not so black as this letter sounds—for instance I'm now going to break off and hear the Louis and Godoy fight which will prove Black Supremacy or Red Indian Supremacy or South American Inca Supremacy or something. I hope you are swimming a lot. I can't exercise even a little any more; I'm best off in my room. But I love to think of you two diving from great heights and being very trim and graceful in the water.

> With dearest love to all,
>
> Scott
> [Daddy

> 1403 North Laurel Avenue
> Hollywood, California
> June 29, 1940

Dearest Scottie:

There's no time to write you a long letter or to answer yours. Only about the summer school:

It seems important that either you take what will tend to give you a definite credit at Vassar or else have a practical tinge. You mentioned economics—I don't know what kind of economics are taught there but the whole science is in such process of dissolution with new laws being built up overnight that if you take it be sure and get a smart man—I mean a brilliant man and preferably a young one. I know a month is a very short time or there are several suggestions I might make. Not being on the spot I can't advise you but only say that I hope it won't be any form of intellectual needlework.

As soon as you get a minute, write me your circumstances there.

> With dearest love,
>
> Daddy

1403 North Laurel Avenue
Hollywood, California

July 12, 1940

Dearest Scottie:

Jib is not spelt gyb. And beyond everything you have sinned in omission by not giving me the correct financial data and I expect an apology. Literally I had $12.00 in the bank for most of that week and it was very unpleasant.

Max Perkins writes me that Jane and three classmates are coming here and want to see something of the movies. I don't know who to introduce them to except Shirley Temple with whom I spent the day yesterday. (Her mother was there so it was all right.) She really is a sweet little girl and reminds me of you at 11½ when you hadn't succumbed to the wiles of Fred Astaire, lovey dovey and the radio crooners. But I told her mother it wouldn't be long now. I don't know whether she's going to do my picture or not.

Haven't you got a carbon of the *New Yorker* article? I've heard that John Mason Brown is a great favorite as a lecturer and I think it's very modern to be taking dramatic criticism though it reminds me vaguely of the school for Roxy ushers. It seems a trifle detached from drama itself. I suppose the thing's to get *really* removed from the subject, and the final removal would be a school for teaching critics of teachers of dramatic criticism.

Isn't the world a lousy place?—I've just finished a copy of *Life* and I'm dashing around to a Boris Karloff movie to cheer up. It is an inspirational thing called *The Corpse in the Breakfast Food*.

Once I thought that Lake Forest was the most glamorous place in the world. Maybe it was.

With dearest love,

Daddy

[*1403 North Laurel Avenue*]
[*Hollywood, California*]
July 18, 1940

Dearest Scottie:

This summer has shown among other things that your education to date is entirely theoretical. I have no general quarrel with this and I believe it is as it should be in preparing for any sort of literary work. However the odds are against your having the type of talent that matures very quickly—most of my contemporaries did not get started at twenty-two, but usually at about twenty-seven to thirty or even later, filling in the interval with anything from journalism [or] teaching [to] sailing a tramp-schooner and going to wars. The talent that matures early is usually of the poetic [type], which mine was in large part. The prose talent depends on other factors—assimilation of material and careful selection of it, or more bluntly: having something to say and an interesting, highly developed way of saying it.

Looking at the problem from short range only, you see how difficult it was to get a job this summer. So let's see what Vassar's got. The first thing that occurs to me is Spanish, which is simply bound to be of enormous value in the next ten years. Every junior-high-school child in California gets a taste of it and could beat you out of a job in South America if we expand that way. It is enough like French so that you have few alphabetical troubles, is pronounced as written, and has a fairly interesting literature of its own. I mean it's not like studying Bulgarian or Chippewa or some strange dialect in which no one had ever had anything to say. Don't you think this would be a much wiser move than the Greek and Latin culture?—the which shocks me that Vassar has such a namby-pamby "course."

I wonder if you've read anything this summer—I mean any one good book like *The Brothers Karamazov* or *Ten Days That Shook the World* or Renan's *Life of Christ*. You never speak of your reading except the excerpts you do in college, the little short bits that they must perforce give you. I know you have read a few of the books I gave you last summer—then I have heard nothing from you on the subject. Have you ever, for example, read *Pere Goriot* or *Crime and Punishment* or even *The Doll's House* or *St.*

Matthew or *Sons and Lovers?* A good style simply doesn't form unless you absorb half a dozen top-flight authors every year. Or rather it *forms* but, instead of being a subconscious amalgam of all that you have admired, it is simply a reflection of the last writer you have read, a watered-down journalese.

Don't be too hard on Princeton. Harvard produced John Reed but they also produced Richard Whitney who I like to believe would have been spotted as a punk at Princeton. The Honor System sometimes has a salutary effect on light-fingered gentry.

With dearest love,

Daddy

[1403 North Laurel Avenue]
[Hollywood, California]
July 29, 1940[1]

I am still on the Temple picture and will continue on if a very avaricious gent named _____ will loosen up. If he doesn't, I will rest for a week, and can stand it as my cough has become a public nuisance.

I wonder who was the ex-Westover woman you met. I wasn't responsible for Ginevra getting fired but that's the way of a legend—it was some Yale boys.

This job has given me part of the money for your tuition and it's come so hard that I hate to see you spend it on a course like "English Prose since 1800." Anybody that can't read modern English prose by themselves is subnormal—and you know it. The chief fault in your style is its lack of distinction—something which is inclined to grow with the years. You had distinction once—there's some in your diary—and the only way to increase it is to cultivate *your own garden.* And the only thing that will help you is poetry which is the most concentrated form of style.

Example: You read *Melanctha* which is practically

[1] The first part of this letter is missing.

poetry and sold a *New Yorker* story—you read ordinary novels and sink back to a Kitty-Foyle-diary level of average performance. The only sensible course for you at this moment is the one on English Poetry—Blake to Keats (English 241). I don't care how clever the other professor is, one can't raise a discussion of modern prose to anything above tea-table level. I'll tell you everything she knows about it in three hours and guarantee that what *each* of us tells you will be largely wrong, for it will be almost entirely conditioned by our responses to the subject matter. It is a course for clubwomen who want to continue on from *Rebecca* and Scarlett O'Hara.

Strange Interlude is good. It was good the first time, when Shaw wrote it and called it *Candida.* On the other hand, you don't pass an hour of your present life that isn't directly influenced by the devastating blast of light and air that came with Ibsen's *Doll's House.* Nora wasn't the only one who walked out of the Doll's House—all the women in Gene O'Neill walked out too. Only they wore fancier clothes.

Well, the old master wearies—the above is really good advice, Pie, in a line where I know my stuff. Unless you can break down your prose a little it'll stay on the ill-paid journalistic level. And you can do better.

Love,

Daddy

P.S. Understand me, I think the poetry courses you took in school (and I read the booklets) were utterly sissified drool. But a real grasp of Blake, Keats, etc., will bring you something you haven't dreamed of. And it should come now.

1403 North Laurel Avenue
Hollywood, California
August 3, 1940

Dear Scottie:

Jane Perkins passed through and happened to mention that she had taken that Blake-to-Keats course—I became less enthusiastic about it because she said they studied Amy Lowell's biography which is a saccharine job compared to Colvin's. However, in the catalogue I see a course called #217 in verse writing. It says, "limited to twelve members—permission required" and it gives only one point. Is that at all practical? I imagine there would be some latitude in the poets that you would read. There is also that Shakespeare course (165) and one in French Poetry (240), one point. Some of the history and philosophical courses look good to me but—oh, hell I can't advise you from this distance. I'm just sorry you can't read some poetry.

It isn't something easy to get started on by yourself. You need, at the beginning, some enthusiast who also knows his way around—John Peale Bishop performed that office for me at Princeton. I had always dabbled in "verse" but he made me see, in the course of a couple of months, the difference between poetry and non-poetry. After that one of my first discoveries was that some of the professors who were teaching poetry really hated it and didn't know what it was about. I got in a series of endless scraps with them so that finally I dropped English altogether.

Poetry is either something that lives like fire inside you —like music to the musician or Marxism to the Communist —or else it is nothing, an empty, formalized bore around which pedants can endlessly drone their notes and explanations. "The Grecian Urn" is unbearably beautiful with every syllable as inevitable as the notes in Beethoven's Ninth Symphony or it's just something you don't understand. It is what it is because an extraordinary genius paused at that point in history and touched it. I suppose I've read it a hundred times. About the tenth time I began to know what it was about, and caught the chime in it and the exquisite inner mechanics. Likewise with "The Nightingale" which I can never read through without tears in my eyes; likewise the "Pot of Basil" with its great stanzas about the two brothers, "Why were they proud, etc."; and "The Eve of St. Agnes," which has the richest, most sensuous imagery in English, not excepting Shakespeare. And finally his three or four great sonnets, "Bright Star" and the others.

Knowing those things very young and granted an ear, one could scarcely ever afterwards be unable to distinguish between gold and dross in what one read. In themselves those eight poems are a scale of workmanship for anybody who wants to know truly about words, their most utter value for evocation, persuasion or charm. For awhile after you quit Keats all other poetry seems to be only whistling or humming.

You still have that French typewriter in storage, haven't you? Would it be any good? We rent one here and it costs only $5.00 for three months. You threaten to send *me* money! If you have any extra, pay your bills in Poughkeepsie. My suggestion is that after you visit Miss Doyle, you go to Lake Forest and from there go South to Montgomery. I'm afraid the latter seems to be necessary. Your mother most particularly asked to see you again and the only alternative would be to send her North to see you, which means sending *two* people. I know it will be dull going into that hot little town early in September—but you are helping me. Even invalids like your mother have to have mileposts—things to look forward to and back upon. It gives her more pride there in Montgomery if you come to see her, something to talk about. Only think how empty her life is and you will see the importance of your going there. Will you figure out what the fare to Chicago will be?

You wrote me such a full letter that I haven't answered it all even now. When we get some breathing space here I'll have Frances figure how much you cost this year.

Dearest love.

Daddy

P.S. Be careful about showing my letters—I mean to your mother for instance. I write you very freely.

1403 North Laurel Avenue
Hollywood, California

August 12, 1940

Dearest Scottina:

I'm sorry I didn't mention the story—I'm *glad* you sold it but I thought you were disappointed that you didn't sell it to a big magazine. I suggested disposing of it to some Vassar paper—do you remember?—just for the sake of getting into print and getting some opinions on it. I'm glad you got some money too. I thought of it as a sort of practice composition but I felt a personal interest in it, not having forgotten the nights we worked over it.

I saw your picture in *Harper's Bazaar* and I'm glad you got the job. Working among the poor has differing effects on people. If you're poor yourself you get their psychology and it's broadening—for example, when a boy of the bourgeoise ships before the mast on a tramp-schooner where he has to endure the same privations as the seaman, undoubtedly he achieves something of their point of view forever. On the contrary, a Bennington girl spending a month in slum work and passing weekends at her father's mansion in Long Island gets nothing at all except a smug feeling that she is Lady Bountiful.

I was interested in your Cape Cod conquest. Theoretically a girl has her widest range of choice from about 19 years, 6 months, to 20 years, 6 months—or so I figure. The 18-year-old girl *seems* to have, because she has a stag line after her, but actually she has probably collected less *eligibles* than a slightly older girl. Of course, with the war there may be a tendency among your generation to rush into things. There were lots of quick marriages in 1918. Most of the men came back—but there are a few "class boys" from my class at Princeton who never saw their fathers.

Enclosed is a Vassar paper about the Spanish. Do remember that, with a new language, the first week *when you learn the structure* is the important time. I believe that if you study Spanish hard for a fortnight, even at the expense of everything else, you can coast along on it pretty easily the rest of the year, but if you don't get the verb forms right and the declensions it will start getting mountainously hard inside of a month and will become your cross. I discovered this in Italian at Princeton—neglecting it and then trying to catch up too late. Result: I flunked it hopelessly and never did learn it. However, I'm glad you're taking a chance.

With dearest love, always,

Daddy

1403 North Laurel Avenue
Hollywood, California

August 24, 1940

Dearest Scottina:

I can imagine the dinner party. I remember taking Zelda to the young _____'s when we were first married and it was a pretty frozen dish, though in general the places we went to even from the beginning were many flights up from the average business man's *menage*. Business is a dull game and they pay a big price in human values for their money. They are "all right when you get to know them." I liked some of the young Princeton men in business but I couldn't stand the Yale and Harvard equivalents because we didn't even have the common ground of the past. The women are empty twirps mostly, easy to seduce and not good for much else. I am not talking about natural society women like Mary Harriman Rumsey and Sara Murphy and some others who made their lives into pageants, almost like actresses.

However, you seem wise enough to see that there is something in _____'s angle. College gives you a head start, especially a girl, and people are not in any hurry to live and think your way. It's all a question of proportion: if you married an army officer you would live half a lifetime of kow-towing to your inferiors until your husband made his way to the top. If, as the chances are, you marry a business man—because for the present business absorbs most of the energetic and attractive boys—you will have to play your cards properly in the business hierarchy. That was why I have always hoped that life would throw you among lawyers or men who were going into politics or big-time journalism. They lead rather larger lives.

Advertising is a racket, like the movies and the brokerage business. You cannot be honest without admitting that its constructive contribution to humanity is exactly minus zero. It is simply a means of making dubious promises to a credulous public. (But if you showed this letter to _____ it would be the end of everything in short order, for a man must have his pride and the *more* he realizes such a situation the *less* he can afford to admit it.) If I had been promoted when I was an advertising man, given enough money to marry your mother in 1920, my life might have been altogether different. I'm not sure though. People often struggle through to what they are in spite of any detours—and possibly I might have been a writer sooner or later anyhow.

You haven't given me much idea of _____. Would he object to your working—outside the house I mean? Excluding personal charm, which I assume, and the more conventional virtues which go with success in business, is he his own man? Has he any force of character? Or imagination and generosity? Does he read books? Has he any leaning toward the arts and sciences or anything beyond creature comfort and duck-shooting? In short, has he the possibilities of growth that would make a lifetime with him seem attractive? These things don't appear later—they are either there latently or they will never be there at all.

I'm *not* asking these questions to be answered, but only to suggest again that if he is a fairly standardized article, you will find plenty of them during the next year—more than you ever met before—and eighteen is still young to commit yourself.

I think I have a job with 20th Century, which may be a long one. I will know Monday. I'm deducing that you received some money from *Harper's* because you give me no idea of the state of your finances. Anyhow I'm enclosing $15.00. When you get this letter please night letter me how much it will cost to get to Montgomery. I would suggest that you go as follows: take the evening boat from New York to Norfolk, spending a day or night with Ceci, and then go from there to Montgomery or to Atlanta as you like. Certainly before you see all those walking neuroses you can spend a day with the Taylors who have always liked you so much. The trip to Norfolk by boat from New York is really damn nice. You come into Chesapeake Bay and Hampton Roads from a different angle—almost like an ocean voyage and the ship is larger and nicer than the little ferry boats from Baltimore. Also the price is reasonable—less than railroad.

Dear, even in joking I don't like to use the expression "nervous breakdown" about any emotional struggle you may have to pass through in the next couple of years. Is your generation so soft that they talk of going to pieces if life doesn't always present itself in terms of beautiful, easy decisions? Most girls of your generation and your mother's and your grandmother's have had to decide difficult things at your age and it is silly to think that it is any strain peculiar to yourself. The young men are just as bad—some of them talk about having nervous breakdowns if they are conscripted. But *you* didn't cut your milk teeth on an aspirin tablet and I hate that raspberry sundae diction. Face what you've got to face and keep your chin where it belongs.

> With dearest love, always,
>
> Daddy

P.S. In your telegram please say also *if* you are going to Norfolk, and *when*.

> *1403 North Laurel Avenue*
> *Hollywood, California*
> *September 5, 1940*

Dearest Scottie:

I'm going into a huddle on this script and probably won't be able to write you again at length before Vassar starts. I read the story in *College Bazaar* and was very pleased with it. You've put in some excellent new touches and its only fault is the jerkiness that goes with a story that has often been revised. Stories are best written in either one jump or three, according to the length. The three-jump story should be done on three successive days, then a day or so for revise and off she goes. This of course is the ideal—in many stories one strikes a snag that must be hacked at but, on the whole, stories that drag along or are terribly difficult (I mean a difficulty that comes from a poor conception and consequent faulty construction) never flow quite as well in the reading. However, I'm glad you published this one. It was nice to see your name.

About names, I don't know what to do. You calling yourself Frances Scott Fitzgerald does push me a little into the background. It calls attention to my being of my generation, which is not too good since I hope to have a big book out in a year. That is my only objection. There are three Van Dorens who write and people have long ago given up telling which is Rita, which is Mark, and which is Carl. I'm afraid that Frances Scott Fitzgerald is likely to lead to a certain confusion. What do you think?

You never told me why you stayed in New York so long—I rather gather somebody was married, possibly my Favorite Glamorist. All girls from 18 to 19 take the marriage of a friend as a heavy body blow but don't let it worry you, kid. Remember your old book, "Men Are Like Street Cars." Anyhow panic about such things is completely endemic to your age and has no basis in reality. God willing, you will have at least fifteen more years of being highly attractive to attractive men. And all this because you've never shaved your legs, plucked your eyebrows or criticized your father! . . . .

A last thought about other people's weddings—you don't have to be *right* about your objectives at the moment —only about your ways and means, learning Spanish, for instance, getting to know poetry. Honestly the ends will take care of themselves.

> With dearest love,
>
> Daddy

P.S. Also saw your account of a weekend at Yale, Harvard and Princeton. It was very colorful. Things don't seem to have changed much. Have you ever been to Cornell? Aw, tell me the truth, I won't dock your allowance. How much does *College Bazaar* pay you? If you remember, will you write me the name of a picture-frame store at Vassar and I'll have those Princeton etchings of Don Swann's framed for you before college starts.

> [*1403 North Laurel Avenue*]
> [*Hollywood, California*]
> *September 17, 1940*

Dearest Scottina:

I hope they won't gun for you at college this year but from the tenor of the letter they sent about your work

improving, I gather that they will. There was just a hint in
it. You must try to realize their point of view and compromise with it. They feel they give you a lot and don't
want you to use the place as simply a proving ground for
individual egotisms—

—which, of course, is what you and I would like it to
be. I went back to junior year with Princeton in my pocket
and it took them four months to take it all away from me
—stripped of every office and on probation—the phrase
was "ineligible for extra-curricular activities." I was in the
hospital besides.

Don't let it happen to you. It isn't necessary. *Start well*
with your work—the old "initial impression." But if you took
the whole play on your shoulders, as you threaten, you'll
have to get straight B's to make them think you're doing
any studying—can't you find some bright sophomores to
do the work while you play the executive—bring them
along "to inherit," so to speak? If any one man tried to
do the Triangle he'd have a beautiful breakdown—it's a
complex organization built up over years.

This is really such sensible advice—you've founded the
club, you want to perpetuate it. All right—draw up an organization that will *really* divide the creative work, which
is to say the hard work. For you to write, cast, direct,
ballyhoo and *manage*—and do any work or reading besides is an idiotic program. I know what effort is and I respect it but aren't you verging on the extravagant—you
who pride yourself on your common sense?

When I set out to write a big novel at 21 it was ambitious and difficult—but when your mother started to
catch up with Pavlova at 28 it was fantastic and impossible.
Your trying to juggle this thing without a director or organization, with your *Harper's Bazaar* and your admirers
and the games and parties, would lead to disaster. It doesn't
take any prophet to make that observation—it just takes
the most casual onlooker. No possible triumph is worth the
loss of your health.

I could almost bet that you've done very little work on
the play this summer—that it's uppermost on your mind
now. That is just the beginning of the great confusion in
which you will find yourself if you don't sit down *now*
and decide what you can do and what you *can't*—and find
others to delegate it to. Believe me—they'll let you do all

the work—and heartily admire you—like they did me. They sent flowers too—but not to the footlights, where I expected them—only to the infirmary.

Your affectionate but somewhat concerned

Daddy

P.S. This is an advance on your next week's allowance as I know all your trips leave you penniless.

[1403 North Laurel Avenue]
[Hollywood, California]
October 5, 1940

Dearest Scottie:

Glad you like *Death in Venice*. I don't see any connection between that and *Dorian Gray* except that they both have an implied homosexuality. *Dorian Gray* is little more than a somewhat highly charged fairly tale which stimulates adolescents to intellectual activity at about seventeen (it did the same for you as it did for me). Sometime you will re-read it and see that it is essentially naive. It is in the lower ragged edge of "literature," just as *Gone with the Wind* is in the higher brackets of crowd entertainment. *Death in Venice*, on the other hand, is a work of art, of the school of Flaubert—yet not derivative at all. Wilde had two models for *Dorian Gray:* Balzac's *Le Peau de Chagrin* and Huysman's *A Rebours*.

After which literary lecture I can only sympathize with the practically desolate state of Vassar and assure you that many of those that have left will lament through their lives that they didn't go on. In that connection, by the way, aren't there many transfers from other colleges in junior year? I should think after this past year everything would indeed be anti-climax. You've had almost everything you wanted—in Vassar, in Baltimore, and in general. But it's rather lucky that in life we don't go on repeating. Certainly you should have new objectives now—this of all years ought to be the time of awakening for the nascent mind of yours. Once one is caught up into the material world not one person in ten thousand finds the time to form literary taste, to examine the validity of philosophic concepts for himself, or to form what, for lack of a better phrase, I might call the wise and tragic sense of life.

By this I mean the thing that lies behind all great careers, from Shakespeare's to Abraham Lincoln's, and as far back as there are books to read—the sense that life is essentially a cheat and its conditions are those of defeat, and that the redeeming things are not "happiness and pleasure" but the deeper satisfactions that come out of struggle. Having learned this in theory from the lives and conclusions of great men, you can get a hell of a lot more enjoyment out of whatever bright things come your way.

You speak of how good your generation is, but I think they share with every generation since the Civil War in America the sense of being somehow about to inherit the earth. You've heard me say before that I think the faces of most American women over thirty are relief maps of petulant and bewildered unhappiness.

Well, and fare thee well. You never answer the specific questions in my letters. You tell me about your courses in general, but not in particular. And that was an important question about your literary name—I'm against your using *two* names of mine, like in the *College Bazaar*.

With dearest love,

Daddy

1403 North Laurel Avenue
Hollywood, California

November 2, 1940

Dearest Scottina:

Listening to the Harvard-Princeton game on the radio with the old songs reminds me of the past that I lived a quarter of a century ago and that you are living now. I picture you as there though I don't know whether you are or not.

I remember once a long time ago I had a daughter who used to write me letters but now I don't know where she

is or what she is doing, so I sit here listening to Puccini—
"Someday she'll write *(Pigliano edda ciano)*."

> With dearest love,
>
> Daddy

> 1403 North Laurel Avenue
> Hollywood, California
> November 29, 1940

Dearest Scottie:

I started Tom Wolfe's book on your recommendation.[1]
It seems better than *Time and the River*. He has a fine inclusive mind, can write like a streak, has a great deal of
emotion, though a lot of it is maudlin and inaccurate, but
his awful secret transpires at every crevice—he did not
have anything particular to say! The stuff about the
GREAT VITAL HEART OF AMERICA is just simply
corny.

He recapitulates beautifully a great deal of what Walt
Whitman said and Dostoevski said and Nietzsche said and
Milton said, but he himself, unlike Joyce and T. S. Eliot
and Ernest Hemingway, has nothing really new to add. All
right—it's all a mess and it's too bad about the individual—
so what? Most writers line themselves up along a solid
gold bar like Ernest's courage, or Joseph Conrad's art, or
D. H. Lawrence's intense cohabitations, but Wolfe is too
"smart" for this and I meant smart in its most belittling
and most modern sense. Smart like Fadiman in *The New
Yorker*, smart like the critics whom he so pretends to despise. However, the book doesn't commit the cardinal sin:
it doesn't fail to live. But I'd like you to think sometime
how and in what way you think it is superior to such a
piece of Zolaesque naturalism as Maugham's *Of Human
Bondage*, or if it is superior at all. Did you like the description of Max Perkins as "Foxhall?" I believe Max had mixed
emotions.

I'm taking a day off from my novel to go to the dentist,

[1] *You Can't Go Home Again.*

the doctor, and my agent, to the latter in order to discuss
picture business when and if I go back to it in February.
And I have saved an hour to rush in where angels fear to
tread. I don't know _____ and have had to piece him together from what you have told me and from a letter you
showed me and so forth. But it sounds to me as if he had
a perceptible dash of lavender. I know exactly what you
mean about the Dwight Fiske attitude—sometimes the Harvard manner approaches that deceptively as a pose—but
when a man is tired of life at 21 it indicates that he is
rather tired of something in himself. One thing I'm sure
of. There are plenty of absolutely first-rate men who will
be within your range in the next two years. I remember
that Lois Moran used to worry because all the attractive
men she knew were married. She finally inverted it into
the credo that if a man *wasn't* married and inaccessible,
he wasn't a first-rate man. She gave herself a very bad
time. The sea is still as full as ever of sharks, whales, trout
and tuna. The real handicap for a girl like you would have
been to have worn herself out emotionally at sixteen. I
think we cut that by about two-thirds by keeping you
comparatively busy in those two very crucial years. Life
should be fun for you and there's plenty of time. All I
care for is that you should marry someone who is not too
much a part of the crowd.

Lanahan is wrong about your disposition. You take ad-
versity very well, but you are utterly dependent on sleep.
Your extraordinary performance out here two years ago
was directly attributable to the fact that you hadn't slept
since getting off the boat, if you slept on board of it! It
amounts almost to an idiosyncracy in you and you should
never make important decisions when you are extremely
tired.

                    With dearest love,

                    Daddy

P.S. It's O.K. about the Xmas money but go slow. The
phone rang after I finished this letter and the doctor after
seeing my cardiogram has confined me to the house. So at
this moment I *couldn't* go to the studios if I wanted to. Try
to save your fare to Baltimore and back.

1403 North Laurel Avenue
Hollywood, California
December 7, 1940

Dearest Scottie:

I'm sending the check you asked for next week. Will that be time enough? Also will send railroad fare, etc. I'm still in bed but managing to write and feeling a good deal better. It was a regular heart attack this time and I will simply have to take better care of myself. I've been living two floors up and will probably have to move, though not immediately.

It interests me what you are doing for Peaches. I should certainly think of nothing else but Peaches while you are writing it so it will be absolutely honest. But afterwards I would very much like to see a copy of it. Littauer, the editor of *Colliers*, came through here last week and liked your *New Yorker* piece very much. He might pay you more than almost anyone else. While I'm on the subject, remember that Harold Ober's advice is only good up to a point. He is "the average reader" and about one third of the stories that I sold to *The Saturday Evening Post* were stories which he did not think they would buy. Like all agents, he is clogged with too much of the kind of reading trained to smell the money in the page—so I should never ask his advice on any literary matter, though of course in other regards he is an excellent agent.

My novel is something of a mystery, I hope. I think it's a pretty good rule not to tell what a thing is about until it's finished. If you do you always seem to lose some of it. It never quite belongs to you so much again.

Your Xmas plans seem O.K. to me.

                                        With dearest love,

                                        [Daddy]

[*1403 North Laurel Avenue*]
[*Hollywood, California*]
[*December, 1940*]

Dearest Scottie:

There has reached you by this time, I hope, a little coat. It was an almost never-worn coat of Sheilah's that she wanted to send you. It seemed very nice to me—it may fill out your rather thin wardrobe. Frances Kroll's father is a furrier and he remade it *without charge!*

So you must *at once please* write the following letters:

(1) To Sheilah, not stressing Mr. Kroll's contribution
(2) To Frances, praising the style.
(3) To me (in the course of things) in such a way that I can show the letter to *Sheilah* who will certainly ask me if you liked the coat.

You make things easier for me if you write these letters promptly. A giver gets pleasure in a letter acknowledging a gift three weeks' late even though it crawls with apologies—you will have stolen pleasure from one who has tried to give it to you. (Ecclesiastes Fitzgerald)

Lastly, drum up some story for Alabama that you bought the coat from some girl. Don't say it came through me.

For the rest, I am still in bed—this time the result of twenty-five years of cigarettes. You have got two beautiful bad examples for parents. Just do everything we didn't do and you will be perfectly safe. But be sweet to your mother at Xmas despite her early Chaldean rune-worship which she will undoubtedly inflict on you at Xmas. Her letters are tragically brilliant on all matters except those of central importance. How strange to have failed as a social creature—even criminals do not fail that way—they are the law's "Loyal Opposition," so to speak. But the insane are always mere guests on earth, eternal strangers carrying around broken decalogues that they cannot read.

I am still not through Tom Wolfe's novel and can't finally report it but the story of the fire is magnificent. Only I'm afraid that after the grand character-planting nothing is going to come of it all. The picture of "Amy Carleton" (Emily Davies Vanderbilt who used to come

to our apartment in Paris—do you remember?), with the
cracked grey eyes and the exactly reproduced speech, is
just simply perfect. She tried hard to make Tom—*sans
succès*—and finally ended by her own hand in Montana
in 1934 in a lonely ranch house. The portrait of Mrs. Jack
is grand too. I believe her absolutely.

> With dearest love,
>
> Daddy

P.S. In the name of Somerset Maugham, the *letter!*

[UNDATED FRAGMENTS FROM LETTERS TO SCOTTIE]

All good writing is *swimming under water* and holding
your breath.

The conclusion is: it will not win you either financial in-
dependence or immortality. But you will be wise to publish it, if you can—if for no gain and only in a college
magazine. It will give you a sense of your own literary
existence, and put you in touch with others trying the
same thing. In a literary way I cannot help you beyond
a point. I might say that I don't think anyone can write
succinct prose unless they have at least tried and failed to
write a good iambic pentameter sonnet, and read Browning's short dramatic poems, etc.—but that was my personal approach to prose. Yours may be different, as Ernest
Hemingway's was. But I wouldn't have written this long
letter unless I distinguished, underneath the sing-song lilt
of your narrative, some traces of a true rhythm that is earmarked Scottina. There is as yet no honesty—the reader
will say "so what?" But when in a freak moment you will
want to give the low-down, not the scandal, not the merely
reported but the *profound* essence of what happened at a
prom or after it, perhaps that honesty will come to you—
and then you will understand how it is possible to make
even a forlorn Laplander *feel* the importance of a trip to
Cartier's!

The first thing I ever sold was a piece of verse to *Poet
Lore* when I was twenty.

I shall somehow manage not to appear in a taxi-cab on Thanksgiving and thus disgrace you before all those "nice" girls. Isn't it somewhat old-fashioned to describe girls in expensive backgrounds as "nice?" I will bet two-thirds of the girls at Miss Walker's school have at least one grandparent that peddled old leather in the slums of New York, Chicago or London, and if I thought you were accepting the standards of the cosmopolitan rich, I would much rather have you in a southern school, where scholastic standards are not so high and the word "nice" is not debased to such a ludicrous extent. I have seen the whole racket, and if there is any more disastrous road than that from Park Avenue to the Rue de la Paix and back again, I don't know it.

They are homeless people, ashamed of being American, unable to master the culture of another country; ashamed, usually, of their husbands, wives, grandparents, and unable to bring up descendants of whom they could be proud, even if they had the nerve to bear them, ashamed of each other yet leaning on each other's weakness, a menace to the social order in which they live—oh, why should I go on? You know how I feel about such things. If I come up and find you gone Park Avenue, you will have to explain me away as a Georgia cracker or a Chicago killer. God help Park Avenue.

Madame Curie progresses and it is a relief to be working on something that the censors have nothing against. It will be a comparatively quiet picture—as was *The Barretts of Wimpole Street,* but the more I read about the woman the more I think about her as one of the most admirable people of our time. I hope we can get a little of that into the story.

You must have some politeness toward ideas. You can neither cut through, nor challenge nor beat the fact that there is an organized movement over the world before which you and I as individuals are less than the dust. Sometime when you feel very brave and defiant and haven't been invited to one particular college function, read the terrible chapter in *Das Kapital* on "The Working Day," and see if you are ever quite the same.

So many writers, Conrad for instance, have been aided by being brought up in a métier utterly unrelated to literature. It gives an abundance of material and, more important, an attitude from which to view the world. So much writing nowadays suffers both from lack of an attitude and from sheer lack of any material, save what is accumulated in a purely social life. The world, as a rule, does not live on beaches and in country clubs.

PART TWO

Letters to
Zelda Fitzgerald

[5521 Amestoy Avenue]
[Encino, California]
May 6, 1939

Dearest Zelda:

Excuse this being typewritten, but I am supposed to lie in bed for a week or so and look at the ceiling. I objected somewhat to that regime as being drastic, so I am allowed two hours of work every day.

You were a peach throughout the whole trip and there isn't a minute of it when I don't think of you with all the old tenderness and with a consideration that I never understood that you had before. Because I can never remember anything else but consideration from you, so perhaps that sounds a little too much like a doctor or someone who knew you only when you were ill.

You are the finest, loveliest, tenderest, most beautiful person I have ever known, but even that is an understatement because the length that you went to there at the end would have tried anybody beyond endurance. Everything that I said and that we talked about during that time stands—I had a wire from daughter in regard to the little Vassar girl, telling me her name, and saying that the whole affair was washed out, but I don't feel at home with the business yet.

There was a sweet letter waiting here from you for me when I came.

With dearest love,

[Scott]

[5521 Amestoy Avenue]
[Encino, California]
June 8, 1939

Dearest Zelda:

I have two letters from you, one the airmail in regard to Scottie's operation and the other evidently posted before you had received mine. While she is in Baltimore I am having a re-check by my old friend, Dr. Louis Hamman. I gather that she has had several "attacks." On the other hand, I want to be absolutely sure that the operation is imperative. I tell you this because though she will come to Asheville in any case—I think you'd better not make absolute arrangements until I get the report from Dr. Hamman. She reaches Baltimore today the 8th (unless she stays over a day with Harold Ober or someone else in New York) and I should get the report from Dr. Hamman about the 15th or 16th—that is a few days before she is due to arrive in Asheville. I will airmail you immediately and then you can clinch whatever arrangements you find advisable.

Remember, I will take care of the business of notifying her, breaking the news by airmail as soon as I hear how long she expects to remain in Baltimore. I am glad, just as you are, that, since this seems to be necessary, you will be able to be at her side.

I am awfully sorry about the news concerning your mother. This seems to be a big year for illness in our family. I shall certainly plan for you to go down to see her around your birthday time as soon as the matter of Scottie's visit—with or without operation—is disposed of. Perhaps if by chance Dr. Hamman doesn't think the operation advisable we can think up some combination scheme.

In the meantime I see from your last letter you were still worried about my health. Only last night I saw the doctor who tells me that I am already 60% better (I quote him exactly) than I was a month ago—and during that time I have blocked out a novel, completed and sold a story to *Colliers* magazine and over half-finished what will be a two-parter for *The Saturday Evening Post*—so you see I cannot possibly be very sick. What is the matter with me is quite definite and quite in control—the cause was overwork at the studios, and the cause being removed the illness should decrease at a faster rate than that at which it was contracted.

I am sitting outdoors as I dictate this and the atmosphere has just a breath of the back country plains in it, dry and hot, though the surrounding landscaped gardens are green and cool, very different from Asheville mountains, but I never had your gift for seeing nature plainly and putting her into vivid phrasing so I am afraid I can't explain to you exactly what kind of country it is until you come here and see. Now Hollywood seems far away though it is just over the mountains and you seem very near always.

Devotedly,

[Scott]

[5521 Amestoy Avenue]
[Encino, California]

[August, 1939]

Dearest:

I know you're going to miss Scottie and I hope August passes quickly for you. It seems strange that it's here—this last month has been too much of a hell for me to help much, but now I can see light at the end of the passage. It was like 1935–1936 when no one but Mrs. Owens and I knew how bad things were and all my products were dirges and elegies. Sickness and no money are a wretched combination. But, as I told you, there has *not* at least been an accumulation of debt and there are other blessings. I see that only the rich now can do the things you and I once did in Europe—it is a tourist-class world—my salary out here during those frantic 20 months turned out to be an illusion once Ober and the governments of the U.S. and Canada were paid and the doctors began.

Keep well. I'm going to try to. I'm glad your mother's illness was a false alarm.

Have arranged for Scottie to have a piano nearby, tho not in this cottage. She seems to have had a happy time with you. I have written two long and two short stories and wait daily for Swanson to find me a studio job that won't be too much of a strain—no more 14-hour days at *any* price. By the time you get this I hope I'll be paying the small (not formidable) array of bills that have accumulated. Here is another check to be used most sparingly—not on presents but necessities of Scottie's departure, etc. Her tickets and traveling money will reach there Tuesday morning if all goes well. Her rail fare, round trip, is only $78.50 round trip, with $5.00 extra fare both ways.

Dearest love.

[Scott]

Of course you can count on going South in September. We could even meet you there.
And the editorial comment about your paintings was a real thrill to me. We must do something about that soon.

5521 Amestoy Avenue
Encino, California
August 4, 1939

Dearest:

Scottie arrives tomorrow and I hope she'll enjoy the weeks out here. She doesn't like heat much and of course this is subtropical, but there is a pool nearby belonging to the landlord and as I wrote you there are boys from the East, at least for the present.

Perhaps I was unwise in telling her so succinctly that she had no home except Vassar. On the other hand, she doesn't see the matter in relation to the past. When I tried to make a home for her she didn't want it, and I have a sickman's feeling that she will arrive in a manner to break up such tranquillity as I have managed to establish after this illness. Perhaps she has changed—but this is the first time in many years that you yourself have expressed pleasure in her filial behavior. I too, have had that, though in short doses, ever since the spring of 1934. Perhaps the very shortness of the doses has been the fault and I hope this visit will be a remedy.

In theory I tend to disagree with you about doing her

harm to know where she stands. Scottie at her best is as she is now with a sense of responsibility and determination. She is at her absolute worst when she lies on her back and waves her feet in the air—so incapable of gratitude of things arranged for (the golf at Virginia Beach, for instance, or the moving picture stuff here, has been accepted as her natural right as a princess). I was sorry for the women of fifty who applied for that secretarial job in Baltimore in 1932—who had never before in their lives found that a home can be precarious. But I am not particularly sorry for a youngster who is thrown on his own at 14 or so and has to make his way through school and college, the old sink or swim spirit—I suppose, *au fond,* the difference of attitude between the North and the old South.

Anyhow, we shall think of you and talk of you a lot and look forward to seeing you and wish you were with us. I will have done something by the time you get this about your expense money there.

Dearest love.

[Scott]

5521 Amestoy Avenue
Encino, California
August 18, 1939

Dearest Zelda:

Got your letter from Saluda. Will absolutely try to arrange the Montgomery trip early in September. Your letter made me sad, and I wish I could say "Yes, go where you want right away"—but it doesn't take into consideration the situation here. I will be much better able to grapple with the problem and with Dr. Carroll two weeks from now. A severe illness like mine is liable to be followed by a period of shaky morale and at the moment I am concerned primarily with keeping us all alive and comfortable. I'm working on a picture at Universal and the exact position is that if I can establish their confidence in the next week that I am of value on this job it will relieve financial pressure through the fall and winter.

Scottie is very pleasant and, within the limits of her age, very cooperative to date—on the other hand, she's one more responsibility, as she learns to drive and brings me her work and this summer there is no Helen Hayes to take her on a glamor tour of Hollywood. All of which boils down to the fact that my physical energy is at an absolute minimum without being definitely sick and I've got to conserve this for my work. I am as annoyed at the unreliability of the human body as you are at the vagaries of the nervous system. Please believe always that I am trying to do my best for us all. I have many times wished that my work was of a mechanical sort that could be done or delegated irrespective of morale, for I don't want or expect happiness for myself—only peace enough to keep us all going. But your happiness I want exceedingly, just as I want Scottie's safety.

I am writing Dr. Carroll a long letter in a week's time of which I will send you a carbon. I have already written Dr. Suitt about the swimming.

> With dearest love,
>
> [Scott]

> 5521 Amestoy Avenue
> Encino, California
> October 6, 1939

Dearest Zelda:

Living in the flotsam of the international situation as we all are, work has been difficult. I am almost penniless—I've done stories for *Esquire* because I've had no time for anything else with $100.00 bank balances. You will remember it took me an average of six weeks to get the mood of a *Saturday Evening Post* story.

But everything may be all right tomorrow. As I wrote you—or did I?—friends sent Scottie back to college. That seemed more important than any pleasure for you or me. There is still two hundred dollars owing on her tuition— and I think I will probably manage to find it somewhere. After her, you are my next consideration; I was properly moved by your mother's attempt to send for you—but not enough to go overboard. For you to go on your first excursion *without* a nurse, *without* money, without even enough to pay your fare back, when Dr. Carroll is backing you, and when Scottie and I are almost equally as helpless in the press of circumstances as you—well, it is the ruse of a clever old lady whom I respect and admire and who loves you dearly but not wisely. . . .

I ask only this of you—leave me in peace with my hemorrhages and my hopes, and what eventually will fight through as the *right* to save you, the *permission* to give you a chance.

Your life has been a disappointment, as mine has been too. But we haven't gone through this sweat for nothing. Scottie has got to survive and this is the most important year of her life.

With dearest love always,

[Scott]

5521 Amestoy Avenue
Encino, California
January 31, 1940

Dearest Zelda:

The article arrived and from a first brief glance I shall say that it is going to be rather difficult to sell. However, I will read it thoroughly tonight and report. Even a very intellectual magazine like the *Forum* or the *Atlantic Monthly* prefers their essays to contain some certain number of anecdotes or some dialogue or some cohesive and objective events. Of course, you might claim that your whole article was conversation and in a sense it is, but it is one person's conversation and thus does not contain much conflict. However, I think it is damn good considering that your pen has been rusty for so long. Shall I suggest you some ideas which you might handle with more chance of realizing on them? Tell me.

Dear, I know no one in Asheville except a couple of

secretaries and nurses and the clerks at the hotel. I was ill all the time I was there and confined to my room most of the time so I have no idea how you would make business contacts. This seems to be a great year for art and I wish you would drop a line to Cary Ross or someone about your new paintings and see if there is some interest. That would be a more practical way of gettings things in motion than taking up something you're unfamiliar with.

All is the same here. I think I have a job for next week. I know I've finished a pretty good story—the first one adequate to the *Post* in several years. It was a hard thing to get back to. My God, what a fund of hope and belief I must have had in the old days! As I say, I will write you more about the story tomorrow.

                              Dearest love.

                              [Scott]

                              5521 Amestoy Avenue
                              Encino, California
                              February 6, 1940

Dearest Zelda:

I understand your attitude completely and s mpathize with it to a great extent. But the mood which considers any work beneath their talents doesn't especially appeal to me in other people, though I acknowledge being sometimes guilty of it myself. At the moment I am hoping for a job at Republic Studios, the lowest of the low, which would among other things help to pay your hospital bill. So the fact that anything you do can be applied on your bill instead of on our jaunt to the Isles of Greece doesn't seem so tough.

However, I am disappointed, with you, that the future Ruskins and Elie Faures and other anatomists of art will have to look at your windows instead of the mail hall. But something tells me that by the time this letter comes you will have changed your point of view. It is those people that have kept your talent alive when you willed it to sink into the dark abyss. Granted it's a delicate thing—mine is so scarred and buffeted that I am amazed that at times is still runs clear. (God, what a mess of similes.) But the awful thing would have been some material catastrophe that would have made it unable to run at all.

Dearest love.

[Scott]

5521 Amestoy Avenue
Encino, California
March 19, 1940

Dearest:

It seems to me best not to hurry things.

(a) I'd like you to leave with the blessings of Dr. Carroll (you've consumed more of his working hours than one human deserves of another—you'd agree if you'd see his correspondence with me). Next to Forel [1] he has been your eventual best friend—better even than Meyer [2] (though this is unfair to Meyer who never claimed to be a clinician but only a diagnostician).

But to hell with all that, and with illness.

(b) Also, you'd best wait because I will *certainly* have more money three weeks from now than at present, and

(c) *If* things develop fast Scottie can skip down and see you for a day during her vacation—otherwise you won't see her before summer. This is an *if!*

I don't think you fully realize the extent of what Scottie has done at Vassar. You wrote rather casually of two years being enough but it isn't. Her promise is unusual. Not only did she rise to the occasion and get in young but she has raised herself from a poor scholar to a very passable one; sold a professional story at eighteen; and moreover in very highbrow, at present very politically minded Vassar she has

[1] Dr. Oscar Forel at the Prangins Sanitarium in Switzerland.
[2] Dr. Adolf Meyer at the Phipps Clinic in Baltimore.

introduced with some struggle a new note. She has written and produced a musical comedy and founded a club called the Omgim to perpetuate the idea—almost the same thing that Tarkington did in 1893 when he founded the Triangle at Princeton. She did this against tough opposition—girls who wouldn't let her on the board of the daily paper because, though she could write, she wasn't "politically conscious."

We have every reason at this point to cheer for our baby. I would do anything rather than deny her the last two years of college which she has now earned. There is more than talent there—a real genius for organization.

Nothing has developed here. I write these "Pat Hobby" stories—and wait. I have a new idea now—a comedy series which will get me back into the big magazines—but my God I am a forgotten man. *Gatsby* had to be taken out of the Modern Library because it didn't sell, which was a blow.

> With dearest love always,
>
> [Scott]

> [*5521 Amestoy Avenue*]
> [*Encino, California*]
> *April 11, 1940*

Dearest Zelda:

I got your wire today asking for $5.00 and simultaneously one came from Dr. Carroll saying you were coming out. I don't know what the rail fare to Montgomery is, but I am sending you herewith $60.00, which I hope will take care of your ticket, baggage, etc. You are leaving bills behind you, I know, which I will try to take care of as soon as I can. I have sent Jean West $25.00 on account. Moreover I have sent a check to your mother for your expenses when you get to Montgomery.

Now as to the general arrangement: I am starting to work on this "speculation" job. That is, they are giving me very little money but if the picture is resold when finished the deal will be somewhat better. I hesitated about accepting it but there have been absolutely no offers in many months and I did it on the advice of my new agent. It is a job that should be fun and suitable to my still uneven state of health. (Since yesterday I seem to be running a fever again.) In any case we can't go on living indefinitely on those *Esquire* articles. So you will be a poor girl for awhile and there is nothing much to do about it. I can manage to send you $30.00 a week of which you should pay your mother about $15.00 for board, laundry, light, etc. The rest will be in checks of alternately $10.00 and $20.00— that is, one week the whole sum will amount to $35.00, one week $25.00, etc. This is a sort of way of saving for you so that in alternate weeks you will have a larger lump sum in case you need clothes or something.

You will be cramped by this at first—more so than in the hospital, but it is everything that I can send without putting Scottie to work which I absolutely refuse to do. I don't think you can promise a person an education and then snatch it away from them. If she quit Vassar I should feel like quitting all work and going to the free Veterans Hospital where I probably belong.

The main thing is not to run up bills or wire me for extra funds. There simply aren't any and as you can imagine I am deeply in debt to the government and everyone else. As soon as anything turns up I will naturally increase your allowance so that you will have more mobility, clothes, etc. I am moving in town to be near my work. For the present, will you address me care of my new agent, Phil Berg, 9484 Wilshire Boulevard, Beverly Hills, California? If you forget, "General Delivery, Encino" will be forwarded to me also. As soon as I have a new permanent address I will write you. I do hope this goes well. I wish you were going to brighter surroundings but this is certainly not the time to come to me and I can think of nowhere else for you to go in this dark and bloody world. I suppose a place is what you make it but I have grown to hate California and would give my life for three years in France.

So bon voyage and stay well.

Dearest love.

[Scott]

[5521 Amestoy Avenue]
[Encino, California]
May 4, 1940

Dearest Zelda:

I sympathize with your desire to do something. Why can't you hire a cool room somewhere for a studio? All you'd need is an easel, a chair and a couch and I think you have an easel somewhere. I think with Marjorie's help you could get it for almost nothing and perhaps after next week I can help more (I go according to the fever—if it says around 99 I feel rash, if it runs up over a degree at a daily average I get alarmed and think we mustn't get stony broke like last fall). My ambition is to pay the government who've laid off me so far. I don't know what they'd annex except my scrapbook.

Will return the clipping Monday—she's a smooth enough enough kid[1] (for which I take most of the credit except for the mouth, legs and personal charm, and barring the wit which comes from us both)—anyhow she's the best kind a good deal of figuring out could do. She's not as honest as either you or me but maybe she didn't have as much to conceal.

I hope you're happy. I wish you read books (you know those things that look like blocks but come apart on one side)—I mean loads of books and not just early Hebrew metaphysics. If you did I'd advise you to try some more short stories. You never could plot for shocks but you might try something along the line of Gogol's "The Cloak" or Chekhov's "The Darling." They are both in the Modern Library's *Best Russian Short Stories* which the local Carnegie may have in stock.

Don't waste your poor little income on wires to me—unless the money *doesn't* come.

Yours at about 99.7,

[Scott]

P.S. Love to all. Excuse the bitter tone. I've overworked on the goddamn movie and am in bed for the day.

[1] Scottie.

[*5521 Amestoy Avenue*]
[*Encino, California*]
May 11, 1940

Dearest Zelda:

Sorry I wrote you such a cross letter last week and I miss getting an answer from you. Things are better. The awful cough I had died down, the temperature fell and I've worked hard this week with apparently no ill effect except that I'm looking forward tomorrow to a peaceful Sunday spent in bed with Churchill's *Life of Marlborough*. Funny that he should be Prime Minister at last. Do you remember luncheon at his mother's house in 1920 and Jack Churchill who was so hard to talk to at first and turned out to be so pleasant? And Lady Churchill's call on the Countess of Byng whose butler was just like the butler in *Alice in Wonderland?* I thank God they've gotten rid of that old rapscallion, Chamberlain. It's all terribly sad and as you can imagine I think of it night and day.

Also I think I've written a really brilliant continuity.[1] It had better be for it seems to be a last life line that Hollywood has thrown me. It is a strong life line—to write as I please upon a piece of my own and if I can make a reputation out here (one of those brilliant Hollywood reputations which endure all of two months sometimes) now will be the crucial time.

Have a cynical letter from Scottie about the Princeton prom. Thank God I didn't let her start to go at sixteen or she would be an old jade by now. Tell me something of your life there—how you like your old friends, your mother's health, etc., and what you think you might do this summer during the hottest part. I should have said in my letter that if you want to read those stories upon which I think you might make a new approach to writing some of your own, order *Best Russian Stories*, Modern Library edition, from Scribners and they will charge it to me.

Next week I'll be able to send you what I think is a permanent address for me for the summer—a small apartment in the heart of the city. Next fall if the cough is still

[1] A script based on his short story, "Babylon Revisited."

active I may have to move again to some dry inland atmosphere.

Love to all of you and especially yourself.

Dearest love.

[Scott]

[*5521 Amestoy Avenue*]
[*Encino, California*]
May 18, 1940

Dearest Zelda:

It's hard to explain about the *Saturday Evening Post* matter. It isn't that I haven't tried, but the trouble with them goes back to the time of Lorimer's retirement in 1935. I wrote them three stories that year and sent them about three others which they didn't like. The last story they bought they published last in the issue and my friend, Adelaide Neil on the staff, implied to me that they didn't want to pay that big price for stories unless they could use them in the beginning of the issue. Well, that was the time of my two-year sickness, T.B., the shoulder, etc., and you were at a most crucial point and I was foolishly trying to take care of Scottie and for one reason or another I lost the knack of writing the particular kind of stories they wanted.

As you should know from your own attempts, high-priced commercial writing for the magazines is a very definite trick. The rather special things that I brought to it, the intelligence and the good writing and even the radicalism all appealed to old Lorimer who had been a writer himself and liked style. The man who runs the magazine now is an up-and-coming young Republican who gives not a damn about literature and who publishes almost nothing except escape stories about the brave frontiersmen, etc., or fishing, or football captains—nothing that would even faintly shock or disturb the reactionary bourgeois. Well, I simply can't do it and, as I say, I've tried not once but twenty times.

As soon as I feel I am writing to a cheap specification

my pen freezes and my talent vanishes over the hill, and
I honestly don't blame them for not taking the things that
I've offered to them from time to time in the past three
or four years. An explanation of their new attitude is that
you no longer have a chance of selling a story with an
unhappy ending (in the old days many of mine *did* have
unhappy endings—if you remember). In fact the standard
of writing from the best movies, like *Rebecca,* is, believe
it or not, much higher at present than that in the commercial magazines such as *Colliers* and the *Post.*

Thank you for your letter. California is a monotonous
climate and already I am tired of the flat, scentless tone of
the summer. It is fun to be working on something I like
and maybe in another month I will get the promised bonus
on it and be able to pay last year's income tax and raise
our standard of living a little.

> Love to you all and dearest love to you.

> [Scott]

P.S. I am sending you the copy of the article you sent me
about Scottie. You said something about giving it to Mrs.
McKinney.

> [*1403 North Laurel Avenue*]
> [*Hollywood, California*]
> *June 7, 1940*

Dearest Zelda:

The Harvard Summer School idea seemed better for
Scottie than her going to Virginia. You remember your old
idea that people ought to be born on the shores of the North
Sea and only in later life drift south toward the Mediterranean in softness? Now all the Montague Normans, Lady
Willerts, Guinnesses, Vallambrosas, etc., who loafed with
us in the South of France through many summers seem to
have dug themselves into an awful pit. I want Scottie to
be hardy and keen and able to fight her own battles and
Virginia didn't seem to be the right note—however charming.

I'll be sending you a semi-permanent address any day now.

Dearest love.

[Scott]

1403 North Laurel Avenue
Hollywood, California

June 14, 1940

Dearest Zelda:

At the moment everything is rather tentative. Scottie is coming South about the 20th and after that wants to go to summer school at Harvard. If I can possibly afford it I want her to go. She wants an education and has recently shown that she has a right to it. You will find her very mature and well-informed. My feeling is that we are in for a ten-year war and that perhaps one more year at Vassar is all she will have—which is one reason why the summer school appeals to me. If I can manage that for a month, then perhaps I can manage the seashore for you in August—by which time you will have had a good deal of Montgomery weather. A lot depends on whether my producer is going to continue immediately with "Babylon Revisited"—or whether any other picture job turns up. Things are naturally shot to hell here with everybody running around in circles yet continuing to turn out two-million-dollar tripe like *All This and Heaven Too*.

Twenty years ago *This Side of Paradise* was a best seller and we were settled in Westport. Ten years ago Paris was having almost its last great American season but we had quit the gay parade and you were gone to Switzerland. Five years ago I had my first bad stroke of illness and went to Asheville. Cards began falling badly for us much too early. The world has certainly caught up in the last four weeks. I hope the atmosphere in Montgomery is tranquil and not too full of war talk.

Love to all of you.

[Scott]

1403 North Laurel Avenue
Hollywood, California

July 6, 1940

Dearest Zelda:

I enjoyed reading the interview given out by our learned Scottie. I'm glad to know she spends her time thinking about strikes, relief and starvation while feeling no slightest jealousy of the girls with silver foxes who choose to recline on country club porches. It shows that we have hatched a worthy egg and I do not doubt that someday, like George Washington, she will "raise that standard to which all good men can repair."

Seriously, I never heard such a bunch of hokum in my life as she sold that newspaper reporter but I'm glad she has one quality which I have found almost as valuable as positive originality, viz.: she can make the most of what she has read and heard—make a few paragraphs from Marx, John Stuart Mill, and *The New Republic* go further than most people can do with years of economic study. That is one way to grow learned, first pretend to be—then have to live up to it.

She has just shown her keenness in another way by taking me for $100.00 more advance money for the summer school than I had expected to pay, leaving me with a cash balance of $11.00 at date. Don't bawl her out for this. Leave it to me because it most certainly will come out of her allowance and it was honestly nothing but carelessness in getting the exact data from the summer school. However, it affects you to this extent—that I'm going to ask you that if these checks reach you Monday not to cash them until Tuesday. It will be perfectly safe to cash them Tuesday because I'm getting a payment on the story at which I am back at work. The majority of the payment ($900.00) goes to Uncle Sam. $300.00 goes against a loan already made against it and the rest will be distributed for our needs during the next three weeks—so please if you have any extra funds save them for any emergency. We have done our share of lending and giving over many years and we must all watch our money.

Tell me what you do. Cousin Ceci writes that my Aunt Elise died last April at the age of ninety. I was fond of that old woman and I hadn't yet assimilated her passing.

With dearest love always,

[Scott]

1403 North Laurel Avenue
Hollywood, California
July 12, 1940

Dearest Zelda:

You never tell me if you are painting or not, or what you are writing if anything. I spent a silly day yesterday with Shirley Temple and her family. They want to do the picture and they don't want to do the picture, but that's really the producer's worry and not mine. She's a lovely little girl, beautifully brought up, and she hasn't quite reached the difficult age yet—figuring the difficult age at twelve. She reminds me so much of Scottie in the last days at La Paix, just before she entered Bryn Mawr. You weren't there the day of the Maryland Hunt Cup Race in the spring of '34 when Scottie got the skirt and coat from my mother which suddenly jumped her into adolescence. You may remember that she wore the little suit till she was about sixteen.

It's hot as hell here today and I haven't been able to work. I too have had only one letter from Scottie, but she seems to like Boston.

With dearest love,

[Scott]

1403 North Laurel Avenue
Hollywood, California
July 20, 1940

Dearest Zelda:

Thanks for your letter about what you are doing. I do wish you were sketching a little if only to keep your hand

in. You've never done any drawing at all in Alabama and
it's so very different in flora and general atmosphere than
North Carolina that I think it would be worthwhile to
record your moods while down there. When times are a
little calmer I think you ought to have a really inclusive
exhibition of your pictures. Perhaps if the war is over next
year it would be a good summer's job for Scottie to arrange
it—I mean fill the place that Cary Ross did six years ago. She
would meet all sorts of interesting people doing it and I
had an idea of suggesting it as her work for this August,
but the war pushes art into the background. At least people
don't buy anything.

I am sending you Gertrude Stein's new book which Max
Perkins sent me. I am mentioned in it on some page—
anyhow I've underlined it. On the back of the wrapping
paper I've addressed it and stamped it to Scottie. She
might like to look it over too. It's a melancholy book now
that France has fallen, but fascinating for all that.

Ten days more to go on the Temple picture.

With dearest love,

[Scott]

PRIVATE AND PERSONAL[1]

Please write me a few lines about your mother's health. Is
she well in general? Is she active? I mean does she still go
downtown, etc., or does she only go around in automobiles?
And tell me why you didn't go to Carolina this year. Was it
lack of funds or is the trip a little too much for her?

1403 North Laurel Avenue
Hollywood, California

August 24, 1940

Dearest Zelda:

By the time you get this Scottie will have leisurely started
South—with two or three stops. I've missed seeing her this

---

[1] This postscript was on a separate sheet of paper.

summer but we've exchanged long letters of a quite intimate character in regard to life and literature. She is an awfully good girl in the broad fundamentals. Please see to one thing —that she doesn't get into any automobiles with drunken drivers.

I think I have a pretty good job coming up next week— a possibility of ten weeks' work and a fairly nice price at 20th Century-Fox. I have my fingers crossed but with the good Shirley Temple script behind me I think my stock out here is better than at any time during the last year.

> With dearest love,
>
> [Scott]

> *1403 North Laurel Avenue*
> *Hollywood, California*
>
> *September 5, 1940*

Dearest Zelda:

Here's ten dollars extra as I thought that due to Scottie's visit it might come in handy. Also I'm sending you Craven's *Art Masterpieces,* a book of extraordinary reproductions that is a little art gallery in itself.

Don't be deceived by this sudden munificence—as yet I haven't received a cent from my new job, but in a wild burst of elation of getting it, I hocked the car again for $150.00.

> With dearest love, always,
>
> [Scott]

> *1403 North Laurel Avenue*
> *Hollywood, California*
>
> *September 14, 1940*

Dearest Zelda:

Am sending you a small check next week which you

should really spend on something which you need—a winter coat, for instance—or, if you are equipped, to put it away for a trip when it gets colder. I can't quite see you doing this, however. Do you have extra bills, dentist's, doctors', etc., and, if so, they should be sent to me as I don't expect you to pay them out of the thirty dollars. And I certainly don't want your mother to be in for any extras. Is she?

This is the third week of my job and I'm holding up very well but so many jobs have started well and come to nothing that I keep my fingers crossed until the thing is in production. Paramount doesn't want to star Shirley Temple alone on the other picture and the producer can't find any big star who will play with her so we are temporarily held up.

As I wrote you, Scottie is now definitely committted to an education and I feel so strongly about it that if she wanted to go to work I would let her really do it by cutting off all allowance. What on earth is the use of having gone to so much time and trouble about a thing and then giving it up two years short of fulfillment. It is the last two years in college that count. I got nothing out of my first two years—in the last I got my passionate love for poetry and historical perspective and ideas in general (however superficially); it carried me full swing into my career. Her generation is liable to get only too big a share of raw life at first hand.

Write me what you do?

With dearest love,

[Scott]

P.S. Scottie may quite possibly marry within a year and then she is fairly permanently off my hands. I've spent so much time doing work that I didn't particularly want to do that what does one more year matter? They've let a certain writer here direct his own pictures and he has made such a go of it that there may be a different feeling about that soon. If I had that chance, I would attain my real goal in coming here in the first place.

1403 North Laurel Avenue
Hollywood, California

September 21, 1940

Dearest Zelda:

So glad you like the art book. I would like to hear of your painting again and I meant it when I said next summer if the war is settled down you ought to have another exhibition.

Scottie went to Baltimore as she planned and I finally got a scrap of a note from her but I imagine most of her penmanship was devoted to young men. I think she's going back with the intention, at least, of working hard and costing little.

I don't know how this job is going. It may last two months—it may end in another week. Things depend on such hairlines here—one must not only do a thing well but do it as a compromise, sometimes between the utterly opposed ideas of two differing executives. The diplomatic part in business is my weak spot.

However, the Shirley Temple script is looking up again and is my great hope for attaining some real status out here as a movie man and not a novelist.

With dearest love,

[Scott]

1403 North Laurel Avenue
Hollywood, California

September 28, 1940

Dearest Zelda:

Autumn comes—I am forty-four—nothing changes. I have not heard from Scottie since she got to Vassar and from what I deduce she is extremely happy, needs nothing, is rich—obviously prosperous, busy and self-sufficient. So what more could I want? A letter might mean the opposite of any of these things.

I'm afraid Shirley Temple will be grown before Mrs. Temple decides to meet the producer's terms of this picture. It wouldn't even be interesting if she's thirteen.

Tomorrow I'm going out into society for the first time in some months—a tea at Dottie Parker's (Mrs. Alan Campbell), given for Don Stewart's ex-wife, the Countess Tolstoy. Don't know whether Don will be there or not. Ernest's book is the "Book-of-the-Month." [1] Do you remember how superior he used to be about mere sales? He and Pauline are getting divorced after ten years and he is marrying a girl named Martha Gellhorn. I know no news of anyone else except that Scottie seems to have made a hit in Norfolk.

Dearest love.

[Scott]

1403 North Laurel Avenue
Hollywood, California
October 5, 1940

Dearest Zelda:

Enjoyed your letter—especially the consoling line about the Japanese being a nice clean people. A lot of the past came into that party. Fay Wray, whose husband, John Monk Saunders, committed suicide two months ago; Deems Taylor, whom I hadn't seen twice since the day at Swope's[2]; Frank Tuttle of the old Film Guild. There was a younger generation there too and I felt very passé and decided to get a new suit.

With dearest love,

[Scott]

---

[1] *For Whom the Bell Tolls.*
[2] Herbert Bayard Swope, the sportsman-journalist, whom Fitzgerald had known at Great Neck in the early Twenties.

1403 North Laurel Avenue
Hollywood, California

October 11, 1940

Dearest Zelda:

Another heat wave is here and reminds me of last year at the same time. The heat is terribly dry and not at all like Montgomery and is so unexpected. The people feel deeply offended, as if they were being bombed.

A letter from Gerald yesterday. He has no news except a general flavor of the past. To him, now, of course, the Riviera was the best time of all. Sara is interested in vegetables and gardens and all growing and living things.

I expect to be back on my novel any day and this time to finish, a two months' job. The months go so fast that even *Tender Is the Night* is six years' away. I think the nine years that intervened between *The Great Gatsby* and *Tender* hurt my reputation almost beyond repair because a whole generation grew up in the meanwhile to whom I was only a writer of *Post* stories. I don't suppose anyone will be much interested in what I have to say this time and it may be the last novel I'll ever write, but it must be done now because, after fifty, one is different. One can't remember emotionally, I think, except about childhood but I have a few more things left to say.

My health is better. It was a long business and at any time some extra waste of energy has to be paid for at a double price. Weeks of fever and coughing—but the constitution is an amazing thing and nothing quite kills it until the heart has run its entire race. I'd like to get East around Christmas-time this year. I don't know what the next three months will bring further, but if I get a credit on either of these last two efforts things will never again seem so black as they did a year ago when I felt that Hollywood had me down in its books as a ruined man—a label which I had done nothing to deserve.

With dearest love,

[Scott]

1403 North Laurel Avenue
Hollywood, California
October 19, 1940

Dearest Zelda:

I'm trying desperately to finish my novel by the middle of December and it's a little like working on *Tender Is the Night* at the end—I think of nothing else. Still haven't heard from the Shirley Temple story but it would be a great relaxation of pressure if she decides to do it, though an announcement in the paper says that she is going to be teamed with Judy Garland in *Little Eva,* which reminds me that I saw the two _____ Sisters both grown enormously fat in the Brown Derby. Do you remember them on the boat with Viscount Bryce and their dogs?

My room is covered with charts like it used to be for *Tender Is the Night,* telling the different movements of the characters and their histories. However, this one is to be short, as I originally planned it two years ago, and more on the order of *Gatsby.*

With dearest love,

[Scott]

1403 North Laurel Avenue
Hollywood, California
October 23, 1940

Dearest Zelda:

Advising you about money at long distance would be silly but you feel we're both concerned in the Carroll matter. Still and all I would much rather you'd leave it to me and *keep* your money. I sent them a small payment last week. The thing is I have budgeted what I saved in the weeks at 20th [Century-Fox] to last until December 15th so I can go on with the novel with the hope of having a full draft by then. Naturally I will not realize anything at once (except on the very slim chance of a serial) and though I will try to make something immediately out of pictures or *Esquire* it may be a pretty slim Christmas. So my advice is to put the hundred and fifty away against that time.

I am deep in the novel, living in it, and it makes me happy. It is a *constructed* novel like *Gatsby*, with passages of poetic prose when it fits the action, but no ruminations or side-shows like *Tender*. Everything must contribute to the dramatic movement.

It's odd that my old talent for the short story vanished. It was partly that times changed, editors changed, but part of it was tied up somehow with you and me—the happy ending. Of course every third story had some other ending, but essentially I got my public with stories of young love. I must have had a powerful imagination to project it so far and so often into the past.

Two thousand words today and all good.

With dearest love,

[Scott]

1403 North Laurel Avenue
Hollywood, California

October 26, 1940

Dearest Zelda:

Ernest sent me his book and I'm in the middle of it. It is not as good as the *Farewell to Arms*. It doesn't seem to have the tensity or the freshness nor has it the inspired poetic moments. But I imagine it would please the average type of reader, the mind who used to enjoy Sinclair Lewis, more than anything he has written. It is full of a lot of rounded adventures on the *Huckleberry Finn* order and of course it is highly intelligent and literate like everything he does. I suppose life takes a good deal out of you and you never can quite repeat. But the point is, he is making a fortune out of it—has sold it to the movies for over a hundred thousand dollars and as it's the Book-of-the-Month selection he will make $50,000 from it in that form. Rather a long cry from his poor rooms over the saw mill in Paris.

No news except that I'm working hard, if that is news,

and that Scottie's story appears in *The New Yorker* this week.

> With dearest love,
>
> [Scott]

> 1403 *North Laurel Avenue*
> *Hollywood, California*
> *November 2, 1940*

Dearest Zelda:

Listening to the Harvard and Princeton game on the radio reminds me of the past that I lived a quarter of a century ago and Scottie is living now. I hear nothing from her though I imagine she is at Cambridge today.

The novel is hard as pulling teeth but that is because it is in its early character-planting phase. I feel people so less intently than I did once that this is harder. It means welding together hundreds of stray impressions and incidents to form the fabric of entire personalities. But later it should go faster. I hope all is well with you.

> With dearest love.
>
> [Scott]

> 1403 *North Laurel Avenue*
> *Hollywood, California*
> *November 9, 1940*

Dearest Zelda:

Got into rather a fret about Scottie last week, which however came out all right. She went to the infirmary with grippe and then in spite of my telegrams to everyone there, including the dean, Scottie and the infirmary itself, darkness seemed to close about her. I could get no information. Her weekly letter was missing. As I say, it turned out all right. She had been discharged and was probably out of town but I wrote her a strong letter that she must keep me informed of her general movements—not that I have any control over them or want any because she is after all of age and capable of looking after herself but one resents the breaking of a habit and I was used to hearing about her once a week.

I'm still absorbed in the novel which is growing under my hand—not as deft a hand as I'd like—but growing.

> With dearest love always,
>
> [Scott]

> 1403 North Laurel Avenue
> Hollywood, California
> November 16, 1940

Dearest Zelda:

I'm still listening to Yale-Princeton, which will convince you I spend all my time on the radio. Have had to lay off Coca-Cola, hence work with an attack of avitaminosis, whatever that is—it's like a weight pressing on your shoulders and upper arms. Oh for the health of fifteen years ago!

I'd love to see anything you write so don't hesitate to send it. I got the doctor's bill which has been paid today. I liked Scottie's little sketch, didn't you?

> With dearest love,
>
> [Scott]

> 1403 North Laurel Avenue
> Hollywood, California
> November 23, 1940

Dearest Zelda:

Enclosed is Scottie's little story—she had just read Gertrude Stein's *Melanctha* on my recommendation and the influence is what you might call perceptible.

The odd thing is that it appeared in eastern copies of *The New Yorker* and not in the western, and I had some bad moments looking through the magazine she had designated and wondering if my eyesight had departed.

The editor of *Colliers* wants me to write for them (he's here in town), but I tell him I'm finishing my novel for myself and all I can promise him is a look at it. It will, at any rate, be nothing like anything else as I'm digging it out of myself like uranium—one ounce to the cubic ton of rejected ideas. It is a novel *à la Flaubert* without "ideas" but only people moved singly and in mass through what I hope are authentic moods.

The resemblance is rather to *Gatsby* than to anything else I've written. I'm so glad you're well and reasonably happy.

> With dearest love,
>
> Scott

P.S. Please send Scottie's story back in your next letter—as it seems utterly impossible to get duplicates and I shall probably want to show it to authors and editors with paternal pride.

> *1403 North Laurel Avenue*
> *Hollywood, California*
>
> *December 6, 1940*

Dearest Zelda:

No news except that the novel progresses and I am angry that this little illness has slowed me up. I've had trouble with my heart before but never anything organic. This is not a major attack but seems to have come on gradually and luckily a cardiogram showed it up in time. I may have to move from the third to the first floor apartment but I'm quite able to work, etc., if I do not overtire myself.

Scottie tells me she is arriving South Xmas Day. I envy you being together and I'll be thinking of you. Everything is my novel now—it has become of absorbing interest. I hope I'll be able to finish it by February.

> With dearest love,
>
> [Scott]

1403 North Laurel Avenue
Hollywood, California
December 13, 1940

Dearest Zelda:

Here's why it would be foolish to sell the watch. I think I wrote you that over a year ago when things were very bad indeed I did consider pawning it as I desperately needed $200.00, for a couple of months. The price offered, to my astonishment, was $20.00, and of course I didn't even consider it. It cost, I believe, $600.00. The reason for the shrinkage is a purely arbitrary change of taste in jewelry. It is actually artificial and created by the jewelers themselves. It is like the Buick we sold in 1927—for $200.00—to come back to America in '31 and buy a car of the same year and much more used for $400.00. If you have no use for the watch I think it would be a beautiful present for Scottie. She has absolutely nothing of any value and I'm sure would prize it highly. Moreover she never loses anything. If you preferred you could loan it to her as I think she'd get real pleasure out of sporting it.

The novel is about three-quarters through and I think I can go on till January 12 without doing any stories or going back to the studio. I couldn't go back to the studio anyhow in my present condition as I have to spend most of the time in bed where I write on a wooden desk that I had made a year and a half ago. The cardiogram shows that my heart is repairing itself but it will be a gradual process that will take some months. It is odd that the heart is one of the organs that does repair itself.

I had a letter from Katharine Tighe the other day, a voice out of the past. Also one from Harry Mitchell who was my buddy at the Barron G. Collier Advertising Agency. And one from Max Perkins who is keen to see the novel and finally one from Bunny Wilson who is married now to a girl named Mary McCarthy who was an editor of *The New Republic*. They have a baby a year old and live in New Canaan.

I will write you again early next week in time for Christmas.

Dearest love.

[Scott]

P.S. I enclose the letter from Max, in fact two letters only I can't find the one that just came. They will keep you *au courant* with the publishing world and some of our friends.

1403 North Laurel Avenue
Hollywood, California

December 19, 1940

Dearest Zelda:

This has to be a small present this year but I figure Scottie's present as a gift to you both and charge it off to you accordingly.

I am very anxious for Scottie to finish this year of college at least, so please do not stress to her that it is done at any inconvenience. The thing for which I am most grateful to my mother and father are my four years at Princeton, and I would be ashamed not to hand it on to another generation so there is no question of Scottie quitting. Do tell her this.

I hope you all have a fine time at Christmas. Much love to your mother and Marjorie and Minor and Nonny and Livy Hart and whoever you see.

Dearest love.

[Scott]

PART THREE

Letters to
Maxwell Perkins

599 Summit Avenue
St. Paul, Minnesota
July 26, 1919

Dear Mr. Perkins:

After four months' attempt to write commercial copy by day and painful half-hearted imitations of popular literature by night I decided that it was one thing or another. So I gave up getting married and went home.

Yesterday I finished the first draft of a novel called

THE EDUCATION OF A PERSONAGE [1]

It is in no sense a revision of the ill-fated *Romantic Egotist* but it contains some of the former material, improved and worked over, and bears a strong family resemblance besides.

But while the other was a tedious, disconnected casserole this is definite attempt at a big novel and I really believe I have hit it, as immediately I stopped disciplining the muse she trotted obediently around and became an erratic mistress if not a steady wife.

Now what I want to ask you is this—if I send you the book by August 20th and you decide you could risk its publication (I am blatantly confident that you will) would it be brought out in October, say, or just what would decide its date of publication?

This is an odd question I realize, especially since you haven't even seen the book, but you have been so kind in the past about my stuff that I venture to intrude once more upon your patience.

Sincerely,

F. Scott Fitzgerald

[1] Afterward, *This Side of Paradise*.

599 Summit Avenue
St. Paul, Minnesota
September 4, 1919

Dear Mr. Perkins:

I sent the book today under a separate cover. I want to discuss a few things in connection with it.

You'll notice that it contains much material from *The Romantic Egotist*.

(1) Chapter II, Book I of the present book contains material from "Spires and Gargoyles," "Ha-Ha Hortense," "Babes in the Wood," and "Crescendo"—rewritten in third person, cut down, and re-edited.

(2) Chapter III, Book I contains material from "Second Descent of the Egotist" and "The Devil," rewritten, etc.

(3) Chapter IV, Book I contains material from "The Two Mystics," "Clara," and "The End of Many Things."

(4) Chapter III, Book II is a revision of Eleanor in third person—with that fur incident left out.

Chapter I, Book I, and Chapters I, II, IV, and V of Book II are entirely new.

You'll see that of the old material there is all new use, outside the revision in the third person. For instance the Princeton characters of *The R.E.*—Tom, Tump, Lorry, Lumpy, Fred, Dick, Jim, Burne, Judy, McIntyre and Jesse —have become in this book Fred, Dick, Alec, Tom, Kerry and Burne. Isabelle and Rosalind of *The R.E.* have become just Isabelle while the new Rosalind is a different person.

Beatrice is a new character. Dr. Dudley becomes Monsignor Darcy; is a much better done—in fact every character is in better perspective.

The preface I leave to your discretion—perhaps it's a little too clever-clever; likewise you may object to the literary personalities in Chapter II and Book II and to the length of the socialistic discussion in the last chapter. The book contains a little over ninety thousand words. I certainly think the hero gets somewhere.

I await anxiously your verdict.

Sincerely,
F. Scott Fitzgerald

P.S. Thornton Hancock is Henry Adams—I didn't do him thoroughly, of course—but I knew him when I was a boy.

599 Summit Avenue
St. Paul, Minnesota
September 18, 1919

Dear Mr. Perkins:

Of course I was delighted to get your letter and I've been in a sort of trance all day; not that I doubted you'd take it but at last I have something to show people. It has enough advertisement in St. Paul already to sell several thousand copies and I think Princeton will buy it. (I've been a periodical, local Great-Expectations for some time in both places.)

Terms, etc., I leave to you but one thing I can't relinquish without at least a slight struggle. Would it be utterly impossible for you to publish the book Xmas—or, say, by February? I have so many things dependent on its success —including of course a girl—not that I expect it to make me a fortune but it will have a psychological effect on me and all my surroundings and besides open up new fields. I'm in that stage where every month counts frantically and seems a cudgel in a fight for happiness against time. Will you let me know more exactly how that difference in time of publication influences the sale and what you mean by "early spring?"

Excuse this ghastly handwriting but I'm a bit nervous today. I'm beginning (last month) a very ambitious novel called *The Demon Lover* which will probably take a year. Also I'm writing short stories. I find that what I enjoy writing is always my best—every young author ought to read Samuel Butler's *Notebooks*.

I'm writing quite a marvelous after-the-war story. Does Mr. Bridges[1] think that they're a little passé or do you think he'd like to see it?

I'll fix up data for advertising and have a photo taken next week with the most gigantic enjoyment (I'm trying H. G. Wells' use of vast Garagantuan [sp.] words).

Well, thank you for a very happy day and numerous other favors and let me know if I've any possible chance for earlier publication, and give my thanks or whatever is in order to Mr. Scribner or whoever else was on the deciding committee.

[1] Robert Bridges, editor of *Scribner's Magazine*.

Probably be East next month or November.

Sincerely,

F. Scott Fitzgerald

P.S. Who picks out the cover? I'd like something that could be a set—look cheerful and important like a Shaw book. I notice Shaw, Galsworthy and Barrie do that. But Wells doesn't—I wonder why. No need of illustrations, is there? I knew a fellow at college who'd have been a wonder for books like mine—a mixture of Aubrey Beardsley, Hogarth and Montgomery Flagg. But he got killed in the war.

Excuse this immoderately long and rambling letter but I think you'll have to allow me several days for recuperation.

599 Summit Avenue
St. Paul, Minnesota

October 25, [1919]

Dear Mr. Bridges:[1]

This is a query. I have a project. It is a work of about 20,000 words and more on the order of my novel than like these stories I've been doing. But it's the sort of thing that will require a full month's work and as *The New Republic, Scribner's* and possibly the *Atlantic Monthly* are the only magazines that would publish it I don't want to start until you assure me that there's *nothing* in the project which seems to bar it from *Scribner's* if it be *sufficiently* interesting and well done.

It is a literary forgery purporting to be selections from the notebooks of a man who is a complete literary radical from the time he's in college thru two years in New York —finally he goes to training camp, gets bored, and enlists as a private. This is the end of the book—a note by me will say that he served in Companies E and G of the Twenty-eighth Infantry and died of appendicitis in Paris in 1918.

---

[1] A few letters not addressed to Max Perkins but bearing on Fitzgerald's relations with Scribners are included in this group.

It will be in turns cynical, ingenuous, life-saturated, critical and bitter. It will be racy and startling with opinions and personalities. I have a journal I have kept for 3½ years which my book didn't begin to exhaust, which I don't seem to be able to draw on for stories but which certainly is, I think, highly amusing. This, thoroughly edited and revised, plus some imagination and ½ dozen ingredients I have in mind will be the bulk of it. It would take 2 or possibly 3 parts to publish it.

The tremendous success of Butler's *Notebooks* and of Barbellion's (Wells'?) *Disappointed Man* makes me think that the public loves to find out the workings of active minds in their personal problems. It will be bound to have that streak of coarseness that both Wells and Butler have but there won't be any James Joyce flavor to it.

Of course you can't possibly commit yourself until you've seen it but as I say I'd want to know before I start if a work of that nature would be intrinsically hostile to the policy of *Scribner's Magazine*. With apologies for intruding upon your patience once again I am

Sincerely,

F. Scott Fitzgerald

[*599 Summit Avenue*]
[*St. Paul, Minnesota*]
[circa *January 10, 1920*]

Dear Mr. Perkins:

I was delighted to hear from you—and tickled to death that W. E. Hill liked my book and has done the cover. I admire him more than any artist in the country. I can hardly wait to see it.

I came home in a thoroughly nervous alcoholic state and revised two tales that went the complete rounds of the magazines last April. I did 'em in four days and sent 'em to Reynolds[1] in the hopes he could get enough for 'em so that I could go South, because I'm afraid I'm about to develop tuberculosis. Last Monday he sent me a check for a thousand from the *Post* for 'em so I'm leaving for New Orleans tomorrow night. I'll write you my address when

---

[1] Paul Revere Reynolds, Fitzgerald's literary agent.

I have one—meanwhile, anything sent here will be forwarded.

Now for several questions. When would a novel have to be finished to have it published serially and then brought out by you for the fall season? Do you think a book on the type of my first one would have any chance of being accepted for serial publication by any magazine? I want to start it but I don't want to get broke in the middle and start in and have to write short stories again—because I don't enjoy it and just do it for money. There's nothing in collections of short stories is there? About how many copies of *John O'May* were sold?

Everything goes serenely except that I feel written out on this short stuff. I've had two vaudeville offers for my current play in *Smart Set* and I've just sent $1000 worth of movies to the Metro people. I have two stories for Mr. Bridges, both stuck in the middle, and two *Post* stories cut off in their first paragraphs.

My *Drunkard's Holiday* and *Diary of a Literary Failure* are also defunct.

The more I think of that advertisement I wrote for my book the more I dislike it. Please don't use it unless you have it already set up in which case I'll make a few small changes in proof and it'll have to go.

I'm deadly curious to see if Hill's picture looks like the real "Rosalind." [1] I suppose he did either the boudoir scene or the mellow parting. May be in New York in March if I can get rid of this damn cough. By the way, I liked Maxwell Burt's "Cup of Tea" [2] so well that I wrote him a note about it and got a very pleasant one in return. He's sort of Richard Harding Davis, only literary instead of journalistic —but he's the only real romanticist there is. We have the daughters of Henry James—Gerould, Glaspell [3] and the other female psychological hair-splitters and the Yiddish descendants of O. Henry—Fanny and Edna[4] and that's all —except Burt, so I like him.

As Ever,

F. Scott Fitz_____

[1] Rosalind in *This Side of Paradise* was modeled on Zelda.
[2] Short story by Maxwell Struthers Burt, in his collection, *John O'May*.
[3] Novelists Katharine Fullerton Gerould and Susan Glaspell.
[4] Fannie Hurst and Edna Ferber.

2900 Prytania Street
New Orleans, Louisiana
January 21, 1920

Dear Mr. Perkins:

I am returning herewith the first batch of proofs, corrected. There is one change I would like to have you make if you can possibly see your way clear to doing it. It is in regard to the type used in those subheadings throughout the chapters, such as "A kiss for Amory" and "Preparatory to the great adventure"—you know what I mean.

Now I have a very strong instinct about having those in a different sort of type. It may seem a small point but I got the idea originally from the Shaw prefaces and the exact sort of type *does* make a difference. Those subheadings are intended as commentaries, sort of *whimsical commentaries* rather more than they are intended as titles, and the correct type would be that sort used in the first two words of the book. The words "Amory Blaine" that begin Chapter one are in exactly the sort of type I mean. I don't know what you call it but it has capitals slightly bigger than the ones in the present subheadings and the first letter of the important words is slightly bigger.

I should have explained that to you before—you see, I think that this sort of type I mean gives the sort of effect of a marginalia—really doesn't break it up as much as these small, severe headings you're using now.

Of course this is my fault but I feel very strongly about [it] so if it can be done without inconvenience I wish you'd have it fixed up.

As ever,

Scott Fitzgerald

P.S. It looks damn good. Thanks for your letter. O. Henry said this was a story town—but it's too consciously that— just as a Hugh Walpole character is too consciously a character.

2900 Prytania Street
New Orleans, Louisiana
February 3, [1920]

Dear Mr. Perkins:

I certainly touched the depths of depression tonight. The action on that book, *Madeline,* has knocked hell out of my new novel, *Darling Heart,* which turned completely on the seduction of the girl in the second chapter. I was afraid all along because of *Susan Lennox,*[1] and the agitation against Dreiser but this is the final blow. I don't know what I'll do now—what in hell is the use of trying to write decent fiction if a bunch of old women refuse to let anyone hear the truth!

I've fallen lately under the influence of an author who's quite changed my point of view. He's a chestnut to you, no doubt, but I've just discovered him—Frank Norris. I think *McTeague* and *Vandover* are both excellent. I told you last November that I'd read *Salt* by his brother Charles and was quite enthusiastic about it. Odd! There are things in *Paradise* that might have been written by Norris—those drunken scenes, for instance—in fact, all the realism. I wish I'd stuck to it throughout! Another of my discoveries is H. L. Mencken who is certainly a factor in present day literature. In fact I'm not so cocksure about things as I was last summer—this fellow Conrad seems to be pretty good after all.

I've decided I'd rather not use Nathan's[2] name at all in connection with my book and in fact that whole foreword strikes me as being rather weak. Couldn't one of your advertising men write it?

I'm glad you're fixing it up about those subtitles. I'm anxiously awaiting the cover.

Those stories I sold the *Post* will start to appear February 21st. I have "Dalyrimple" and "Benediction" in the current *Smart Set* and I had a one-act play in the January number which got several vaudeville offers. Read it if you can. It was called "Porcelain and Pink" and it's excellent. *Smart Set, Scribner's* and *Post* are the only three magazines.

I'm going to break up the start of my novel and sell it

[1] By David Graham Phillips.
[2] Critic George Jean Nathan.

as three little character stories to *Smart Set*. I'll only get
$40.00 a piece but no one else would take them, I don't
think—and besides I want to have Mencken and Nathan
hot on my side when my book comes out. As soon as I've
done that I'm going to do two or three stories for Mr.
Bridges. If I give up the idea of *Darling Heart* which I've
practically decided to do, at least as a serial, and plan
not to start my fall novel until June and finish it in
August, my idea will be to do 3 stories a month, one for
Smart Set, one for *Scribner's*, and one for the *Post*. The
latter are now paying me $600.00 which is a frightful in-
ducement since I'm almost sure I'll get married as soon
as my book is out.

Have you any idea of the date yet? And when my short
stories will begin to appear?

Faithfully yours,

F. Scott Fitzgerald

P.S. Please forward any mail that may come there for me.
I expect to be in New York about the 24th—leave here
the 20th.

Westport, Connecticut

August 12, 1920

Dear Mr. Scribner:[1]

Again I am immensely obliged to you. I should certainly feel much more business-like and less profligate if
you would tell your bookkeeper when our reckoning
comes this autumn to charge me full interest on the advances you've made me.

My new novel, called *The Flight of the Rocket*,[2] concerns the life of one Anthony Patch between his 25th and
33d years (1913–1921). He is one of those many with
the tastes and weaknesses of an artist but with no actual
creative inspiration. How he and his beautiful young wife
are wrecked on the shoals of dissipation is told in the

---

[1] Charles Scribner II, then head of the firm.
[2] Afterward, *The Beautiful and Damned*.

story. This sounds sordid but it's really a most sensational book and I hope won't disappoint the critics who liked my first one. I hope it'll be in your hands by November 1st.

Sincerely,

F. Scott Fitzgerald

38 West 59th Street
New York City
December 31, 1920

Dear Mr. Perkins:

The bank this afternoon refused to lend me anything on the security of stock I hold—and I have been pacing the floor for an hour trying to decide what to do. Here, with the novel within two weeks of completion, am I with six hundred dollars' worth of bills and owing Reynolds $650.00 for an advance on a story that I'm utterly unable to write. I've made a half dozen starts yesterday and to-day and I'll go mad if I have to do another debutante, which is what they want.

I hoped that at last being square with Scribners I could remain so. But I'm at my wit's end. Isn't there some way you could regard this as an advance on the new novel rather than on the Xmas sale which won't be due me till July? And at the same interest that it costs Scribners to borrow? Or could you make it a month's loan from Scribner & Co. with my next ten books as security? I need *$1600.00*.

Anxiously,

F. Scott Fitzgerald

6 Pleasant Avenue
Montgomery, Alabama
July 30, 1921

Dear Mr. Perkins:

I have been intending to write you the following letter

for some months and I've been deterred for many causes—
chief among which were the facts that any letter from me
on this subject would sound like impertinent and unsolicited criticism and secondly because I have been the recipient of so many favors and courtesies from Scribners
that is was scarcely my place to cavil at what I considered
ultra-conservatism in their marketing and editorial policies.
But in most businesses nowadays a box is set aside for
employees' suggestions and so perhaps even from outside
you won't resent it if I speak what's on my mind.

What prompted this letter was the clipping on page D[1]
which I took from the *Tribune.* I happen [to] know that
two weeks ago *Mooncalf* had not reached 50,000 copies
and I know also that it has not had nearly the vogue of
my book in the libraries as is apparent from *The Bookman's* monthly score. Yet my novel so far as I have seen
got not *one* newspaper ad, not one *Times* or *Tribune* ad
or Chicago ad since *six months* after publication. And
Knopf has forcibly kept *Mooncalf* in the public eye for
twice that long. What notoriety my book has preserved
as well as what notoriety it got in the beginning, it got
almost unaided. Its ads were small and undistinguished
and confined almost entirely to college magazines and to
Scribner's. The only ad from among my nine or ten suggestions that was used (except the "novel about flappers
written for philosophers") was ruined by Black's "make it
a Fitzgerald Christmas." The ads gotten up in the office
were small and so scattered as to have no follow-up or
reiterative punch. Don't gather from this that I have the
idea that my book was slighted: on the contrary I think
Whitney Darrow and Rodgers and everyone who had anything to do with it there gave it much more personal attention than any book they were handling. Nevertheless the
following facts remain:

(1) *Mooncalf,* on its issue, was advertised in *Montgomery,
Alabama. This Side of Paradise,* tho it sold fifty or more
copies here on Zelda's reputation, was *not once* advertised.
Mooncalf was advertised *two months* in St. Paul. *This
Side of Paradise* appeared in the papers *3 times* in ads. It

---

[1] A Knopf advertisement of *Zell* and *Mooncalf,* in which the latter was
called "the most brilliantly successful first novel of many years." Fitzgerald commented, "You've let everyone forget that my book once had
this title. Knopf's statement goes quite unchallenged."

sold itself largely on personal home-town unsolicited notices about me. This was also true to a great extent in Chicago —from the advertising section of the *Chicago Daily News* which I have on file together with the numbers of *Chicago Tribune* during the week when my book was heading the list, I discover about eleven ads. It ran 18 weeks as best seller in Chicago. During that time it should have been advertised in 2 papers *at least* every other week. From my slight experience in advertising I know that much about campaigns. *Mooncalf* (not to mention *Lulu Bett* [and] *The Age of Innocence,* neither of which had one-tenth the initial publicity of my book and both of which are still selling) has been advertised almost every week for 8 months in Chicago papers and usually in both. Knopf runs almost daily ads for books that *he believes in* that may not sell 10,000 copies (like *Zell* for instance) in the *Tribune.* The greatest selling point my book had, Mencken's statement quoted on the wrapper (together with an entirely neutral statement from Phelps) was allowed to be forgotten with *one* exception, *one* ad. Knopf would be using it still, and keeping the book talked about by means of it. Sinclair Lewis's remark in the *Tribune,* "In Scott Fitzgerald we have an author who will be the equal of any young European," was *absolutely* unused.[1]

> *Dellwood*
> *White Bear Lake, Minnesota*
> *August 25, 1921*

Dear Mr. Perkins:

Excuse the pencil but I'm feeling rather tired and discouraged with life tonight and I haven't the energy to use ink—ink, the ineffable destroyer of thought, that fades an emotion into that slatternly thing, a written-down mental excretion. What ill-spelled rot!

About the novel—which after my letters I should think you'd be so bored with you'd wish it had never existed— I'd like very much if it came out in England simultaneously

[1] The letter breaks off here, unsigned.

with America. You have the rights to it, have you not?
If you do not intend to place it would you be willing to
turn them over to me on the same 10% basis as *Paradise*
so I could place it either with Collins' or thru Reynolds?

Hope you're enjoying New Hampshire—you probably
are. I'm having a hell of a time because I've loafed for 5
months and I want to get to work. Loafing puts me in this
particularly obnoxious and abominable gloom. My third
novel, if I ever write another, will I am sure be black as
death with gloom. I should like to sit down with ½ dozen
chosen companions and drink myself to death but I am
sick alike of life, liquor and literature. If it wasn't for
Zelda I think I'd disappear out of sight for three years.
Ship as a sailor or something and get hard—I'm sick of
the flabby semi-intellectual softness in which I flounder
with my generation.

                                                Scott Fitz

                              Dellwood
                              White Bear Lake, Minnesota
                              [*Before October 7, 1921*][2]

Dear Mr. Perkins:

I appreciate your courtesy and thoughtfulness in telegraphing me. Zelda received the letter and is awaiting the
book with interest. In setting up the book are they including that table "By F. Scott Fitzgerald" with my mul-
titudinous and voluminous [notes] numbered beneath?

I have not seen *one single review* for 2 months but here
are my prognostications for the fall. I have only read the
first of these books.

(1) *Brass* by Charles Norris. Worthy, honest, thorough,
    but fundamentally undistinguished.
(2) *Three Soldiers* by John Dos Passos. The book of
    the autumn.

---

[1] William Collins Sons & Co., the English publisher.
[2] Meaning that in the Scribners' files this undated letter immediately pre-
cedes Perkins' letter to Fitzgerald dated October 7, 1921.

(3) *Eric Dorn* by Ben Hecht. Probably the second best book of the autumn.

(4) *The Beginning of Wisdom* by Stephen Vincent Benet. Beautifully written but too disjointed and patternless. Critics will accuse him of my influence but unjustly as his book was written almost simultaneously with mine.

(5) *The Briary Bush.* Another rotten novel by Floyd Dell, which, because it is without a touch of grace or beauty or wit, will be hailed as a masterpiece by by all the ex-policemen who are now critics.

Will you send me that Brentano sketch when it appears?

Sincerely,

F. Scott Fitz——

626 *Goodrich Avenue*
St. Paul, Minnesota
[*Before December 12, 1921*]

Dear Mr. Perkins:

Have just received your letter in re Bible anecdote in novel [1] and I'm rather upset about it. You say:

"Even when people are wrong you cannot but respect those who speak with such passionate sincerity about it."

Now in that remark lies, I think, the root of your objection—except to substitute *"be intimidated by"* for "respect." I don't suppose any but the most religious-minded people in the world believe that such interludes as *The Song of Solomon* [or] the story of *Ruth* have or ever had *even in the minds of the original chroniclers* the faintest religious significance. The Roman Church insists that in *The Song of Solomon* the bride is the church and the lover is Christ but it is almost universally doubted if any such thing was even faintly intended.

Now I feel sure that most people will know that my

[1] The passage in *The Beautiful and Damned* where Maury Noble debunks the Bible as the work of ancient skeptics, whose sole aim was the literary immortality they achieved.

sketch refers to the *Old* Testament, and to Jehovah, the
cruel Hebrew God, against whom such writers as even
Mark Twain not to mention Anatole France and a host of
others have delivered violent pyrotechnics from time to
time.

As to the personal side of it don't you think all changes in
the *minds* of people are brought about by the *assertion* of a
thing—startling perhaps at first but later often becoming,
with the changes of the years, bromidic. You have read
Shaw's preface to *Androcles and the Lion*—that made no
great stir—in fact to the more sophisticated of the critics
it was a bit bromidic. His preface, moreover, is couched
with very little reverence even tho it treats of *Christ* who
is much less open to discussion than merely that beautiful
epic of the Bible. If you object to my phrasing I could
substitute "deity" for "godalmighty" and get a better word
than bawdy—in fact make it more dignified—but I would
hate to cut it out as it's very clever in its way and Mencken
—who saw it—and Zelda were very enthusiastic about it.
It's the sort of thing you find continually in Anatole
France's *Revolt of the Angels*—as well as in *Jurgen* and
in Mark Twain's *Mysterious Stranger*. The idea, refusing
homage to the Bible and its God, runs thru many of Mark
Twain's essays and all through Paine's biography.[1]

In fact, Van Wyck Brooks in *The Ordeal*[2] criticizes
Clemens for allowing many of his statements to be toned
down at the request of William Dean Howells or Mrs.
Clemens. If it was an incident which I felt had no particular literary merit I should defer to your judgment
without question, but that passage belongs beautifully to
that scene and is exactly what was needed to make it more
than a beautiful setting for ideas that fail to appear. You
say:

"Even when people are altogether wrong you cannot but
respect those who speak with such passionate sincerity."

I can imagine that remark having been made to Galileo
and Mencken, Samuel Butler and Anatole France, Voltaire
and Bernard Shaw, George Moore and even, if you will
pardon me, in this form once upon a time.

"You don't like these scribes and pharisees. You call

[1] *Mark Twain* by Albert Bigelow Paine.
[2] *The Ordeal of Mark Twain* by Van Wyck Brooks.

them whitened sepulchres but even when people are altogether wrong—etc."

I haven't seen the proof with your notation and have
only read your letter. But I do feel that my judgment is
right in this case. I do not expect in any event that I am
to have the same person-for-person public this time that
Paradise had. My one hope is to be endorsed by the intellectually élite and thus be *forced* onto people as Conrad
has. (Of course I'm assuming that my work grows in sincerity and proficiency from year to year as it has so far.)
If I cut this out it would only [be] because I would be
afraid and I haven't done that yet and dread the day when
I'll have to.

Please write me frankly as I have you—and tell me if
you are speaking for yourself, for the Scribner Company,
or the public. I am rather upset about the whole thing.
Will wait until I hear from you.

As ever,

F. Scott Fitzgerald

P.S. Besides, as to the position of the thing in the story, it
is necessary to show the growth of Maury's pessimism and
to do this I have invented a fable in which the *hoi poloi*
do more than refuse to believe their wise men—but they
twist the very wisdom of the wise into a justification of
their own maudlin and self-satisfactory creeds. This would
discourage *any*one.

626 Goodrich Avenue
St. Paul, Minnesota
[*Before December 21, 1921*]

Dear Mr. Perkins:

Your second letter came and I want to apologize to
you for mine. I might have known you did not mean what
in haste I imagined you did. The thing *was* flippant—I
mean it was the sort of worst of George Jean Nathan. I
have changed it now—changed "godalmighty" to "deity,"

cut out "bawdy," and changed several other words, so I think it is all right.

Why, really, my letter was so silly, with all those absurd citations of Twain, Anatole France, Howells, etc., was because I was in a panic because I was afraid I might have to cut it out and, as you say, it does round out the scene.

I hope you'll accept my apology.

Is the girl *beautiful* in the W. E. Hill picture? Are you going to have a light blue background on the jacket as I suggested—I mean like you had for your Lulu Ragdale book two years ago? And did you catch that last correction I sent you before it was too late?

I have put a new ending on the book—that is, on the last paragraph, instead of the repetition of the Paradise scene of which I was never particularly fond. I think that now the finish will leave the "taste" of the whole book in the reader's mouth as it didn't before—if you know what I mean.

I can't tell you how sorry I am about that silly letter. I took that "Oh Christ" out as you suggested. As you say, "Oh, God" won't fill the gap but "Oh my God" does it pretty well.

With my changing of the extreme last and fixing up the symposium I am almost, but not quite, satisfied with the book. I prophesy that it will go about 60,000 copies the first year—that is, assuming that *Paradise* went about 40,000 the first year. Thank God I'm thru with it.

                                        As ever,

                                        F. Scott Fitzg——

                                        [*626 Goodrich Avenue*]
                                        [*St. Paul, Minnesota*]
                                        [circa *January 31, 1922*]

Dear Mr. Perkins:

The books came[1] and I'm delighted with the blurb on

[1] Advance copies of *The Beautiful and Damned*.

the back which I suspect you wrote yourself. I think it strikes exactly the right note, gives a moral key to the stupider critics on which to go, and justifies the book to many who will think it is immoral! Thank you.

I like the way it is got up—it surprised me to find that it is half again as long as *Paradise*.

I wired you last night about the color of the jacket, which has come out, in my copies at least, a sickly yellow. It was a deep reddish orange, you remember, in the jacket you sent me before.

The more I think of the picture on the jacket the more I fail to understand his drawing that man. The girl is excellent of course—it looks somewhat like Zelda—but the man, I suspect, is a sort of debauched edition of me. At any rate the man is utterly unprepossessing and I do not understand an artist of Hill's talent and carefulness going quite contrary to a detailed description of the hero in the book.

Note these divergencies—

1. Anthony is "just under six feet"— Here he looks about Gloria's height with ugly short legs.

2. Anthony is dark-haired— This bartender on the cover is light-haired.

3. Anthony's general impression is described on page 9 —in not a single trait does this person on the jacket conform to that impression. He looks like a sawed-off young tough in his first dinner-coat.

Everybody I've talked to agrees with me and I'm a little sore. When a book has but one picture to give the impression, the illustrator ought to be careful. The *Metropolitan* illustrations were bad enough, God knows, but at least the poor botcher of an illustrator tried to give Anthony the physique and atmosphere assigned to him.

As you can see I'm an ill-natured crabber. I ought not to be. The girl is excellent and I suppose Hill thought it would please me if the picture looked like Zelda and me. But I'd rather have the man on the *Paradise* jacket even with his tie tucked neatly under his collar in the Amherst fashion. Hill has done about 9 figures for my covers altogether and I suppose 8 good out of 9 is a good average.

Excuse this letter—it's just to get rid of an inhibition of anger so I can get back to my play this morning. Wilson's article about me in the March 1st *Vanity Fair* is superb.

It's no blurb—not by a darn sight—but it's the first time I've been done *at length* [by] an intelligent and sophisticated man and I appreciate it—jeers and all.

As ever,

F. Scott Fitzgerald

626 Goodrich Avenue
St. Paul, Minnesota

[circa *March 5, 1922*]

Dear Mr. Perkins:

This is to thank you for the money. I was in a tight place—had actually cashed a bad check and didn't know it. However, the *Metropolitan* had begun to pay a little and I think I'm out of the woods.

When I wrote you about *The Mind in the Making*[1] I'd only read two chapters. I have finished it and entirely changed my views on its importance. I think it's a thoroughly excellent book. It states the entire case for modernity's lingering hope of progress. It is a depressing book, I think, as are Wells' and Shaw's late things, and all those of that brave company who started out in the 90's so full of hope and joy in life and faith in science and reason. Thomas Hardy survives them all. I think when I read Upton Sinclair's *The Brass Check* I made my final decision about America—that freedom has produced the greatest tyranny under the sun. I'm still a socialist but sometimes I dread that things will grow worse and worse the more the people nominally rule. The strong are too strong for us and the weak too weak. I shall not write another novel for a year but when I do it will not be a realistic one. At least I don't think it will.

The more I think of *The B. and D.'s* chances the more I think that your blurb will save it if anything can.

Nathan writes me: "A very substantial performance. There is a wealth of sound stuff in it. You are maturing rapidly. It pleases me to have so good a piece of work dedicated in part to me. You have done a first rate job."

[1] By James Harvey Robinson.

I don't want to use this though as he's funny about that sort of thing.

I've read my book over and I've decided that I like it fine. I think it is as good as *Three Soldiers*—which is high praise from me.

The Knopf man was here a while ago and I had quite a talk with him in Boyd's bookstore. It seemed to me that he was personally dishonest and utterly disloyal to his company—that is, he was trying to sell one of his sample books and he said that Knopf was as honest as any publisher with a wink! I doubt if Knopf gives his authors a full 15% on those $2.50 books—of course he shouldn't as they cost more. I had an interesting time with Hergesheimer —he came through and came to dinner. However, what I started to say was how favorably Knapp compared with the Knopf man.

Please don't get the impression that I was fooled by the size of the St. Paul orders. I knew they were chiefly "on sale." I think I'm going to have a great non-fiction book ready for you about next January. And if my play is a big success, will you bring it out in book form—or do you think it best to wait until I have three of them, as O'Neill has done, following Shaw and Barrie and Galsworthy?

I'm glad you liked *In One Reel*.[1] Wait till you see the stories. You haven't seen half of them. Read *Chrome Yellow*. Best to Roger. Knapp seemed devoted to you, which was our chief bond of union.

Yours ever,

F. Scott Fitzg_____

626 Goodrich Avenue
St. Paul, Minnesota
April 19, 1922

Dear Mr. Scribner:

I am consumed by an idea and I can't resist asking you about it. It's probably a chestnut, but it might not have occurred to you before in just this form.

[1] Evidently Fitzgerald's proposed title for his next volume of short stories. He repudiates it in the letter after this.

No doubt you know of the success that Boni and Liveright have made of their Modern Library. Within the last month Doubleday, Page & Company have withdrawn the titles that were theirs from Boni's Modern Library, and gone in on their own hook with a Lambskin Library. For this they have chosen so far about 18 titles from their past publications—some of them books of merit (Frank Norris and Conrad, for instance) and some of them trashy, but all books that at one time or another have been sensational either as popular successes or as possible contributions to American literature. The Lambskin Library is cheap, bound uniformly in red leather (or imitation leather), and makes, I believe, a larger appeal to the buyer than the A. L. Burt reprints, for its uniformity gives it a sort of permanence, a place of honor in the scraggly library that adorns every small home. Besides that, it is a much easier thing for a bookseller to display and keep up. The titles are numbered and it gives people a chance to sample writers by one book in this edition. Also it keeps before the public such books as have once been popular and have since been forgotten.

Now my idea is this: the Scribner Company have many more distinguished years of publishing behind them than Doubleday, Page. They could produce a list twice as long of distinguished and memorable fiction and use no more than one book by each author—and it need not be the book by that author most in demand.

Take for instance *Predestined* and *The House of Mirth.* I do not know, but I imagine that those books are kept upstairs in most bookstores, and only obtained when someone is told of the work of Edith Wharton and Stephen French Whitman. They are almost as forgotten as the books of Frank Norris and Stephen Crane were five years ago, before Boni's library began its career.

To be specific, I can imagine that a Scribner library containing the following titles and selling for something under a dollar would be an enormous success:

1. *The House of Mirth*   Edith Wharton
   (or *Ethan Frome*)
2. *Predestined*   Stephen French Whitman
3. *This Side of Paradise*   F. Scott Fitzgerald

4. *The Little Shepherd of Kingdom Come* — John Fox, Jr.
5. *In Ole Kentucky* — Thomas Nelson Page
6. *Sentimental Tommy* — J. M. Barrie
7. Some Civil War book by — George Barr Cable
8. Some novel by — Henry Van Dyke
9. Some novel by — Jackson Gregory
10. *Saint's Progress* — John Galsworthy
11. *The Ordeal of Richard Feverel* — George Meredith
12. *Treasure Island* — Robert Louis Stevenson
13. *The Turn of the Screw* — Henry James
14. *The Stolen Story* (or *The Frederic Carrolls*) — Jesse Lynch Williams
15. *The Damnation of Theron Ware* (I think Stone use to own this.) — Harold Frederick
16. *Soldiers of Fortune* — Richard Harding Davis
17. Some book by — Mary Raymond Shipman Andrews
18. *Simple Souls* — John Hastings Turner

Doubtless a glance at your old catalogues would suggest two dozen others. I have not even mentioned less popular writers such as Burt and Katharine Gerould. Nor have I gone into the possibilities of such non-fiction as a volume of Roosevelt, a volume of Huneker, or a volume of Shane Leslie.

As I say, this is quite possibly an idea which has occurred to you before and been dismissed for reasons which would not appear to me, an outsider. I am moved to the suggestion by the success of the experiments I have mentioned. They have been made possible, I believe, by the recent American strain for "culture" which expresses itself in such things as uniformity of bindings to make a library. Also the selective function of this library would appeal to many people in search of good reading matter, new or old.

One more thing and this interminably long letter is done. It may seem to you that in many cases I have chosen novels whose sale still nets a steady revenue at $1.75—and that it would be unprofitable to use such property in this way. But I have used such titles only to indicate my idea— *Gallagher* (which I believe is not in your subscription sets of Davis) could be substituted for *Soldiers of Fortune*, *The Wrong Box* for *Treasure Island*, and so on in the case of Fox, Page and Barrie. The main idea is that the known titles in the series should "carry" the little known or forgotten. That is: from the little-known writer you use his best novel, such as *Predestined*—from the well-known writer you use his more obscure, such as *Gallagher*.

I apologize for imposing so upon your time, Mr. Scribner. I am merely mourning that so many good or lively books are dead so soon, or only imperfectly kept alive in the cheap and severe impermanency of the A. L. Burt editions.

I am, sir,

Most sincerely,
F. Scott Fitzgerald

626 Goodrich Avenue
[St. Paul, Minnesota]
May 11, [1922]

Dear Mr. Perkins:

After careful consideration by the Fitzgerald menage, two booksellers and several friends, I am strongly in favor of keeping the *Jazz Age* title.[1] Here's my line of reasoning:

(1) If it were a novel I should say the salesmen were undoubtedly right—the word flapper, or jazz, would be passé and kill a big sale.

(2) Short stories do not sell and *Flappers* was an exception chiefly on account of my first novel and what was then the timeliness of the title.

(3) I do not expect the new collection to have an advance sale of more than four or five thousand, and the total will never reach more than nine or ten thousand (that is, the first year or so).

(4) It will be bought by *my own personal public*—that

[1] *Tales of the Jazz Age*, Fitzgerald's second volume of short stories.

is, by the countless flappers and college kids who think I am a sort of oracle.

(5) The question of *Jazz* or *not Jazz* is Scylla and Charybdis anyhow. If I use such a title as *Half Portions*, etc., or *Chance Encounters*, no one will buy it anyhow— it will just be another book of short stories. It is better to have a title and a title-connection that is a has-been than one that is a never-will-be. The splash of the flapper movement was too big to have quite died down—the outer rings are still moving.

(6) If I could think of a wonderful selling title uncon- nected with jazz I'd use it but I can't, so we better use a safe one that has a certain appeal. Short story collections are the hardest things on earth to name—to get a title which is at once arresting, inviting, applicable and inclusive, and doesn't sound like a rehash of the titles of O. Henry, or isn't an anemic namby-pamby wishy-washy phrase.

(7) In any case I think it will be wise to undersell the booksellers—a few, I fear from your silence, are going to be stuck with *The B. and D.* and, though *Flappers* seems to be still trickling along, there are two bookstores in St. Paul that have quite a few left.

(8) The only possible other title I can think of is *The Diamond as Big as the Ritz and Other Stories*. I hate titles like *Sideshow* and *In One Reel* and *Happy End*. They have begun to sound like veils and apologies for bringing out collections at all. Only good short story titles lately are *Limbo* and *Seven Men*. I might possibly call my book *Nine Humans and Fourteen Dummies* if you'd permit such a long title (in this case I'd have to figure out how many dummies there are in the collection)—but if you feel aw- fully strongly against *Jazz Age*, I insist that it be an arrest- ing title if it spreads over half the front cover.

Please let me know at once what you think.

I'm sure in any case the stories will be reviewed a great deal, largely because of the Table of Contents.

Wire me if necessary.

As ever,

Scott Fitzg——

If you are really considering the library, don't forget *The White Mice* by Gouverneur Morris.

626 Goodrich Avenue
St. Paul, Minnesota

[*Before May 13, 1922*]

Dear Mr. Bridges:

As Mr. Perkins has no doubt told you I was aghast and horrified at that silly anecdote sprung from God knows whither which Burton Rascoe had the ill-taste to reprint in his column.[1] I wrote him an indignant letter about it but I haven't heard from him.

I can only tell you what I have long suspected—that any strange happening in the new literary generation is at once attributed to me. When we returned from Europe last summer there were legends enough current to supply three biographers.

Needless to say I regret the indignity done to you by the association with your name of such a piece of unwarranted vulgarity—and believe me.

As ever sincerely,

F. Scott Fitzgerald

The Yacht Club
White Bear Lake, Minnesota

[circa *August 11, 1922*]

Dear Mr. Perkins:

I've labored over these proofs for a week and feel as if I never want to see a short story again. Thanks [for] the information about Canadian and Australian publishers. You ought to penalize the lighted-match-girl twenty yards.

Now as to "Tarquin of Cheapside." It first appeared in the *Nassau Literary Magazine* at Princeton and Katharine Fullerton Gerould reviewing the issue for the *Daily Princetonian* gave it high praise, called it "beautifully writ-

[1] Rascoe wrote, "Fitzgerald, during a conversation with Robert Bridges, had leaned over and plucked a hair from Dr. Bridges' beard with the comment that it was grey, and the dignified gentleman had been so nonplussed by this amazing performance that he did not remonstrate until Fitzgerald had plucked out six hairs."

ten," and tickled me with the first public praise my writing has ever had. When Mencken printed it in the *Smart Set* it drew letters of praise from George O'Neill, the poet, and Zoe Atkins. Structurally it is almost perfect and next to "The Offshore Pirate" I like it better than any story I have ever written.

If you insist I will cut it out, though very much against my better judgment and Zelda's. It was even starred by O'Brien in his yearbook of the short story and mentioned by Blanche Colton Williams in the preface to the last O. Henry memorial collection. Please tell me what you think.

As to another matter, my play, *Gabriel's Trombone*[1] is now in the hands of Arthur Hopkins. It is, I think, the best American comedy to date and undoubtedly the best thing I have ever written. Noting that *Harper's* are serializing *The Intimate Strangers*, a play by Booth Tarkington, I wonder if *Scribner's Magazine* would be interested in serializing *Gabriel's Trombone*—that is, of course, on condition that it is to be produced this fall. Will you let me know about this or shall I write Bridges?

Also, last but not least, I have not yet received a statement from you. I am awfully hard up. I imagine there's something over $1000 still in my favor. Anyway will you deposit $1000 for me when you receive this letter? If there's not that much due me will you charge off the rest as advance on *Tales of the Jazz Age?* After my play is produced I'll be rich forever and never have to bother you again.

Also let me know about the "Tarquin" matter and about *Gabriel's Trombone*.

As ever,

F. Scott Fitzgerald

P.S. Thanks for the *Fair & Co.* check.

---

[1] Afterward, *The Vegetable*.

Great Neck, [Long Island]
[Before November 7, 1923]

Dear Max:

I have got myself into a terrible mess. As you know, for the past month I have been coming every day to the city to rehearsals[1] and then at night writing and making changes on the last act and even on the first two. It's in shape at last and everybody around the theater who has seen it says it's a great hit. I put aside the novel three weeks ago and wrote a short story but it was done under such pressure that it shows it and Hovey[2] doesn't want it. I am so hard pressed now for time trying to write another for him that I'm not even going [to] the Harvard-Princeton game Saturday. The show opens in Atlantic City a week from Monday.

I went up to the American Play Company yesterday and tried to get some money on the grounds that the show was in rehearsal. They sighed and moaned a little but said firmly that it was against their rules.

I'm at the end of my rope—as the immortal phrase goes. I owe the Scribner Company something over $3500, even after deducting the reprint money from *The Beautiful and Damned*. I owed them more than that before *The B. and D.* was published but that was guaranteed by the book being actually in your hands.

Could this be done? Could I assign the first royalty payments on the play to you to be paid until the full amount be cleared up? I meant to pay some of it if there was a margin anyhow on account of the delay in the novel. But this would at least guarantee it.

What I need to extricate myself from the present hole is $650.00 which will carry me to the 15th when Hovey will have my next story. And the only grounds on which I can ask for this additional is for me to assign you those rights up to the figure outstanding and to include also the interest on the whole amount I owe you.

If I don't in some way get $650.00 in the bank by Wednesday morning I'll have to pawn the furniture. Under the assignment of the royalties to you, the full amount would be paid back at between $500.00 and $1100 a week, before January 15th.

---

[1] Of *The Vegetable*.
[2] Carl Hovey, editor of *Metropolitan Magazine*.

I don't even dare come up there personally but for God's sake try to fix it.

Yours in Horror,

F. Scott F.

Great Neck, [*Long Island*]
[*Before April 16, 1924*]

Dear Max:

A few words more, relative to our conversation this afternoon. While I have every hope and plan of finishing my novel [1] in June, you know how those things often come out, and even if it takes me ten times that long I cannot let it go out unless it has the very best I'm capable of in it, or even, as I feel sometimes, something better than I'm capable of. Much of what I wrote last summer was good but it was so interrupted that it was ragged and, in approaching it from a new angle, I've had to discard a lot of it—in one case, 18,000 words (part of which will appear in the *Mercury* as a short story).[2] It is only in the last four months that I've realized how much I've, well, almost *deteriorated* in the three years since I finished *The Beautiful and Damned*. The last four months of course I've worked but in the two years—over two years—before that, I produced exactly *one* play, *half a dozen* short stories and three or four articles—an average of about *one hundred* words a day. If I'd spent this time reading or traveling or doing anything—even staying healthy—it'd be different, but I spent it uselessly, neither in study nor in contemplation but only in drinking and raising hell generally. If I'd written *The B. and D.* at the rate of one hundred words a day, it would have taken me *4 years,* so you can imagine the moral effect the whole chasm had on me.

What I'm trying to say is just that I'll have to ask you to have patience about the book and trust me that at last, or at least for the first time in years, I'm doing the best I

---

[1] *The Great Gatsby.*
[2] "Absolution."

can. I've gotten in dozens of bad habits that I'm trying to get rid of

1. Laziness
2. Referring everything to Zelda—a terrible habit; nothing ought to be referred to anybody until it's finished
3. Word consciousness and self-doubt, etc., etc., etc., etc.

I feel I have an enormous power in me now, more than I've ever had in a way, but it works so fitfully and with so many bogeys because I've *talked so much* and not lived enough within myself to develop the necessary self-reliance. Also I don't know anyone who has used up so much personal experience as I have at 27. *Copperfield* and *Pendennis* were written at past 40, while *This Side of Paradise* was three books and *The B. and D.* was two. So in my new novel I'm thrown directly on purely creative work—not trashy imaginings as in my stories but the sustained imagination of a sincere yet radiant world. So I tread slowly and carefully and at times in considerable distress. This book will be a consciously artistic achievement and must depend on that as the first books did not.

If I ever win the right to any leisure again, I will assuredly not waste it as I wasted this past time. Please believe me when I say that now I'm doing the best I can.

Yours ever,

Scott F._____

Villa Marie, Valescure
St. Raphael, France
June 18, 1924

Dear Max:

Thanks for your nice long letter. I'm glad that Ring's[1] had good reviews but I'm sorry both that he's off the wagon and that the book's not selling. I had counted on a sale of 15 to 25 thousand right away for it.

[1] *How to Write Short Stories.*

Shelley was a God to me once. What a good man he is compared to that colossal egotist Browning! Haven't you read *Ariel* yet? For heaven's sake read it if you like Shelley. It's one of the best biographies I've ever read of anyone and it's by a Frenchman. I think Harcourt publishes it. And who "thinks *badly*" of Shelley now!

We are idyllically settled here and the novel is going fine—it ought to be done in a month—though I'm not sure as I'm contemplating another 16,000 words, which would make it about the length of *Paradise*—not quite though even then.

I'm glad you liked "Absolution." As you know it was to have been the prologue of the novel but it interfered with the neatness of the plan. Two Catholics have already protested by letter. Be sure and read "The Baby Party" in *Hearst's* and my article in *The Woman's Home Companion*.

Tom Boyd wrote me that Bridges had been a dodo about some Y.M.C.A. man—I wrote him that he oughtn't to fuss with such a silly old man. I hope he hasn't—you don't mention him in your letter. I enjoyed Arthur Train's story in the *Post* but he made three steals on the first page —one from Shaw (the Arab's remark about Christianity), one from Stendahl, and one I've forgotten. It was most ingeniously worked out—I never could have handled such an intricate plot in a thousand years. *War and Peace* came —many thanks, and for the inscription too. Don't forget the clippings. I will have to reduce my tax in September.

As ever, yours,

F. Scott Fitzgerald

P.S. If Struthers Burt comes over here, give me his address.

Villa Marie, Valescure
St. Raphael, France
[circa *July 16, 1924*]

Dear Max:

Is Ring dead? We've written him three times and not a word. How about his fall book? I had two suggestions.

Either a collection called *Mother Goose in Great Neck* (or something nonsensical) to include his fairy tales in *Hearst's,* some of his maddest syndicate articles, his Forty-niners' sketch, his Authors League sketch, etc.

—or *My Life and Loves* (privately printed for sub-scribers only—on sale at all bookstores). I believe I gave you a tentative list for that but he'd have to eke it out by pointing some new syndicate articles that way. I thought his short story book was *great*—"Alibi Ike," "Some Like 'em Cold" and "My Roomy" are as good almost as "The Golden Honeymoon." Mencken's review was great. Do send me others. Is it selling?

Would you do me this favor? Call up Harvey Craw, Fifth Ave.—he's in the book—and ask him if my house is rented. I'm rather curious to know and letters bring me no response. He is the Great Neck agent.

I'm not going to mention my novel to you again until it is on your desk. All goes well. I wish your bookkeeper would send me the August statement even tho no copies of my books have been sold. How about Gertrude Stein's novel? I began *War and Peace* last night. Do write me a nice long letter.

As ever,

Scott

Villa Marie, Valescure
St. Raphael, France
[*Before August 27, 1924*]

Dear Max:

(1) The novel will be done next week. That doesn't mean however that it'll reach America before October 1st as Zelda and I are contemplating a careful revision after a week's complete rest.

(2) The clippings have never arrived.

(3) Seldes[1] has been with me and he thinks *For the Grimalkins* is a wonderful title for Ring's book. Also

---

[1] Critic Gilbert Seldes.

I've got great ideas about *My Life and Loves* which I'll tell Ring when he comes over in September.

(4) How many copies has his short stories sold?

(5) Your bookkeeper never did send me my royalty report for August 1st.

(6) For Christ's sake, don't give anyone that jacket you're saving for me. I've written it into the book.[1]

(7) I think my novel is about the best American novel ever written. It is rough stuff in places, runs only to about 50,000 words, and I hope you won't shy at it.

(8) It's been a fair summer. I've been unhappy but my work hasn't suffered from it. I am grown at last.

(9) What books are being talked about? I don't mean best sellers. Hergesheimer's novel in the *Post* seems vile to me.

(10) I hope you're reading Gertrude Stein's novel in the *Transatlantic Review*.

(11) Raymond Radiguet's last book (he is the young man who wrote *Le Diable au Corps* at sixteen [untranslatable]) is a great hit here. He wrote it at 18. It's called *Le Bal du Comte d'Orgel* and though I'm only half through it I'd get an opinion on it if I were you. It's cosmopolitan rather than French and my instinct tells me that in a good translation it might make an enormous hit in America, where everyone is yearning for Paris. Do look it up and get at least one opinion on it. The preface is by the dadaist Jean Cocteau but the book is not dada at all.

(12) Did you get hold of Ring's other books?

(13) We're liable to leave here by October 1st so after the 15th of September I wish you'd send everything care of Guaranty Trust Co., Paris.

(14) Please ask the bookstore, if you have time, to send me Havelock Ellis' *Dance of Life* and charge to my account.

(15) I asked Struthers Burt to dinner but his baby was sick.

(16) Be *sure* and answer *every* question, Max.

I miss seeing you like the devil.

                                                        Scott

[1] The dust jacket of *The Great Gatsby* showed two huge eyes, intended to be those of Daisy Fay, brooding over New York City, and this had been Fitzgerald's inspiration for the eyes of Dr. T. J. Eckleburg.

Villa Marie, Valescure
St. Ralphael, France
[Before October 18, 1924]

Dear Max:

The royalty was better than I'd expected. This is to tell you about a young man named Ernest Hemingway, who lives in Paris (an American), writes for the *Transatlantic Review* and has a brilliant future. Ezra Pound published a collection of his short pieces in Paris, at some place like the Egotist Press. I haven't it here now but it's remarkable and I'd look him up right away. He's the real thing.

My novel goes to you with a long letter within five days. Ring arrives in a week. This is just a hurried scrawl as I'm working like a dog. I thought Stallings' book was disappointingly rotten.[1] It takes a genius to whine appealingly. Have tried to see Struthers Burt but he's been on the move. More later.

                                          Scott

P.S. *Important.* What chance has a smart young Frenchman with an intimate knowledge of French literature in the bookselling business in New York? Is a clerk paid much and is there any opening for one specializing in French literature? Do tell me as there's a young friend of mine here just out of the army who is anxious to know.

                                          Sincerely,

                                          Scott

Villa Marie, Valescure
St. Raphael, France
(After Nov. 3d care of
American Express Co., Rome, Italy)
October 27, 1924

Dear Max:

Under separate cover I'm sending you my third novel,

---
[1] *Plumes* by Laurence Stallings.

The Great Gatsby. (I think that at last I've done something really my own, but how good "my own" is remains to be seen.)

I should suggest the following contract.

15% up to 50,000
20% after 50,000

The book is only a little over fifty thousand words long but I believe, as you know, that Whitney Darrow[1] has the wrong psychology about prices (and about what class constitute the book-buying public now that the lowbrows go to the movies) and I'm anxious to charge two dollars for it and have it a *full-size book.*

Of course I want the binding to be absolutely uniform with my other books—the stamping too—and the jacket we discussed before. This time I don't want any signed blurbs on the jacket—not Mencken's or Lewis' or Howard's[2] or anyone's. I'm tired of being the author of *This Side of Paradise* and I want to start over.

About serialization. I am bound under contract to show it to *Hearst's,* but I am asking a prohibitive price, Long[3] hates me, and it's not a very serialized book. If they should take it—they won't—it would put publication in the fall. Otherwise you can publish it in the spring. When Hearst turns it down, I'm going to offer it to *Liberty* for $15,000 on condition that they'll publish it in ten weekly installments before April 15th. If they don't want it, I shan't serialize. *I am absolutely positive Long won't want it.*

I have an alternative title: *Gold-hatted Gatsby.*

After you're read the book, let me know what you think about the title. Naturally I won't get a night's sleep until I hear from you, but do tell me the absolute truth, *your first impression of the book,* and tell me anything that bothers you in it.

As ever,
Scott

I'd rather you wouldn't call Reynolds as he might try to act as my agent.

[1] Sales manager at Scribners.
[2] Playwright Sidney Howard.
[3] Ray Long, editor of *Hearst's International.*

Hotel Continental
St. Raphael, France
(leaving Tuesday)

[circa *November 7, 1924*]

Dear Max:

By now you've received the novel. There are things in it I'm not satisfied with, in the middle of the book—Chapters 6 and 7. And I may write in a complete new scene in proof. I hope you got my telegram.

I have now decided to stick to the title I put on the book. *Trimalchio in West Egg.*

The only other titles that seem to fit it are *Trimalchio* and *On the Road to West Egg.* I had two others, *Goldhatted Gatsby* and *The High-bouncing Lover,* but they seemed too light.

We leave for Rome as soon as I finish the short story I'm working on.

As ever,

Scott

I was interested that you've moved to New Canaan. It sounds wonderful. Sometimes I'm awfully anxious to be home.

But I am confused at what you say about Gertrude Stein. I thought it was one purpose of critics and publishers to educate the public up to original work. The first people who risked Conrad certainly didn't do it as a commercial venture. Did the evolution of startling work into accepted work cease twenty years ago?

Do send me Boyd's (Ernest's) book when it comes out. I think the Lardner ads are wonderful. Did the *Dark Cloud* flop?

Would you ask the people downstairs to keep sending me my monthly bill for the encyclopedia?

Hotel des Princes
Piazza di Spagna
Rome, Italy
[circa *December 1, 1924*]

Dear Max:

Your wire and your letters made me feel like a million dollars—I'm sorry I could make no better response than a telegram whining for money. But the long siege of the novel winded me a little and I've been slow on starting the stories on which I must live.

I think all your criticisms are true.

(a) About the title. I'll try my best but I don't know what I can do. Maybe simply *Trimalchio* or *Gatsby*. In the former case, I don't see why the note shouldn't go on the back.

(b) Chapters VI and VII I know how to fix.

(c) Gatsby's business affairs I can fix. I get your point about them.

(d) His vagueness I can repair by *making more pointed* —this doesn't sound good but wait and see. It'll make him clear.

(e) But his long narrative in Chapter VIII will be difficult to split up. Zelda also thought it was a little out of key, but it is good writing and I don't think I could bear to sacrifice any of it.

(f) I have 1000 minor corrections which I will make on the proof and several more large ones which you didn't mention.

Your criticisms were excellent and most helpful, and you picked out all my favorite spots in the book to praise as high spots. Except you didn't mention my favorite of all— the chapter where Gatsby and Daisy meet.

Two more things. Zelda's been reading me the cowboy book[1] aloud to spare my mind and I love it—tho I think he learned the American language from Ring rather than from his own ear.

Another point—in Chapter II of my book when Tom and Myrtle go into the bedroom while Carraway reads

[1] *Cowboys North and South* by Will James.

Simon Called Peter—is that raw? Let me know. I think it's pretty necessary.

I made the royalty smaller because I wanted to make up for all the money you've advanced these two years by letting it pay a sort of interest on it. But I see by calculating I made it too small—a difference of 2000 dollars. Let us call it 15% up to 40,000 and 20% after that. That's a good fair contract all around.

By now you have heard from a smart young French woman who wants to translate the book. She's equal to it intellectually and linguistically, I think—had read all my others—if you'll tell her how to go about it as to royalty demands, etc.

Anyhow thanks and thanks and thanks for your letters. I'd rather have you and Bunny[1] like it than anyone I know. And I'd rather have you like it than Bunny. If it's as good as you say, when I finish with the proof it'll be perfect.

Remember, by the way, to put by some cloth for the cover uniform with my other books.

As soon as I can think about the title, I'll write or wire a decision. Thank Louise[2] for me, for liking it. Best regards to Mr. Scribner. Tell him Galsworthy is here in Rome.

As ever,

Scott

Hotel des Princes
Piazza di Spagna
Rome, Italy
[circa *December 20, 1924*]

Dear Max:

I'm a bit (not very—not dangerously) stewed tonight and I'll probably write you a long letter. We're living in a small, unfashionable but most comfortable hotel at $525.00 a month, including tips, meals, etc. Rome does *not* particu-

[1] Edmund Wilson.
[2] Mrs. Maxwell Perkins.

larly interest me but it's a big year here, and early in the spring we're going to Paris. There's no use telling you my plans because they're usually just about as unsuccessful as to work as religious prognosticators are as to the End of the World. I've got a new novel to write—title and all— that'll take about a year. Meanwhile, I don't want to start it until this is out and meanwhile I'll do short stories for money (I now get $2000 a story but I hate worse than hell to do them) and there's the never-dying lure of another play.

Now! Thanks enormously for making up the $5000. I know I don't technically deserve it, considering I've had $3000 or $4000 for as long as I can remember. But since you force it on me (inexecrable [or is it execrable] joke) I will accept it. I hope to Christ you get 10 times it back on *Gatsby*—and I think perhaps you will.

For:

I can now make it perfect but the proof (I will soon get the immemorial letter with the statement "We now have the book in hand and will soon begin to send you proof." What is "in hand?" I have a vague picture of everyone in the office holding the book in the right hand and reading it.) will be one of the most expensive affairs since *Madame Bovary*. *Please* charge it to my account. If it's possible to send a second proof over here I'd love to have it. Count on 12 days each way—four days here on first proof and two days on the second. I hope there are other good books in the spring because I think now the public interest in *books* per se rises when there seems to be a group of them, as in 1920 (spring and fall), 1921 (fall), 1922 (spring). Ring's and Tom's (first) books,[1] Willa Cather's *Lost Lady*, and in an inferior, cheap way Edna Ferber's are the only American fiction in over two years that had a really excellent press (say, since *Babbitt*).

With the aid you've given me I can make *Gatsby* perfect. The Chapter 7 (the hotel scene) will never quite be up to mark—I've worried about it too long and I can't quite place Daisy's reaction. But I can improve it a lot. It isn't imaginative energy that's lacking—it's because I'm automatically prevented from thinking it out over again

[1] Thomas Boyd, best known for his war novel, *Through the Wheat*.

because I must get all those characters to New York in order to have the catastrophe on the road going back, and I must have it pretty much that way. So there's no chance of bringing the freshness to it that a new free conception sometimes gives.

The rest is easy and I see my way so clear that I even see the mental quirks that queered it before. Strange to say, my notion of Gatsby's vagueness was O.K. What you and Louise and Mr. Charles Scribner found wanting was that:

I myself didn't know what Gatsby looked like or was engaged in and you felt it. If I'd known and kept it from you you'd have been *too impressed with my knowledge to protest*. This is a complicated idea but I'm sure you'll understand. But I know now—and as a penalty for not having known first, in other words to make sure, I'm going to tell more.

It seems of almost mystical significance to me that you thought he was older—the man I had in mind, half-unconsciously, *was* older (a specific individual) and evidently, without so much as a definite word, I conveyed the fact. Or rather I must qualify this Shaw Desmond trash by saying that I conveyed it without a word that I can at present or for the life of me trace. (I think Shaw Desmond was one of your bad bets—I was the other.)

Anyhow after careful searching of the files (of a man's mind here) for the Fuller Magee case and after having had Zelda draw pictures until her fingers ache I know Gatsby better than I know my own child. My first instinct after your letter was to let him go and have Tom Buchanan dominate the book (I suppose he's the best character I've ever done—I think he and the brother in *Salt* and Hurstwood in *Sister Carrie* are the three best characters in American fiction in the last twenty years, perhaps and perhaps not) but Gatsby sticks in my heart. I had him for awhile, then lost him, and now I know I have him again. I'm sorry Myrtle is better than Daisy. Jordan of course was a great idea (perhaps you know it's Edith Cummings) but she fades out. It's Chapter VII that's the trouble with Daisy and it may hurt the book's popularity that it's *a man's book*.

Anyhow I think (for the first time since *The Vegetable*

failed) that I'm a wonderful writer and it's your always wonderful letters that help me to go on believing in myself.

Now some practical, very important questions. Please answer every one.

1. Montenegro has an order called the Order of Danilo. Is there any possible way you could find out for me there what it would look like—whether a courtesy decoration given to an American would bear an English inscription—or anything to give verisimilitude to the medal which sounds horribly amateurish?
2. Please have *no blurbs of any kind on the jacket!!!* No Mencken or Lewis or Sid Howard or anything. I don't believe in them *one bit* any more.
3. Don't forget to change name of book in list of works.
4. Please shift exclamation point from end of third line to end of fourth line in title page poem. *Please!* Important!
5. I thought that the whole episode (2 paragraphs) about their playing the "Jazz History of the World" at Gatsby's first party was rotten. Did you? Tell me your frank *reaction—personal.* Don't *think!* We can all think!

Got a sweet letter from Sid Howard—rather touching. I wrote him first I thought *Transatlantic* was great stuff—a really gorgeous surprise. Up to that I never believed in him specially and I was sorry because he did in me. Now I'm tickled silly to find he has power, and his own power. It seemed tragic too to see *Mrs. Vietch* wasted in a novelette when, despite Anderson, the short story is at its lowest ebb as an art form. (Despite Ruth Suckow, Gertrude Stein, Ring, there is a horrible impermanence on it *because* the overwhelming number of short stories are impermanent.)

Poor Tom Boyd! His cycle sounded so sad to me—perhaps it'll be wonderful but it sounds to me like sloughing in a field whose first freshness has gone.

See that word?[1] The ambition of my life is to make that use of it correct. The temptation to use it as a neuter is one of the vile fevers in my still insecure prose.

Tell me about Ring! About Tom—is he poor? He seems

[1] Fitzgerald had encircled "whose" in the sentence before.

to be counting on his short story book, frail cane! About Biggs[1]—did he ever finish the novel? About Peggy Boyd [2]— I think Louise might have sent us her book!

I thought *The White Monkey* was stinko. On second thoughts I didn't like *Cowboys, West and South* either. What about *Bal du Comte d'Orgel?* and Ring's set? and his new book? and Gertrude Stein? and Hemingway?

I still owe the store almost $700.00 on my encyclopedia, but I'll pay them on about January 10th—all in a lump as I expect my finances will then be on a firm footing. Will you ask them to send me Ernest Boyd's book?[3] Unless it has about my drinking in it that would reach my family. However, I guess it'd worry me more if I hadn't seen it than if I had. If my book is a big success or a great failure (financial—no other sort can be imagined I hope) I *don't* want to publish stories in the fall. If it goes between 25,000 and 50,000 I have an excellent collection for you. This is the longest letter I've written in three or four years. Please thank Mr. Scribner for me for his exceeding kindness.

Always yours,

Scott Fitz———

Hotel des Princes
Rome, Italy
(But address the American Express
Co. because it's damn cold here
and we may leave any day.)
January 24, 1925

Dear Max:

This is a most important letter so I'm having it typed. Guard it as your life.

1) Under a separate cover I'm sending the first part of the proof. While I agreed with the general suggestions in your first letters I differ with you in others. I *want* Myrtle

---

[1] Fitzgerald's college friend, John Biggs.
[2] Mrs. Thomas Boyd.
[3] *Portraits Real and Imaginary.*

Wilson's breast ripped off—it's exactly the thing, I think, and I don't want to chop up the good scenes by too much tinkering. When Wolfsheim says "sid" for "said," it's deliberate. "Orgastic" is the adjective for "orgasm" and it expresses exactly the intended ecstasy. It's not a bit dirty. I'm much more worried about the disappearance of Tom and Myrtle on galley 9—I think it's all right but I'm not sure. If it isn't please wire and I'll send correction.

2) Now about the page proof—under certain conditions never mind sending them (unless, of course, there's loads of time, which I suppose there isn't. I'm keen for late March or early April publication).

The conditions are two.

a) That someone reads it *very carefully twice* to see that every one of my inserts are put in correctly. There are so many of them that I'm in terror of a mistake.

b) That no changes *whatsoever* are made in it except in the case of a misprint so glaring as to be certain, and that only by you.

If there's some time left but not enough for the double mail, send them to me and I'll simply wire O.K. which will save two weeks. However don't postpone for that. In any case send me the page proof as usual just to see.

3) Now, many thanks for the deposit. Two days after wiring you I had a cable from Reynolds that he'd sold two stories of mine for a total of $3750, but before that I was in debt to him and after turning down the $10,000 from *College Humor* I was afraid to borrow more from him until he'd made a sale. I won't ask for any more from you until the book has earned it. My guess is that it will sell about 80,000 copies but I may be wrong. Please thank Mr. Charles Scribner for me. I bet he thinks he's caught another John Fox[1] now for sure. Thank God for John Fox. It would have been awful to have had no predecessor.

4) This is very important. Be sure not to give away *any* of my plot in the blurb. Don't give away that Gatsby *dies* or is a *parvenu* or *crook* or anything. It's a part of the suspense of the book that all these things are in doubt until the end. You'll watch this, won't you? And remember about having no quotations from critics on the jacket—*not even about my other books!*

---

[1] A Scribner novelist who had written some runaway best sellers.

5) This is just a list of small things.
   a) What's Ring's title for his spring book?
   b) Did O'Brien star my story "Absolution" or any of my others on his trash-album?[1]
   c) I wish your bookkeeping department would send me an account on February first. Not that it gives me pleasure to see how much in debt I am but that I like to keep a yearly record of the sales of all my books.

Do answer every question and keep this letter until the proof comes. Let me know how you like the changes. I miss seeing you, Max, more than I can say.

As ever,

Scott

P.S. I'm returning the proof of the title page, etc. It's O.K. but my heart tells me I should have named it *Trimalchio*. However against all the advice I suppose it would have been stupid and stubborn of me. *Trimalchio in West Egg* was only a compromise. *Gatsby* is too much like *Babbitt* and *The Great Gatsby* is weak because there's no emphasis even ironically on his greatness or lack of it. However let it pass.

Hotel Tiberio
Capri, Italy
(new address)
[circa *February 18, 1925*]

Dear Max:

After six weeks of uninterrupted work the proof is finished and the last of it goes to you this afternoon. On the whole it's been very successful labor.
   (1) I've brought Gatsby to life.
   (2) I've accounted for his money.
   (3) I've fixed up the two weak chapters (VI and VII).
   (4) I've improved his first party.

---

[1] *Best American Short Stories*, collected annually by Edward J. O'Brien.

(5) I've broken up his long narrative in Chapter VIII.

This morning I wired you to *hold up the galley of Chapter X*. The correction—and God! it's important because in my other revision I made Gatsby look too mean—is enclosed herewith. Also some corrections for the page proof.

We're moving to Capri. We hate Rome. I'm behind financially and have to write three short stories. Then I try another play, and by June, I hope, begin my new novel.

Had long interesting letters from Ring and John Bishop. Do tell me if all corrections have been received. I'm worried.

                                                                Scott

I hope you're setting publication date at first possible moment.

                                        Hotel Tiberio
                                        Capri, [*Italy*]
                                        March 31, 1925

Dear Max:

As the day approaches, my nervousness increases. To-morrow is the 1st and your wire says the 10th. I'll be here until the 25th, probably later, so if the book prospers I'll expect some sort of cable before I leave for Paris. All letters that you write after the 15th of April should be addressed to the Guaranty Trust Co., Paris, but if there's any dope in the first two or three days of publication I'd love a reassuring line here, even if the success doesn't justify a cable.

I enclose you a picture of a naked woman, which you may add to your celebrated pornographic collection from Sumatra, Transylvania, and the Polynesian Islands.

This place is full of fairies—one of them, a nice young man my own age, is a writer of promise and performance on the Aldous Huxley type. I like his books (his name is ———— ————) and suggested that I send some to you as you are shy on young English of recent years, but Knopf had signed him up three weeks before!

I think Tom Boyd's book is excellent—the preface is faintly pretentious but the stories themselves are great. By the way I think my new collection will be called *Dear Money*. It ought to be awfully good and there will be no junk in it.

> Yours in a Tremble,
>
> Scott

Will you have a copy of my book sent to Miss Willa Cather, care of Knopf?

When should my book of short stories be in?[1]

I had, or rather saw, a letter from my uncle who had seen a preliminary announcement of the book. He said: "It sounded as if it were very much like his others."

This is only a vague impression of course but I wondered if we could think of some way to advertise it so that people who are perhaps weary of assertive jazz and society novels might not dismiss it as "just another book like his others." I confess that today the problem baffles me—all I can think of is to say in general to avoid such phrases "a picture of New York life," or "modern society" —though as that is exactly what the book is it's hard to avoid them. The trouble is so much superficial trash has sailed under those banners. Let me know what you think.

> *14 rue de Tilsitt*
> *Paris, France*
> *(permanent address)*
>
> [circa *April 22, 1925*]

Dear Max:

I suppose you've sent the book to Collins. If not, please do, and let me know right away. If he won't take it because of its flop we might try Cape's.[2] I'm miserable at

---

[1] *All the Sad Young Men.*
[2] Jonathan Cape, the English publisher.

owing you all that money—if I'd taken the serial money I could at least have squared up with you.

I've had enthusiastic letters from Mencken and Wilson —the latter says he's reviewing it for that *Chicago Tribune* syndicate he writes for. I think all the reviews I've seen, except two, have been absolutely stupid and lousy. Someday they'll eat grass, by God! This thing, both the effort and the result, have hardened me and I think now that I'm much better than any of the young Americans *without exception*.

Hemingway is a fine, charming fellow and he appreciated your letter and the tone of it enormously. If Liveright doesn't please him he'll come to you, and he has a future. He's twenty-seven.

Bishop sent me *The Apple of the Eye*[1] and it seemed pretty much the old stuff that D. H. Lawrence, Anderson, Suckow and Cather did long ago and Hardy before them. I don't think such peasantry exists in America—Ring is much closer to the truth. I suspect tragedy in the American countryside because all the people capable of it move to the big towns at twenty. All the rest is pathos. However maybe it's good, a lot of people seem to think so.

I will send *All the Sad Young Men* about June 1st or 10th. Perhaps the deferred press on *Gatsby* will help it but I think now there's no use even sending it to that crowd, Broun, F.P.A., Ruth Hale, etc. Incidentally my being over here and consequent delay in the proofs and review copies undoubtedly hurt the effect of the book's appearance. Thanks again for your kind letters and all you've done. Let me know about Collins.

Scott

Please let me know how many copies sold and whether the sale is now dead.

Marseille, en route to Paris

[circa *April 24, 1925*]

Dear Max:

Your telegram depressed me—I hope I'll find better news

---

[1] A novel by Glenway Wescott.

in Paris and am wiring you from Lyons. There's nothing
to say until I hear more. If the book fails commercially
it will be from one of two reasons or both.

First, the title is only fair, rather bad than good.

Second *and most important,* the book contains no important woman character, and women control the fiction
market at present. I don't think the unhappy end matters
particularly.

I will have to sell 20,000 copies to wipe out my debt to
you. I think it will do that all right—but my hope was it
would do 75,000. This week will tell.

Zelda is well, or almost, but the expense of her illness
and of bringing this wretched little car of ours back to
France, which has to be done, by law, has wiped out what
small progress I'd made in getting straight financially.

In all events I have a book of good stories for the fall.
Now I shall write some cheap ones until I've accumulated
enough for my next novel. When that is finished and published I'll wait and see. If it will support me with no more
intervals of trash I'll go on as a novelist. If not, I'm going
to quit, come home, go to Hollywood and learn the movie
business. I can't reduce our scale of living and I can't
stand this financial insecurity. Anyhow there's no point in
trying to be an artist if you can't do your best. I had my
chance back in 1920 to start my life on a sensible scale and
I lost it, and so I'll have to pay the penalty. Then perhaps
at 40 I can start writing again without this constant worry
and interruption.

> Yours in great depression,
>
> Scott

P.S. Let me know about Ring's book. Did I tell you I
thought "Haircut" was mediocre?
P.S. (2) Please refer any movie offers to Reynolds.

> *c/o Guaranty Trust Co.*
> *Paris, France*
>
> *May 1, [1925]*

Dear Max:

There's no use for indignation against the long suffering

public when even a critic who likes the book fails to be fundamentally held—that is, Stallings who has written the only intelligent review so far—but it's been depressing to find how quick one is forgotten, especially unless you repeat yourself *ad nauseam*. Most of the reviewers floundered around in a piece of work that obviously they completely failed to understand and tried to give it reviews that committeed them neither pro or con until someone of culture had spoken. Of course I've only seen *The Times* and the *Tribune*—and, thank God, Stallings, for I had begun to believe no one was even glancing at the book.

Now about money. With the $1000 for which I asked yesterday (and thank you for your answer) I owe you about $1200, or, if the book sells 12,000, about $4000. If there is a movie right, I will pay you all I owe—if not, all I can offer you at present is an excellent collection of stories for the fall entitled *All the Sad Young Men*—none of the stories appeared in the *Post*—I think "Absolution" is the only one you've read. Thank you for all your advertising and all the advances and all your good will. When I get ahead again on trash I'll begin the new novel.

I'm glad Ring is getting such a press and hope he's selling. The boob critics have taken him up and always take a poke at the "intelligentsia" who patronize him. But the "intelligentsia," Seldes and Mencken, discovered him (after the people) while the boob critics let *The Big Town* and *Gullible's Travels* come out in dead silence. Let me know the sale.

A profound bow to my successor, Arlen[1]—when I read *The London Venture* I knew he was a comer and was going to tell you but I saw the next day that Doran had already published *Piracy*. That was just before I left New York.

Which reminds me—it seems terrible that all the best of the young Englishmen have been snapped up. I tried to get ———— for you in Capri but he'd signed a rotten cash contract with Knopf a week before. Also they've just signed Brett Young who might have been had any time in the last two years and who'll be a big seller and now I see *The Constant Nymph*[2] is taken. Wouldn't it pay you to have

[1] Michael Arlen, author of *The Green Hat*.
[2] By Margaret Kennedy.

some live young Londoner watch the new English books? I imagine Kingsley[1] gets his information a month late out of *The London Times Supplement*. This sounds ill-natured but I am really sorry to see you lose so many new talents when they are appearing as fast now in England as they did here in 1920. Liveright has got Hemingway! How about Radiguet?

We have taken an apartment here from May 12th to January 12th, eight months, where I shall do my best. What a six months in Italy! Christ!

I'm hoping that by some miracle the book will go up to 23,000 and wipe off my debt to you. I haven't been out of debt now for three years and with the years it grows heavy on my aging back. The happiest thought I have is of my new novel—it is something really NEW in form, idea, structure—the model for the age that Joyce and Stein are searching for, that Conrad didn't find.

Write me any news—I haven't had [a] written line since publication except a pleasant but not thrilling note from the perennial youth, Johnny Weaver. I am bulging with plans for—however, that's later. Was Ring's skit which was in Mencken's *American Language* incorporated into *What Of It?* If not it should have been—it's one of his best shorter things. And doesn't it contain his famous World's Series articles about Ellis Lardner's Coat? If not they'd be a nucleus for another book of nonsense. Also his day at home in imitation of F.P.A.'s diary.

My address after the 12th is *14 rue de Tilsitt*. If you have my *Three Lives* by Gertrude Stein don't let anybody steal it.

> Many thanks to Mr. Scribner and to
> all the others and to you for
> all you've done for me and for the book.
> The jacket was a hit anyhow.

Scott

P.S. And Tom Boyd's book?

[1] Charles Kingsley, Scribners' London representative.

14 rue de Tilsitt
Paris, France

[circa *June 1, 1925*]

Dear Max:

This is the second letter I've written you today—I tore up my first when the letter in longhand from New Canaan telling me about Liveright arrived. I'm wiring you today as to that rumor—but also it makes it necessary to tell you something I didn't intend to tell you.

Yesterday arrived a letter from T. R. Smith[1] asking for my next book—saying nothing against the Scribners but just asking for it: if I happened to be dissatisfied they would be delighted, etc., etc. I answered at once, saying that you were one of my closest friends and that my relations with Scribners had always been so cordial and pleasant that I wouldn't think of changing publishers. That letter will reach him at about the time this reaches you. I have never had any other communication *of any sort* with Liveright or any other publisher except the *very definite and explicit letter* with which I answered their letter yesterday.

So much for that rumor. I am both angry at Tom[2] who must have been in some way responsible for starting it and depressed at the fact that you could have believed it enough to mention it to me. Rumors start like this—

Smith *(a born gossip):* I hear Fitzgerald's book isn't selling. I think we can get it, as he's probably blaming it on Scribners.

The Next Man: It seems Fitzgerald is dissatisfied with Scribners and Liveright is after him.

The Third Man: I hear Fitzgerald has gone over to Liveright.

Now, Max, I have told you many times that you are my publisher, and permanently, as far as one can fling about the word in this too mutable world. If you like I will sign a contract with you immediately for my next

---

[1] An editor with the firm of Boni & Liveright.
[2] Thomas Boyd.

three books. The idea of leaving you has never for *one single moment* entered my head.

First. Tho, as a younger man, I have not always been in sympathy with some of your publishing ideas (which were evolved under the pre-movie, pre-high-literacy-rate conditions of twenty to forty years ago), the personality of you and Mr. Scribner, the tremendous squareness, courtesy, generosity and open-mindedness I have always met there and, if I may say it, the special consideration you have all had for me and my work, much more than make up the difference.

Second. You know my own idea on the advantage of one publisher who backs you and not your work. And my feeling about uniform books in the matter of house and binding.

Third. The curious advantage to a rather radical writer in being published by what is now an ultra-conservative house.

Fourth (and least need of saying). Do you think I could treat with another publisher while I have a debt, which is both actual and a matter of honor, of over $3000?

If Mr. Scribner has heard this rumor please show him this letter. So much for Mr. Liveright & Co.

Your letters are catching up with me. Curtis in *Town & Country* and Van Vechten in *The Nation* pleased me. The personal letters—Cabell, Wilson, Van Wyck Brooks, etc. —have been the best of all. Among people over here, Ernest Hemingway and Gertrude Stein are quite enthusiastic. Except for Rascoe it has been, critically only, a clean sweep.

Ring's book has been a terrible disappointment to everyone here. He didn't even bother to cut out the connecting tags at the end of his travel articles and each of the five plays contain the same joke about "his mother—afterwards his wife." I shouldn't press him about his new collection if I were you because if you just took the first nine stories he writes, they couldn't be up to the others *and you know how reviewers are quick to turn on anyone in whom they have believed and who now disappoints them.* Of course I've only read "Haircut" and I may be wrong. I do want him to believe in his work and not have any blows to take away his confidence. The reviews I have seen of *What of It?* were sorry imitations of Seldes' stuff and all of them went out of their way to stab Seldes in the back. God, cheap reviewers are low swine—but one must live.

As I write, word has just come by cable that Brady has made an offer for the dramatic rights of *Gatsby,* with Owen Davis, king of professional play doctors, to do dramatization. I am, needless to say, accepting, but please keep it confidential until the actual contract is signed.

As you know, despite my admiration for *Through the Wheat,* I haven't an enormous faith in Tom Boyd either as a personality or an artist—as I have, say, in E. E. Cummings and Hemingway. His ignorance, his presumptuous intolerance and his careless grossness, which he cultivates for vitality as a man might nurse along a dandelion with the hope that it would turn out to be an onion, have always annoyed me. Like Rascoe he has never been known to refuse an invitation from his social superiors—or to fail to pan them with all the venom of a James Oliver Curwood he-man when no invitations were forthcoming.

All this is preparatory to saying that his new book sounds utterly lousy—Sheila Kaye-Smith has used the stuff about the farmer having girls instead of boys and being broken up about it. The characters you mention have every one become stock-props in the last ten years— "Christy, the quaint old hired man" after a season in such stuff as Owen Davis' *Ice Bound* must be almost ready for the burlesque circuit.

History of the Simple Inarticulate Farmer and His Hired Man Christy
(Both guaranteed to be utterly full of the Feel of the Soil)

First Period
1855—English Peasant discovered by George Eliot in *Mill on the Floss, Silas Marner,* etc.

1888—Given intellectual interpretation by Hardy in *Jude* and *Tess.*

1890—Found in France by Zola in *Germinal.*

1900—Crowds of Scandinavians—Hamsun, Bojer, etc.—

tear him bodily from the Russian, and, after a peep at Hardy, Hamlin Garland finds him in the Middle West.

(Most of that, however, was literature. It was something pulled by the individual out of life and only partly with the aid of models in other literatures.)

Second Period

1914—Sheila Kaye-Smith frankly imitates Hardy, produces two good books and then begins to imitate herself.

1915—Brett Young discovers him in the coal country.

1916—Robert Frost discovers him in New England.

1917—Sherwood Anderson discovers him in Ohio.

1918—Willa Cather turns him Swede.

1920—Eugene O'Neill puts him on the boards in *Different* and *Beyond* [*the*] *Horizon*.

1922—Ruth Suckow *gets* in before the door closes.

(These people were all good second-raters [except Anderson]. Each of them brought something to the business—but they exhausted the ground, the type was set. All was over.)

Third Period

The Cheapskates discover him—bad critics and novelists, etc.

1923—Homer Croy writes *West of the Water Tower*.

1924—Edna Ferber turns from her flip Jewish saleswoman for a strong silent earthy carrot grower and the Great Soul of Charley Towne thrills to her passionately Real and Earthy Struggle.

1924—*Ice Bound* by the author of *Nellie the Beautiful Cloak Model* wins Pulitzer Prize. *The Abel McLaughlins* wins $10,000 prize and is forgotten the following week.

1925—*The Apple of the Eye* pronounced a masterpiece.

1926—TOM, BOYD, WRITES, NOVEL, ABOUT, IN-ARTICULATE, FARMER, WHO, IS, CLOSE, TO SOIL, AND, HIS, HIRED, MAN CHRISTY! "STRONG! VITAL! REAL!"

As a matter of fact the American peasant as "real" material scarcely exists. He is scarcely 10% of the population, isn't bound to the soil at all as the English and Russian peasants were—and, if [he] has any sensitivity whatsoever (except a most sentimental conception of himself, which our writers persistently shut their eyes to), he is in the towns before he's twenty. Either Lewis, Lardner and myself have been badly fooled, or else using him as typical American material is simply *a stubborn seeking for the static in a world that for almost a hundred years had simply not been static.* Isn't it a fourth rate imagination that can find only that old property farmer in all this amazing time and land? And anything that ten people a year can do well enough to pass muster has become so easy that is isn't worth doing.

I can not disassociate a man from his work. That . . . . [1] are going to tell us mere superficial "craftsmen" like Hergesheimer, Wharton, Tarkington, and me about the Great Beautiful Appreciation they have of the Great Beautiful Life of the Manure Widder rather turns my stomach. The real people like Gertrude Stein (with whom I've talked) and Conrad (see his essay on James) have a respect for people whose materials may not touch theirs *at a single point.* But the fourth-rate and highly derivative people like Tom are loud in their outcry against any subject matter that doesn't come out of the old, old bag which their betters have used and thrown away.

For example there is an impression among the thoughtless (including Tom) that Sherwood Anderson is a man of profound ideas who is "handicapped by his inarticulateness." As a matter of fact Anderson is a man of practically no ideas—*but he is one of the very best and finest writers in the English language today.* God, he can write! Tom could never get such rhythms in his life as there are on the pages of *Winesburg, Ohio.* Simple! The words on the lips of critics make me hilarious: Anderson's style is about as simple as an engine room full of dynamos. But Tom flatters himself that he can sit down for five months and by dressing up a few heart throbs in overalls produce literature.

It amazes me, Max, to see you with your discernment and your fine intelligence fall for that whole complicated

[1] Fitzgerald here mentioned three writers whose private lives were distasteful to him.

fake. Your chief critical flaw is to confuse mere earnestness with artistic sincerity. On two of Ring's jackets have been statements that he never wrote a dishonest word (maybe it's one jacket). But Ring and many of the very greatest artists have written thousands of words in plays, poems and novels which weren't even faintly sincere or earnest and were yet *artistically sincere*. The latter term is *not* a synonym for plodding earnestness. Zola did not say the last word about literature nor the first.

I append all the data on my fall book, and in closing I apologize for seeming impassioned about Tom and his work when neither the man or what he writes has ever been personally inimical to me. He is simply the scapegoat for the mood Rascoe has put me in and, tho I mean every word of it, I probably wouldn't have wasted all this paper on a book that won't sell and will be dead in a month, and an imitative school that will be dead by its own weight in a year or so, if the news about Liveright hadn't come on top of the Rascoe review and ruined my disposition. Good luck to *Drummond*.[1] I'm sure one of two critics will mistake it for profound stuff—maybe even Mencken, who has a weakness in that direction. But I think you should look closer.

With best wishes as always, Max,

Your friend,

Scott

DATA ON NEW FITZGERALD BOOK

Title: *All the Sad Young Men*

(9 Short Stories)

Print list of previous books as before with addition of this title under "Stories." Binding uniform with others. Jacket plain, as you suggest, with text instead of picture. Dedication: To Ring and Ellis Lardner.

The stories (now under revision) will reach you by July 15th. No proofs need be sent over here.

[1] *Samuel Drummond,* a novel by Thomas Boyd.

It will be fully up to the other collections and will contain only one of those *Post* stories that people were so snooty about. You have read only one of the stories ("Absolution")—all the others were so good that I had difficulty in selling them, except two.

They are, in approximate order to be used in book:

1. "The Rich Boy" (just finished—serious story and very good)	13,000	words
2. "Absolution" (from *Mercury*)	6,500	"
3. "Winter Dreams" (a sort of first draft of the *Gatsby* idea from *Metropolitan* 1923)	9,000	"
4. "Rags Martin-Jones and the Pr-nce of Wales" (fantastic jazz, so good that Lorimer and Long refused it—from *McCall's*)	5,000	"
5. "The Baby Party" (from *Hearst's*—a fine story)	5,000	"
6. "Dice, Brassknuckles and Guitar" (from *Hearst's*—exuberant jazz in my early manner)	8,000	"
7. "The Sensible Thing" (story about Zelda and me, all true, from *Liberty*)	5,000	"
8. "Hot and Cold Blood" (good story, from *Hearst's*)	6,000	"
9. "Gretchen's Forty Winks" (from *Post*—Farrer, Christian Gauss and Jesse Williams thought it my best—it isn't)	7,000	"

Total—about   64,500

(And possibly one other short one)

This title is because seven stories deal with young men of my generation in rather unhappy moods. The ones to mention on the outside wrap are the first five or the first three stories.

Rather not use advertising appropriation in *Times*—people who read *Times Book Review* won't be interested in me. Recommend *Mercury*, the F.P.A. page of the *World*, *Literary Review*, and Fanny Buckler page of *Chicago Tribune*.

No blurbs in ad as I think the blurb doesn't help any more. Suggestion:

Charles Scribner's Sons
announce a new book of short stories
by
F. Scott Fitzgerald

Advertising Notes

Suggested line for jacket: "Show transition from his early exuberant stories of youth which created a new type of American girl and the later and more serious mood which produced *The Great Gatsby* and marked him as one of the half-dozen masters of English prose now writing in America. . . . What other writer has shown such unexpected developments, such versatility, changes of pace," etc., etc., etc. I think that, toned down as you see fit, is the general line. Don't say "Fitzgerald has done it!" and then in the next sentence that I am an artist. People who are interested in artists aren't interested in people who have "done it." Both are O.K. but don't belong in the same ad. This is an author's quibble. All authors have one quibble.

However, you have always done well by me (except for Black's memorable excretion in the *Alumni Weekly,* do you remember—"Make it a Fitzgerald Christmas!") and I leave it to you. If 100,000 copies are not sold I shall shift to Mitchell Kennerley.

By the way what has become of Black? I hear he has written a very original and profound novel. It is said to be about an inarticulate farmer and his struggles with the "soil" and his sexual waverings between his inarticulate wife and an inarticulate sheep. He finally chooses his old pioneering grandmother as the most inarticulate of all but finds her in bed with none other than our old friend THE HIRED MAN CHRISTY.

CHRISTY HAD DONE IT!

[In 1962 Fitzgerald's famous letter to Perkins was sold at auction at Chrystie's (not old man Christy's) for £7000.][1]

---

[1] These are Fitzgerald's words.

14 rue de Tilsitt
Paris, France
[circa *July 1, 1925*]

Dear Max:

This is another one of those letters with a thousand details in them, so I'll number the details and thus feel I'm getting them out of the way.

(1) Will you have an account (bi-yearly statement) sent me as soon as you can? I don't know how much I owe you but it must be between 3 and 4 thousand dollars. I want to see how much chance *All the Sad Young Men* has of making up this difference. Thanks many times for the $700.00. It will enable me to go ahead next month with *Our Type*[1] which is getting shaped up both [on] paper and in my head. I'd rather not tell about it just yet.

(2) Is *Gatsby* to be published in England? I'm awfully anxious to have it published there. If Collins won't have it, can't you try Jonathan Cape? Do let me know about this.

(3) Will you tell me the figures on Ring's books? Also on *Through the Wheat*. I re-read the latter the other day and think it's marvelous. Together with *The Enormous Room* and, I think, *Gatsby*, it's much the best thing that has come out of American fiction since the war. I exclude Anderson because since reading *Three Lives* and his silly autobiography my feeling about him has entirely changed. He is a short story writer only.

(4) I spent $48.00 having a sketch of me done by Ivan Opfer. It was lousy and he says he'll try another. If it's no good I'll send a photo. The stories for the book leave here day after tomorrow.

(5) I think the number of Americans in Europe has hurt the market. *Gatsby* is the last principal book of mine that I want to publish in the spring. I believe that from now on fall will be much the best season.

(6) I'm sorry about that burst at Tom [Boyd]. But I am among those who suffer from the preoccupation of literary America with the drab as subject matter. Seldes points this out in a great review of *Gatsby* for the *London*

[1] His new novel.

Criterion. Also he says, "Fitzgerald has certainly the best chance at present of becoming our finest artist in fiction." Quite a bit from Gilbert who only likes Ring, Edith Wharton, Joyce and Charlie Chaplin. Please get Meyer to put it on the cover of the new book and delete the man who says I "deserve the huzzas of those who want to further a worthy American Literature." Perhaps I deserve their huzzas but I'd rather they'd express their appreciation in some less boisterous way.

(7) I'm sending back the questionnaire.

(8) I suppose that by now *Gatsby* is over 18,000. I hope to God it reaches 20,000. It sounds so much better. Shane Leslie thought it was fine.

No news, Max. I was drinking hard in May but for the last month I've been working like a dog. I still think *Count Orgel's Ball* by Radiguet would sell like wildfire. If I had the time I'd translate it myself.

                                                            Scott

                                        14 rue de Tilsitt
                                        Paris, France
                                        [circa *October 6, 1925*]

Dear Max:

Your letter of September 28th doesn't answer my question about *Gatsby* in England. Is there some reason why Chatto & Windus can't publish in the spring? —And if they believe in it so little that they'll defer it a year and a half wouldn't they be willing to hand it over to Cape? I hate to be a crabby old woman about this, Max, but it means a lot to me. *Gatsby* is just the sort of book which the English say that Americans can't write, which they praise Hergesheimer for *almost* writing; I know half a dozen influential people there who will go to bat for it right now and it seems to me that it should have a chance. I am further confused when your letter says "Chatto & Windus and other publishers admired it but they thought it too American in its scene to be understood in England."

Does that mean Chatto & Windus aren't going to publish it? I'm disgruntled and up-in-the-air about the whole thing.

Isn't Ernest Hemingway's book fine?[1] Did you read the last story?

I'm having Reynolds send you 6 tickets to the opening of *Gatsby* if it gets to New York. Distribute them as you like and if you want more let him know.

I'm anxiously awaiting the figure on *Gatsby* (how many sold, I mean); also on Ring's reprints as I feel sort of responsible to you on that idea. If he'd have a litle pep and interest he might have devoted enough care to *What of It?* to make it sell as well as *The Illiterate Digest*.

Who has the American rights to Paul Morand's *Open All Night* and *Closed All Night?* Guy Chapman publishes them in England. They're *great*—and would sell like wildfire. Isn't Anderson's new book *lousy?*[2]

As ever,

Scott

14 rue de Tilsitt
Paris, France

[circa *December 27, 1925*]

Dear Max:

I write to you from the depth of one of my unholy depressions. The book is wonderful—I honestly think that when it's published I shall be the best American novelist (which isn't saying a lot) but the end seems far away. When it's finished I'm coming home for awhile anyhow though the thought revolts me as much as the thought of remaining in France. I wish I were twenty-two again with only my dramatic and feverishly enjoyed miseries. You remember I used to say I wanted to die at thirty —well, I'm now twenty-nine and the prospect is still welcome. My work is the only thing that makes me happy—

[1] *In Our Time.*
[2] *Dark Laughter.*

except to be a little tight—and for those two indulgences
I pay a big price in mental and physical hangovers.

I thank you for your newsy letter—by the way we got
and hugely enjoyed Louise's beautiful book and I wrote
and thanked her care of Scribners. I liked too your idea
about *Representative Men* but it seems remote to me. Let
me know if it comes to something and I'll contribute.[1]

That was a sweet slam from Ellen Mackey. Is it true that
she and Irving Berlin have signed up to play a permanent
engagement in *Abie's Irish Rose?* I hope the short stories
sell seven or eight thousand or so. Is *Gatsby* dead? You
don't mention it. Has it reached 25,000? I hardly dare to
hope so. Also I deduce from your silence that Tom Boyd's
book was a flop. If so I hope he isn't in financial difficulties.
Also I gather from reviews that the penciled frown came a
cropper. I wish Liveright would lose faith in Ernest.
Through the whole year only the following American
novels have seemed worth a damn to me:

> The Spring Flight
> Perennial Bachelor
> In Our Time
> The Great Gatsby

I thought the books by *Lewis, Van Vechten, Edith
Wharton, Floyd Dell, Tom Boyd* and *Sherwood Anderson*
were just *lousy!*

And the ones by *Willa Cather* and *Cyril Hume* almost as
bad.

Dos Passos and *Ruth Suckow* I haven't yet read.

The press Anderson got on *Dark Laughter* filled me
with a much brighter shade of hilarity. You notice it wasn't
from those of us who waited for the Winesburg stories one
by one in the *Little Review* but by Harry Hansen, Stallings,
etc., and the other boys who find a new genius once a
week and at all cost follow the fashions.

It's good you didn't take my advice about looking up
Gertrude Stein's new book *(The Making of Americans)*.
It's bigger than *Ulysses* and only the first parts, the parts

---

[1] Perkins had proposed a burlesque biographical dictionary, with fictional
biographies of various American types to be written by Fitzgerald,
Lardner, Benchley and others.

published in the *Transatlantic,* are intelligible at all. It's published privately here.

The best English books of the fall are *The Sailor's Return* by David Garnett and *No More Parades* by Ford Madox Ford (a sequel to *Some Do Not*).

(Speaking of Gertrude Stein I hope you are keeping my precious *Three Lives* safe for me.) Ring's book sounds good. Send me a copy—also the wrap of mine.

I told Ober to send you half a dozen seats for the *Gatsby* opening to distribute to the Scribners as you think best. If you want more phone him.

No, Zelda's not entirely well yet. We're going south next month to Salies-les-Bains to see if we can cure her there. *So from the time of receiving this letter address all mail to me care of*

> *The Guaranty Trust Co.*
> *1 rue des Italiens*
> *Paris, France*

Why was Jack Wheeler kicked out of *Liberty?*

My novel should be finished next fall.

Tell me all the gossip that isn't in *The New Yorker* or the *World*—isn't there any regular dirt?

I called on Chatto & Windus in London last month and has a nice talk with Swinnerton, their reader. (It was he, it seems, who was strong for the book.) Saw Leslie[1] also and went on some very high-tone parties with Mountbattens and all that sort of thing. Very impressed, but not very, as I furnished most of the amusement myself. *Please* write! Best to Louise.

Your friend,

Scott Fitzg_____

Has story book had good advance sale? Or hasn't it been the rounds yet? What's its date?

[1] Shane Leslie.

14 rue de Tilsitt
(New address: Guaranty Trust Co.
1 rue des Italiens)

[circa *December 30, 1925*]

Dear Max:

(1) To begin with, many thanks for all deposits, to you and to the Scribners in general. I have no idea now how I stand with you. To set me straight, will you send me my account *now* instead of waiting till February 1st? It must be huge, and I'm miserable about it. The more I get for my trash, the less I can bring myself to write. However this year is going to be different.

(2) Hemingway's book (not his novel) is a 28,000 word satire on Sherwood Anderson and his imitators called *The Torrents of Spring*. I loved it, but believe it wouldn't be popular, and Liveright have refused it—*they are backing Anderson* and the book is almost a vicious parody on him. You see I agree with Ernest that Anderson's last two books have let everybody down who believed in him—I think they're cheap, faked, obscurantic and awful. Hemingway thinks, but isn't yet sure to my satisfaction, that their refusal sets him free from his threebook (letter) agreement with them. In that case I think he'll give you his novel (on condition you'll publish satire first—probable sale, 1000 copies) which he is now revising in Austria. Harcourt has just written Louis Bromfield that to get the novel they'll publish satire, sight unseen (utterly confidential) and Knopf is after him via Aspinwall Bradley.

He and I are very thick and he's marking time until he finds out how much he's bound to Liveright. If he's free I'm almost sure I can get satire to you first and then if you see your way clear you can contract for the novel *tout ensemble*. He's anxious too to get a foot-hold in your magazine—one story I've sent you, the other, to my horror, he'd given for about $40 to an "arty" publication called *This Quarter*, over here.

He's *dead set* on having the satire published first. His idea has always been to come to you and his only hesitation has been that Harcourt might be less conservative in regard to certain somewhat broad scenes. His address is:

Herr Ernest Hemingway   Don't even tell him

Hotel Taube   I've discussed his
Schrunns   Liveright and Harcourt
Vorarlburg   relations with you.
Austria

As soon as he has definite dope I'll pass it on to you. I wanted a strong wire to show you were as interested, and more, than Harcourt. Did you know your letter just missed by two weeks getting *In Our Time?* It had no sale of course but I think the novel may be something extraordinary— Tom Boyd and E. E. Cummings and Biggs combined.

Wasn't Dos Passos' book astonishingly good? [1] I'm very fond of him but I had lost faith in his work.

(3) Tell me all about my play.

(4) I can't wait to see the book you're sending me. Zelda says it might be *Gatsby* but I don't think so.

(5) Poor Elinor Wylie! Poor Bill Benét! Poor everybody!

(6) My novel is wonderful.

(7) The translation of *Gatsby* sounds wonderful.

(8) Will you ask the bookstore to send *The Beautiful and Damned* to *M. Victor Llona, 106 rue de la Tour, Paris?* Thanks. Charge to my account, of course.

(9) I thought Dunn's remark about Biggs' book was wonderful. Tell me about it. Also about Tom Boyd's work and Ring's. You never do.

As ever,

Scott

c/o Guaranty Trust Co.
Paris, France
[circa *January 19, 1926*]

Dear Max:

Your thoughtful cablegram came today and I can't imagine how the rumor got started—unless from Zelda us-

---

[1] *Manhattan Transfer.*

ing an imaginary illness as a protection against the many
transients who demand our time. Somehow if one lives in
Paris one is fair game for all the bores one wouldn't look at
and who wouldn't look at one in New York. (If there's
one thing I hate it's a sentence full of "ones.")

We have escaped to a small town in the Pyrenees where
Zelda is to take a cure. Our address for cables is Fitzgerald, Bellevue, Salies-de-Béarn, France, but for letters the
Guaranty, Paris, is best. We are living in an absolutely de-
serted hotel. We move on to Nice the first of March. Here
are my usual list of things.

(1) Thanks a million times for the bound copy of my
book—it is beautiful and, Max, I'm enormously obliged. I
wish you'd written in the front—but that will wait till I
get home. Your thought of me touched me more than
I can say.

(2) Now about the many deposits. They are past all
reckoning but must total $5000 which is a record advance
(?) on a book of short stories. I'm terribly sorry, Max.
Could he send me my account this year on the 1st of
February *really* instead of February 15th? We won't be
able to tell about *The Sad Young* anyhow and I'm frantic
to know if I'm helplessly in debt.

(3) What is the date of the book? How are advance
sales, compared with *Gatsby?* Did the latter ever reach
25,000?

(4) Now, confidentially, as to Hemingway. He wrote a
satire 28,000 words long on Sherwood Anderson, very
funny but very cerebral, called *The Torrents of Spring.* It is
biting on Anderson—so Liveright turns it down. Hemingway's contract *lapses when Liveright turns down a book,
so Hemingway says.* But I think Horace will claim this isn't
a book and fight it like the devil, according to a letter I
saw which he wrote Ernest, because he's crazy to get
Ernest's almost completed novel *The Sun Also Rises.* It is
such a mess that Ernest goes to N.Y. next month.

Meanwhile Harcourt and Knopf are after him but he's
favorably disposed toward you because of your letters, and
of the magazine. He's very excitable, though, and I can't
promise he'll know his own mind next month. I'll tip you
off the moment he arrives. Of course if Bridges likes his
work and if you'll take *Torrents* he's yours absolutely—

contingent, of course, on the fact that he isn't bitched by some terrible contract with Liveright. To hear him talk you'd think Liveright had broken up his home and robbed him of millions—but that's because he knows nothing of publishing, except in the cuckoo magazines, is very young and feels helpless so far away. You won't be able to help liking him—he's one of the nicest fellows I ever knew.

In addition to the critics will you send my new book to the following people and charge my account (except in cases like Hergesheimer and Van Vechten, who actually reviewed *Gatsby*)? Send me only 3 copies.

Thanks again for my beautiful copy.

> As ever,
> Scott

South of France
February 20, 1926

Dear Max:

Two things have just occurred to me—or rather three.

(1) You'll get this letter about the 3rd of March. My book of stories may, at that time, have been out three weeks or three days—you've not told me the date. Will you in any case write me immediately forecasting roughly the approximate sale? I know it can be only guesswork and you'll be afraid of overestimating but I'd like to know *at least* the sale to that date. It has something to do with my income tax which must leave here the 14th. Also, would you send me an income tax blank?

My God! If it should sell 10,000 copies I'd be out of debt to you for the 1st time since 1922. Isn't that a disgrace, when I get $2500 for a story as my regular price? But trash doesn't come as easily as it used to and I've grown to hate the poor old debauched form itself.

How about Tom Boyd? Is he still going to be one of the barnyard boys? Or has he got sense and decided to write about the war, or seducing married women in St. Paul, or life in a bum Kentucky military school, or something he knows about. He has no touch of genius like Hemingway and Cummings but like Dos Passos he has a strong, valuable talent. He must write about the external world, as vividly and acutely and even brilliantly as he can, but let him stop there. He is almost without the power of clear ratiocination and he has no emotional depths whatsoever. His hide is so thick that only battle itself could really make an impression on him—playing with the almost evanescent spiritual material of Anderson he becomes an ox to public view. I wish to God I could see him and talk to him. For heaven's sake, Max, curb your usual (and, generally, sagacious) open-mindedness and don't help him to ruin his future by encouraging his stupidest ambitions—he'll turn bitter with failure.

(2) Has the play's success helped the book *Gatsby?* My theory, you know, is that nowadays there's not the faintest connection. That's why I wouldn't allow a movie edition of *The Beautiful and Damned.* By the way I don't imagine those little 75 cent books sell any more. They shouldn't. Do they? I mean did Jesse Williams', Arthur Train's, Wilson's addresses, etc., sell like *The Perfect Tribute* and *The Third Wise Man?*

Now, confidential: T. S. Eliot, for whom you know my profound admiration—I think he's the greatest living poet in any language—wrote me he'd read *Gatsby* three times and thought it was *the first step forward American fiction had taken since Henry James.*

Wait till they see the new novel!

Did you get Hemingway?

There was something else I wanted to ask you. What was it, damn it?

We're coming home in the fall, but I don't want to. I'd like to live and die on the French Riviera.

What's the inside dope on the Countess Cathcart case?

I can't remember my other question and it's driving me frantic. Frantic! (Half an hour later) *Frantic!*

FRANTIC!!!

If you see anybody I know tell 'em I hate 'em all, him especially. Never want to see 'em again.

Why shouldn't I go crazy? My father is a moron and my mother is a neurotic, half insane with pathological nervous worry. Between them they haven't and never have had the brains of Calvin Coolidge.

If I knew anything I'd be the best writer in America.

Scott Fitzg——

Eureka! Remembered! Refer my movie offers to Reynolds.

> *Villa Paquita*
> *Juan-les-Pins*
> *Alpes Maritime*
> *France*
> *(address till June 15)*
> [circa *February 25, 1926*]

Dear Max:

Thanks very much for your nice letter and the income blank. I'm delighted about the short story book. In fact with the play going well and my new novel growing absorbing and with our being back in a nice villa on my beloved Riviera (between Cannes and Nice) I'm happier than I've been for years. It's one of those strange, precious, and all too transitory moments when everything in one's life seems to be going well.

Thanks for the Arthur Train legal advice.

I'm glad you got Hemingway. I saw him for a day in Paris on his return and he thought you were great. I've brought you two successes (Ring and Tom Boyd) and two failures (—— and ——). Ernest will decide whether my opinions are more of a hindrance or a help.

Why not try *College Humor* for his story? They published one thing of mine.

Poor Tom Boyd! First I was off him for his boneheadedness. Now I'm sorry for him.

Your friend,

Scott

I am out of debt to you for the first time in four years.

Will you get the enclosure for me, open it, and write me? Think of that horse's ass F.P.A. coming around to my work after six years of neglect. I'd like to stick his praise up his behind, God knows it's no use to me now.

> *Villa Paquita*
> *Juan-les-Pins*
> *France*
> [*Before April 27, 1926*]

Dear Max:

Why in God's name did the advertising department broadcast a rotten sketch of me that makes me look like a degenerate? It's come to me in a dozen clippings and will probably haunt me for the next five years. As it appears in *Scribner's Magazine* I suppose Meyer sent it out—otherwise I would have thought it originated with some country newspaper that needed space in an awful hurry. I know it's partly my own fault for not sending you one and I suppose this sounds vain and unpleasant but if you knew how it has taken the joy out of the press on my book to have that leering, puffy distortion reach me at the head of almost every review you'd know the way I've gotten worked up over it.

Thanks many times for *Our Times*.[1] I read every word of it and loved it. Thoroughly interesting. About Mary Colum's article: I thought that the more solid parts were obvious and pedantic, and that a good half of it was the sort of nonsense I didn't expect from her. What on earth is the connection between Cocteau and Cummings? What does she mean by form? Does she think *King Lear* lacks it, while Marianne Moore has it? She uses it in the sense of successful conscious organization (so one thinks) and then it develops that she means mere novelty. Says she:

"How profoundly true to their race, period and the needs of their public are the great artists—Goethe, Dante, Shakespeare, Moliere! You can from their work pick out all

---

[1] By Mark Sullivan.

the qualities, all the thoughts, all the ideals of the time that needed expression."

How in the devil does she know that? How does anyone know that? There may have been whole elements in each of their times (John Donne, Roger Bacon in Shakespeare's and Dante's respective times for example) whose ideals and spirits were not even faintly summed up by the powerful but fallible and all-too-human titan who succeeded in forcing on us his picture. Don't you agree?

I disliked the essay chiefly because it's so plausible, and so dead, like (whisper it not, because I like him) the critical work of Ernest Boyd. Perhaps because I've just finished Chekhov's *Letters on Literature*. God, there's a book!

You owe me a long letter.

> As ever,
>
> Scott

> *Villa Paquita*
> *Juan-les-Pins*
> *France*
> [*Before May, 10, 1926*]

Dear Max:

Thanks many times for all the books. The *Hickey*[1] I loved, having read the other three volumes of it. The war book too was great—God, what bad luck Tom Boyd had! Stallings made the killing with the play and movie; now Thomason makes a contract with Hearst, for a lot, I guess, and Tom who came first came too early, I suppose. Yet *What Price Glory* would never have been written, I suppose, except for *Through the Wheat*. Not that Tom's novel wasn't a success in a way but to make about $6000 as an originator and see others rake it in like croupiers later—I know how bitter it must make him.

The _____ book was tedious. I'm allowing for having seen it all at least three times but it *was* tedious. Un-

---

[1] *Memoirs of William Hickey.*

doubted power and a great gift of prose but you can't arbitrarily patch together shreds of fine writing and call it a novel. And parts of it were merely sensational bombast. I'm sorry.

Nor, I'm afraid, will Ring's book add to his reputation. Several stories were fine, none were cheap, but—God, I wish he'd write a more or less personal novel. Couldn't you persuade him? The real history of an American manager, say Ziegfeld or a theatrical girl. Think how far Anita Loos got with a mere imitation of him.

I'm enclosing a letter. If you are willing I'd like to have them use "May Day" from *Tales of the Jazz Age* and "The Rich Boy" from *All the Sad Young Men*.

If it is too soon, in your judgment, to use the latter I could substitute "The Diamond as Big as the Ritz." If you act as my agent in a case like this will you take it up with them? If not, let me know immediately and I will.

Also Charlie Bailey of Henry Holt wants to use "The Camel's Back" in an anthology. I suppose it's all right, good advertising, etc. I'd rather have him use "The Curious Case of Benjamin Button" if [he] would. Both are in *Tales of the Jazz Age*.

The reviews of *All the Sad Young Men* have been pleasant, mostly, but, after the book and the play, rather tame. Did it go to 12,000 as you suggested? We've had some good nibbles for the the movie rights of *Gatsby* but they want $45,000, I hear. I get one-third of the gross price.

See my article on Hemingway in *The Bookman*—it's pretty good.

In *absolute confidence* I've received an offer of $3500 per short story from *Liberty*. I'm considering it.

My book is *wonderful*. I don't think it'll be interrupted again. I expect to reach New York about December 10th with the manuscript under my arm. I'll ask between $30,000 and $40,000 for the serial rights and I think *Liberty* will want it. So book publication would be late spring 1927 or early fall.

No news. Do write. Tell me if *Torrents of Spring* gets a press. I doubt it will sell. Again thank you for the books.

Ever and always your friend,

Scott Fitzg_____

Why don't you come over for a month this summer? You
and Louise and the two oldest children! Has your depression of last December gone?

> *Villa St. Louis*
> *Juan-les-Pins*
> *France*
>
> [circa *May 10, 1926*]

Dear Max:

The mistral is raging outside like the end of the world
and the idea of writing is anathema to me. We are won-
derfully situated in a big house on the shore with a beach
and the Casino not 100 yards away and every prospect of
a marvelous summer.

I'm sorry about Van Wyck Brooks. You yourself
sounded a bit depressed.[1]

Dreiser would be crazy to leave Liveright, tho I can
understand how Horace would get on his nerves. I heard
that the movie rights of *An American Tragedy* brought
$90,000 but I don't believe it. *Gatsby*, so it now appears,
sold for $50,000. An agent on the coast got 10% and
Davis, Brady and I split the $45,000. Then I had to pay
Reynolds 10% more, so instead of $16,666.66 I received
$13,500—or $3,166.66 went in agents' commissions. However I shouldn't kick. Everybody sells movies through an
agent and the Reynolds part was necessary since I'm
away. I thought the drawings for *The Sad Young Men*
ads were fine. By the way I'm sending two negatives for
pictures. Do send them out right away to replace the
others.

Thanks for the O'Brien anthology information. You
have never mentioned a cheap edition of *Gatsby*. Not
that I care, for I'm rather skeptical about it, but I'm
curious to know if it were ever put up to the trade. Tell
me what you think of *The Sun Also Rises*.

I'm not surprised at Galsworthy not being responsive
to my stuff. I've found that if you don't respond to an-

---

[1] Perkins had told of Van Wyck Brooks losing confidence in the book he
was writing.

other man's writings the chances are it's mutual—and except for "The Apple Tree" and, oddly enough, *Saint's Progress,* he leaves me cold. I suspect he had some unfortunate idyllic love affair in his youth and whenever that crops into his work it comes alive to me. The subject matter of *The Forsyte Saga* seemed stuffy to me. I entirely "approve" of him though and liked him personally.

Have you considered coming over?

Always your friend,

Scott

> *Villa Paquita*
> *Juan-les-Pins*
> *Alpes Maritime*
> *France*
> [circa *June 10, 1926*]

Dear Mr. Scribner:

For the first time in over four years I am no longer in financial debt to you—or rather I won't be when the money from my short story book becomes due me. But in another sense I shall always be in your debt—for your unfailing kindness and confidence and obligingness to me in all my exigencies during that time. Never once was I reminded of my obligations, which were sometimes as high as $4000, with no book in sight.

With every assurance of my deep respect and very real gratitude, I remain

> Faithfully yours,
>
> F. Scott Fitzgerald

> *Villa St. Louis*
> *Juan-les-Pins*
> *France*
> [circa *June 25, 1926*]

Dear Max:

Thanks for both letters. We were in Paris having Zelda's

appendix neatly but firmly removed or I would have answered before.

First as to Ernest's book.[1] I liked it but with certain qualifications. The fiesta, the fishing trip, the minor characters were fine. The lady I didn't like, perhaps because I don't like the original. In the mutilated man I thought Ernest bit off more than can yet be chewn between the covers of a book, then lost his nerve a little and edited the more vitalizing details out. He has since told me that something like this happened. Do ask him for the absolute minimum of necessary changes, Max— he's discouraged about the previous reception of his work by publishers and magazine editors (tho he loved your letter). From the latter (magazine editors) he has had a lot of words and, until Bridges' offer for the short story (from which he had even before cut out a thousand words on my recommendation), scarcely a single dollar. From the *Torrents* I expect you'll have little response. Do you think the *Bookman* article did him any good?

I roared at the idea of you and the fish in the tree.

O.K. as to Haldeman-Julius.

Will you ask them (your accounting department) to send me an account the 1st of August? I'd love to see what a positive statement looks like for the first time in three years.

I am writing Bridges today. I have an offer now for a story at $3500 (rather for six stories). To sell one for $1000 would mean a dead loss of $2500 and as I average only six stories a year I don't see how I can do it. I hope he'll understand.

The novel, in abeyance during Zelda's operation, now goes on apace. This is confidential but *Liberty,* with certain conditions, has offered me $35,000 sight unseen. I hope to have it done in January.

Do send out a picture to everyone that got that terrible one.

Ever your friend,

Scott

[1] *The Sun Also Rises.*

Villa St. Louis
Juan-les-Pins
France

[circa *June 28, 1926*]

Dear Mr. Bridges:

It isn't a question of contracts—it's frankly a question of money. I hate writing short stories, as you know, and only do my six a year to have the leisure to write my novels at leisure. And since my price has risen to $3500 per story it would mean a dead loss to me of $2500. I'm terribly sorry. If it comes about that a story develops, as they sometimes do, into the type that the big circulation magazines can't print I'll send it on to you but that's all I can promise, because it's become a sort of chore to me to write a short story having had to cook up so [many] tasteless morsels under the whip of the national advertisers. I do hate to refuse, Mr. Bridges. I hope you'll understand.

Sincerely,

F. Scott Fitzgerald

Villa St. Louis
Juan-les-Pins
France

[circa *August, 10, 1926*]

Dear Max:

As to your questions:

(1) Unless the Americans are first driven out of France (as at present seems not unlikely)—I'll be home with the finished manuscript of my book about mid-December. We'll be a week in New York, then south to Washington and Montgomery to see our respective parents and spend Xmas—and back in New York in mid-January to spend the rest of the winter. Whether the spring will see us back on Long Island or returning to Europe depends on politics, finances and our personal desires.

(2) The only censorable thing I found in Ernest's book

was the "balls" conversation. I didn't find the James thing objectionable but then he seems to me to have been dead fifty years.

(3) I'm sorry *Torrents* hasn't done better and delighted about *The Sad Young Men.* Have you sounded out Curtis Brown about an anthology of my stories in England? Still, that better wait till my novel. Don't forget the August statement.

(4) God, how much I've learned in these two and a half years in Europe. It seems like a decade and I feel pretty old but I wouldn't have missed it, even its most unpleasant and painful aspects.

(5) About the Scribners' story I wrote Bridges. If another "Absolution" turns up he shall have first look.

I do want to see you, Max.

Always your friend,

Scott

Ellerslie
Edgemoor, Delaware
[circa *May 12, 1927*]

Dear Max:

The cane was marvelous. The nicest one I ever saw and *infinitely* superior to the one mislaid. Need I say I value the inscription? This is the cane I shall never lose.

It seems a shame to put business into a letter thanking you for such a gift but just a line about Ernest. It is all bull that he left Liveright about that story. One line *at least* is pornographic, though *please* don't bring my name into the discussion. The thing is—what is a seduction story with the seduction left out? Yet if that is softened it is quite printable. However I trust your judgment, as he should.

I'm sorry about O'Hara.[1] I imagined that this book wasn't as good as his first—however he doesn't seem to

---

[1] Unidentifiable.

me now to be an indisputably good risk—he's mature and developed and ought to be doing first rate things, if ever.

(Explain to Hemingway, why don't you, that while such an incident might be lost in a book, a story centering around it *points* it. In other words the material *raison d'être* as opposed to the artistic *raison d'être* of the story is, in part, to show the physiological details of a seduction. If that were possible in America, 20 publishers would be scrambling for James Joyce tomorrow.)

Thanks many times for looking for the old cane. It doesn't matter. I want to put off the pamphlet for a month until I make up some misunderstandings with the men who wrote the articles.

Many, many sincere thanks, Max. I was touched when I found it at the station.

                                                            Scott

                                              Ellerslie
                                              Edgemoor, Delaware
                                              [*Before January 3, 1928*]

Dear Max:

Patience yet a little while, I beseech thee, and thanks eternally for the deposits. I feel awfully about owing you that money—all I can say is that if book is serialized I'll pay it back immediately. I work at it all the time but that period of sickness set me back—made a break both in the book and financially so that I had to do those *Post* stories—which made a further break. Please regard it as a safe investment and not as a risk.

I have no news. I like *Some People* by Nicolson and *The Bridge of San Luis Rey*. Also I loved John's book[1] and I saw your letter agreement that it's his best thing, and the most likely to go. It's really thought out—oddly enough its least effective moments are the traces of his old manner, tho on the whole it's steadily and cumulatively effective throughout. From the first draft, which was the one

[1] *Seven Days Whipping* by John Biggs.

I saw, I thought he could have cut 2000 or 3000 words that were mere Conradian stalling around. Whether he did or not I don't know.

No news from Ernest. In the latest *Transition* (Volume 9) there is some good stuff by Murray Goodwin (unprintable here) and a fine German play.

Always your afft. friend,

Scott

Except for a three day break last week (Xmas) I have been on the absolute wagon since the middle of October. Feel simply grand. Smoke only Sanos. God help us all.

c/o Guaranty Trust Co.
[*Paris, France*]
[circa *July 1, 1928*]

Dear Max:

We are settled and not a soul in the world knows where we are; on the absolute wagon and working on the novel, the whole novel and nothing but the novel. I'm coming back in August with it or on it. Thank you so much for the money—by this time Reynolds will have sold my last story and that, at French prices, will carry us through.

Please advise me as to the enclosure. Why not let's do it—you acting as my agent directly with him and keeping 10% thus saving Curtis Brown's 10%? Anyhow please advise me—I'd like to be published by him as he's done better than anyone in England with Americans.

I strongly advise your obtaining immediately the translation rights to

> *Les Hommes de la Route*
> by André Chamson
> (Published by Bernard Grasset)

He's young, not salacious, and apparently is destined by all the solid literary men here to be the great novelist of France—no flash in the pan like Crevel, Radiguet, Aragon, etc. He has a simply astonishing reputation in its enthusiasm and solidity.

Yours as ever devotedly,

Scott

Thanks for the books at the boat—many thanks!

[*58 rue Vaugirard*]
[*Paris, France*]
[circa *July 15, 1928*]

Dear Max:

I read John Bishop's novel. Of course it's impossible. All the people who were impressed with Norman Douglas' *South Wind* and Beerbohm's *Zuleika Dobson* tried to follow them in their wretched organization of material—without having either the brilliant intelligence of Douglas or the wit of Beerbohm. *Vide* the total collapse of Aldous Huxley. Conrad has been, after all, the healthy influence on the technique of the novel.

Anyhow at the same time Bishop gave me a novelette to read—and to my great astonishment, as a document of the Civil War, it's right up to Bierce and Stephen Crane—beautifully written, thrilling, and water tight as to construction and interest. He's been so discouraged over the hash he made of the novel that he's been half afraid to send it anywhere, and I told him that now that tales of violence are so popular I thought *Scribner's Magazine* would love to have a look at it.

So I'm sending it—no one has seen it but me. His address is Chateau de Tressancourt, Orgeval, Seine et Oise. I'm working hard as hell.

As ever your friend,

Scott

[*58 rue Vaugirard*]
[*Paris, France*]
[circa *July 21, 1928*]

Dear Max:

(1) The novel goes fine. I think it's quite wonderful and I think those who've seen it (for I've read it around a little) have been quite excited. I was encouraged the other day, when James Joyce came to dinner, when he said, "Yes, I expect to finish my novel in three or four years more at the *latest*," and he works 11 hours a day to my intermittent 8. Mine will be done *sure* in September.

(2) Did you get my letter about *André Chamson?* Really, Max, you're missing a great opportunity if you don't take that up. Radiguet was perhaps obscene—Chamson is absolutely *not*—he's head over heels the best young man here, like Ernest and Thornton Wilder rolled into one. This *Hommes de la Route* (Road Menders) is his second novel and all but won the Prix Goncourt—the story of men building a road, with all of the force of K. Hamsun's *Growth of the Soil*—not a bit like Tom Boyd's bogus American husbandmen. Moreover, tho I know him only slightly and have no axe to grind, I have every faith in him as an extraordinary personality, like France and Proust. Incidentally King Vidor (who made *The Crowd* and *The Big Parade*) is making a picture of it next summer. If you have any confidence in my judgment do at least get a report on it and let me know what you decide. Ten years from now he'll be beyond price.

(3) I plan to publish a book of those Basil Lee stories after the novel. Perhaps one or two more serious ones to be published in *The Mercury* or with Scribners, if you'd want them, combined with the total of about six in the *Post* series would make a nice *light* novel, almost to follow my novel in the season *immediately* after, so as not to seem in the direct line of my so-called "work." It would run to perhaps 50 or 60 thousand words.

(4) Do let me know any plans of (a) Ernest, (b) Ring, (c) Tom (reviews poor, I notice), (d) John Biggs.

(5) Did you like Bishop's story? I thought it was grand.

(6) Home September 15th, I think. Best to Louise.

(7) About Cape—won't you arrange it for me and take

the 10% commission? That is if I'm not committed *mor-ally* to Chatto & Windus who did, so to speak, pick me up out of the English gutter. I'd *rather* be with Cape. Please decide and act accordingly if you will. If you don't I'll just ask Reynolds. As you like. *Let me know.*

> Ever your devoted and grateful friend,
>
> Scott

> [*Ellerslie*]
> *Edgemoor,* [*Delaware*]
> [*November, 1928*]

Dear Max:

It seems fine to be sending you something again, even though it's only the first fourth of the book (2 chapters, 18,000 words). Now comes another short story, then I'll patch up Chapters 3 and 4 the same way, and send them, I hope, about the 1st of December.

Chapter 1 here is good.

Chapter 2 has caused me more trouble than anything in the book. You'll realize this when I tell you it was once 27,000 words long! It started its career as Chapter 1. I am far from satisfied with it even now, but won't go into its obvious faults. I would appreciate it if you jotted down any criticisms—and *saved them until* I've sent you the whole book, because I want to *feel* that each part is finished and not worry about it any longer, even though I may change it enormously at the very last minute. All I want to know now is if, in general, you like it and this will have to wait, I suppose, until you've seen the next batch which finishes the first half. (My God, it's good to see those chapters lying in an envelope!)

I think I have found you a new prospect of really ex-traordinary talent in a Carl Van Vechten way. I have his first novel at hand—unfortunately it's about Lesbians. More of this later.

I think Bunny's title[1] is *wonderful!*

---

[1] *I Thought of Daisy*, a novel by Edmund Wilson.

Remember novel is confidential, even to Ernest.

> Always yours,
>
> Scott

[*Ellerslie*]
[*Edgemoor, Delaware*]
[circa *March 1, 1929*]

Dear Max:

I am sneaking away like a thief without leaving the chapters—there is a week's work to straighten them out and, in the confusion of influenza and leaving, I haven't been able to do it. I'll do it on the boat and send it from Genoa. A thousand thanks for your patience—just trust me a few months longer, Max—it's been a discouraging time for me too but I will never forget your kindness and the fact that you've never reproached me.

I'm delighted about Ernest's book—I bow to your decision on the Modern Library without agreeing at all. $100.00 or $50.00 advance is better than one-eighth of $40.00 for a year's royalty, and Scribner collection sounds vague and arbitrary to me. But it's a trifle and I'll give them a new and much inferior story as I want to be represented with those men, i.e., Forster, Conrad, Mansfield, etc.

Herewith a manuscript I promised to bring you—I think it needs cutting but it just might sell with a decent title and no foreword. I don't feel certain tho at all—

Will you watch for some stories from a young Holger Lundberg who has appeared in *The Mercury?* He is a man of some promise and I headed him your way.

I hate to leave without seeing you—and I hate to see you without the ability to put the finished ms. in your hands. So for a few months goodbye, and my affection and gratitude always.

> Scott

[*Somewhere in France*]

[circa *April 1, 1929*]

Dear Max:

This letter is too hurried to thank you for the very kind and encouraging one you wrote me. It's only to say— watch for a book on *Baudelaire* by Pierre Loving which Madeleine Boyd will bring you. I believe another one has been published but this man once did me a service and I promised to call your attention to it, before knowing it had a rival in the market.

I'm delighted about Ernest's novel.[1] Will be here in Paris, trying as usual to finish mine, till July 1st, c/o The Guaranty Trust, rue des Italiens. Then the seashore.

A Frenchman here (unfortunately I haven't his book at hand but he's a well-known writer on aviation) has written a book called *Evasions d'Aviateurs* dealing with aviators' escapes during the war—all true and to me fascinating. It's a best seller here now. In three months will come a sequel which will include some escapes of German and American aviators (as you know it was the tradition of all aviators to escape) which will include that of Tommy Hitchcock.

What would you say to the two-in-one oversized volume, profusely illustrated with photographs? I believe *Liberty* had a great success with Richthofen and as a record of human ingenuity *Les Evasions d'Aviateurs* is astounding. To swell the thing a third book he has just published called *Special Missions of Aviators During the War* might be added. What do you think? It might just make a great killing, like *Trader Horn*—it has a certain bizarre quality to divert the bored.

Unfortunately I haven't the man's name.

Again thank you for your kind and understanding letter. I'm ashamed of myself for whining about nothing and never will again.

Scott F.

---

[1] *A Farewell to Arms.*

Villa Fleur des Bois
Boulevard Eugene Gazagnaire
(Till October 1st)
Cannes, France

[circa *June, 1929*]

Dear Max:

A line in haste to say

(1) I am working night and day on novel from new angle that I think will solve previous difficulties.

(2) Dotty Parker, whose "Big Blonde" won O. Henry prize, is writing a novelette or novel. She has been getting bad prices and I think, if she interested you, she'd be glad to find a market in Scribners. Just now she's at a high point as a producer and as to reputation. You'd better get her Paris bank address from *Bookman* or *New Yorker* and have them forward, as I don't know when she'll leave here, where she's at Hotel Beau Rivage, Antibes. I wouldn't lose any time about this if it interests you.

(3) Ernest's last letter a little worried, but I don't see why. To hell with the toughs of Boston. I hope to God *All Quiet on the Western Front* won't cut in on his sales. My bet is the book will pass 50,000.

(4) Deeply sorry about Ring. *Why* won't he write about Great Neck, a sort of Odyssey of man starting in theatre business?

(5) Do send me Bunny's book. I heard about his breakdown. I hope his poems include "Our Autumns were unreal with the new—" *Please* ask him about it—it's haunted me for 12 years.

(6) Sorry about John's leg—am writing him as I want news of the play.

(7) Tom Boyd has apparently dropped from sight, hasn't he? Do give me any news.

Always your afft. friend,

Scott

10 rue Pergolèse
Paris, France
[circa *November 15, 1929*]

Dear Max:

For the first time since August I see my way clear to a long stretch on the novel, so I'm writing you as I can't bear to do when it's in one of its states of postponement and seems so in the air. We are not coming home for Xmas, because of expense and because it'd be an awful interruption now. Both our families are raising hell but I can't compromise the remains of my future for that.

I'm glad of Ring's success tho—at least it's for something new and will make him think he's still alive and not a defunct semi-classic. Also Ernest's press has been marvelous and I hope it sells. By the way McAlmon[1] is a bitter rat and I'm not surprised at anything he does or says. He's failed as a writer and tries to fortify himself by tying up to the big boys like Joyce and Stein and despising everything else. Part of his quarrel with Ernest some years ago was because he assured Ernest that I was a fairy—God knows he shows more creative imagination in his malice than in his work. Next he told Callaghan[2] that Ernest was a fairy. He's a pretty good person to avoid.

Sorry Bunny's book didn't go—I thought it was fine, and more interesting than better, or at least more achieved, novels.

Congratulations to Louise.

Oh, and what the *hell* is this book I keep getting clippings about, with me and Struthers Burt and Ernest, etc.? As I remember, you refused to let "The Rich Boy" be published in the Modern Library in a representative collection where it would have helped me, and here it is in a book obviously foredoomed to oblivion that can serve no purpose than to fatigue reviewers with the stories. I know it's a small matter but I am disturbed by the fact that you didn't see fit to discuss it with me.

However that's a rather disagreeable note to close on when I am forever in your debt for countless favors and valuable advice. It is because so little has happened to me

---

[1] American writer and publisher, Robert McAlmon.
[2] Canadian writer, Morley Callaghan.

lately that it seems magnified. Will you, by the way, send the Princeton book by Edgar—it's not available here. Did Tom Boyd elope? And what about Biggs' play?

Ever your afft. friend,

Scott

10 rue Pergolèse
Paris, France
January 21, 1930

Dear Max:

This has run to seven long close-written pages so you better not read it when you're in a hurry.[1] There is so much to write you— or rather so many small things that I'll write, first the personal things, and then on another sheet a series of suggestions about books and authors that have accumulated in me in the last six months.

(1) To begin with, because I don't mention my novel it isn't because it isn't finishing up or that I'm neglecting it— but only that I'm weary of setting dates for it till the moment when it is in the post office box.

(2) I was very grateful for the money—it won't happen again but I'd managed to get horribly into debt and I hated to call on Ober,[2] who's just getting started, for another cent.

(3) Thank you for the documents in the Callaghan case. I'd rather not discuss it except to say that I don't like him and that I wrote him a formal letter of apology. I never thought he started the rumor and never said nor implied such a thing to Ernest.

(4) Delighted with the success of Ernest's book. I took the responsibility of telling him that McAlmon was at his old dirty work around New York. McAlmon, by the way, didn't have anything to do with founding *Transition*. He

---

[1] This was written above the greeting.
[2] Harold Ober, Fitzgerald's literary agent, had recently left the firm of Paul Revere Reynolds to start his own firm.

published Ernest's first book over here and some books of his own and did found some little magazine but of no importance.

(5) Thank you for getting *Gatsby* for me in foreign languages.

(6) . . . .

(7) Tom Boyd seems far away. I'll tell you one awful thing tho. Laurence Stallings was in the West with King Vidor at a *huge* salary to write an equivalent of *What Price Glory*. King Vidor told me that Stallings, in despair of showing Vidor what the war was about, gave him a copy of *Through the Wheat*. And that's how Vidor made the big scenes in *The Big Parade*. Tom Boyd's profits were a few thousand—Stallings were a few hundred thousands. Please don't connect my name with this story but it is the truth and it seems to me rather horrible.

(8) Lastly and most important. For the English rights of my next book Knopf made me an offer so much better than any in England (advance $500.00; royalties sliding from ten to fifteen and twenty; guaranty to publish next book of short stories at same rate) that I accepted of course. My previous talk with Cape was encouraging on my part but conditional. As to Chatto & Windus—since they made no overtures at my *All the Sad Young Men* I feel free to take any advantage of a technicality to have my short stories published in England, especially as they answered a letter of mine on the publication of the book with the signature *(Chatto & Windus, per Q)*, undoubtedly an English method of showing real interest in one's work.

I must tell you (and privately) for your own amusement that the first treaty Knopf sent me contained a clause that would have required me to give him $10,000 on date of publication—that is: 25% of *all* serial rights (not specifying only *English* ones) for which *Liberty* have contracted, as you know, for $40,000. This was pretty . . . ., or maybe an error in his office, but later I went over the contract with a fine tooth comb and he was very decent. Confidential! Incidentally he said to me as Harcourt once did to Ernest that you were the best publishers in America. I told him he was wrong—that you were just a lot of royalty-doctorers and short changers.

No more for the moment. I liked Bunny's book and

am sorry it didn't go. I thought those Day Edgar stories made a nice book, didn't you?

Ever your devoted friend,

Scott

I append the sheet of brilliant ideas of which you may find one or two worth considering. Congratulations [on] the Eddy book.

(Suggestion List)

(1) Certainly if the ubiquitous and ruined McAlmon deserves a hearing then John Bishop, a poet and a man of really great talents and intelligence, does. I am sending you under another cover a sister story of the novelette you refused, which together with the first one and three shorter ones will form his Civil-War-civilian-in-invaded-Virginia book, a simply grand idea and a new, rich field. The enclosed is the best thing he has ever done and the best thing about the *non-combatant* or rather behind-the-lines war I've ever read. I *hope* to God you can use this in the magazine—couldn't it be run into small type carried over like Sew Collins did with *Boston* and you *Farewell to Arms?* He *needs* the encouragement and is *so* worth it.

(2) In the new *American Caravan* amid much sandwiching of Joyce and Co. is the first work of a 21 year old named *Robert Cantwell*. Mark it well, for my guess is that he's learned a better lesson from Proust than Thornton Wilder did and has a destiny of no mean star.

(3) Another young man therein named *Gerald Sykes* has an extraordinary talent in the line of heaven knows what, but very memorable and distinguished.

(4) Third (and these three are all in the whole damn book) there is a man named Erskine Caldwell, who interested me less than the others because of the usual derivations from Hemingway and even Callaghan—still, read him. He and Sykes are 26 years old. I don't know any of them.

If you decide to act in any of these last three cases I'd do it within a few weeks. I know none of the men but Cantwell will go quick with his next stuff if he hasn't gone already. For some reason young writers come in groups— Cummings, Dos Passos and me in 1920–21; Hemingway,

Callaghan and Wilder in 1926–27—and no one in between and no one since. This looks to me like a really new generation.

(5) Now a personal friend (but he knows not that I'm [writing] you)—Cary Ross (Yale 1925)—poorly represented in this *American Caravan,* but rather brilliantly by poems in *The Mercury* and *Transition,* studying medicine at Johns Hopkins, and one who at the price of publication or at least examination of his poems might prove a valuable man. Distinctly *younger* than *post* war, later than my generation, sure to turn to fiction and worth corresponding with. I believe these are the cream of the young people.

(6) Dos Passos wrote me about the ms. of some protégée of his but as I didn't see the ms. or know the man the letter seemed meaningless. Did you do anything about Murray Godwin (or Goodwin)? Shortly I'm sending you some memoirs by an ex-marine, doorman at my bank here. They might have some documentary value as true stories of the Nicaraguan expedition, etc.

(7) In the foreign (French) field there is besides Chamson one man, and at the opposite pole, of great talent. It is not Cocteau nor Aragon but young *René Crevel.* I am opposed to him for being a fairy but in the last *Transition* (Number 18) there is a *translation* of the beginning of his current novel which simply knocked me cold with its beauty. The part in *Transition* is called *"Mr. Knife and Miss Fork"* and I wish to God you'd read it immediately. Incidentally the novel is a great current success here. I know it's not yet placed in America and if you're interested *please* communicate with me *before* you write Bradley.

(8) Now, one last, much more elaborate idea. In France any military book of real tactical or strategical importance, theoretical or fully documented (and usually the latter) (and I'm not referring to the one-company battles between "Red" and "Blue" taught us in the army under the name of Small Problems for Infantry)—they are mostly published by Payot here and include such works as *Ludendorf's Memoirs;* and the *Documentary Preparations for the German Break-through in 1918*—how the men were massed, trained, brought up to the line in 12 hours in 150 different technical groups from flame throwers to field kitchens, the whole inside story *from captured orders* of the greatest *tactical* attack in history; a study of *Tannenburg*

(German); several, both French and German, of the first Marne; a thorough study of gas warfare, another of tanks; no dogmatic distillations compiled by some old dotard, but original documents.

Now—believing that so long as we have service schools and not much preparation (I am a political cynic and a big-navy-man, like all Europeans) English translations should be available in all academies, army service schools, staff schools, etc. (I'll bet there are American army officers with the rank of captain that don't know what "infiltration in depth" is or what Colonel Bruckmuller's idea of artillery employment was)—it seems to me that it would be a great patriotic service to consult the war-department bookbuyers on some subsidy plan to bring out a tentative dozen of the most important as "an original source tactical library of the lessons of the great war." It would be a parallel, but *more* essentially *military* rather than *politico-military,* to the enclosed list of Payot's collection. I underline some of my proposed inclusions. This, in view of some millions of amateurs of battle now in America, might be an enormous popular success as well as a patriotic service. Let me know about this because if you shouldn't be interested I'd like to make the suggestion for my own satisfaction to someone else. Some that I've underlined may be already published.

My God—this is 7 pages and you're asleep and I want to catch the *Olympic* with this so I'll close. Please tell me your response to *each* idea.

Does Chamson sell at all? Oh, for my income tax will you have the usual statement of lack of royalties sent me—and for my own curiosity to see if I've sold a book this year except to myself.

[*10 rue Pergolèse*]
[*Paris, France*]

[circa *May 1, 1930*]

Dear Max:

I was delighted about the Bishop story—the acceptance has done wonders for him. The other night I read him a good deal of my novel and I think he liked it. Harold Ober wrote me that if it wouldn't be published this fall I should publish the Basil Lee stories, but I know too well by whom reputations are made and broken to ruin myself completely by such a move—I've seen Tom Boyd, Michael Arlen, and too many others fall through the eternal trap-door of trying to cheat the public, no matter what their public is, with substitutes—better to let four years go by. I wrote young and I wrote a lot and the pot takes longer to fill up now but the novel, my novel, is a different matter than if I'd hurriedly finished it up a year and a half ago. If you think Callaghan hasn't completely blown himself up with this deathhouse masterpiece just wait and see the pieces fall. I don't know why I'm saying this to you who have never been anything but my most loyal and confident encourager and friend but Ober's letter annoyed me today and put me in a wretched humor. *I know what I'm doing*— honestly, Max. How much time between *The Cabala* and *The Bridge of St. Luis Rey*, between *The Genius* and *The American Tragedy*, between *The Wisdom Tooth* and *Green Pastures*? I think it seems to go by quicker there in America but time put in is time eventually taken out—and whatever this thing of mine is it's certainly not a mediocrity like *The Woman of Andros* and *The Forty-Second Parallel*. "He's through" is an easy cry to raise but it's safer for the critics to raise it at the evidence in print than at a long silence.

Ever yours,

Scott

[*10 rue Pergolèse*]
[*Paris, France*]
[*May, 1930*]

Dear Max:

First let me tell you how shocked I was by Mr. Scribner's death. It was in due time of course but nevertheless [I shall miss] his fairness toward things that were of another generation, his general tolerance and simply his being there as titular head of a great business.

Please tell me how this affects you—if at all.

The letter enclosed has been in my desk for three weeks as I wasn't sure whether to send it when I wrote it. Then Powell Fowler and his wedding party arrived and I got unfortunately involved in dinners and night clubs and drinking; then Zelda got a sort of nervous breakdown from overwork and consequently I haven't done a line of work or written a letter for twenty-one days.

Have you read *The Building of St. Michele* and D. H. Lawrence's *Fantasia of the Unconscious?* Don't miss either of them.

Always yours,

Scott

What news of Ernest?
Please don't mention the enclosed letter to Ober as I've written him already.

[*Switzerland*]

[circa *July 8, 1930*]

Dear Max:

I'm asking Harold Ober to offer you these three stories which Zelda wrote in the dark middle of her nervous breakdown. I think you'll see that apart from the beauty and richness of the writing they have a strange haunting and evocative quality that is absolutely new. I think too that there is a certain unity apparent in them—their actual unity is a fact because each of them is the story of her life when things for a while seemed to have brought her to the edge of madness and despair. In my opinion they are literature tho I may in this case read so much between the lines that my opinion is valueless. (By the way Caldwell's stories were a thorough disappointment, weren't they—more crimes committed in Hemingway's name.)

Ever yours,

Scott

[*Switzerland*]

[circa *July 20, 1930*]

Dear Max:

Zelda is still sick as hell, and the psychiatrist who is devoting almost his entire time to her is an expensive proposition. I was so upset in June when hopes for her recovery were black that I could practicaly do no work and got behind—then arrived a wire from Ober that for the first time he couldn't make me the usual advance up to the price of a story. So then I called on you. I am having him turn over to you $3000 from the proceeds of the story I am sending off this week, as it's terrible to be so in debt. A thousand thanks and apologies.

Yours as ever (if somewhat harassed and anxious about life),

Scott

Geneva, Switzerland

[circa *September 1, 1930*]

Dear Max:

All the world seems to end up in this flat and antiseptic smelling land—with an overlay of flowers. Tom Wolfe is the only man I've met here who isn't sick or hasn't sickness to deal with. You have a great find in him—what he'll do is incalculable. He has a deeper culture than Ernest and more vitality, if he is slightly less of a poet that goes with the immense surface he wants to cover. Also he lacks Ernest's quality of a stick hardened in the fire—he is more susceptible to the world. John Bishop told me he needed advice about cutting, etc., but after reading his book I thought that was nonsense. He strikes me as a man who should be let alone as to length, if he has to be published in five volumes. I liked him enormously.

I was sorry of course about Zelda's stories—possibly they mean more to me than is implicit to the reader who doesn't know from what depths of misery and effort they sprang. One of them, I think now, would be incomprehensible without a waste-land footnote. She has those series of eight portraits that attracted so much attention in *College Humor* and I think in view of the success of Dotty Parker's *Laments* (25,000 copies) I think a book might be got together for next spring if Zelda can add a few more during the winter.

Wasn't that a nice tribute to C.S. from Mencken in *The Mercury?*

The royalty advance or the national debt as it might be called shocked me. The usual vicious circle is here—I am now exactly $3000 ahead which means 2 months on the encyclopedia. I'd prefer to have all above the $10,000 paid back to you off my next story (in October). You've been so damn nice to me.

Zelda is almost well. The doctor says she can never drink again (not that drink in any way contributed to her collapse), and that I must not drink anything, not even wine, for a year, because drinking in the past was one of the things that haunted her in her delirium.

Do please send me things like Wolfe's book when they appear. Is Ernest's book a history of bull-fighting? I'm sending you a curious illiterate ms. written by a chasseur at my bank here. Will you skim it and see if any parts, like the marines in Central America, are interesting as pure data? And return it, if not, directly to him? You were absolutely right about the dollar books—it's a preposterous idea and I think the Authors League went crazy.

Always yours,

Scott

This illness has cost me a fortune—hence that telegram in July. The biggest man in Switzerland gave all his time to her—and saved her reason by a split second.

Grand Hotel de la Paix
Lausanne, Switzerland
[*Before, May 21, 1931*]

Dear Max:

An idea:
Princeton has had lots of books, too many in the last
ten years (on a cursory inspection I'm not so much impressed with Burnham's book which leans heavily on so
many of us greybeards), but—
There's been no Harvard book since Charlie Flandrau
and Philosophy Four. I'm very impressed with a series of
Harvard-Boston society stories by Bernard De Voto which
have been running in the *Post* the last year. They're light,
romantic and *exceedingly witty*. I think that under some
such title as *Outside the Yard* the as yet unsaturated Harvard public would lap them up. (I don't dare suggest you
call them *Recent Researches at Cambridge*.)
The new avant-garde magazines are not up to *Transition*, and this *Caravan* has nothing new except some good
poetry. The Jazz Age is over. If Mark Sullivan is going on,
you might tell him I claim credit for naming it and that it
extended from the suppression of the riots on May Day
1919 to the crash of the stock market in 1929—almost
exactly one decade.
Zelda is *so* much better. I'm taking her on a trip tomorrow—only for the day. But she's herself again now, tho
not yet strong. *Please* send that proof of hers.

Always yours,

Scott Fitz

Don Ce-Sar Hotel
St. Petersburg, Florida
(for three days only)
[circa *January 15, 1932*]

Dear Max:

At last for the first time in two years and a half I am
going to spend five consecutive months on my novel. I am

actually six thousand dollars ahead. Am replanning it to include what's good in what I have, adding 41,000 new words and publishing. Don't tell Ernest or anyone—let them think what they want—you're the only one who's ever consistently felt faith in me anyhow.

Your letters still sound sad. For God's sake take your vacation this winter. Nobody could quite ruin the house in your absence, or would dare to take any important steps. Give them a chance to see how much they depend on you and when you come back cut off an empty head or two. Thalberg did that with Metro-Goldwyn-Mayer.

Which reminds me that I'm doing that "Hollywood Revisited" in the evenings and it will be along in, I think, six days—maybe ten.

Have Nunnally Johnson's humorous stories from the *Post* been collected? Everybody reads them. Please at least look into this. Ask Myers—he ought to search back at least a year which is as long as I've been meaning to write you about it.

Where in hell are my Scandinavian copies of *The Great Gatsby?*

You couldn't have sent me anything I enjoyed more than the Churchill book.

Always yours devotedly,

Scott Fitzg———

Hotel Rennert
Baltimore, Maryland
[*Before May 2, 1932*]

Dear Max: ....

Zelda's novel [1] is now good, improved in every way. It is new. She has largely eliminated the speakeasy-nights-and-our-trip-to-Paris atmosphere. You'll like it. It should reach you in ten days. I am too close to it to judge it but it may be even better than I think. *But* I must urge you two things.

[1] *Save Me the Waltz.*

(1) If you like it please *don't* wire her congratulations and please keep whatever praise you may see fit to give *on the staid side*—I mean, *as you naturally would,* rather than yield to a tendency one has with invalids to be extra nice to cheer them up. This seems a nuance but it is rather important at present to the doctors that Zelda does not feel that the acceptance (always granted you like it) means immediate fame and money. I'm afraid all our critical tendencies in the last decade got bullish; we discovered one Hemingway to a dozen Callaghans and Caldwells (I think the latter is a wash-out) and probably created a lot of spoiled geniuses who might have been good workmen. Not that I regret it— if the last five years uncovered Ernest, Tom Wolfe and Faulkner it would have been worthwhile, but I'm not certain enough of Zelda's present stability of character to expose her to any superlatives. If she has a success coming she must associate it with work done in a workmanlike manner for its own sake, and part of it done fatigued and uninspired, and part of it done when even to remember the original inspiration and impetus is a psychological trick. She is not twenty-one and she is not strong, and she must not try to follow the pattern of my trail which is of course blazed distinctly on her mind.

(2) Don't discuss contract with her until I have talked to you.

Ring's last story in the *Post* was pathetic, a shade of himself, but I'm glad they ran it first and I hope it'll stir up his professional pride to repeat.

Beginning the article for you on Monday. You can count on it for the end of next week.

Now *very important.*

(1) I must have a royalty report for 1931 for my income tax—they insist.

(2) I borrowed $600 in 1931. $500 of this was redeemed by my article. The other hundred should show in royalty report.

(3) Since *Gatsby* was not placed with Grosset or Burt, I'd like to have it in the Modern Library. This is my own idea and have had no approach but imagine I can negotiate it. Once they are interested would of course turn negotiations over to you. But I feel, should you put obstacles in the way, you would be doing me a great harm and injustice. *Gatsby* is constantly mentioned among

memorable books but the man who asks for it in a store on the basis of such mention does not ask twice. Booksellers do not keep such an item in stock and there is a whole new generation who cannot obtain it. This has been on my mind for two years and I must insist that you give me an answer that doesn't keep me awake nights wondering why it possibly benefited the Scribners to have me represented in such an impersonal short story collection as that of the Modern Library by a weak story, and Ring, etc., by none at all. That "they would almost all have been Scribner authors" was a most curious perversion of what should have been a matter of pride into an attitude of dog-in-the-manger.

Excuse that outburst, Max. Please write, answering all questions. Tell Louise I liked her story and hope she's better. Things go all right with me now. What news of Ernest? And his book?

Ever your friend,

Scott

[*Hotel Rennert*]
[*Baltimore, Maryland*]
[circa *May 14, 1932*]

Dear Max:

Here is Zelda's novel. It is a good novel now, perhaps a very good novel—I am too close to tell. It has the faults and virtues of a first novel. It is more the expression of a powerful personality, like *Look Homeward, Angel,* than the work of a finished artist like Ernest Hemingway. It should interest the many thousands interested in dancing. It is *about something* and absolutely new, and should sell.

Now, about its reception. If you refuse it, which I don't think you will, all communication should come through me. If you accept it write her directly and I withdraw all restraints on whatever meed of praise you may see fit to give. The strain of writing it was bad for her but it had to be written—she needed relaxation afterwards and I was afraid that praise might encourage the incipient egomania the doctors noticed, but she has taken such a sane common-sense view lately—(At first she refused to revise—then she revised completely, added on her own suggestion and has changed what was a rather flashy and self-justifying "true confessions" that wasn't worthy of her into an honest piece of work. She can do more with the galleys but I can't ask her to do more now.)—But now praise will do her good, within reason. But she mustn't write anything more on the *personal* side for six months or so until she is stronger.

Now a second thing, more important than you think. You haven't been in the publishing business over twenty years without noticing the streaks of smallness in very large personalities. Ernest told me once he would "never publish a book in the same season with me," meaning it would lead to ill-feeling. I advise you, if he is in New York (and always granting you like Zelda's book), *do not praise it, or even talk about it to him!* The finer the thing he has written, the more he'll expect your entire allegiance to it as this is one of the few pleasures, rich and full and new, he'll get out of it. I know this, and I think you do too and probably there's no use warning you. There is no possible conflict between the books but there has always been a subtle struggle between Ernest and Zelda, and any apposition might have curiously grave consequences—curious, that is, to un-jealous men like you and me.

One thing more. Please, in your letter to Zelda (if of acceptance) do not mention contracts or terms. I will take it up immediately on hearing from you.

Thanks about the Modern Library. I don't know exactly what I shall do. Five years have rolled away from me and I can't decide exactly who I am, if anyone. . . .

Ever your friend,

Scott

La Paix, Rodgers' Forge
Towson, Maryland
January 19, 1933

Dear Max:

I was in New York for three days last week on a terrible

bat. I was about to call you up when I completely collapsed and laid in bed for twenty-four hours groaning. Without a doubt the boy is getting too old for such tricks. Ernest told me he concealed from you the fact that I was in such rotten shape. I send you this, less to write you a *Rousseau's Confession* than to let you know why I came to town without calling you, thus violating a custom of many years' standing.

Thanks for the books that you have had sent to me from time to time. They comprise most of the reading I do because like everybody else I gradually cut down on expenses. When you have a line on the sale of Zelda's book let us know.

Found New York in a high state of neurosis, as does everybody else, and met no one who didn't convey the fact to me: it possibly proves that the neurosis is in me. All goes serenely down here. Am going on the water-wagon from the first of February to the first of April but don't tell Ernest because he has long convinced himself that I am an incurable alcoholic due to the fact that we almost always meet on parties. I am *his* alcoholic just like Ring is mine and do not want to disillusion him, tho even *Post* stories must be done in a state of sobriety. I thought he seemed in good shape, Bunny less so, rather gloomy. A decision to adopt Communism definitely, no matter how good for the soul, must of necessity be a saddening process for anyone who has ever tasted the intellectual pleasures of the world we live in.

For God's sake can't you lighten the pall of gloom which has settled over *Scribner's* [*Magazine*]—Erskine Caldwell's imitations of Morley Callaghan's imitations of Ernest, and Stuart Chase's imitations of Earl Browder imitating Lenin? Maybe Ring would lighten your volume with a monthly article. I see he has perked up a little in *The New Yorker*.

All goes acceptably in Maryland, at least from the window of my study, with distant gun flashes on the horizon if you walk far out of the door.

Ever your old friend,

F. Scott Fitzgerald

La Paix, Rodgers' Forge
Towson, Maryland
September 25, 1933

Dear Max:

The novel has gone ahead faster than I thought. There was a little setback when I went to the hospital for four days but since then things have gone ahead of my schedule which, you will remember, promised you the whole manuscript for reading November 1, with the first one-fourth ready to shoot into the magazine (in case you can use it) and the other three-fourths to undergo further revision. I now figure that this can be achieved by about the 25th of October. I will appear in person, carrying the manuscript and wearing a spiked helmet.

There are several points and I wish you would answer them categorically.

1. Did you mean that you could get the first fourth of the story into the copy of the magazine appearing late in December and therefore that the book could appear early in April? I gathered that on the phone but want to be sure. I don't know what the ocean travel statistics promise for the spring but it seems to me that a May publication would be too late if there was a great exodus and I should miss being a proper gift book for it. The story, as you know, is laid entirely in Europe—I wish I could have gotten as far as China but Europe was the best I could do, Max (to get into Ernest's rhythm).

2. I would not want a magazine proof of the first part, though of course I would expect your own proofreaders to check up on blatant errors, but would want to talk over with you any small changes that would have to be made for magazine publication—in any case to make them myself.

3. Will publication with you absolutely preclude that the book will be chosen by the Literary Guild or the Book-of-the-Month? Whatever the answer, the serial will serve the purpose of bringing my book to the memory and attention of my old public and of getting straight financially with you. On the other hand, it is to both our advantages to capitalize if possible such facts as that the editors of those book leagues might take a fancy to such a curious idea that the author, Fitzgerald, actually wrote a book

after all these years (this is all said with the reservation that the book is good). Please answer this as it is of importance to me to know whether I must expect my big returns from serial and possibly theatrical and picture rights or whether I have as good a chance at a book sale, launched by one of those organizations, as any other best seller.

Ober is advancing me the money to go through with it (it will probably not need more than $2000 though he has promised to go as far as $4000) and in return I am giving him 10% of the serial rights. I plan to raise the money to repay him (if I have not already paid him by *Post* stories) by asking a further advance on the book royalties or on my next book which might be an omnibus collection of short stories or those two long serial stories about young people that I published some time ago in the *Post* as the Basil stories and the Josephine stories—this to be published in the fall.

You are the only person who knows how near the novel is to being finished. *Please don't say a word to anyone.*

4. How will you give a month's advance notice of the story—slip a band on the jacket of the December issue? I want to talk to you about advertising when I see you in late October so please don't put even the publicity man at any work yet. As to the photographs I have a snapshot negative of the three of us with a surfboard, which enlarges to a nice 6 x 10 glossy suitable for rotogravures, and also have a fine double profile of Zelda and me in regular cabinet photograph size and have just gotten figures from the photographer. He wants $18.00 for twelve, $24.00 for twenty-four and $35.00 for fifty and says he does not sell the plates, though I imagine he could be prevailed upon if we give him a "take it or leave it" offer. How many would you need? These two photographs are modern. I don't want any of the old ones sent out and I don't want any horrors to be dug up out of newspaper morgues.

Tell me how many you would need to cover all the press? Would it be cheaper if I sat when I came up there—the trouble is that in only one out of any three pictures is my pan of any interest.

5. My plan, and I think it is very important, is to prevail upon the Modern Library, even with a subsidy, to bring out *Gatsby* a few weeks after the book publication

of this novel. Please don't say that anybody would possibly have the psychology of saying to themselves "one of his is in the Modern Library, therefore I will not buy another," or that the two books could be confused. The people who buy the Modern Library are not at all the people who buy the new books. *Gatsby*—in its present form, not actually available in sight to book buyers—will only get a scattering sale as a result of the success of this book. I feel that every time your business department has taken a short-sighted view of our community of interest in this matter, which is my reputation, there has been no profit on your part and something less than that on mine. As, for example, a novel of Ernest's in the Modern Library and no novel of mine, a good short story of Ernest's in their collection of the *Great Modern Short Stories* and a purely commercial story of mine. I want to do this almost as much as I want to publish this novel and will cooperate to the extent of sharing the cost.

There will be other points when I see you in October, but I will be greatly reassured to have some sort of idea about these points so that I can make my plans accordingly. I will let you know two or three days in advance when you may expect me.

One last point: unlike Ernest I am perfectly agreeable to making any necessary cuts *for serial publication* but naturally insist that I shall do them myself.

You can imagine the pride with which I will enter your office a month from now. *Please do not have a band as I do not care for music.*

Ever yours,

F. Scott Fitzgerald

La Paix, Rodgers' Forge
Towson, Maryland
September 29, 1933

Dear Max:

Since talking to you and getting your letter another angle has come up. Ober tells me that Burton of *Cosmo-*

politan is very interested in the novel and if he took it would, in Ober's opinion, pay between $30,000 and $40,000 for it. Now against that there are the following factors:

1. The fact that though Burton professes great lust for my work the one case in which I wrote a story specifically for him, that movie story that you turned down and that Mencken published, he showed that he really can't put his taste into action; in that case the Hearst policy man smeared it.

2. The tremendous pleasure I would get from appearing in *Scribner's*.

3. The spring publication.

4. My old standby, the *Post*, would not be too pleased to have my work running serially all spring and summer in the *Cosmopolitan*.

On the other hand, the reasons why it must be considered are between thirty and forty thousand, and all of them backed by the credit of the U.S. Treasury. It is a purely hypothetical sum I admit and certainly no serial is worth it, yet if Willie Hearst is still pouring gold back into the desert in the manner of 1929 would I be stupid not to take some or would I be stupid not to take some? My own opinion is that if the thing is offered to Burton, he will read it, be enthusiastic, and immediately an Obstacle will appear. On the other hand, should I even offer it to them? Should I give him a copy on the same day I give you a copy asking an answer from him within three days? Would the fact that he refused it diminish your interest in the book or influence it? Or, even, considering my relations with you would it be a dirty trick to show it to him at all? What worries *me* is the possibility of being condemned to go back to *The Saturday Evening Post* grind at the exact moment when the book is finished. I suppose I could and probably will but I will need a damn good month's rest outdoors or traveling before I can even do that.

Can you give me any estimate as to how much I could expect from you as to payment for the serial and how much of that will be in actual cash? It seems terrible to ask you this when it is not even decided yet whether or not you want it; but what I want to do is to see if I can *not* offer it at all to Burton. I wish to God I had never talked to Harold about it and got these upsetting commercial ideas in my head.

I am taking care of the picture matter. I certainly would like to be on your cover and stare down Greta Garbo on the news-stands. I figure now that it should reach you, at the latest, on the 25th, though I am trying for the 23rd.

Ring's death was a terrible blow. Have written a short appreciation of him for *The New Republic*.

Please answer.

> Ever yours,
>
> Scott

La Paix, Rodgers' Forge
Towson, Maryland

October 7, 1933

Dear Max:

I had already thought of your point and talked to John Lardner about it.[1] My idea was that Gilbert Seldes could do it and was the ideal man for the job; also my idea was that the articles that Ring wrote over that series of time could be made into a sort of Ring's history of the world. Whoever edits it should make it into a unit as far as possible. (Naturally I am not referring to the achieved facts of the stories.) I think that a big book of nonsense could be got up based on all the writings, apart from fiction, that Ring did, from his early newspaper days until the present. I have already taken it up with Seldes and John Lardner (the latter of whom is still under the spell of his father's obsequies and will probably not get around to any action for a week or so) that it must be *edited*. When I say edited, I mean edited; if you want to have a volume of Ring's that would properly represent him you should commission such a man as Gilbert to go through *everything* which is not fiction and make a sort of story out of it. Pay him high, 35 to 45% of the total royalties, and publish the book as a standard book of nonsense; no thin little volume such as

---

[1] A selected edition of Ring Lardner's writings.

the *Story of a Wonderman* (though what meat was in that should be used) but a real monument of American nonsense.

Any collection of Benchley, Corey Ford or Thurber would be merely a selection of incidents, in my opinion, while this collection of Ring's could be made the story of a whole period, not up to the present, for toward the end he was a sick man and did not record very well; but during the period in which Ring functioned rationally he got everything that was going and that might be of interest to many people.

Why not get in touch with Gilbert and talk it over, showing him this letter, or else telling him the equivalent of the opinions here expressed? I know what I could do with the material and have faith in the hypothetical result, but it is simply impossible for me to undertake such work under present circumstances. This publication, mind you, would have to be utterly unlike the hasty compilations of Ring's nonsense that you have put out—it would have to be a new dealing with it; it would take an intelligent appreciator's whole time for a month to put it out in any other form than that would do harm to his reputation. My idea is that this nonsense cannot be spotted like Lear's nonsense but must be organized like Lewis Carroll's nonsense. All of it that is still funny (except the parts that were merely timely) should be included, but *it must be made consecutive*—well, consult with Gilbert and see if he has anything to suggest; this is the best I can offer.

> Ever yours,
>
> Scott

> *La Paix, Rodgers' Forge*
> *Towson, Maryland*
> *October 19, 1933*

Dear Max:

All goes well here. The first two chapters are in shape and am starting the third one this afternoon. So the first section comprising about 26,000 words will be mailed to you Friday night or Saturday morning.

Naturally I was delighted by your gesture of coming up two thousand. I hope to God results will show in the circulation of the magazine and I have an idea they will. Negotiations with *Cosmopolitan* were of course stopped and Ober is sure that getting the release from *Liberty* is merely a matter of form which he is attending to. I think I will need the money a little quicker than by the month, say $1000 on delivery of the first section and then the other $3000 every fortnight after that. This may not be necessary but the first $2000 will. As you know, I now owe Ober two or three thousand and he should be reimbursed so he can advance me more to carry me through the second section and a *Post* story. Naturally, payments on the serial should be made to him.

I am saying this now and will remind you later. My idea is that the book form of the novel should be set up from the corrected proof of the serial—in that I will re-insert the excisions which I am making for the serial.

If you have any way of getting French or Swiss railroad posters it would be well for you to try to. Now as to the blurbs: I think there should not be too many; I am sending you nine. . . .[1]

> *"The Great Gatsby* is undoubtedly a work of art."
> *The London Times*

As to T. S. Eliot: What he said was in a letter to me—that he'd read it several times, it had interested and excited him more than any novel he had seen, either English or American, for a number of years, and he also said that it seemed to him that it was the first step forward in the American novel since Henry James.

I know him slightly but I would not dare ask him for an endorsement. If it can be managed in any way without getting a rebuff, even some more qualified statement would be the next best thing to an endorsement by Joyce or Gertrude Stein.

Of course I think blurbs have gotten to be pretty much the bunk, but maybe that is a writer's point of view and the lay reader does not understand the back-scratching that is at the root of most of them. However, I leave it in

[1] The first eight are missing.

your hands. Don't quote all of these unless you think it is advisable.

We can talk over the matter of *Gatsby* in the Modern Library after your announcement has appeared.

Again thanks for the boost in price and remember the title is a secret to the last.

> Ever your friend,
>
> Scott Fitzgerald

I should say to be careful in saying it's my first book in seven years *not to imply that it contains seven years' work*. People would expect too much in bulk and scope.

This novel, my fourth, completes my story of the boom years. It might be wise to accentuate the fact that it does *not* deal with the depression. *Don't* accentuate that it deals with Americans abroad—there's been too much trash under that banner.

No exclamatory "At last, the long awaited, etc." That merely creates the "Oh yeah" mood in people.

> *1307 Park Avenue*
> *Baltimore, Maryland*
> *Xmas, 1933*

Dear Fritz:[1]

Section III (Chapters VI to IX inclusive) is being typed and goes off special delivery Wednesday evening. I was foolish to have come South as there was inevitable Xmas confusion and I only got through by working all night and all the night before. It began by being 40,000 words but I judge it will turn out between 24,000 and 29,000 after all.

While it is not weak it is perhaps a let-down from the two love affairs of Sections I and II. This was a hurried business and I intend to do the polishing on the proof. The month I lost in Bermuda was damn costly.

Now give me a real date and not a precautionary one for Section IV so I can make my plans with some ration-

---

[1] Alfred Dashiell, editor of *Scribner's Magazine*.

ality. You have nothing to fear—at the worst you could publish that section as it stands.

If this doesn't arrive too late "beyed" is better Deep South for "bird" than either "bed" or "buhd." As for the "Ah guess, etc."—better change the one dialect line to "I reckon" and let it go at that.

I appreciate your interest which I feel is in the piece as well as in the magazine. Don't hesitate to pass on any comments but I'd rather get them in bulk than piecemeal. I'll probably have rewritten the whole thing by spring. Very best of Xmas greetings and tell Max only shame has prevented me thanking him for the extra loan.

                                        Scott Fitzgerald

The psychiatrist at Hopkins says that not only is the medical stuff in II accurate but it seems the only good thing ever written on psychiatry and the—oh what the hell. Anyhow, that part's O.K.

My mother wasn't interested so it must have *some* merit.

                                        1307 Park Avenue
                                        Baltimore, Maryland
                                        January 13, 1934

Dear Max:

What do you think of the idea of using twenty-four of those woodcuts, which illustrate the serial, as head and tail pieces for chapters in the book or, alternatively, interspersing them through the novel? I think it is comparatively an innovation in recent fiction and might give the book a certain distinction. I've gotten very fond of the illustrations. Who the hell is the illustrator? If it is too expensive a process let me know, but since the cuts are already made I thought it might not be.

Please do not send me any book galley for the present, just hold it there. I am already confused by the multiplicity of the irons I have in the fire and as far as possible would prefer to do the book galley in one or two long stretches.

I did not thank you over the phone for the further

advance, which does not mean that I did not appreciate it, but only that I have so much to thank you for.

Tell Dashiell that I cannot promise not to make changes in Section III, but under no conditions will it be lengthened. Section IV is taking longer than I thought and it may be the middle of next week before you get it.

Ever yours,

Scott Fitz‒‒‒‒

P.S. 1. Will you ask Dashiell to strike off as many as half a dozen additional proofs because I have always a use for them in passing them around for technical advice. Again, this request is conditioned by not wanting it to be exorbitantly expensive.

P.S. 2. Don't forget my suggestion that the jacket flap should carry an implication that though the books starts in a lyrical way, heavy drama will presently develop.

P.S. 3. Any contract you suggest will probably be O.K. You might bring one with you when you come down, an event to which I look forward eagerly.

P.S. 4. Also remember that upon due consideration I would prefer the binding to be uniform with my other books. If these were prosperous times and there were any prospect of a superior reissue of my whole tribe I'd say "Let it begin here," to quote the famous commander of the Minutemen, but there isn't, so I prefer to stick to my undistinguished green uniform—I mean even to the point of the gilt stampings being uniform to the others.

P.S. 5. I don't want to bore you by reiterating but I do think the matter of *Gatsby* in the Modern Library should be taken up as shortly as possible after the appearance of installment II.

P.S. 6. Am getting responses only from a few writers and from the movies. The novel will certainly have *succès d'estime* but it may be slow in coming—alas, I may again have written a novel for novelists with little chance of its lining anybody's pockets with gold. The thing is perhaps too crowded for story readers to search it through for the story but it can't be helped, there are times when you have to get every edge of your fingernails on paper. Anyhow I think this serial publication will give it the best chance it can possibly have because it is a book that only gives its full effect on its second reading. Almost every part of it now has been revised and thought out from three to six times.

P.S. 7. What is the name of a functioning press clipping bureau?

> *1307 Park Avenue*
> *Baltimore, Maryland*
> *February 5, 1934*

Dear Max:

Isn't there any mechanical means by which you can arrange to include the 1400 words of the arrest in Cannes? The more I think of it the more I think that it is absolutely necessary for the unity of the book and the effectiveness of the finale to show Dick in the dignified and responsible aspect toward the world and his neighbors that was implied so strongly in the first half of the book. It is all very well to say that this can be remedied in book publication but it has transpired that at least two dozen important writers and newspaper men are reading the book in the serial and will form their impressions from that. I have made cuts in Section IV—a good bit of the last scene between Dick and Tommy—but also the proof has swollen somewhat in revision which counteracts that, nor can I reduce the 1250 words of that scene to 800. I am saying 1400 because I know there will be a slight expansion. Couldn't you take out some short piece from the number? Surely it hasn't crystallized at this early date. Even with this addition the installment is shorter than the others, as I promised Fritz.

If I do not hold these two characters to the end of the book it might as well never have been written. It is legitimate to ruin Dick but it is by no means legitimate to make him an ineffectual. In the proof I am pointing up the fact that his intention dominated all this last part but it is not enough and the foreshortening without the use of this scene, which was a part of the book structure from the first, does not contain enough of him for the reader to reconstruct his whole personality as viewed as a unit throughout—and the reason for this is my attempt to tell the last part entirely through Nicole's eyes. I was even going to have her in on the Cannes episode but decided against it because of the necessity of seeing Dick alone.

My feeling about this was precipitated by the remarks of the young psychiatrist who is the only person who had read all the magazine proof and only the magazine proof. He felt a sharp lesion at the end which those who had read the whole novel did not feel.

While I am writing you I may as well cover some other points:

1. Please don't forget the indentation of title and author on the front cover as in previous books. There are other Fitzgeralds writing and I would like my whole name on the outside of the book, and also I would prefer uniformity.

2. Would you please strike off at least three book proofs for me, all to be used for revisions such as medical, linguistic, etc.? Also, I would like an extra galley of book proof Section IV when you have it, for Ober to pass on to Davis in order to supply the missing material.

3. In advertising the book some important points are: Please do not use the phrase "Riviera" or "gay resorts." Not only does it sound like the triviality of which I am so often accused, but also the Riviera has been thoroughly exploited by E. Phillips Oppenheim and a whole generation of writers and its very mention invokes a feeling of unreality and unsubstantiality. So I think it would be best to watch this and reduce it only to the statement that the scenes of the book are laid in Europe. If it could be done, a suggestion that, after a romantic start, a serious story unfolds would not be amiss; also it might be mentionable that for exigencies of serialization a scene or two was cut. In general, as you know, I don't approve of great ballyhoo advertisements, even of much quoted praise. The public is very, very, very weary of being sold bogus goods and this inevitably reacts on solider manufactures.

I find that revising in this case is pulling up the weaker

section of the book and then the next weakest, etc. First
Section III was the weakest and Section IV the strongest,
so I bucked up III; then IV was the weakest and is still,
but when I have fixed that Section I will be the weakest.
The section that has best held up is Section II.

I was tremendously impressed with *South Moon Under*[1]
until I read her prize short story, "Gal Young Un." I suddenly saw the face of Ethan Frome peering out from under
a palmetto hat. The heroine is even called Matt in tribute
to the power of the subconscious. Well, well, well, I often
think of Picasso's remark "You do it first, then other people can come along and do it pretty and get off with a big
proportion of the spoils. When you do it first you can't do
it pretty." So I guess Miss Rawlings is just another writer
after all, just when I was prepared to welcome her to the
class of 1896 with Ernest, Dos Passos and myself.

Please wire about the inclusion of the Cannes episode,
and *don't* sidetrack these advertising points.

Ever yours,

Scott

1307 Park Avenue
Baltimore, Maryland
February 7, 1934

Dear Max:

The fear of being dependent again on *The Saturday
Evening Post* promoted this idea and led me to a consideration of publishing in general; and, from that, the notion
developed in the half-baked way that I told you. I began
by thinking of the publishing devices of the early 18th century, with special reference to Dickens' *Household Words*.

Now, just as *Scribner's Magazine* has changed its character several times between being primarily a fiction magazine, or primarily an open forum, so there is no reason in
its tradition why it should not consider a radical step. I
do not underestimate the value of the present *Scribner's*

[1] A novel by Marjorie Kinnan Rawlings.

in the humanitarian way, but nowadays ventures must be self-sustaining, and competing journals can also muster the same quantity and quality of uneasy liberal thinking—*viz.* *Harper's* and *Atlantic Monthly.* This innovationary policy has, of course, been exemplified in your regime, not only by encouraging the short novels, or novelettes, but also in this new departure about long novels. Pursuing this policy to its logical end, I am inclined to think that sooner or later you will be faced with the decision of choosing (temporarily at least) between being a magazine of fiction or being a magazine of opinion, and that the opinions eventually must be yours. I am Communist enough to distrust the idea of an "open forum," which usually means a forum in which a Roman citizen can appear and talk as much as he wants within the range of Roman opinion— in despite of the apparent radicalism of your publishing John Strachey.

By and large I see the problems that confront you, yet I wonder whether you or I, or any of us, can really print a synthesis of opinions in the air as a policy; and in the same breath, I reiterate that in all common sense this tack will sooner or later amount to a compromise that, like all compromises, will have neither force nor vitality. The other idea, on the contrary, has the following advantages: from the editorial point of view it would give you the opportunity of going into a specialization that, substituted for the somewhat vague economic views (and here I refer to the whole staff of Scribners publishing house, from Charles to the printer's devil, indeed, to all of us insofar as we are associated with you, with the accumulated taste embodied in the publishing house), would be a line for which you are perhaps better equipped than anybody in America.

A second argument in favor of the idea is that you have at your disposal almost anybody that you want. When you say, as you did the other night, that you cannot count on writers delivering on time, God knows I understand, but you have so many *good* young writers, and I am counting on the idea attracting so many others who otherwise cannot publish except in book form. I think your difficulties, once the idea was launched, would be on the contrary, a question of deciding betwixt good things offered.

My idea, as I told you, would be a cover, which would

say, for example: first part of Hemingway, second part of Fleming, third part of Fitzgerald, fourth part of Wolfe. You would be dealing with two or three established authors and perhaps one newcomer that you happened to like, and the money that you paid out would serve to keep those people going. In these days any author would rather have a modest fee for his serial than not to serialize at all. In a sense, they would develop a feeling that they were partners in a corporate enterprise and I think that I can speak for many of us when I say that we would welcome the idea of a forum which is as open for long fiction as it is for the most casual opinionated shreds of political opinion.

A fourth point: while I don't know the mechanics of the magazine's make-up, this policy should not preclude the inclusion of a certain number of opinionated articles upon public affairs, used almost as editorials. From your experience you must have seen that out of half a dozen articles in *Scribner's,* or for that matter in any other quality magazine, about six a year have the value of what the Victorians would call essays and the rest is mere timely journalism, moribund almost with its appearance; after a few months how many of such articles are of more literary or humanitarian importance than the spreads in Hearst's Sunday supplement? And, practically, if the consumer can get *The New York Sunday Times Book Review* and *Magazine Section* what distinction can he make between that and a quality magazine except for the name and the colored jacket?

As I mentioned last night, almost all the editorial magazine successes have depended on young men, if I can flatter you and Charles Scribner, me, Ernest, Tom Wolfe, as being young men. Crowninshield [1] grows old and Ross comes up with *The New Yorker; The Literary Digest* grows old and *Time* comes along; Lorimer,[2] who has been for a long time my bread (*Scribner's* being considered the meat of my survival), is growing old, and then that bread will inevitably go stale.

It is not beyond the limits of imagination to suppose that

[1] Frank Crowninshield, editor of *Vanity Fair.*
[2] George Horace Lorimer, editor of *The Saturday Evening Post.*

this condition, in which only the choices of the Book-of-the-Month get across big, may be a permanent condition. It is conceivable that the local bookstore, except as represented by such as yours and Brentano's, will become as obsolete as the silent picture. For one thing the chain-store buying and the job-lot-buying department stores seem to condemn the independent bookstores to the situation that they have reached in Baltimore where, considering the outlay involved, they can only be compared to the fallow antique shops. There is also the library question, which, in a socializing world, will become bigger and bigger.

In résumé, let me line up the elements for and against the idea.

Present procedure: dignified presentation of a, perhaps, good book with sale of 3000 copies, and not much profit to anybody.

Attitude toward the author's surrendering dramatic and movie rights correct in the 90s when conditions were different but now archaic.

Futility of issuing books that, either from inefficiency in writing or being-over-the-heads-of-the-crowd, clutter up the remnant counter. Essentially this is not a service to writers as was the case in the past. Take, for example, my recommendation to you, rather half-hearted, of Woodward Boyd's *The Love Legend.* Why the hell should she have the right to publish a poor book? As things tighten up I think that more harm is done by encouraging inefficient amateurs than would be done if they were compelled to go through a certain professional apprenticeship. The one man or woman aspirant out of a hundred who has some quality of genius is another matter, but those who show "promise" had probably better be relegated immediately to doing other things in the world, or else working on their own guts for professional advancement, rather than be coddled along on the basis that they may eventually make a fortune for themselves and everybody concerned.

Therefore, a weariness in the reviewers, and, except for the presentation, no realistic cooperation.

Now to consider conditions as they are: there is, first, the selection by the book leagues, whether we like it or not; there is the reprinting of either quality stuff in the Modern Library or drug-store stuff in the reprint houses, with the publishers frankly taking a share in other rights, specifically including movie rights.

Now why shouldn't incipient writers have to prove themselves? Why shouldn't an issue of a book between boards be contingent upon the ability of the work to arouse interest? And isn't a magazine-printing a cheaper and more advantageous test all around?

If this comes out at the proper end of the horn as the note I intended to blow when I blew, it reduces itself to the following propositions:

1. That *Scribner's* is much better equipped now to handle fiction, travel, etc., than to handle politics.

2. That, unless you have some big axe to grind, politics are of only transitory interest.

3. That traditionalism is, in this case, a policy to which one can fairly attach the odium of archaism, because just as an author's main purpose is "to make you see," so a magazine's principal purpose is to be read.

4. Perhaps I am the proverbial fool rushing in, and if it so appears to you simply forget the whole suggestion. However, I have a hunch that within a year somebody will adopt such a policy. And may I reiterate that the idea was suggested originally by a policy which you have already inaugurated, and that this is simply a radical urge to hasten it toward what I think is an inevitable outcome, an effort to meet the entertainment business on its own predetermined grounds.

Ever yours,

F. Scott Fitzgerald

1307 Park Avenue
Baltimore, Maryland
March 4, 1934

Dear Max:

Confirming our conversation on the phone this morning, I wish you could get some word to the printers that they should not interfere with my use of italics. If I had made a mess of a type face, that would be another matter. I know exactly what I am doing, and I want to use italics for *emphasis*, and not waste them on the newspaper convention laid down by Mr. Munsey in 1858. Of course, always you have been damned nice in having your printers follow my specifications, but in this case, and under the very pressing conditions under which we are working, it worries me that the book galleys came back with exactly the same queries that the magazine galleys had. Could you tip them the wink some way so that they would please follow my copy exactly as they used to, as this is my last chance at the book? Whoever has been in charge of it must be very patient because I know at the ninth revision that the very sight of any part of it fills me with nausea. However, I have to go on in this particular case while they don't, and so are liable to get careless.

Going over the other points, I hope both (1) that the review copies will go out in plenty of time, and (2) that they will get the version of the novel as it will be published because there is no doubt that each revision makes a tremendous difference in the impression that the book will leave. After all, Max, I am a plodder. One time I had a talk with Ernest Hemingway, and I told him, against all the logic that was then current, that I was the tortoise and he was the hare, and that's the truth of the matter, that everything that I have ever attained has been through long and persistent struggle while it is Ernest who has a touch of genius which enables him to bring off extraordinary things with facility. I have no facility. I have a facility for being cheap, if I wanted to indulge that. I can do cheap things. I changed Clark Gable's act at the moving picture theatre here the other day. I can do that kind of thing as quickly as anybody but when I decided to be a serious man, I tried to struggle over every point until I have made myself into a slow-moving behemoth (if that is the correct spelling), and so there I am for the rest of my life. Anyhow, these points of proofreading, etc., are of tremendous importance to me, and you can charge it all to my account, and I will realize all the work you have had on it.

As I told you on the phone, I enjoyed Marjorie Rawlings' praise, but it was somewhat qualified by her calling my people trivial people. Other stuff has drifted in from writers from all over America, some of it by telegram, which has been complimentary.

Now, about advertising. Again I want to tell you my theory that everybody is absolutely dead on ballyhoo of any kind, and for your advertising department to take up any interest that the intellectuals have so far shown toward the book, and exploit that, would be absolutely disastrous. The reputation of a book must grow from within upward, must be a natural growth. I don't think there is a comparison between this book and *The Great Gatsby* as a seller. *The Great Gatsby* had against it its length and its purely masculine interest. This book, on the contrary, is a woman's book. I think, given a decent chance, it will make its own way insofar as fiction is selling under present conditions.

Excuse me if this letter has a dogmatic ring. I have lived so long within the circle of this book and with these characters that often it seems to me that the real world does not exist but that only these characters exist, and, however pretentious that remark sounds (and my God, that I should have to be pretentious about my work), it is an absolute fact—so much so that their glees and woes are just exactly as important to me as what happens in life.

Zelda is better. There is even a chance of her getting up for the exhibition of her paintings at Easter, but nothing certain. Do you still think that idea of piling the accumulated manuscript in the window[1] is a valid one? My instinct does not quite solve the problem. What do you think? Would it seem a little phony?

> With best wishes,
>
> Scott

> *1307 Park Avenue*
> *Baltimore, Maryland*
> *March 5, 1934*

Dear Max:

The stout arrived this morning and I am sampling it for lunch. I think I'd better have my photograph taken first for if I become as swollen as you intend my thousands

[1] The Scribner's display window on Fifth Avenue.

and thousands of younger admirers will just leave the sinking ship.

By the way, when you and Louise left here did you, by any chance, take with you 12 spoons, 12 forks, 12 knives (fish), 12 knives (dinner), 1 silver salver, 1 revolver, 1 platinum and diamond wrist-watch? I don't like to accuse *anybody* of *anything* but there is a very curious coincidence. I may say if it's all sent back within the week I shall take no further steps in the matter. We assure you, sir, that we returned the wrong trousers and we are having our agent look into the matter. With a business as large as ours and trousers as small as yours such things will happen.

In any case, Max, if the stout kills me I protected myself by a new clause in my will based on the old Maryland Poison Act—Md.362 XX: 1, 47.

Yours very truly,

F. Scott Fitzgerald
(Bart)

1307 Park Avenue
Baltimore, Maryland
June 26, 1934

Dear Max:

Am sending along Number 1 of the stories[1] because I feel it's going to be the devil to set up. There are two others all corrected, but the slow thing is to look through *Tender Is the Night* and see what phrases I took out of the stories. This is confused by the fact that there were so many revisions of *Tender* that I don't know what I left in it and what I didn't leave in it finally. I am going to have trouble with two of the stories you suggested. In "The Captured Shadow," I'll have to make up a whole new ending which is almost like writing a new story. Secondly, the Josephine story, "A Nice Quiet Place," has some awfully phony stuff in the middle that I'll have to find a substitute for. So can't I send the stories in their original order, and

[1] For his collection *Taps at Reveille*.

have them set up *separately*, and then sandwich between them these last two if I can think of some way of fixing them in time?

Nothing new about the title.

By the time you get this, you will have gotten a begging telegram asking for a thousand dollars. How I ever got so deep in debt I don't know unless it's been this clinic business, because I've written regularly a story a month since finishing the last proof of *Tender* and they have been sold. I have also fixed up and sold some of Zelda's little articles besides. Debt is an odd thing and it seems if you ever get started in it is very difficult to get disentangled. I have put the movie possibilities of the novel out of mind for the present though the young man I told you about who went from here to the coast is still trying further treatments in hopes that they will buy it. My best chance now is that if Phyllis Bottome's psychiatric story goes, they may all rush to buy whatever else is available in that line. Looks now as if I will be here until well into the summer, but I am going to try damn hard to get a month off somewhere if I can get clear of debt and clear of the work to which I committed myself. I can well understand all your difficulties working in the office by day and with Tom Wolfe by night because until ten days ago, when I collapsed and took to my bed, I have been doing about the same thing. I am all right now and once I get this *Post* story off should be out of the worst.

Zelda does much better. Morrow read her stuff but turned down the plan.

Ever yours,

Scott

1307 Park Avenue
Baltimore, Maryland
July 30, 1934

Dear Max:

The bottom sort of fell out of things after you left. We sat around for a few hours and talked a lot about you. The only flaw in the evening was the fact that afterwards I didn't seem to be able to sleep any better in Virginia than I did in Maryland, so, after reading an old account of Stuart's battles for an hour or so, I got dressed in despair and spent the small hours of the morning prowling around the place, finally snatching two hours of sleep between seven and nine. The next day—it being our hostess' custom to sleep late—Anne took me over to meet the fabled Harden, who was as interesting as promised by the discussions about him. Returning to "Welbourne," [1] a whole slew of Virginians appeared and to my regret I didn't have much more chance to talk to Elizabeth, because my conscience had begun to worry me and I decided to take the three o'clock bus back to Washington. However, one of the guests took dictation and I managed to have my joke about Grant and Lee taken down on paper. Then last night I had it faked up by the *Sun* here in Baltimore and I am going to send one to Elizabeth framed. Please return the one herewith enclosed for your inspection.

I thought Elizabeth Lemmon was charming. . . . The whole atmosphere of that countryside made me wonder about many things. It seems to me more detached than any place I have ever visited in the Union except a few remote towns in Alabama and Georgia during the war before the radio came. By the way, I have never ridden in a bus before and thought it was rather a horrible experience after the spacious grace of that house.

This morning before breakfast I read Tom Wolfe's story in *Scribner's*.[2] I thought it was perfectly beautiful and it had a subtlety often absent from his work, an intense poetry rather akin to Ernest (though naturally you won't tell Tom that because he wouldn't take it as a compliment). What family resemblance there is between we three as writers is the attempt that crops up in our fiction from time to time to recapture the exact feel of a moment in time and space, exemplified by people rather than by things —that is, an attempt at what Wordsworth was trying to do rather than what Keats did with such magnificent ease, an attempt at a mature memory of a deep experience. Any-

[1] A pre-Civil War mansion in Middleburg, Virginia, where Fitzgerald was visiting.
[2] "The House of the Far and Lost."

how please congratulate him for me with all my heart.

This letter is dragging out. Hope you found Louise all right. A thousand thanks for taking me into that very novel and stimulating atmosphere. I had been in a hell of a rut.

Ever yours,

Scott

P.S. Here's the money I owe you. I made it twelve instead of eleven because I had forgotten that expensive wine that I insisted upon ordering and which I drank most of, and anyhow twelve is a more symmetrical number than eleven.

1307 Park Avenue
Baltimore, Maryland
August 24, 1934

Dear Max:

This is a sort of postscript to my letter of yesterday: I do think that you were doing specious reasoning in part of your letter. The fact that Ernest has let himself repeat here and there a phrase would be no possible justification for my doing the same. Each of us has his virtues and one of mine happens to be a great sense of exactitude about my work. He might be able to afford a lapse in that line where I wouldn't be and after all I have got to be the final judge of what is appropriate in these cases. Max, to repeat for the third time, this is in no way a question of laziness. It is a question absolutely of self-preservation. It is not going to be a money book in any case and is not going to go very far toward reimbursing the money I still owe you, and so I think in view of everything that my suggestion of waiting until after Christmas is the best.

Besides, it is not only the question of the repetitions but there are certain other stories in the collection that I couldn't possibly *think* of letting go out in their current form. I fully realize that this may be a very serious inconvenience to you but for me to undertake anything

like that at this moment would just mean sudden death
and nothing less than that.

Ever yours,

Scott

P.S. I have just gotten a royalty report and don't know
whether the sum of my debit is on the red page or on the
regular royalty report. Please have someone let me know.

1307 Park Avenue
Baltimore, Maryland
October 17, 1934

Dear Max:

The mood of terrible depression and despair is not going to become a characteristic and I am ashamed and felt
very yellow about it afterwards. But to deny that such
moods come increasingly would be futile.

I took you at your word and went down to Welbourne
for an afternoon to prance before Elizabeth and found
her in her usual good form, and also Mary Rumsey. But
the trouble about women is that when you need them
most they are never in a receptive mood (not that both
Elizabeth and Mary were not hospitable, it's just the old
story that when you feel like weeping on somebody's
shoulder you're usually in such a state of mind and body
that nobody wants you to weep on their shoulder).

The country was beautiful, however. Will write at length
later. They missed you, and I added to their chagrin by
telling them how I urged you to go down the night before.

Feel somewhat refreshed and am finishing my story today.

Ever yours,

Scott

1307 Park Avenue
Baltimore, Maryland
November 8, 1934

Dear Max:

In further reference to my telegram of Tuesday night: first, I am sending you the third story in its proper place ready to go into the book. The thing that worried me when I did it was whether the proofreader is going to be able to release a lot of type, because, due to the fact that the end of one story and the beginning of another were run on one galley, he will have to scrap half the type in the galley and yet retain the other half—this because the stories were not set up in proper order. I know this is a terrible and costly mess and I take full responsibility; nevertheless, I did think the stories would be set up separately and getting at them is as if the chapters of a book were set up any which way, like I, VII, II, V, III, VI, and it all has to be straightened out each time. As you know that is fatiguing work and can best be done when one is fresh, and is hard to do at night.

My big mistake was in thinking I could possibly deliver this collection for this fall. I should have known perfectly well that, in debt as I was to the tune of about $12,000 on finishing *Tender,* I should have to devote the summer and most of the fall to getting out of it. My plan was to do my regular work in the daytime and do one story every night, but as it works out, after a good day's work I am so exhausted that I drag out the work on a story to two hours when it should be done in one and go to bed so tired and wrought up, toss around sleepless, and am good for nothing next morning except dictating letters, signing checks, tending to business matters, etc.— but to work up a creative mood there is nothing doing until about four o'clock in the afternoon. Part of this is because of ill health. It would not have seemed so difficult to me ten years, or even five years ago, but now just one more straw would break the camel's back.

I have about half a dozen of these done but I am determined this time to send them in only in the proper order and not add further confusion either in my own mind or that of the printer's. The trouble began when I sent you two stories to be set up which were nowhere near each other in the book. If I told a story about a boy of sixteen years old and sixty pages on the reader came upon a story of the same boy at thirteen it would make no sense to him and look like careless presentation, and which, as you know, I dislike nothing more.

As you may have seen I took out "A New Leaf" and put in "Her Last Case." You didn't tell me whether or not you read it or liked it.

I know you have the sense that I have loafed lately but that is absolutely not so. I have drunk too much and that is certainly slowing me up. On the other hand, without drink I do not know whether I could have survived this time. In actual work since I finished the last proof of the novel in the middle of March, eight months ago, I have written and sold three stories for the *Post,* written another which was refused, written two and a half stories for the *Redbook,* rewritten three articles of Zelda's for *Esquire* and one original for them to get emergency money, collaborated on a 10,000-word treatment of *Tender Is the Night,* which was no go, written an 8000-word story for Gracie Allen, which was also no go, and made about five false starts on stories which went from 1000 to 5000 words, and a preface to the Modern Library edition of *The Great Gatsby,* which equalizes very well what I have done in other years. I am good for just about one good story a month or two articles. I took no vacation this summer except three or four one-night trips to Virginia and two business trips to New York, each of which lasted about four or five days. Of course this is no excuse for not making more money, because in harder times you've got to word harder, but as it happens I am in a condition at the moment where to work extra hard means inevitably that I am laid up for a compensatory time either here or in the hospital. All I can say is that I will try to do two or three of these all at once after finishing each piece of work, and as I am now working at the rate of a story each ten days for the *Redbook* series I should finish up the ten I have left to do in about one hundred days and deliver the last of them in mid-February. Perhaps if things break better it may be a month sooner.

Thanks immensely for the Henry James which I thought was wonderful and which is difficult reading as it must have been to write, and for "At Sea."

The London press on my book has been spotty but *The London Times* gave it a good review as did G. B. Stern in *The Daily Telegraph,* and so did *The Manchester Guardian* and *The Spectator,* and those I guess are the four most important ones in England and I got a column in each of them. A letter says that it hasn't reached a thousand copies yet.

I hope you'll be down here soon. It was rather melancholy to think of "Welbourne" being closed for the winter but the last time I saw Elizabeth she seemed quite reconciled at visiting here and there, though such a prospect would drive me nuts. Hope you have sent off the carbon of the Table of Contents.

Best ever,

Scott

1307 Park Avenue
Baltimore, Maryland
November 26, 1934

Dear Max:

The real thing that decided me about "Her Last Case" was that it was a *place* story and just before seeing it in *published form* I ran across Thomas Wolfe's "The House of the Far and Lost" and I thought there was no chance of competing with him on the same subject, when he had brought off such a triumph. There would inevitably have been invidious comparisons. If my story had anything to redeem it, except atmosphere, I would not hesitate to include it but most of it depends on a mixture of hysteria and sentiment—anyhow, I did not decide without some thought.

I think by this time you will have read and liked "The Fiend" which, spare and meager as it may be, has, I believe, a haunting quality. At least the tale in itself had enough poignancy to haunt me long enough, to keep in my skull for six years. Whether I've given it the right treatment, or disparaged it by too much peeling away of accessories, I can't say. That's one reason that I asked you to set it up, because maybe I am not too clear about it myself and maybe I can do something with the proof if it seems advisable.

I throw out most of the stuff in me with delight that it is gone. That statement might be interesting to consider in relation with Ernest's article in last month's *Esquire;* an unexpressed idea is often a torment, even though its expression is liable to leave an almost crazy gap in the continuity of one's thoughts. And it would have been absolutely impossible for me to have stretched "The Rich Boy" into anything bigger than a novelette.

That statement was something that Ring got off; he never knew anything about composition, except as it concerned the shorter forms; that is why he always needed advice from us as to how to organize his material; it was his greatest fault—the fault of many men brought up in the school of journalism—while a novelist with his sempiternal sigh can cut a few breaths. It is a hell of a lot more difficult to build up a long groan than to develop a couple of short coughs!

Glad Ernest isn't doing the Crusading story, now, because it would be an unfortunate competition.

Josephine goes along and I think I will be in the clear about her this week, and—as I told you—two or three of the others have already been done and just have to be glanced at.[1]

Your suggestion to go to Key West is tempting as hell but I don't know whether it would be advisable on either Ernest's account or mine. We can talk about that later.

A short note from Beth acknowledged an invitation that I gave her to meet Gertrude Stein if she should be in the vicinity, and said that she had a long letter from you. Outside of that, life has gone along at what would seem to most people a monotonous routine: entertained Lovestone "the Opposition Communist" Saturday and put him up for the night but haven't quite made up my mind what I think of him.

Am so fascinated with the medieval series that my problem is making them into proper butcher's cuts for monthly consumption. I have thought of the subject so long that an actual fertility of invention has become even a liability.

Ever yours,

Scott

[1] The Josephine stories.

1307 Park Avenue
Baltimore, Maryland
December 18, 1934

Dear Max:

Tremendously obliged for the fifty dollars. The *Red-book* is stalling on these medieval stories, much to my disgust, and that is slowing up things and also it may put a crimp in the series so far as serialization is concerned. They have taken three and can't seem to decide about the fourth, so temporarily I am going to return to the *Post* and make some larger money until that straightens out. This was the reason for the financial emergency.

Now I've got to blow up because an incident of this proof has upset my entire morning. You know how irascible I am when I am working and it increases with the years, but I have never seen a proofreader quite as dumb as the one who has looked over this second galley. In the first place I did not *want* a second galley and did not ask for it —these stories have been corrected *once* for myself, *once* for the *Post* and the third time on your first galleys and *that is all I can do*. I expected to have the page proofs made up from the corrected first galley and requested that not even these be sent to me. I first understand that it is an advantage to make *no more* corrections, then along comes a set of completely superfluous galleys marked with the most idiotic and disturbing queries.

Example: this proofreader calmly suggests that I correct certain mistakes of construction in the characters' dialogue. My God, he must be the kind who would rewrite Ring Lardner, correcting his grammar, or fix up the speeches of Penrod to sound like Little Lord Fauntleroy. Who is it? Robert Bridges?

His second brilliant stroke of Victorian genius was to query all the split infinitives. If, on a fourth version, I choose to let them stand I am old enough to know what I am doing. On this proof I simply struck off the queries and am sending the rest back without looking at it. My worry is that I didn't look at the Basil stories at all before returning them, and if he has corrected all Basil's language, spoiling some of my jokes—well, it just gives me the feeling of wanting to send back the whole mass of first galleys and saying set it up.

Honestly, Max, I have worked like a dog on these galleys and it is costing me money to make these changes, and to have some cluck fool with them again is exasperating beyond measure. They should have gone right into page proof from my first galleys—I would a hundred times rather have half a dozen errors creep in than have half a dozen humorous points and carefully considered rhythms spoiled by some school marm. This may seem vehement but I tell you it will haunt me in my sleep until you write reassuring me that no such thing happened in the case of the Basil stories.

Again thanks for the money. It was a life-saver. There will be another story coming along tomorrow.

Ever yours,

Scott

1307 Park Avenue
Baltimore, Maryland
March 9, 1935

Dear Max:

The book arrived. It was fine to see. I liked the get-up and thought it was an excellent blurb on the back, but—

—is it, alas, too late to do anything about the jacket? It is pretty God-awful and about six people have commented on it. I don't know who Miss Doris Spiegal is but it's rather discouraging to spend many hours trying to make the creatures in a book charming and then have someone who can't draw as well as Scottie cover five square inches with daubs that make them look like morons. The first jacket was very much better.

This sounds ungrateful in view of the trouble my books have always been, but I do want to record the fact that of late I have been badly served by your art department. To take a perfectly good photograph and debauch it into a toothless old man on the back of *Tender* was not so good, but I do think a jacket like this has the absolute opposite effect of those fine attractive jackets that Hill and Held used to draw for my books. I always believed that eternal care about titles and presentation was a real element in their success.

I've seen Jim Boyd and we've had several meals together. He's an awfully nice fellow.

I am still hesitating about sending this letter because I know what a lot more important things you have in your mind and how busy you are at this season, but I am sending it on the off-chance that it *might* have been a sample jacket and that something *might* be done.

Ever yours,

Scott

P.S. I was glad that Tom got nice reviews in *Time* and *The New Yorker* and that they gave him space in proportion to the time and effort that went into his volume.[1] I'm going to give it a more thorough reading next week.

1307 Park Avenue
Baltimore, Maryland
March 11, 1935

Dear Max:

The second annoyance to you in two days—pretty soon I'm going to be your most popular author. (By the way, we had sort of a Scribner congeries here last night. Jim Boyd and Elizabeth came to supper and George Calverton dropped in afterwards. Your name came up frequently and you would have probably wriggled more than at Wolfe's dedication. To prolong this parenthesis unduly I am sorry I mentioned Tom's book. I hope to God I won't be set up as the opposition for there are fine things in it, and I loved reading it, and I am delighted that it's a wow, and it may be a bridge for something finer. I simply feel a certain disappointment which I would, on no account, want Tom to know about, for, responding as he does to criticism, I know it would make us life-long enemies and we might do untold needless damage to each other, so please be careful how you quote me. This is in view of Calverton's saying he heard from you that I didn't like it.

[1] *Of Time and the River.*

It has become increasingly plain to me that the very excellent organization of a long book or the finest perceptions and judgment in time of revision do not go well with liquor. A short story can be written on a bottle, but for a novel you need the mental speed that enables you to keep the whole pattern in your head and ruthlessly sacrifice the sideshows as Ernest did in *A Farewell to Arms.* If a mind is slowed up ever so little it lives in the indivdual part of a book rather than in a book as a whole; memory is dulled. I would give anything if I hadn't had to write Part III of *Tender Is the Night* entirely on stimulant. If I had one more crack at it cold sober I believe it might have made a great difference. Even Ernest commented on sections that were needlessly included and as an artist he is as near as I know for a final reference. Of course, having struggled with Tom Wolfe as you did all this is old hat to you. I will conclude this enormous parenthesis with the news that Elizabeth has gone to Middleburg to help Mrs. White open up her newly acquired house.)

This letter is a case of the tail (the parenthesis) wagging the dog. Here is the dog. A man named John S. Martens writes me wanting to translate *Tender Is the Night* or *This Side of Paradise* or *The Great Gatsby* into Norwegian. He has written Scribners and met the same blank wall of silence that has greeted me about all publishing of my books in other countries. I am quite willing to handle continental rights directly but I cannot do it when I do not know even the name of the publisher of my books, having never had copies of them or any information on that subject. Isn't there somebody in your office who is especially delegated to seeing to such things? It is really important to me and if I should write a book that had an international appeal it would be of great advantage to have a foothold with translators and publishers in those countries. All I want from you is the status of *The Great Gatsby* in Scandinavia, Germany, etc., and a word as to whether I shall go ahead and make arrangements myself for the future in that regard.

I'd be glad to get a dozen or so copies of *Taps at Reveille* as soon as available.

Ever yours,

Scott

P.S. I haven't had a drink for almost six weeks and haven't had the faintest temptation as yet. Feel fine in spite of the fact that business affairs and Zelda's health have never been worse.

1307 Park Avenue
Baltimore, Maryland
April 15, 1935

Dear Max:

You don't say anything about *Taps* so I gather it hasn't caught on at all. I hope at least it will pay for itself and its corrections. There was a swell review in *The Nation;* did you see it?

I went away for another week but history didn't repeat itself and the trip was rather a waste. Thanks for the message from Ernest. I'd like to see him too and I always think of my friendship with him as being one of the high spots of life. But I still believe that such things have a mortality, perhaps in reaction to their very excessive life, and that we will never again see very much of each other. I appreciate what he said about *Tender Is the Night*. Things happen all the time which makes me think that it is not destined to die quite as easily as the boys-in-a-hurry prophesied. However, I made many mistakes about it from its delay onward, the biggest of which was to refuse the Literary Guild subsidy.

Haven't seen Beth since I got back and am calling her up today to see if she's here. I am waiting eagerly for a first installment of Ernest's book. When are you coming South? Zelda, after a terrible crisis, is somewhat better. I am, of course, on the wagon as always, but life moves at an uninspiring gait and there is less progress than I could wish on the medieval series—all in all an annoying situation as these should be my most productive years. I've simply got to arrange something for this summer that will bring me to life again, but what it should be is by no means apparent.

About 1929 I wrote a story called "Outside the Cabinet-Maker's," which ran in the *Century Magazine*. I either lost it here or else sent it to you with the first batch of se-

lected stories for *Taps* and it was not returned. Will you
(a) see if you've got it? or (b) tell me what and where
the Century Company is now and whom I should address
to get a copy of the magazine?

I've had a swell portrait painted at practically no charge
and next time I come to New York I am going to spend
a morning tearing out of your files all those preposterous
masks with which you have been libeling me for the last
decade.

Just found another whole paragraph in *Taps*, top of page
384, which appears in *Tender Is the Night*. I'd carefully
elided it and written the paragraph beneath it to replace it,
but the proofreaders slipped and put them both in.

                                        Ever yours,

                                        Scott

                                1307 Park Avenue
                                Baltimore, Maryland
                                April 17, 1935

Dear Max:

Reading Tom Wolfe's story in the current *Modern
Monthly*[1] makes me wish he was the sort of person you
could talk to about his stuff. It has all his faults and virtues.
It seems to me that with any sense of humor he could see
the Dreiserian absurdities of how the circus people "ate
the cod, bass, mackerel, halibut, clams and oysters of the
New England coast, the terrapin of Maryland, the fat
beeves, porks and cereals of the middle west," etc., etc.,
down to the "pink meated lobsters that grope their way
along the sea-floors of America." And then (after one of
his fine paragraphs which sounds a note to be expanded
later) he remarks that they leave nothing behind except
"the droppings of the camel and the elephant in Illinois."
A few pages further on his redundance ruined some paragraphs (see the last complete paragraphs on page 103) that

---

[1] "Circus at Dawn."

might have been gorgeous. I sympathize with his use of repetition, of Joyce-like words, endless metaphor, but I wish he could have seen the disgust in Edmund Wilson's face when I once tried to interpolate part of a rhymed sonnet in the middle of a novel, disguised as prose. How he can put side by side such a mess as "With chitterling tricker fast-fluttering skirrs of sound the palmy honied birderies came" and such fine phrases as "tongue-trilling chirrs, plumbellied smoothness, sweet lucidity" I don't know. He who has such infinite power of suggestion and delicacy has absolutely no right to glut people on whole meals of caviar. I hope to Christ he isn't taking all these emasculated paeans to his vitality very seriously. I'd hate to see such an exquisite talent turn into one of those muscle-bound and useless giants seen in a circus. Athletes have got to learn their games; they shouldn't just be content to tense their muscles, and if they do they suddenly find when called upon to bring off a necessary effect they are simply liable to hurl the shot into the crowd and not break any records at all. The metaphor is mixed but I think you will understand what I mean, and that he would too—save for his tendency to almost feminine horror if he thinks anyone is going to lay hands on his precious talent. I think his lack of humility is his most difficult characteristic, a lack oddly enough which I associate only with second or third rate writers. He was badly taught by bad teachers and now he hates learning.

There is another side of him that I find myself doubting, but this is something that no one could ever teach or tell him. His lack of feeling other people's passions, the lyrical value of Eugene Gant's love affair with the universe —is that going to last through a whole saga? God, I wish he could discipline himself and really plan a novel.

I wrote you the other day and the only other point of this letter is that I've made now a careful plan of the medieval novel as a whole (tentatively called *Philippe, Count of Darkness—confidential*) including the planning of the parts which I can sell and the parts which I can't. I think you could publish it either late in the spring of '36 or early in the fall of the same year. This depends entirely on how the money question goes this year. It will run to about 90,000 words and will be a novel in every sense with the episodes unrecognizable as such. That is my only plan. I wish I had these great masses of manuscripts stored away like Wolfe and Hemingway but this goose is beginning to be pretty thoroughly plucked I am afraid.

A young man has dramatized *Tender Is the Night* and I am hoping something may come of it. I may be in New York for a day and a night within the next fortnight.

Ever yours,

Scott

Later—went to N.Y. as you know, but one day only. Didn't think I would like Cape that day. Sorry you and Nora Flynn didn't meet. No news here—I think Beth is leaving soon.

1307 Park Avenue
Baltimore, Maryland
May 11, 1935

Dear Max:

It was fine seeing you but I was in a scrappy mood about Tom Wolfe. I simply cannot see the sign of achievement there yet, but I see that you are very close to the book and you don't particularly relish such an attitude.

I am closing the house and going away somewhere for a couple of months and will send you an address when I get one.

Did you ever find that copy of "Outside the Cabinet-Maker's?"

I'd like to see Ernest but it seems a long way and I would not like to see him except under the most favorable of circumstances because I don't think I am the pleasantest company of late. Zelda is in very bad condition and my own mood always somehow reflects it.

Katy Dos Passos was here and in *her* version the bullet bounced off the side of the boat, but I suppose when Ernest's legend approaches the Bunyan type it will have bounced off the moon, so it is much the same thing.

Had a nice letter from Jim Boyd agreeing with me about Clara but not about the weak writing at the end. I am quite likely to see him this summer.

Ever yours,

Scott

Hotel Stafford
Baltimore, Maryland
[circa *June 25, 1935*]

Dear Max:

I feel I owe you a word of explanation: first, as to the health business. I was given what amounted to a death sentence about 3 months ago. It was just before I last saw you—which was why, I think, I got into that silly quarrel with you about Tom Wolfe that I've regretted ever since. I was a good deal dismayed and probably jealous, so forget all I said that night. You know I've always thought there was plenty [of] room in America for more than one good writer, and you'll admit it wasn't like me.

Anyhow what upset me most was that it came just two months after the liquor question was in hand at last—and I was quite reconciled, simply cross and upset at the arbitrary change of plan. (I never felt emotional about it until a fortnight ago when I learned that the Great Scene *wasn't* coming off. It seemed such a shame after such good rehearsals that one grew suddenly sentimental and sorry for oneself.)

Second. Came up to Baltimore for five days to see Zelda who seems hopeless and send Scottie to camp. I had 24 hours with nothing to do and went to N.Y. to see a woman I'm very fond of—it's a long peculiar story. . . . one of a curious series of relationships that run through a man's life. Anyhow she'd given up the weekend at the last minute to meet me and it was impossible to leave her to see you.

Putting Scottie on train in 10 minutes. In haste,

Always yours,

Scott

I wish Struthers Burt would decide on a name—I call him everything but Katherine!

1 East 34th Street
Baltimore, Maryland
March 17, 1936

Dear Max:

A kid named Vincent McHugh has written me asking me to recommend him to you. Ordinarily I would not do such things any more but he has been a sort of unknown protégé of mine for some time. He has published a book called *Sing Before Breakfast* which I thought was a remarkable book and showed a very definite temperament. I'm not promising you that he is as strong a personality as Ernest or Caldwell or Cantwell or the men that I have previously recommended, but I do wish you would get hold of this earlier book *Sing Before Breakfast* published by Simon and Schuster in 1933 and consider that as much as what he has to offer at the moment in making your decision.

I know that due to your experience with Tom Boyd, you place a great deal of emphasis on vitality, but remember that a great deal of the work in this world has been done by sick men and people who at first sight seem to have no vitality will suddenly exhibit great streaks of it. I've never seen this young man but potentially he seems capable of great efforts.

Things are standing still here. I am waiting to hear this afternoon about a *Saturday Evening Post* story, which, if it is successful, will continue a series.

Best wishes always,

Scott

Asheville, North Carolina
September 19, 1936

Dear Max:

This is my second day of having a minute to catch up with correspondence. Probably Harold Ober has kept you in general touch with what has happened to me but I will summarize:

I broke the clavicle of my shoulder, diving—nothing heroic, but a little too high for the muscles to tie up the efforts of a simple swan dive. At first the doctors thought that I must have tuberculosis of the bone, but x-ray showed nothing of the sort, so (like occasional pitchers who throw their arms out of joint with some unprepared-for effort) it was left to dangle for twenty-four hours with a bad diagnosis by a young intern; then an x-ray and found broken and set in an elaborate plaster cast.

I had almost adapted myself to the thing when I fell in the bathroom reaching for the light, and lay on the floor until I caught a mild form of arthritis called "myotosis," which popped me in the bed for five weeks more. During this time there were domestic crises: Mother sickened and then died and I tried my best to be there but couldn't. I have been within a mile and half of my wife all summer and have seen her about half dozen times. Total accomplished for one summer has been one story, not very good, two *Esquire* articles, neither of them very good.

You have probably seen Harold Ober and he may have told you that Scottie got a remission of tuition at a very expensive school where I wanted her to go (Miss Ethel Walker's School in Connecticut). Outside of that I have no good news, except that I came into some money from my mother, not as much as I had hoped, but at least $20,000 in cash and bonds at the materialization in six months—for some reason, I do not know the why or where-fore of it, it requires this time. I am going to use some of it, with the products of the last story and the one in process of completion, to pay off my bills and to take two or three months' rest in a big way. I have to admit to myself that I haven't the vitality that I had five years ago.

I feel that I must tell you something which at first seemed better to leave alone: I wrote Ernest about that story of his,[1] asking him in the most measured terms not

[1] In "The Snows of Kilimanjaro," published in *Esquire* (August, 1936), Hemingway had his hero musing, "The rich were dull and they drank too much, or they played too much backgammon. They were dull and they were repetitious. He remembered poor Scott Fitzgerald and his romantic awe of them and how he had started a story once that began, 'The very rich are different from you and me.' And how someone had said to Scott, Yes, they have more money. But that was not humorous to Scott. He thought they were a special glamorous race and when he found they weren't it wrecked him just as much as any other thing that wrecked him."

to use my name in future pieces of fiction.[1] He wrote me back a crazy letter, telling me about what a great Writer he was and how much he loved his children, but yielding the point—"If I should outlive him—" which he doubted. To have answered it would have been like fooling with a lit firecracker.

Somehow I love that man, no matter what he says or does, but just one more crack and I think I would have to throw my weight with the gang and lay him. No one could ever hurt him in his first books but he has completely lost his head and the duller he gets about it, the more he is like a punch-drunk pug fighting himself in the movies.

No particular news except the dreary routine of illness. Scottie excited about the wedding.

As ever yours,

Scott Fitz

Grove Park Inn
Asheville, North Carolina
October 16, 1936

Dear Max:

As I wired you, an advance on my mother's estate from a friend makes it unnecessary to impose on you further.

I do not like the idea of the biographical book. I have a novel planned, or rather I should say conceived, which fits much better into the circumstances, but neither by this inheritance nor in view of the general financial situation do I see clear to undertake it. It is a novel certainly as long as *Tender Is the Night,* and, knowing my habit of endless corrections and revisions, you will understand that I figure it at two years. Except for a lucky break you see how difficult it would be for me to master the leisure of the two years to finish it. For a whole year I have been

---

[1] See Fitzgerald's letter on p. 338. "Scott Fitzgerald" was changed to "Julian" in subsequent printing of "The Snows of Kilimanjaro."

counting on such a break in the shape of either Hollywood buying *Tender* or else of Grisman getting Kirkland or someone else to do an efficient dramatization. (I know I would not like the job and I know that Davis who had every reason to undertake it after the success of *Gatsby* simply turned thumbs down from his dramatist's instinct that the story was not constructed as dramatically as *Gatsby* and did not readily lend itself to dramatization.) So let us say that all accidental, good breaks can not be considered. I can not think up any practical way of undertaking this work. If you have any suggestions they will be welcomed, but there is no likelihood that my expenses will be reduced below $18,000 a year in the next two years, with Zelda's hospital bills, insurance payments to keep, etc. And there is no likelihood that after the comparative financial failure of *Tender Is the Night* that I should be advanced such a sum as $36,000. The present plan, as near as I have formulated it, seems to be to go on with this endless *Post* writing or else go to Hollywood again. Each time I have gone to Hollywood, in spite of the enormous salary, has really set me back financially and artistically. My feelings against the autobiographical book are:

First: that certain people have thought that those *Esquire* articles[1] did me definite damage and certainly they would have to form part of the fabric of a book so projected. My feeling last winter that I could put together the articles I had written vanished in the light of your disapproval, and certainly when so many books have been made up out of miscellaneous material and exploited material, as it would be in my case, there is no considerable sale to be expected. If I were Negley Farson and had been through the revolutions and panics of the last fifteen years it would be another story, or if I were prepared at this moment to "tell all" it would have a chance at success, but now it would seem to be a measure adopted *in extremis,* a sort of period to my whole career.

In relation to all this, I enjoyed reading *General Grant's Last Stand,* and was conscious of your particular reasons for sending it to me. It is needless to compare the difference in force of character between myself and General Grant,

---

[1] Three essays known collectively as "The Crack-Up."

the number of words that he could write in a year, and the absolutely virgin field which he exploited with the experiences of a four-year life under the most dramatic of circumstances. What attitude on life I have been able to put into my books is dependent upon entirely different field of reference with the predominant themes based on problems of personal psychology. While you may sit down and write 3000 words one day, it inevitably means that you write 500 words the next. . . .

I certainly have this one more novel, but it may have to remain among the unwritten books of this world. Such stray ideas as sending my daughter to a public school, putting my wife in a public insane asylum, have been proposed to me by intimate friends, but it would break something in me that would shatter the very delicate pencil-end of a point of view. I have got myself completely on the spot and what the next step is I don't know.

I am going to New York around Thanksgiving for a day or so and we might discuss ways and means. This general eclipse of ambition and determination and fortitude, all of the very qualities on which I have prided myself, is ridiculous, and, I must admit, somewhat obscene.

Anyhow, thank you for your willingness to help me. Thank Charlie for me and tell him that the assignments he mentioned have only been waiting on a general straightening up of my affairs. My God, debt is an awful thing!

Yours,

F. Scott Fitzgerald

Heard from Mrs. Rawlings and will see her.

Grove Park Inn
Asheville, North Carolina
October 22, 1936

Dear Mr. Kerr:[1]

There is one great publisher in America, and that is

[1] Hugh F. B. Kerr, a Baltimorean who had met Fitzgerald casually and had written to ask his advice about getting a novel published.

Charles Scribner's Sons. Their list includes, as you must know, Hemingway, Wolfe, etc., and has included at most times young Erskine Caldwell and (for the magazine, at least) William Faulkner. There is no question that they are more open to talent than any other publisher because of their resources, first, and because of the tradition of taking a chance on a talent that has not yet got itself an audience.

I am out of Baltimore in Asheville where I have been ill and I am unable to see you or read your manuscript or estimate what you have to offer, but I think by all odds the wisest thing to do is to send your manuscript to Maxwell Perkins, where you will be read carefully and with imagination by a staff of three or four men who have managed to pick out some of the most extraordinary books of our time, after other publishers have turned them down.

If they should decide that it was not to their advantage to publish your manuscript, send copies of this correspondence to my agent, Harold Ober, at 40 East 49th Street, New York City, and he might be able to give you better advice. If in the future your novel is published and makes a success, I should suggest that you put all rights in his hands. He will charge you ten per cent, but in sixteen years of professional writing he has saved me much more than ten per cent.

Now, have I told you anything you want to know? Again, I am sorry that I cannot read your novel until it is in type, but I am laboring under tremendous obligations here and there is simply not the physical time. This is exactly the same advice that I gave Ernest Hemingway many years ago and is based on a long career which has touched the publishing business in general.

Sincerely yours,

F. Scott Fitzgerald

[*Oak Hall Hotel*]
[*Tryon, North Carolina*]
[*February, 1937*]

Dear Max:

Thanks for your note and the appalling statement. Odd

how enormous sums of $10,000 have come to seem lately—
I can remember turning down that for the serialization of
The Great Gatsby—from *College Humor*.

Well, my least productive and lowest general year since
1926 is over. In that year I did 1 short story and 2 chapters of a novel—that is, two chapters that I afterwards
used. And it was a terrible story. Last year, even though
laid up 4 months, I sold 4 stories and 8 *Esquire* pieces,
a poor showing God knows. This year has started slowly
also, some damn lack of interest, staleness, when I have
every reason to want to work if only to keep from thinking. Haven't had a drink since I left the North (about six
weeks, not even beer) but while I feel a little better nervously, it doesn't bring back the old exuberance. I honestly
think that all the prize fighters, actors, writers who live
by their own personal performance ought to have man-
agers in their best years. The ephemeral part of the talent
seems when it is in hiding so apart from one, so "otherwise," that it seems it ought to have some better custodian
than the poor individual with whom it lodges and who is
left with the bill. My chief achievement lately has been
in cutting down my and Zelda's expenses to rock bottom;
my chief failure is my inability to see a workable future.
Hollywood for money has much against it, the stories are
somehow mostly out of me unless some new source of
material springs up, a novel takes money and time—I am
thinking of putting aside certain hours and digging out a
play, the ever-appealing mirage. At 40 one counts carefully one's remaining vitality and resources, and a play
ought to be within both of them. The novel and the autobiography have got to wait till this load of debt is lifted.

So much, and too much, for my affairs. Write me of
Ernest and Tom and who's new and does Ring still sell and
John Fox and *The House of Mirth*. Or am I the only best
seller who doesn't sell?

The account, I know, doesn't include my personal debt
to you. How much is it please?

I don't know at all about Brookfield. Never have heard
of it but there are so many schools there. Someone asked
me about Oldfields where Mrs. Simpson went and I'd never
heard of that. Please write me—you are about the only
friend who does not see fit to incorporate a moral lesson, especially since "The Crack-Up" stuff. Actually I hear from

people in Sing Sing and Joliet all comforting and advising me.

> Ever your friend,
>
> Scott

> [*Oak Hall Hotel*]
> [*Tryon, North Carolina*]
> [*Before March 19, 1937*]

Dear Max:

Thanks for the book—I don't think it was very good but then I didn't go for Sheean or Negley Farson either. Ernest ought to write a swell book now about Spain—real Richard Harding Davis reporting or better. (I mean not the sad jocosity of P.O.M. passages or the mere calendar of slaughter.) And speaking of Ernest, did I tell you that when I wrote asking him to cut me out of his story he answered, with ill grace, that he would—in fact he answered with such unpleasantness that it is hard to think he has any friendly feeling to me any more. Anyhow please remember that he agreed to do this if the story should come in with me still in it.

At the moment it appears that I may go to Hollywood for awhile, and I hope it works out. I was glad to get news of Tom Wolfe though I don't understand about his landlady. What?

> Ever yours,
>
> Scott

Write me again—I hear no news. On the wagon since January and in good shape physically.

> [*Oak Hall Hotel*]
> [*Tryon, North Carolina*]
> [*Before May 20, 1937*]

Dear Max:

Thanks for your letter—and the loan. I hope Ober will be able to pay you in a few weeks.

All serene here and would be content to remain indefinitely save that for short stories a change of scene is better. I have lived in tombs for years it seems to me—a real experience like this first trip to Loudon County usually means a story. As soon as I can, I want to travel a little— it's fine not having Scottie to worry over, love her as I do. I want to meet some new people. (I do constantly but they seem just the old people over again but not so nice.)

Ever your friend,

Scott

Thanks for the word about Ernest. Methinks he does protest too much.[1]

[The Garden of Allah Hotel]
[Hollywood, California]
[Before July 19, 1937]

Dear Max:

Thanks for your letter—I was just going to write you. Harold has doubtless told you I have a nice salary out here tho until I have paid my debts and piled up a little security so that my "catastrophe at forty" won't be repeated I'm not bragging about it or even talking about it. The money is budgeted by Harold, as someone I believe Charlie Scribner recommended years ago. I'm sorry that the Scribner share will only amount to $2500 or so the first year but that is while I'm paying back Harold who like you is an individual. The second year it will be better.

There are clauses in the contract which allow certain off-periods but it postpones a book for quite a while.

Ernest came like a whirlwind, put Ernst Lubitsch the great director in his place by refusing to have his picture prettied up and remade for him à la Hollywood at various cocktail parties. I feel he was in a state of nervous tensity,

---

[1] Perkins had written Fitzgerald about Hemingway, ". . . his feelings towards you are different from what you seem to suspect. I think he had some queer notion that he would give you a 'jolt' and that it might be good for you or something like that."

that there was something almost religious about it. He
raised $1000 bills won by Miriam Hopkins fresh from the
gaming table, the rumor is $14,000 in one night.

Everyone is very nice to me, surprised and rather relieved that I don't drink. I am happier than I've been
for several years.

Ever your friend,

Scott

[The Garden of Allah Hotel]
[Hollywood, California]

[Before August 24, 1937]

Dear Max:

Have heard every possible version[1] save that Eastman
has fled to Shanghai with Pauline.[2] Is Ernest on a bat—
what has happened? I'm so damn sorry for him after my
late taste of newspaper bastards. But is he just being stupid
or are they after him politically? It amounts to either great
indiscretion or actual persecution.

Thanks for my "royalty" report. I scarcely even belong
to the gentry in that line. All goes beautifully here. So far
Scottie is having the time of her young life, dining with
Crawford, Shearer, etc., talking to Fred Astaire and her
other heroes. I am very proud of her. And a *grand-
daughter*, Max! Do you feel a hundred?

Ever your friend,

Scott

---

[1] Of a scrap between Hemingway and Max Eastman in the Scribner office
which had brought Hemingway bad publicity.

[2] Mrs. Ernest Hemingway.

Metro-Goldwyn-Mayer Corporation
Culver City, California
September 3, 1937

Dear Max:

Thanks for your long, full letter.[1] I will guard the secrets as my life.

I was thoroughly amused by your descriptions, but what transpires is that Ernest did exactly the asinine thing that I knew he had it in him to do when he was out here. The fact that he lost his temper only for a minute does not minimize the fact that he picked the exact wrong minute to do it. His discretion must have been at low ebb or he would not have again trusted the reporters at the boat.

He is living at the present in a world so entirely his own that it is impossible to help him, even if I felt close to him at the moment, which I don't. I like him so much, though, that I wince when anything happens to him, and I feel rather personally ashamed that it has been possible for imbeciles to dig at him and hurt him. After all, you would think that a man who has arrived at the position of being practically his country's most eminent writer could be spared that yelping.

All goes well—no writing at all except on pictures.

Ever your friend,

Scott

The Schulberg book[2] is in all the windows here.

The Garden of Allah Hotel
Hollywood, California
March 4, 1938

Dear Max:

Sorry I saw you for such a brief time while I was in New York and that we had really no time to talk.

[1] Perkins had written Fitzgerald a detailed account of the Hemingway-Eastman affair.
[2] *They Cried a Little* by Sonya Schulberg.

My little binge lasted only three days, and I haven't had a drop since. There was one other in September, likewise three days. Save for that, I haven't had a drop since a year ago last January. Isn't it awful that we reformed alcoholics have to preface everything by explaining exactly how we stand on that question?

The enclosed letter is to supplement a conversation some time ago. It shows quite definitely how a whole lot of people interpreted Ernest's crack at me in "Snows of K." When I called him on it, he promised in a letter that he would not reprint it in book form. Of course, since then, it has been in O'Brien's collection, but I gather he can't help that. If, however, you are publishing a collection of his this fall, do keep in mind that he has promised to make an elision of my name. It was a damned rotten thing to do, and with anybody but Ernest my tendency would be to crack back. Why did he think it would add to the strength of his story if I had become such a negligible figure? This is quite indefensible on any grounds.

No news here. I am writing a new Crawford picture, called *Infidelity*. Though based on a magazine story, it is practically an original. I like the work and have a better producer than before—Hunt Stromberg—a sort of one-finger Thalberg, without Thalberg's scope, but with his intense power of work and his absorption in his job.

Meanwhile, I am filling a notebook with stuff that will be of more immediate interest to you, but please don't mention me ever as having any plans. *Tender Is the Night* hung over too long, and my next venture will be presented to you without preparation or fanfare.

I am sorry about the Tom Wolfe business.[1] I don't understand it. I am sorry for him and, in another way, I am sorry for you for I know how fond of him you are.

I may possibly see you around Easter.

Best to Louise.

Ever yours,

Scott

All this about "The Snows" is confidential.

[1] Wolfe had left Scribners and gone to Harper's.

The Garden of Allah Hotel
Hollywood, California

April 23, 1938

Dear Max:

I got both your letters and appreciate them and their fullness, as I feel very much the Californian at the moment and, consequently, out of touch with New York.

The Marjorie Rawlings' book fascinated me.[1] I thought it was even better than *South Moon Under* and I envy her the ease with which she does action scenes, such as the tremendously complicated hunt sequence, which I would have to stake off in advance and which would probably turn out to be a stilted business in the end. Hers just simply flows; the characters keep thinking, talking, feeling and don't stop, and you think and talk and feel with them.

As to Ernest, I was fascinated by what you told me about the play, touched that he remembered me in his premonitory last word, and fascinated, as always, by the man's Byronic intensity. The *Los Angeles Times* printed a couple of his articles, but none the last three days, and I keep hoping a stray Krupp shell hasn't knocked off our currently most valuable citizen.

In the mail yesterday came a letter from that exquisitely tactful co-workers of yours, _____ _____. I've never had much love for the man since he insisted on selling *This Side of Paradise* for a dollar fifty, and cost me around five thousand dollars; nor do I love him more when, as it happened the other day, I went into a house and saw someone reading the Modern Library's *Great Modern Short Stories* with a poor piece of mine called "Act Your Age" side by side with Conrad's "Youth," Ernest's "The Killers" because _____ _____ was jealous of a copyright.

His letter informs me that *This Side of Paradise* is now out of print. I am not surprised after eighteen years (looking it over, I think it is now one of the funniest books since *Dorian Gray* in its utter spuriousness—and then, here and there, I find a page that is very real and living), but I know to the younger generation it is a pretty remote business, reading about the battles that engrossed us then and the things that were startling. To hold them I would have to

[1] *The Yearling.*

put in a couple of abortions to give it color (and probably would if I was that age and writing it again). However, I'd like to know what "out of print" means. Does it mean that I can make my own arrangements about it? That is, if any publisher was interested in reprinting it, could I go ahead, or would it immediately become a valuable property to _____ again?

I once had an idea of getting Bennett Cerf to publish it in the Modern Library, with a new preface. But also I note in your letter a suggestion of publishing an omnibus book with *Paradise, Gatsby* and *Tender*. How remote is that idea, and why must we forget it? If I am to be out here two years longer, as seems probable, it certainly isn't advisable to let my name sink so out of sight as it did between *Gatsby* and *Tender*, especially as I now will not be writing even the *Saturday Evening Post* stories.

I have again gone back to the idea of expanding the stories about Philippe, the Dark Ages knight, but when I will find time for that, I don't know, as this amazing business has a way of whizzing you along at a terrific speed and then letting you wait in a dispirited, half-cocked mood when you don't feel like undertaking anything else, while it makes up its mind. It is a strange conglomeration of a few excellent overtired men making the pictures, and as dismal a crowd of fakes and hacks at the bottom as you can imagine. The consequence is that every other man is a charlatan, nobody trusts anybody else, and an infinite amount of time is wasted from lack of confidence.

Relations have always been so pleasant, not only with you but with Harold and with Lorimer's *Saturday Evening Post*, that even working with the pleasantest people in the industry, Eddie Knopf and Hunt Stromberg, I feel this lack of confidence.

Hard times weed out many of the incompetents, but they swarm back—Herman Mankiewicz, a ruined man who hasn't written ten feet of continuity in two years, was finally dropped by Metro, but immediately picked up by Columbia! He is a nice fellow that everybody likes and has been brilliant, but he is being hired because everyone is sorry for his wife—which I think would make him rather an obstacle in the way of making good pictures. Utter toughness toward the helpless, combined with super-sentimentality—Jesus, what a combination!

I still feel in the dark about Tom Wolfe, rather frightened for him; I cannot quite see him going it alone, but neither can I see your sacrificing yourself in that constant struggle. What a time you've had with your sons, Max—Ernest gone to Spain, me gone to Hollywood, Tom Wolfe reverting to an artistic hill-billy.

Do let me know about *This Side of Paradise*. _____ _____'s letter was so subtly disagreeable that I felt he took rather personal pleasure in the book being out of print. It was all about buying up some second-hand copies. You might tell him to do so if he thinks best. I have a copy somewhere, but I'd like a couple of extras.

> Affectionately always,
>
> Scott

> *Metro-Goldwyn-Mayer Corporation*
> *Culver City, California*
> *September 29, 1938*

Dear Max:

I feel like writing to you about Tom as to a relation of his, for I know how deeply his death must have touched you, how you were so entwined with his literary career and the affection you had for him. I know no details. Shortly after I got your letter that he was in Seattle, I read in the paper that he was starting East sick. This worried me and it seemed a very forlorn and desolate and grievous experience, yet something which his great vitality would somehow transcend and dominate—and then the end at Baltimore and that great pulsing, vital frame quiet at last. There is a great hush after him—perhaps even more than after the death of Ring who had been moribund so long.

I would like to know something about the situation. You, as his literary executor, are I suppose oddly enough more in control of his literary destiny than when he was alive. I don't suppose that his "million words" rounds out his great plan but I am not so sure that that matters because the plan must have been a mutating and progressive thing. The more valuable parts of Tom were the more lyrical parts or, rather, those moments when his lyricism was best combined with his powers of observation—those fine blends such as the trip up the Hudson in *Of Time and the River*. I am curious to know what his very last stuff was like, whether he had lost his way or perhaps found it again.

With deepest sympathy for you and also for his family. Do you think it would do any good to write them a letter, and to whom should I address it?

Ever, your friend

Scott

P.esses: I am more than delighted about Zippy's boy. Which of your daughters went to Vassar? You speak vaguely of some plans of Ernest's, but you leave me in the dark. Glad he cut me out of "The Snows." Thanks for "The Captain's Chair." Also for the news about Elizabeth.

Metro-Goldwyn-Mayer Corporation
Culver City, California
December 24, 1938

Dear Max:

Since the going-out-of-print of *Paradise* and the success (or is it one?) of *The Fifth Column* [1] I have come to feel somewhat neglected. Isn't my reputation being allowed to let slip away? I mean what's left of it. I am still a figure to many people and the number of times I still see my name in *Time* and *The New Yorker,* etc., makes me wonder if it should be allowed to casually disappear—when there are memorial double deckers to such fellows as Farrell and Steinbeck.

I think something ought to be published this spring. You had a plan for the three novels and I have another plan, of which more hereafter, for another big book; the recession is over for awhile and I have the most natural ambition to see my stuff accessible to another generation. Ben-

---

[1] *The Fifth Column* [play] *and the First Forty-Nine Stories* by Ernest Hemingway.

nett Cerf obviously isn't going to move about *Tender* and it seems to me things like that need a spark from a man's own publisher. It was not so long ago that *Tender* was among the dozen best of a bad season and had an offer from the Literary Guild—so I can't be such a long chance as, say, Callaghan. Either of the two books I speak of might have an awfully good chance to pay their way. A whole generation now has never read *This Side of Paradise*. (I've often thought that if Frank Bunn at Princeton had had a few dozen copies on his stands every September he could have sold them all by Christmas.)

But I am especially concerned about *Tender*—that book is not dead. The *depth* of its appeal exists—I meet people constantly who have the same exclusive attachment to it as others had to *Gatsby* and *Paradise*, people who identified themselves with Dick Diver. Its great fault is that the *true* beginning—the young psychiatrist in Switzerland—is tucked away in the middle of the book. If pages 151–212 were taken from their present place and put at the start, the improvement in appeal would be enormous. In fact the mistake was noted and suggested by a dozen reviewers. To shape up the ends of that change would, of course, require changes in half a dozen other pages. And as you suggested, an omnibus book should also have a preface or prefaces—besides my proposed glossary of absurdities and inaccuracies in *This Side of Paradise*. This last should attract some amused attention.

The other idea is this:

A Big collection of stories leading off with *Philippe*—entirely rewritten and pulled together into a 30,000-word novelette. The collection could consist of:

1. *Philippe*
2. Pre-war (Basil and Josephine)
3. "May Day"
4. The Jazz Age (the dozen or so best jazz stories)
5. About a dozen others including "Babylon"

The reason for using *Philippe* is this: he is to some extent completed in the fourth story (which you have never read) and, in spite of some muddled writing, he is one of the best characters I've ever "drawn." He should be a long book—but whether or not my M-G-M contract is renewed

I'm going to free-lance out here another year to lay by some money, and then do my modern novel. So it would be literally *years* before I got to *Philippe* again—if ever.

In my work here I can find time for such a rewrite of *Philippe* as I contemplate—I could finish it by the first of February. The other stories would go into the collection unchanged. Unlike Ernest I wouldn't want to put in *all* the stories from all four books but I'd like to add four or five never published before.

I am desperately keen on both these schemes—I think the novels should come first and, unless there are factors there you haven't told me about, I think it is a shame to put it off. It would not sell wildly at first but unless you make some gesture of confidence I see my reputation dying on its feet from lack of nourishment. If you could see the cards for my books in the public libraries here in Los Angeles continually in demand even to this day, you would known I had never had wide distribution in some parts of the country. When *This Side of Paradise* stood first in *The Bookman's Monthly List* it didn't even appear in the score of the Western States.

You can imagine how distasteful it is to blow my own horn like this but it comes from a deep feeling that something could be done, if it is done at once, about my literary standing—always admitting that I have any at all.

Ever your friend,

Scott

Metro-Goldwyn-Mayer   Corporation
Culver City, California
January 4, 1939

Dear Max:

Your letter rather confused me. I had never clearly understood that it was the Modern Library who were considering doing my three books as a giant volume. I thought it was an enterprise of yours. If they show no special enthusiasm about bringing out *Tender* by itself, I don't see how they would be interested in doing a giant anyhow. You spoke of it last year as something only the recession kept you from doing.

What I don't like is the out-of-print element. In a second I'm going to discuss the *Philippe* business with you, but first let me say that I would rather have *This Side of Paradise* in print, if only in that cheap American Mercury book edition than not in print at all. I see they have just done Elliot Paul's *Indelible*. How do you think they would feel about it? And what is your advice on the subject?

Now about *Philippe*. When I wrote you I had envisaged another year of steady work here. At present, while it is possible that I may be on the coast for another year, it is more likely that the work will be from picture to picture with the prospect of taking off three or four months in the year, perhaps even more, for literary work. *Philippe* interests me. I am afraid, though, it would have to be supported by something more substantial. I would have to write 10,000 or 15,000 more words on it to make it as big a book as *Gatsby* and I'm not at all sure that it would have a *great* unity. You will remember that the plan in the beginning was tremendously ambitious—there was to have been Philippe as a young man founding his fortunes—Philippe as a middle-aged man participating in the Capetian founding of France as a nation—Philippe as an old man and the consolidation of the feudal system. It was to have covered a span of about sixty years from 880 A.D. to 950. The research required for the second two parts would be quite tremendous and the book would have been (or would be) a piece of great self-indulgence, though I admit self-indulgence often pays unexpected dividends.

Still, if periods of three or four months are going to be possible in the next year or so I would much rather do a modern novel. One of those novels that can only be written at the moment and when one is full of the idea—as *Tender* should have been written in its original conception, all laid on the Riviera. I think it would be a quicker job to write a novel like that between 50 and 60,000 words long than to do a thorough revision job with an addition of 15,000 words on *Philippe*. In any case I'm going to decide within the next month and let you know.

Thanks for your letter. I wish you'd send me a copy of the Tom Wolfe article because I never see anything out here. John wrote about me in the *Virginia Quarterly,* too.

Ever your friend,

Scott

P.S. I hope Jane and Scottie see a lot of each other if Scottie stays in, but as I suspected, she has tendencies toward being a play-girl and has been put on probation. I hope she survives this February.

5521 Amestoy Avenue
Encino, California
February 25, 1939

Dear Max:

I was sorry that a glimpse of you was so short but I had a hunch that you had wanted to talk over something with your daughter and that I was rather intruding. How pretty she was—she seemed a little frightened of me for some reason, or maybe it was one of my self-conscious days.

One of the things I meant to tell you was how much I enjoyed the book *Cantigny* by Evarts, whom I gather is a cousin of yours—or is that true? It seemed to me very vivid. It reminded me of one of the best of Tom Boyd's stories in *Point of Honor* though the attitude was quite satisfactorily different.

No doubt you have talked to Harold in regard to that life insurance business. Of course, he thinks I am rash, but I think it would be morally destructive to continue here any longer on the factory worker's basis. Conditions in the industry somehow propose the paradox: "We brought you here for your individuality but while you're here we insist that you do everything to conceal it."

I have several plans, and within a day or so will be embarked on one of them. It is wonderful to be writing again instead of patching—do you know in that *Gone with the Wind* job I was absolutely forbidden to use any words except those of Margaret Mitchell; that is, when new phrases had to be invented one had to thumb through as if it were

Scripture and check out phrases of hers which would cover the situation!

Best wishes always.

Scott

P.S. I am, of course, astonished that Tom Wolfe's book did what you told me. I am sure that if he had lived and meant to make a portrait of you he would at least have given it a proper tone and not made you the villain. It is astonishing what people will do though. Ernest's sharp turn against me always seemed to have pointless childish quality—so much so that I really never felt any resentment about it. Your position in the Wolfe matter is certainly an exceedingly ironic one.

5521 Amestoy Avenue
Encino, California
May 22, 1939

Dear Max:

Just had a letter from Charlie Scribner—a very nice letter and I appreciated it and will answer it. He seemed under the full conviction that the novel was about Hollywood and I am in terror that this misinformation may have been disseminated to the literary columns. If I ever gave any such impression it is entirely false: I said that the novel was about some things that had happened to me in the last two years. It is distinctly *not* about Hollywood (and if it were it is the last impression that I would want to get about).[1]

It is, however, progressing nicely, except that I have been confined to bed for a few weeks with a slight return of my old malady. It was nice getting a glimpse of you, however brief—especially that last day. I caught the plane at half past four and had an uneventful trip west.

I have grown to like this particular corner of California where I shall undoubtedly stay all summer. Dates for a

---

[1] *The Last Tycoon* was in fact about Hollywood.

novel, are, as you know, uncertain, but I am blocking this out
in a fashion so that, unlike *Tender,* I may be able to put
it aside for a month and pick it up again at the exact spot
factually and emotionally where I left off.

Wish I had some news, but what I have seen lately is only
what you can see outside a window. With very best to all
—and please do correct that impression which Charlie
seems to have.

Ever your friend,

Scott

5521 Amestoy Avenue
Encino, California
November 20, 1939

Dear Max:

A lot depends on this week. I've about decided to show
him (Littauer)[1] the first nine or ten thousand words and I
think it's literally about fifty-fifty whether he'll want it or
not. The material is definitely "strong." As soon as I hear
anything from him I'll let you know.

Of course, if he will back me it will be a life-saver, but
I am by no means sure that I will ever be a popular writer
again. This much of the book, however, should be as fair
a test as any. Thanks for your letter.

Ever yours,

F. Scott Fitzgerald

5521 Amestoy Avenue
Encino, California
December 19, 1939

Dear Max:

The opinion about the novel seems half good and half

---

[1] Editor of *Colliers.* Perkins had written Fitzgerald to ask whether *Colliers*
would give him an advance for the right to serialize his novel-in-progress.

bad. In brief, about four or five people here like it immensely, Leland likes it and you like it. *Colliers,* however, seems indifferent to it though they like the outline. My plan is to just go ahead and dig it out. If I could interest any magazine, of course, it would be a tremendous help but today a letter from the *Post* seems to indicate that it is not their sort of material. The plan has changed a bit since I first wrote the outline, but it is essentially as you know it.

Your offering to loan me another thousand dollars was the kindest thing I ever heard of. It certainly comes at the most opportune time. The first thing is this month's and last month's rent and I am going to take the liberty of giving my landlady a draft on you for $205.00, for January 2nd. This with the $150.00 that you have already sent me is $355.00. For the other $645.00, will you let me know when it is available?

I am not terribly in debt as I was in 1935–7, but uncomfortably so. I think though my health is getting definitely better and if I can do some intermittent work in the studios between each chapter of the novel instead of this unprofitable hacking for *Esquire,* I shall be able to get somewhere by spring.

Max, you are so kind. When Harold withdrew from the questionable honor of being my banker, I felt completely numb financially and I suddenly wondered what money was and where it came from. There had always seemed a little more somewhere and now there wasn't.

Anyhow, thank you.

Ever your friend,

Scott

5521 Amestoy Avenue
Encino, California
February 21, 1940

Dear Max:

Thanks for sending the release on "Babylon." I haven't yet gotten the money but it will be something over $800.00, very little as Hollywood prices go. However, it will give me a chance to try another short story and if either that or the one that is out now finds a home I ought to produce a few chapters of the novel. Meanwhile things do not move here at all in a moving-picture way, but one makes a certain adjustment.

I am glad John Bishop is in good spirits. The affairs of the world never really worried him much. The fact fills me with great envy. I can see ahead no further than finishing this book and getting Scottie through Vassar. The rest looks no brighter than it has for a long time. The greatest privilege would be to be able to do work so absorbing that one could forget the trouble abroad and at home.

I will keep you informed.

Ever yours,

Scott

c/o Phil Berg Agency
9484 Wilshire Boulevard
Beverly Hills, California
May 20, 1940

Dear Max:

I've owed you a decent letter for some months. First— the above is my best address though at the moment I'm hunting for a small apartment. I am in the last week of an eight week movie job for which I will receive $2300. I couldn't pay you anything from it, nor the government, but it was something, because it was my own picture *Babylon Revisited* and may lead to a new line up here. I just couldn't make the grade as a hack—that, like everything else, requires a certain practiced excellence.

The radio has just announced the fall of St. Quentin! My God! What was the use of my wiring you that André Chamson has a hit when the war has now passed into a new stage, making his book a chestnut of a bygone quiet era.

I wish I was in print. It will be odd a year or so from now when Scottie assures her friends I was an author and finds that no book is procurable. It is certainly no fault of yours. You (and one other man, Gerald Murphy) have been a friend through every dark time in these five years. It's funny what a friend is—Ernest's crack in "The Snows," poor John Bishop's article in the *Virginia Quarterly* (a nice return for ten years of trying to set him up in a literary way) and Harold's sudden desertion at the wrong time, have made them something less than friends. Once I believed in friendship, believed I *could* (if I didn't always) make people happy and it was more fun than anything. Now even that seems like a vaudevillian's cheap dream of heaven, a vast minstrel show in which one is the perpetual Bones.

Professionally, I know, the next move must come from me. Would the 25-cent press keep *Gatsby* in the public eye —or *is the book unpopular?* Has it *had* its chance? Would a popular reissue in that series with a preface *not* by me but by one of its admirers—I can maybe pick one—make it a favorite with classrooms, profs, lovers of English prose —anybdy? But to die, so completely and unjustly after having given so much! Even now there is little published in American fiction that doesn't slightly bear my stamp—in a *small* way I was an original. I remember we had one of our few and trifling disagreements because I said that to anyone who loved "When Lilacs Last," Tom Wolfe couldn't be such a *great original.* Since then I have changed about him. I like "Only the Dead" and "Arthur, Garfield, etc.," right up with the tops. And where are Tom and I and the rest when psychological Robespierres parade through American letters elevating such melo as *Christ in Concrete* to the top, and the boys read Steinbeck like they once read Mencken! I have not lost faith. People will *buy* my new book and I hope I shan't again make the many mistakes of *Tender.*

Tell me the news if you have time. Where is Ernest and what doing? . . . .

Love to all of you, of all generations.

Scott

1403 Laurel Avenue
Hollywood, California
(new address)

June 6, 1940

Dear Max:

Thanks for your nice long letter, and for the book[1]—or did I thank you for the book? I was fascinated, not only by the excellent coverage of the battles (though the man's extreme bias and the necessity of compression threw some of them out of focus), but by the curious philosophic note which began to run through it, from the discussion of Pharsalla on.

The note was reminiscent, exultant and dumb, but not until I found the name Spengler did his psychology become clear to me. Up to then I had thought: "What a wide range for a military man!" Then the truth became plain. Poor old Spengler has begotten Nazis that would make him turn over in his grave, and Fuller makes his own distortion. Spengler believed that the Western world was dead, and he believed nothing else but that—though he had certain ideas of a possible Slavic rebirth. This did *not* include Germany, which he linked with the rest of western Europe as in decline. And that the fine flower of it all was to be the battle of Vittorio Veneto and the rise of Mussolini —well, Spengler's turn in his grave must have been like that of an airplane propeller.

In his last four chapters Fuller begins to get ridiculous. I wonder how he feels now when that *admirable* Mr. Franco is about to batter down Gibraltar. This of course does not detract from the interest of the book, especially through the Napoleonic era. Did you ever read Spengler —specifically including the second volume? I read him the same summer I was writing *The Great Gatsby* and I don't think I ever quite recovered from him. He and Marx are the only modern philosophers that still manage to make sense in this horrible mess—I mean make sense by themselves and not in the hands of distorters. Even Mr. Lenin looks now like a much better politician than a philosopher. Spengler, on the other hand, prophesied gang rule, "young peoples hungry for spoil," and more particularly "the

---

[1] *Decisive Battles: Their Influence upon History and Civilization,* by J. F. C. Fuller.

world as spoil" as an idea, a dominant supercessive idea.

Max, what becomes of copyrights when a book goes out of print? For example, in the case of *Flappers*. For the sake of possible picture rights and so forth should I renew that copyright now? I haven't an idea about this.

How does Ernest feel about things? Is he angry or has he a philosophic attitude? The Allies are thoroughly licked, that much is certain, and I am sorry for a lot of people. As I wrote Scottie, many of her friends will probably die in the swamps of Bolivia. She is all right now, by the way. . . .

Do let me know about the copyright business, and I would be interested in at least a clue to Ernest's attitude.

Ever your friend,

Scott

[*1403 North Laurel Avenue*]
[*Hollywood, California*]
December 13, 1940

Dear Max:

Thanks for your letter. The novel progresses—in fact progresses fast. I'm not going to stop now till I finish a first draft which will be sometime after the 15th of January. However, let's pretend that it doesn't exist until it's closer to completion. We don't want it to become—"a legend before it is written," which is what I believe Wheelock[1] said about *Tender Is the Night*. Meanwhile will you send me back the chapters I sent you as they are all invalid now, must be completely rewritten, etc. The essential idea is the same and it is still, as far as I can hope, a secret.

Budd Schulberg, a very nice, clever kid out here, is publishing a Hollywood novel with Random House in January. It's not bad but it doesn't cut into my material at all. I've read Ernest's novel and most of Tom Wolfe's[2] and have been doing a lot of ruminating as to what this whole profession is about. Tom Wolfe's failure to really explain why you and he parted mars his book but there are great things

---

[1] Scribners editor, John Hall Wheelock.
[2] *You Can't Go Home Again.*

in it. The portraits of the Jacks (who are they?), Emily
Vanderbilt are magnificent.

No one points out how Saroyan has been influenced by
Franz Kafka. Kafka was an extraordinary Czechoslovakian
Jew who died in '36. He will never have a wide public but
The Trial and *America* are two books that writers are never
able to forget.

This is the first day off I have taken for many months
and I just wanted to tell you the book is coming along and
that comparatively speaking all is well.

Ever your friend,

Scott

P.S. How much will you sell the plates of *This Side of
Paradise* for? I think it has a chance for a new life.

PART FOUR

Letters to
Ernest Hemingway

14 rue de Tilsitt
[Paris, France]

[Postmarked November 30, 1925]

Dear Ernest:

I was quite ashamed of the other morning. Not only in disturbing Hadley,[1] but in foisting that _____alias_____ upon you. However it is only fair to say that the deplorable man who entered your apartment Saturday morning was *not* me but a man named Johnston who has often been mistaken for me.

Zelda, evidences to the contrary, was not suffering from lack of care but from a nervous hysteria which is only relieved by a doctor bearing morphine. We both went to Belleau Wood next day to recuperate.

For some reason I told you a silly lie—or rather an exaggeration—silly because the truth itself was enough to make me sufficiently jubilant. *The Saturday Evening Post* raised me to $2750 and not $3000, which is a jump of $750.00 in one month. It was probably in my mind that I could not get $3000 from the smaller magazines. The *Post* merely met the Hearst offer, but that is something they seldom do.

What garbled versions of the McAlmon episode or the English orgy we lately participated in I told you, I don't know. It is true I saved McAlmon from a beating he probably deserved and that we went on some wild parties in London with a certain Marchioness of Milford Haven whom we first met with Talluah Bankhead. She was about half royalty. I think. Anyhow she was very nice—anything

---

[1] Mrs. Ernest Hemingway.

else I may have added about the relations between the Fitzgeralds and the house of Windsor is pure fiction.

I'm crazy to read the comic novel. Are you going to the MacLeishes' Tuesday? I hope Hadley is well now. Please believe me that we send our

> Best wishes to
> Ernest M. Hemingway.
>
> [Scott]

> [*Villa St. Louis*]
> [*Juan-les-Pins*]
>
> [*August or September, 1926*]

Dear Ernest:

Sorry we missed you and Hadley. No news. I'm on the wagon and working like hell. Expect to sail for N.Y. December 10th from Genoa on the *Conte Biancamano*. Will be here till then. Saw bullfight in Fréjus. Bull was euneuch (sp.). House barred and dark. Front door chained. Have made no enemies for a week. _____ domestic row ended in riot. Have new war books by Pierrefeu. God is love.

> Signed,
>
> Ernestine Murphy

Did you read in the *N.Y. Herald* about ". . . Henry Carpenter, banker, and Willie Stevens, half-wit, . . ."

> [*Villa St. Louis*]
> [*Juan-les-Pins*]
>
> [*Fall, 1926*]

We were in a back-house in Juan-les-Pins. Bill had lost control of his sphincter muscles. There were wet *MaFins* in the rack beside the door. There were wet *Eclaireurs de*

Nice in the rack over his head. When the King of Bulgaria came in, Bill was just firing a burst that struck the old limeshit twenty feet down with a *splat-tap*. All the rest came just like that. The King of Bulgaria began to whirl round and round.

"The great thing in these affairs—" he said.
Soon he was whirling faster and faster. Then he was dead.

At this point in my letter my 30th birthday came and I got tight for a week in the company of such fascinating gents as Mr. Theodore Rousseau and other ornaments of what is now a barren shore.

Ernest of little faith, I hope the sale of "The Killers" will teach you to send every story either to Scribners or an agent. Can't you get "Today Is Friday" back? Your letter depressed and rather baffled me. Have you and Hadley permanently busted up, and was the necessity of that what was on your soul this summer? Don't answer this unless you feel like it. Anyhow I'm sorry everything's such a mess and I do want to see you if you come to Marseille in October.

We saw the _____s before they left, got stewed with them (at their party)—that is we got stewed—and I believe there was some sort of mawkish reconciliation. However they've grown dim to me and I don't like them much any more. _____s to have grown shadowy—he's *so* nice, but she's a club woman at heart and made a great lot of trouble in subtle ways this summer. We saw _____ the day she left and the huge Garoupe standing desolate, and her face, and the pathetic bales of *chiclets* for the Garoupe beach in her bedroom are the strongest impression I have left of a futile and petty summer. It might all have happened at Roslyn, Long Island.

Swimming's almost over now. We have our tickets for America December 10th on the *Conte Biancamano*—we'll spend the winter in New York. _____ was here with his unspeakably awful wife. He seems anemic and washed out, a memory of the past so far as I'm concerned.

I'm glad as hell about the story and I hope it's the first of many. I feel too much at loose ends to write any more tonight. Remember—if I can give you any financial help let me know.

Always your friend,

Scott

I had a lot more to say but it's 3:30 A.M. and I've been working since 11 this morning and it's very hazy. Have you read *The Spanish Farm* and *Sixty-four, ninety-four!* by Mottram? *Wonderful* war books. Much better than Ford Madox Ford. In fact the best thing I've read this summer. Met your cousin from Princeton!

Villa St. Louis
Juan-les-Pins
[*December, 1926*]

Dear Ernest:

We leave this house Tuesday for Genoa and New York. I hope everything's going better for you. If there is anything you need done here as in America—anything about your work, or money, or human help under any head— remember you can always call on

Your devoted friend,

Scott

S.S. Conte Biancamano
[*En route New York*]
[*Postmarked December 23, 1926*]

Dear Ernest:

Your letter depressed me—illogically because I knew more or less what was coming.[1] I wish I could have seen you and heard you, if you wished, give some sort of version of

---

[1] Hemingway's divorce.

what happened to you. Anyhow I'm sorry for you and for Hadley and for Bumby and I hope some way you'll all be content and things will not seem so hard and bad.

I can't tell you how much your friendship has meant to me during this year and a half—it is the brightest thing in our trip to Europe for me. I will try to look out for your interests with Scribners in America, but I gather that the need of that is past now and that soon you'll be financially more than on your feet.

I'm sorry you didn't come to Marseille. I go back with my novel still unfinished and with less health and not much more money than when I came, but somehow content, for the moment, with motion and New York ahead and Zelda's entire recovery—and happy about the amount of my book that I've already written.

I'm delighted with what press I've already seen of *The Sun, etc.* Did not realize that you had stolen it all from me but am prepared to believe that it's true and shall tell everyone. By the way I liked it in print even better than in manuscript.

1st printing was probably 5000. 2nd printing may mean that they've sold 4500 so have ordered up 3000 more. It may mean any sale from 2500 to 5000, tho.

College Humor pays fine. No movie in *Sun Also* unless book is big success or scandal. That's just a guess.

We all enjoyed *"La vie est beau avec Papa."* We agree with Bumby.

Always yours affectionately,

Scott

Write me care of Scribners.

Hotel Roosevelt
Washington, D.C.
[March, 1927]

Dear Ernest:

A line in terrible haste. Lunched with Mencken in Baltimore yesterday. He is just starting reading *The Sun, etc.*

—has no recollection of having seen "Big Two-Hearted River" and admits confusion about two *In Our Times*. Got him to say he'd pay you $250.00 for anything of yours he could use. So there's another market.

Told him about how you were going to beat him up. He's a "peach of a fellow" (no irony; just a slip of the pen). He's thoroughly interested and utterly incapable of malice. Whole thing was simply rather sloppy, as he's one of the busiest men in America.

"The Killers" was fine.

> Your devoted friend,
>
> Scott

> [*Ellerslie*]
> [*Edgemoor, Delaware*]
> [*Postmarked April 18, 1927*]

Dear Ernest:

Your stories were great (in April *Scribner's*). But like me you must beware Conrad rhythms in direct quotation from characters, especially if you're pointing a single phrase and making a man live by it.

"In the fall the war was always there but we did not go to it any more" is one of the most beautiful prose sentences I've ever read.

So much has happened to me lately that I despair of ever assimilating it—or forgetting it, which is the same thing.

I hate to think of your being hard up. Please use this if it would help. *The Atlantic* will pay about $200.00, I suppose. I'll get in touch with Perkins about it when he returns from vacation (1 week). Won't they advance you all you need on the book of stories? Your title is fine by the way. What chance of your crossing this summer?

My novel is to be finished July 1st.

> With eager and anxious good wishes,
>
> Scott

Address for a year—Ellerslie Mansion, Edgemoor, Delaware. Huge old house on Delaware River. Pillars, etc. I am called "Colonel." Zelda "de old Missus."

Ellerslie
Edgemoor, Delaware
[*November, 1927*]

Dear Ernest:

Thousands will send you this clipping.[1] I should think it would make you quite conscious of your public existence. It's well meant—he praised your book a few days before.

The book is fine. I like it quite as well as *The Sun*, which doesn't begin to express my enthusiasm. In spite of all its geographical and emotional rambling, it's a unit, as much as Conrad's books of Contes were. Zelda read it with fascination, liking it better than anything you've written. Her favorite was "Hills Like White Elephants," mine, barring "The Killers," was "Now I Lay Me." The one about the Indians was the only one that left me cold and I'm glad you left out "Up in Michigan." They probably belong to an earlier and almost exhausted vein.

"In the fall the war was always there but we did not go to it any more." God, what a beautiful line. And the waking dreams in "Now I Lay Me" and the whole mood of "Hills Like."

Did you see the pre-review by that . . . . Rascoe who obviously had only read three stories but wanted to be up to the minute?

Max says it's almost exhausted 7500—however that was five days ago. I like your title—*All the Sad Young Men Without Women*—and I feel my influence is beginning to tell. Manuel Garcia is obviously Gatsby. What you haven't learned from me you'll get from Good Woman Bromfield and soon you'll be Marching in the Van of the Younger Generation.

No work this summer but lots this fall. Hope to finish the novel by 1st December. Have got nervous as hell lately

[1] A parody of Hemingway in F.P.A.'s column, "The Conning Tower."

—purely physical but scared me somewhat—to the point of putting me on the wagon and smoking denicotinized cigarettes. Zelda is ballet dancing three times a week with the Phila Symphony—painting also. I think you were wise not jumping at *Hearst's* offer. I had a contract with them that, as it turned out, did me unspeakable damage in one way or another. Long is a sentimental scavenger with no ghost of taste or individuality, not nearly so much as Lorimer for example. However, why not send your stories to Paul Reynolds? He'll be glad to handle them and will get you good prices. The *Post* now pays me $3500—this detail so you'll be sure who's writing this letter.

I can't tell you how I miss you. May cross for 6 weeks March or April. *The Grandmothers*[1] was respectable but undistinguished, and are you coming home? Best to Pauline.[2] With good wishes and affection,

                                        Scott

                              Ellerslie
                              Edgemoor, Delaware
                              [*December, 1927*]

Dear Ernest:

Perkins sent me the check for 800 bits (as we westerners say), indicating, I hope, that you are now comfortably off in your own ascetic way. I am almost through my novel, got short and had to do three *Post* stories but as I am now their pet exhibit . . . . to the tune of 32,000 bits per felony it didn't take long to come to the surface.

(This tough talk is not really characteristic of me—it's the influence of *All the Sad Young Men Without Women in Love.*) Louis Golding stepped off the boat and said you and I were the hope of American Letters (if you can find them) but aside from that things look black, "old pard"— Brommy is sweeping the West, Edna Ferber is sweeping the East and Paul Rosenfeld is sweeping what's left into a large ornate waste-basket, a gift which any Real Man would like, to be published in November under the title, *The Real*

---

[1] A novel by Glenway Wescott.
[2] Hemingway's second wife.

Leisure Class, containing the work of one-story Balzacs and poets so thin-skinned as to be moved by everything to exactly the same degree of mild remarking.

Lately I've enjoyed *Some People, Bismark* (Ludwig's), *Him* (in parts) and the *Memoirs* of Ludendorff. I have a new German war book, *Die Krieg Against Krieg,* which shows men who mislaid their faces in Picardy and the Caucasus—you can imagine how I thumb it over, my mouth fairly slithering with fascination.

If you write anything in the line of an "athletic" story please try the *Post* or let me try them for you, or Reynolds. You were wise not to tie up with *Hearst's.* They are absolute bitches who feed on contracts like vultures, if I may coin a neat simile.

I've tasted no alcohol for a month but Xmas is coming.

Please write me at length about your adventures—I hear you were seen running through Portugal in used B.V.D.s, chewing ground glass and collecting material for a story about boule players; that you were publicity man for Lindbergh; that you have finished a novel a hundred thousand words long consisting entirely of the word "balls" used in new groupings; that you have been naturalized a Spaniard, dress always in a wine-skin with "zipper" vent and are engaged in bootlegging Spanish Fly between St. Sebastian and Biarritz where your agents sprinkle it on the floor of the Casino. I hope I have been misinformed but, alas!, it all has too true a ring. For your own good I should be back there, with both of us trying to be good fellows at a terrible rate. Just before you pass out next time think of me.

This is a wowsy country but France is [illegible] and I hope to spend March and April, or April and May, there and elsewhere on the continent.

How are you, physically and mentally? Do you sleep? "Now I Lay Me" was a fine story—you ought to write a companion piece, "Now I Lay Her." Excuse my bawdiness but I'm oversexed and am having saltpeter put in my *Pâté de Foie Gras au Truffles Provençal.*

Please write news. My best to Pauline—Zelda's also to you both. God will forgive everybody—even Robert McAlmon and Burton Rascoe.

Always afftly,

Scott

[Ellerslie]
Edgemoor, Delaware
[Postmarked December 28, 1928]

Dear Ernest:

I'm terribly sorry about your trouble. I guess losing parents is just one of the things that happens to one in the thirties—every time I see my father now I think it's the last time.

Thank Pauline for the really beautiful Xmas card. It was great to have you both here, even when I was intermittently unconscious.

I send you what may be news, and what a nice precedent for beating up Mencken. Saw the Murphys for an hour in New York. We're sailing March 1st and I hope to have the novel here. (Confidential about sailing though, until I'm sure—won't go unless novel's finished.) Ring thought you were fine—he was uncharacteristically enthusiastic.

I'm bored and somewhat depressed tonight so I won't continue. Oh, yes—I met old H. Stearns just before leaving Paris and feeling drunk and Christ-like suggested a title to him, "Why I Go On Being Poor in Paris," told him to write it as an informal letter to me and I'd sell it. In a burst of energy he did and I sent it to Max who wrote a check for $100.00 for it. Now Harold writes me that $100 isn't very much (as a matter of fact it isn't much of a letter either) and exhibits such general dissatisfaction that I think he thinks I held out on him. You've got to be careful who you do favors for—within a year you'll probably hear a story that what started him on his downward path was my conscienceless theft of his royalties.

Spengler's second volume is marvelous. Nothing else is any good—when will you save me from the risk of memorizing your works from over-reading them by finishing another? Remember, Proust is dead—to the great envy of

Your crony and gossip,

Scott

[Paris, France]
[Postmarked May 17, 1929]

Dear Herr Hemophile: or "Bleeding Boy" as I sometimes call you.

Will you take salt with us on Sunday or Monday night? Would make great personal whoopee on receipt of favorable response. Send me a pneu or answer me in person, save between 3 and 7. Highest references, willing to travel— *gens du monde, cultivé, sympathique cherche hôte pour dimanche ou lundi*—answer because I shall probably ask Bishop, if you can come. . . .

> God Save us, Preserve us, Bless us.
>
> Yrs, in Xt.
>
> Fitzg——

> *12 Blvd. Eugène Gazagnaire*
> *Cannes, France*
> *August 23, 1929*

Dear Ernest:

I've been working like hell, better than for four years, and now am confident of getting old faithful off before the all-American teams are picked—hence the delay.

I wrote Max (not mentioning your letter) one of these don't-lose-your-head notes, though I, like you, never thought there was more than an outside chance of his being forced to let you down. I felt sure that if it came to a crisis he'd threaten to resign and force their hand.

The book sticks with me, by the way; I'm sure it's all I thought at first and can't wait to read it in printing letters.

It's been gay here but we are, thank God, desperately unpopular and not invited anywhere. See the Murphys once a week or so—Gerald is older, less gay, more social, but not so changed as many people in five years. D. Parker is on the crest—tho I didn't see her as much as I'd liked.

Now—Ruth Goldbeck Voallammbbrrossa not only had no intention of throwing you out in any case, but has even promised *on her own initiative* to speak to whoever it is (she knows her) has the place. She is a fine woman, I think; one of the most attractive in evidence at this moment, in every sense, and is not deserving of that nervous bitterness.

Not knowing whether you've left Spain I'm sending this to Paris. Hoping you'll be here in September for a week or so.

Bunny Wilson's book[1] has a fascinating portrait of Dos in it, and is full of good things, and to me interesting throughout. Oddly enough what it lacks is his old bogey, form. It is shapeless as Wells at his wildest, or almost.

Have read nothing good recently save a book on the Leopold-Loeb case and Harold Nicholson's *Tennyson*, neither recent.

This is a dull letter but it's late and what's left of the mind is tired.

Always afftly yours,

Scott

Best to Pauline.

Villa Fleur des Bois
Cannes, France
September 9, 1929

Dear Ernest:

I'm glad you decided my letter wasn't snooty—it was merely hurried (incidentally I thought you wanted a word said to Ruth G. if it came about naturally—I merely remarked that you'd be disappointed if you lost your apartment—never a word that you'd been exasperated). But enough of pretty dismal matters—let us proceed to the really dismal ones. First tho let me say that from Perkins' last your book like Pickwick has become a classic still in serial form. Everything looks bright as day for it and I envy you like hell but would rather have it happen to you than to anyone else.

Just taken another chapter to typist's and it's left me in a terrible mood of depression as to whether it's any good or not. In 2½ months I've been here I've written 20,000 words on it and one short story, which is superb for me of late years. I've paid for it with the usual nervous depres-

[1] *I Thought of Daisy.*

sions and such drinking manners as the lowest bistro
(bistrot?) boy would scorn. My latest tendency is to collapse about 11:00 and, with the tears flowing from my
eyes or the gin rising to their level and leaking over, tell
interested friends or acquaintances that I haven't a friend
in the world and likewise care for nobody, generally including Zelda, and often implying current company—
after which the current company tend to become less current and I wake up in strange rooms in strange palaces.
The rest of the time I stay alone working or trying to work
or brooding or reading detective stories—and realizing
that anyone in my state of mind, who has in addition never
been able to hold his tongue, is pretty poor company. But
when drunk I make them all pay and pay and pay.

Among them has been ——— ———. Naturally she, having been in an equivalent state, lacks patience—(this isn't
snooty—no one likes to see people in moods of despair
they themselves have survived). Incidentally the Murphys
have given their whole performance for her this summer
and I think, tho she would be the last to admit it, she's had
the time of her life.

We're coming to Paris for 2 months the 1st of October.

Your analysis of my inability to get my serious work
done is too kind in that it leaves out the dissipation, but
among acts of God it is possible that the 5 years between
my leaving the army and finishing *Gatsby* (1919–1924)
which included 3 novels, about 50 popular stories and a
play and numerous articles and movies may have taken all
I had to say too early, adding that all the time we were
living at top speed in the gayest worlds we could find. This
au fond is what really worries me—tho the trouble may be
my inability to leave anything once started. I have worked
for 2 months over a popular short story that was foredoomed to being torn up when completed. Perhaps the
house will burn down with this ms. and preferably me in it.

Always your stinking old friend,

Scott

I have no possible right to send you this gloomy letter.
Really if I didn't feel rather better with one thing or another I couldn't have written it. Here's a last flicker of the
old cheap pride: the *Post* now pays the old whore $4000

a screw. But now it's because she's mastered the 40 positions—in her youth one was enough.

> *1307 Park Avenue*
> *Baltimore, Maryland*
> *May 10, 1934*

Dear Ernest:

Did you like the book?[1] For God's sake drop me a line and tell me one way or another. You can't hurt my feelings. I just want to get a few intelligent slants at it to get some of the reviewers' jargon out of my head.

> Ever your friend,
>
> Scott

All I meant about the editing was that if I'd been in Max's place I'd have urged you to hold the book[2] for more material. It had neither the surprise of *I.O.T.*[3] *(nessessessarily)* nor its unity, and it did not have *as large a proportion* of first-flight stories as *M.W.W.*[4] I think in a "general presentation" way this could have been atoned for by sheer bulk. Take that opinion for what it's worth.

On the other hand you can thank God you missed this publishing season! I am 5th best seller in the country and haven't broken 12,000.

> *1307 Park Avenue*
> *Baltimore, Maryland*
> *June 1, 1934*

Dear Ernest:

Your letter crossed, or almost crossed, one of mine

[1] *Tender Is the Night.*
[2] *Winner Take Nothing.*
[3] *In Our Time.*
[4] *Men Without Women.*

which I am glad now I didn't send, because the old charming frankness of your letter cleared up the foggy atmosphere through which I felt it was difficult for us to talk any more.

Because I'm going egoist on you in a moment. I want to say that just exactly what you suggested, that the addition of that Chinamen-running story in the *Cosmopolitan* would have given *Winner Take Nothing* the weight that it needed, was in my head too. Allow me one more criticism, that while I admire your use of purely abstract titles I do not think that one was a particularly fortunate choice.

Next to go to the mat with you on a couple of technical points. The reason I had written you a letter was that Dos dropped in in passing through and said you had brought up about my book what we talked about once in a café on the Avenue de Neuilly about composite characters. Now, I don't entirely dissent from the theory but I don't believe you can try to prove your point on such a case as Bunny using his own father as the sire of John Dos Passos, or in the case of this book that covers ground that you personally paced off about the same time I was doing it. In either of those cases how could you trust your own detachment? If you had never met any of the originals then your opinion would be more convincing.

Following this out a little farther, when does the proper and logical combination of events, cause and effect, etc., end and the field of imagination begin? Again you may be entirely right because I suppose you were applying the idea particularly to the handling of the creative faculty in one's mind rather than to the effect upon the stranger reading it. Nevertheless, I am not sold on the subject, and especially to account for the big flaws of *Tender* on that ground doesn't convince me. Think of the case of the Renaissance artists, and of the Elizabethan dramatists, the first having to superimpose a medieval conception of science and archeology, etc., upon the Bible story; and, in the second, of Shakespeare's trying to interpret the results of his own observation of the life around him on the basis of Plutarch's *Lives* and Hollinshed's *Chronicles*. There you must admit that the feat of building a monument out of three kinds of marble was brought off. You can accuse me justly of not having the power to bring it off, but a theory that it can't be done is highly questionable. I make this point with such persistence because such a conception, if you stick to it, might limit your own choice of materials. The idea can be reduced simply to: you can't say *accurately* that composite characterization hurt my book, but that it only hurt it for you.

To take a case specifically, that of Gerald and Sara. I don't know how much you think you know about my relations with them over a long time, but from certain remarks that you let drop, such as one "Gerald threw you over," I guess that you didn't even know the beginning of our relations . . . .

I think it is obvious that my respect for your artistic life is absolutely unqualified, that save for a few of the dead or dying old men you are the only man writing fiction in America that I look up to very much. There are pieces and paragraphs of your work that I read over and over—in fact, I stopped myself doing it for a year and a half because I was afraid that your particular rhythms were going to creep in on mine by process of infiltration. Perhaps you will recognize some of your remarks in *Tender*, but I did every damn thing I could to avoid that. (By the way, I didn't read the Wescott story of Villefranche sailors till I'd done my own version. Think that was the wisest course, for me anyhow, and got a pleasant letter from him in regard to the matter.)

To go back to my theme song, the second technical point that might be of interest to you concerns direct steals from an idea of yours, an idea of Conrad's and a few lines out of David-into-Fox-Garnett. The theory back of it I got from Conrad's preface to *The Nigger*, that the purpose of a work of fiction is to appeal to the lingering after-effects in the reader's mind as differing from, say, the purpose of oratory or philosophy which respectively leave people in a fighting or thoughtful mood. The second contribution to the burglary was your trying to work out some such theory in your troubles with the very end of *A Farewell to Arms*. I remember that your first draft—or at least the first one I saw—gave a sort of old-fashioned Alger book summary of the future lives of the characters: "The priest became a priest under Fascism," etc., and you may remember my suggestion to take a burst of eloquence from anywhere in the book that you could find it and tag off with that; you were against this idea because you felt that the true line of a work of fiction was to take a reader up to a high emotional pitch but then let him down or ease him off. You gave no aesthetic reason for this—nevertheless, you convinced me. The third piece of burglary contributing to this symposium was my admiration of the dying fall in the aforesaid Garnett's book and I imitated it as accurately as it is humanly decent in my own ending of *Tender*, telling the reader in the last pages that, after all, this is just a casual event, and trying to let *him* come to bat for *me* rather than going out to shake his nerves, whoop him up, then leaving him rather in a condition of a frustrated woman in bed. (Did that ever happen to you in your days with MacCallagan or McKisco, Sweetie?)

Thanks again for your letter which was damned nice, and my absolute best wishes to all of you. (By the way, where did you ever get the idea that I didn't like Pauline, or that I didn't like her as much as I should?) Of all that time of life the only temperamental coolness that I ever felt toward any of the people we ran around with was toward _____, and even in that case it was never any more than that. I have honestly never gone in for hating. My temporary bitternesses toward people have all been ended by what Freud called an inferiority complex and Christ called "Let him without sin"—I remember the day he said it. We were justlikethat then; we tossed up for who was going to go through with it—and he lost.

I am now asking only $5000 for letters. Make out the check to Malcolm Republic, *c/o The New Cowlick*.

Ever your friend,

[Scott]

P.S. Did you ever see my piece about Ring in *The New Cowlick*—I think you'd have liked it.

P.S.S. This letter and questions require no answers. You are "write" that I no longer listen, but my case histories seem to go in largely for the same magazines, and with simple people I get polite. But I listen to you and would like damn well to hear your voice again.

[*Grove Park Inn*]
[*Asheville, North Carolina*]
[*August, 1936*]

Dear Ernest:

Please lay off me in print. If I choose to write *de profundis* sometimes[1] it doesn't mean I want friends praying aloud over my corpse. No doubt you meant it kindly but it cost me a night's sleep. And when you incorporate it (the story) in a book would you mind cutting my name?

It's a fine story[2]—one of your best—even though the "Poor Scott Fitzgerald, etc." rather spoiled it for me.

Ever your friend,

Scott

Riches have *never* fascinated me, unless combined with the greatest charm or distinction.

[*On the train, traveling to some point in the South*]
June 5, 1937

It was fine to see you so well and full of life, Ernest. I hope you'll make your book fat—I know some of that *Esquire* work is too good to leave out. All best wishes to your Spanish trip—I wish we could meet more often. I don't feel I know you at all.

Ever yours,

Scott

Going South always seems to me rather desolate and fatal and uneasy. This is no exception. Going North is a safe dull feeling.

[1] "The Crack-Up."
[2] "The Snows of Kilimanjaro."

[*1403 North Laurel Avenue*]
[*Hollywood, California*]
November 8, 1940

Dear Ernest:

It's a fine novel,[1] better than anybody else writing could do. Thanks for thinking of me and for your dedication. I read it with intense interest, participating in a lot of the writing problems as they came along and often quite unable to discover how you brought off some of the effects, but you always did. The massacre was magnificent and also the fight on the mountain and the actual dynamiting scene. Of the side shows I particularly liked the vignette of Karkov and Pilar's Sonata to death—and I had a personal interest in the Moseby guerilla stuff because of my own father. The scene in which the father says goodbye to his son is very powerful. I'm going to read the whole thing again.

I never got to tell you how I liked *To Have and Have Not* either. There is observation and writing in that that the boys will be imitating with a vengeance—paragraphs and pages that are right up with Dostoevsky in their undeflected intensity.

Congratulations too on your new book's great success. I envy you like hell and there is no irony in this. I always like Dostoevsky with his wide appeal more than any other European—and I envy you the time it will give you to do what you want.

With old affection,

[Scott]

P.S. I came across an old article by John Bishop about how you lay four days under dead bodies at Caporetto and how I flunked out of Princeton (I left on a stretcher in November—you can't flunk out in November) and how I am an awful suck about the rich and a social climber. What I started to say was that I do know something about you on the Italian front, from a man who was in your unit—how you crawled some hellish distance pulling a wounded man with you and how the doctors stood over you wondering

---

[1] *For Whom the Bell Tolls.* Hemingway had sent Fitzgerald a copy inscribed "To Scott with affection and esteem."

why you were alive with many perforations. Don't worry
—I won't tell anybody. Not even Alan Campbell who
called me up and gave me news of you the other day.
P.S. (2) I hear you are marrying one of the most beautiful
people I have ever seen. Give her my best remembrance.[1]

[1] Martha Gellhorn.

PART FIVE

Letters to
Edmund Wilson

593 Summit Avenue
St. Paul, Minnesota

September 26, 1917

Dear Bunny:

You'll be surprised to get this but it's really begging for an answer. My purpose is to see exactly what effect the war at close quarters has on a person of your temperament. I mean I'm curious to see how your point of view has changed or not changed—

I've taken regular army exams but haven't heard a word from them yet. John Bishop is in the second camp at Fort Benjamin Harrison in Indiana. He expects a 1st Lieutenancy. I spent a literary month with him (July) and wrote a terrific lot of poetry mostly under the Masefield-Brooke influence.

Here's John's latest.

BOUDOIR

The place still speaks of worn-out beauty of roses,
    And half retrieves a failure of Bergamotte,
Rich light and a silence so rich one all but supposes
    The voice of the clavichord stirs to a dead gavotte

For the light grows soft and the silence forever
    quavers,
    As if it would fail in a measure of satin and lace,
Some eighteenth century madness that sighs and
    wavers
    Through a life exquisitely vain to a dying grace.

This was the music she loved; we heard her often

Walking alone in the green-clipped garden outside.
It was just at the time when summer begins to soften
    And the locust shrills in the long afternoon that
        she died.

The gaudy macaw still climbs in the folds of the
        curtain;
    The chintz-flowers fade where the late sun strikes
        them aslant.
Here are her books too: Pope and the earlier Burton,
    A worn Verlaine; *Bonheur* and the *Fêtes Galantes*.

Come—let us go—I am done. Here one recovers
    Too much of the past but fails at the last to find
Aught that made it the season of loves and lovers;
    Give me your hand—she was lovely—mine eyes
        blind.

Isn't that good? He hasn't published it yet. I sent twelve
poems to magazines yesterday. If I get them all back I'm
going to give up poetry and turn to prose. John may publish a book of verse in the spring. I'd like to but of course
there's no chance. Here's one of mine.

TO CECILIA

When Vanity kissed Vanity
    A hundred happy Junes ago,
He pondered o'er her breathlessly,
    And that all time might ever know
He rhymed her over life and death,
    "For once, for all, for love," he said . . .
Her beauty's scattered with his breath
    And with her lovers she was dead.

Ever his wit and not her eyes,
    Ever his art and not her hair.
"Who'd learn a trick in rhyme be wise
    And pause before his sonnet there."
So all my words however true
    Might sing you to a thousandth June
And no one ever *know* that you
    Were beauty for an afternoon.

It's pretty good but of course fades right out before John's. By the way I struck a novel that you'd like, *Out of Due Time* by Mrs. Wilfred Ward. I don't suppose this is the due time to tell you that, though. I think that *The New Machiavelli* is the greatest English novel of the century. I've given up the summer to drinking (gin) and philosophy (James and Schopenhauer and Bergson).

Most of the time I've been bored to death— Wasn't it tragic about Jack Newlin? I hardly knew poor Gaily.[1] Do write me the details.

I almost went to Russia on a commission in August but didn't so I'm sending you one of my passport pictures—if the censor doesn't remove it for some reason— It looks rather Teutonic but I can prove myself a Celt by signing myself

Very sincerely,

F. Scott Fitzgerald

Cottage Club
Princeton, New Jersey
[*Fall, 1917*]

Dear Bunny:

I've been intending to write you before but as you see I've had a change of scene and the necessary travail thereof has stolen time.

Your poem came to John Biggs, my room-mate, and we'll put it in the next number—however it was practically illegible so I'm sending you my copy (hazarded) which you'll kindly correct and send back—

I'm here starting my senior year and still waiting for my commission. I'll send you the *Lit*[2] or no—you've subscribed, haven't you?

Saw your friend Larry Noyes in St. Paul and got beautifully stewed after a party he gave. —He got beautifully full of canned wrath—I don't imagine we'd agree on much—

[1] Princetonians who died in the war.
[2] *The Nassau Literary Magazine.*

Do write John Bishop and tell him not to call his book *Green Fruit*.

Alec is an ensign. I'm enclosing you a clever letter from Townsend Martin which I wish you'd send back.

Princeton is stupid but Gauss and Gerould are here. I'm taking naught but Philosophy and English—I told Gauss you'd sailed (I'd heard as much) but I'll contradict the rumor.

Have you read Wells' *Boon, the Mind of the Race* (Doran, 1916). It's marvelous! (Debutante expression.)

The *Lit* is prosperous—Biggs and I do the prose—Creese and Keller (a junior who'll be chairman) and I the poetry. However any contributions would be etc., etc.

Young Benét (at New Haven) is getting out a book of verse before Xmas that I fear will obscure John Peale's. His subjects are less *precieuse* and decadent. John is really an anachronism in this country at this time—people want ideas and not fabrics.

I'm rather bored here but I see Shane Leslie occasionally and read Wells and Rousseau. I read Mrs. Gerould's *British Novelists Limited* and think she underestimates Wells but is right in putting Mackenzie at the head of his school. She seems to disregard Barrie and Chesterton whom I should put above Bennett or in fact anyone except Wells.

Do you realize that Shaw is 61, Wells 51, Chesterton 41, Leslie 31 and I 21? (Too bad I haven't a better man for 31. I can hear your addition to this remark.)

Oh and that awful little _____ _____ (a sort of attenuated superfruit) is still around (ex '16—now '17½). He belongs to a preceptorial where I am trying to demolish the Wordsworth legend—and contributes such elevating freshman-cultural generalities as "Why I'm suah that romanticism is only a cross-section of reality, Dr. Murch."

Yes—Jack Newlin is dead—killed in ambulance service. He was, potentially, a great artist.

Here is a poem I just had accepted by *Poet Lore*.

THE WAY OF PURGATION

A fathom deep in sleep I lie
    With old desires, restrained before;
To clamor life-ward with a cry
    As dark flies out the greying door.

And so in quest of creeds to share
  I seek assertive day again;
But old monotony is there—
  Long, long avenues of rain.

Oh might I rise again! Might I
  Throw off the throbs of that old wine—
See the new morning mass the sky
  With fairy towers, line on line—
Find each mirage in the high air
  A symbol, not a dream again!
But old monotony is there—
  Long, long avenues of rain.

No—I have no more stuff of John's—I ask but never receive.

If Hillquit gets the mayoralty of New York it means a new era. Twenty million Russians from South Russia have come over to the Roman Church.[1]

I can go to Italy if I like as private secretary of a man (a priest) who is going as Cardinal Gibbons' representative to discuss the war with the Pope (American Catholic point of view—which is most loyal—barring the Sinn Fein—40% of Pershing's army are Irish Catholics). Do write.

Gaelically yours,

Scott Fitzgerald

I remind myself lately of Pendennis, Sentimental Tommy (who was not sentimental and whom Barrie never understood), Michael Fane, Maurice Avery and Guy Hazelwood.[2]

---

[1] In the margin beside this paragraph Fitzgerald wrote, "News Jottings (unofficial)."
[2] The last three of these names refer to characters in Compton Mackenzie's early novels.

[*Fort Leavenworth, Kansas*]

January 10, [*1918*]

Dear Bunny:

Your last refuge from the cool sophistries of the shattered world is destroyed! I have left Princeton. I am now Lieutenant F. Scott Fitzgerald of the 45th Infantry (regulars). My present address is

c/o Q. P.O.B.

Ft. Leavenworth, Kansas

After February 26th

593 Summit Avenue

St. Paul, Minnesota

will always find me, forwarded.

—So the short, swift chain of the Princeton intellectuals (Brooks clothes, clean ears and, withal, a lack of mental priggishness . . . Whipple, Wilson, Bishop, Fitzgerald . . .) have passed along the path of the generation—leaving their shining crown upon the gloss and unworthiness of John Biggs' head.

One of your poems I sent on to the *Lit* and I'll send the other when I've read it again. I wonder if you ever got the *Lit* I sent you . . . so I enclosed you two pictures; well, give one to some poor motherless Poilu fairy who has no dream. This is smutty and forced but in an atmosphere of cabbage . . .

John's book came out in December and though I've written him reams (Rheims) of praise, I think he's made poor use of his material. It is a thin Green Book.

GREEN FRUIT

(One man here remarked that he didn't read it because Green Fruit always gave him a pain in the a——!)

by JOHN PEALE BISHOP

1st Lt. Inf. R.C.

SHERMAN FRENCH CO.

BOSTON

In section one ("Souls and Fabrics") are "Boudoir," "The Nassau Inn" and of all things "Fillipo's Wife," a relic

of his decadent sophomore days. "Claudius" and other
documents in obscurity adorn this section.

Section two contains the Elspeth poems—which I think
are rotten. Section three is "Poems out of Jersey and
Virginia" and has "Campbell Hall," "Millville" and much
saccharine sentiment about how much white bodies pleased
him and how, nevertheless, he was about to take his turn
with crushed brains (this slender thought done over in
poem after poem). This is my confidential opinion, however; if he knew what a nut I considered him for leaving
out "Ganymede" and "Salem Water" and "Francis Thompson" and "Prayer" and all the things that might have given
body to his work, he'd drop me from his writing list. The
book closed with the dedication to Townsend Martin
which is on the circular I enclose. I have seen no reviews
of it yet.

THE ROMANTIC EGOTIST

by F. Scott Fitzgerald

". . . the Best is over
You may complain and sigh
Oh Silly Lover . . ."
Rupert Brooke

"Experience is the name Tubby gives to his mistakes."
Oscar Wilde

Chas. Scribner's Sons (Maybe!)
MCMXVIII

There are twenty-three chapters, all but five are written, and it is poetry, prose, *vers libre* and every mood of
a temperamental temperature. It purports to be the picares-
que ramble of one Stephen Palms from the San Francisco
fire thru school, Princeton, to the end, where at twenty-
one he writes his autobiography at the Princeton aviation
school. It shows traces of Tarkington, Chesterton, Chambers, Wells, Benson (Robert Hugh), Rupert Brooke and
includes Compton-Mackenzie-like love affairs and three
psychic adventures including an encounter with the devil
in a harlot's apartment.

It rather damns much of Princeton but it's nothing to

what it thinks of men and human nature in general. I can most nearly describe it by calling it a prose, modernistic *Childe Harold* and really if Scribners takes it I know I'll wake some morning and find that the debutantes have made me famous overnight. I really believe that no one else could have written so searchingly the story of the youth of our generation. . .

In my right hand bunk sleeps the editor of *Contemporary Verse* (ex), Devereux Josephs, Harvard '15 and a peach— on my left side is G. C. King, a Harvard crazy man who is *dramatizing War and Peace;* but you see I'm lucky in being well protected from the Philistines.

The *Lit* continues slowly but I haven't received the December issue yet so I can't pronounce on the quality.

This insolent war has carried off Stuart Walcott in France, as you may know, and really is beginning to irritate me—but the maudlin sentiment of most people is still the spear in my side. In everything except my romantic Chestertonian orthodoxy I still agree with the early Wells on human nature and the "no hope for Tono Bungay" theory.

God! How I miss my youth—that's only relative of course but already lines are beginning to coarsen *in other people* and that's the sure sign. I don't think you ever realized at Princeton the childlike simplicity that lay behind all my petty sophistication and my lack of a real sense of honor. I'd be a wicked man if it wasn't for that and now that's disappearing. . .

Well I'm overstepping and boring you and using up my novel's material so goodbye. Do write and let's keep in touch if you like.

God bless you.

Celtically,

F. Scott Fitzgerald

Bishop's address:
  Lieut. John Peale Bishop (He's a 1st Lt.)
    334th Infantry
    Camp Taylor, Kentucky

599 Summit Avenue
St. Paul, Minnesota
August 15, [1919]

Dear Bunny:

Delighted to get your letter. I am deep in the throes of a new novel.

Which is the best title?

(1) *The Education of a Personage*
(2) *The Romantic Egotist*
(3) *This Side of Paradise*

I am sending it to Scribners—they liked my first one. Am enclosing two letters from them that might amuse you. Please return them.

I have just finished the story for your book.[1] It's not written yet. An American girl falls in love with an officer Francais at a southern camp.

Since I last saw you I've tried to get married and then tried to drink myself to death but foiled, as have been so many good men, by the sex and the state I have returned to literature.

Have sold three or four cheap stories to Amuricun magazines.

Will start on story for you about 25th *d'Aout* (as the French say or do not say) which is about 10 days off.

I am ashamed to say that my Catholicism is scarcely more than a memory—no, that's wrong, it's more than that; at any rate I go not to the church nor mumble stray nothings over crystalline beads.

May be in N'York in September or early October.

Is John Bishop *in hoc terrain?*

Remember me to Larry Noyes. I'm afraid he's very much off me. I don't think he's seen me sober for many years.

For God's sake, Bunny, write a novel and don't waste your time editing collections. It'll get to be a habit.

That sounds crass and discordant but you know what I mean.

Yours in the Holder[2] group,

Scott Fitzgerald

[1] Wilson was trying to get together a collection of realistic stories about the war.
[2] This refers to Holder Hall, one of the Princeton dormitories.

599 Summit Avenue
St. Paul, Minnesota

[*Probably September, 1919*]

Dear Bunny:

Scribners has accepted my book for publication late in the winter. You'll call it sensational but it really is neither sentimental nor trashy.

I'll probably be East in November and I'll call you up or come to see you or something. Haven't had time to hit a story for you yet. Better not count on me as the w. of i. or the E.S. are rather dry.

Yrs. faithfully,

Francis S. Fitzgerald

Hotel Cecil
London, England

[*May, 1921*]

Dear Bunny:

Of course I'm wild with jealousy! Do you think you can indecently parade this obscene success [1] before my envious disposition, with *equanimity?* You are mistaken.

God damn the continent of Europe. It is of merely antiquarian interest. Rome is only a few years behind Tyre and Babylon. The negroid streak creeps northward to defile the Nordic race. Already the Italians have the souls of blackamoors. Raise the bars of immigration and permit only Scandinavians, Teutons, Anglo-Saxons and Celts to enter. France made me sick. Its silly pose as the thing the world has to save. I think it's a shame that England and America didn't let Germany conquer Europe. It's the only thing that would have saved the fleet of tottering old wrecks. My reactions were all philistine, antisocialistic, provincial and racially snobbish. I believe at last in the white man's burden. We are as far above the modern

---

[1] Wilson had published an essay on Mencken in *The New Republic,* and Mencken had praised it in a letter to Wilson.

Frenchman as he is above the Negro. Even in art! Italy
has no one. When Anatole France dies French literature
will be a silly jealous rehashing of technical quarrels.
They're thru and done. You may have spoken in jest
about New York as the capital of culture but in 25 years
it will be just as London is now. Culture follows money
and all the refinements of aestheticism can't stave off its
change of seat (Christ! what a metaphor). We will be the
Romans in the next generations as the English are now.

Alec sent me your article. I read it half a dozen times
and think it is magnificent. I can't tell you how I hate
you. I don't hate Don Stewart half as much (tho I find
that I am suddenly and curiously irritated by him) because I don't really dread him. But *you!* Keep out my
sight. I want no more of your articles!

Enclosed is 2 francs with which you will please find a
French slave to make me a typed copy of your letter from
Mencken. Send *here* at once, if it please you. I will destroy
it on reading it. Please! I'd do as much for you. I haven't
gotten hold of a *Bookman*.

Paradise is out here. Of 20 reviews about half are
mildly favorable, a quarter of them imply that I've read
"*Sinister Street*" once too often" and the other five (including *The Times*) damn it summarily as artificial. I doubt
if it sells 1500 copies.

Mencken's first series of *Prejudices* is attracting attention here. Wonderful review in *The Times*.

I'm delighted to hear about *The Undertaker*.[1] . . . Edna
has no doubt told you how we scoured Paris for you. Idiot!
The American Express mail department has my address.
Why didn't you register? We came back to Paris especially
to see you. Needless to say our idea of a year in Italy was
well shattered and we sail for America on the 9th and
thence to the "Sahara of Bozart" (Montgomery) for life.

With envious curses and hopes of an immediate response,

      F. Scott Fitzgerald—author of *Flappers and
      Philosophers* (juvenile)

---

[1] *The Undertaker's Garland,* prose and verse by Wilson and John Peale
Bishop.

626 Goodrich Avenue
St. Paul Minnesota

[*Postmarked November 25, 1921*]

Dear Bunny:

Thank you for your congratulations.[1] I'm glad the damn thing's over. Zelda came through without a scratch and I have awarded her the croix-de-guerre with palm. Speaking of France, the great general with the suggestive name is in town today.

I agree with you about Mencken—Weaver and Dell are both something awful. I like some of John's criticism but Christ! he is utterly dishonest. Why does he tell us how rotten he thinks *Mooncalf* is and then give it a "polite bow" in his column. Likewise he told me personally that my "book just missed being a great book" and how I was the most hopeful, etc., etc., and then damned me with faint praise in two papers six months before I'm published. I am sat with a condescending bow "halfway between the post of Compton Mackenzie and Booth Tarkington." So much for that!

I have almost completely rewritten my book.[2] Do you remember you told me that in my midnight symposium scene I had sort of set the stage for a play that never came off—in other words when they all began to talk none of them had anything important to say. I've interpolated some recent ideas of my own and (possibly) of others. See enclosure at end of letter.[3] Having disposed of myself, I turn to you. I am glad you and Ted Paramore are together. I was never crazy about the oboist nor the accepter of invitations and I imagine they must have been small consolation to live with. I like Ted immensely. He is a little too much the successful Eli to live comfortably in his mind's bed-chamber but I like him immensely.

What in hell does this mean? My control must have dictated it. His name is Mr. Ikki and he is an Alaskan orange-grower.

Nathan and me have become reconciled by letter. If

---

[1] On the birth of his daughter.
[2] *The Beautiful and Damned.*
[3] These enclosures included the greater part of Maury Noble's monologue in the chapter called "Symposium."

the baby is ugly she can retire into the shelter of her full name, Frances Scott.

I hear strange stories about you and your private life. Are they all true? What are you going to do? Free-lance? I'm delighted about *The Undertaker's Garland*. Why not have a preface by that famous undertaker in New York, say just a blurb on the cover? He might do it if he had a sense of humor.

St. Paul is dull as hell. Have written two good short stories and three cheap ones.

I like *Three Soldiers* immensely and reviewed it for the *St. Paul Daily News*. I am tired of modern novels and have just finished Paine's biography of Clemens. It's excellent. Do let me see it if you do me for *The Bookman*. Isn't *The Triumph of the Egg* a wonderful title? I liked both John's and Don's articles in *Smart Set*. I am lonesome for New York. May get there next fall and may go to England to live. Yours in this hell-hole of life and time, the world.

F. Scott Fitz

626 *Goodrich Avenue*
St. Paul, Minnesota

[*Postmarked January 24, 1922*]

Dear Bunny:

Farrar tells a man here that I'm to be in the March "Literary Spotlight." [1] I deduce that this is your doing. My curiosity is at fever heat—for God's sake send me a copy immediately.

Have you read Upton Sinclair's *The Brass Check?*

Have you seen Hergesheimer's movie *Tol'able David?*

Both are excellent. I have written two wonderful stories and get letters of praise from six editors with the addenda that "our readers, however, would be offended." Very discouraging. Also discouraging that Knopf has put off the *Garland* till fall. I enjoyed your da-daist article in *Vanity Fair*—also the free advertising Bishop gave us.

[1] A series of portraits of contemporary writers published in *The Bookman.*

Zelda says the picture of you is "beautiful and bloodless."

I am bored as hell out here. The baby is well—we dazzle her exquisite eyes with gold pieces in the hopes that she'll marry a millionaire. We'll be East for ten days early in March.

I have heard vague and unfathomable stories about your private life—not that you have become a pervert or any-thing—romantic stories. I wish to God you were not so reticent!

What are you doing? I was tremendously interested by all the data in your last letter. I am dying of a sort of emotional anemia like the lady in Pound's poem. *The Briary Bush* is stinko. *Cytherea* is Hergesheimer's best but it's not quite.

Yours,

John Grier Hibben[1]

626 Goodrich Avenue
St. Paul, Minnesota

[*January, 1922*]

Dear Bunny:

Needless to say I have never read anything with quite the uncanny fascination with which I read your article.[2] It is, of course, the only intelligible and intelligent thing of any length which has been written about me and my stuff —and like everything you write it seems to me pretty generally true. I am guilty of its every stricture and I take an extraordinary delight in its considered approbation. I don't see how I could possibly be offended at anything in it—on the contrary it pleases me more to be compared to "standards out of time," than to merely the usual scape-goats of contemporary criticism. Of course I'm going to carp at it a little but merely to conform to convention. I like it, I think it's an unprejudiced diagnosis and I am con-

---

[1] John Grier Hibben, then president of Princeton.
[2] This letter and the letter after it refer to Wilson's essay, "F. Scott Fitzgerald," in the March, 1922, *Bookman* (reprinted in Wilson's collec-tion, *The Shores of Light*).

siderably in your debt for the interest which impelled you to write it.

Now as to the liquor thing—it's true, but nevertheless I'm going to ask you take it out. It leaves a loophole through which I can be attacked and discredited by every moralist who reads the article. Wasn't it Bernard Shaw who said that you've either got to be conventional in your work or in your private life or get into trouble? Anyway the legend about my liquoring is terribly widespread and this thing would hurt me more than you could imagine— both in my contact with the people with whom I'm thrown —relatives and respectable friends—and, what is much more important, financially.

So I'm asking you to cut.

1. "when sober" on page one. I have indicated it. If you want to substitute "when not unduly celebrating" or some innuendo no more definite than that, all right.

2. From "This quotation indicates . . ." to ". . . sets down the facts" would be awfully bad for me. I'd much rather have you cut it or at least leave out the personal implication if you must indicate that my characters drink. As a matter of fact I have never written a line of any kind while I was under the glow of so much as a single cocktail and tho my parties have been many it's been their spectacularity rather than their frequency which has built up the usual "dope-fiend" story. Judge and Mrs. Sayre would be crazy! And they never miss *The Bookman*.

Now your three influences, St. Paul, Irish (incidentally, though it doesn't matter, I'm not Irish on Father's side— that's where Francis Scott Key comes in) and liquor are all important I grant. But I feel less hesitancy asking you to remove the liquor because your catalogue is not complete anyhow—the most enormous influence on me in the four and a half years since I met her has been the complete, fine and full-hearted selfishness and chill-mindedness of Zelda.

Both Zelda and I *roared* over the Anthony-Maury incident. You've improved mine (which was to have Muriel go blind) by 100%—we were utterly convulsed.

But Bunny, and this I hate to ask you, *please* take out the soldier incident. I am afraid of it. It will not only utterly spoil the effect of the incident in the book but will give rise to the most unpleasant series of events imaginable.

Ever since *Three Soldiers, The New York Times* has been itching for a chance to get at the critics of the war. If they got hold of this I would be assailed with the most violent vituperation in the press of the entire country (and you know what the press can do, how they can present an incident to make a man upholding an unpopular cause into the likeness of a monster—*vide* Upton Sinclair). And, by God, they would! Besides the incident is not correct. I didn't apologize. I told the Colonel about it very proudly. I wasn't sorry for months afterwards and then it was only a novelist's remorse.

So for *God's sake* cut that paragraph. I'd be wild if it appeared! And it would without doubt do me serious harm.

I note from the quotation from "Head and Shoulders" and from reference to "Bernice" that you have plowed through *Flappers* for which conscientious labor I thank you. When the strain has abated I will send you two exquisite stories in what Professor Lemuel Ozuk in his definitive biography will call my "second" or "neo-flapper" manner.

But one more carp before I close. Gloria and Anthony *are* representative. They are two of the great army of the rootless who float around New York. There must be thousands. Still, I didn't bring it out.

With these two cuts, Bunny, the article ought to be in my favor. At any rate I enjoyed it enormously and shall try to reciprocate in some way on *The Undertaker's Garland* though I doubt whether you'd trust it to my palsied hands for review. Don't change the Irish thing—it's much better as it is—besides the quotation hints at the whiskey motif.

Forever,

Benjamin Disraeli

I am consoled for asking you to cut the soldier and alcoholic paragraphs by the fact that if you *hadn't* known me you couldn't or wouldn't have put them in. They have a critical value but are really personal gossip.

I'm glad about the novelette in *Smart Set*. I am about to send them one. I am writing a comedy—or a burlesque or something. The "romantic stories" about you are none of my business. They will keep until I see you.

Hersesassery—*Quelque* mot!

How do you like echolalia for "meaningless chatter?"

Glad you like the title motto— Zelda sends best— Remember me to Ted.[1] Did he say I was "old woman with jewel?"

> *626 Goodrich Avenue*
> *St. Paul, Minnesota*
>
> *February 6, [1922]*

Dear Bunny:

I read your letter in a chastened mood. My whole point was that you read the book a long time ago in its informal condition, before its final revision and before your own criticisms had strained out some of the broken cork—that, therefore, while as a critic seeing the book for the first time you would, of course, have to speak the truth whether it hurt me financially or not, still that this case was somewhat different and that a pre-publication review which contained private information destined (in my opinion) to hurt the sale of my book was something of which I had a legitimate right to complain. My specification of "financial" injury is simply a private remark to you—it would be absurd for me to pretend to be indifferent to money, and very few men with a family they care for can be. Besides you know that in these two novels I have not suppressed anything with the idea of making money by the suppression but I think I am quite justified in asking you to suppress a detail of my private life—and it seems to me that a financial reason is as good as any, rather better in fact, according to Samuel Butler, than to spare my family.

I had forgotten, as a matter of fact, that those "Spotlight" things are supposed to be personal. Please don't think that I minded the Maury thing. I was simply congratulating you on inventing a more witty parody than I thought I had made. Still I was tight that night and may

---

[1] Ted Paramore. Actually it was Edna Millay who had said that to meet Fitzgerald was to think of a stupid old woman with whom someone had left a diamond (his talent), and Wilson had quoted the remark at the beginning of his *Bookman* essay.

have said it. The actual quotation from my first draft is quite correct—I didn't say it wasn't.

This is a quibbling letter and I hope it doesn't sound ill-natured. It isn't. I simply felt that your letter put me in a bad light and I hasten to explain my objections.

As a matter of fact I am immensely grateful to you for the article and tried to tell you so in my letter. Despite the fact that I am *not* quite insane about *What Maisie Knew* as you prophesied I would be I admire your judgments in almost every way more than those of anyone else I know, and I value your opinion on my stuff. In your first letter you said yourself that it was O.K. to object to the booze thing and your quarrel with me seems to be that I gave you a perfectly unaffected and honest answer when I told you I feared financial injury.

As you have a first edition of the book I won't send you another but will give it my invaluable autograph when I reach New York. I had intended that Perkins should send me the novel to autograph first.

I think it's too bad that you have gone to all this trouble over the article and I'm afraid I have put you to it. Anyway it's a complicated subject and I can excuse myself better when I see you sometime next month. But I feel quite sure that if Mencken in doing a "Literary Spotlight" on Dreiser had remarked in dead earnest that Dreiser's having four wives had had a considerable influence on his work, Dreiser would have raised a slight howl. And if he had remarked that Dreiser was really the hero of all the seductions mentioned in *The Titan* I think Dreiser would have torn his hair—and complained, at least, that he wanted to save such data for his privately printed editions.

As ever,

F. Scott Fitz-Hardy

626 Goodrich Avenue
St. Paul, Minnesota

[*Spring, 1922*]

Dear Bunny:

From your silence I deduce that either you decided that

the play[1] was not in shape to offer to the Guild or that they refused it.

I have now finished the revision. I am forwarding one copy to Harris and, if you think the Guild would be interested, will forward them the other. Your play should be well along by now. Could you manage to send me a carbon?

I'm working like a dog on some movies at present. I was sorry our meetings in New York were so fragmentary. My original plan was to contrive to have long discourses with you but that interminable party began and I couldn't seem to get sober enough to be able to tolerate being sober. In fact the whole trip was largely a failure.

My compliments to Mary Blair, Ted Paramore and whomsoever else of the elect may cross your path.

We have no plans for the summer.

                                        Scott Fitz——

F. SCOTT FITZGERALD
HACK WRITER AND PLAGIARIST
SAINT PAUL, MINNESOTA[2]

626 Goodrich Avenue
[Postmarked May 30, 1922]

Dear Bunny:

Your delightful letter, of which I hope you have kept a copy, arrived this A.M. and the Fitzgeralds perused it ferociously, commending especially your hope that ——— gets a good screw in France.

I am so discouraged about the play that it has cheered me to know it's still under consideration. I thought they'd burn it up.

I think you overestimate the play—tho Act I is a gem. Also I think you're wrong about the soldier scene. Zelda,

[1] *The Vegetable.*
[2] This was a printed letterhead.

George Nathan, Miller, Townsend and I think John all thought it should come out. Still I should not object to it being reinserted. Do you like my letterhead? I have jazzed up the millionaire scene in the revised version. I have not read *Ulysses* but I'm wild to—especially now that you mention some coincidence. Do you know where I can get it at any price? Sorry about your *Smart Set* novelette. . . .

I am enormously interested in your play. Send me a copy when you can.

I'd like to meet Dos Passos— God, this is a dull letter. I didn't read your *Double Dealer* poem tho I heard about it and it seems to have achieved fame. The magazine is unprocurable out here.

We're going to the country for the summer, but write me here *immediately*. I wish I could close in a rhapsody like yours but the fire is out for the night. Harris sent back the play to Reynolds without comment. If you can think of a title for it, jot it down and let me know.

Yield to your country complex. Zelda says how-de-do.

Ever thine,

F. Scott F_____

St. Paul, Minnesota

[*Postmarked June 4, 1922*]

Dear Bunny:

You will be looked up by Thomas A. Boyd, a very clever kid who conducts the best book page west of New York, in a newspaper here. I do not ask you to wine or dine him as I personally dislike people sent to me with letters. I do ask you to see him tho and give him half an hour or so of your valuable time. He's quite a friend of mine.

Scott Fitz_____

[*The Yacht Club*]
[*White Bear Lake, Minnesota*]
June 25, 1922

Dear Bunny:

Thank you for giving the play to Craven—and again for your interest in it in general. I'm afraid I think you overestimate it—because I have just been fixing up "Mr. Icky".[1] for my fall book and it does not seem very good to me. I am about to start a revision of the play—also to find a name. I'll send it to Hopkins next. So far it has only been to Miller, Harris and the Theatre Guild. I'd give anything if Craven would play that part. I wrote it, as the text says, with him in mind. I agree with you that *Anna Christie* was vastly overestimated. . . .

Am going to write another play whatever becomes of this one. *The Beautiful and Damned* has had a very satisfactory but not inspiring sale. We thought it'd go far beyond *Paradise* but it hasn't. It was a dire mistake to serialize it. *Three Soldiers* and *Cytherea* took the edge off it by the time it was published. . . .

Did you like "The Diamond as Big as the Ritz" or did you read it. It's in my new book anyhow.

What do you think of Rascoe's page? It's excellent, of course, compared to *The Times* or *Herald* but I think your criticism of his Frank-Harassment of his conversations hit the mark. There is something faintly repellent in his manner—in writing I mean. Who is this professionally quaint Kenhelm Digby? He is kittenish beyond credibility and I hate his guts. Is it Morley or Benét?

I have *Ulysses* from the Brick Row Bookshop and am starting it. I wish it was laid in America—there is something about middle-class Ireland that depresses me inordinately—I mean gives me a sort of hollow, cheerless pain. Half of my ancestors came from just such an Irish strata or perhaps a lower one. The book makes me feel appallingly naked. Expect to go either South or to New York in October for the winter.

Ever thine,

F. Scott Fitz

[1] Wilson had been telling him how funny he thought this burlesque, which first appeared in the *Smart Set* and was afterwards included in *Tales of the Jazz Age*.

The Yacht Club
White Bear Lake, Minnesota
[*Postmarked July 13, 1922*]

Dear Bunny:

Zelda and I have concocted a wonderful idea for Act II of the play. So when Craven returns it will you send it to me—or hold on to it, either one?

I read your article on *Ulysses,* the only criticism yet I could make head or tail of. Also your article on Byron in *the Tribune.* You are an incomparable egg and I wish I could see you. Life is damn dull.

In God's name,

F. Scott Fitzgerald

The Yacht Club
White Bear Lake, Minnesota
[*Postmarked August 1, 1922*]

Dear Bunny:

Just a line to tell you I've finished my play and am sending it to Nathan to give to Hopkins or Selwyn. It is now a wonder. I'm going to ask you to destroy the 2 copies you have as it makes me sort of nervous to have them out. This is silly but so long as a play is in an actor's office and is unpublished as my play at Craven's I feel lines from it will soon begin to appear on Broadway.

I want to thank you again for all you did for it and the time it took. I don't know anything that involves more labor than trying to place someone else's ms. I did it for _____ so I know and I am enormously obliged.

Write me any gossip if you have time. No news or plans have I.

Thine,

Fitz

[*The Yacht Club*]
[*White Bear Lake, Minnesota*]
[*Postmarked August 5, 1922*]

Dear Bunny:

Fitzgerald howled over "Quintilian."[1] He is glad it was
reprinted as he couldn't get the *Double Dealer* and feared
he had missed it. It's excellent especially the line about
Nero and the one about Dr. Bishop.

The play with an absolutely new second act has gone to
Nathan who is giving it to Hopkins or Selwyn. Your description of John leaving was fine. Zelda and I both enjoyed it with dramatic[?] and, what would have been
gratifying to you, awe. Thank you for taking it to Ames &
Elkins. I'm rather glad now that none of them took it as
I'd have been tempted to let them do it—and my new
version is much better. Please do not bother to return the
2 mss. you have as it's a lot of trouble. I have copies of
them and no use for them. Destruction will save the same
purpose—it only worries me to have them knocking
around.

I read sprigs of the old oak that grew from the marriage of Mencken and Margaret Anderson (Christ! What
a metaphor!) and is known as the younger genitals. It
bored me. I didn't read yours—but Rascoe is getting worse
than Frank Harris with his elaborate explanations and
whitewashings of himself. There's no easier way for a
clever writer to become a bore. It turns the gentle art of
making enemies into the East Aurora Craft of making
people indifferent . . . in the stunned pause that preceded
this epigram Fitzgerald bolted his aspic and went to a
sailor's den.

"See here," he said, "I want some new way of using the
great Conradian vitality, the legend that the sea exists without Polish eyes to see it. Masefield has spread it on iambics
and downed it; O'Neill has sprinkled it on Broadway; Mc-
Fee has added an Evenrude motor—"

But I could think of no new art form in which to fit
him. So I decided to end the letter. The little woman, my

---

[1] A nonsense poem of Wilson's published in the New Orleans *Double
Dealer*.

best pal and, I may add, my severest critic, asked to be remembered.[1]

Would you like to see the new play? Or are you fed up for awhile? Perhaps we better wait till it appears. I think I'll try to serialize it in *Scribner's*—would you?

Scott F.

Am undecided about *Ulysses* application to me—which is as near as I ever come to forming an impersonal judgment.

> *The Yacht Club*
> *White Bear Lake, Minnesota*
> [*Postmarked August 28, 1922*]

Dear Bunny:

The *Garland* arrived and I have re-read it. Your preface is perfect—my only regret is that it wasn't published when it was written almost two years ago. "The Soldier" of course I read for about the fifth time. I think it's about the best short war story yet—but I object violently to "pitched forward" in the lunch-putting anecdote. The man would have said "fell down" or "sorta sank down." Also I was delighted as usual by "The Efficiency Expert." Your poems I like less than your prose—"The Lake" I do not particularly care for. I like "The Centaur" and the "Epilogue" best—but all your poetry seems to flow from some source outside or before the romantic movement even when its intent is mostly lyrical.

I like all of John's except the play, which strikes me as being obvious, and "Resurrection" which despite its excellent idea and title and some spots of good writing is pale and without any particular vitality.

Due to you, I suppose, I had a wire from Langner. I referred him to George Nathan.

Many thanks for the book. Would you like me to re-

---

[1] In the margin beside this paragraph Fitzgerald had written, "Cribbed from Harry Leon Wilson."

view it? If so suggest a paper or magazine and I'll be glad
to.

Thine,

F. Scott Fitz

The format of the book is most attractive. I grow envious every time I see a Knopf binding.

*Villa Marie, Valescure
St. Raphael, France*

[*Postmarked October 7, 1924*]

Dear Bunny:

The above will tell you where we are, as you proclaim
yourself unable to find it on the map.[1] We enjoyed your
letter enormously, colossally, stupendously. It was epochal,
acrocryptical, categorical. I have begun life anew since
getting it and Zelda has gone into a nunnery on the
Peloponnesus. . . .

The news about the play is grand and the ballet too. I
gather from your letter that O'Neill and Mary had a great
success. But you are wrong about Ring's book.[2] My title
was the best possible. You are always wrong—but always
with the most correct possible reasons. (This statement is
merely acrocritical, hypothetical, diabolical, metaphori-
cal.) . . . .

You speak of _____ _____'s wife. I didn't see her—but
stay, there was a woman there—but what she said and did
and looked like I can not tell. Is she an elderly, gross
woman with hair growing in her ears and a red, porous
forehead? If so, I remember her. Or stay—there was a
rumor that he had married an Ethiop and took her to
bleach beside the fjord. . . .

I had a short curious note from the latter[3] yesterday,
calling me to account for my *Mercury story*.[4] At first I

---

[1] Fitzgerald had drawn a map of the French coast between Hyères and
Nice.
[2] Ring Lardner's *How to Write Short Stories.*
[3] A friend just mentioned in a sentence not printed here.
[4] "Absolution."

couldn't understand this communication after seven bless-
edly silent years—behold: he was a Catholic. I had broken
his heart.

This is a dumb letter but I have just been reading the advertisements of whore-houses in the French magazines. I
seethe with passion for a "bains-massage," with *volupté*
[for] oriental delights *(tout un)* in a Hotel Particular, or
else I long to go with a young man (intell., *bonne famille,
affectueux*) for a paid amorous weekend to the coast of
[illegible]. Deep calling to deep.

I will give you now the Fitz touch without which this
letter would fail to conform to your conception of my
character.

Sinclair Lewis sold his new novel to the *Designer* for
$50,000 (950,000.00 francs)—I never did like that fel-
low. (I do really.)

My book is wonderful,[1] so is the air and the sea. I have
got my health back—I no longer cough and itch and roll
from one side of the bed to the other all night and have a
hollow ache in my stomach after two cups of black coffee.
I really worked hard as hell last winter—but it was all
trash and it nearly broke my heart as well as my iron constitution.

Write to me of all data, gossip, event, accident, scandal,
sensation, deterioration, new reputation—and of yourself.

Our love,

Scott

14 rue de Tilsitt
Paris, France
[*Spring, 1925*]

Dear Bunny:

Thanks for your letter about the book.[2] I was awfully
happy that you liked it and that you approved of the design. The worst fault in it, I think is a BIG FAULT: I

[1] *The Great Gatsby.*
[2] *The Great Gatsby.*

gave no account (and had no feeling about or knowledge of) the emotional relations between Gatsby and Daisy from the time of their reunion to the catastrophe. However, the lack is so astutely concealed by the retrospect of Gatsby's past and by blankets of excellent prose that no one has noticed it—tho everyone has felt the lack and called it by another name. Mencken said (in a most enthusiastic letter received today) that the only fault was that the central story was trivial and a sort of anecdote (that is because he has forgotten his admiration for Conrad and adjusted himself to the sprawling novel) and I felt that what he really missed was the lack of any emotional backbone at the very height of it.

Without making any invidious comparisons between Class A and Class C, if my novel is an anecdote so is *The Brothers Karamazov*. From one angle the latter could be reduced into a detective story. However, the letters from you and Mencken have compensated me for the fact that of all the reviews, even the most enthusiastic, not one had the slightest idea what the book was about and for the even more depressing fact that it was, in comparison with the others, a financial failure (after I'd turned down fifteen thousand for the serial rights!). I wonder what Rosenfeld thought of it.

I looked up Hemingway. He is taking me to see Gertrude Stein tomorrow. This city is full of Americans—most of them former friends—whom we spend most of our time dodging, not because we don't want to see them but because Zelda's only just well and I've got to work; and they seem to be incapable of any sort of conversation not composed of semi-malicious gossip about New York courtesy celebrities. I've gotten to like France. We've taken a swell apartment until January. I'm filled with disgust for Americans in general after two weeks' sight of the ones in Paris—these preposterous, pushing women and girls who assume that you have any personal interest in them, who have all (so they say) read James Joyce and who simply adore Mencken. I suppose we're no worse than anyone, only contact with other races brings out all our worst qualities. If I had anything to do with creating the manners of the contemporary American girl I certainly made a botch of the job.

I'd love to see you. God. I could give you some laughs.

There's no news except that Zelda and I think we're pretty good, as usual, only more so.

                                                    Scott

Thanks again for your cheering letter.

                                        Ellerslie
                                        Edgemoor, Delaware
                                        [*February, 1928*]

Dear Bunny: . . . .

All is prepared for February 25th. The stomach pumps are polished and set out in rows, stale old enthusiasms are being burnished with that zeal peculiar only to the British Tommy. My God, how we felt when the long slaughter of Passchendaele had begun. Why were the Generals all so old? Why were the Fabian society discriminated against when positions on the general staff went to Dukes and sons of profiteers? Agitators were actually hooted at in Hyde Park and Anglican divines actually didn't become humanitarian internationalists overnight. What is Britain coming to—where is Milton, Cromwell, Oates, Monk? Where are Shaftesbury, Athelstane, Thomas à Becket, Margot Asquith, Iris March? Where are Blackstone, Touchstone, Clapham-Hopewellton, Stoke-Poges? Somewhere back at G.H.Q. handsome men with grey whiskers murmured, "We will charge them with the cavalry," and meanwhile boys from Bovril and the black country sat shivering in the lagoons at Ypres writing memoirs for liberal novels about the war. What about the tanks? Why did not Douglas Haig or Sir John French (the big smarties—look what they did to General Mercer) invent tanks the day the war broke out, like Sir Phillip Gibbs, the weeping baronet, did or would, had he thought of it?

This is just a *sample* of what you will get on the 25th of February. There will be small but select company, coals, blankets, "something for the inner man."

Please don't say you can't come the 25th but would like to come the 29th. We never receive people the 29th.

It is the anniversary of the 2nd Council of Nicea when our Blessed Lord, our Blessed Lord, our Blessed Lord, our Blessed Lord—

It always gets stuck in that place. Put on "Old Man River" or something of Louis Bromfield's.

Pray gravity to move your bowels. It's little we get done for us in this world. Answer.

Scott

Enjoyed your Wilson article *enormously*. Not so Thompson affair.[1]

c/o Guaranty Trust
4 Place de la Concorde
Paris, [*France*]

[*Summer, 1930*]

Dear Bunny:

Congratulations on your marriage and all real hopes for your happiness. We heard, through Mary, long after the event of your collapse[2] and the thought that you'd survived it helped me through some despairing moments in Zelda's case. She is now almost "well," which is to say the psychosis element is gone. We must live quietly for a year now and to some extent forever. She almost went permanently crazy—four hours' work a day at the ballet for two years, and she 27 and too old when she began. I'm relieved that the ballet was over anyhow as our domestic life was cracking under the strain and I hadn't touched my novel for a year. She was drunk with music that seemed a crazy opiate to her and her whole cerebal tradition was something locked in such an absolutely impregnable safe inside her that it was months after the break before the doctors could reach her at all. We hope to get home for Christmas.

I have seen no one for months save John in Paris . . . . the brief spell of work I nagged him into during Margaret's pregnancy has now given way to interminable talk

---

[1] An article by W. G. Thompson, counsel for Sacco and Vanzetti, which appeared in the *Atlantic Monthly* of February, 1928.

[2] Fitzgerald refers to Wilson's having had a nervous breakdown.

about a well on their property. . . . Also a man named Thomas Wolfe, a fine man and a fine writer. Paris swarms with fairies and I've grown to loathe it and prefer the hospital-like air of Switzerland where nuts are nuts and coughs are coughs. Met your friend Allen Tate, liked him. . . .

Salute the new Mrs. Wilson for me. . . . and remember you're never long absent from the solicitudes of

Your old friend,

Scott

It was nice of you, and like you, to write Zelda.

La Paix (My God!)
Towson, Maryland

[*Probably March, 1933*]

Dear Bunny:

Your letter with the head of Vladimir Ulianov[1] just received. Please come here the night of the inauguration and stay at least the next day. I want to know with what resignation you look forward to your role of Lunacharsky and whether you decided you had nothing further worth saying in prose fiction or whether there was nothing further to say. Perhaps I should draw the answer to the last question from *Axel's Castle* yet I remember stories of yours that anticipated so much that was later said that it seemed a pity. (Not that I don't admire your recent stuff—particularly I liked "Hull House.")

We had a most unfortunate meeting. I came to New York to get drunk and swinish and I shouldn't have looked up you and Ernest in such a humor of impotent desperation. I assume full responsibility for all unpleasantness—with Ernest I seem to have reached a state where when we drink together I half bait, half truckle to him; and as for bringing up the butcher boy matter—my God! making trouble between friends is the last thing I had ever thought

---

[1] A stamp with Lenin's head which Wilson had put on his letter to Fitzgerald.

myself capable of. Anyhow, plenty of egotism for the moment.

Dos was here, and we had a nice evening—we never quite understand each other and perhaps that's the best basis for an enduring friendship. Alec came up to see me at the Plaza the day I left (still in awful shape but not conspicuously so). He told me to my amazement that you had explained the fundamentals of Leninism, even Marxism, the night before, and Dos tells me that it was only recently made plain thru the same agency to *The New Republic*. I little thought when I left politics to you and your gang in 1920 you would devote your time to cutting up Wilson's shroud into blinders! Back to Mallarmé.

—Which reminds me that T. S. Eliot and I had an afternoon and evening together last week. I read him some of his poems and he seemed to think they were pretty good. I liked him fine. . . .

However, come in March. Don't know what time the inauguration takes place but you find out and tell us the approximate time of your arrival here. Find out *in advance* for we may go to it too and we might all get lost in the shuffle.

> Always your friend,
>
> Scott

P.S. Please not a word to Zelda about anything I may have done or said in New York. She can stand literally nothing of that nature. I'm on the water-wagon but there'll be lots of liquor for you.

> *1307 Park Avenue*
> *Baltimore, Maryland*
> [*Postmarked March 12, 1934*]

Dear Bunny:

Despite your intention of mild criticism[1] in our conversation, I felt more elated than otherwise—if the char-

1 Of *Tender Is the Night.*

acters got real enough so that you disagreed with what I chose for their manifest destiny the main purpose was accomplished. (By the way, your notion that Dick should have faded out as a shyster alienist was in my original design, but I thought of him, in reconsideration, as an "homme épuisé," not only an "homme manqué." I thought that, since his choice of a profession had accidentally wrecked him, he might plausibly have walked out on the profession itself.)

Any attempt by an author to explain away a partial failure in a work is of course doomed to absurdity—yet I could wish that you, and others, had read the book version rather than the magazine version which in spots was hastily put together. The last half for example has a *much* more polished facade now. Oddly enough several people have felt that the surface of the first chapters was *too* ornate. One man even advised me to "coarsen the texture," as being remote from the speed of the main narrative!

In any case when it appears I hope you'll find time to look it over again. Such irrelevancies as Morton Hoyt's nose-dive and Dick's affair in Innsbruck are out, together with the scene of calling on the retired bootlegger at Beaulieu, and innumerable minor details. I have driven the Scribner proofreaders half nuts but I think I've made it incomparably smoother.

Zelda's pictures go on display in a few weeks and I'll be meeting her in N.Y. for a day at least. Wouldn't it be a good time for a reunion?

It was good seeing you and good to think that our squabble, or whatever it was, is ironed out.

With affection always,

Scott Fitzgerald

1307 Park Avenue
Baltimore, Maryland
September 7, 1934

Dear Bunny:

I've had a big reaction from your last two articles in *The*

New Republic.[1] In spite of the fact that we always approach material in different ways there is some fast-guessing quality that, for me, links us now in the work of the intellect. Always the overtone and the understatement.

It was fun when we all believed the same things. It was more fun to think that we were all going to die together or live together, and none of us anticipated this great loneliness, where one has dedicated his remnants to imaginative fiction and another his slowly dissolving trunk to the Human Idea. Nevertheless the stress that you put upon this in your *New Republic* article—of forces never still, of rivers never ending, of clouds shifting their prophecies at evening, afternoon or morning—this sense of things has kept our courses loosely parallel, even when our references to data has been so disparate as to throw us miles apart.

The purport of this letter is to agree passionately with an idea that you put forth in a discussion of Michelet: that conditions irretrievably change men and that what looks purple in a blue light looks, in another spectrum, like green and white bouncing snow. I want you to know that one among many readers is absolutely alert to the implications and substrata of meaning in this new work.

> Ever affectionately yours,
>
> Scott

> *5521 Amestoy Avenue*
> *Encino, California*
> *May 16, 1939*

Dear Bunny:

News that you and Mary had a baby reached me rather late because I was out of California for several months. Hope he is now strong and crawling. Tell him if he grows up any bigger I shall be prepared to take him for a loop when he reaches the age of twenty-one at which time I shall be sixty-three. I don't know any girl in the last sev-

---

[1] On Michelet.

eral years with more charm than Mary. It was a delight to
meet her and spend an evening with you all. If I had
known about the news in time, I would have wired you.

I called up Louise Fort in San Diego, but couldn't get
her number and imagine she had left before I came back
to California. However, I am sending on your letter to Ted
Paramore who may have more luck.

Believe me, Bunny, it meant more to me than it could
possibly have meant to you to see you that evening. It
seemed to renew old times learning about Franz Kafka and
latter things that are going on in the world of poetry, because I am still the ignoramus that you and John Bishop
wrote about at Princeton. Though my idea is now, to
learn about a new life from Louis B. Mayer who promises
to teach me all about things if he ever gets around to it.

                    Ever your devoted friend,

                    Scott

                    1403 North Laurel Avenue
                    Hollywood, California
                    October 21, 1940

Dear Bunny:

I am deep into the *Finland Station* and I break off to
write you that some of the reviews especially *The New
Yorker* and *New Republic* made me sick. . . .

I suppose they wanted you to produce a volume on the
order of John Strachey, and they had a few labels prepared
with which to quarantine you. Why otherwise they should
quarrel with your historical approach is inexplicable to me.

It is a magnificent book—just as it promised to be in
The New Republic. My very best to you both and to the
young one.

                    Ever,

                    [Scott]

P.S. Am somewhere in a novel.

*1403 North Laurel Avenue
Hollywood, California*

November 25, 1940

Dear Bunny: . . . .

Two years after it was published I ran across an article by John Bishop in the *Virginia Quarterly*. His war story about Ernest under the corpses is pure crap. Also he says that I flunked out of Princeton, though in the year referred to I went to my last class November 28th, when it is somewhat unusual to flunk out. Also he reproached me with being a suck around the rich. I've had this before but nobody seems able to name these rich. I always thought my progress was in the other direction—Tommy Hitchcock and the two Murphys are not a long list of rich friends for one who, unlike John, grew up among nothing else but. I don't even *know* any of the people in "café society." It seems strange from John. I did more than anyone in Paris to help him finish his Civil War book and get it published. It can't be jealousy for there isn't much to be jealous of any more. . . .

I think my novel is good. I've written it with difficulty. It is completely upstream in mood and will get a certain amount of abuse but is first hand and I am trying a little harder than I ever have to be exact and honest emotionally. I honestly hoped somebody else would write it but nobody seems to be going to.

With best to you both,

[Scott]

P.S. This sounds like such a bitter letter—I'd rewrite it except for a horrible paucity of time. Not even time to be bitter.

PART SIX

Letters to
John Peale Bishop

626 Goodrich Avenue
[St. Paul, Minnesota]

[Late February or early March, 1922]

Dear John:

I'll tell you frankly what I'd rather you'd do. Tell specifically what you like about the book[1] and don't. The
characters—Anthony, Gloria, Adam Patch, Maury, Bloeck-
man, Muriel Dick, Rachael, Tana, etc., etc., etc.—exactly
whether they're good or bad, convincing or not. What you
think of the style—too ornate (if so quote) good (also
quote) rotten (also quote). What emotion (if any) the
book gave you. What you think of its humor. What you
think of its ideas. If ideas are bogus hold them up specifically and laugh at them. Is it boring or interesting? How interesting? What recent American books are more so? If
you think my "Flash-Back in Paradise" in Chapter I is like
elevated moments of D. W. Griffith say so. Also do you
think it's imitative, and of whom? What I'm angling for is
a specific definite review. I'm tickled both that they've asked
for such a lengthy thing and that you're going to do it [it].
You cannot hurt my feelings about the book—tho I did resent in your Baltimore article being definitely limited at 25
years old to a place between Mackenzie who wrote 2½
good (but not wonderful) novels and then died—and
Tarkington who if he has a great talent has the mind of a
school boy. I mean, at my age they'd done nothing.

As I say I'm delighted that you're going to do it and, as
you wrote asking me to suggest a general mode of attack,
I am telling you frankly what I would like. I'm so afraid
of all the reviews being general and I devoted so much

---

[1] *The Beautiful and Damned.*

more care myself to the *detail* of the book than I did to thinking out the *general* scheme that I would appreciate a detailed review. If it is to be that length article it could scarcely be all general anyway.

I'm awfully sorry you've had the flu. We arrive East on the 9th. I enjoy your book page in *Vanity Fair* and think it is excellent.

The baby is beautiful.

As ever,

Scott

[*Capri, Italy*]

[*March, 1925*]

Dear John:

I am quite drunk. I am told that this is Capri; though as I remember Capri was quieter.[1] As the literary wits might say, your letter received and contents quoted. Let us have more of the same—I think it showed a great deal of power and the last scene—the dinner at the young Bishops—was handled with admirable restraint. I am glad that at last Americans are producing letters of their own. The climax was wonderful and the exquisite irony of the "Sincerely yours" has only been equaled in the work of those two masters Flaubert and Ferber. . . .

I will now have two copies of Wescott's *Apple* as in despair I ordered one—a regular orchard. I shall give one to Brooks here whom I like. Do you know Brooks? He's just a fellow here . . .

Excuse the delay. I have just been working on the envelope . . .

That was a caller. His name was Mussolini, I think, and he says he is in politics here. And besides I have lost my pen so I will have to continue in pencil . . .[2] It turned up—

---

[1] This was written above the date.
[2] This sentence was written in pencil. The rest of the letter is in ink.

I was writing with it all the time and hadn't noticed. That is because I am full of my new work, a historical play based on the life of Woodrow Wilson.

Act I. *At Princeton*

Woodrow seen teaching philosophy. Enter Pyne. Quarrel scene—Wilson refuses to recognize clubs. Enter woman with Bastard from Trenton. Pyne re-enters with glee club and trustees. Noise outside. "We have won—Princeton 12, Lafayette 3." Cheers. Football team enter and group around Wilson. "Old Nassau." Curtain.

Act II. *Gubernatorial Mansion at Paterson*

Wilson seen signing papers. Tasker Bliss and Marc Connelly come in with proposition to let bosses get control. "I have important papers to sign—and none of them legalize corruption." Triangle Club begins to sing outside window. Enter woman with Bastard from Trenton. President continues to sign papers. Enter Mrs. Galt, John Grier Hibben, Al Jolson and Grantland Rice. Song "The Call to Larger Duty." Tableau. Coughdrop.

Act III (optional). *The Battlefront 1918.*

Act IV

The peace congress. Clemenceau, Wilson and Jolson at table. The Bastard from Trenton now grown up but still a baby, in the uniform of the Prussian Guard, is mewling and pewking in Wilson's lap. . . . The junior prom committee comes in through the skylight. Clemenceau: "We want the Sarre." Wilson: "No, Sarre, I won't hear of it." Laughter . . . Enter Marilyn Miller, Gilbert Seldes and Irish Meusel. Tasker Bliss falls into the cupsidor . . .

Oh Christ! I'm sobering up! Write me the opinion you may be pleased to form of my *chef d'oeuvre* and others' opinion. *Please!* I think it's great but because it deals with much debauched materials, quick deciders like Rascoe may mistake it for Chambers. To me it's fascinating. I never get tired of it. . . .

Zelda's been sick in bed for five weeks, poor child, and is only now looking up. No news except I now get $2000 a story and they grow worse and worse and my ambition is to get where I need write no more but only novels. Is Lewis' book any good? I imagine that mine is infinitely better—what else is well reviewed this spring? Maybe my book[1] is rotten but I don't think so.

What are you writing? Please tell me something about your novel. And if I like the idea maybe I'll make it into a short story for the *Post* to appear just before your novel and steal the thunder. Who's going to do it? Bebe Daniels? She's a wow!

How was Townsend's first picture? Good reviews? What's Alec doing? And Ludlow? And Bunny? Did you read Ernest Boyd's account of what I might ironically call our "private" life in his *Portraits?* Did you like it? I rather did.

Scott

I am quite drunk again and enclose a postage stamp.

c/o American Express Company
Rome, Italy
[April, 1925]

Dear John:

Your letter was perfect. It told us everything we wanted to know and the same day I read your article (very nice too) in *Vanity Fair* about cherching the past. But you disappointed me with the quality of some of it (the news)— for instance that Bunny's play failed, that Townsend has got the swelled head and that you and Margaret find life dull and depressing there. We want to come back but we want to come back with money saved and so far we haven't saved any—tho I'm one novel ahead and book of pretty good (seven) short stories. I've done about 10 pieces of horrible junk in the last year tho that I can never republish or bear to look at—cheap and without the spon-

---

[1] *The Great Gatsby.*

taneity of my first work. But the novel I'm sure of. It's marvelous.

We're just back from Capri where I sat up (tell Bunny) half the night talking to my old idol Compton Mackenzie. Perhaps you met him. I found him cordial, attractive and pleasantly mundane. You get no sense from him that [he] feels his work has gone to pieces. He's not pompous about his present output. I think he's just tired. The war wrecked him as it did Wells and many of that generation.

To show how well you guessed the gossip I wanted, we were wondering where _____ got the money for Havana, whether the Film Guild finally collapsed. (Christ! You should have seen their last two pictures—one from my story.) But I don't doubt that _____ and _____ will talk themselves into the Cabinet eventually. I'd do it myself if I could but I'm too much of an egotist and not enough of a diplomat ever to succeed in the movies. You must begin by placing the tongue flat against the posteriors of such worthys as _____ _____ and _____ _____ and commence a slow caressing movement. Say what they may of Cruze—Famous Players is the product of two great ideas, DeMille and Gloria Swanson, and it stands or falls not [on] their "conference methods" but on those two and the stock pictures that imitate them. The Cruze winnings are usually lost on such expensive experiments as _____ _____. (Needless to say this letter is not for T.M. or Alec, but for your ears alone.)

Is Dos Passos' novel any good? And what's become of Cummings' work? I haven't read *Some Do Not* but Zelda was crazy about [it]. I glanced through it and kept wondering why it was written backward. At first I thought they'd sewn the cover on upside down. Well—these people *will* collaborate with Conrad.

Do you still think Dos Passos is a genius? My faith in him is somehow weakened. There's so little time for faith these days.

_____ _____ is a damned attractive woman and, while the husband's a haberdasher, he's at least a Groton haberdasher (he went there, I mean, to school). . . .

The Westcott book will be eagerly devoured. A personable young man of that name from Atlantic introduced himself to me after the failure of *The Vegetable*. I wonder if he's the same. At any rate your Wescott, so

Harrison Rhodes tells me, is coming here to Rome.

I've given up Nathan's books. I liked the fourth series of *Prejudices*. Is Lewis' new book good? Hergesheimer's was awful. He's all done.

Merrit Hemingway—I have a dim memory that he and I admired Ginevra King at the same time once in those palmy days.

The cheerfulest things in my life are first Zelda and second the hope that my book has something extraordinary about it. I want to be extravagantly admired again. Zelda and I sometimes indulge in terrible four-day rows that always start with a drinking party but we're still enormously in love and about the only truly happily married people I know.

Our very best to Margaret.

Please write!
Scott

In the Villa d'Este at Tivoli all that ran in my brain was:

> An alley of dark cypresses
>   Hides an enrondured pool of light
> And there the young musicians come
>   With instruments for her delight
> ....locks are bowed
>   Over dim lutes that sigh aloud
> Or else with heads thrown back they tease
>   Reverberate *ec*hoes from the drum
> The stiff folds *etc.*

It was wonderful that when you wrote that you'd never seen Italy—or, by God, now that I think of it, never lived in the 15th century.

But then I wrote *T.S. of P.* without ever having been to Oxford.

14 rue de Tilsitt
Paris, France
[*August 9, 1925*]

Dear John:

Thank you for your most pleasant, full, discerning and

The novel is just something you've learned from and profited by. It has occasional spurts—like the conversations frequently of Brakespeare, but it is terribly tepid—I refrain—rather I don't refrain but here set down certain facts which you are undoubtedly quite as aware of as I am.

1. Pp. 1–28. Elaborate preparation. Baby born *without a scene*. Only announcement. Monsignor feeble. A Catholic bishop does not rank above monsignor—his ambition to be a bishop is as incomprehensible as the idea of a staff captain to have a company.

2. You have now all but lost the reader. He will not face the mass of detail 28 et sequitur. Italian theme strained—your ignorance of the Catholic Church fascinates me. Did you ever meet Mrs. Winthrop Chanler? Madden good idea but observed thinly.

Your combination of leaning on a great thing for your color and simultaneously trying to patronize it—!

At end something happens—child cries—feeble—has no significance except the strained one of making the reader think—"Well, after all *that* climb it must mean more than I think it does!"

P. 48 Et sequitur.

First really fine page—my novel has same idea (shorter) about an English whore. However when this sixth *Who's Who* commences all interest finally vanishes. No life is that dull. Did you ever see those midwestern books of the eighties-nineties, *Our Pioneers*, or *Mid-Western Military Men—A Compilation?* Even lists of dates, with their suggestion, are more alive.

(I'm taking you for a beating, but do you remember your letters to me about *Gatsby?* I suffered, but I got something—like I did out of your friendly tutelage in English poetry.)

You ought never to use an unfamiliar word unless *you've had to* search for it to express a delicate shade—where in effect you have recreated it. This is a damn good prose rule I think. *Cf. andrognous (sic)*, etc. Exceptions: (a) need to avoid repetition (b) need of rhythm, etc. (c) etc.

P. 62. Story interest again begins.

P.71. Gone again. Reader's effort, like writer's, was too much.

P.79, etc. (Incidentally in this novel you have (a) sug-

gestion that Gettysburg was fought before Chancellorsville
(b) that retreat from Gettysburg and from Antietam was
in same campaign (c) that Colonels were often locally
elected in southern armies—which contrast sharply with
your profound knowledge of the Civil War in story.)

A big person can make a much bigger mess than a little
person and your impressive stature converted a lot of
pottery into pebbles during the three years or so you were
in the works. Luckily the pottery was never very dear to
you. Novels are not written, or at least begun, with the
idea of making an ultimate philosophical system—you tried
to atone for your lack of confidence by a lack of humility
before the form.

The main thing is: no one in our language possibly excepting Wilder has your talent for "the world," your culture and acuteness of social criticism as implied in the
story. There the approach (second and third person, etc.)
is considered, full scope in choice of subject for your
special talents (descriptive power, sense of *le pays,* ramifi-
cations of your special virtues such as loyalty, conceal-
ment of the sensuality, that is your *bête noire* to such an
extent that you can no longer see it black, like me my
drunkenness).

Anyhow it's (the story) marvelous. Don't be mad at this
letter. I have the horrors tonight and perhaps am taking it
out on you. Write me when I could see you here in Paris
in the afternoon between 2:30 and 6:30 and talk—and
name a day and a café at your convenience—I have no
dates save on Sunday so any day will suit me. Meanwhile
I'll make one more stab at your novel to see if I can think
of any way by a miracle of cutting it could be made pre-
sentable. But I fear there's neither honor nor money in it
for you.

> Your old and always affectionate friend,
>
> Scott

Excuse Christ-like tone of letter. Began tippling at page
2 and am now positively holy (like Dostoevski's non-
stinking monk).

Grand Hotel de la Paix
Lausanne

April, 1931

Dear John:

Read *Many Thousands* over again (the second time) and like it *enormously*. I think it hangs together as a book too. I like the first story—I think it's damn good. I'd never read it before. "Death and Young Desire" doesn't come off—as for instance the handling of the same theme in *The Story of St. Michele*. Why I don't know. My favorite is "The Cellar"—I am still fascinated by the Conradian missing man—that's real fiction. "Bones" seems even better in the respect-inspiring light thrown by Bunny's opinion. I'm taking it to Zelda tomorrow.

Ever your friend,

Scott

1307 Park Avenue
Baltimore, Maryland

April 2, 1934

Dear John:

Somebody (I've forgotten who after an overcrowded and hectic twenty-four hours in New York) quoted you to me as saying that this current work[1] is "no advance on what he's done before." That's a legitimate criticism, but I can't take it as a slam. I keep thinking of Conrad's *Nigger of the Narcissus* preface—and I believe that the important thing about a work of fiction is that the essential reaction shall be profound and enduring. And if the ending of this one is not effectual I should be gladder to think that the effect came back long afterwards, long after one had forgotten the name of the author.

All this makes it more necessary to see you and do some doping on the practice of the novel while you're in process of revision. I'll be up in New York toward the

[1] *Tender Is the Night.*

beginning of next week. Will you keep that in mind and if your plans change suddenly let me know?

Pleasant thoughts to you all.

As ever,

Scott

Two things I forgot to say—

1. There's a deliberate choice in my avoidance of a dramatic ending—I deliberately did not want it.

2. Without making apologies, I'd prefer to *fade off* my book, like the last of *The Brothers Karamazov,* or *Time Regained,* and let the belly carry my story, than to resort [to] the arbitrary blood-letting of Flaubert, Stendahl and the Elizabethans.

You see we must talk—no room in a letter.

1307 Park Avenue
Baltimore, Maryland
April 7, 1934

Dear John:

On receiving your first letter with its handsome tribute and generous praise I realized that I had been hasty in crediting that you would make such a criticism as "this book is no advance on *Gatsby*." You would be the first to feel that the intention in the two books was entirely different, that (to promote myself momentarily) *Gatsby* was shooting at something like *Henry Esmond* while this was shooting at something like *Vanity Fair*. The dramatic novel has canons quite different from the philosophical, now called psychological, novel. One is a kind of *tour de force* and the other a confession of faith. It would be like comparing a sonnet sequence with an epic.

The point of my letter which survives is that there were moments all through the book where I could have pointed up dramatic scenes, and I *deliberately* refrained from doing so because the material itself was so harrowing and highly charged that I did not want to subject the reader to a series of nervous shocks in a novel that was inevitably close to whoever read it in my generation.

Contrariwise, in dealing with figures as remote as are a bootlegger and crook to most of us, I was not afraid of heightening and melodramatizing any scenes; and I was thinking that in your novel I would like to pass on this theory to you for what it is worth. Such advice from fellow-craftsmen has been a great help to me in the past, indeed I believe it was Ernest Hemingway who developed to me, in conversation, that the dying fall was preferable to the dramatic ending under certain conditions, and I think we both got the germ of the idea from Conrad.

With affection always,

Scott

1307 Park Avenue
Baltimore, Maryland
January 30, 1935

Dear John:

Your book[1] had an extraordinary effect on me. Let me be frank to say that I took it up with some misgivings due to the fact that I felt that you had decided to deal with somewhat drab material, and that to make it colorful you might be inclined to lean over into melodrama—but more of that later. From the first I got completely under the spell of the exquisite prose, the descriptions of the Shenandoah country, and as one by one the characters began to unfold, the whole scene became tense and exciting. I think the way that you built up the character of Marston on the foundation of old Mason was fine—contrary to Ernest's dictum as to synthetic characters not being plausible.

Charlie emerges as an almost heroic figure early in the book, your young narrator is sympathetic but suffers insomuch as he partakes of the vague artist-as-a-young-man quality that distinguishes our time from the Werther-Byron-Stendahl character of a hundred years ago.

Virginia is the least achieved character to me. There

---

[1] Bishop's novel, *Act of Darkness.*

are the fine passages describing her bedroom hysteria after the event, but, because it was never clear in your own mind exactly how she was, the courtroom scene in which she appeared did not hang fire with the intensity of similar scenes in *High Wind in Jamaica* or *An American Tragedy* or *Sanctuary*.

Your minor characters were fine, the comic aunt, the nigger pansy, the decayed Job's counselor (female), the ghost of the poetic judge—all in all, the book is packed full of beauty and wisdom and richness of perception. I read through the first half in one night and was so excited that I had to call up somebody (it turned out to be Elizabeth Lemmon) to tell them how much I liked it, how good it was, and how *delighted I* was that it was good!

Yet when I finished the book there was a certain sense of unfulfillment and now I am going to permit myself to play papa for a moment.

When your heart was in poetry your inclination was to regard prose fiction as merely a stop-gap, a necessary nuisance. Time showed you the error of that early evaluation and it cost you a pretty penny in years. There are things in this book which are still typical of one who cannot light his way around and who has got to, for these are the years for you during which the best ammunition has to be fired off. Let me list, not too categorically, what I consider the faults of execution in the opus:

First, conscientiously you must try to cut all traces of other people out of yourself. If you were twenty-one it wouldn't matter; it was all right for Tom Wolfe in *Look Homeward, Angel* to make one chapter practically a parody of a chapter in *Ulysses*. It was forgivable for me to have done an equivalent thing half a dozen times in *This Side of Paradise,* but for anybody over forty to do it *is simply not in the picture of one who has to make himself a personality*.

Vide: Page 148, Frank Norris, speaking of Kipling, said, "the little colonial, to whose pipe we must all dance"—but by that general admission of the tremendous power of certain stylists he announced that he, for one, would fight shy of any effect that he might gain by using their rhythms to cradle his ideas or to fill gaps with reminiscent echolalia. Several times I saw patterns in this book which derived background and drama from Faulkner, or cadence from Hemingway, and each time you might have produced something much stronger by having more of a conscience, by fighting against that tendency, cutting out the passage no matter how satisfactory it may have been in itself, and building up the structure with something that *is* yourself. In any case, that has been my experience, and I pass it on to you for what it's worth.

Let's call that the first point— There are only two. The second is purely a matter of structure. You once wrote me about Conrad's ability to build his characters into such a reality, commonplace reality, that any melodrama that afterwards occurred would be palatable. The first half of your book is so heavy with stimuli and promises, that the later catastrophe of the rape is minimized—both in itself and in its consequences. Charlie's whole wild day should have been telescoped and much cut, insofar as the intervening episodes are concerned, such as the bathers hearing the shots. The title should not have given away so much of the plot. You had put out so many leads by that time that the reader was practically expecting the World War, and the actual fact that Charlie violated a spinster is anticlimactical as is her ensuing denunciation of him. When you plant a scene in a book the importance of the scene cannot be taken as a measure of the space it should occupy, for it is entirely a special and particular artistic problem. If Dreiser, in *The American Tragedy,* plans to linger over the drowning in upper New York well and good, but I could tell you plenty [of] books in which the main episode, around which swings the entire drama, is over and accomplished in four or five sentences.

There is, after all, a third point. I think the book is a little too rough. The insistence on sex-in-the-raw occupies more space than the phenomenon usually does in life. Insofar as this is the story of a boy's awakening to the world of passion, it is justified, but when you launch yourself into an account of the brutal fate that haunts us the balance is not what it should be. Much of the testimony in the trial seemed to be *arbitrarily* introduced from Krafft-Ebing.

Now as a peroration let me congratulate you again. It is beautifully made, beautifully written and *one* of your three characters emerges as a creation. I liked Charlie, and would like to have met him, and he will stay with me when most of the fictional history of many years is forgotten. I congratulate you with all my heart.

> With best to you both,

> Scott

P.S. Aside from the fun of the above strictures it gives me great pleasure to tell you that the word "demean" does *not* mean "debase." The phrase "to demean" means only "to conduct one's self" and does not imply that the conduct is either good or bad. It is a common error. Other quibbles: On the jacket the Shenandoah Valley is placed in tidewater Virginia and the story in the 90s. When did people roll around so casually in cars in the late 90s? It seems to me that you would be justified in asking Max to correct these errors in further printings.

> *Grove Park Inn*
> *Asheville, North Carolina*
>
> [*May, 1935*]

Dear John:

Here's a letter of uncalled-for advice. I think though it's good. All right—into the lion's mouth.

Act of Darkness must be written off. It was a good novel—*it had high points* (I'm coming back to that), it showed that your long phase of being self-conscious in prose is over. You've got ten good years—two or three fine novels left. Now, here's my inventory.

From the wildest fantasy (which you did not and could not handle through lack of readiness and incisiveness of wit, profuseness of it, and through other reasons like Hergesheimeric tendency to take it easy doing still-lives) you went (and I was all for it) to the most complete realism, taking in passing the Civil War. The part taken in passing came closest to being your natural field. *You jumped over it too quickly*—I don't mean the war in particular—I mean the blend. *Because you're two people* —you are not yet your work as in a sense I am mine.

You are

a. a person of conventional background and conduct with tendency almost to drabness, non-resistance, uxoriousness, bourgeois-respectable, etc., etc., etc., etc.

b. a poet with sense of wonder and color of life expressed in men, women, and words; and grand gestures, grand *faits accomplis,* parades.

1. *Setting.* I should use a sensational set, probably costume set using some such character as the Lost Dauphin—I mean it—*not a fulfilled Renaissance character or you'll just make a picture book.* Something enormous, gross, obvious, untouched by *fine* hands. Some *great* stone the sculptors have rejected. Your background had better shimmer, not be static or peaceful.

2. *Plot.* Advice on this is no good. You handle it well but I advise a change of pace—I find so many good enough books are in the same key, i.e., *Appointment in Samarra.* Life is not so smooth that it can't go over suddenly into melodrama. That's the other face of much worry about inevitability. Everything's too beautifully caused—one can guess ahead. Even the movies know this and condemn a story as "too straight." My own best solution to date is the to-and-fro, keep-facts-back mystery stuff, but it's difficult. Of course it's the Dickens-Dostoevski thing. *Act of Darkness* was much too straight, and tempo too even. Only a very short piece wants complete tempo, *one breath, Ethan Frome.* It's short story technique. Even *Pride and Prejudice* walks and runs like life.

3. Try and find more "bright" characters; if the women are plain make them millionairesses or nymphomaniacs, if they're scrubwomen, give them hot sex attraction and charm. This is such a good trick I don't see why it's not more used—I always use it just as I like to balance a beautiful word with a barbed one.

There is tremendous comedy inherent in your relations with Hurlock and Feustman. You can do more with minor characters—your perverted Negroes, etc., are good enough but you're rich with stuff. You dredge yourself with difficulty.

I'd like to see some gaiety in your next book to help sell it. Can't you find some somewhere?

Anyhow all this care for shimmering set, active plot, bright characters, change of pace and gaiety should *all show in the plan.* Leave *out* any two, and your novel is weaker, any three or four and you're running a department store with only half the counters open.

All this is a presumption. Max Perkins told me the book hadn't gone and while I know it had a good press and the season was bad still I do worry about you and would hate to see you either discouraged or apathetic about your future as a novelist.

Best to your huge clan.

Scott

P.S. Address as on envelope till about June 25th.
Haven't had a drink this year—not even wine or beer—are you surprised?

PART SEVEN

Letters to
Shane Leslie

Ft. Leavenworth, Kansas
December 22, 1917

My dear Mr. Leslie:

Your letter followed me here— My novel isn't a novel in verse. It merely shifts rapidly from verse to prose but it's mostly in prose.

The reason I've abandoned my idea of a book of poems is that I've only about twenty poems and can't write any more in this atmosphere—while I can write prose, so I'm sandwiching the poems between reams of autobiography and fiction. It makes a potpourri, especially as there are pages in dialogue and in *vers libre*, but it reads as logically for the times as most public utterances of the prim and prominent. It is a tremendously conceited affair. The title page looks (will look) like this:

THE ROMANTIC EGOTIST

by

F. SCOTT FITZGERALD

"The Best is over.
You may remember now and think and sigh
Oh silly lover!"
—Rupert Brooke

"Ou me coucha banga loupa
Domalumba guna duma . . ."
—Gilbert Chesterton

"Experience is the name Tubby gives to all
his mistakes."
—Oscar Wilde

I'll send you a chapter or two to look over if you would. I'd like it a lot if you would. I'm enclosing you a poem that *Poet Lore* a magazine of verse has just taken.

Yours,

F. Scott Fitzgerald
2nd Lt., U.S., Co. Q

Ft. Leavenworth, Kansas
February 4, 1918

Dear Mr. Leslie:

This is just a note to inform you that the first draft of *The Romantic Egotist* will be ready for your inspection in three weeks altho I'm sending you a chapter called "The Devil" next week.

Think of a romantic egotist writing about himself in a cold barracks on Sunday afternoons . . . yet that is the way this novel has been scattered into shape—for it has no form to speak of.

Dr. Fay told me to send my picture that he wants through you. Whether he meant for you to forward it to him or put it away until he returns I didn't comprehend.

I certainly appreciate your taking an interest in my book . . . By the way I join my regiment, the 45th Infantry, at Camp Taylor, Kentucky, in three weeks.

Faithfully,

F. Scott Fitzgerald

[Ft. Leavenworth, Kansas]
[Early February, 1918]

Dear Mr. Leslie:

Here's Chapter XVI "The Devil" and Chapter XIII. I picked it out as a chapter you could read without knowing the story. I wish you'd look it over and see what you think of it. It's semi-typical of the novel in its hastiness and scrubby style.

I have a week's leave before joining my regiment and I'm going up to Princeton to rewrite. Now I can pass thru Washington and see you about this novel either on the seventh or eighth or ninth of February. Will you tell me which of these days you'd be liable to have an afternoon off? Any one of them [is] convenient as far as I'm concerned. I could bring you half a dozen chapters to look at and I'd like to know whether you think it would have any chance with Scribner.

The novel begins nowhere as most things do and ends with the war as all things do. Chapter XIII will seem incoherent out of its setting. Well—I leave here Monday the 26th. After that my address will be Cottage Club—Princeton, N.J.

I'd be much obliged if you'd let me know which afternoon would be most convenient for you.

Faithfully,

F. Scott Fitzgerald

Did you ever notice that remarkable coincidence? Bernard Shaw is 61 years old, H. G. Wells is 51, G. K. Chesterton 41, you're 31, and I'm 21—all the great authors of the world in arithmetical progression.

45th Infantry
Camp Gordon, Georgia
May 8, 1918

Dear Mr. Leslie:

Your letter filled me with a variety of literary emotions . . . you see, yours is the first pronouncement of any kind that I've received upon my first born . . .

That it is crude, incredibly dull in places is too true to be pleasant . . . I have no idea why I hashed in all that monotonous drivel about childhood in the first part and would see it hacked out like an errant appendix without a murmur . . . There are too many characters and too much local social system in the Princeton section . . . and in all places all through, the verses are too obviously lugged in . . .

At any rate I'm tremendously obliged [to you] for taking an interest in it and writing that awfully decent letter to Scribner . . . If he thinks that a revision would make it at all practicable I'd rather do it than not, or if he despairs of it I might try some less conservative publisher than Scribner is known to be . . .

We have no news except that we're probably going inside of two months and, officers and men, we're wild to go . . .

I wonder if you're working on the history of Martin Luther or are on another tack . . . Do write a novel with young men in it, and kill the rancid taste that the semi-brilliant *Changing Winds*[1] left on so many tongues. Or write a thinly disguised autobiography . . . or something. I'm wild for books and none are forthcoming . . . I wrote mine (as Stevenson wrote *Treasure Island*) to satisfy my own craving for a certain type of novel. Why are all the truish novels written by the gloomy half-twilight realists like Beresford and Walpole and St. John Ervine? Even the *Soul of a Bishop* is colorless . . . Where are the novels of five years ago: *Tono Bungay, Youth's Encounter, Man Alive, The New Machiavelli?* Heavens, has the war caught all literature in the crossed nets of Galsworthy and George Moore?

Well . . . May St. Robert (Benson) appear to Scribner in a dream . . .

Faithfully,

F. Scott Fitzgerald

P.S. Much obliged for mailing on Dr. Fay's letter.

---

[1] A novel by St. John Ervine.

17th Infantry, Brig. Headquarters
Camp Sheridan, Alabama

January 13, [1919]

Dear Mr. Leslie:

I can't tell you how I feel about Monsignor Fay's death— He was the best friend I had in the world and last night he seemed so close and so *good* that I was almost glad—because I think he wanted to die. Deep under it all he had a fear of that blending of the two worlds, that sudden change of values that sometimes happened to him and put a vague unhappiness into the stray corners of his life.

> But selfishly dam sorry. Never more
> "will we drink with the sunlight for lamp
> Myself and the dead"

I know how you feel too and Stephen Parrott and Mrs. Leslie and Mrs. Chanler and Father Hemmick and Delbos and O'Kelly and Sanderson and the fifty people that must somehow have felt a great security in him. He was such a *secure* man: one *knows* that he is happy now— Oh God! I can't write—

I just wanted to talk to someone who knew him as I knew him.

Sincerely,

F. Scott Fitzgerald

American Red Cross Base Hospital
Camp Sheridan, Alabama

[Late January, 1919]

Dear Mr. Leslie:

Your letter seemed to start a new flow of sorrows in me. I've never wanted so much to die in my life. Father Fay always thought that if one of us died the other would, and now how I've hoped so.

Oh, it all seemed so easy—life, I mean, with people

who understood and satisfied needs. Even the philistines seemed very good and quiet, always ready to be duped or influenced or something, and now my little world made to order has been shattered by the death of one man.

I'm beginning to have a horror of *people:* I can quite sympathize with your desire to be a Carthusian.

This has made me nearly sure that I will become a priest. I feel as if in a way his mantle has descended upon me—a desire, or more, to some day recreate the atmosphere of him. I think he was the sort of man St. Peter was, so damned human.

Think of the number of people who in a way looked to him and depended on him. His faith shining thru all the versatility and intellect.

I think I did feel him but I can't tell you of it in a letter.[1] It was rather ghastly.

I'm coming to New York in February or March to write or something. I'll come and see you then.

If there's anything about him in any magazine I wish you'd send them.

I've been here in the hospital with influenza.

As ever,

F. Scott Fitzgerald

Westport, Connecticut
August 6, 1920

Dear Mr. Leslie:

Your letter came today and I hasten to assure you that you were one of the half dozen chosen to whom I sent autographed first editions. I am sorry as the deuce, not to say humiliated, that it never reached you as you were my first literary sponsor, godfather to this book, and my original intention was to dedicate it to both of you.[2] I sent it to your New York address as I'd lost your letter from Ireland.

[1] Fitzgerald thought he had seen Monsignor Fay's ghost the day of his death.
[2] *This Side of Paradise* was dedicated to Monsignor Fay.

I am married and living rustically in Connecticut—working on a second novel. I married the Rosalind of the novel, the southern girl I was so attached to, after a grand reconciliation.

The book has sold 30,000 copies here and will be published immediately in England and Australia.

I apologize for the spelling of Dr. Fay's name; also—did you notice—for an almost excerpt from one of your letters with an account of the funeral. I didn't see it myself and had to describe it. I credited you with it in the copy I sent you.

I have written numerous short stories to be published by Scribners this fall, under the title of *Flappers and Philosophers*. I am living royally off the moving picture rights of these same stories.

I will certainly send you a first edition of my new book which includes that story "Benediction," since published in the *Smart Set*—and next time I'm in New York I'll send you the 7th edition of *This Side of Paradise* just to show you I'm not like republics ungrateful, and that the correction in Dr. Fay's name has been corrected.

Stephen Parrott was staying with us last week and we talked much of both you and Dr. Fay. I certainly made use of his letters and the poem in the book but I'm sure he would fully approve, don't you?

When are [*you*] coming to America?

Sincerely,

F. Scott Fitzgerald

P.S. My best regards to Mrs. Leslie.

The Catholic papers here seem to think my book was a subtle attack on the American clergy. I can't think why! I'm sure the most sympathetic character in it was Monsignor Darcy.

Westport, Connecticut
September 17, 1920

Dear Mr. Leslie:

The book is appearing in England next spring. William

Collins Sons & Co. are bringing it out. Did I tell you? I sent a tracer after the book I sent you last spring and today I forwarded an 8th edition of *Paradise* and a first of my new one, *Flappers and Philosophers,* a collection of short stories. I am now working on my second novel—much more objective this time and hence much harder sledding. But the bourgeoisie are going to stare!

The three letters and the poem of Dr. Fay's possibly should not have followed the dedication but I really don't think he'd have minded. I was married quite liturgically and canonically—I mean only the latter, tho, for it took place in the rectory of St. Patrick's Cathedral.

We are coming abroad in January and will certainly come and have a long talk with you. "Rosalind" was tremendously impressed with "10, Talbot Square, Hyde Park, London, England." And I would like to see Fr. Hemmick again. How I'll watch for that review in the *Dublin Review!*

I liked Tom Kettle's poem but I really don't think it's extraordinary. I'm trying to get hold of his book.

I'm taking your advice and writing very slowly and paying much attention to form. Sometimes I think that this new novel has nothing much else but form.

There's no use concealing the fact that my reaction a year ago last June to apparent failure in every direction did carry me rather away from the church. My ideas now are in such wild riot that I would flatter myself did I claim even the clarity of agnosticism. If you knew the absolute dirth of Catholic intelligentsia in this country! One Catholic magazine, *America,* had only one prim comment on my book—"a fair example of our non-Catholic college's output." My Lord! Compared to the average Georgetown alumnus Amory is an uncanonized saint. I think I laundered myself shiny in the book!

Faithfully,

F. Scott Fitzgerald

38 West 59th Street
New York City
November 16, 1920

Dear Mr. Leslie:

Thanks for the article. It seems a pity that something even more exhaustive can't be written about Dr. Fay. He always told me to save his letters and some day we'd all publish them anonymously in some form. I found, however, that he'd written me less than he thought so the three letters that occur in the book are largely pieced together and even considerably added to from memories of remarks he'd made to me plus even a few things I thought he might have said.

The entire funeral description you quoted was culled from your letter except that "he would have enjoyed his own funeral" and "making all religion a thing of lights and shadows, etc." I apologize most humbly. I think the influences of your style on me are traceable in various other portions of the book.

I met Fr. Hemmick in the Biltmore and he looked at me as tho he saw the horns already sprouting. Do you know that the story "Benediction" that I sent you and that also received the imprimatur of the most intelligent priest I know has come in for the most terrible lashing from the American Catholic intelligentsia? It's too much for me. It seems that an Englishman like Benson can write anything but an American had better have his works either pious tracts for nuns or else disassociate them from the church as a living issue.

I am coming to see you when we cross this winter.

Yours ever,

F. Scott Fitzgerald

Paris, France
May 24, 1921

Dear Mr. Leslie:

Just a word to thank you for your courtesies to us. I

think Zelda enjoyed her trip through Wapping more than anything that's happened so far.

We had dinner with Galsworthy the night before we left and I was rather disappointed in him. I can't stand pessimism with neither irony nor bitterness. Incidentally, I tried all over London to get you *The Mysterious Stranger* by Twain but evidently it's not published in England. I am almost through with *Manning*[1] and intend to review him in *The Bookman*.

France is a bore and a disappointment, chiefly, I imagine, because we know no one here. Italy on Wednesday.

Faithfully,

F. Scott Fitzgerald

[1] Leslie's biography of Cardinal Manning.

PART EIGHT

Letters to Christian Gauss

Edgemoor, Delaware
Ellerslie

February 1, 1928

Dear Dean Gauss:

This is in elaboration of my excited telegram. As it happened I left Princeton in company with two different types and in both cases I worked the discussion around to the honor system. The freshman, a football man with whom I rode to the Junction, told me specifically (for I didn't ask for opinions) that his roommate knew of two cases of absolute violations during tests, one man twice and another once, and "didn't know whether to report it or not." He had known for some months. In other words the honor system no longer included his personal honor but seemed opposed to it.

I rode from the Junction to Phila with the president of a very prominent club, not my own, a Princetonian of the rather old-line, conservative, very gentlemanly type. He said he'd often participated in discussions as to whether he would report a case—and his conclusion was he didn't know. But he knew of cases where violations had *not* been reported. The implication was that these were many. The utter stupidity of the business on the part of the undergraduates is what excited and depressed me to the extent of wiring you. I wanted to come back and see you but there was a whole house party here at home.

Now it seems to me that if one complete generation goes through with this attitude, that is if next year there is no class which hasn't felt it as part of them, the chain is eternally broken and something has gone out of the life and pride of every Princeton man. But I can't believe it could happen surreptitiously. What is behind it? I heard some talk about the "spirit of the honor system" and an implication that it was being stretched too far, to cover themes, etc. If this has been done then I can understand it and the people who stretched it have, I believe, been in grave error. For after all it was a bargain, as all honor is until it becomes a tradition, and if it applied to themes what does the undergraduate get out of it? The other way he gets freedom from supervision, but themes were never written under supervision. As delicate a thing as the honor system is not at anyone's willful and arbitrary control.

Don't you think that, if that is so, it means that it should be *redefined in its original and simplest form?* Then perhaps an appeal might be made all at once, in the *Prince,* student council, by alumni (my occasionally eloquent pen is at your service) to show them the utterly perverted stupidity of what they are doing?

I feel helpless and ignorant. Please enlighten me.

Always yours cordially and admiringly,

Scott Fitz———

P.S. I'm so sorry you were let in for my "speech" the other night. It was my first and last public appearance and the awful part of it was that I really did have something to say.

La Paix, Rodgers' Forge
Towson, Maryland
February 2, 1933

Dear Dean Gauss:

I had no special reason for calling you beyond that of friendship. I was up there for a couple of days because Gregg Dougherty was checking over some chemistry data I had in a story. I observed the disappearance of the rah-rah boy and thought Princeton in sweaters was quite becoming to itself. If this depression wasn't so terrible it wouldn't be so bad at all.

I am still at the novel and hope to God it can be finished this spring as I am very tired of being Mr. Lorimer's little boy year after year, though I don't know what I'd do without him.

Will certainly call on you when I next come to Princeton. With best regards to Mrs. Gauss and your beautiful red-headed progeny, I am, as always,

Your friend,

F. Scott Fitzgerald

1307 Park Avenue
Baltimore, Maryland
April 23, 1934

Dear Mr. Gauss:

Your full and generous letter reached me just before I went off on a three-day vacation. I cannot tell you how it pleased me.[1] There comes a time when a writer writes only for certain people and where the opinion of the others is of little less than no importance at all and you are one of the people for whom I, subconsciously, write. From the time that you put in a good word for my first book, then bound for Scribners, I have appreciated your opinion and advice. I remember the one thing you said against *The Great Gatsby* in Paris some seven years ago when we saw something of each other with Ernest Hemingway; the fact that I had over-used the expression of "windows blooming with light" has stuck with me to the present day, and I think had a large and valuable influence in some of my problems.

I wish to God I could join you and Bunny on your junket but I am simply swamped by the hangover of the book and with domestic affairs so I don't think I will see Princeton before June, and, believe me, I regret it very much because there is much more that I want to talk to you about than literature.

Scribners writes that they are sending me your book which I think I have read almost entire in its scattered form

---

[1] Gauss had written to congratulate Fitzgerald on *Tender Is the Night*.

but which I will pursue again with deep pleasure.

With best regards to Mrs. Gauss and admiration for your beautiful red-headed progeny, I am

> Ever yours,
>
> (even in red crayon,
> the only thing available)
> Scott Fitzg_____

> 1307 Park Avenue
> Baltimore, Maryland
> September 7, 1934

Dear Dean Gauss:

This is a wild idea of mine, conditioned by the fact that my physician thinks I am in a solitary rut and that I ought to have outside interests. Well, outside interests generally mean for me women, liquor or some form of exhibitionism. The third seems to be most practical at the present moment, wherefore I would like to give a series of lectures at Princeton, say eight, on the actual business of creating fiction. There would be no charge and I would consider it a favor if I were allowed to do this in a University lecture hall. (Incidentally, to safeguard you from my elaborate reputation, I would pledge my word to do no drinking in Princeton save what might be served at your table if you should provide me with luncheon before one of these attempts.)

The lectures I've not planned but they would be, in general, the history of say:

1. What Constitutes the Creative Temperament.
2. What Creative Material Is.
3. Its Organization.
And so forth and so on.

This would be absolutely first-hand stuff and there might be a barrier to crash in regard to the English Department, and if you don't think this is the time to do it don't hesitate to let me know frankly. So many bogus characters have shown up in Princeton trying to preach what they have never been able to practice, that I think even if I reach only half a dozen incipient talents the thing might be worthwhile from the scholastic point of view, and will be selfishly worthwhile to me—I would like to time these lectures so that they would come on the afternoon or eve of athletic events that I would like to see.

You will know best how to sound out the powers-that-be in the English Department. I have a hunch that Gerould rather likes me and I like Root whether he likes me or not. . . .

This is an arrow in the dark. I feel I never knew so much about my stuff as I now know, about the technique concerned, and I can't think of anywhere I would like to disseminate this egotistic feeling more than at Princeton.

This all might come to something, you know!

Hope you had a fine summer abroad. With my respects to Mrs. Gauss.

                                                    Ever yours,

                                                    F. Scott Fitzg

P.S. Naturally, after my wretched performance at the Cottage Club you might be cynical about my ability to handle an audience, but my suggestion is that the first lecture should be announced as a single, and *if* there is further demand we could go from thence to thither.

                                        1307 Park Avenue
                                        Baltimore, Maryland
                                        September 26, 1934

Dear Dean Gauss:

I know about "The Club" and they asked me last year to come and lecture. What I have against that is that it is sponsored by undergraduates which detracts from speaking under the authoritative aegis of the University, and second, because my plan was a series of lectures and not one that I could develop in a single evening. Also they were meant to be pretty serious stuff, that is, written out rather than spoken from notes, straight lectures rather than preceptorials. However, if the powers-that-be feel it inadvisable I can only yield the point and postpone the idea until a more favorable year.

Glad you enjoyed your rest abroad and escaped Miriam Hopkins' jumping out of the second-story window onto your shoulders. But I suppose you've been kidded to death about that already and I know you took it with your usual sense of humor.

Best wishes always,

F. Scott Fitzgerald

Hotel Stafford
Baltimore, Maryland
September 30, 1935

Dear Dean Gauss:

This is an imposition coming at the very beginning of the term when I know you are busy, so if you can grant this favor please do it at your leisure. As you know my daughter was brought up in France and I have conscientiously labored to keep her bilingual. This is now reduced to fortnightly conversations with a French woman and to supplement this I wanted some work in grammar— I mean advanced grammar. She is rather widely read in French (Hugo, Dumas, Molière. etc., and the classic poets) and I'd like to have for her some junior and senior French examination papers which I can have administered to her here. Is it within your power to have a sheaf of old ones dug up for me, or can you tell me where I can find some?

This is an odd request coming from such a wretched linguistic scholar as I was.

With best wishes to you always and with high hopes of seeing you sometime this fall,

Ever yours,

Scott Fitzg

PART NINE

Letters to
Harold Ober

*599 Summit Avenue
St. Paul, Minnesota*

January 8, [1920]

Dear Mr. Ober:

You could have knocked me over with a feather when you told me you had sold "Myra"—I never was so heartily sick of a story before I finished it as I was of that one.[1]

Enclosed is a new version of "Barbara," called "Bernice Bobs Her Hair" to distinguish it from Mary Rinehart's "Bab" stories in the *Post*. I think I've managed to inject a snappy climax into it. Now this story went to several magazines this summer—*Scribner's, Woman's Home Companion* and the *Post*—but it was in an entirely different, *absolutely unrecognizable* form, *single-spaced* and none of 'em kept it more than three days except *Scribner's*, who wrote a personal letter on it.

Is there any money in collections of short stories?

This *Post* money comes in very handy—my idea is to go South—probably New Orleans—and write my second novel. Now my novels, at least my first one, are not like my short stories at all, they are rather cynical and pessimistic—and therefore I doubt if as a whole they'd stand much chance of being published serially in any of the uplift magazines at least until my first novel and those *Post* stories appear and I get some sort of a reputation.

Now I published three incidents of my first novel in *Smart Set* last summer and my idea in the new one is to sell such parts as might go as units separately to different magazines, as I write them, because it'll take ten weeks to write it and I don't want to run out of money. There will be

---

[1] "Myra Meets His Family," *The Saturday Evening Post*, March 20, 1920.

one long thing which might make a novelette for the *Post* called *The Diary of a Popular Girl,* half a dozen cynical incidents that might do for *Smart Set* and perhaps a story or two for *Scribner's* or *Harper's.* How about it—do you think this is a wise plan—or do you think a story like C. G. Norris' *Salt* or Cabell's *Jurgen* or Dreiser's *Jennie Gerhardt* would have one chance in a million to be sold serially? I'm asking you for an opinion about this beforehand because it will have an influence on my plans.

Hoping to hear from you I am

Sincerely,

F. Scott Fitzgerald

P.S. The excellent story I told you of probably won't be along for two or three weeks. I'm stuck in the middle of it.

Salies de Béarn
God knows where

[*Received March 15, 1926*]

Dear Ober:

This is one of the lousiest stories I've ever written.[1] Just *terrible!* I lost interest in the middle (by the way the last part is typed triple-space because I thought I could fix it—but I couldn't).

Please—and I mean this—don't offer it to the *Post.* I think that as things are now it would be *wretched* policy. Nor to the *Redbook.* It hasn't *one redeeming touch* of my usual spirit in it. I was desperate to begin a story and invented a business plot— the kind I can't handle. I'd rather have $1000 for it from some obscure place than twice that and have it seen. *I feel very strongly about this!*

Am writing two of the best stories I've ever done in my life.

As ever,

Scott Fitz——

[1] "Your Way and Mine," *The Woman's Home Companion,* May, 1927.

Villa St. Louis
Juan-les-Pins
Alpes Maritime
France
[*Received June 3, 1926*]

Dear Ober:

Well, it's rather melancholy to hear that the run was over.[1] However as it was something of a *succès d'estime* and put in my pocket seventeen or eighteen thousand without a stroke of work on my part I should be, and am, well content.

A thousand thanks for your courtesy to my father. You went out of your way to be nice to him and he wrote me a most pleased and enthusiastic letter. He misses me, I think, and at his age such an outing as that was an exceptional pleasure. I am, as usual, deeply in your debt, and now for a most pleasant and personal reason. His own life after a rather brilliant start back in the seventies has been a "failure"—he's lived always in mother's shadow and he takes an immense vicarious pleasure in any success of mine. Thank you.

Yours always,

Scott Fitzgerald

No stories sent since "Your Way and Mine."

10 rue Pergolèse
Paris, France
[*Received November 16, 1929*]

Dear Harold:

Sorry this has been so delayed. I had another called "The Barnaby Family" that I worked on to the point of madness and may yet finish, but simply lost interest. The en-

---

[1] The Broadway production of *Gatsby* which Ober had gone to with Fitzgerald's father.

closed (I mean to say separate package) is heavy but, I think, good. Is it too heavy?

Now to answer questions, etc.

(1) As to Hemingway. You (I speak of you personally, not the old firm) made a mistake not to help sell his stuff personally 2 years ago—if any success was more clearly prognosticated I don't know it. I told him the present situation and I know from several remarks of his that he thought at first he was being approached by the same agents as mine—but he is being fought over a lot now and is confused and I think the wisest thing is to do nothing at present. If any offer for moving pictures of his books for $20,000 or more came to you however don't hesitate to wire him as he's not satisfied with present picture offers. Simply wire him Garritus—he knows quite well who you are, etc. *Please* don't in any correspondence with him use my name—you see my relations with him are entirely friendly and not business and he'd merely lose confidence in me if he felt he was being hemmed in by any coalition. My guess is, and I'm not sure, that he is pretty much deferring definite action for the present on stories and serials but this may not be true by the time this reaches you and may not be at this moment.

(2) I note cable formula and will save $25 or $50 a year thereby.

(3) *Post* stories all available here—don't send *Post*.

(4) *World* offer seems small ($300). Will answer refusing it politely myself.

(5) Of new authors this Richard Douglass[1] author of *The Innocent Voyage* (called *High Wind in Bermuda*) in England is much the best bet but a lot of editors may have thought of that. Maybe not though! Will try to keep you informed at the same time I usually do Scribners of anybody new I hear of as, if he interests me, I like to give him a chance for a hearing; but there's nobody now—but may write about that later! America will from now on give about one-half its book-buying ear to *serious* people or at any rate to people who have a backing from the sophisticated minority.

(6) *New Yorker* offers O.K. but uninteresting—as for

---

[1] Fitzgerald must have meant Richard Hughes, author of *High Wind in Jamaica*.

Mrs. _____ _____¹ (whoever she is) I will gladly modify my style and subject matter for her but she will have to give me her beautiful body first and I dare say the price is too high.

(7) Did *McCall's* like the article "Girls Believe in Girls?"

(8) Now I have two uninterrupted months on the novel and will do my best. There is no question of my not trying for the serial right and never has been.

(9) About *The Woman's Home Companion,* you know.

Yours ever in Masonry and Concubinage,

Scott Fitzg

> 4 rue Herran
> Paris, France
> [*Received May 13, 1930*]

Dear Harold:

First, I will be mailing a new story about the 25th. Glad you liked "A Nice Quiet Place." Did you ask about the corrected proof of "First Blood?" (Addenda of letter covers this.)—I do so want to have it. Glad you put up a kick about the illustrations—they were awful, with all the youthful suggestion of a G.A.R. congress.

Thanks for the statements. I'm about where I feared I was.

Zelda was delighted with your compliments about "The Millionaire's Girl."

Now—about the novel²—the other night I read one great hunk of it to John Peale Bishop, and we both agreed that it would be ruinous to let *Liberty* start it uncompleted. Here's a hypothetical possibility. Suppose (as may happen in such cases) they didn't like the end and we quarreled about it—then what the hell! I'd have lost the *Post,* gained an enemy in *Liberty*—who would we turn to—Ray Long? Suppose *Liberty* didn't like even the first part and went

---

¹ A *New Yorker* editor.
² Which Fitzgerald had been working on since *The Great Gatsby.*

around saying it was rotten before it was even finished. I want to be in New York if possible when they accept it for there's that element of cutting, never yet discussed—are they going to cut it? Are they going to cut my stories to 5000 words or not? Are they going to pay $3500 or $4000? At one time I was about to send four chapters out of eight done to you. Then I cut one of those chapters absolutely to pieces. I know you're losing faith in me and Max too but God knows one has to rely in the end on one's own judgment. I could have published four lousy, half-baked books in the last five years and people would have thought I was at least a worthy young man not drinking myself to pieces in the south seas—but I'd be dead as Michael Arlen, Bromfield, Tom Boyd, Callaghan and the others who think they can trick the world with the hurried and the second-rate. These *Post* stories *in* the *Post* are at least not any spot on me—they're honest and if their *form* is stereotyped people know what to expect when they pick up the *Post*. The novel is another thing—if, after four years, I published the Basil Lee stories as a book I might as well get tickets for Hollywood immediately.

Well, that's how things are. If you'll have confidence in me I think you'll shortly see I knew what I was doing.

Ever yours,

Scott Fitz——

This letter sounds cross but I'm stupid-got with work today and too tired to rewrite it. Please forgive it—it has to get tomorrow's boat.

Addenda

Zelda's been sick—not dangerously but seriously—and then I got involved in a wedding party and after 2 weeks just got to work on new story yesterday but 3000 words already done—about as many as I must owe you dollars.

Meanwhile I acknowledge:

(1) The account
(2) News about *The Beautiful and D*——
(3) Costain's suggestion (incidentally he can go to hell). The only way I can write a decent story is to imagine no one's going to accept it and who cares. Self-consciousness

about editors is *ruinous* to me. They can make their criticisms afterwards. I'm not going to do another Josephine thing until I can get that out my head. I tore up the beginning of one. You might tell him pleasantly, of course, that I just can't work that way. Still there's no use telling him—the harm's done but if he has any other ideas about writing stories please don't tell me.

(4) I'm sorry the proof's destroyed on "First Blood." Could you get me a copy of the magazine it's in—I've lost mine. I want to fix it while I remember. By the way I don't mind not having [proofs of] my own stories [sent me] when I'm here—but when I've worked on a proof it's like losing a whole draft of a thing.

Yours always,

Scott

Last Word

I understand the movies are buying short stories again. Do you know a good agent in Hollywood you might persuade to interest himself in "Majesty?" It's constructed dramatically like a play and has some damn good dramatic scenes in it.

1307 Park Avenue
Baltimore, Maryland
December 8, 1934

Dear Harold:

After rereading your letter there were some things I felt hadn't been sufficiently answered. The first is that I have a deep suspicion that you and Max got together at some point and decided I needed disciplining. Now I know of my fondness for you both and assume that it is reciprocated and I know also that when one man is in debt to another he is rather helpless in such matters. Nevertheless, the assumption that all my troubles are due to drink is a little too easy. Gliding over my domestic difficulties and my self-indulgence on that score and not deciding which one has caused the trouble—whether the hen preceded the egg or the egg preceded the hen—I want to get down to a few facts: a compact "apologia pro sua vita" after all the horrors in Montgomery and the winter of '30 and '31, the return of Zelda's trouble, attacked by the family, etc. (and you will find that this coincides almost exactly with my remissness in getting out mss. on specification). It became apparent to me that my literary reputation, except with the *Post* readers, was at its very lowest ebb. I was completely forgotten and this fact was rubbed in by Zelda's inadvertently written book. From that time on until early this spring my chief absorption was to get my book published at any cost to myself and still manage to keep the ball rolling. With yours and Max's help and some assistance from Mother the thing was accomplished but at the end it left me in the black hole of Calcutta, mentally exhausted, physically exhausted, emotionally exhausted, and, perhaps, morally exhausted. There seemed no time or space for recuperation. My expedition to Bermuda was a washout because of the pleurisy; Zelda collapsed again shortly after the holidays. The necessary "filling up" that a writer should be able to do after great struggles was impossible. No sooner did I finish the last galley on the last version of the last proof of the book proof of *Tender Is the Night* than it was necessary to sit down and write a *Post* story.

Of course any *apologia* is necessarily a whine to some extent; a man digs his own grave and should, presumably, lie in it, and I know that the fault for this goes back to those years, which were really years of self-indulgence. . . .[1]

> *Hotel Stafford*
> *Baltimore, Maryland*
>
> [*Received July 2, 1935*]

Dear Harold:

I'm still here—at the last moment it appears that there is a suggestion about Zelda (three days ago was a most discouraging time) and it means finding a very special nurse.

[1] The rest of the letter is missing.

So I won't leave till tomorrow. On an impulse I'm sending you a letter from Zelda that came today—a letter from which you can gauge the awful strangling heart-rending quality of this tragedy that has gone on now more than six years, with two brief intervals of hope. I know you'll understand the intrusion of sending it to you—please mail it back to me; with things so black I hang on to every scrap that is like things used to be.

And with its precise irony life continues—I went to N.Y. after all Saturday afternoon to meet a girl—stayed 20 hours and got back here Sunday night to put Scottie on the train to camp.

Now as to business—or rather finances. I owe you still somewhere around $6500 (?) and should be paying you back at the rate of $1500 per story. But this has been a slow 6 weeks—first illness, then unsuccessful attempt at revise of *Medieval IV*,[1] then a false start, then "What You Don't Know." Considering that story alone for a minute and supposing it sold for $3000. You've given me

$500 advance
$500   "
_____
+ 300 commission
_____
$1300

Normally that would leave me $1700. And I need *$1000* for bills due (that doesn't solve them but is "on account") and I'll need $700 on the 12th for life insurance. Of course I hope to have a new story in your hands by the 15th but I hope you can see your way clear to letting me have the whole sum this time—with the understanding that on the *next* story I will surely be able to reimburse you $1500. (Won't need the $700 till the *12th* but need the $1000 this week, by Friday, say, if the *Post* accepts and will put a check through.)

All this raises the ugly head of *Medieval IV*. Granted that *Post* pays $3000 and you can complete paying me the

[1] A series of stories about a ninth century Frankish knight named Philippe.

whole sum this time—that is $1700 more—

Then shall I do *Redbook* revise IV first (it's, alas, paid
for!) and make Balmer[1] believe in me again? (He's already published III and it reads well), or shall I do a *Post*
story and begin to square things with you? Only you can
decide this. I told you: *Redbook* IV *can't* be revised but
must be rewritten, and that *and* a new *Post* story will take
to the end of July. I can survive till then but will it be too
much of a drain on you to wait till then for further
payments?

There is no use of me trying to rush things. Even in
years like '24, '28, '29, '30, all devoted to short stories, I
could not turn out more than 8–9 top-price stories a year.
It simply is impossible—all my stories are conceived like
novels, require a special emotion, a special experience—
so that my readers, if such there be, know that each time
it'll be something new, not in form but in substance. (It'd
be far better for me if I could do pattern stories but the
pencil just goes dead on me. I wish I could think of a line
of stories like the Josephine or Basil ones which could go
faster and pay $3000. But no luck yet. If I ever get out
of debt I want to try a second play. It's just possible I
could knock them cold if I let go the vulgar side of my
talent.)

So that covers everything. Will you let me know by
straight wire as soon as you've read this if I can count on
these advances ($1000 this week—$700 on the 12th) *if*
the *Post* buys?

Then I can sign the checks and get off South with a clear
conscience.

I want to see you and have a long talk with you under
better conditions than we've found of late. You haven't
seen me since I've been on my no-liquor regime.

Yours ever,

Scott Fitz———

Mail Zelda's letter to Asheville. Thanks for your nice wire
about story. It set me up.

[1] Edwin Balmer, editor of *Redbook*.

Cambridge Arms Apartments
Charles & 34th Streets
Baltimore, Maryland
December 31, 1935

Dear Harold:

I'd have gone to Hollywood a year ago last spring. I don't think I could do it now but I might. Especially if there was no choice. Twice I have worked out there on other people's stories—on an "original" with John Considine telling me the plot twice a week and on the Katharine Brush story—it simply fails to use what qualities I have. I don't blame you for lecturing me since I have seriously inconvenienced you, but it would be hard to change my temperament in middle-life. No single man with a serious literary reputation has made good there. If I could form a partnership with some technical expert it might be done. (That's very different from having a supervisor who couldn't fit either the technical or creative role but is simply a weigher of completed values.) I'd need a man who knew the game, knew the people, but would help me tell and sell my story—*not his*. This man would be hard to find, because a *smart* technician doesn't want or need a partner, and an uninspired one is inclined to have a dread of ever touching tops. I could work best with a woman, because they haven't any false pride about yielding a point. I could have worked with old Bess Meredith if we hadn't been in constant committees of five. I'm afraid unless some such break occurs I'd be no good in the industry.

The matter will probably solve itself—I'll either pull out of this in the next few months or else go under—in which case I might start again in some entirely new way of my own.

I know what you would do now in my situation and what the Ideal Way would be, but it simply isn't in me to do my duty blindly. I have to follow my fate with my eyes wide open.

Scottie is so well and happy. She has such faith in me and doesn't know what's happening. Tonight she and two of her admirers decorated a tree. I hope Dick is better and

has a happy Christmas even out there away from his
family.

Yours,

Scott Fitzgerald

P.S. Do you think *The New Yorker* could use poem attached?

The Cambridge Arms
Charles & 34th Streets
Baltimore, Maryland
February 8, 1936

Dear Harold:

The man Braun is a plain, simple man with a true instinct toward the arts. He is of complete financial integrity
and we were awfully nice to him once during a journey
through North Africa and I think he is honestly fond of
both Zelda and me.

I start with this because I don't want to mess up this
chance with any of the inadvertencies and lack of fore-
sight that lost me the sale of *Tender Is the Night* and
ruined the Gracie Allen venture. You are now in touch
with Hollywood in a way that you were not several years
ago. This is obviously a job that I can do expertly—but it
is also obviously a job that a whole lot of other people can
do fairly well. Now it seems to me that the point can be
sold that I am equipped to do this treatment, which is the
whole gist of this letter.

He has gone out there[1] and they will put some hack on
the thing and in two minutes will have a poor imitation of
Lily Pons deserting the stage for a poor country boy or a
poor country girl named Lily Pons astounding the world
in ten minutes. A hack will do exactly that with it, thinking
first what previous stories dealing with the ballet and
theatre have been about, and he will try to write a reason-

[1] To Hollywood.

able imitation about it. As you know Zelda and I have been through hell about the whole subject and you'll know, too, that I should be able to deliver something entirely authentic in the matter full of invention and feeling.

It seems odd having to sell you such a suggestion when once you would have taken it at my own valuation, but after these three years of reverses it seems necessary to reassure you that I have the stuff to do this job and not let this opportunity slide away with the rumor that "Scott is drinking" or "Scott is through."

You know that the merest discussion of ideas among the Yids would mean that they were public property. You know also as in the case of radio, Columbia, that they want a sample. Now how on earth you can both sell the idea that I can do this job, that is, write a 5000-word story with cash in advance, and yet be sure that the plot won't leak out, I don't know. That seems to be your problem. You remember that I lost the whole month of October on that false radio come-on where they were obviously kidding. Isn't there some way to determine whether these people are kidding or not? This man has, in a sense, come to me and I think the idea ought to be caught and trapped right now because as you may well imagine I have little energy to dissipate.

A list of suggestions follows:

First I enclose something which I wish you would read last because it has nothing to do with the present offer, but it is something that I wrote gratuitously for a Russian dancer some years ago. Please consider that last and featuring, as it does, a male dancer rather than a female, it would certainly not fit Spessivtzewa's requirements. The other ideas which follow are the basis of a moving picture while that was for an actual ballet.

1. Zelda's awful experience of trying a difficult art too late in life to culminate with the irony that just before she cracked up she had been hoping to get little "bits" in Diaghilev's ballet and that people kept coming to the studio who she thought were emissaries of his and who turned out to be from the Folies Bergères and who thought they might make her into an American shimmy dancer. This was about like a person hoping to lead the Philadelphia Symphony being asked to be assistant conductor of Ben Bernie's band.

Please don't have anybody read Zelda's book because it is a bad book![1] But by glancing over it yourself you will see that it contains all the material that a tragedy should have, though she was incapable as a writer of realizing where tragedy lay as she was incapable of facing it as a person. Of course the tragic ending of Zelda's story need not be repeated in the picture. One could concede to the picture-people the fact that the girl might become a popular dancer in the Folies Bergères. One could conceive of a pathetic ending à la Hepburn in which because of her idealism she went on being a fifth-rate "figurine" in ballets all over Europe—this to be balanced by a compensatory love story which would make up for her the failure of her work. This would seem to me to be much the best treatment of this story.

2. This idea has to do with an episode of some memoirs of Pavlova. It begins with a little girl briefly glimpsed and dancing in the Imperial Ballet before the war. A scene later in Paris at the height of the flurry over the ballet and stranded finally with a ballet company in either Australia or Brazil for lack of funds. The climax would hinge on the catastrophe of the death of Diaghilev. The sorrow of it that Zelda felt, as did many others, who seemed to feel also that the ballet was ended; the old Imperial school was dead and now Diaghilev who had personally kept it alive in Paris had gone to his grave. There seemed to them no future and I know how strong that feeling was among the ballet people in '30 and '31, a sort of utter despair, a sense that they had once been under patronage of the Czar and later of an entrepreneur and that now nobody was taking care of them. They are like children to a ridiculous extent and have less practical ideas than the wildest musician imaginable. This story would end up in New York or in Hollywood, the ballet having a new renaissance under an American growing delight in that particular art, as is practically true with Masine's ballet in New York and with Trudy Shoop's successful little trek around the country. That's idea number two.

The third idea is more difficult in its selling aspects. In 1920 I tried to sell to D. W. Griffith the idea that people were so interested in Hollywood that there was money in

<hr />

[1] Her novel, *Save Me the Waltz*.

a picture about that and romance in the studio. He was immediately contemptuous of it, but of course a year later *Merton of the Movies* mopped up the country. The movies seem willing always to romanticize anything from a radio broadcasting room to a newspaper office as far as the entertainment world is concerned, but are so shy about themselves that another picture can be got out of Hollywood, which is certainly one of the most romantic cities in the world. A sort of mental paralysis came over them. Do you remember how the Hearst publicity men killed my story "Crazy Sunday" for *Cosmopolitan?* That was in case someone should get hurt, that it might offend Norma Shearer, Thalberg, John Gilbert or Marion Davies, etc., etc. As a matter of fact I had mixed up those characters so thoroughly that there was no character who could have been identified except possibly King Vidor and he would have been very amused by the story.

Let me repeat that this is the most difficult idea to sell but in some ways the most interesting of the three. A Russian ballet dancer finds herself in the extra line in Hollywood; they pick her out of the crowd for her good looks, give her bits of one kind or another but always on some other basis than the fact that she is a ballet dancer. This treatment of the general subject would have to close with a crash, at least I haven't thought any further than that. It would turn entirely on the essential tonal background of the adventures of Europeans who develop their metier in a Yiddish world (only you don't use that word except in Germany) that would be interesting to the people in the same rococo sense that the demand for pictures about places like Shanghai and the Trans-Siberian Railroad have in the American people. Combined with it is the always fascinating Hollywood story.

I've spent the morning writing this letter because I am naturally disappointed about the *Post's* not liking the Gwen story and must rest and go to work this afternoon to try to raise some money somehow, though I don't know where to turn.

Scott

[*Oak Hall Hotel*]

[*Tryon, North Carolina*]

[*Received March 23, 1937*]

Dear Harold:

Here, or herewith, is the revision of "Thumbs Up." Maybe it'll go. It's an odd story—one editor says cut the thumbs episode, another says cut everything else—I've done the latter and shortened it to about 5500 words (from 8000) *and* revised it thoroughly and written a new scene.

Thanks for the money—as time passes my position becomes more and more ludicrous, I mean generally. I just got a book *(Books and Battles of the Twenties)* in which I am practically a leading character; my birthday is two-column front page news as if I were 80 instead of 40—and I sit worrying about next week's $35.00 hotel bill! I really mean it that I'd like to go to Hollywood and let them *see* me. I wish you could see me. Weight 160 instead of 143 which was it last Xmas. And the dullest dogs making $1000 a week in Hollywood. Something has got to be done—this will end in slow ruination. Anyhow I've begun the football story but God knows where the next two weeks' rent comes from. I will owe $105 by Thursday and will need cash—all in all $150. I was going to Max as a last resource but you have tapped that. What in hell shall I do? I want to write the football story unworried and uninterrupted. Since going on the wagon I will have written two originals, rewritten two stories ("Thumbs" and the cartoon story) and written 3 little *Esquire* pieces (two of them mediocre) to live on. That will be a hard two and a half months' work. But reward, there is none.

In fatalistic optimism,

Scott

Going to country dog-shows isn't my daily occupation—it was my single appearance of that kind. I wanted you to see how different I look from Xmas.

Look at this _____ _____[1] next to me—covered with rings, lives in a mansion and owns it. Ah me—well, perhaps I've learned wisdom at 40 at last. If I ever get out of this mess!

[1] A successful woman writer.

5521 Amestoy Avenue
Encino, California
August 2, 1939

Dear Harold:

I have been and still am somewhat shocked by your sudden and most determined reversal of form. Only six months ago you were telling me "not to be in too much of a hurry to pay you back" but instead try to save some money. It was something of a counter-blast to find that my credit was now worth much less than I loaned Charles Warren and other young authors last year.

Your advice that I should have "taken on some movie work" with a lung cavity and a temperature of 102° was a new slant. The cavity evidently began to form about the time I started on *Air Raid,* and your implication that I had been loafing must have been based on those two-day binges in New York, several months apart. Anyhow, when the temperature was still a hundred and the cavity still crackling I was asking Swanie[1] to get me work and meanwhile putting in five hours a day on a bed-desk.

Being in need, I make no apology for having sent the original of the enclosed directly to the *Post,* with the request that they communicate by wire to me as well as by letter to you. I had a fifteen-day wait on "Temperature"— it is hard to remember there was a time your cables reached me in North Africa. Sending a story direct may be bad policy but one doesn't consider that when one is living on money from a hocked Ford—every day counts, less in the material matter of eating than in the inestimable question of morale. Swanie turned down a dozen jobs for me when I was sick in bed—but there just haven't been any since the cavity began to heal.

I don't have to explain that even though a man has once saved another from drowning, when he refuses to stretch out his arm a second time the victim has to act quickly and desperately to save himself. For change you did, Harold, and without warning—the custom of lending up to the probable yield of a next short story obtained between us for a dozen years. Certainly you haven't just discovered that I'm not any of the things a proper business man should

[1] H. N. Swanson, Hollywood agent.

be? And it wasn't even a run-around—it was a walk-around that almost made me think the New York telegraph was closed. Finally I had to sell a pair of stories to *Esquire*, the longer one of which (2800 words) might have brought twice as much from *Liberty*.

Whatever I am supposed to guess, your way of doing it, and the time you chose, was as dispiriting as could be. I have been all too hauntingly aware during these months of what you did from 1934 to 1937 to keep my head above water after the failure of *Tender*, Zelda's third collapse and the long illness. But you have made me sting nonetheless. Neither Swanson nor Sheilah nor Eddie Knopf have any idea but that I have labored conscientiously out here for twenty months and every studio (except Wanger, but including Metro!) asked for, according to Swanson, me at some time during April and May.

Your reasons for refusing to help me were all good, all praiseworthy, all sound—but wouldn't they have been equally so any time within the past fifteen years? And they followed a year and a half in which I fulfilled all my obligations.[1]

If it is of any interest to you I haven't had a drink in two months but if I was full of champagne I couldn't be more confused about you than I am now.

                                        Ever yours,

                                        Scott

P.S. "Temperature" turned up yesterday at the Van Nuys Railway Express—and in case you think that's incredible I forward the evidence.

> 5521 Amestoy Avenue
> Encino, California
> October 7, 1939

Dear Harold:

Thanks for your letter. Thanks for taking care of Scottie. And your saying that you had written me several letters

---

[1] Fitzgerald refers to his having paid off about $25,000 worth of debts with his M-G-M salary.

and torn them up did something to clarify what I had begun to interpret as some sadistic desire to punish me. I sent the stories to *Colliers* for the simple reason that it seemed difficult to deal with someone who treats you with dead silence. Against silence you can do nothing but fret and wonder. Your disinclination to back me is, of course, your own business, but representing me without communication (such as returning a story to me without even an airmail stamp) is pretty close to saying you were through with me.

I communicated directly with *Colliers* and wrote a series of pieces for *Esquire* because we have to live and eat and nothing can interfere with that. Can't you regard this trouble as a question of a man who has had a bad break and leave out the moral problem as to whether or not or how much it is his own fault? And if you think I can't write, read these stories. They brought just two hundred and fifty apiece from *Esquire,* because I couldn't wait to hear from you, because I had bank balances of five, ten and fifteen dollars.

Anyhow I have "lived dangerously" and I may quite possibly have to pay for it, but there are plenty of other people to tell me that and it doesn't seem as if it should be you.

I don't think there is any chance of fixing up that other story. It just isn't good.

Sincerely,

Scott

P.S. Could you mail me back these stories? I have no copies. Don't you agree that they are worth more than $250.00? One of them was offered to *Colliers* in desperation—the first Pat Hobby story—but Littauer wired that it "wasn't a story." Who's right?

PART TEN

Letters to
Mrs. Richard Taylor

[*Princeton University*]
[*Princeton, New Jersey*]
June 10, 1917

Dear Cousin Ceci:

Glad you liked the poem. Here are two others.

ON THE SAME PLAY—TWICE SEEN

Here in the figured dark I watch once more
  There with the curtain rolls a year away
  A year of years— There was an idle day
Of ours when happy endings didn't bore
Our unfermented souls—and rocks held ore,
  Your little face beside me, wide-eyed, gay,
  Smiled its own repertoire, while the poor play
Reached me as a faint ripple reaches short—

Yawning and wondering an evening thru
  I watch alone and chatterings of course
    Spoil the one scene which somehow *did* have charms

You wept a bit, and I grew sad for you
  Right there—where Mr. K. defends divorce
    And What's-her-name falls fainting in his arms.

Here's another one, very recent, that's rather better. It's called:

WHEN WE MEET AGAIN

  The little things we only know
              We'll have forgotten,
              Put away

Words that have melted with the snow
    And dreams begotten
     This today
And dawns and days we used to greet
That all could see and none could share
Will be no bond—and when we meet
 We shall not care— We shall not care.

And not a tear will fall for this
    A little while hence
     No regret
Will rise for a remembered kiss
    Nor even silence
     When we've met
Can give old ghosts a waste to roam
Or stir the surface of the sea
If grey shapes drift beneath the foam
 We shall not see— We shall not see.

When life leaps deathward as a flame
    Love at the scorching
     Of its breath
Casts his mad heart into the same
    Fires that are torching
     Life to Death
Though cracks may widen in the tomb
Chords from still heart to moving ear
Tremble and penetrate the gloom
 We shall not hear— We shall not hear

Colours of mine have filled your eyes,
    Light from the morn
     Of our last sea
Has gathered to you till the wise
    Think love so born
     Eternity.
But wisdom passes—yet the years
Will feed you wisdom; age will go
Back to the old— For all your tears
 We shall not know— We shall not know.

I can't resist putting in two more.

ON A CERTAIN MAN

He loved me too much, I could not love him
    Opened so wide my eyes I could not see,
For all I left unsaid I might not move him
    He did not love himself enough for me.

He kissed my hand and let himself, unruddered,
    Drift on the surface of my "youth" and "sin"
His was the blameless life, and still I shuddered
    Seeing the dark spot where his lips had been.

"How you must hate me, you of joy and brightness
    Who have no sentiment— Ah—I'm a bore—"
I smile and lie and pray the God, politeness;
    I'll sicken if his curled hair nears once more.

Trembling before the fire, I gasp and rise,
    Yawn some and drawl of sleep, profess to nod,
And weird parallels image on my eyes
    A devil screaming in the arms of God.

He'd gone too far, had merged his heart somewhere
    In my mean self, and all that I could see
Was a raw soul that labored, grovelled there.
    I loathed him for that soul—that love of me.

Here's the last one. Do you remember what I said about
my capacity for hero worship? Well—

CLAY FEET

Still on clear mornings I can see them sometimes—
    Men, gods and ghosts, queens, girls and graces,
Then that light fades, noon sickens, and there come times
    When I can see but pale and ravaged places
That they have left in exodus; and seeing
    My whole soul falters, as an invalid
Too often cheered. Did something in their being
    That *was* fine pass when my ideal did?

Men, gods and ghosts, damned so by my own damning,

Whether you knew or no, saw or nay,
Either were weak or failed a bit in shamming—
    Yet had I known a freedom that could weigh
So much, hung round the heart, I'd sought protection
    Once more in those warm dreams, lest you should fall
From that great height to this great imperfection—
    So do I mourn—so do I hate you all.

I'm writing a lot now—especially poetry—also drilling and preparing to go to this second camp— Damn this war!

Had I met Shane Leslie when I last saw you? Well, I've seen a lot more of him— He's an author and a perfect knockout— On the whole I'm having a fairly good time— but it looks as if the youth of me and my generation ends sometime during the present year, rather summarily— If we ever get back, and I don't particularly care, we'll be rather aged—in the worst way. After all, life hasn't much to offer except youth and I suppose for older people the love of youth in others. I agree perfectly with Rupert Brooke's men of Grantchester

> "Who when they get to feeling old
>   They up and shoot themselves I'm told."

Every man I've met who's been to war—that is this war—seems to have lost youth and faith in man unless they're wine-bibbers of patriotism which, of course, I think is the biggest rot in the world.

Updike of Oxford or Harvard says "I die for England" or "I die for America"—not me. I'm too Irish for that— I may get killed for America—but I'm going to die for myself.

I'm going to visit in West Virginia and I may stop by Norfolk for a day. Will you give me lunch on say about the twentieth—or will you be away?

Do read *The End of a Chapter* and *The Celt and the World* by Shane Leslie—you'd enjoy them both immensely.

I suppose Tom[1] has come and gone— I hear reports of him all over the country. He certainly seems to carry faith and hope with him. He's the old-fashioned Jesuit—the kind they got continually when the best men in the priesthood were all Jesuits.

[1] Cousin Ceci's brother, Thomas Delihant, was a Jesuit priest.

Went to a reception last week at the Duke de Richelieu's in New York where I consumed great quantities of champagne and fraternized with most of the prominent Catholics —due to champagne. I used to wonder how terribly stiff and formal receptions were possible but I see now that it is the juice of the grape.

One more thing—the most sincere apologies for the cold you got listening to my inane ramblings (of course I don't *really* think they were inane) on the porch of the Cairo.

Give my best to
    Sally
        Cecilia
           Tommy
              Ginny.[1]
And love to Aunt Elise.

                          Yours, etc.,

                          F. Scott Fitz

                      The Ambassador Hotel
                      Los Angeles, California
                      [Winter, 1927]

Dear Cousin Ceci:

If you can imagine the rush from France to Italy to New York to Montgomery to New Orleans and then to— to be plunged immediately into movie-making you'll understand this delayed Christmas card. Please believe how much I want to see you all. And do send me Sally's address because we want to send her our delayed wedding present when we get back to New York.

My God! how hard they work out here! This is a tragic city of beautiful girls—the girls who mop the floor are beautiful, the waitresses, the shop ladies. You never want to see any more beauty. (Always excepting yours.)

                          Love,

                          Scott

[1] Cousin Ceci was a widow with four daughters.

S.S. Olympic

February 23, 1931

My dearest Ceci:

I don't know what in hell I'd have done unless you had come up. The trip South was not so fortunate as it might have been, but it didn't blot out my sense of you and how much I have always loved you and depended on you. Thank you for your second note. I have always wanted, if anything happened to me while Zelda is still sick, to get you to take care of Scottie.

All those days in America[1] seem sort of blurred and dream-like now. Sometimes I think of Father, but only sentimentally; if I had been an only child I would have liked those lines I told you about of William McFee over his grave:—

"O staunch old heart that toiled so long for me:
I waste my years sailing along the sea."

Life got very crowded after I left you, and I am damned glad to be going back to Europe where I am away from most of the people I care about, and can *think* instead of feeling.

Gigi wrote me such a sweet letter, especially because it said that you liked me.

Dearest love to you.

Scott

[*1307 Park Avenue*]
[*Baltimore, Maryland*]

[*Postmarked August 17, 1934*]

Dearest Ceci:

Mrs. Owen says you asked her about the picture—I *did* get it. Didn't you get yours? Let me know.

Everything here goes rather badly. Zelda no better—

[1] Fitzgerald had come back from Europe for his father's funeral.

your correspondent in rotten health and two movie ventures gone to pot—one for Gracie Allen and George Burns
that damn near went over and took 2 weeks' work and *they*
liked and wanted to buy—and Paramount stepped on.
It's like a tailor left with a made-to-order suit—no one
to sell it to. So back to the *Post.*

(By the way I have a new series in the *Redbook.*)

Hope to hell the whoopies are well, and all the kids.

Love always,

Scott

P.S. Apropos of our conversation it will interest you to
know that I've given up politics. For two years I've gone
half haywire trying to reconcile my double allegiance to
the class I am part of, and the Great Change I believe in—
considering at last such crazy solutions as the one I had in
mind in Norfolk. I have become disgusted with the party
leadership and have only health enough left for my
literary work, so I'm on the sidelines. It had become a
strain making speeches at "Leagues Against Imperialistic
War," and their treatment of the Negro question finished
me. This is confidential, of course.

Grove Park Inn
Asheville, North Carolina
June 11, 1935

Dearest Ceci:

By now the Result-of-an-Irresistible-Impulse will be
among you. I am enclosing a check with which I hope you
will buy her as much gayety as she deserves. Don't let her
go out with any sixteen-year-old boys who have managed
to amass a charred keg and an automobile license as their
Start-in-Life. Really I mean this. My great concern with
Scottie for the next five years will be to keep her from
being mashed up in an automobile accident.

I love you as always—and that is no perfunctory statement.

Isn't Mother a funny old wraith? Didn't you get a sug-

gestion of the Witches' Cave from several of the things
that she said that night at 2400?

                    Always affectionately,

                    Scott

P.S. I mean that, about any unreliable Virginia boys taking my pet around. I will never forget that it was a Norfolk number (later drowned in the South American
swamps) who gave me my first drink of whiskey. Scottie
hasn't got three sisters—she has only got me. Watch her
please!
What a typist this one turned out to be!

                    Old Hall [Hotel]
                    [Tryon, North Carolina]
                    [Spring, 1937]

Dearest Ceci:

   Zelda is at Highland's Hospital, Asheville, N.C.
   She is much much better. So am I. I stopped drinking
in January and have been concentrating on other mischief, such as work, which is even duller, or seems so to
me at present. But Scottie must be educated and Zelda
can't starve. As for me I'd had enough of the whole
wretched mess some years ago and seen thru a sober eye
find it more appalling than ever.

                    With dearest love always,

                    Scott

                    [En route to Hollywood]
                    [Postmarked July 5, 1937]

Dearest Ceci:

   Just a line about my whereabouts. I'm going out here for
two years on a big contract financially. My health's equal

to it now and the movie people are convinced I'm on the wagon and worth buying.

It's a hell of a prospect in every other way except money but for the present and for over 3 years the creative side of me has been dead as hell. Scottie is in New York; Helen Hayes and Charlie MacArthur are bringing her out to me in July. Helen isn't working, as she has 40 more weeks as Queen Victoria on the road, so she's keeping an eye on Scottie out here while Charlie and I work.

Could Scottie spend a few days with you in September? I think you'd like her a lot now. She took her preliminaries for Vassar this spring.

Dearest love always.

Scott

1403 North Laurel Avenue
Hollywood, California
August 14, 1940

Dearest Ceci:

Aunt Elise's death was a shock to me. I was very fond of her always—I was fond of Aunt Annabel and Aunt Elise, who gave me almost my first tastes of discipline, in a peculiar way in which I wasn't fond of my mother who spoiled me. You were a great exception among mothers—managing by some magic of your own to preserve both your children's love and their respect. Too often one of the two things is sacrificed.

With Father, Uncle John and Aunt Elise a generation goes. I wonder how deep the Civil War was in them—that odd childhood on the border between the states with Grandmother and old Mrs. Scott and the shadow of Mrs. Suratt. What a sense of honor and duty—almost eighteenth century rather than Victoria. How lost they seemed in the changing world—my father and Aunt Elise struggling to keep their children in the *haute bourgeoisie* when their like were sinking into obscure farm life or being lost in the dark boarding houses of Georgetown.

I wrote Scottie to stop by and say hello to you on her

way South to see her mother next month. I would so like to see you all myself. Gigi wrote me such a nice letter from Richmond.

                         With dearest love always,
                         [Scott]

PART ELEVEN

Letters to
Gerald and Sara Murphy

Grove Park Inn
Sunset Mountain
Asheville, North Carolina

August 15, 1935

Dearest Sara:

Today a letter from Gerald, a week old, telling me this and that about the awful organ music around us, made me think of you, and I mean *think* of you (of all people in the world you know the distinction). In my theory, utterly opposite to Ernest's, about fiction, i.e., that it takes half a dozen people to make a synthesis strong enough to create a fiction character—in that theory, or rather in despite of it, I used you again and again in *Tender:*

"Her face was hard and lovely and pitiful"

and again

"He had been heavy, belly-frightened with love of her for years"

—in those and in a hundred other places I tried to evoke not *you* but the effect that you produce on men—the echoes and reverberations—a poor return for what you have given by your living presence, but nevertheless an artist's (what a word!) sincere attempt to preserve a true fragment rather than a "portrait" by Mr. Sargent. And someday, in spite of all the affectionate skepticism you felt toward the brash young man you met on the Riviera eleven years ago, you'll let me have my little corner of you where I know you better than anybody—yes, even better than Gerald. And if it should perhaps be your left ear (you hate anyone to examine any single part of your person, no matter how appreciatively—that's why you wore bright clothes) on June evenings on Thursdays from 11:00 to 11:15 here's what I'd say.

That not one thing you've done is for nothing. If you lost everything you brought into the world—if your works were burnt in the public square the law of compensation would still act (I am too moved by what I am saying to write it as well as I'd like). You are part of our times, part of the history of our race. The people whose lives you've touched directly or indirectly have reacted to the corporate bundle of atoms that's you in a *good* way. *I have seen you again and again at a time of confusion take the hard course almost blindly because long after your powers of ratiocination were exhausted you clung to the idea of dauntless courage.* You were the one who said:

"All right, I'll take the black checker men."

I know that you and Gerald are one and it is hard to separate one of you from the other, in such a matter for example as the love and encouragement you chose to give to people who were full of life rather than to others, equally interesting and less exigent, who were frozen into rigid names. I don't praise you for *this*—it was the little more, the little immeasurable portion of a millimeter, the thing at the absolute top that makes the difference between a World's Champion and an also-ran, the little glance when you were sitting with Archie on the sofa that you threw at me and said:

"And—Scott!"

—taking me in too, and with a heart so milked of compassion by your dearest ones that no person in the world but you would have that little more to spare.

Well—I got somewhat excited there. The point is: I rather like you, and I *think* that perhaps you have the makings of a good woman.

Gerald has invited me to come up for a weekend in the fall—probably September.

It's odd that when I read over this letter it seems to convey no particular point, yet I'm going to send it. Like Cole's eloquent little song

"I think it'll tell you how *great* you are."

From your everlasting friend,

Scott

Cambridge Arms Apts.
Baltimore, Maryland
[*Postmarked March 30, 1936*]

Dearest Sara (and Gerald too, if he's not in London):

I want news of you. The winter has presented too many problems here for me to come North, even as far as New York, and my last word of you was by kindness of Archie —and not too encouraging.

If you read the little trilogy I wrote for *Esquire*[1] you know I went through a sort of "dark night of the soul" last autumn, and again and again my thoughts reverted to you and Gerald, and I reminded myself that nothing had happened to me with the awful *suddenness* of your tragedy of a year ago,[2] nothing so utterly conclusive and irreparable. I saw your face, Sara, as I saw it a year ago this month, and Gerald's face last fall when I met him in the Ritz Bar, and I felt very close to you—and correspondingly detached from Ernest, who has managed to escape the great thunderbolts, and Nora Flynn whom the gods haven't even shot at with much seriousness. She would probably deny that, and she helped me over one black week when I thought this was probably as good a time to quit as any, but as I said to her the love of life is essentially as incommunicable as grief.

I am moving Zelda to a sanitarium in Asheville—she is

---

[1] "The Crack-Up."
[2] The Murphys' son Baoth had died of spinal meningitis.

no better, though the suicidal cloud has lifted. —I thought over your Christian Science idea and finally decided to try it but the practitioner I hit on wanted to begin with "absent treatments," which seemed about as effectual to me as the candles my mother keeps constantly burning to bring me back to Holy Church—so I abandoned it. Especially as Zelda now claims to be in direct contact with Christ, William the Conqueror, Mary Stuart, Apollo and all the stock paraphernalia of insane-asylum jokes. Of course it isn't a bit funny but after the awful strangulation episode of last spring I sometimes take refuge in an unsmiling irony about the present *exterior* phases of her illness. For what she has really suffered, there is never a sober night that I do not pay a stark tribute of an hour to in the darkness. In an odd way, perhaps incredible to you, she was always my child (it was not reciprocal as it often is in marriages), my child in a sense that Scottie isn't, because I've brought Scottie up hard as nails (perhaps that's fatuous, but I *think I* have). Outside of the realm of what you called Zelda's "terribly dangerous secret thoughts" I was her great reality, often the only liaison agent who could make the world tangible to her—

The only way to show me you forgive this great outpouring is to write me about yourselves. Some night when you're not too tired, take yourself a glass of sherry and write me as lovely and revealing [a] letter as you did before. Willy-nilly we are still in the midst of life and all true correspondence is necessarily sporadic but a letter from you or Gerald always pulls at something awfully deep in me. I want the best news, but in any case I want to know.

> With dearest affection to you all,
>
> Scott

> Oak Hall Hotel
> Tryon, North Carolina
> *January 31, 1937*

Dearest Gerald and Sara:

The telegram came today and the whole afternoon was

so sad with thoughts of you and the past and the happy times we had once. Another link binding you to life is broken and with such insensate cruelty that [it] is hard to say which of the two blows was conceived with more malice.[1] I can see the silence in which you hover now after this seven years of struggle and it would take words like Lincoln's in his letter to the mother who had lost four sons in the war to write you anything fitting at the moment. The sympathy you will get will be what you have had from each other already and for a long, long time you will be inconsolable.

But I can see another generation growing up around Honoria and an eventual peace somewhere, an occasional port of call as we all sail deathward. Fate can't have any more arrows in its quiver for you that will wound like these. Who was it said that it was astounding how the deepest griefs can change in time to a sort of joy? The golden bowl is broken indeed but it *was* golden; nothing can ever take those boys away from you now.

Scott

[*Metro-Goldwyn-Mayer Corporation*]
[*Culver City, California*]
March 11, 1938

Dear Gerald:

Your letter was a most pleasant surprise. The telegram I sent you was prompted by one of those moments when you see people as terribly alone—a moment in the Newark airport. It was entirely a piece of sentimentality because, of course, Sheilah[2] has lots of friends in New York; and I realize now that it was a bad time to ask anything. You were awfully damn kind, in any case, and as a friend you have never failed me.

Alas, I wish I could say the same for myself. I don't gather from your letter whether you were going to look

---

[1] The Murphys' other son, Patrick, had died of tuberculosis.
[2] Sheilah Graham.

upon the antique world of Sara, Dos and Katy.[1] I wish I was, but with the sort of wishing that is remote and academic. I don't care much where I am any more, nor expect very much from places. You will understand this. To me, it is a new phase, or, rather, a development of something that began long ago in my writing—to try to dig up the relevant, the essential, and especially the dramatic and glamorous from whatever life is around. I used to think that my sensory impression of the world came from outside. I used to actually believe that it was as objective as blue skies or a piece of music. Now I know it was within, and emphatically cherish what little is left.

I am writing a picture called *Infidelity* for Joan Crawford. Writing for her is difficult. She can't change her emotions in the middle of a scene without going through a sort of Jekyll and Hyde contortion of the face, so that when one wants to indicate that she is going from joy to sorrow, one must cut away and then cut back. Also, you can never give her such a stage direction as "telling a lie," because if you did, she would practically give a representation of Benedict Arnold selling West Point to the British. I live a quiet life here, keeping regular hours, trying to get away every couple of weeks for days in the sun at La Jolla, Santa Barbara. King Vidor appeared for a day or so, asked about you and is off for England. Eddie[2] and I talk of you. Sheilah, of course, was fascinated by you both, and I looked up old pictures in old scrapbooks for her. *Tender Is the Night* has been dramatized and may go on the stage next fall. I shall obtain you gallery seats for the first night where you can blush unseen.

[Scott]

[*5521 Amestoy Avenue*]
[*Encino, California*]

[*Spring, 1940*]

Honey—that goes for Sara too:

I have written a dozen people since who mean nothing

[1] Mrs. John Dos Passos.
[2] Edwin Knopf.

to me—writing you I was saving for good news. I suppose pride was concerned—in that personally and publicly dreary month of September last about everything went to pieces all at once and it was a long uphill pull.

To summarize: I don't have to tell you anything about the awful lapses and sudden reverses and apparent cures and thorough poisoning effect of lung trouble. Suffice to say there were months with a high of 99.8, months at 99.6 and then up and down and a stabilization at 99.2 every afternoon when I could write in bed—and now for two and a half months and one short week that may have been grip—nothing at all. With it went a psychic depression over the finances and the effect on Scottie and Zelda. There was many a day when the fact that you and Sara did help me at a desperate moment . . . seemed the only pleasant human thing that had happened in a world where I felt prematurely passed by and forgotten. The thousands that I'd given and loaned—well, after the first attempts I didn't even worry about that. There seem to be the givers and the takers and that doesn't change. So you were never out of my mind—but even so no more present than always because this was only one of so many things.

In the land of the living again I function rather well. My great dreams about this place are shattered and I have written half a novel and a score of satiric pieces that are appearing in the current *Esquires* about it. After having to turn down a bunch of well-paid jobs while I was ill there was a period when no one seemed to want me for duck soup—then a month ago a producer asked me to do a piece of my own for a small sum ($2000) and a share in the profits. The piece is "Babylon Revisited" an old and not bad *Post* story of which the child heroine was named Honoria![1] I'm keeping the name.

It looks good. I have stopped being a prophet (third attempt at spelling this) but I think I may be solvent in a month or so if the fever keeps subservient to what the doctors think is an exceptional resistance. . . .

So now you're up to date on me and it won't be so long again. I might say by way of counter-reproach that there's no word of any of *you* in your letter. It is sad about _____.

[1] After the Murphys' daughter.

Writing you today has brought back so much and I could weep very easily.

With dearest love,

Scott

Twentieth Century-Fox Film Corporation
Beverly Hills, California
September 14, 1940

Dear Gerald:

I suppose anybody our age suspects what is emphasized—so let it go. But I was flat in bed from April to July last year with day and night nurses. Anyhow as you see from the letterhead I am now in official health.

I find, after a long time out here, that one develops new attitudes. It is, for example, such a slack *soft* place—even its pleasure lacking the fierceness or excitement of Provence—that withdrawal is practically a condition of safety. The sin is to upset anyone else, and much of what is known as "progress" is attained by more or less delicately poking and prodding other people. This is an unhealthy condition of affairs. Except for the stage-struck young girls people come here for negative reasons—all gold rushes are essentially negative—and the young girls soon join the vicious circle. There is no group, however small, interesting as such. Everywhere there is, after a moment, either corruption or indifference. The heroes are the great corruptionists or the supremely indifferent—by whom I mean the spoiled writers, Hecht, Nunnally Johnson, Dotty,[1] Dash Hammett, etc. That Dotty has embraced the church and reads her office faithfully every day does not affect her indifference. So is one type of Commy Malraux didn't list among his categories in *Man's Hope*—but nothing would disappoint her so vehemently as success.

I have a novel pretty well on the road. I think it will baffle and in some ways irritate what readers I have left. But it is as detached from me as *Gatsby* was, in intent

[1] Dorothy Parker.

anyhow. The new Armageddon, far from making everything unimportant, gives me a certain lust for life again.
This is undoubtedly an immature throw-back, but it's the
truth. The gloom of all causes does not affect it—I
feel a certain rebirth of kinetic impulses—however mis-
directed. . . .

I *would* like to have some days with you and Sara. I
hear distant thunder about Ernest and Archie and their
doings but about you not a tenth of what I want to know.

With affection,

Scott

PART TWELVE

Letters to
Mrs. Bayard Turnbull

La Paix, [Rodgers' Forge]
[Towson, Maryland]
September 10, 1932

Dear Mrs. Turnbull:

Thanks for your quotation from the Emperor.[1] It is a great thesis and even the Communists are working it—claiming that no man not under a religious spell (in their case, Communism) can have a focal point from which to orientate his work. I think that it is largely a question of the age in which one lives and I am not philosopher enough to think it through for myself.

Thanks too for the Lawrence item which I will read tonight. Later: Read it and enjoyed the Murray letter hugely.

With unjustified egotism I am sending you two articles on the American novel that have appeared in the last year. I know Munson by reputation—Leighton I haven't heard of. One is pleasantly disposed toward me—the other not—and both articles seem to me mostly bunk. I send them because Lewisohn treats with interest his own generation and dismisses mine so entirely, because we deal with the post-war world which he does not understand. To give, for example, Hergesheimer's stories of ladies' laundry and picturesque peasants, all got up in the questionable later stylistics of Henry James, more importance than Hemingway's work is simply to say, "Well, that's the world *I* like and I'm a pacifist liberal Jew and you can't expect me to understand new tendencies in a social system I didn't get with my mother's milk anyhow." He allows to his own

[1] Napoleon.

generation the right to report the traditionally unimportant, but in the *new* one, the observed truth has got to fit in with his own crystallized conceptions. Well, well—I shall be like that sometime.

The young men turn to us (I don't mean, God forbid! my *Post* stories, but to my generation). The bow they made to Cabell, for example, is purely formal. I believe that if one is interested in the world into which willy-nilly one's children will grow up the most accurate data can be found in the European leaders, such as Lawrence, Jung and Spengler, and after that in the very sincere young Americans emerging one by one, and least in the attempts to make logical and palatable the current world scene. I think we are all a little sick but the logic of history won't permit us to go backward.

Again thanks for sending me the Lawrence, which I'd have otherwise missed. With very best wishes,

Sincerely,

F. Scott Fitzgerald

La Paix, Rodgers' Forge
[*Towson, Maryland*]
September 21, 1932

Dear Mrs. Turnbull:

I'm afraid I was dogmatic last night on a subject about which it is silly to be dogmatic. But I do know that I'd prefer Scottie to marry a man of the world even if he was not of her world—a man six or eight years older than herself. The value of every year of experience he brings to the marriage is enormous. I have heard so many college girls complain about their young husbands not *knowing* anything, by which they didn't mean formal education but the lack of any approach to life except the social or the modern big-business approach. They have never been to sea, or to the wars, robbed a bank, hunted to live, supported a chorus girl, founded a religion, or dealt directly with other men in some rough school such as politics. If she marries for a whole lot of money that is a different matter for with enough money one can change husbands or live in Paris and not even bother. I am referring to the young couple who will have to meet the usual problems together, such as the money one. And I think if a suitor of Scottie's was entirely innocent in his past life I'd be inclined to make the old remark: "Well, I don't want you to practice on her."

Of course nowadays with so much knowledge available the chances are that women know when they're being cheated but fifty years ago, so numerous doctors have revealed, there were many marriage tragedies beneath what seemed a happy surface.

Of course, I don't believe in the double standard—I believe it's disappearing anyhow—I only meant that it was possible for a man to be far from a saint and yet be wildly jealous of his wife, as I am.

Just a last word and I am through boring you with this interminable discussion—I don't think it matters what a boy's politics are before he is sixteen but I hope the colleges will cover about all the current economic theories, if only that the boy should know where he stands and what he's fighting. When a United States Senator *after his election* has to look up the principles of Marxism by which one-sixth of the world is governed it shows he's a pretty inadequate defender of his own system.

Again, excuse this long letter—couldn't get down to work this morning and simply had to argue about something.

Sincerely,

F. Scott Fitzgerald

I'm sorry I lent you the Hemingway book[1]—there's a streak of vulgarity in it I would find quite offensive except I know that he does it as a protest against censorship.

[1] *The Sun Also Rises.*

[*La Paix, Rodgers' Forge*]
[*Towson, Maryland*]

[*Probably Spring, 1933*]

Dear Mrs. Turnbull:

I can't resist adding a word of qualification to the opinions I expressed so freely last night.

1st   Ford Madox Ford once said, "Henry James was the greatest writer of his day; therefore for me the greatest man." That is all I meant by superiority. T. S. Eliot seems to me a very great person—Mrs. Lanier seems to me a very fine character. To me the conditions of an artistically creative life are so arduous that I can only compare to them the duties of a soldier in war-time. I simply cannot admire, say, a merchant or an educator with the intensity I reserve for other professions, and in a sense the world agrees with me. Of the Elizabethans we remember the Queen and Drake, a ruler and a captain—only *two* "people of affairs" in contrast to Bacon, Sidney, Shakespeare, Marlowe, Jonson, Raleigh. You may say that is because history is written by writers—I think it is more than that.

2nd   Please believe that, within the limits of the frame you have chosen, I know no children better brought up than yours. My somewhat tactless bursts of criticism of the frame itself are prompted by my faith in a sort of sixth sense that I think I have about the way the world is going.

3rd   I cannot permit my silence of last night when you spoke of yourself as being "shallow, etc." [to] pass as a tacit acceptance of the truth of that. I simply meant that for me the test of human values is conformity to the strictest and most unflinching rationality, while in your case it is based on standards of conduct. I don't mean that because Rousseau's life was disordered an intellectual should use that to justify his own weaknesses, nor even that my criteria necessarily subsume yours, but I must *think* they do even though I continually check up by seeing the lives of "orderly" people, judging what's fake and what's real. This by the way doesn't excuse the arrogance and bad manners of which I was guilty last night.

4th   In résumé I owe you an apology, because I value your friendship, but not a retraction if I can persuade you that even my definitions are different from yours. With great admiration and respect for you and your way of life let me sign myself as your

> Erratic but sincere tenant,
>
> F. Scott Fitzgerald

> [*La Paix, Rodgers' Forge*]
> [*Towson, Maryland*]
> [*September, 1933*]

Dear Mrs. Turnbull:

I am going to have to not come to dinner Friday[1] (all of us, I mean), though naturally will come up in evening or afternoon to pay my respects to your mother with great pleasure—and curiosity and interest—at your convenience. We have dined out exactly four times in two years: twice with you, once at the Ridgelys, once on a ship. Without going into the whys of the precedent, it has become one, so with many thanks, I remain your friend (in this case regretful),

> Scott Fitzgerald

P.S. I have some documents of yours which I will cherish for a few days, unless you want them back immediately: one magazine article, one clipping, 2 letters of Andrew's (or do you save letters—if not I will file them as they seem interesting to me and form part of a series).

> [*La Paix, Rodgers' Forge*]
> [*Towson, Maryland*]
> [*September, 1933*]

Dear Mrs. Turnbull:

How would this plan seem to you? for the school trek, beginning Thursday.

[1] Beside these words Fitzgerald wrote in the margin, "What a sentence!"

You to take Thursday and Friday; then:

Our week, your week, our week, your week, your week
Our week, "   "   "   "   "   "   "   "

                          etc.

—This arrangement because this year your children have the far mileage to cover. Is it Oak? (I believe the dictionary spelling is "Oke.")

Your mother is utterly charming. I have never known a woman of her age to be so alive (I retract: there was also Mrs. Winthrop Chanler). I enjoyed our hour together *so much*. Tell her so.

Ever your chattel,

F. Scott Fitzgerald

1307 Park Avenue
Baltimore, Maryland
May 31, 1934

Dear Margaret:

I know it was very annoying for me to have lost my temper in public and I want to apologize to you both, for the discomfort that I know I gave you. There are certain subjects that *simply do not belong to an afternoon tea* and, while I still think that Mrs. Perce's arguments were almost maddening enough to justify homicide, I appreciate that it was no role of mine to intrude my intensity of feeling upon a group who had expected a quiet tea party.

Ever yours faithfully,

Scott Fitzgerald

P.S. I'm sorry this is typed but I seem to have contracted Scottie's poison ivy and my hands are swathed in bandages.

1307 Park Avenue
Baltimore, Maryland
May 11, 1935

Dear Margaret:

The lilies are wonderful. First I gave them to Scottie and then I took them back. I rushed to my window and called you just as your Ford rolled out of sight. I wanted to see you before I left, which is now, for a protracted sojourn in the country, probably Carolina, still seeking to get back the hours of sleep that I lost in '33 and '34. I am closing the house but am coming back in June to pack Scottie off to camp.

I think of you all so often and I miss keeping up with Andrew and Eleanor, their woes and joys and changes. Through Scottie's eyes they lack reality, Andrew becomes a schemer of Machiavellian hue, Eleanor remains the child who just never will be as old as Scottie no matter how hard she tries, as though she were an Alice who had just perversely lost her growing cake. I still hear the wings of a career beating about her. As for Andrew I shall have to catch up as much as possible when I take him to the football games next autumn, though I wish I knew what he was going to do this summer.

I have a fair story in the current *McCall's* if you run into it. La Paix must be grand now—I wish Zelda could walk through it, but alas, she is far too sick. When she is a little better and can go outside will you call on her sometime? I will let you know. She will be pretty lonesome when I am away and I hate like the devil to leave her but it is doctor's orders.

Always affectionately,

Scott

[Grove Park Inn]
[Asheville, North Carolina]
[June, 1935]

Dear Margaret:

What a nice letter you write! I quoted to Zelda tonight

(in a letter) the part about "Scottie in yellow ruffles . . . with Andrew, Jack and Clarence . . . forming the dark half of the design."

Also the inevitable fatalism that creeps into all womanhood, the almost lust for death as the culmination of experience; to quote you again, "life being made up of hope, and a little fulfillment." The hell it is—too much fulfillment from a man's point of view, if he has been one of those who wanted to identify himself with it utterly. It's so fast, so sweeping along, that he walks stumbling and crying out, wondering sometimes where he is, or where the others are, or if they existed, or whether he's hurt anybody, but not much time to wonder, only sweeping along again with his only choice being between blindness or being muscle-bound from caution-conservatism-cowardice, the three great C's I've tied up together, though God knows I'm capable of all three. . . .

I became so metaphysical there that I had to destroy what I'd written. Anyhow I think that the fatalism of women can be confused with radicalism but is neither radical nor conservative to any extent. But a man's life is a more gorgeous thing, I think, if he's one of the fortunate. Oh, well—these generalities set ill upon a man of my age.

Thank you for asking Scottie out. You have been good to her. I like it when she goes to your house and gets a sense of the continuity of life that her own choppy existence hasn't given her. I want her to be pretty hard but if she has to be a *condottiere* to a certain extent, I like her to know that all people don't.

I am benefiting by my rest here, gaining weight, exuberance. But living alone leaves so many loopholes for brooding and when I do face the whole tragedy of Zelda it is simply a day lost. I think I feel it more now than at any time since its inception. She seems so helpless and pitiful. Liquor used to help put it out of mind, and it was one of the many services my old friend Barleycorn did me. However he had outlived his usefulness in that as well as all other regards.

I hear it is beautiful here, but without people all places are the same to me. I'd rather be at La Paix watching thru my iron grille one of your tribe moving about the garden, and wondering if Zelda had yet thrown the tennis racquet at Mr. Crosley.[1]

What a ten months this has been for Frances—good God! a lifetime for some people. Blessings on her—she is a fine person.

All my affectionate good wishes to you and yours,

Scott Fitz

Cambridge Arms
Baltimore, Maryland

[*Fall, 1935*]

Dear Margaret:

Pardon! We moved. I wrote. And wrote. And wrote. All *politesse* ceased to exist for a thick week during which I lived in a haze of cigarette smoke and nervous querulousness. I don't even know why I wrote you about Scottie save that on my occasional emergencies all matters in the outside world seemed of equally vital importance—or unimportance: the N.R.A. and the Princeton-Williams game, the decline of the democratic dogma and the faint worry of a child. Anyhow, thanks.

I destroyed Andrew's letter—he is so level-headed in his analyses and he keeps growing. I wish I knew him better but I won't though, until he is about 19. He might know *me* but I won't know *him* because until then he will give me a *presentation* of himself that he thinks will impress or please me. This will not prevent him, I repeat, from finding out more and more about me if we meet often.

I know this Pell's brother who was in '28. This one[2] had a school in New England for awhile, didn't he, or was assistant headmaster somewhere or taught at St. Mark's? I've heard well of him. He was in Ivy, I think, and well liked, but on principle I'm against schoolmarms, male or female—though there's just the ghost of one in me. Common sense tells me that there are rules but, like all modern

---

[1] A tennis pro who gave Zelda lessons on the grass court at La Paix.
[2] Walden Pell, headmaster of St. Andrew's School.

men, the shade of Rousseau haunts me. (Bertrand Russell's Rousseau school is a flop—I know that at practically first hand—I've seen and talked to both parents and products.) That's too big a subject for a letter and we've probably talked of it before.

Zelda is much much better—I've taken her out twice; suicidal tendency vanishing—interest in life returning.

Please enclose this to Andrew when you write.

Oh—I know what I wanted to tell you—I think I'm about to write a series of sketches for radio about father and daughter—I'll tell you about it when we meet. In a week we'll be in our real apartment (this is a substitute) in the same building, and you and Frances must come and give us your benediction, or are there only dates and cotillions now? We talk about you all a lot.

Always affectionately,

Scott Fitzg——

The Harvard game is November 9th—just a reminder.

[*The Cambridge Arms*]
[*Baltimore, Maryland*]
[*Spring, 1936*]

Dear Margaret:

Just a footnote to our conversation: you of course recognized the allusion to William James' remark when I spoke of "tender-minded" and "tough-minded" and said that I was the former and you the latter. It has no relation to *sensitiveness* but rather to *sensibility*. And I am not at all sure which I am. I think perhaps the creative worker has the privilege of jumping from one attitude to the other, or of balancing on the line. I am continually surprised both by my softness and by my hardiness.

Ever yours,

Scott Fitz

Read the article by Antheil if you get the last *Esquire*.

Grove Park Inn
Asheville, North Carolina
November 11, 1936

Dear Margaret:

Only the fact that I have been incapacitated by a broken shoulder has broken the tradition of taking Andrew to a game beside the hall of his grandfather ("Pepper Constable").[1] I am sending him two tickets to the last Princeton game and if he doesn't want to use them he can give them to someone else who wants to.

Andrew is a brave fighter and I admire, sometimes, his stubbornness and his reticence just as much as I would like him in the sunshine when I have tried to give him what I have found from life. He has the potentialities of being absolutely first-rate. I hope he read *War and Peace;* and I wish I had had the advantage when I was a child of parents and friends who knew more than I did.

With dearest love to you all,

Scott Fitzgerald

Oak Hall [Hotel]
Tryon, North Carolina
[Spring, 1937]

Dear Margaret:

What a lovely letter you write. I am timorous in answering you, having no flair for letters—my old ones reread make me wince.

And now, assuming that there are 20 intelligent women in Baltimore (isn't the proper word "bright" or "clever?") I spring to answer you.

I think your first topic is the best of the two[2] (the second embraces all feminism and will lead to triteness) but it's not perfect. It's awfully yes or no—has the aristo-

[1] A Princeton football star.
[2] Margaret Turnbull had asked Fitzgerald's advice about topics for a discussion group to which she belonged.

crat got money?—if "it" hasn't it had better be born into the middle of the middle classes in a small town. If you had money and were not Russian or Spanish it was certainly an advantage to be an aristocrat up to now. One might not be invited out much or have a king give up his throne in one's honor or be as well known as Harlow and Low outside the county, and certainly one had to kneel to the monied nobility, but it had its compensations. Tories have such true-and-tried indignations that they are practically formed at ten.

Oh, well—Tolstoi didn't like it—which leads me to ask if Andrew finished *War and Peace* or has D. H. Lawrence come between them? He seemed fine at Xmas. The time will come when all adults will spend the holidays in bed as I did and you apparently. I came down here and went on the white list for another long stretch and am finding it dull and not even conducive to work. Not that I miss the liquor which gives me but little elation in my old age but it is gloomy to see how few things I really care about when I see clearly. I support Zelda's contention that it were best to begin at the pole and work south to the Riviera and likewise add that one should have first drunk at 35 and progress to a champagne-pink three score and ten.

I should think Andrew would love *Look Homeward, Angel* and *A Farewell to Arms*.

Reading over Eleanor's sweet little note gave me pleasure. Scottie does well, leading the school in French and English and apparently being very serious after her Xmas debauch.

I think of you often in your garden. Hasn't my ghost become pretty dim at La Paix?

Always affectionately,

Scott

Metro-Goldwyn-Mayer Corporation
Culver City, California
[Fall, 1937]

Dear Margaret:

I have owed you a letter for so long but these have

been crowded months. I suppose Scottie told you the general line-up—after almost 3 years of intermittent illness it's nice to be on a steady job like this—a sort of tense crossword puzzle game, creative only when you want it to be, a surprisingly interesting intellectual exercise. You mustn't miss my first effort, *Three Comrades,* released next winter.

I'm sorry you were ill last March—a blood transfusion—that sounds serious! The news about Frances is strange and loyal and profound. I hope she finds it again—it's not very easy if you have "anything to you." I know—though I've often tried desperately hard to be light of love.

Antony[1] is a fine book—odd I almost sent it to you! Also an odd comment—several people who were "tops" in English society—and I don't mean the fast set but the inner-of-inner Duke-of-York business—told me he was "rather a bounder." I wonder what they meant—I can sort of understand.

I have sent Andrew two seats to Harvard-Princeton and two to Navy-Princeton. They will arrive in a few weeks *addressed to me care of you* with Princeton University Athletic Association *stamped on the envelope. Just open them and send them to Andrew* with my enduring affection.

And reserve a bushel for yourself.

                                                                Scott

                                                    [*5521 Amestoy Avenue*]
                                                    [*Encino, California*]
                                                    November 13, 1939

Dear Margaret:

The enclosed letter explains itself.[2] I am not allowed to communicate with Andrew in this regard by the club convention, nor should you send him this letter, but it would be perfectly proper for you to tell him that if a delegation of

---

[1] By James Lytton, Viscount Knebworth.
[2] A letter in behalf of Andrew Turnbull to the Chairman of the Elections Committee of Cottage Club.

Cottage boys call on him, he might at least exchange appraising glances with them. Of *course*, he may be already set with a crowd joining some other organization—and most especially I want him to be happy in his choice of companions for his last two years.

In general my views are somewhat contrary to yours, insofar as the advantage of belonging to a larger than to a smaller corporate body. You remember how I argued, almost to the point of presumption, against your selection of Williams for him as against one of the Big Three. In the same manner, it seems to me that it would be a little better for Andrew's future if he joined one of the so-called "big clubs" at Princeton than one of the others. They are called big not because they necessarily have more members, but because they divide among themselves the leadership in most undergraduate policy. The Charter Club and the Quadrangle Club are notably among the nicer "small" clubs, but only a few months ago Jimmy Stewart was telling me how it wrankled throughout his whole Princeton career that he had joined Charter instead of Cottage, which had been his father's club. The larger group, it seems to me, though it may make for stiffer going, pays off better at the end.

Nothing would please me better than that the whole snobbish system be abolished. But it is thoroughly entrenched there, as Woodrow Wilson saw, and to boys of that impressionable age assumes an importance all out of proportion to its reality. And boys have gone through college without joining any club at all with no loss of self-respect.

In general: if Andrew goes into naturally, say Cap and Gown, with the crowd he has always known, that is all in all probably the best thing. Failing that, it would be better to go into Cottage with two or three friends than to go with some larger group into any of the lesser clubs. I haven't seen Andrew for years now (though I've had pleasant glimpses of him from Scottie and from several letters which he's written me). So this is pretty much work in the dark. One thing that distinguished "big clubs" from the others is that the boys are slightly older, and more sophisticated, and rather more endowed with front. I had my choice of two of the bigger clubs and two of the smaller ones and though I might have been more *comfortable* in

Quadrangle, for instance, where there were lots of literary minded boys, I was never sorry about my choice. My ideas of education still go in the direction that college like the home should be an approximation of what we are likely to expect in the world.

Let me hear some news of you and yours. Scottie seems to be settling down at last at Vassar, but I would never again want to undertake the education of a girl of whom boys have made a sort of adolescent fetish. I don't think that down in her heart she likes it much either.

With affection,

[Scott]

PART THIRTEEN

Miscellaneous
Letters

TO MRS. EDWARD FITZGERALD

Camp Chatham
Orillia, Ontario
July 18, 1907

Dear Mother,[1]

I received your letter this morning and though I would like very much to have you up here I don't think you would like it as you know no one here except Mrs. Upton and she is busy most of the time. I don't think you would like the accommodations as it is only a small town and no good hotels. There are some very nice boarding houses but about the only fare is lamb and beef. Please send me a dollar because there are a lot of little odds and ends I need. I will spend it cautiously. All the other boys have pocket money besides their regular allowance.

Your loving son,

Scott Fitzgerald

TO ALIDA BIGELOW [2]

Cottage Club
Princeton, New Jersey
[Postmarked January 10, 1917]

Dear Alida:

I never felt so depressed in my life as I do this afternoon

---

[1] This letter, written when Fitzgerald was ten, is his earliest on record.
[2] Alida Bigelow had grown up with Fitzgerald in St. Paul.

and what should I do in the middle and lowest point of it but pick up *North of Boston*.[1]—It made me still gloomier; but it's well worth reading and for the most part good poetry. The first poem, the one about mending the wall, is the best thing in it I think.

—Much obliged—you were very good to send it. Even the "platitudinous remark" seemed satirical on a day like this however.

I'll send you a one-act play by me when it comes out in the next *Nassau Lit*. It's called "The Debutante." —It's a knockout!

Just had a scrap with my English preceptor—he's a simple bone-head and I'm not learning a thing from him. I told him so!

I never had such a simple Christmas vacation as this one. The only two parties I enjoyed particularly were the German and the Lamda Sigma dance. Perhaps there was a reason—tho incidentally I've cut out all drinking for one year. (Good old New Year's resolution.) I suppose you've regaled Ruth with an account of my exploits at the first-named affair—but what bother I!

Isn't it a shame about Mrs. S! I hear from Elkins Owlliphant, however, that she's now back at school.

I wonder if Sandy is going to marry _____! Wouldn't this be a suitable pair to travel around the streets of St. Paul! He must have some strange power over woming!

Haven't heard a word from home since I got back here— Gee! Honestly! Never did I feel so low.

It's four o'clock and I have the electric light on—you can imagine what kind of day it [is].

If you can receive books and you won't be shocked I'll send you a knockout called *The Confessions of an Inconstant Man*. One part of it is rather mean, tho!! You'll have to send it back as another copy is unprocurable for Love or Money. —Tell me whether you want to read it or not.

I got the funniest letter from a girl in New York whom I'd never heard of saying that she had light brown hair and brown eyes and that she wanted to meet me. She said she's seen that picture (awful chromo) of *moi* in *The Times*.

1 By Robert Frost.

Well Alida I'm sorry this letter is so gloomy but that's the form I'm in so it can't be helped.

Give my best to Virginia Sweat and tell her I'm sorry I've got such [a] weak line. I am

Yours till deth,

F. Scott Fitzgerald

TO MRS. EDWARD FITZGERALD

University Cottage Club
Princeton, New Jersey
November 14, 1917

Dear Mother:

You were doubtless surprised to get my letter but I certainly was delighted to get my commission.

My pay started the day I signed the Oath of Allegiance and sent it back which was yesterday— Went up to Brooks Brothers yesterday afternoon and ordered some of my equipment.

I haven't received any orders yet but I think I will be ordered to Fort Leavenworth within a month—I'll be there three months and would have six additional months' training in France before I was ordered with my regiment to the trenches.

I get $141 a month ($1700 a year) with a 10% increase when I'm in France.

My uniforms are going to cost quite a bit so if you haven't sent me what you have of *my own money* please do so.

I'm continuing here going to classes until I get orders. I am Second Lieutenant in the *regular* infantry and *not* a reserve officer—I rank with a West Point graduate.

Things are stupid here—I hear from Marie and Catherine Tighe occasionally and got a letter from Non two weeks ago—I hear he's been ordered to Texas.

Went down to see Ellen Stockton in Trenton the other night. She is a perfect beauty.

About the army, please let's not have either tragedy or

Heroics because they are equally distasteful to me. I went into this perfectly cold-bloodedly and don't sympathize with the

"Give my son to country" etc.

etc.

etc.

or

"Hero stuff"

because *I just went* and purely for *social reasons*. If you want to pray, pray for my soul and not that I won't get killed—the last doesn't seem to matter particularly and if you are a good Catholic the first ought to.

To a profound pessimist about life, being in danger is not depressing. I have never been more cheerful. Please be nice and respect my wishes.

Love,

Scott

TO SALLY POPE TAYLOR[1]

45th Infantry
Camp Taylor, Kentucky
March 10, 1918

Dear Sally Pope:

Much obliged for the Easter postcard—I'd have loved to have come down for Easter but as you know we haven't much say as to what we can do and what we can't.

My first novel is now in the hands of Scribner and Co. Whether they'll publish it for me I don't know yet. It's called *The Romantic Egotist* and most of the adventures in it have happened to me in my short but eventful life. Your mother probably won't let you read it until you're sixteen, Sally, and she's perfectly right. However this is premature as it hasn't been accepted yet.

I often think of you all down there and it's good to think that in this muddled hurly-burly of a world some little corners still preserve their peace and sanity. We're going to be moved from Camp Taylor soon but where we're go-

---

[1] A daughter of Mrs. Richard Taylor (Cousin Ceci).

ing I don't know. I'm anxious to get to France but probably won't for a long, long time. Tell your mother to read
Changing Winds [by] St. John Ervine. It is anti-Catholic
rather, but Rupert Brooke is one of the characters in it and
I rather think she'd like it.

I hope you read a most tremendous lot, Sally—you've
got a keen mind and just feed it with every bit of reading
you can lay your hands on, good, poor or mediocre. A
good mind has a good separator and can peck the good
from the bad in all it absorbs.

My best wishes to everyone.

Love,

Scott F.

TO SALLY POPE TAYLOR

45th Infantry
Camp Sheridan, Alabama
June 19, [1918]

I did enjoy your letter, Sally, and I believe you're going
to be quite a personage. A personage and a personality are
quite different—I wonder if you can figure the difference.
Your mother, Peter the Hermit, Joan of Arc, Cousin Tom,
Mark Antony and Bonnie Prince Charlie were personalities.
You and Cardinal Newman and Julius Caesar and Elizabeth Barrett Browning and myself and Mme. de Staël
were personages. Does the distinction begin to glimmer
on you? Personality may vanish at a sickness; a personage
is hurt more by a worldly setback. Of you four sisters,
you and Tommy are personages, Celia is a personality and
Virginia may be either—or both, as Disraeli was.

Do you know, Sally, I believe that for the first time in
my life I'm rather lonesome down here—not lonesome for
family and friends or anyone in particular but lonesome
for the old atmosphere—a feverish crowd at Princeton
sitting up until three discussing pragmatism or the immortality of the soul—for the glitter of New York with a
tea dance at the Plaza or lunch at Sherries—for the quiet
respectable boredom of St. Paul.

What a funny way to write a girl of thirteen, or is it fourteen?

Thy cousin,

Scott

TO RUTH STURTEVANT

67th Infantry
Camp Sheridan, Alabama
1st of Winter
Nineteen hundred and Eighteen
[*Postmarked December 4, 1918*]

Dear Ruth:

Just a line to tell you how much I enjoyed *Sonia*— If you like that sort of book you should read *Youth's Encounter* (Mackenzie), *Changing Winds* (Ervine), and *The New Machiavelli* and *Tono Bungay* (H. G. Wells)—

My affair still drifts[1]— But my mind is firmly made up that I will not, shall not, can not, should not, must not marry—still, she *is* remarkable—I'm trying desperately *exire armis*—

As ever,

Scott Fitzg_____

TO C. EDMUND DELBOS [2]

17th Brig. Headquarters
Camp Sheridan, Alabama
January 13, [*1919*]

Dear Mr. Delbos:

Your telegram was the greatest shock I have ever known. Like so many others I looked to Dr. Fay before anyone in the world—and I'll think of the days when I came back to school to join his circle before the fire as the happiest of my life.

---

[1] Fitzgerald had made Ruth Sturtevant a confidante in his romance with Zelda.
[2] Delbos had succeeded Fay as headmaster of the Newman School which Fitzgerald attended.

I can't realize that he has gone—that all of us who loved him have lost him forever and that that side of life is over, the great warmth and atmosphere he could cast over youth —the perfect understanding. —When I begin to think about him and what he meant to me I can hardly see the paper.

I can't get leave, but all day Tuesday I'll devote to his memory just as I suppose I will all my life.

The best is over—I feel like the dregs of a cup.

Sincerely,
F. Scott Fitzgerald

TO MRS. EDWARD FITZGERALD

Fort Leavenworth, [Kansas]
[Winter, 1919]

Dear Mother:

I wrote you a letter yesterday but lost it somewhere.

(1) Candy was fine but best not send it in a long box as it gets smashed a little.
(2) Checks came— Thanks.
(3) Am very well.
(4) My novel is autobiographical in point of view but I've borrowed incidents from all my friends' experience.
(5) It's too much trouble to send my flannels home to be washed.
(6) I want suitcase back.
(7) Will you ask father to show you those quotations about "Lord Alfred" in "Lucille"—and copy them out and send them to me— I need them in my book.
(8) I am bored but not weary.
(9) This is the coldest state in the Union.

Love,
Scott

TO RUTH STURTEVANT

[New York City]
June 24, [1919]

Dear Ruth:

I feel I ought to tell you something because you're the

only person in the world that knows the other half. I've
done my best and I've failed—it's a great tragedy to me
and I feel I have very little left to live for because until
everything is as it should be I'll have that sense of vacancy
that only this can give.

I wish you'd tear up this letter and I know you'll never
say what I told you in an hour of depression. Unless someday she will marry me I will never marry.

As ever,

Scott

TO ALIDA BIGELOW

1st Epistle of St. Scott to the Smithsonian
Chapter the I
Verses the I to the last—

(599 Summit Ave.)

In a house below the average
    Of a street above the average
        In a room below the roof
            With a lot above the ears
I shall write Alida Bigelow
    Shall indite Alida Bigelow
        As the world's most famous goof
            (This line don't rhyme)

(September 22, 1919)

What's a date!   Stop this rot. What's a date,
    Mr. Fate   Keep a date,   Mr. Fate?
        Can't berate   Father time,   S'ever
            Mr. Scott.   Such a lot   Scott
                He is not   To berate;
                    Marking time: Tho I hate
                        It's too late   To the dot!
                            So, in rhyme,

Most beautiful, rather-too-virtuous-but-entirely-enchanting Alida:

Scribners has accepted my book. Ain't I smart!

But *hic jubilatio erat totam* spoiled for *meum par lisant une livre, une novellum (novum) nomine* Salt *par* Herr C. G. Morris—a most astounding piece of realism, it makes *Fortitude* look like an antique mental ash-can and is quite as good as *The Old Wives' Tale.*
Of course I think Walpole is a weak-wad anyhow.
Read *Salt,* young girl, so that you may know what life B.
In a few days I'll have lived one score and three days in this vale of tears. On I plod—always bored, often drunk, doing no penance for my faults—rather do I become more tolerant of myself from day to day, hardening my crystal heart with blasphemous humor and shunning only tooth-picks, pathos, and poverty as being the three unforgivable things in life.
Before we meet again I hope you will have tasted strong liquor to excess and kissed many emotional young men in red and yellow moonlights—these things being chasteners of those prejudices which are as *gutta percha* to the niblicks of the century.
I am frightfully unhappy, look like the devil, will be famous within one 12-month and, I hope, dead within 2.
Hoping you are the same, I am

With excruciating respect,

F. Scott Fitzgerald

P.S. If you wish, you may auction off this letter to the gurls of your collidge[1]—on condition that the proceeds go to the Society for the Drownding of Armenian Airedales.

Bla!

[1] Alida Bigelow was at Smith.

TO RUTH STURTEVANT

The Allerton
East 39th Street
New York City
[February, 1920]

Dear Ruth:

I should have written you many moons ago to congratulate you but life sort of picked me up and whirled me along beginning last June and it's only recently that I'm on my feet—so I'm hoping you'll forgive me and sending you a belated wedding present. I have a vague memory of writing you a wild letter when my world collapsed last June— I wonder if you ever got it.

I seem, at present, to be a fairly well established author, with six stories appearing in *The Saturday Evening Post* beginning with the issue of February 21st, stories regularly in *Smart Set* and some in *Scribner's,* and a novel coming out in April, published by Scribners. I'm probably going to get married in March—the same girl, of course—but we haven't any idea where we're going to live. I am immeasurably older, Ruth; I rather want to talk to you sometime—maybe we'll be able to have an eventual bicker while our respective husband and wife chatter of the weather in the corner.

I told you an astounding thing last April—I shouldn't have told you but at the time I simply had to tell someone. Life is so damn odd!

Faithfully,

F. Scott Fitz———

P.S. Is that your right name—"Curt"—or is it "Curtis?" Or maybe it's Kirt, Kurt or Kirk.

TO RUTH STURTEVANT

University Cottage Club
Princeton, New Jersey
March 26, 1920

Dear Ruth:

I certainly was glad to get your letter because you are a

good egg, Ruth, and Sam Kauffman who is at my elbow agrees with me. You may laugh when I tell you I am getting married April Fools' Day but as a matter of fact I think I am. I have no idea where we'll live—we're going to the Biltmore for a week or so but my pocketbook wouldn't stand that long, so we may take a cottage at Rye or somewhere like that. My book came out today and of course I'm frightfully excited. I am quite jubilant because I sold the movie rights of my first *Post* story, "Head and Shoulders" for $2500 to the Metro people. Doesn't that sound good? It was in the February 21st issue and was much better than the one last week.

Next time you're in New York I want you to meet Zelda because she's very beautiful and very wise and very brave as you can imagine—but she's a perfect baby and a more irresponsible pair than we'll be will be hard to imagine. My address for the next ten years will probably be c/o Charles Scribner's Sons and be sure and let me know next time you come or sometime and we can have luncheon or dinner or some darn thing— (You can see from this how out of my depths, I am.)

Well, Ruth, read my book.

As ever,

Scott Fitz——

TO THE BOOKSELLERS' CONVENTION

[*The Biltmore Hotel*]
[*New York City*]
[*Early April, 1920*]

THE AUTHOR'S APOLOGY

I don't want to talk about myself because I'll admit I did that somewhat in this book. In fact to write it, it took three months; to conceive it—three minutes; to collect the data in it—all my life. The idea of writing it came on the first of last July; it was a substitute form of dissipation.

My whole theory of writing I can sum up in one sentence. An author ought to write for the youth of his own generation, the critics of the next, and the schoolmasters of ever afterward.

So, gentlemen, consider all the cocktails mentioned in this book drunk by me as a toast to the Booksellers' Convention.

Sincerely yours,

[F. Scott Fitzgerald]

TO MARIE HERSEY [1]

*The Commodore Hotel
New York City*
[*May, 1920*]

Dear Bug:

Well, you may go to Princeton but we never will again. We were there three days, Zelda and five men in Harvey Firestone's car, and not one of us drew a sober breath. Just ask anybody about it when you go down there—ask your friend Ollie Rogers—he was on the party. It was the damnedest party ever held in Princeton and everybody in the University will agree.

We are going around in a circle but at last seem to have a plan. We have purchased an ancient Marmon—not very ancient, 1917—and we're going to tour north to Lake Champlain and see if we can get a cottage there for the summer. We didn't like Rye at all and we can't live in Princeton after our celebration.

So you are going to see Bet. My Gawd! I can imagine anyone married but not she.

I'm glad you and Jim are going to have another chance to cause each other's doom and I certainly hope that if you decide you do want him you won't change your mind again. I'm still mad about marriage—if we could only find a place to live.

---

[1] Marie Hersey had grown up with Fitzgerald in St. Paul.

Zelda sends her best and says to come back to New York and help her buy some more clothes.

                              Best to Bet and Heine.

                              Love,

                              F. Scott F——

TO RUTH STURTEVANT

                              c/o Mrs. Wakeman
                              Westport, Connecticut
                              [*May 14, 1920*]

Dear Ruth:

In acute agony and despair we at last forcibly left the Commodore, bought a car, threw our bags in the back seat and set out. We discovered the alarming fact our first day on the road from the people we had lunch with that *there's no swimming in Lake Champlain because it's too cold.* That was the shock of our lives, Ruth, because if Zelda can't swim she's miserable. I feel I'm a terrible piker to have put you to all that trouble but honestly it never occurred to me that there was no swimming there. We turned down a slick cottage on the coast of Maine last month for that very reason.

So we bore East, arrived here at nine o'clock this morning and immediately found the slickest little cottage on the Sound. We signed the lease on it at noon. There's a beach here and loads of seclusion and just about what we're looking for. We'd just about given up hope so now we're in the most jovial mood imaginable.

Thank Curt for me, Ruth, and tell him I'm mighty indebted and awfully sorry we were so stupid in our geography. He wrote that you weren't well. I hope you're lots better now.

                              As ever,

                              F. Scott Fitzgerald

TO JOHN GRIER HIBBEN [1]

> *Wakeman's*
> *Westport, Connecticut*
> [*June 3, 1920*]

My dear President Hibben:

I want to thank you very much for your letter and to confess that the honor of a letter from you outweighed my real regret that my book gave you concern. It was a book written with the bitterness of my discovery that I had spent several years trying to fit in with a curriculum that is after all made for the average student. After the curriculum had tied me up, taken away the honors I'd wanted, bent my nose over a chemistry book and said "No fun, no activities, no offices, no Triangle trips—no, not even a diploma if you can't do chemistry"—after that I retired. It is easy for the successful man in college, the man who has gotten what he wanted to say.

"It's all fine. It makes men. It made me, see"—

—but it seems to me it's like the captain of a company when he has his men lined up at attention for inspection. He sees only the tightly buttoned coat and the shaved faces. He doesn't know that perhaps a private in the rear rank is half crazy because a pin is sticking in his back and he can't move, or another private is thinking that his wife is dying and he can't get leave because too many men in the company are gone already.

I don't mean at all that Princeton is not the happiest time in most boys' lives. It is, of course—I simply say it wasn't the happiest time in mine. I love it now better than any place on earth. The men—the undergraduates of Yale and Princeton are cleaner, healthier, better-looking, better dressed, wealthier and more attractive than any undergraduate body in the country. I have no fault to find with Princeton that I can't find with Oxford and Cambridge. I simply wrote out of my own impressions, wrote as honestly as I could a picture of its beauty. That the picture is cynical is the fault of my temperament.

[1] Hibben, president of Princeton, had written Fitzgerald a letter lamenting the portrayal of the University in *This Side of Paradise*. At the same time he praised Fitzgerald's story, "The Four Fists," for showing "human nature at its best."

My view of life, President Hibben, is the view of the Theodore Dreisers and Joseph Conrads—that life is too strong and remorseless for the sons of men. My idealism flickered out with Henry Strater's anti-club movement at Princeton. "The Four Fists," latest of my stories to be published, was the first to be written. I wrote it in desperation one evening because I had a three-inch pile of rejection slips and it was financially necessary for me to give the magazine what they wanted. The appreciation it has received has amazed me.

I must admit however that *This Side of Paradise* does overaccentuate the gayety and country club atmosphere of Princeton. For the sake of the reader's interest that part was much overstressed, and of course the hero, not being average, reacted rather unhealthily I suppose to many perfectly normal phenomena. To that extent the book is inaccurate. It is the Princeton of Saturday night in May. Too many intelligent classmates of mine have failed to agree with it for me to consider it really photographic any more, as of course I did when I wrote it.

Next time I am in Princeton I will take the privilege of coming to see you.

I am, sir,

Very respectfully yours,

F. Scott Fitzgerald

TO BURTON RASCOE

38 West 59th Street
New York City
November 17, 1920

Dear Mr. Rascoe:

Thanks for the pamphlet. I enjoyed your essay on Mencken—I think it's a clever touch: his "being the only true American," just as Anatole France "is the only living Catholic." Also I agree with you that he is a great man and bum critic of poetry. Why has no one mentioned to him or of him that he is an intolerably muddled syllogism with several excluded middles on the question of aristocracy? What on earth does he mean by it? Every aristocrat of every race has come in for scathing comment yet he holds out the word as a universal panacea for art.

He and Nathan were up in the apartment drinking with us the other night and he was quite enthusiastic about *Main Street*.

This *Mooncalf* is a wretched thing without a hint of glamor, utterly undistinguished, childhood impressions dumped into the reader's lap with a profound air of importance, and the sort of thing that Walpole and Beresford (whom I abominate) turn out twice a year with great bawlings about their art. I'd rather be Tarkington or David Graham Phillips and cast at least some color and radiance into my work! Wouldn't you?

> Thanks again.
> Yours,
>
> F. Scott Fitzgerald

TO JAMES BRANCH CABELL

> *38 West 59th Street*
> *New York City*
> *Christmas, 1920*

Dear Mr. Cabell:

It was the surprise of my life when Zelda handed me an autographed first edition of *Jurgen* this morning. You can imagine how I felt when I tell you I haven't even been able to borrow it. Whenever I go to George Nathan's I finger it covetously but I could never get farther than the door with it. People have a way of regarding it as infinitely precious. I want to see anyone try to borrow mine!

I once fingered a copy of it in a New Orleans bookstore one year ago and I've been cursing myself ever since for not buying it. I'd seen Mencken's review but was very broke at the time. I read a wretched article on you in *The Bookman* by someone last month. Mencken and water. It must amuse you to have whole book review sections devoted to you after years of comparative neglect. Do you remember Samuel Butler's

> "Oh critics, cultured critics
> Who will praise me after I am dead

>   Who will see in me either more or less
>   than I intended
>   How I should have hated you."

—only you have the ironic good fortune of being alive.

I have just finished an extraordinary novel called *The Beautiful Lady Without Mercy*[1] which shows touches of your influence, much of Mencken, and not a little of Frank Norris. Up to now such diverse writers as you, Mencken, Dreiser, and so forth have been held together more or less by the common enemy, philistia, but now that good books are, for the moment, selling almost as well as bad ones I wish Mencken would take a crack at such bogus masterpieces as *Mooncalf,* a book without glamor, without ideas, with nothing except a timorously uninteresting report of a shoddy and uninteresting life. I'm all for *Salt, The Titan* and *Main Street.* At *Poor White* I grow weary—but at *Mooncalf*—my God!

The only two books I've ever known my wife to weep over were *Ethan Frome* and *The Rivet in Grandfather's Neck.*[2] I appreciated your qualified tribute to Tarkington in *Beyond Life.* I agree with it perfectly.

I hope we'll meet in the near future and meanwhile I'm looking forward to *Jurgen* as I have never looked forward to a book before.

>   Most admiringly and gratefully,
>
>   F. Scott Fitzgerald

TO MR. AND MRS. PHILIP McQUILLAN[3]

>   *38 West 59th Street*
>   *New York City*
>   *December 28, 1920*

Dear Aunt Lorena and Uncle Phil:

The steak set is fine! We were in a furnished cottage all summer so we bought no silver so this will come in awfully handy whenever we have dinner in our apartment. We

---

[1] Afterward *The Beautiful and Damned.*
[2] By Cabell.
[3] Philip McQuillan was a younger brother of Fitzgerald's mother.

won't have to bring the bread knife on the table any more. We certainly are much obliged.

I am just putting the finishing touches on my novel, *The Beautiful Lady Without Mercy*, which is the story of a young couple who rapidly go to pieces. It is much more carefully written than the first one and I have a good deal of faith in it tho it's so bitter and pessimistic that I doubt if it'll have the popular success of the first. Still, as you know, I really am in this game seriously and for something besides money and if it's necessary to bootlick the pet delusions of the inhabitants of *Main Street* (Have you read it? It's fine!) to make money I'd rather live on less and preserve the one duty of a sincere writer—to set down life as he sees it as gracefully as he knows how.

I have a contract you know with the *Metropolitan Magazine* to serialize my next novel for $7000 but I'm sure if they tried to do this one their circulation would drop. You know the stuff they want! My current idol, H. L. Mencken, says about it:

"If you yearn to uplift and like a happy comfortable sobbing, an upward rolling of eyes and a vast blowing of noses it will please you—on the other hand if you are a carnal fellow as I am, with a stomach ruined by alcohol, it will gag you."

So within several years you'll probably hear that I've been hung by an earnest delegation of 100% Americans.

I am waiting to hear from a scenario I outlined on Griffith's order for _____ _____ —who is a colorless wench in the life as is her pal, _____ _____. But I am not averse to taking all the shekels I can garner from the movies. I'll roll them joy pills (the literary habit) till doomsday because you can always say, "Oh, but they put on the movie in a different spirit from the way it was written!"

When I collect from Scribners this winter we expect to go abroad and spend a year or so. Why don't you come East? The best liquor in New York is only $8.00 a quart. I thought of sending you and Uncle Alley and Father a bottle each but I decided it was too risky. I imagine you'd pay about $18.00 for anything drinkable out there.

Thanks again and luck to the redoubtable David.

As ever,

Scott

TO JAMES BRANCH CABELL

38 West 59th Street
New York City
December 30, 1920

Dear Mr. Cabell:

Can't resist telling you that I have finished *Jurgen* and think on the whole that it's a finer novel than *The Revolt of the Angels*—tho at present I'm inclined to rank your work as a whole below both Conrad and Anatole France. However you're a much younger man.

My wife doesn't agree—you are by all odds her favorite novelist.

Please don't bother to answer this but if you'd let us know next time you're in New York we'd both be very flattered.

Yours,

F. Scott Fitzgerald

". . . Then Joe * read us . . . his poem at which both David † . . . and I laughed appreciatively

> "I'm sending a cable to Cabell
> To cavil at callow callants
> Who callously carped at the rabble
> For caring for amours gallantes
>
> For each pious burg out in Bergen
> (a county in Jersey) has spoke
> For jerking the joy out of *Jurgen*
> And judging *The Genius* a joke!"

(From Margot Asquith's Diary, Vol. 9, p. 273)

* King Joseph III of Patagonia.
† David Balfour, M.D., D.D.

TO SINCLAIR LEWIS

38 West 59th Street
New York City
January 26, 1920 [*1921*]

Dear Mr. Lewis:

I want to tell you that *Main Street* has displaced *Theron Ware* in my favor as the best American novel. The amount of sheer data in it is amazing! As a writer and a Minnesotan let me swell the chorus—after a third reading.

With the utmost admiration,

F. Scott Fitzgerald

TO JAMES BRANCH CABELL

[*38 West 59th Street*]
New York City
February 23, [*1921*]

Dear Mr. Cabell:

I was delighted to get *Figures of Earth.* I had just ordered it at the bookstore, which copy I shall present to some unworthy charity.

I am cancelling all engagements to read it today and tomorrow.

Having finished my second novel née *The Beautiful Lady Without Mercy* but now known as *The Beautiful and Damned* I am about to sell my soul. . . . and go to the coast to write one moving picture. . . . "Well," as Codman says in his touching monograph on Anchovies, "there is no movie in *Jurgen.* It just won't fillum." Incidentally given free rein, wouldn't it be a treat to see it unexpurgated in the movies?

That was an idiotic review of *The Cords of Vanity* by Richard Le Gallienne—which reminds me I must order France's new book, *The Fall of the Angels.* It must be a sequel to *The Revolt of the Angels.*

Still hoping that we may meet soon.

Faithfully,

F. Scott Fitzgerald

38 West 59th Street
New York City
February 26, 1921

My dear Miss Newman:

While it astonished me that so few critics mentioned the influence of *Sinister Street* on *This Side of Paradise*, I feel sure that it was much more in intention than in literal fact. It occurred to me to write an American version of the history of that sort of young man—in which, no doubt, I was hindered by lack of perspective as well as by congenital shortcomings.

But I was also hindered by a series of resemblances between my life and that of Michael Fane which, had I been a more conscientious man, might have precluded my ever attempting an autobiographical novel. I have five copies of *Youth's Encounter* at present in my library, sent me by people who stumbled on the book and thought that it was an amazing parallel to my own life. When I was twenty-one and began *This Side of Paradise* my literary taste was so unformed that *Youth's Encounter* was still my "perfect book." My book quite naturally shows the influence to a marked degree. However, I resent your details. Both Shane Leslie in the *Dublin Review* and Maurice Francis Egan in the *Catholic World* took me to task for painting "Monsignor Darcy" from the life. He was, of course, my best friend, the Monsignor Sigourney Fay to whom the book was dedicated. He was known to many Catholics as the most brilliant priest in America. The letters in the book are almost transcriptions of his own letters to me.

Amory Blaine's mother was also an actual character, the mother of a friend of mine, whose name I cannot mention. There is such an obvious connection between her early career and that of the cook in *Youth's Encounter* that I appreciate your pointing it out. You see I object to being twice blamed—once for transcribing a character from life and once for stealing him from another author. I have had numerous comments from Princeton about putting J——[1]

[1] John Peale Bishop.

into the book as "Thomas P. D'Invilliers," and now I am
told that I borrowed the dilettante aesthete Wilmot from
Mackenzie. "Spires and Gargoyles" was possibly suggested
by "Dreaming Spires" but the terms "slicker" and "big
men" were in use at Princeton when I first went there—
before *Youth's Encounter* was written.

It seems to me that you have marred a justified criticism
by such pettinesses as comparing the names "Blaine" and
"Fane," and by remarking on the single occurrence of the
word "narcissus" in *Sinister Street*. You seem to be unconscious that even Mackenzie had his sources such as
Dorian Gray and *None Other Gods* and that occasionally
we may have drunk at the same springs. Incidentally Michael's governess did *not* tease him about G. A. Henty.

This is the first letter of any kind I have ever written to a critic of my book and I shall probably regret this
one before the day is over. I sent the novel to Mencken
with the confession that it derived itself from Mackenzie,
Wells and Tarkington, with half a dozen additional overtones, but there are comparisons you brought up that make
me as angry as my book evidently made you. It is as if I
accused Floyd Dell of being a plagiarist because both our
mooncalfs wrote poetry and both walked toward a dark
town at the last, whispering of their lost loves—or said that
Cabell's *Jurgen* is an imitation of *The Revolt of the Angels*, or even, to use another Tristan and Irene comparison,
compared your article with p. 138 of Mencken's *Prejudices,
1st Series*.

                                        Yours very truly,

                                        F. Scott Fitzgerald

TO MISS VAS

                                Dellwood
                                White Bear Lake, Minnesota
                                September 14, 1921

My dear Miss Vas:

Your teacher is probably an ass—most of them are, I've
found. Your details about me are correct but your spelling

is as incorrect as mine. There were *125* misspellings in the 1st printing of *Paradise*.

I would enjoy seeing your review—also your novel. There is no such thing "getting your values straightened out" except for third-class minds who are willing to accept the latest jitney interpretation of the universe by some Illinois or South Carolina messiah.

Sincerely,

F. Scott Fitzgerald

TO GEORGE JEAN NATHAN

626 Goodrich Avenue
St. Paul, Minnesota

[Winter, 1922]

Dear George:

Thanks for your note. In the same mail came a letter from Harris' office about my play.[1] I suppose they would be best as, according to Zoe Akin, Hopkins is a bad financier and John Williams is on the rocks. The play is, like most of my stuff, a very bad performance full of exceedingly good things. It varies between comedy and burlesque and is composed of three intermediate fanciful scenes strung together not too securely between a very solid first and last act.

I shall probably be sending you an exquisite novelette within the month—the best thing I've ever done—something really remarkable.

By now you've read my book and though I know it amused and entertained you I'd give anything to talk with you and hear what you thought of its artistic merits. Bunny (Edmund B.) Wilson is doing an article on me for the March *Bookman* in which he dissects me cruelly and completely. I can't tell you how I enjoyed it. He has a fine mind, George, and except for Aldous Huxley and Dos Passos he's worth all the rest of the "younger generation" put together.

[1] *The Vegetable.*

A long time ago when Donald Stewart first met you he wondered if you recognized him as the man whom we brought to your apartment once and who went on a party with Ruth, Zelda, you and me.

We're coming East for a fortnight in March. I read *The Critic and the Drama* with the greatest interest, though I had read most if not all of it in the *Smart Set*. Best to Mencken.

As ever,

F. Scott Fitzgerald

TO JAMES BRANCH CABELL

626 Goodrich Avenue
St. Paul, Minnesota
[*February, 1922*]

Dear Mr. Cabell:

I feel that by asking your permission to quote a private letter I have not acted in the best of taste. There have been, of course, innumerable precedents of late, but that does not excuse it. I appreciate your exceeding kindness and courtesy.

It seems that Perkins of Scribners had heard from some editor in Richmond that you liked the book. He had tried to get in touch with that editor to see if it was quotable—realizing how invaluable a word from you might be. For some reason he evidently failed, and he wired me Monday night—or Sunday—asking me if I had a letter from you which was quotable. I wired you immediately.

I've had the pleasure of a three day amour with an Exquisite Case of Spanish Influenza, and like all such illicit affairs it has left me weak and chastened. I hope you are *not* the same.

Faithfully,

F. Scott Fitzgerald

TO JAMES BRANCH CABELL

626 Goodrich Avenue
St. Paul, Minnesota
March 4, 1922

Dear Mr. Cabell:

Thank you for your letter. I am tremendously sorry you followed *The Beautiful and Damned* in the serial because it was cut to pieecs. But I appreciate the compliment of your doing so. And the final book version was considerably revised. However it isn't worth going through again, for you, I mean.

Hergesheimer, that charming egotist, came through this swollen Main Street awhile back. He didn't like it.

When do we meet?

I have just finished a comedy for the commercial stage.[1]

When do you publish another book? Please do soon as I am bored with all current fiction including my own.

Yours faithfully,[2]

F. Scott Fitzgerald

I appreciate your kindness in saying those things about the book. I cut part of the ending in the final revision, as you notice. I hope it wasn't the part you liked. I liked the other ending but it seemed to spoil the general *hardness* of the book.

TO JAMES BRANCH CABELL

The Plaza
New York City
March 27, 1922

Dear Mr. Cabell:

Am dictating this and it is the most profound agony I have ever gone through. The stenographer embarrasses me

[1] *The Vegetable.*
[2] Concerning this farewell Fitzgerald wrote in the margin, "This is yours. I believe I'll use it for awhile."

because I feel that I have got to think quickly and in consequence everything comes in broken clauses. But I simply cannot let your very kind letter go unanswered any longer. You were very nice to allow me to place such an endorsement in the advertisements of my book. It has gone up beyond 30,000, in fact it will touch 40,000 within the week, but I doubt very much if as many people will like it who liked *This Side of Paradise*. I saw Mencken and Nathan for a minute the other morning. Mencken seemed nervous and tired, but Nathan is his usual self, albeit developing a paunch and losing a bit of his remarkable youthfulness. Why do not you publish a geography of the lands of your own creating on the inside, front and back covers of your next book, much as Conrad has in the last edition of *Victory?* I think it would be very amusing both for you and for your public, or would it, in the case of an imaginative country, appear too obvious?

Am in New York, having rather a poor time and will return to St. Paul Sunday.

As ever,

F. Scott Fitzgerald

TO JOHN V. A. WEAVER

626 Goodrich Avenue
St. Paul, Minnesota

[*Probably May, 1922*]

Dear John:

I was tickled to write the review.[1] I saw Broun's and F.P.A.'s reviews but you know how they love me and how much attention I pay to their dictums.

This is my new style of letter writing.[2] It is to make it easy for comments and notes to be put in when my biographer begins to assemble my collected letters.

The *Metropolitan* isn't here yet. I shall certainly read

[1] Of *Margery Wins the Game* by Weaver.
[2] The letter was written in a very small hand in the middle of a sheet of paper.

"Enamel." I wish to Christ I could go to Europe.

Thine,

F. Scott Fitzgerald

TO MISS PAXTON

Great Neck, Long Island
[Fall, 1922–Spring, 1924]

Dear Miss Paxton:

As I have nothing but respect for Theta Sigma Phi it would be a mean trick for me to agree to make a speech for them. How would you like to have a collapsed novelist wandering wildly over the campus of the University of Illinois? I suggest Mr. Bryant or Mr. Cone as an alternate.

Seriously I'd love to do it but I'm absolutely incapable through constitutional stagefright. With appreciation of the honor of being asked, I am

Most sincerely,

F. Scott Fitzgerald

P.S. My price for lectures is 12,000 louis d'or or when lecturing in Guatemala, I accept my fee in rubber.

TO MR. MAURICE

Great Neck, Long Island
[February, 1923]

Dear Mr. Maurice:

I don't know how to apologize for my delay—but the fault is Sherwood Anderson's. It's an amazing book[1] and affected me profoundly. It reached me Friday and I didn't get to reading it until Sunday—finished it late Sunday night—intending to review it Monday morning. Well, I

[1] *Many Marriages.*

sat down at nine and wrote about 1500 words of the worst drivel ever launched. My wife read it, we decided it'd be criminal to hand it in. The book is the full flowering of Anderson's personality and wants the most careful consideration else one is tempted to say the wildest things about it.

This is the first time I can remember having failed to live up to my word on a thing like this—but it seemed simply out of my power. My review will reach you Friday. I suppose that's plenty of time as it's already two days too late for the issue of February 24th.

> With sincere apologies, I am
> Yours,
> F. Scott Fitzgerald

TO SHERWOOD ANDERSON

> *Great Neck, Long Island*
> [*April, 1923*]

Dear Sherwood:

Just as I was asking the girl in *Vanity Fair* to save me an autograph of yours if one ever happened in there, your letter came. I liked *Many Marriages* much more fully than I could express in that review— It stays with me still. It's a haunting book and, it seems to me, ahead of *Poor White* and even of the two books of short stories.

I don't quite get you about Tom Boyd—he's a great fellow, incidentally, and a strong admirer of your work. His own first book out this month is an excellent piece of work.

> Yours,
> F. Scott Fitzgerald

TO THE EDITOR OF *THE LITERARY DIGEST* [1]

[1] Fitzgerald wrote this statement in reply to a circular from *The Literary Digest* asking "the leaders of thought in literature, drama, and religion" to express their views on censorship in the arts. Fitzgerald stipulated, "If used at all this is not to be cut or changed in any way."

[*Great Neck, New York*]
[*Probably late April, 1923*]

The clean-book bill will be one of the most immoral measures ever adopted. It will throw American art back into the junk heap where it rested comfortably between the Civil War and the World War. The really immoral books like *Simon Called Peter* and *Mumbo Jumbo* won't be touched—they'll attack Hergesheimer, Dreiser, Anderson and Cabell whom they detest because they can't understand. George Moore, Hardy and Anatole France who are unintelligible to children and idiots will be suppressed at once for debauching the morals of village clergymen.

F. Scott Fitzgerald

TO CARL VAN VECHTEN

Great Neck, New York
[*Postmarked March 1, 1924*]

Dear Carl:

Thanks for the kind telegram. I'm always glad when anyone likes *The Beautiful and Damned*—most people prefer *This Side of Paradise* and while I do myself I hate to see one child preferred above another—you know the feeling. We both want to see you soon and are going to haul or drag you out here by "hook or crook" (if I may be allowed to coin a new phrase).

Thine,

F. Scott Fitz_____

TO CARL VAN VECHTEN

Villa Marie, Valescure
St. Raphael, France
[*Probably June, 1924*]

Dear Carl:

Your letter was one of the nicest compliments I've ever

had. Thank you for a most cheerful half hour while I basked in the warmth of such generous praise. We shall be here until November 1st so *don't* neglect to send *The Tattooed Countess*[1] down to the last sardonic gargoyle on her navel.

We are living here in a sort of idyllic state among everything lovely imaginable in the way of Mediterranean delights. Unlike you I have only an occasional lust for the exotic streets of the metropolis—at present I am content to work and become excruciatingly healthy under Byron's and Shelley's and Dickens' sky. I will try to dig up a picture though God knows where. I have just received two furious letters from papists referring to "Absolution." But yours is worth ten thousand of them.

Zelda sends her admiration and love to you both and I do too.

F. Scott Fitz———

TO ERNEST BOYD

Hotel des Princes
Rome, Italy
February 1, 1925

Dear Ernest:

Your picture of me in *Portraits, Real and Imaginary* truly touched me. I was honestly delighted that I, or we, had pleased anybody enough so they could write about me (or us) like that. Of course it was indiscreet (you should see the letter I got today from Mother: "Who is this Ernest Boyd who seems to know so much about my boy?") but it is so delicately done that I'm sure it will fill the gay cafés with everybody who reads it. It made Zelda and I horribly homesick for New York. We'd love to go shooting out into space with you and Madeline. We're tired of black shirts and dirty teeth and the parades of Pope ——— the Sixth—tho, contrary to Madeleine's prediction, we thoroughly enjoyed St. Raphael last summer. Paris in the spring, as they say!

[1] A novel by Van Vechten.

I read the whole book with the greatest pleasure, regretting that the "impressions" were so short, and liking especially A. E., Nathan, myself, Aesthete, Yeats and Beer. And, least, the critic. But God, it all sounded like home—and the $100,000 we're trying to save over here is still about $99,000 away.

My new novel appears in late March: *The Great Gatsby*. It represents about a year's work and I think it's about ten years better than anything I've done. All my harsh smartness has been kept ruthlessly out of it—it's the greatest weakness in my work, distracting and disfiguring it even when it calls up an isolated sardonic laugh. I don't think this has a touch left. I wanted to call it *Trimalchio* (it's laid on Long Island) but I was voted down by Zelda and everybody else.

Best love to you and Madeleine from both of us—and thank you for writing about me so pleasantly. I feel like an infinitely more genial soul than I did a week ago.

Scott Fitzg——

TO ROGER BURLINGAME [1]

[*Bound from Naples to Marseille en route to Paris*]

April 19, 1925

Dear Roger:

I think that's about the nicest letter I ever received about my work. I was tremendously pleased that it moved you in that way—"made you want to be back somewhere so much"—because that describes, better than I could have put it myself, whatever unifying emotion the book has, either in regard to the temperament of Gatsby himself or in my own mood while writing it. Thank you so much for taking the trouble to write.

As yet I know nothing. Zelda has been too sick for the long overland trip to Paris in our French Ford so we had to catch a boat on a day's notice to get the car back to France within the 6 months' period of the International

[1] An editor at Scribners.

touring arrangement. (She's better now—Italy depressed us both beyond measure—a dead land where everything that could be done or said was done long ago—for whoever is deceived by the pseudo-activity under Mussolini is deceived by the spasmodic last jerk of a corpse. In these days of criticism it takes a weak bunch of desperates to submit for 3 years to a tyrant, even a mildly beneficent one.)

—But leaving suddenly I have heard nothing about *Gatsby*—nothing except you and Ring since Perkins' letters three months ago. I don't know how many were printed or what advance orders or what notices or advertising, not to mention reviews, tho by this time all that information is probably waiting for me in Paris, having been forwarded from Capri. (By the way, will you ask Max to pass on any movie nibbles to Reynolds?)

Thank you again and again for your letter. I shall always keep it.

                                                    Scott Fitz——

TO H. L. MENCKEN

                                            14 rue de Tilsitt
                                            Paris, France
                                            May 4, 1925

Dear Menck:

Your letter was the first outside word that reached me about my book. I was tremendously moved both by the fact that you liked it and by your kindness in writing me about it. By the next mail came a letter from Edmund Wilson and a clipping from Stallings, both bulging with interest and approval, but as you know I'd rather have you like a book of mine than anyone in America.

There is a tremendous fault in the book—the lack of an emotional presentment of Daisy's attitude toward Gatsby after their reunion (and the consequent lack of logic or importance in her throwing him over). Everyone has felt this but no one has spotted it because it's concealed beneath elaborate and overlapping blankets of prose. Wilson complained: "The characters are so uniformly unpleasant"; Stallings: "a sheaf of gorgeous notes for a novel"; and you say: "The story is fundamentally trivial." I think the smooth, almost unbroken pattern makes you feel that. Despite your admiration for Conrad you have lately— perhaps in reaction against the merely well made novels of James' imitators—become used to the formless. It is in protest against my own formless two novels, and Lewis' and Dos Passos' that this was written. I admit that in comparison to *My Antonia* and *The Lost Lady* it is a failure in what it tries to do but I think in comparison to *Cytherea* or *Linda Condon* it is a success. At any rate I have learned a lot from writing it, and the influence on it has been the masculine one of *The Brothers Karamazov*, a thing of incomparable form, rather than of the feminine one of *The Portrait of a Lady*. If it seems trivial or "anecdotal" (sp) it is because of an aesthetic fault, a failure in one very important episode, and not a frailty in the theme. At least I don't think so. Did you ever know a writer to calmly take a just criticism and shut up?

Incidentally, I had hoped it would amuse the Mencken who wrote the essay on New York in the last book of *Prejudices*—tho I know nothing in the new Paris streets that I like better than Park Avenue at twilight.

I think the book is so far a commercial failure, at least it was two weeks after publication—hadn't reached 20,000 yet. So I rather regret (but not violently) the fact that I turned down $15,000 for the serial rights. However I have all the money I need and was growing rather tired of being a popular author. My trash for the *Post* grows worse and worse as there is less and less heart in it. Strange to say, my whole heart was in my first trash. I thought that "The Offshore Pirate" was quite as good as "Benediction." I never really "wrote down" until after the failure of *The Vegetable* and that was to make this book possible. I would have written down long ago if it had been profitable —I tried it unsuccessfully for the movies. People don't seem to realize that for an intelligent man writing down is about the hardest thing in the world. When people like Hughes and Stephen Whitman go wrong after one tragic book, it is because they never had any real egos or attitudes but only empty bellies and cross nerves. The bellies full and the nerves soothed with vanity they see life rosily and would be violently insincere in writing anything but the happy trash they do. The others, like Owen Johnson, just get tired. There's nothing the matter with some of Johnson's later books, they're just rotten that's all. He was tired and his work is no more writing in the sense that the work [of] Thomas Hardy and Gene Stratton Porter is writing than were Dreiser's dime novels.

However I won't bore you any longer. I expect to spend about two years on my next novel and it ought to be more successful critically. It's about myself—not what I thought of myself in *This Side of Paradise*. Moreover it will have the most amazing form ever invented.

With many, many thanks,

F. Scott Fitz——

P.S. This is simply an acknowledgment and expects no answer.

Italy (but not France) is full of Pilsen and Munich beer of fine quality. There is less than there was when I got there.

TO H. L. MENCKEN

*14 rue de Tilsitt
Paris, France*

[*May or June, 1925*]

Dear Menck:

The idea is fascinating and I'll try it when we go to Brussels in July. I've got two pieces of hack work to do first. I thought the *Spring Flight* [1] was great—it needed some cutting tho, and I have no feeling that he has another book in him. That must have all been true. Also I liked *The Constant Nymph* [2] but I thought *The Apple of the Eye* was lousy.

By the way you mention in your review of *Sea Horses* that Conrad has only two imitators. How about

[1] By Lee J. Smits.
[2] By Margaret Kennedy.

O'Neill in *Emperor Jones*	*(Heart of Darkness)*
Hergesheimer in *Bright Shawl*	*(Java Head)*
Me in *Gatsby*	(God! I've learned a lot from him)
Maugham in *The Moon and Sixpence*	(You mentioned it in your own review, five years ago)

But his (Conrad's) approach and his prose is naturally more imitated than his material, tho he did send [at] least O'Neill and Masefield to sea in ships.

As ever,

Robert Chambers Fitzgerald
(according to Rascoe)

TO CARL VAN VECHTEN

14 rue de Tilsitt
Paris, France

[*Postmarked June 6, 1925*]

Dear Carl:

I met Fanya[1] on the streets of this not unpress-agented hamlet, looking lovely as usual (Fanya—not Paris) and she told me you like *Gatsby* and had written me. The letter must have gone astray but last week arrived *The Nation* with your review of my book. Carl, it made me feel awfully high to have anyone whose work I admire and enjoy as much as I do yours feel that way and write that way about my book. A dozen or more people have been very complimentary about it, largely on account of the writing, but only three or four seemed to have cared to notice what I was driving at and whether or not I approached realizing my intention—but I am consoled by the fact that those three or four have been the people whose appreciation I would rather have than any other Americans. And when

[1] Mrs. Carl Van Vechten.

one of them goes to the trouble not only of writing a letter but of reviewing it—well, you can't ask much more in the way of courtesy or friendliness. I can't tell you how deeply I am in your debt.

Scott Fitz_____

TO GILBERT SELDES

14 rue de Tilsitt
[*Paris, France*]
[*June, 1925*]

Dear Gilbert:

Your letter made me feel awfully good. Please come over! We dined with Gerald [1] last night and had such a good time that I must shift to pencil or my trembling hand will spread the high hint of hangover over the page.

If you get a proof of your *Dial* review please send it to me as I can't wait to see the magazine—having had only three even decent reviews.

Burton Rascoe says *The Great Gatsby* is just Robert Chambers with overtones of *Nedra* by Harold Nigrath. So I think I'll write a "serious" novel about the Great Struggle the Great American Peasant has with the Soil. Everyone else seems to be doing it. Burton will be the hero as I'm going to try to go to "life" for my material from now on.

Best from us both to you both.

Scott

TO GERTRUDE STEIN

14 rue de Tilsitt
[*Paris, France*]
June, 1925

Dear Miss Gertrude Stein:

Thank you. None of your letter was "a bad compliment"

[1] Gerald Murphy.

and all of it "was a comfort." Thank you very much. My wife and I think you a very handsome, very gallant, very kind lady and thought so as soon as we saw you, and were telling Hemingway so when you passed us searching your car on the street. Hemingway and I went to Lyons shortly after to get my car and had a slick drive through Burgundy. He's a peach of a fellow and absolutely first-rate.

I am so anxious to get *The Making of Americans* and learn something from it and imitate things out of it which I shall doubtless do. That future debt I tried so hard to repay by making the Scribners read it in the *Transatlantic* convinced one, but the old man's mind was too old.

You see, I am content to let you, and the one or two like you who are acutely sensitive, think or fail to think for me and my kind artistically (their name is not legend but the word like it), much as the man of 1901, say, would let Nietche (sp!) think for him intellectually. I am a very second-rate person compared to first-rate people—I have indignation as well as most of the other major faults—and it honestly makes me shiver to know that such a writer as you attributes such a significance to my factitious, meritricous (metricous?) *This Side of Paradise*. It puts me in a false position, I feel. Like Gatsby, I have only hope.

Thank you enormously for writing me.

Scott Fitzg——

TO GILBERT SELDES

14 rue de Tilsitt
Paris, France
[*June or July, 1925*]

Dear Gilbert:

Thank you a thousand times for your enthusiasm about *Gatsby*. I believe I'd rather [have] your discriminating enthusiasm than anyone's in America (did I tell you this before?), and to be really believed-in again, to feel "exciting," is tremendously satisfactory. My new novel may be my last for ten years or so—that is if it sells no better than *Gatsby* (which has only gone a little over 20,000 copies) for I may go to Hollywood and try to learn the moving picture business from the bottom up.

We leave for Antibes on August 4th—Zelda and I in our car (the same one) and nurse and baby by train. There we shall spend one month growing brown and healthy— then return here for the fall. Beyond January our plans are vague—Nice followed by Oxford or Cambridge for the summer perhaps. _____ _____ has been here—he seemed horribly pretentious to me and more than usually wrong— in fact it was a shock to see the change in him. I see Hemingway a great deal and, before you left, something of Gerald—both of them are thoroughly charming.

If you and Amanda come over in the spring we may have a villa big enough for you to visit us in Nice. God, I'm wild for the Riviera. Love from us to you both.

Scott

TO H. L. MENCKEN

14 rue de Tilsitt
[*Paris, France*]
[*Fall, 1925*]

Dear Menck:

Thank you for your most kind, just and illuminating review of *Gatsby*. I am amused at the later reviews coming in from the West, some of them containing whole paraphrases from it (your review) needless to say unacknowledged. I think it has had the effect of swinging the expression of opinion from a sort of suspicious bewilderment to a grudging, but on the whole deferential, bewilderment.

Once more I am in your debt for the interest you have shown in dedicating that much space and consideration to me.

I have met most of the American literary world here (the crowd that centers about Pound) and find them mostly junk-dealers; except a few like Hemingway who are doing rather more thinking and working than the young men around New York. Best regards to George.

Sincerely,
F. Scott Fitzgerald

TO ALEXANDER WOOLLCOTT

14 rue de Tilsitt
Paris, France
[Fall, 1925]

Dear Alec:

This is to ask you a peculiar favor and to add hastily that if it is any trouble please don't hesitate to neglect it. It is the case of a newspaperman here named Harold Stearns, whom you may know, and who is down and out through, so he claims and so others claim, a sort of persecution on the part of Sinclair Lewis. To what extent Lewis has gone after him I don't know but he came to me (he meaning Stearns) with the story that he could *get no answer of any kind* from the stuff he has sent the *World* or *The New Yorker,* stuff that was to some extent solicited.

He has been helped here by various people (for the last month his typewriter has been in pawn in Deauville) but he is terribly depressed by what he imagines is a sort of universal blackball against him. The favor I want to ask you is to find out if there is stuff of his lying unused and unpaid for in the *World* office. He says he's written and written and written and can't get an answer.

This is of course confidential and any answer I get from you I will communicate to no one but him. It is terribly sad to see a man of his age and intelligence going to pieces because of what may possibly be a series of accidents and coincidences. This possibility is what I'd like to clear up.

Your friend,

F. Scott Fitzgerald

TO CARL VAN VECHTEN

14 rue de Tilsitt
Paris, France
[Fall, 1925]

Dear Carl:

Firecrackers came and Zelda and I read it with the

greatest delight. You have never done anything better than the acrobats, the whole roadhouse scene at the end and attempted seduction by the broker (character of the girl was marvelously managed). With *The Blind Bow Boy* I like it best of your four novels—it seems to me that this rather than *The Tattooed Countess* is your true line of genius—in Campaspe for example you suggest so much more than you say—she is the embodiment of New York, mysterious and delicate and entirely original, while Countess Natorini, for all the amazing and virtuosic details about her past, was really a "character." Gunnar was fine also, and a brilliant conception—the least successful part of a very brilliant book were the relations between Gunnar and Campaspe.

I wish you could personally create a new form for that sort of novel, something lying between the almost unbearable sequence of humor in *Zuleika* and the almost equally annoying diffuseness of *South Wind*. You in *The Blind Bow Boy* have come nearer to doing it, so far, than either Huxley or Firbank.

As ever your friend,

Scott Fitzgerald

TO MARYA MANNES

14 rue de Tilsitt
Paris, France
[October, 1925]

Dear Marya:

Thank you for writing me about *Gatsby*—I especially appreciate your letter because women, and even intelligent women, haven't generally cared much for it. They do not like women to be presented as *emotionally* passive—as a matter of fact I think most women are, that their minds are taken up with a sort of second-rate and unessential bookkeeping which their apologists call "practicality"—like the French, they are centime-savers in the business of magic. (You see I am a Schopenhauerian, not a Shavian.)

You are thrilled by New York—I doubt you will be after five more years when you are more fully nourished from within. I carry the place around the world in my heart but sometimes I try to shake it off in my dreams. America's greatest promise is that something is going to happen, and after awhile you get tired of waiting because nothing happens to people except that they grow old, and nothing happens to American art because America is the story of the moon that never rose. Nor does the "minute itself" ever come to life either, the minute not of unrest and hope but of a glowing peace—such as when the moon rose that night on Gerald and Sara's garden and you said you were happy to be there. No one ever makes things in America with that vast, magnificent, cynical disillusion with which Gerald and Sara make things like their parties.

(They were here, last week, and we spent six or seven happy days together.)

My new novel is marvelous. I'm in the first chapter. You may recognize certain things and people in it.

The young people in America are brilliant with second-hand sophistication inherited from their betters of the war generation who to some extent worked things out for themselves. They are brave, shallow, cynical, impatient, turbulent and empty. I like them not. The "fresh, strong river of America!" My God, Marya, where are your eyes—or are they too fresh and strong to see anything but their own color and contour in the glass? America is so decadent that its brilliant children are damned almost before they are born. Can you name a single American artist except James and Whistler (who lived in England) who didn't die of drink? If it is fresh and strong to be unable to endure or tolerate things-as-they-are, to shut your eyes or to distort and lie—then you're right, Marya Mannes, and no one has ever so misinterpreted the flowers of civilization, the Greek or Gallic idea, as

Your sincere admirer,

F. Scott Fitzgerald

TO GERTRUDE STEIN

14 rue de Tilsitt
Paris, France
[*December 27, 1925*]

Dear Miss Gertrude Stein:

It was so good to hear from you again—especially as I am in the geographical center of *The Making of Americans* and have been so fascinated by it and have been thinking of you so much lately.

About Tuesday: We leave for Salies-les-Bains January 7th or 8th to try and cure my wife who has been ill now in bed for over a week. She gets up tomorrow but it's too soon for her to go out as she must save for the trip and we've been forced to decline all invitations. But she's so anxious to see you again that instead of accepting for my-self alone I'm going to be so bold as to ask you if we can't come some afternoon between this Friday (1st) and next Thursday (6th)—any one of those afternoons we'd be so happy to come. Can we?

Yours, always admiringly and respectfully,
F. Scott Fitzgerald

TO HENRY ALBERT PHILLIPS

Hotel Bellevue
Salies de Béarn
Basses-Pyrénées
France
[*Winter, 1926*]

Dear Mr. Phillips:

As you see we're in this out-of-the-way hole; taking a cure and getting very healthy. That is: my wife's taking a cure and I'm merely getting healthy. The other inhabitants are two goats and a paralytic. We'll be in Nice however from the 1st of March on, where our address will be c/o American Express. Can't we meet there?

Sincerely,
F. Scott Fitzgerald

TO CARL VAN VECHTEN

Villa St. Louis
Juan-les-Pins
France
[Summer, 1926]

Dear Carl:

Nigger Heaven is great! Your best to date, though my affection for *The Bow Boy* will never die. I can't tell you of our enthusiasm, but suffice to say I read it in one night and Zelda read it the next. It seems, outside of its quality as a work of art, to sum up subtly and inclusively, all the *direction* of the northern nigger or, rather, the nigger in New York. Our civilization imposed on such virgin soil takes on a new and more vivid and more poignant horror as if it had been dug out of its context and set down against an accidental and unrelated background. This is a lousy sentence but I hope it expresses a small part of our delight in the book.

Always your friend,

Scott Fitz———

TO CECILIA TAYLOR[1]

Ellerslie
Edgemoor, Delaware
[August, 1927]

Dear Cecilia:

This is to remind you about September. We'll be having some sort of party here and then we'll go to New York for a day or two and see some shows. So save a week for us. When is your vacation?

We're just leaving for Long Island to visit Tommy Hitchcock and watch the polo (Zelda prays nightly that the Prince of Wales will come down from Canada), then we're visiting some people in Genesee and back here by the eighteenth. We talk of you all so often—I can't tell you

---

[1] A daughter of Mrs. Richard Taylor (Cousin Ceci).

how proud of you I am for being such exceptionally gorgeous people, or how much I enjoyed being with you and feeling pleasantly linked up with you. I know when I say how few people in the world really count at all, it seems to you a mere piece of snobbishness, but to me it's simply a bare, cold, unpleasant fact. People have always subconsciously recognized this by letting vitality atone for many more sins than charity can. You five[1] are among those "for whom the physical world exists." * For most people it simply glides by in a half-comprehended and unenjoyed dream. And

> *We Both Love You.*
>
> Scott

* Remy de Gourmont.

TO GILBERT SELDES

> *Ellerslie*
> *Edgemoor, Delaware*
> [*Probably Fall, 1927*]

Dear Gilbert:

The doll was beautiful. I sleep with it. You are the dearest grandmother a little girl ever had.

As I sit here in my spacious twenty-room mansion, hearing the howling of the winds outside and the groans of my toiling servants below, I think of how wonderful it is to be born a German princelet. The letter I wrote is in our very owniest dialect, Iranian-Ruthanian, or, allowing for the Cyrillic alphabet, Chinese Basque, altho some philologists and restaurateurs admit nothing of the sort.

Tell Amanda that we have not taken up Behaviorism but are going to govern our child's life by the cipher concealed in the Sears, Roebuck catalogue which proves that Julian Rosenwald wrote the works of Edgar Guest. I don't blame either of you for being disgusted with our public brawl the other day—but the manhole is on again; we are sober and almost the nicest people I ever met.

[1] Cousin Ceci and her four daughters.

How about the Dial reprints for $30.00! Have you forgotten—we are yearning for them and if you send them I can sell two other sets.

We'd love to have you for Christmas or New Year's or both. We are on the wagon till then and our difference of opinion, which had been going on for a miserable fortnight for two weeks before we came to New York and led to all the unpleasantness, is settled and forgotten.

Zelda wrote you a letter [but] mailed it to 82nd St. without the number.

Love to you both,

Scott

TO THOMAS LINEAWEAVER[1]

Ellerslie
Edgemoor, Delaware
[1927 or 1928]

Dear Tom:

I've been meaning to write you for months. I'm afraid I was the world's greatest bore last night. I was in the insistent mood—you know the insistent mood? I'm afraid I irritated both you and Eleanor, and I wanted to please you more than anyone there. It's all very dim to me but I remember a lot of talk about fairies and the managing kind of American woman, whatever that means. It's possible that I may be apologizing to the wrong people—anyway if I was lousy, please forgive me and tell Eleanor I can be almost human when sober.

We are on the wagon. If you come down to Roseleaf or Rosenbloom or whatever that place is please come over! We are always here weekends. I'm awfully anxious to see you and bicker with you under more favorable circumstances. Tell Eleanor I love her and I want to marry her. Does that fix everything?

Scott

[1] Lineaweaver, a college friend, and his wife Eleanor had been to a party at the Fitzgeralds'.

TO ZOË AKINS

> *Ellerslie*
> *Edgemoor, Delaware*
> [*February, 1928*]

Dear Zoe: Darling Zoe:

Are you, by any chance, so to speak, here? If you are, perhaps you'd come out Sunday to lunch—Thornton Wilder and some others are coming down.

Perhaps, even, you and Miss Taylor[1] would come out after the performance for a small revel Saturday night—? If we sent the car for you? We are just five minutes from the Dupont Hotel.

Will you phone 5859? We do so want to see you.

> Always Your Slave,
>
> F. Scott Fitzgerald

Zelda is in Philadelphia at ballet school for the afternoon so I'm writing this for her.

I hear *The Furies*[2] is great. We are seeing it tonight—

Friday.

TO JULIAN STREET

> *c/o Guaranty Trust*
> (*en route* [*to Paris*])
> [*Postmarked July 1, 1928*]

Dear Julian Street:

My best to you! My contempt for Tarkington extends only to his character of being ashamed of his early sins and thus cutting out of his experience about one-half of life. He woke up one morning sober and 40, and thought that no one had ever been lascivious or drunk or vain except himself, and turned deliberately back to the illusions of his boyhood.

---

[1] Laurette Taylor.
[2] A play of Zoë Akins which was being tried out in Wilmington.

Delighted that you liked Wilder—do read Hemingway—what do you mean by a *theme?* "Begin with an individual and you have created a type. Begin with a type and you have created nothing," as an humble writer once said.[1] Books called "oil" or "money"—surely the author of *Sunbeams, Inc.*[2] couldn't mean what you seem to mean. *War and Peace* is one man's point of view always.

Excuse this lousy pen.

Yours cordially,

Scott Fitzgerald

That clipping was fine and am having it duplicated to send to young writers who ask for advice.

TO BETTY MARKELL

c/o Guaranty Trust
4 Place de la Concorde
Paris, France

September 16, 1929

Dear Betty Markell:

I haven't answered your letter before because it's one of the nicest letters I've ever received, and it came when I was in a mood of tremendous dejection and I wanted to wait until I was a human being again before answering it. About five years ago I became, unfortunately, interested in the insoluble problems of personal charm and have spent the intervening time on a novel that's going to interest nobody and probably alienate the remaining half dozen who are kind enough to be interested in my work. Unfortunately my sense of material is much superior to my mind or my talent and if I ever survive this damned thing I shall devote my life to musical comedy librettos or become swimming instructor to the young Mikadesses of Japan.

The Basil Lee stories were a mistake—it was too much good material being shoved into a lousy form. I'm glad you liked them—I thought they were rather better than the response they had. I am going to be in New York from January 5th–March 1st. If you make trips East and can

[1] Fitzgerald in "The Rich Boy."
[2] By Julian Street.

stand disillusion about people I'd love to meet you. I have
no address yet, save care of my publishers. With most sincere hopes of meeting you,

> Yours,
>
> F. Scott Fitzgerald

TO MRS. EDWARD FITZGERALD

> *Beau-Rivage Palace*
> *Ouchy-Lausanne*
> [*June, 1930*]

Dear Mother:

My delay in writing is due to the fact that Zelda has been
desperately ill with a complete nervous breakdown and is
in a sanitarium near here. She is better now but recovery
will take a long time. I did not tell her parents the seriousness of it so say nothing—the danger was to her sanity
rather than her life.

Scottie is in the apartment in Paris with her governess.
She loved the picture of her cousins. Tell Father I visited
the

> "—seven pillars of Gothic mould
>   in Chillon's dungeons deep and old" [1]

and thought of the first poem I ever heard, or was [it]
"The Raven?"

Thank you for the Chesterton.

> Love,
>
> Scott

[1] From Byron's "Prisoner of Chillon" which Fitzgerald's father had read
aloud to him.

TO MRS. EDWARD FITZGERALD

[*Switzerland*]

[*June, 1930*]

Dear Mother:

I've thought of you both a lot lately and I hope Father is better after his indigestion. Zelda's recovery is slow. Now she [has] terrible eczema—one of those mild but terrible diseases that don't worry relations but are a living hell for the patient. If all goes as well as it did up to a fortnight ago we will be home by Thanksgiving.

According to your poem I am destined to be a failure. I re-enclose it.

(1) All big men have spent money freely. I hate avarice or even caution.

(2) I have never forgiven or forgotten an injury.

(3) This is the only one that makes sense.

(4) If it's worth doing. Otherwise it should be thrown over immediately.

(5) No man's criticism has ever been worth a damn to me.

These would be good rules for a man who wanted to be a chief clerk at 50.

Thanks for the check but really you mustn't. I re-enclose it. The snap I'll send to Scottie. The children are charming. Address me care of my Paris bank though I'm still by Father's Castle of Chillon. Have you read Maurois' *Life of Byron?* And Thomas Wolfe's *Look Homeward, Angel?*

Much love to you both,

Scott

TO DAYTON(?) KOHLER

819 Felder Avenue
Montgomery, Alabama
January 25, 1932

Dear Mr. Kohler:

The reason for my long delay in writing you is this— shortly after receiving your letter I left France for Switzerland in terrible confusion because of the sickness of my wife. My current correspondence was packed by mistake in a crate—which has only just been opened. I am terribly sorry.

I was delighted naturally with your article about me. You cover me with soothing oil and make me feel more important than I have for ages.

I am mid-channel now in a double-decker novel which I hope will justify some of the things that you say. Perhaps Swanson of *College Humor* or someone there might be interested—for the moment I am *vieux jeu* and completely forgotten by the whole new generation which has grown up since I published my last book in '26. So since there has been no published development since then, I think the article would be for the present hard to sell.

I am doubly grateful for your interest and again I apologize for my apparent discourtesy in not answering you before.

If you are ever in Montgomery, Alabama, I would love to see you. My address is 819 Felder Avenue.

Sincerely,

F. Scott Fitzgerald

TO GERTRUDE STEIN

Hotel Rennert
Baltimore, Maryland
April 28, 1932

Dear Gertrude Stein:

You were so nice to think of me so far off and send me your book. Whenever I sit down to write I think of the line that you drew for me and told me that my next book should be that thick. So many of your memorable remarks come often to my head, and they seem to survive in a way that very little current wisdom does.

I read the book, of course, immediately, and was half through it for the second time (learning a lot as we all do from you) when my plans were upset by my wife's illness, and by an accident it was consigned to temporary storage.

I hope to be in Europe this summer and to see you. I have never seen nearly as much of you as I would like.

Yours always, admiringly and cordially,

F. Scott Fitzgerald

TO ANDREW TURNBULL

La Paix, Rodgers' Forge
Towson, Maryland
August 2, 1932

Reputed Bantling:

In deponing and predicating incessantly that you were a "Shakespearean clown" I did not destinate to signify that you were a wiseacre, witling, dizzard, chowderhead, Tom Nody, nizy, radoteur, zany, oaf, loon, doodle, dunderpate, lunkhead, sawney, gowk, clod-poll, wise man of Boeotia, jobbernowl or mooncalf but, subdititiously, that you were intrinsically a longhead, luminary, "barba tenus sapientes," pundit, wrangler, licentiate learned Theban and sage, as are so many epigrammatists, wit-worms, *droles de corp*, sparks, merry-andrews, mimes, posturemasters, pucinellas, scaramouches, pantaloons, pickle-herrings and persifleurs that were pullulated by the Transcendent Skald.

Unequivocally,

F. Scott Fitzgerald

TO ANDREW TURNBULL

La Paix, Rodgers' Forge
Towson, Maryland
August 18, 1932

Dear Andronio:

Upon mature consideration I advise you to go no farther with your vocabulary. If you have a lot of words they will become like some muscle you have developed that you are compelled to use, and you must use this one in expressing yourself or in criticizing others. It is hard to say who will punish you the most for this, the dumb people who don't know what you are talking about or the learned ones who do. But wallop you they will and you will be forced to confine yourself to pen and paper.

Then you will be a writer and may God have mercy on your soul.

No! A thousand times no! Far, far better confine yourself to a few simple expressions in life, the ones that served billions upon countless billions of our forefathers and still serve admirably all but a tiny handful of those at present clinging to the earth's crust. Here are the only expressions you need:

"*Yeah*"
"*Naw*"
"*Gimme de meat*"

and you need at least one good *bark* (we all need one good bark) such as:

"*I'll knock your back teeth down your throat!*"

So forget all that has hitherto attracted you in our complicated system of grunts and go back to those fundamental ones that have stood the test of time.

With warm regards to you all,

Scott Fitz_____

TO RICHARD KNIGHT

La Paix, Rodgers' Forge
Towson, Maryland
September 29, 1932

Dear Dick:

That was swell praise you gave Zelda and needless to say delighted her and set her up enormously. She revised the book so much that she lost contact with it and yours is the first word that gives it public existence. My own opinions on it were as disjointed as hers.

I'm sorry I used the word fairy and that you found it offensive. I have never in my wildest imaginings supposed you were a fairy, and I admit that under similar circumstances I would be inclined probably to bristle if the word were thrown around by someone whose attitude toward me was not unchallengeable. It is a lousy word to anyone not a member of the species. I offer you my sincere apologies and put it down to the fact that I was half asleep when you came and subsequently a little tight.

However, there must have been some desire to wound in using such a word, however trivially. You annoyed me—specifically by insisting on a world which we will willingly let die, in which Zelda can't live, which damn near ruined us both, which neither you nor any of our more gifted friends are yet sure of surviving; you insisted on its value, as if you were in some way holding a battlefront, and challenged us to join you. If you could have seen Zelda, as the most typical end-product of that battle, during any day from the spring of '31 to the spring of '32 you would have felt about as much enthusiasm for the battle as a doctor at the end of a day in a dressing station behind a blood battle.

So for the offensive and inapplicable phrase read *neurotic,* and take it or leave it, whatever the bulk concerned. We have a good way of living, basically, for us; we got through a lot and have some way to go; our united front is less a romance than a categorical imperative and when you criticize it in terms of a bum world, no matter how big you face it, it is annoying to me, and seems to negate on purpose both past effort and future hope and I reserve the right to be annoyed.

Of course I like you, as who wouldn't, and appreciate your lavish generosity with yourself, and much more about you than I can express in a letter. I feel that any unpleasantness between us has all been on the basis of liking Zelda, and the sincerity of your feeling toward her shouldn't offend anybody except the most stupid and churlish of husbands. In another year, *Deus volens,* she will be well. For the moment she must live in a state of Teutonic morality, far from the exploits of the ego on its own. In other words, when you city fellows come down you can't put ideas in the heads of our farm girls, without expecting resistance.

I lay myself open to your discovery of my most blatant hypocrisies. God knows that the correctness of our life preys on such a one as old Fitzgerald, but there we are, or rather here we are. With all good wishes,

Your most obedient servant,

[Scott]

TO MALCOLM COWLEY

La Paix, Rodgers' Forge
Towson, Maryland
June 1, 1933

Dear Malcolm:

It was good to hear from you and we certainly enjoyed your brief visit. Dos is cured and has left to bask in the sun at Antibes and I certainly do envy him. I am working like hell.

As to using a part of my article in your book, go ahead, but I am using certain parts of it myself in my new book, in particular, parts about Antibes, so I will ask you to say, as it were, "Fitzgerald says" instead of "Fitzgerald says in an article on the Jazz Age" because I do not want to call attention to the fact that I piece shorter things into long things though I suppose we all do. Would you mind arranging this?

Hope you manage to come back this way and let us know in advance.

Sincerely,

[Scott]

TO CHARLES W. DONAHOE [1]

La Paix, Rodgers' Forge
Towson, Maryland
June 26, 1933

Dear Sap:

The rush from the house[2] included not only the butler, the second butler, the two footmen, the first and second trained nurse, my mother, aunt, three first cousins, my four children, my secretary, who is very fat and weighs 250 pounds, the illegitimate children, J. P. Morgan and myself but ten other members of my household who may perhaps not be known to you by name. I extinguished the fire myself by an act of tremendous valor. Among the objects of art saved were "The Last Supper," the bat with which Babe Ruth batted his first home run, and the baby spoon with which you presented Scottie at her birth. (Let me take this occasion to congratulate you on what the West Coast does to growing boys. I cannot see Mrs. Sap's face in the picture but gather all goes beautifully.)

Seriously, the fire was greatly overexaggerated—so was the implication that old Fitzgerald was keeping up an elaborate household. We are struggling along like everybody else though I must confess with a pretty good break so far.

It was a coincidence that I heard from all my Princeton friends of which there are about a dozen—of which you, my dear sir, happen to be the most cherished—have turned up lately without even going to a reunion. From our class I heard from Non, two letters from Henry, one from you, none from Paul Dickey; in 1918 the record is not good on second thought; in 1919 however I crossed with Dave Bruce and a year ago Tom Lineaweaver turned up here in Baltimore and we spent two good days together.

---

[1] One of Fitzgerald's closest friends at Newman and Princeton.
[2] La Paix had recently caught fire.

Insofar as upperclassmen are concerned I saw a rather depressed runt at the Yale game and leave out _____ _____, a professional fairy. Even Dean Clarke, Bob Clarke's brother (class of '27), has been here in Baltimore this winter which is like seeing Bob again.

All this list of names is put in for what provocative powers may be on you, and with a further wish that it may suggest to you the personality of your old friend from reading off a list of the people with whom he had dealings.

For yourself, your family and all that are dear to you I tender the old bunk and can't tell you what a kick I got out of your note.

[Scott]

TO JOHN O'HARA

La Paix, Rodgers' Forge
Towson, Maryland
July 18, 1933

Dear O'Hara:

I am especially grateful for your letter. I am half black Irish and half old American stock with the usual exaggerated ancestral pretensions. The black Irish half of the family had the money and looked down upon the Maryland side of the family who had, and really had, that certain series of reticences and obligations that go under the poor old shattered word "breeding" (modern form "inhibitions"). So being born in that atmosphere of crack, wisecrack and countercrack I developed a two-cylinder inferiority complex. So if I were elected King of Scotland tomorrow after graduating from Eton, Magdalene to Guards, with an embryonic history which tied me to the Plantagenets, I would still be a parvenu. I spent my youth in alternately crawling in front of the kitchen maids and insulting the great.

I suppose this is just a confession of being a Gael though I have known many Irish who have not been afflicted by this intense social self-consciousness. If you are interested in colleges, a typical gesture on my part would have been, for being at Princeton and belonging to one of its snootiest clubs, I would be capable of going to Podunk on a visit and being absolutely booed and overawed by its social system, not from timidity but simply because of an inner necessity of starting my life and my self-justification over again at scratch in whatever new environment I may be thrown.

The only excuse for that burst of egotism is that you asked for it. I am sorry things are breaking. . . .[1]

TO ANDREW TURNBULL

La Paix, Rodgers' Forge
Towson, Maryland

August 8, 1933

Dear Andrew:

Nobody *naturally* likes a mind quicker than their own and one more capable of getting its operation into words. It is practically something to conceal. The history of men's *minds has been the concealing of them,* until men cry out for intelligence, and the thing has to be brought into use. Your mother told me that you had written a couple of somber letters home[2] and I am both amused and disgusted. In trouble such as yours (of the reality of which I am by no means convinced) the proper tradition is that the mouth is kept shut, the eyes are lowered; the personality tries to say to itself: "I will adjust and adapt, I can beat anything offered to me; therefore I can beat change." Anything short of that would be dishonor to the past and to whatever you believe in.

The mouth tight, and the teeth and lips together are a hard thing, perhaps one of the hardest stunts in the world, but not a waste of time, because most of the great things you learn in life are in periods of enforced silence. Remember to think straight: the crowd at camp is probably right *socially* and you are probably wrong. I'll tell you a fact to corroborate that: I almost gave up the

[1] The rest of the letter is missing.
[2] From camp.

lease on this house for the simple fact that you persistently clung to the idea that beating down females was a method of establishing superiority over them.

Andrew, this will sound like kicking somebody when he's down, and you wouldn't expect that from a man who pretends to be your friend; nevertheless, we have spent too many hours together for you to doubt that my friendship for you is founded on a mutual understanding that nothing could break—outside of a disagreement in principle. So I presume to suggest: would you examine your conscience and see if you have violated such primary laws as have been laid down for you? Where you haven't—well, to hell with what other people think—better to fight your way out. The only thing that I ever told you definitely was that popularity is not worth a damn and respect is worth everything, and what do you care about happiness—and who does except the perpetual children of this world?

Always your friend,

[F. Scott Fitzgerald]

Postscript: Am sending you a book.

Postscript (2) The poor boys called on me again. I tried to discourage them by making them work but *I think they liked it!*

Postscript (3) Don't leave this letter around—I'm sure you will get what I'm shooting at but it would defeat its own purpose if your contemporaries happened on it.

Postscript (4) Why, if your professed affection for your family is so strong, should you have disturbed your mother enough so that she should have brought up your gloom in conversation to me? Are you a Willie boy after all?

Postscript (5) This letter expects an answer.

TO JOHN LARDNER

La Paix, Rodgers' Forge
Towson, Maryland
September 20, 1933

Dear John:

I was sorry not seeing you in Paris but your residence there coincided with illness in Switzerland. The whole point of calling you up was an idea that I have had for some time, which won't be less good for being old, that those articles that your father wrote could be strung into a very interesting story. Nevertheless, someone would have to work over it. Who to turn to! Much better a contemporary; consequently I have examined the possibilities. I can't do it myself because I am engrossed in work of my own, and it seems to me the next best person would be Gilbert Seldes; consequently I called Gilbert Seldes and he said he would like to do the work. I suggested to him a ten per-cent cut of whatever it nets; even if he asks more I think it would be worth your while because he is a crack editor and I would let stand whatever terms he suggests.

This is a rather difficult situation because, as I said on the phone, your father is the worst editor of his own stuff who ever turned up in a big way of the writing line, with the possible exception of Theodore Dreiser. And your mother is not especially interested in writing as such, and so I will have to turn it over to you, but I would like to turn it over as a complete idea so that you could do it or destroy it as seems fitting to you. Will you let Gilbert Seldes decide? Pass over all the material to him that you get from Wheeler, not in sections, but collect it first yourself even if it takes about a month altogether. Gilbert is one of the very first journalists in America and if anyone can make an interesting and consecutive narrative of it he can do it, and, to repeat, he is interested in the idea. When a Jew is interested he has the strong sense of the track that we other races don't even know the sprinting time of. His task is not merely an editorial one, according to my original conception, but will also include getting the stuff in order so it will tell a *whole* story (as much as Ring wanted to tell) of a certain period in his life. As his happens to be one of the most interesting temperaments of all the Americans of our time somebody is sure to be interested in publishing it, probably Scribners; but there I want to butt into the situation and get it done right. *The Autobiography of Ring W. Lardner* was merely a long short story, all full of personal anecdotes that could only have been of interest to Ring and his friends. That's what I mean by the fact that he has been a poor editor of his own stuff, and probably his sickness has not improved him in that regard, so while you must naturally tell him the idea is in progress it is much wiser for you and me to keep it in our hands. Or rather I hereby hand it over to you, with the opinion that you get from Seldes, and I would like to be called in as the doctor at the last moment when something tangible has been accomplished.

With regards to (Scarface) (Half-Wit) (Red Nose) (Pure Insult) Lardner: please give all of them my very best regards and to yourself with reiterated regrets that we didn't meet in Paris.

Yours,

[F. Scott Fitzgerald]

TO GLENWAY WESCOTT

1307 Park Avenue
Baltimore, Maryland

February 6, 1934

Dear Glenway Wescott (This seems to be the form with which authors insult each other) (this letter is friendly),

About six years [ago] when I was doping out my novel *Tender Is the Night*, which will appear this spring, somebody told me about the departure of an American battleship from Villefranche with the attendant *poules,* etc. I built an episode of my book around it and spoke of it to several people. A year or so later a letter came from Ernest Hemingway telling me that you had used it for a background in a short story. His advice was that I should read it and thus avoid any duplication, but my instinct was to the contrary, and I waited until I had written my own scene before I read *Goodbye to Wisconsin*. There are, unavoidably, certain resemblances, but I think that I will let it stand. This letter is written to you exactly as I wrote one to Willa Cather before publication of *The Great Gatsby* in regard to a paragraph that strangely paralleled one of hers in *The Lost Lady*. I have a cruel hatred of plagiarism of one's contemporaries, and would not want you to think that I had taken to shoplifting.

What the hell did you do to Gertrude Stein that she went harsh on you? I am eagerly awaiting your next book.

With best wishes,

F. Scott Fitzgerald

TO THOMAS WOLFE

*1307 Park Avenue
Baltimore, Maryland*

April 2, 1934

Dear Arthur, Garfield, Harrison and Hayes:[1]

Thanks a hell of a lot for your letter[2] which came at a rather sunken moment and was the more welcome. It is hard to believe that it was in the summer of 1930 we went up the mountainside together—some of our experiences have become legendary to me and I am not sure even if they happened at all. One story (a lie or a truth) which I am in the habit of telling is how you put out the lights of Lake Geneva with a Gargantuan gesture,[3] so that I don't know any more whether I was with you when it happened, or whether it ever happened at all!

---

[1] American presidents who were the subject of Wolfe's story, "The Four Lost Men."
[2] Praising *Tender Is the Night*.
[3] Wolfe, waving his arms as he talked, had snapped an overhead wire and caused a blackout.

I am so glad to hear from our common parent, Max, that you are about to publish. Again thanks for your generous appreciation.

Ever yours,

F. Scott Fitzgerald and
Arthur, Garfield, Harrison and Hayes

TO JOHN JAMIESON

1307 Park Avenue
Baltimore, Maryland
April 7, 1934

Dear Mr. Jamieson:

I thought Leighton's article[1] had a sort of fruity bitterness about it but I was not at the time in a position of answering it—and I was amused by the severe kidding that Ernest Hemingway gave it. I am absolutely sure that more sweat and blood went into the creation of, say, *A Farewell to Arms* than into *Le Bal du Comte d'Orgel*. I agree with you that the latter is not heavily weighted, but to me it sounds less like a rough draft than like a small section of Proust.

I was interested also in your analysis of the influences upon my own books. I never read a French author, except the usual prep-school classics, until I was twenty, but Thackeray I had read over and over by the time I was sixteen, so as far as I am concerned you guessed right.

In any case let me thank you many times for your interest in *Gatsby* (by the way, the Modern Library is bringing it out again this spring) and your courtesy in sending me your observations. With very best wishes in hopes that we may meet in the near future,

Sincerely,

F. Scott Fitzgerald

[1] "An Autopsy and a Prescription" by Lawrence Leighton in *Hound and Horn*, July–September, 1932.

TO JOHN JAMIESON

> 1307 Park Avenue
> Baltimore, Maryland
> April 15, 1934

Dear Mr. Jamieson:

Thank you, immensely, for sending me your article. I agree with you entirely, as goes without saying, in your analysis of Gatsby. He was perhaps created on the image of some forgotten farm type of Minnesota that I have known and forgotten, and associated at the same moment with some sense of romance. It might interest you to know that a story of mine, called "Absolution," in my book *All the Sad Young Men* was intended to be a picture of his early life, but that I cut it because I preferred to preserve the sense of mystery.

Again, thanks!

With very best wishes,

> Yours,
>
> Scott Fitzgerald

TO H. L. MENCKEN

> 1307 Park Avenue
> Baltimore, Maryland
> April 23, 1934

Dear Menck:

I am afraid that I am going to have to violate your favorite code of morals—the breaking of engagements—because I've got to go to New York about trying to capitalize on my novel[1] in the movies.

[1] The whole letter relates to *Tender Is the Night.*

Without wanting to add to your mass of accumulated correspondence just as you've cleared it away, I would like to say in regard to my book that there was a deliberate intention in every part of it except the first. The first part, the romantic introduction, was too long and too elaborated largely because of the fact that it had been written over a series of years with varying plans, but everything else in the book conformed to a *definite intention* and if I had to start to write it again tomorrow I would adopt the same plan, irrespective of the fact of whether I had in this case brought it off or not brought it off. That is what most of the critics fail to understand (outside of the fact that they fail to recognize and identify anything in the book): that the motif of the "dying fall" was absolutely deliberate and did not come from any diminution of vitality but from a definite plan.

That particular trick is one that Ernest Hemingway and I worked out—probably from Conrad's preface to *The Nigger*—and it has been the greatest "credo" in my life ever since I decided that I would rather be an artist than a careerist. I would rather impress my image (even though an image the size of a nickel) upon the soul of a people than be known except insofar as I have my natural obligation to my family—to provide for them. I would as soon be as anonymous as Rimbaud, if I could feel that I had accomplished that purpose—and that is no sentimental yapping about being disinterested. It is simply that, having once found the intensity of art, nothing else that can happen in life can ever again seem as important as the creative process.

With terrific regrets that I probably won't be back in time to hear your harrowing African adventures, and compare them with my own, and with best regards always to my favorite Venus, Sara,[1] I am

As ever,

F. Scott Fitzgerald

---

[1] Mrs. H. L. Mencken.

TO MABEL DODGE LUHAN

1307 Park Avenue
Baltimore, Maryland
May 10, 1934

Dear Mrs. Luhan:

I was tremendously pleased and touched by your letter and by your communication to the *Tribune*.[1] It always strikes me as very strange when I find new people in the world, because I always crystallize any immediate group in which I move as being an all-sufficient, all-inclusive cross-section of the world, at the time I know it (the group)—this all the more because a man with the mobility of the writing profession and a certain notoriety thinks that he has a good deal of choice as to whom he will know. That from the outer bleakness, where you were only a name to me, you should have felt a necessity of communicating an emotion felt about a stranger, gave me again the feeling that Conrad expresses as "the solidarity of innumerable human hearts," at times a pretty good feeling, and your letter came to me at one of those times. Having been compared to Homer and Harold Bell Wright for fifteen years, I get a pretty highly developed delirium tremens at the professional reviewers: the light men who bubble at the mouth with enthusiasm because they see other bubbles floating around, the dumb men who regularly mistake your worst stuff for your best and your best for your worst, and, most of all, the cowards who straddle and the leeches who review your books in terms that they have cribbed out of the book itself, like scholars under some extraordinary dispensation which allows them to heckle the teacher. With every book I have ever published there have always been two or three people, as often as not strangers, who have seen the intention, appreciated it, and allowed me whatever percentage I rated on the achievement of that intention. In the case of this book your appreciation has given me more pleasure than any other, not excepting Gilbert Seldes who

[1]About *Tender Is the Night.*

seemed to think that I had done completely what I started
out to do and that it was worth doing.

With gratitude for that necessity in you which made you
take the special trouble, the extra steps, which reassured
me that even at the moment of popping out something new
I was reaching someone by air mail—and with the added
declaration that I want to see you,

                                    I am

                                    Yours most cordially,

                                    [F. Scott Fitzgerald]

P.S. My excuse for dictating this is a sprained arm.

TO GILBERT SELDES

                                    1307 Park Avenue
                                    Baltimore, Maryland
                                    May 31, 1934

Dear Gilbert:

Just read the Lardner collection. At first I was disappointed because I had expected there would be enough
stuff for an omnibus and I still feel that it could have
stood more weight. However, looking over those syndicate
articles I realize what you were up against—even many
of those which you were compelled to use are rather definitely
dated and I think you did the best you could with the material at hand.

Anyhow, I've had a further hunch on the matter which
is this: the short one-act plays at the end *do* stand up but
they would not play in any conventional sense because so
much of the nonsense is embodied in the stage directions,
but if they were done, as I believe one was, for the Authors
League Fete or the Dutch Treat Club with Benchley and
Stewart clowning the whole business, I believe they would
play very well. Now doping along on the subject, it seems
to me an evening of five nonsense plays would be monotonous no matter how funny they were, but just suppose,
taking over the technique of the Grand Guignol, two of

those plays were alternated with something macabre. When the Grand Guignol failed in New York it seems to me that I remember that all the plays were plays of horror and the minute the novelty wore off it closed up shop. If the fault of too much of a good thing were repeated this whole hunch might flop, but mightn't some enterprising producer be interested in a thoroughly balanced program if we could get the material together? I don't know whether there are any good horror one-acters in America but we might pick up a couple of the Grand Guignol hits very cheaply or get somebody to dredge something out of Edgar Allan Poe. What do you think of this idea? Do you think there's any money in it? If we do it we ought to get started immediately. I am terribly tied up in work and also not being on the spot could not efficiently go into it. I hand you the suggestion for what it is worth and I wish you would let me know what you think of it. In any case I would be glad to aid in any advisory capacity.

My novel seems to go pretty well. I haven't been able to make up my mind entirely how good it is because most of the reviewers have been so entirely cuckoo in their effect of saying in one line that the thing comes off entirely because it is technically so well done and others say it comes off in spite of all its technical faults. No two reviewers—and I am speaking only of the big shots—agree who was the leading character. Malcolm Cowley in *The New Republic* seems to be chiefly impressed by a man who only appears once in the whole picture—in any case my total impression is that a whole lot of people just skimmed through the book for the story and it simply cannot be read that way. In any case, your review and Mabel Dodge Luhan's enthusiasm made it all worthwhile to me.

Love to Amanda and the children.

Ever yours,

[Scott]

TO FRITZ CRISLER[1]

[*1307 Park Avenue*]
[*Baltimore, Maryland*]

[*June, 1934*]

Dear Fritz:

You write me again demanding advice concerning the coming season. I hasten to answer—*again* I insist that using a member of the Board of Trustees at left tackle to replace Charlie ("Asa") Ceppi and Christian ("Dean") Eisenhart would be a mistake. My idea is a backfield composed of Kipke, Eddie Mahan, President Lowell, and anybody we can get for the left side—Pepper Einstein in the center—and then either bring back Light-Horse Harry Lee, or else you will fill in yourself for the last place. Or else shift Kadlic to center and fill in with some member of the 75-lb. team.

Failing that, it *is,* as you suggest in your round-robin, a question of using a member of the Board of Trustees. Then who? and where? There is "Hack" Kalbaugh. There is the late President Witherspoon—but where is he? There is Harkness Hall, but we can't get it unless we pay for the whole expressage *at this end!*

The best suggestion is probably to put Rollo Rulon Roll-on at full, and return to the Houghton system.

Now Fritz, I realize that you and I and Tad know more about this thing than I do—nevertheless I want to make my suggestion: all the end men and backfield men and members of the Board of Trustees start off together—then they all reverse their fields, led by some of the most prominent professors and alumni—Albie Booth, Bob Lassiter, etc.—and almost before we know it we are up against the Yale goal—let me see, where was I? I meant the Lehigh goal—anyhow some goal, perhaps our own. Anyhow the main thing is that the C.W.A. is either dead, or else just beginning, and to use again that variation of the "Mexican" shift that I suggested last year will be just disastrous. Why? Even I can follow it! Martineau comes out of the huddle—or topples back into it—he passes to

[1] This was an open letter to Princeton's football coach, who had sent a questionnaire to alumni.

some member of past years' teams—(who won't be named here because of the eligibility rules) and then—well, from there on we go on to practically anything.

But not *this* year, Fritz Crisler, if you take my advice!

THE TEAM

TO ANDREW TURNBULL

[*Middleburg, Virginia*]

[*Summer, 1934*]

Dear Andrew:

I'm down here in Virginia recuperating from a siege of two stories by fishing and ruminating. Wish to heaven I could see you before you go and would promise to tell you *nothing* about life on a ranch, as Scottie tells me my moralities are becoming a strain. (Ungrateful woman— as if my prophecies have ever been wrong about her.)

Only remember—west of the Mississippi it's a little more look, see, act.

A little less rationalize, comment, talk.

Yours for the Purple Sage,

Scott Fitz——

TO ELIZABETH LEMMON

1307 Park Avenue
Baltimore, Maryland
September 6, 1934

Dearest Beth:

This is the story that I got out of "Welbourne," [1] with my novelist instinct to make copy out of social experience. I don't think for a moment that this does any justice to

---

[1] A pre-Civil War mansion belonging to Elizabeth Lemmon's family in Middleburg, Virginia. The story was "Her Last Case," published in *The Saturday Evening Post*, Nov. 3, 1934.

"Welbourne" but it might amuse you as conveying the sharp impression that the place made on me during a few weekends. Am sorry that this is not a transcription of the final draft as the *Post* will publish it, but in its general outlines it is the story as written.

Of course the detail about the initials of the "Gallant Pelham" [1] will identify the place to such neighbors of yours who read *The Saturday Evening Post*. As the story is so detached from any reality I am sure it won't cause you or family any annoyance.

With love,

Scott Fitz_____

Just wired you the weather killed my Manassas trip. Hope to hell you're all right now.

TO MRS. WILLIAM HAMM [2]

1307 Park Avenue
Baltimore, Maryland
October 4, 1934

Dear Marie:

It seems late to answer your letter. . . .

Scottie has become acclimated to Baltimore but I'd like to have her pull a sort of Gertrude Harris a little later to the extent of having a debut out there. So a few years may see us settled there for at least a summer. This in spite of the fact that having rambled so much I no longer regard St. Paul as my home any more than the eastern seaboard or the Riviera. This is said with no disloyalty but simply because after all my father was an easterner and I went East to college and I never did quite adjust myself to those damn Minnesota winters. It was always freezing my cheeks, being a rotten skater, etc.—though many events

---

[1] Actually it was Jeb Stuart's initials which Major John Pelham, Stuart's chief of artillery, had scratched on one of the window panes at "Welbourne."
[2] The former Marie Hersey.

there will always fill me with a tremendous nostalgia. Anyhow all recent reports paint it as a city of gloom and certainly the ones from the remnants of the McQuillan family are anything but cheerful. Baltimore is very nice and with plenty of cousins and Princetonians, if I were in a social mood, and I can look out the window and see a statue of the great, great uncle,[1] and all three of us like it here. There, have I rambled on long enough?

I send you this letter as a desperate bid for some news of St. Paul and the following people: the Kalmans, Flandraus, Jacksons, Clarks and Kit Ordway. I suppose Dud and Grace are now completely expatriated to Chicago and I know that Joe and Lou will most likely never return. Who runs things now? So many of us have emigrated—Katharine Tighe, etc.—and so many new names keep popping up whenever I get hold of a St. Paul paper that I cling in spirit to the few friends I still have there.

With affection from Zelda and love always from me,

Scott

P.S. Don't omit to add news mostly about yourself.

TO GERTRUDE STEIN

1307 Park Avenue
Baltimore, Maryland
November 23, 1934

Dearest Gertrude Stein:

Ever since you've been in this country I have been looking forward to a meeting with you and ever since news of your arrival became the town topic of Baltimore I had determined that I would give you such pleasures as I could command in these parts. Knowing how you are going to be hymned and sung I leave the details to you. I have a small but efficient establishment here and would be more than delighted to give you lunch alone, dinner alone, lunch alone and a group of your choosing, dinner alone

---

[1] An approximate description of Francis Scott Key. Fitzgerald's great, great, great grandfather and Key's grandfather were brothers.

and a group of your choosing, lunch alone and a group of my choosing, dinner alone and a group of my choosing. Also I offer you tea, breakfast, midnight supper—in fact anything that you can possibly suggest, and as many of them, so you see you have one devoted slave in this vicinity who tenders you material homage. All I ask of you is to tell me in advance how many hours and occasions you will be able to give me.

With affection always,

F. Scott Fitzgerald

TO GERTRUDE STEIN

1307 Park Avenue
Baltimore, Maryland
December 29, 1934

Dearest Gertrude Stein:

It was a disappointment to think that you would not be here for another meeting. I was somewhat stupid-got with the Christmas spirit, but I enjoyed the one idea that you *did* develop and, like everything else you say, it will sing in my ears long after everything else about that afternoon is dust and ashes. You were the same fine fire to everyone who sat upon your hearth—for it was your hearth, because you carry home with you wherever you are—a home before which we have all always warmed ourselves.

It meant so much to Zelda, giving her a tangible sense of her own existence, for you to have liked two of her pictures enough to want to own them. For the other people there, the impression was perhaps more vague, but everyone felt their Christmas Eve was well spent in the company of your handsome face and wise mind—and sentences "that never leak." [1]

All affection to you and Alice,

F. Scott Fitzgerald

[1] On this occasion Gertrude Stein had remarked that sentences must not have bad plumbing—they must not leak.

TO ALICE RICHARDSON

1307 Park Avenue
Baltimore, Maryland
February 28, 1935

Lovely Alicia:

You are in receipt of a communication from a man who has been in the southland and has not touched liquor for a month and, because some things in the last few months are a little hazy, you will have to be more explicit as to what the other letters were.[1] As I remember, the two department store tie-ups that I had were through Brown Wanamaker and Cupid Simon. I am enclosing a letter to my publisher. It seems to me there were other angles that we talked about, but what they were I don't remember. On a long chance I am enclosing one also to Charlie MacArthur. Of course script girls are made, not born. He and Ben Hecht have their own plant now and you might strike him at the right moment. Beyond that I am pretty blank, that is, I could suggest nothing that Carmer couldn't suggest or that you would not find yourself. However, if you remember any further suggestions I made, write them to me and I will come through with the letters.

Now as to the manuscript.[2] It won't do, Alice. It is in part too personal and in part not personal enough. It is really not English to write such a sentence as "Her tonsils were in terrible shape," which gives rather a revolting picture of the lady's throat. I appreciate your sparing me on the alcoholic side, at the same time the picture of a writer living in a dressing gown isn't sufficiently new or startling to give personality interest. Due to the fact that my books no longer have the national circulation they used to have but sell chiefly in big cities, the interest in such articles would be limited to magazines such as *The New Yorker* whose readers would not consider the company of an author very exciting after all. This is sad but true and it was a bad guess of mine to think it could be steered into something marketable. It's like those episodes that are funny when they happen but don't bear telling.

---

[1] Alice Richardson, who had been Fitzgerald's secretary, was job-hunting in New York and had asked him for letters of introduction.
[2] A short memoir by Alice Richardson, describing her experience as Fitzgerald's secretary.

I hope to heaven things go well with you, Alice, and that these letters may, by some chance, bear some fruit.

Faithfully,

Scott Fitzg

TO ALEXANDER WOOLLCOTT

1307 Park Avenue
Baltimore, Maryland
April 24, 1935

Dear Alec:

That was damn nice of you to write me about the poem.[1] I was surprised at the number of people who liked it but I was especially delighted to hear from you after so long. It pleased me too that you liked *Tender Is the Night*.

I thought it was awfully nice of you to have that mention of Patrick Murphy in your broadcast. Sweet Jesus, you have become famous!

I have seen one of the Woollcott girls act at Bryn Mawr School; I have talked to a second one in person about her short stories; and a third one is in the same class at Bryn Mawr with my daughter, so I feel as if I knew the whole family. This is a big city and it is almost as rare to look up people as it would be in New York, but I am looking forward to running into them sometime and I will give your name as a recommendation.

I am engrossed in a new literary project but it will be another year before it develops because I am feeling somewhat plucked and old as I approach forty. I have been for some time a teetotaler with the chief intention of fooling the kind friends who predicted for me an alcoholic grave.

With my very best wishes to you always, Alec,

Your friend,

Scott Fitz——

[1] "Lamp in a Window," *The New Yorker*, March 23, 1935.

TO ZOË AKINS

1307 Park Avenue
Baltimore, Maryland
April 24, 1935

Dearest Zoe:

That was a hell of a nice thing you wrote me about the poem. There was a good deal of emotion in it but I was nevertheless surprised that it was noticed as much as it was, it being the first poem I have written in thirteen years.

Zelda is no better at the moment but spring and summer always represent a hope for improvement; in trying for a cure in these cases the difficult period is always the protecting of her during a readjustment to life when she returns to it, and I fall far short in this regard, being usually an agitated and turbulent sort of person myself. Scottie is fine and I will ask her about the moving picture stars.

I am delighted that *The Old Maid* is still on Broadway. It is still talked about here by those who went to it with me. No news with me except that I don't drink any more, many moons now since liquor of any kind has touched these lips. *Tender Is the Night* is being dramatized. I've always thought that the advantageous contract I made in the case of *The Great Gatsby* was thanks to your sound advice.

Always affectionately yours,

Scott Fitz

TO JAMES BOYD

1307 Park Avenue
Baltimore, Maryland
May 2, 1935

Dear Jim:

I started *Roll River* in a copy Max Perkins sent me and recapitulated *The Dark Shore*, of which I missed one issue in *Scribner's,* then in the copy which you were kind enough to send me I read *Toward Morning.*[1] I could say a hell of

[1] *The Dark Shore* and *Toward Morning* were Books I and II of Boyd's *Roll River.*

a lot of nice things about the book—the whole war episode from the landing to the return, the reunion scene with his wife which is one of the best little touches in the book, the mine scene *per se,* the generousness of talent, the sense that you really *do* know about all those people—but in view of the fine press you are beginning to get I want to make a few cavils.

In the first place there is the question of Clara. The obvious model for such a picture of a woman as heroine and later as priestess of accumulated experience is of course Beatrix Esmond, later Madam Bernstein in *Esmond* and *The Virginians.* Madam Bernstein is a projection of Beatrix but she lives in her own right and what we recognize in her is Beatrix's enormous vitality and how life both preserved it and transmuted it. I can't honestly think that the elder Clara has that vividness, or preserves much of the younger Clara, and your failure to bring this off is the biggest fault of the book *as a whole* for she was your strongest thread to draw it together with.

One more point is that I have the same *penchant* as you *at the moment* for letting a theme *unravel* at the end, so to speak, as things do in life rather than to cut it off short, but I feel that this can be achieved without having the writing *itself* become exhausted. It is my old contention that tiredness, boredom, exhaustion, etc., must not be conveyed by the symbols which they show in life, in fact, can't be so conveyed in literature because boredom is essentially boring and tiredness is essentially tiring. For example: your rag-tag-and-bob-tail of continental troops filing past in the dark latter days of the Revolution were for the most part somewhat discouraged farmers, and the *impression* of a dogged discouragement was beautifully conveyed because you had the vitality to invent a tremendously vivid picture which wasn't a bit discouraging artistically. You did not let their state dampen your power to describe, nor their exhaustion drag you down; but in the last part of *Toward Morning* both the foreshortening and the lack of any such writing as there is in the best passages of *The Dark Shore* show that you have let the *oldness* of your protagonists communicate itself to you. This may be nonsense. It is one of those things that is easy to say after the event. This letter should be really to congratulate you on a fine book and to thank you for the enjoyment it gave me.

All quiet here. In a week or so I am off for the summer. You made a conquest in Elizabeth Lemmon who was very enthusiastic about *Roll River* and who has returned to The Old Dominion.

As your sister-in-law has probably told you I tried like hell to get you at the Belvedere. The Ed Poes wanted to have you for dinner.

I have been in Tryon since I saw you and found Southern Pines a surprisingly long distance away from it, but I shall be in Carolina again this summer, will you?

With the most cordial good wishes,

Scott Fitzgerald

TO ARNOLD GINGRICH [1]

1307 Park Avenue
Baltimore, Maryland

May 8, 1935

Dear Arnold:

Scottie was delighted to get the check from Abramson. I don't know what in God's name he wants it for but he's welcome to it. It's a nice little piece for that age so you have pleased her immensely and don't reproach yourself.

As to health, the body had been gradually sliding toward annihilation for two years but the process didn't get acute until about six months ago, and when it did, it went fast. I was doing my stuff on gin, cigarettes, bromides, and hope. Finally, the stuff itself was getting rather watery so I decided to get away while I was still on my feet. I laid up, or rather down, in Tryon, North Carolina, recuperated quickly, decided to quit drinking for a few years (which has honestly been no trouble so far) and am back here feeling quite myself.[2] I tell you these dull details at length because your letter seemed really interested, and an inquiry about health is practically irresistible at my age.

I've followed the career of *Cast Down the Laurel* [3] with

---

[1] Editor of *Esquire*.
[2] The winter and spring of 1935 Fitzgerald made a conscientious effort to overcome his drinking, but he did not succeed until the winter of 1937.
[3] A novel by Gingrich.

interest. You certainly got the top press and I was gratified. (Finished Part III by the way and like it best of all!)

Will be here till heaven knows when, except possibly a short Easter trip somewhere with my daughter.

Ever yours,

Scott Fitz

P.S. I haven't forgotten that I owe you a $200.00 article, but I am sewed up with *S.E.P.* fiction for a few weeks more.

P.S. 2. Again let me tell you that I appreciate that nice little compliment to Scottie about the poem.

TO ARNOLD GINGRICH

[*1307 Park Avenue*]
[*Baltimore, Maryland*]
May 11, 1935

Dear Arnold:

That was a damn nice letter to write me, but my God, I have suddenly reached a change of life in which everything I have written seems terrible, an odd state of things because usually I pore over my own stuff crying aloud from time to time in ecstasy, "What a man!" I don't like anybody else's work either. I wish there was something to do except read. Women and liquor take up so much time and get you into so much trouble. I wish I liked music like you do but it simply makes me want to howl when certain notes are struck.

Esquire holds up beautifully but my dog story was rotten.[1] I have two other short plots which I swear I will do for you within the next two months. I still owe you one. Your literary plans are frightening but of course everybody is always behind; still, it is exceptional to be so particularly far behind.

Best wishes always,

Scott Fitz

[1] "Shaggy's Morning," *Esquire*, May, 1935.

TO ANDREW TURNBULL

> *Grove Park Inn*
> *Asheville, North Carolina*
> *[Summer, 1935]*

Dear Andrew:

Thanks for remembering me with a letter on Frances' new typewriter. Haven't seen you to *really* talk for such a long time that I scarcely know you except thru Scottie. She tells me you are a low-lifer and in trouble with the police for passing some of the Weyerhauser kidnap jack but I say, "Don't believe it—Andrew is all right. There is nothing the matter with the boy except his character, environment, family, body, mind, past and future, and he will probably turn out O.K. in the end." But what an end!

So far as Constable is concerned—*I don't want you to run him down.* He's all right—not as good as his substitute Rulon-Miller but *all right.* And I'm glad. In fact I got him elected captain—I came into the room in a blackbeard disguise during the conclave and pled with them. "See here," I said, "a good back hasn't come out of Gilman since Slagle, and they're starving for somebody to admire, them kids are. Pretty soon they'll begin to turn to dolls like 'Apples' Fitzpatrick and 'Mozart' Hopney—" but I stopped myself at this juncture. I enclose Fritz Crisler's answer.[1]

> Always your friend,
>
> Scott Fitz_____

TO JULIAN STREET

> *Grove Park Inn*
> *Asheville, North Carolina*
> *[Summer, 1935]*

Dear Street:

Thanks for your letter—I mean really *thanks.* It was a

---

[1] The enclosure, an actual letter from Crisler, contained a postscript in Fitzgerald's handwriting which said, "I have had Constable elected captain as a favor to your young friend Turnbull."

most generous gesture and came at a time when I was wondering if anyone I respected read my stories—not that exactly, but if they liked them or if I was losing my grip in that medium—that is, of writing "high-priced" stories and still having them make sense. It was easier when I was young and believed in things and hoped that life might be a happy matter for some people. But as you learn that happiness is a prerogative of the perennial children of this world, and not too many of them, it becomes increasingly difficult.

Again thanks—my mind goes back often to several pleasant afternoons in Paris with you.

Faithfully,

F. Scott Fitzgerald

TO MARGARET CASE HARRIMAN

Hotel Stafford
Baltimore, [*Maryland*]

[*August, 1935*]

. . . .[1]

Anyhow I knew later that *you knew all this.* I started to come to New York yesterday afternoon, to see you, because I thought you'd think I'd run out on *you,* instead of on my own wretched state of mind and health (not a bit helped by a three-hour session with Zelda's doctors), got as far as *Philadelphia,* phoned from there to the Algonquin to change my forwarding address to The Stafford instead of my house, and took the train back to Baltimore. When I see you again I want everything to be right—even if I find you engrossed in a love affair with Geo V. and have no time for me.

I am still swollen up like a barrel but have reduced my beer consumption to nine bottles today. My spots are fading, but I still have a faint hope they may turn out to be leprosy and end my exigent private life forever so I can go on writing unperturbed.

---

[1] The first page of this letter is missing.

Sweet Jesus! They have now disappeared from the torso and appeared on the sides of my neck! The end has come! Oh, if I had but known!

While I think of it—in regard to Joe Hergesheimer. *Of course* he is more established than I am, in the same way that Hugh Walpole is more "established" than D. H. Lawrence—established with whom? And I like his talent in half a dozen fine scenes and don't compare Walpole to him intellectually. But it is simply *another sort of writing*. Almost everything I write in novels goes, for better or worse, into the subconscious of the reader. People have told me years later things like "The Story of Benjamin Button" in the form of an anecdote, having long forgotten who wrote it. This is probably the most egotistic thing about my writing I've ever put into script or even said (it's one of those matters like the question of being a l.l. that *has* to be left to demonstration—but in the former case [literary] the matter takes a spread of years). Everyone who has read *Java Head* knows that Hergesheimer wrote it—even those who remember a fairly novel torch cry from *Cytherea,* "I *want* to be outraged," will remember Hergesheimer. But his two highest flights, the only two that really became part of the conscience of our race, probably wouldn't be remembered. The awful loneliness of the girl and the man in the forest in Episode I of the *Three Black Pennies* (the rest of the 3 legged thing was n.g. pretentious and superimposed form)—

and the other was the burning of Linda's mother's hair in a permanent.

Surely that is a very mild contribution to have made to the human consciousness!

This letter is getting as long as the other. I remember so many things you said—about how New Yorkers' lives were spaced to have always something, there was no time left for loneliness—oh, there's so much to hear you say, no matter how much I'd be cynical about—

Affectionately,

Scott

I may be North again in three weeks—I must go to Carolina first and write one story or two.

Postscript: In the morning.

I sent a telegraph. I feel *so* sick—I'm lying in a gallon of sweat as I write this—that I'd call a doctor except I've been through this before and would be ashamed to ask him what to do when I *know!* I hope the telegram was coherent. Will try to lie here and discipline myself and note down what goes thru my head in fever and make something out of these lost three days.

And I can all too well see us sitting together in "one of those outdoor cafés or whatever they call them."

Whatever they call them!

TO JAMES BOYD

> [*Grove Park Inn*]
> [*Asheville, North Carolina*]
>
> [*August, 1935*]

Dear Jim:

Long Hunt came. I read it immediately. I liked it—it has the same quality of all your books, and yourself is in it. (To digress for a minute—I've had several clippings lately that found qualities in common between your work and mine. I was trying to think what they were, for God knows our subject matter, pasts, etc., have been miles apart, but I think I know—it's a sort of nostalgic sadness that runs through them. I don't know whether it's because we both read Keats a lot when we were young, or because we neither of us have been entirely well men throughout a large part of our maturity but there is undoubtedly a similarity of mood between *The Dark Shore* and *Tender Is the Night*. God what a parenthesis.)

Anyhow *Long Hunt* is a haunting book. I have quarrels with it as I have with every book ever written, including one's own, of course, but I like it because of its sharp individuality that follows it through the—wait a minute, let me start that sentence over. You have a strong sense of the common good, the common weal, whether in tribes, frontier cities, "society," etc., but the individuality never deserts you. They are both you.

I have just emerged not totally unscathed, I'm afraid, from a short violent love affair which will account for the somewhat sentimental cadence of this letter and for the lack of ink in the vicinity.[1] It's no one I ever mentioned to you but it was in the bag when I came to Southern Pines and I had done much better to let it alone because this was scarcely a time in my life for one more emotion. Still it's done now and tied up in cellophane and—and maybe someday I'll get a chapter out of it. God, what a hell of a profession to be a writer. One is one simply because one can't help it. Much better to follow the Long Hunt.

With all regards and good wishes to you both—hope we meet again this summer. You write a nice letter—I wish I did.

Your Friend,

Scott Fitzg

TO ————— —————[2]

[Grove Park Inn]
[Asheville, North Carolina]
[Early September, 1935]

—————:

This is going to be as tough a letter to read as it is to write. When I was young I found a line in Samuel Butler's Notebooks—the worst thing that can happen to a man is the loss of his health, the second worst the loss of his money. All other things are of minor importance.

This is only a half truth but there are many times in life when most of us, and especially women, must live on half truths. The utter synthesis between what we want and what we can have is so rare that I look back with a sort of wonder on those days of my youth when I had it, or thought I did.

[1] The letter was written in pencil.
[2] This letter was written to a young married woman with whom Fitzgerald had had an affair the summer of 1935.

The point of the Butler quotation is that in times of unhappiness and emotional stress that seemed beyond endurance, I used it as a structure, upon which to build up
a hierarchy of comparative values:

—This comes first.

—This comes second.

This is what you, _____, are not doing!

Your charm and the heightened womanliness that makes
you attractive to men depends on what Ernest Hemingway once called (in an entirely different connection)
"grace under pressure." The luxuriance of your emotions
under the strict discipline which you habitually impose on
them makes that tensity in you that is the secret of all
charm—when you let that balance become disturbed,
don't you become just another victim of self-indulgence?—
breaking down the solid things around you and, moreover,
making *yourself* terribly vulnerable?—imagine having to
have had to call in Doctor Cole in this matter! The *indignity!* I have plenty [of] cause to be cynical about women's
nervous resistance, but frankly I am concerned with my
misjudgment in thinking you were one of the strong—
and I can't believe I was mistaken.

The tough part of the letter is to send you this enclosure
—which you should read now [a loving, dependent letter
from Zelda]—

—now you've read it?

There are emotions just as important as ours running
concurrently with them—and there is literally no standard
in life other than a sense of duty. When people get mixed
up they try to throw out a sort of obscuring mist, and then the
sharp shock of a *fact*—a collision seems to be the only thing
to make them sober-minded again. You once said, "Zelda
is your *love!*" (only you said "lu-uv"). And I gave her all
the youth and freshness that was in me. And it's a sort of
investment that is as tangible as my talent, my child, my
money. That you had the same sort of appeal to me, deep
down in the gut, doesn't change the other.

The harshness of this letter will have served its purpose
if on reading it over you see that I have an existence outside you—and in doing so remind you that you have an
existence outside of me. I don't belittle your fine intelligence
by supposing that anything written here *need* be said, but

I thought maybe the manner of saying it might emphasize those old dull truths by which we live. We can't just let our worlds crash around us like a lot of dropped trays.

—*You have got to be good.*

—Your sense of superiority depends upon the picture of yourself as being *good,* of being large and generous and all-comprehending, and just and brave and all-forgiving. But if you are not *good,* if you don't preserve a sense of comparative values, those qualities turn against you—and your love is a mess and your courage is a slaughter.

Scott

TO LAURA GUTHRIE [1]

Hotel Stafford
[Baltimore, Maryland]
September 23, 1935

Dear Laura:

The news from the West is pretty terrible—I have seen plenty of people disappointed in love, from old maids who thought they had lost their only chance, to ____ ____ who tried to kill herself when ____ ____ threw her over —but I never saw a girl [2] who *had so much* take it all so hard. She knew from the beginning there would be nothing more, so it could scarcely be classed even as a *disappointment*—merely one of these semi-tragic facts that must be faced. It's very strange and sad. I have nothing from her except the wire.

For myself all goes *well.* I woke up on the train after a fine sleep, came to the hotel and went to work with Mrs. Owens before noon. We discussed all the "ifs" and will decide nothing before a week. Scottie arrived like a sun goddess at 5 o'clock, all radiant and glowing. We had a happy evening walking and walking the dark streets. The next morning she was invited to visit in the country for

---

[1] Mrs. Guthrie was Fitzgerald's secretary in Asheville the summer of 1935.
[2] The recipient of the preceding letter.

the weekend and I continued my picking up of loose ends. First Zelda—she was fine, almost herself, has only one nurse now and has no more intention of doing away with herself. It was wonderful to sit with her head on my shoulder for hours and feel as I always have even now, closer to her than to any other human being. This is not a denial of other emotions—oh, you understand.

I have stopped all connections with M. Barleycorn. The eczema is almost gone but not quite. Baltimore is warm but pleasant. I love it more than I thought—it is so rich with memories—it is nice to look up the street and see the statue of my great uncle and to know Poe is buried here and that many ancestors of mine have walked in the old town by the bay. I belong here, where everything is civilized and gay and rotted and polite. And I wouldn't mind a bit if in a few years Zelda and I could snuggle up together under a stone in some old graveyard here. That is really a happy thought and not melancholy at all.

[Scott]

TO JOSEPH HERGESHEIMER

[*Baltimore, Maryland*]

[*Probably Fall, 1935*]

Dear Joe:

You talked to someone who didn't like this book[1]—I don't know who, or why they didn't. But I could tell in the Stafford Bar that afternoon when you said that it was "almost impossible to write a book about an actress" that you hadn't read it thru because the actress fades out of it in the first third and is only a catalytic agent.

Sometime will you open it at the middle, perhaps at page 155, and read on for five or ten minutes—? If it were not for my sincere admiration for your judgment I would

---

[1] *Tender Is the Night.* This letter was Fitzgerald's inscription to Hergesheimer.

forego this plea. You were not the only one repelled by the apparent triviality of the opening—I would like this favorite among my books to have another chance in the crystal light of your taste.

Ever yours,

F. Scott Fitzgerald

Page 155—*et seq.*

TO JULIAN STREET

Cambridge Arms Apartments
1 East 34th Street
Baltimore, Maryland
February 24, 1936

Dear Mr. Street:

That was an awfully nice letter. Like the other it has made me think that you are indeed a friend even though we have seldom met. There is a third article which completes the trilogy of depression.[1] Of course now that things seem a little brighter, or at least the intensity of that despair is fading, I can see that the writing of them was a sort of catharsis but at the time of writing them what I said seemed absolutely real. And may I add that this is no claim to being completely out of the woods except that I would not be inclined to write that way again under the present circumstances. I see, too, that an unfriendly critic might damn the series as the whining of a spoilt baby, but in that case so is most poetry the complaints of the eternally youthful thing that persists in the writer and merely the fact that this is prose separates it from a great many of the mutterings of Shelley, Stephen Crane and Verlaine. I am not comparing this in quality with great poems of lamentation. I am simply saying that it is not essentially different in mood.

Thank you again for your letter. I wish we could meet

[1] The "Crack-Up" series.

sometime soon when I have fully emerged from this small abyss.

Ever yours,

F. Scott Fitzgerald

TO ARNOLD GINGRICH

[*The Cambridge Arms*]
[*Baltimore, Maryland*]
March 20, 1936

Dear Arnold:

In my "Ant" satire,[1] phrase

> *Lebanon School for the Blind*
> should be changed to
> *New Jersey School for Drug Addicts.*

It will be an easy change to make, easy to find in such a short piece. It seems important because the former seems in poor taste because of war blind, etc.

This is a good issue—fine piece by Ernest, and I enjoyed the Mex divorce. Haven't got through the issue.

I get letters from all over (mostly from writers) about the "Crack-Up" series: Alec Woollcott, Julian Street, G. B. Stern, Nancy Hoyt, James Boyd, etc., and from old friends, and naturally am rather touched. What the general response is is more questionable but there have been many of those too.

I will have another piece along shortly but I know there's no hurry and I'm doing a ballet story or trying to for Goldwyn and Miriam Hopkins. Let me know when you want it.

Ever yours,

Scott Fitz

Please don't forget this change in "Ants."

[1] "The Ants at Princeton," *Esquire*, June, 1936.

TO ASA BUSHNELL[1]

[*The Cambridge Arms*]
Baltimore, Maryland

April 27, 1936

Dear Asa:

Is this a crazy idea? Perhaps architects will laugh at it but a recent editorial in an *Alumni News* asked for suggestions. My idea is to have as a building for the library a reproduction of what was torn down to make way for the present library. This part of the library would be above ground, and a series of subterranean galleries covered with glass brick radiating therefrom would house the books.

These galleries would (according to the type of book they carried, scientific, cultural, etc.) shoot in the direction of some convenient hall; for example, the gallery served with scientific books would lead toward the laboratories, that with religious books toward the Chapel reading room, etc.

The idea of a sort of subway, served (as I should envisage it) by electric trucks, and passing a series of alcoves, lit overhead by skylights paralleling the present walks, or by the aforementioned glass brick, is certainly revolutionary. But it would keep the library in the center of the campus. It would solve so many problems, and without violating any of the strategical plan for future Princeton architectural development.[2]

What do you think?

Ever yours,

Scott

---

[1] Princeton's graduate manager of athletics and a former clubmate of Fitzgerald.
[2] Fitzgerald accompanied his letter with illustrative diagrams.

TO MRS. CLIFTON SPRAGUE [1]

[The Cambridge Arms]
[Baltimore, Maryland]

[June, 1936]

Dear Annabel:

It has been a rather terrible day and tomorrow promises to be no better, but after that I'm going to—got to—put Mother out of my mind for a day or so. I'll summarize what happened.

It was sad taking her from the hotel, the only home she knew for fifteen years, to die—and to go thru her things. The slippers and corset she was married in, Louisa's dolls in tissue paper, old letters and souvenirs, and collected scrap paper, and diaries that began and got nowhere, all her prides and sorrows and disappointments all come to nothing, and her lugged away like so much flesh the world had got thru with—

Mother and I never had anything in common except a relentless stubborn quality, but when I saw all this it turned me inside out realizing how unhappy her temperament made her and how she clung, to the end, to all things that would remind her of moments of snatched happiness. So I couldn't bear to throw out anything, even that rug, and it all goes to storage. . . . [2]

TO ROBERT R. DUNN [3]

Grove Park Inn
Asheville, North Carolina

[Probably Summer, 1936]

Dear Bob:

This is sheer impulse for no close friend ever passed so completely and abruptly out of my life as you did— except by death. Our whole adult life till now has passed without a single communication, unless I count a few

---

[1] Fitzgerald's sister.
[2] The rest of the letter is unavailable.
[3] Dunn had grown up with Fitzgerald in St. Paul.

chance encounters wth your father fifteen years ago.

Is your mother living? Are you married? Has life been kind or bitter to you? I assume you know something about me from happening on my stuff here and there, but I know nothing about you. I remember a talk with Norma Talmadge (not Nash!) where your name figured, and meeting a fraternity brother of your "delegation" on a bout between Naples and Marseille (name forgotten)—and I sometimes dream of you. In the dream you're always very snooty and high-hat.

Life's too short for you not to answer this. If your mother lives, give her my eternal homage, unqualified by the fact that she was always skeptical of me. She was one of the most fascinating women I ever knew.

Your old friend,

Scott

TO BENNETT CERF

Grove Park Inn
Asheville, North Carolina
July 23, 1936

Dear Bennett:

Temporarily I am no longer a Baltimorean, so I am afraid we will not be able to talk personally unless you are this far South. From your letter I guess that you are a little cagey about shooting at *Tender Is the Night* at the moment and I have no idea how many of a Modern Library edition of a book it is necessary to sell to make it pay its way.

I have an idea that even among your clientele the actual bulk of a book, the weight of it in the hand, has something to do with buyer psychology. That is, that you would do better with, say, Willa Cather's *My Antonia* than you would with *Lost Lady*. All the first Modern Library books were small. Your tendency toward the giant size shows that you [are] alive to this psychological trait in the potential buyer.

To that extent you might have luck with *Tender Is the Night*. As you may know, *Tender Is the Night* hung around between sixth and twelfth best seller through its publishing season (spring of '34) which was a terrible one, while *The Great Gatsby*, which was a light little volume barely touching 50,000 words, was a rank commercial failure and was only on best-seller lists its first week during a fine season (the spring of 1925). As a *succès d'estime* *Gatsby* outshone *This Side of Paradise* and *Beautiful and Damned* but I do not believe its sale to this day, outside your Modern Library edition, has passed 25,000 copies in America. Of course the Continental sales in German, French and Scandinavian have added a great deal to that.

Since actual distribution of *Tender Is the Night* was small *in spite* of its place on the best-selling list, it might be a much better bet than *The Great Gatsby* and there is always recurrent interest in *This Side of Paradise* (a calling, indeed, by this time).

I would like to have another book on your list, not from vanity (take a bow, Mr. Cerf), but simply because I think that two books would be stronger than one in building up a permanent interest among those whose destiny leads them to accept my observation as part of their cosmology. Do let me hear from you.

Ever yours,

[Scott]

TO JOHN O'HARA

Grove Park Inn
Asheville, North Carolina
July 25, 1936

Dear John:

Your letter got side-tracked in moving and has just turned up. Possibly I may have answered it before and, if I did, everything I said was true, and if what I say now contradicts everything I said before that is all true too. Before I tell you how to write your new novel let me tell you about affairs here.

There are no affairs here.

We will now turn to your new novel. You quoted in your letter a very cryptic passage from the wonderful advice that I give to people. It sounds exactly like the advice that Ernest and I used to throw back and forth at each other, none of which ever had any effect—the only effect I ever had on Ernest was to get him in a receptive mood and say let's cut everything that goes before this. Then the pieces got mislaid and he could never find the part that I said to cut out. And so he published it without that and later we agreed that it was a very wise cut. This is not literally true and I don't want it established as part of the Hemingway legend, but it's just about as far as one writer can go in helping another. Years later when Ernest was writing *Farewell to Arms* he was in doubt about the ending and marketed around to half a dozen people for their advice. I worked like hell on the idea and only succeeded in evolving a philosophy in his mind utterly contrary to everything that he thought an ending should be, and [it] later convinced me that he was right and made me end *Tender Is the Night* on a fade-away instead of a staccato. Didn't we talk about this once before—I seem to see your large ear in the way of my voice.

There is some element that can as well as not be expressed by the dietician's word "roughage" or up-stream by which you can judge yourself as a novelist or as a personality—the fact recently quoted by Middleton Murray that John Keats felt that creative talent is essentially without character, is empiric: the acceptance of disorganization is another matter because it eventually implies a lesion of vitality. I have just written a long letter to an admirer or mourner as to why I do not believe in Psychoanalysis, for the disintegration of that thing, that judgment, the extinction of that light is much more to be dreaded than any material loss.

We are creatures bounding from each other's shoulders, feeling already the feet of new creatures upon our backs bounding again toward an invisible and illusory trapeze (at present played by the short-winded Saroyans). If the calf no longer flexes, the bound will not be so high. In any case the outstretched arms will never catch that swinging thing because when life has been well lived one can make an adjustment and become the second man in the pyramid.

It is when life has been ill lived [that one] is the third man; the first man always falls to his death, a fact that has haunted Ernest all his life.

This is all rather poor metaphysics expressed in ineffectual images. Again and again in my books I have tried to imagize my regret that I have never been as good as I intended to be (and you must know that what I mean by good is the modern don't-hurt-a-hair-of-anybody's-head-and-kill-a-hundred-thousand-people-if-necessary—in other words a personal conscience and meaning by the personal conscience yourself stripped in white midnight before your own God).

To take off with my whole weight (Charlie MacArthur continually urges me) if my suggestion about the bucolic background for a novel makes any sense it is embraced in the paragraph you requoted to me. I certainly think you should undertake something more ambitious and I know to my own sorrow that to contemplate and project a long work is often an excuse for laziness. But let me pass along a suggestion:

Invent a system Zolaesque (see the appendix to Josephson's *Life of Zola* in which he gives Zola's plan for the first Rougon-Maquart book), but buy a file. On the first page of the file put down the outline of a novel of your times enormous in scale (don't worry, it will contract by itself) and work on the plan for two months. Take the central point of the file as your big climax and follow your plan backward and forward from that for another three months. Then draw up something as complicated as a continuity from what you have and set yourself a schedule.

After all who am I to be giving you advice? I dare to do so only because I know that you are at heart a humble man and not resentful of anything said by one who wishes you well.

(This is being taken down by a young man from Brown University who is wilting visibly as he writes after a session with the many concerns that seem to surround a man of forty and the hieroglyphics of a half-done *Post* story to decipher tomorrow. He sends his regards or does he? Do you? No answer. He says he wonders what would

happen if he would write a postscript to this thing.)
So much for tonight. . . .

Ever your friend,

[Scott]

TO BENNETT CERF

Grove Park Inn
Asheville, North Carolina
August 13, 1936

Dear Bennett:

The revision job[1] would take the form, to a large extent,
of a certain new alignment of the scenes—without changing their order in any case. Some such line as this:

That the parts instead of being one, two, and three (they
were one, two, three and four in the magazine serial)
would include in several cases sudden stops and part headings which would be to some extent explanatory; certain
pages would have to be inserted bearing merely headings.
Part two, for example, should say in a terse and graceful
way that the scene is now back on the Riviera in the fall
after these events have taken place, or that this brings us
up to where Rosemary first encounters the Divers. Those
examples are not accurate to my intention nor are they
at all couched as I would have them, but that's the general
idea. (Do you remember the number of subheads I used
in *This Side of Paradise*—at that time a rather novel experiment, the germ of which I borrowed from Bernard
Shaw's preface headings to his plays; indeed that was one
of the few consciously original things in *This Side of
Paradise*.)

There would be certain changes but I would supply the
equivalent line lengths. I have not my plan with me; it
seems to be in Baltimore. But I know how printing costs
are. It was evolved to have a very minimum of replacement. There is not more than one complete sentence that

---

[1] On *Tender Is the Night* for proposed Modern Library edition.

I want to eliminate, one that has offended many people and that I admit is out of Dick's character: "I never did go in for making love to dry loins." It is a strong line but definitely offensive. These are all the changes I contemplated with—in addition some minor spelling corrections such as would disturb nothing but what was within a printed line. There will be no pushing over of paragraphs or disorganization of the present set-up except in the aforesaid inserted pages. I don't want to change anything in the book but sometimes by a single word change one can throw a new emphasis or give a new value to the exact same scene or setting.

Ever yours,

[Scott]

TO BEATRICE DANCE

[*Grove Park Inn*]
Asheville, North Carolina
September 15, 1936

Dear Beatrice:

The last two months have been such a feverish nightmare, day and night, sickness and that sort of thing, that I haven't very clear memories of what letters I have written and what I haven't. Today for the first time, I am really systematizing things under the proper headings of: "Immediate," "Semi-Immediate," "Mother's Death," "Financial," "Scottie's School," "Work," etc., etc.

—so I am by no means sure whether I have to thank you for the fine kimono which I am wearing at present (alas! I have used it so much that you would scarcely know that it is only a month old), or whether only for the gorgeous sweater which I have so reverently laid away to save for more robust days) but really you must not inundate me with such tokens. I am embarrassed. It is impossible for me to send up equivalent incense to your memory—much more than a memory, you know that.

Your letters were bright—and melancholy in the practically arctic night of the past ten months. I have never had so many things go wrong and with such defiant persistence. By an irony which quite fits into the picture, the legacy which I received from my mother's death (after being too ill to go to her death bed or her funeral) is the luckiest event of some time. She was a defiant old woman, defiant in her love for me in spite of my neglect of her, and it would have been quite within her character to have died that I might live.

Thank you for your wire today. People have received this *Esquire* article with mingled feeling—not a few of them think it was a terrific mistake to have written any of them from "Crack-Up." On the other hand, I get innumerable "fan letters" and requests to republish them in the *Reader's Digest*, and several anthologists' requests, which I prudently refused.

My Hollywood deal (which, as it happened, I could not have gone through with because of my shoulder) was seriously compromised by their general tone. It seems to have implied to some people that I was a complete moral and artistic bankrupt.

Now—I come to some things I may have written you before. Did I tell you that I got the broken shoulder from diving from a fifteen-foot board, which would have seemed modest enough in the old days, and the shoulder broke before I hit the water—a phenomenon which has diverted the medicos hereabout to some extent; and that when it was almost well, I tripped over the raised platform of the bathroom at four o'clock one morning when I was still surrounded by an extraordinary plaster cast and I lay on the floor for forty-five minutes before I could crawl to the telephone and get rescued by Mac? It was a hot night, and I was soaking wet in the cast so I caught cold on the tile floor of the bathroom, and a form of arthritis called "myotosis" developed, which involved all of the joints on that side of the body, so back to the bed I went and I have been cursing and groaning without cessation until about three days ago when the devil began to abandon me. During this time Mother died in the North and a dozen other things seemed to happen at once, so that it will take me several months to clear the wreckage of a completely wasted summer, productive of one mediocre short story and two or three shorts. . . .

The summer was to have been devoted to Zelda and I

have seen her exactly five times, her doctors feeling proud
of her improvement and knowing that it would depress her
to see me ill or in pain.

As to Ernest, at first I resented his use of my name in
the story[1] and I wrote him a somewhat indignant letter,
telling him it must not be republished in a book. He answered, agreeing, but rather resentfully, and saying that he
felt that since I had chosen to expose my private life so
"shamelessly" in *Esquire,* he felt that it was sort of an open
season for me, and I wrote him a hell of a letter which
would have been sudden death for somebody the next time
we met, and decided, hell, let it go. Too often literary men
allow themselves to get into internecine quarrels and finish
about as victoriously as most of the nations at the end of
the World War. I consider it an example of approaching
maturity on my part and am proud of my self control. He
is quite as nervously broken down as I am but it manifests
itself in different ways. His inclination is toward megalo-
mania and mine toward melancholy.

I am glad you have had a happy summer and have been
amused by such reports as your running into our Grove
Park Inn friend.

Scott

TO CAMERON ROGERS

Grove Park Inn
Asheville, North Carolina
September 21, 1936

Dear Rogers:

Manila Galleon arrived last week. I was reminded all
through of *Victory,* just as Conrad I suppose was reminded of something when he wrote *Victory.* I loved it.

I have been with a broken shoulder and there were
only two books in the bad times that I could let the nurses
read to me—*Manila Galleon* and Mencken's *American
Language.*

I had the sense of an utterly vacant sky, without the

---

[1] "The Snows of Kilimanjaro."

blue of the Caribbean, sort of a yellow-white. It made me ill at ease and made me want to go back to Europe at all cost, or at least to some seaboard where the only colors were those of my own scars and breeches and the only glint that of my own sword.

Your friend and admirer,

Scott Fitz

TO C. O. KALMAN [1]

Grove Park Inn
Asheville, North Carolina
October 10, 1936

Dear Kallie:

Above and beyond the egotism that seems to descend upon a sick man like a dark cloud, I have been able to appreciate the kindness and friendliness with which you have come to my assistance. I do not know very many rich people well, in spite of the fact that my life has been cast among rich people—certainly only two well enough to have called upon in this emergency, the first personal loan I have ever asked for—though I have made heavy drains on my publishers and agents at times.

I was just about up to the breaking point financially when I came down here to Asheville. I had been seriously sick for a year and just barely recovered and tried to set up a household in Baltimore which I was ill equipped to sustain. I was planning to spend a fairly leisurely summer, keeping my debt in abeyance on money I had borrowed on my life insurance, when I went over with Zelda (who is in a sanitarium near here, better, but still a mental patient, as perhaps she always will be) to a pool near here and tried a high dive with muscles that had not been exercised, by the doctors' orders, for two years, and split my shoulder and tore the arm from its moorings, so that the ball of the ball-and-socket joint hung two and one-half inches below the socket joint. It started to heal after two

---

[1] Mr. and Mrs. C. O. Kalman of St. Paul were old friends of Scott and Zelda.

weeks and I fell on it when it was soaked with sweat inside the plaster cast, and got a thing called "myotosis" which is a form of arthritis. To make a long story short, I was on my back for ten weeks, with whole days in which I was out of bed trying to write or dictate, and then a return to the impotency of the trouble. The more I worried, the less I could write. Being one mile from Zelda, I saw her twice all summer, and was unable to go North when my Mother had a stroke and died, and later was unable to go North to put my daughter in school. (She earned a scholarship to a very expensive school—Miss Walker's, do you know it? She is now in school and apparently very happy.)

The nervous system is pretty well shot. You have probably guessed that I have been doing a good deal of drinking to keep up what morale has been necessary—think of it any way you want to; I know, thank God, you are no moralist. I know you have lent this money on the ask-me-no-question basis, but I feel I owe you this explanation.

For heaven's sake, please try to expedite the loan. The first time in my life I have known what it is to be hog-tied by lack of money, as you know how casually I have always dealt with it.

I want to bring Scottie West at Easter and, seeing her, you will see how much I still have to live for, in spite of a year in a slough of despond.

                                        Ever afftly yours,

                                        Scott Fitz

TO MRS. WILLIAM HAMM

                                Grove Park Inn
                                Asheville, North Carolina
                                October 28, 1936

Dear Marie:

It was damn nice of you to write me. That article in *Time* (not to mention the three "Crack-Up" articles in *Esquire*) brought so many letters from old friends, ranging from such as you—and I think of you as about my oldest real friend, certainly my first love—to men that had been in my Company in the army, addressed to "Dear Lieutenant." Thank you for your thoughtfulness in trying to cheer me up. However, child, life is more complicated than that. There has been some question in my mind whether I should ever have written the *Esquire* articles. Ernest Hemingway wrote me an irritable letter in which he bawled me out for having been so public about what were essentially private affairs and should be written about in fiction or not at all.

As to the article in *Time*, it came from an interview in the *New York Evening Post* written by a man who presumably had come all the way from New York to talk to me about my fortieth birthday. He spread it across three columns in the *Post*, with a picture of me as I was at twenty-one and an entirely faked-up picture of me as I was at forty. None of the remarks attributed to me did I make to him. They were taken word by word from the first "Crack-Up" article. I saw him because he had come a long way, and I had a temperature of 103 with arthritis, after a ten weeks' siege in and out of bed. He was an s. o. b. and I should have guessed it. As soon as the *Time* article came out I wired Miss Walker's School in Simsbury, which Scottie has just entered, to keep it from her if possible, and I think she escaped reading it.

I am leading a dull life convalescing, but am planning to go to New York next month and am actually writing again after a long interval of incapacity to do anything.

Indeed, I do know Lefty and Nora Flynn. We three and Zelda (she is still ill and in and out of sanitariums) went to a football game last week. Yesterday she called me up from downstairs in the hotel to say she was in a fashion show and would I come behind the scenes. Zelda and I are going over to dine with them sometime next week. During the mood of depression that I seem to have fallen into about a year ago she was a saint to me; took care of Scottie for a month one time under the most peculiar circumstances, and is altogether, in my opinion, one of the world's most delightful women. But if you know her, there is no need to tell you that.

Saw something of Joe with the Kalmans in Paris—my God, is it six years ago? But since then they have vanished.

St. Paul contacts have been so infrequent that I am practically determined to go out there next summer for a while and bring the daughter. In spite of a fifteen-year absence, it still is home to me; but the people that make it so are now only such a few—the Kalmans, Nonnie, Bob Clarke and a scattering of others. I don't know what I would have to say to so many people who once meant so much to me. An amazing letter came out of the West from Bob Dunn a few months ago saying that he had tried to get in touch with me the last time I was in Hollywood. We exchanged a little local gossip by correspondence, but the trying to keep alive a friendship at long distance is a difficult business. Do you remember one time at the Cottage Club at Princeton, about 1927, when I came up behind you and grabbed you by the arms in a great crowd and said in your ear, "This is somebody you know very well," but I might have been almost anyone, so far as you knew.

I know you went through hell, Marie, with your first marriage, and all that kidnapping of the children, and of course when my son named, I believe, John Fitzgerald, kidnapped your husband (or was he then your fiance?) I was shocked at his daring to molest you. I wrote him a letter to the penitentiary in which I said that if he wanted to kidnap anybody to leave Marie alone, because she was beginning to have a neurosis on the matter. John has been a good son to me, sending me most of the Weyerhauser ransom money, but the trouble is, I blew it in, Marie.

Well, well, for the rest of the news—my mother died at a ripe old age last summer. If you answer this, tell me how is your mother, who always daily frightened me, and for whom I also had a peculiar admiration because she somehow played the part that Alice Brady plays currently of a completely haywire person who always really had a grip on things.

I thought _____ _____ was not particularly interesting but very nice. Her father is the oldest settler in this hotel, a retired newspaper publisher, and the man she married looked to me like one of his contemporaries.

It seems strange to hear you say you have just moved in from Lake Minnetonka instead of from White Bear. The cities were growing close when we were young, but are they now so close together that such places as White Bear Lake and Minnetonka are the same thing?

> With affection always,
>
> Scott

TO MR. AND MRS. EBEN FINNEY

> [*Oak Hall Hotel*]
> [*Tryon, North Carolina*]
> [*Spring, 1937*]

Dear Pete and Peggy:

It was swell of you to write me and I don't know yet how you found out where my wandering daughter was. Coincidental with your telegram came one from her saying she had expected to wire me tomorrow and is coming by Spartanburg, not Asheville as ordered, with me in the act of leaving a call for six o'clock to meet her in Asheville! Ah, me—or youth, hell, or something.

Still as I let her down Xmas I shall forgive the lapse. There isn't really much I can do about it. She expects it to be dull here but she'll find it quite gay. I want to get to know her again—I'm in fine shape again (for forty)—not so much as a glass-beer since January, and perhaps she'll approve of me.

I think of you often and your kindness to her in the chilling emergencies of the past year. Someday I'm going to write about the series of calamities that led up to the awful state I was in Xmas. A writer not writing is practically a maniac within himself. Because of this—I mean too many anxieties and too much introspection—I'm going to Hollywood next month and extrovert awhile, do a picture on order for Harlow and Robert Taylor and then some other work for Metro if they want me to stay on. I might take Scottie there this summer.

This little town is as full of Princetonians as Baltimore and fuller of sunshine. I was never a part of Baltimore but in spite of much personal unhappiness there, I mean chiefly illnesses, I love the place and am grateful to its general urbanity and sophistication for much kindness—with your kindness to Scottie coming first. I think I like it next to any city except New York but I'm [too] confirmed a wanderer to have been content there.

I hope the Peacherino[1] is as beautiful and blooming as ever and that you, Peggy, are strong enough now to do whatever you want to do. I still think of your lovely house with the June sunlight on the pool and the black-brown children being ravenously happy.

With every good wish to you all,

Ever your friend,

F. Scott Fitzgerald

P.S. I still don't see how you got Scottie's address unless you phoned Miss Walker's. I didn't even know Sally Simmons' father's name!

TO COREY FORD[2]

Oak Hall[3]
Tryon, North Carolina
April, 1937

Dear Corey:

I think you have read or heard that I've been in a somewhat bitter temper for a year, and that led you to say to yourself, "It might cheer the poor bastard up to think he's not forgotten." Whatever was the impulse that made you write it *did* cheer me up and the idea that people have such thoughts and do something so concrete about it is the most cheering thought of all.

I had been sick as hell for a year and took an extra one to get over it morally for, as a child of the bitch goddess, I began trying to fight it with two quarts a day and got into an awful psychological jam. However I came back

---

[1] The Finneys' daughter, Peaches.
[2] Rereading *The Great Gatsby* had prompted Ford to write Fitzgerald a fan letter.
[3] With an arrow pointing to "Oak Hall" Fitzgerald wrote, "That always reminds me of you and your Rover Boys—didn't you read Dave Porter too?"

to life last January after the newspapers began cracking at
me (it was rather a shock—nobody ever tried to interfere
with Ring Lardner's utterly private life, but I had myself
to blame with those indiscreet *Esquire* articles) and decided to be an example to myself. I now admire myself
almost as much as William Seabrook, Mary McLane and
Casanova.

Maybe this has nothing to do with why you wrote me.
Anyhow thank you more than I can say. I'm sorry our
meetings have been so brief—the last at Marice Hamilton's
in February, 1931. My God, where have these six years
gone—whole months go by and nothing seems to happen.
Is that just middle-age? I'd like to do a lot of leisurely
things now but there seems to be no time.

Yours,

F. Scott Fitzgerald

TO C. O. KALMAN

[*Oak Hall Hotel*]
[*Tryon, North Carolina*]
[*June, 1937*]

Dear Kallie:

Well, you certainly gave me a generous helping hand
out of a nightmare and now that it is paid up—as far as
such an obligation can be paid—I want to tell you that I've
been constantly thinking of what you did with gratitude
and appreciation. What got me into the two years' mess
that reached its lowest point in the fall of 1936 was the
usual combination of circumstances. A prejudiced enemy
might say it was all drink, a fond mama might say it was
a run of ill-luck, a banker might say it was not providing
for the future in better days, a psychiatrist might say it was
a nervous collapse—it was perhaps partly all these things
—the effect was to fantastically prevent me from doing
any work at the very age when presumably one is at the
height of one's powers. My life looked like a hopeless mess there for awhile and the point was I didn't
want it to be better. I had completely ceased to give a good
Goddamn.

Luckily a few people had faith in me, or perhaps only kindliness—there was a doctor that was interested and some old friends who simply couldn't believe it was me. I hurt myself professionally no end but did no great damage to private relations—Scottie being away at school, Zelda in a sanitarium, and myself in North Carolina where I saw no people at all. And for six months (I went on the complete wagon, not even beer, in January) I have been steadily coming back, first physically, and finally financially, tho that's only just begun and I'm afraid I'll have to go to Hollywood before accumulating any surplus.

So much for me and I don't think it will ever happen again. I want to come to St. Paul sometime this summer, probably on my way to or from the coast, and I want to be sure you're there, so write me if and when you and Sandy will be gone to Europe to fight with General Franco for the rights of labor and the 20-hour day. Scribners, 597 Fifth Ave., is a permanent address for me, though in person I am usually in Carolina near Zelda. I took her out swimming yesterday and we talked of you. Again my deepest gratitude.

With affection always,

Scott Fitzg_____

TO COREY FORD

Metro-Goldwyn-Mayer Corporation
Culver City, California
[*Early July, 1937*]

Dear Corey:

These Texas lands are like crossing a sea—spiritually I mean, with a fat contract at the end and the loss of something for a year or so. Tho I find that the vast majority of _____ _____s who yelp about that had nothing to lose, either talent or vitality, when they sold out—and at the moment with my play finished I'm no exception. Even Dotty's[1] chief kick was, I imagine, that the precious lazy-bones never had to work so hard in her life. And it amuses

---

[1] Dorothy Parker.

me to see the squirming of one-opus geniuses like Lawson, Hermann and Saroyan who simply have no more to say. How simple to be a Communist under those conditions— one can explain away not only the world's inadequacies but one's own. After _____ _____'s long pull at the mammalia of the Whitneys he ought to be able to swim under a long way. He'll be under something else when the real trouble begins.

The only real holdout against Hollywood is Ernest. O'Neill, etc., are so damn rich that they don't count. Dos Passos has nibbled and Erskine Caldwell, whom I admire a lot, seems to have gone in. It's a pretty unsatisfactory business—I'm trying a special stunt to beat the game. I'm getting up at six and working till nine on my own stuff which I did before under similar circumstances when I was young. (This is confidential.) The boys who try to write creatively at night after a day in the studio or on Saturdays after work there are gypped from the start—also those who write "on vacations." Nobody's ever gotten out that way and I'm not going to perish before one more book.

Oddly enough this book is like *Paradise*. Mine have alternated between being selective and blown up. *Paradise* and *Gatsby* were selective; *The Beautiful and Damned* and *Tender* aimed at being full and comprehensive—either could be cut by one-fourth, especially the former. (Of course they were cut that much but not enough.) The difference is that in these last two I wrote everything, hoping to cut to interest. In *This Side of Paradise* (in a crude way) and in *Gatsby* I selected the stuff to fit a given mood or "hauntedness" or whatever you might call it, rejecting in advance in *Gatsby*, for instance, all of the ordinary material for Long Island, big crooks, adultery theme and always starting from the *small* focal point that impressed me—my own meeting with Arnold Rothstein for instance. All this because you seem to sincerely like some of my work and I dare then assume that above might interest you somewhat.

So our meeting is postponed unless you come West tho I'll keep your address in my "immediate" file in case autumn finds me in New York.

Yours with cordial good wishes,

Scott Fitzgerald

TO THOMAS WOLFE

> [*The Garden of Allah Hotel*]
> [*Hollywood, California*]
> [*July, 1937*]

Dear Tom:

I think I could make out a good case for your necessity
to cultivate an alter ego, a more conscious artist in you.
Hasn't it occurred to you that such qualities as pleasant-
ness or grief, exuberance or cynicism can become a plague
in others? That often people who live at a high pitch often
don't get their way emotionally at the important moment
because it doesn't stand out in relief?

Now the more, the stronger, man's inner tendencies are
defined, the more he can be sure they will show, the more
necessity to rarefy them, to use them sparingly. The novel
of selected incidents has this to be said: that the great
writer like Flaubert has consciously left out the stuff that
Bill or Joe (in his case, Zola) will come along and say
presently. He will say only the things that he alone sees.
So *Madame Bovary* becomes eternal while Zola already
rocks with age. . . .

That, in brief, is my case against you, if it can be called
that when I admire you so much and think your talent is
unmatchable in this or any other country.

> Ever your friend,
>
> Scott Fitzgerald

TO MRS. HAROLD OBER

> [*The Garden of Allah Hotel*]
> [*Hollywood, California*]
> *July 26, 1937*

Dear Anne:

This letter is long overdue. Suffice to summarize: I have
seen Hollywood—talked with Taylor, dined with March,
danced with Ginger Rogers (this will burn Scottie up but
it's true), been in Rosalind Russell's dressing room, wise-

cracked with Montgomery, drunk (ginger ale) with Zukor and Lasky, lunched alone with Maureen O'Sullivan, watched Crawford act, and lost my heart to a beautiful half-caste Chinese girl whose name I've forgotten. So far I've bought my own breakfasts.

And this is to say I'm through. From now on I go nowhere and see no one because the work is hard as hell, at least for me, and I've lost ten pounds. So farewell, Miriam Hopkins, who leans *so* close when she talks, so long, Claudette Colbert, as yet unencountered, mysterious Garbo, glamorous Dietrich, exotic Shirley Temple—you will never know me. Except Miriam who promised to call up but hasn't. There is nothing left, girls, but to believe in reincarnation and carry on.

Tell my daughter she is a vile daughter of Babylon who does not write letters but can charge $25.00 worth of wash dresses at Franklin Simon but nowhere else. Or if she wants, Harold will advance her $25.00 from a check sent today to go to Saks.

I'm glad she is playing tennis. I do want to see the wretched little harpy and don't let her make a mess of it. Helen[1] will be in Nyack after the 29th—and is leaving the 2nd. No Long Island date should prevent Scottie from getting in touch with her and coming with her. All Metro could find for chaperones were the Ritz Brothers and I can't see it. They might vanish her as a practical joke.

> Yours with gratitude and devotion,
>
> Scott

TO HELEN HAYES

> [*The Garden of Allah Hotel*]
> [*Hollywood, California*]
> *September 16, 1937*

Dear Helen:

You left so precipitately (to my mind) that I'm not going to blame myself for not being on hand. Called up Scottie

[1] Helen Hayes.

half an hour after you'd gone to suggest that we make a farewell call on you; then I sent a wire to Mrs. MacArthur on the train, but it was returned—I guess you were just plain Helen Hayes again. (I see, by the way, that the Basil Rathbone story leaked out, to my great delight.)

Helen, I'm not going to overwhelm you with thanks, but if you ever get too old to play *Queen Victoria*, I'm going to write a companion piece to Shaw's *Methuselah* for you that will eke out a living for you and Charlie and Mary during your declining years.

As a sort of a "wake" for you, Scottie and I ran off *Madeleine Claudet* the day you left, in a projection room. Charlie dropped in, and the Fitzgeralds contributed appropriate tears to the occasion—an upshot which, as you will remember, Garbo failed to evoke from this hardened cynic, so I think you have a future. Remember to speak slowly and clearly and don't be frightened—the audience is just as scared as you are. Maxwell Anderson's line should be spoken with a chewing motion and an expression of chronic indigestion.

I'll now tell you all about Mary's education, as I am a licensed nuisance on the subject. I think it is impossible to get a first rate American governess who will not make home a hell. That's reason number one for procuring a French, English or German number who will have a precise knowledge of her so-called "place." The position of a governess, which is halfway between an employee and a servant, is difficult for anyone to keep up with dignity— that is, to be a sort of an ideal friend to the child and yet maintain an unobtrusive position in regard to mama and papa. It is utterly un-American, and I have never seen one of our countrywomen who was really successful at it. They don't succeed in passing on any standards, save those of the last shoddy series of movies. On the contrary, from a European upper servant, a child learns many short cuts, ways to dispose of those ordinary problems that irk us in youth. The business of politeness is usually deftly handled without any nonsense—and what a saving! The self-consciousness, if any, is eradicated smoothly and easily; the nerves are somehow cushioned by a protective pillow of good form, something which would be annoying to a formed adult but for a child is a big saving of wear and tear. We can all manufacture our unconventionality when the time comes and we have earned the right to it, but this country is filled with geniuses without genius, without the faintest knowledge of what work is, who were brought up on the Dalton system or some faint shadow of it. As I told you, it was tried and abandoned in Russia after three years. It is an attempt to let the child develop his ego and personality at any cost to himself or others—a last gasp of the ideas of Jean Jacques Rousseau. As a practice against too much repression, such as sending a shy girl to a strict convent, it had its value, but the world, especially America, has swung so far in the opposite direction that I can't believe it is good for one American child in a hundred thousand. Certainly not for one born in comparatively easy circumstances.

I have said my say on the subject, welcome or not, because I know you will be faced with some such problem soon when Miss X outgrows her usefulness. The pace of American life simply will not permit a first-rate woman to take up such a profession. I think for very young children the *very best* negro nurses in the South are an exception. They at least stand for something and I think a child absolutely demands a standard. Those years can be passed without harm in some uncertainty as to where the next meal is coming from, but they can't be passed in an ethical void without serious damage to the child's soul, if that word is still in use. The human machinery which controls the sense of right, duty, self-respect, etc., must have conscious exercise before adolescence, because in adolescence you don't have much time to think of anything.

I have just come back from eight days in the East where I found Zelda much better than usual—we went to Charleston, South Carolina, for four days—and on my return here learned that the work had pleased the powers-that-be.

Scottie has finished her play and goes back to school with enthusiasm, though she paid me the tribute of a rare tear when I left her. She will remember this summer all her life, and moreover she will be marked by the idealism she has for you. She talked about you constantly—the things that you wisely did and wisely left undone. Do you mind being a shining legend?

Devotedly,

[Scott]

TO MR. AND MRS. EBEN FINNEY

> *Metro-Goldwyn-Mayer Corporation*
> *Culver City, California*
> *October 8, 1937*

Dear Pete and Peggy:

The mystery of the missing daughter solved itself when your telegram came. I might have guessed she was with you, but it was absolutely arranged that she was to go on to New York to do some tutoring before school opened. I had visions of her being up in the pampas of Charles Town with the little Mackie girl, or else shopping herself around from house to house in Baltimore so that she could tear around madly with Bill-the-butcher or Bob-the-baker, or whatever that boy's name is. It seems that she had told her aunt and simply thought that I'd crawled back into my shell hole out here and put her out of my mind. The weakness was that the Obers didn't know where she was either. However, that's ancient history.

So is her trip out here, but I must say that it was an *Alice in Wonderland* experience for her, and both of us kept wishing that Peaches could have shared some of the excitements that were rife. She seems to have a little more poise and made a good impression, though the reports about the talent scouts following her around are somewhat exaggerated.

I have just finished the script of *Three Comrades*[1] (I guess she told you about it) and I'm reconciled to staying out here. It is the kind of life I need. I think I'm through drinking for good now, but it's a help this first year to have the sense that you are under observation—everyone *is* in this town, and it wouldn't help this budding young career to be identified with John Barleycorn. In free-lance writing it doesn't matter a damn what you do with your private life as long as your stuff is good; but I had gotten everything pleasant that drink can offer long ago, and really do not miss it at all and rather think of that last year and a half in Baltimore and Carolina as a long nightmare. A nightmare has its compensations but you wake up at the end of it feeling that life has moved on and left you stand-

---

[1] Based on the novel, *Three Comrades,* by Erich Remarque.

ing still with ever greater problems to meet han before.

Your kindness to Scottie is again appreciated. She has a fixation on Baltimore—partly because it was there that she first became conscious of boys. I think that this time she was old enough to realize that Baltimore boys are no more or less magical than any other boys, but the warm spot will always be there.

> Ever yours with gratitude and affection,
>
> Scott Fitzgerald

TO MRS. ALLEIN OWENS [1]

> *Metro-Goldwyn-Mayer Corporation*
> *Culver City, California*
> *October 8, 1937*

Dear Mrs. Owens:

Thanks for your letter. I think of you often and am enclosing a Christmas present in advance which I wish you would use to buy feed for the puppies.

Regarding the usual mix-up about Scottie, entitled "Where Is She?"—she finally appeared from under a boxcar in the neighborhood of Gramercy Park. So I am proceeding to forget her for a few months. She seemed happy out here and, as you say, has much more poise this year than during her lamentable career as the Belle of Baltimore. She listens to me more willingly. I remember Mark Twain saying, "At fourteen I thought I'd never seen such an awful ignoramus as my father was, but when I got to be twenty, I used to be astonished at how much the old man had learned in the interval."

Three Comrades is almost finished. Joan Crawford is still slated for Pat, but you never can tell. In my version, Taylor has about three lines to her two—perhaps that will discourage her.

Will you do this for me? Go to the storage and find the box which contains my files and abstract file or files which probably contain important receipts, old income tax statements, etc.—not the correspondence file. You will know

---

[1] Fitzgerald's secretary in Baltimore.

the one or ones that I mean—those that would seem to have most to do with current business. I should have taken it or them along. Also I want my scrapbooks—the big ones including Zelda's and the photograph books. This should make quite a sizable assortment, and I'd like the whole thing boxed and sent to me here collect. If they won't send it this way, let me know what the charges will be. I have just sent them a check for $99.00 which covers all bills to date, but maybe they have another statement for me and don't know where to send it.

I like it here very much. I hear the report of my salary has been terrifically exaggerated in Baltimore. Thought at first it was Scottie's doing but she denies it. I like the work which is occasionally creative—most often like fitting together a very interesting picture puzzle. I think I'm going to be good at it.

With affection always,

Scott Fitz

TO TED PARAMORE [1]

[*Metro-Goldwyn-Mayer Corporation*]
[*Culver City, California*]
October 24, 1937

Dear Ted:

I'd intended to go into this Friday but time was too short. Also, hating controversy, I've decided after all to write it. At all events it must be discussed now.

First let me say that in the main I agree with your present angle, as opposed to your first "war" angle on the script, and I think you have cleared up a lot in the short time we've been working. Also I know we can work together even if we occasionally hurl about charges of pedantry and prudery.

But on the other hand I totally disagree with you as to the terms of our collaboration. We got off to a bad start and I think you are under certain misapprehensions

[1] Fitzgerald's collaborator on the script of *Three Comrades*.

founded more on my state of mind and body last Friday than upon the real situation. My script is in a general way approved of. There was not any question of taking it out of my hands—as in the case of Sheriff. The question was who I wanted to work with me on it and for how long. *That was the entire question* and it is not materially changed because I was temporarily off my balance.

At what point you decided you wanted to take the whole course of things in hand—whether because of that day or because when you read my script you liked it much less than did Joe[1] or the people in his office—where that point was I don't know. But it was apparent Saturday that you had and it is with my faculties quite clear and alert that I tell you I *prefer to keep* the responsibility for the script as a a whole.

For a case in point: such matters as to whether to include the scene with Bruer in Pat's room, or the one about the whores in Bobby's apartment, or this bit of Ferdinand Grau's dialogue or that, or whether the car is called Heinrich or Ludwig, are not matters I will argue with you before Joe. I will yield points by the dozen but in the case of such matters, Joe's knowledge that they were in the book and that I did or did not choose to use them are tantamount to his acceptance of my taste. That there are a dozen ways of treating it all, or of selecting material, is a commonplace but I have done my exploring and made my choices according to my canons of taste. Joe's caution to you was not to spoil the Fitzgerald quality of the *script*. He did not merely say to let the good scenes alone—he meant that the *quality* of the script in its entirety pleased him (save the treatment of Kőster). I feel that the quality was obtained in certain ways, that the scene of Pat in Bruer's room, for instance, has a value in suddenly and surprisingly leading the audience into a glimpse of Pat's world, a tail hanging right out of our circle of protagonists, if you will. I will make it less heavy but I can't and shouldn't be asked to defend it beyond that, nor is it your function to attack it before Joe unless a doubt is already in his mind. About the whores, again it is a feeling but, in spite of your current underestimation of my abilities, I think you would be overstepping your functions if you

[1] Joseph Mankiewicz, producer-director of *Three Comrades*.

make a conference-room point of such a matter.

Point after point has become a matter you are going to "take to Joe," more inessential details than I bothered him with in two months. What I want to take to Joe is simply this—the assurance that we can finish the script in three weeks more—you've had a full week to find your way around it—and the assurance that we are in agreement on the main points.

I'm not satisfied with the opening and can't believe now that Joe cared whether the airplane was blown up at the beginning or end of the scene, or even liked it very much—but except for that I think we do agree on the main line even to the sequences.

But, Ted, when you blandly informed me yesterday that you were going to write the whole thing over yourself, kindly including my best scenes, I knew we'd have to have this out. Whether the picture is in production in January or May there is no reason on God's earth why we can't finish this script in three to four weeks if we divide up the scenes and get together on the piecing together and technical revision. If you were called on this job in the capacity of complete rewriter then I'm getting deaf. I want to reconceive and rewrite my share of the weak scenes and I want your help but I am not going to spend hours of time and talent arguing with you as to whether I've chosen the best or second best speech of Lenz's to adorn the dressing-up scene. I am not referring to key speeches which are discussable but the idea of sitting by while you dredge through the book again as if it were Shakespeare—well, I didn't write four out of four best sellers or a hundred and fifty top-price short stories out of the mind of a temperamental child without taste or judgment.

This letter is sharp but a discussion might become more heated and less logical. Your job is to help me, not hinder me. Perhaps you'd let me know before we see Joe whether it is possible for us to get together on this.

This letter is an argument against arguments and certainly mustn't lead to one. Like you, I want to work.

[Scott]

TO MRS. HAROLD OBER

[*The Garden of Allah Hotel*]
[*Hollywood, California*]
[*Christmas, 1937*]

Dear Anne:

Thanks for your note. Scottie will be North again before school opens. As she is obviously destined to be a perpetual guest I do try to split her visits with such easily imposed-on yaps as the Finneys and Obers into reasonable bits lest the golden gooses cease to lay—wait a minute, this metaphor has gotten entirely out of hand. Anyhow all I can think of is for you and Harold to spend your old age with me—and even that won't square things.

These letters or cards for Scottie came to hand—better hold them. I have high hopes of getting East *before* she goes back to school—if not I'll go to her school in January. I love it here. It's nice work if you can get it and you can get it if you try about three years. The point is once you've got it—Screen Credit first, a Hit second, and the Academy Award third—you can count on it forever—like Laurence Stallings does—and know there's one place you'll be fed, without being asked to even wash the dishes. But till we get those three accolades we Hollywood boys keep trying.

That's cynical but I'm not a bit cynical. I'm delighted with screen credit and really hopeful of a hit—the line-up is good, depending on whether or not one of our principals has to have an operation. I hope none of you need even an extraction.

Ever affectionately,

Scott Fitz——

P.S. I recognized the dogs individually in your Christmas card. I'm going to have my suite photographed with the mice in the hall for next Xmas. (I'm getting old and unfertile so will put this crack in my notebook.)

TO JOSEPH MANKIEWICZ

[*New York City*]
January 17, 1938

Dear Joe:

I read the third batch (to page 51) with mixed feelings. Competent it certainly is, and in many ways tighter-knit than before. But my own type of writing doesn't survive being written over so thoroughly and there are certain pages out of which the rhythm has vanished. I know you don't believe the Hollywood theory that the actors will somehow "play it into shape," but I think that sometimes you've changed without improving.

P. 32 The shortening is good.

P. 33 "Tough but sentimental." Isn't it rather elementary to have one character describe another? No audience heeds it unless it's a false plant.

P. 33 Pat's line, "I would, etc.," isn't good. The thing isn't supposed to provoke a sneer at Alois. The pleasant amusement of the other is much more to our purpose. In the other she was natural and quick. Here she's a kidder from Park Avenue. And Erich's "We're in for it, etc.," carries the joke to its death. I think those two lines about it in mid-page should be cut. Also the repeat on next page.

P. 36 Original form of "threw it away like an old shoe" has humor and a reaction from Pat. Why lose it? For the rest, I like your cuts here.

P. 37 The war remark from Pat is as a chestnut to those who were in it—and meaningless to the younger people. In 8 years in Europe I found few people who talked that way. The war became rather like a dream and Pat's speech is a false note.

P. 39 I thought she was worried about Bruer—not her T.B. If so, this paragraph (the second) is now misplaced.

P. 41 I liked Pat's lie about being feverish. People never blame women for social lies. It makes her *more* attractive taking the trouble to let him down gently.

P. 42 Again, Pat's speech beginning "—if all I had, etc.," isn't as good as the original. People don't begin all sentences with *and, but, for* and *if*, do they? They simply break a thought in mid-paragraph, and in both *Gatsby* and *Farewell to Arms* the dialogue tends that way. Sticking in conjunctions makes a *monotonous* smoothness.

The next scene is all much better but—

P. 46 Erich's speech too long at beginning. Erich's line about the bad smell spoils *her* line about spring smell.

P. 48 "Munchausen" is trite. Erich's speech—this repetition from first scene is distinctly self-pity.

I wired you about the flower scene. I remember when I wrote it, thinking whether it was a double love climax, and deciding it wasn't. The best test is that on the first couple of readings of my script *you didn't think so either*. It may not be George Pierce Baker [1] but it's right *instinctively* and I'm all for restoring it. I honestly don't mind when a scene of mine is cut but I think this one is terribly missed.

P. 49 Word "gunman" too American. Also "tried to strong-arm Riebling" would be a less obvious plant.

P. 51 Kőster's tag not right. Suppose they both say, with different meanings, "You see?"

What I haven't mentioned, I think is distinctly improved. New York is lousy this time of year.

Best always,

[Scott]

TO JOSEPH MANKIEWICZ

[*Metro-Goldwyn-Mayer Corporation*]
[*Culver City, California*]
January 20, 1938

Dear Joe:

Well, I read the last part and I feel like a good many writers must have felt in the past. I gave you a drawing and you simply took a box of chalk and touched it up. Pat has now become a sentimental girl from Brooklyn, and I guess all these years I've been kidding myself about being a good writer.

Most of the movement is gone—action that was un-

[1] Professor of playwriting at Harvard and Yale.

expected and diverting is slowed down to a key that will disturb nobody—and now they can focus directly on Pat's death, squirming slightly as they wait for the other picture on the program.

To say I'm disillusioned is putting it mildly. For nineteen years, with two years out for sickness, I've written best-selling entertainment, and my dialogue is supposedly right up at the top. But I learn from the script that you've suddenly decided that it isn't good dialogue and you can take a few hours off and do much better.

I think you now have a flop on your hands—as thoroughly naive as *The Bride Wore Red* but utterly inexcusable because this time you *had* something and you have arbitrarily and carelessly torn it to pieces. To take out the manicurist and the balcony scene and then have space to put in that utter drool out of *True Romances* which Pat gets off on page 116 makes me think we don't talk the same language. God and "cool lips," whatever they are, and lightning and elephantine play on words. The audience's feeling will be "Oh, go on and die." If Ted had written that scene you'd laugh it out of the window.

You are simply tired of the best scenes because you've read them too much and, having dropped the pilot, you're having the aforesaid pleasure of a child with a box of chalk. You are *or have been* a good writer, but this is a job you will be ashamed of before it's over. The little fluttering life of what's left of my lines and situations won't save the picture.

Example number 3000 is taking out the piano scene between Pat and Kőster and substituting garage hammering. Pat the girl who hangs around the garage! And the recasting of lines—I feel *somewhat outraged*.

Lenz and Bobby's scene on page 62 isn't even in the same category with my scene. It's dull and solemn, and Kőster on page 44 is as uninteresting a plodder as I've avoided in a long life.

What does scene 116 mean? I can just hear the boys relaxing from tension and giving a cheer.

And Pat on page 72—"books and music—she's going to teach him." My God, Joe, you must see what you've done. This isn't Pat—it's a graduate of Pomona College or one of more bespectacled ladies in Mrs. Farrow's department. Books and music! Think, man! Pat is a lady—a cultured European—a charming woman. And Bobby playing soldier. And Pat's really *re*-fined talk about the flower garden. They do everything but play ring-around-a-rosie on their Staten Island honeymoon. Recognizable characters they simply are not, and cutting the worst lines here and there isn't going to restore what you've destroyed. It's all so inconsistent. I thought we'd decided long ago what we wanted Pat to be!

On page 74 we meet Mr. Sheriff again, and they say just the cutest merriest things and keep each other in gales of girlish laughter.

On page 93 God begins to come into the script with a vengeance, *but to say in detail what I think of these lines would take a book*. The last pages that everyone liked begin to creak from 116 on, and when I finished there were tears in my eyes, but not for Pat—for Margaret Sullavan.

My only hope is that you will *have a moment of clear thinking. That you'll ask some intelligent* and *disinterested* person to look at the two scripts. Some honest thinking would be much more valuable to the enterprise right now than an effort to convince people you've improved it. I am utterly miserable at seeing months of work and thought negated in one hasty week. I hope you're big enough to take this letter as it's meant—a desperate plea to restore the dialogue to its former quality—to put back the flower cart, the piano-moving, the balcony, the manicure girl—all those touches that were both natural and new. Oh, Joe, can't producers ever be wrong? I'm a good writer—honest. I thought you were going to play fair. Joan Crawford might as well play the part now, for the thing is as groggy with sentimentality as *The Bride Wore Red*, but the true emotion is gone.

[Scott]

TO EDDIE MANNIX AND SAM KATZ[1]

> [*Metro-Goldwyn-Mayer Corporation*]
> [*Culver City, California*]
>
> [*Winter, 1938*]

Dear Sirs:

I have long finished my part in the making of *Three Comrades* but Mank_____[2] has told me what the exhibitors are saying about the ending and I can't resist a last word. If they had pronounced on *Captains Courageous* at this stage, I feel they would have had Manuel the Portuguese live and go out West with the little boy and *Captains Courageous* could have stood that much better than *Three Comrades* can stand an essential change in its story. In writing over a hundred and fifty stories for George Lorimer, the great editor of *The Saturday Evening Post*, I found he made a sharp distinction between a sordid tragedy and a heroic tragedy—hating the former but accepting the latter as an essential and interesting part of life.

I think in *Three Comrades* we run the danger of having the wrong head go on the right body—a thing that confuses and depresses everyone except the ten-year-olds who are so confused anyhow that I can't believe they make or break a picture. To every reviewer or teacher in America, the idea of the comrades going back into the fight in the spirit of "My head is bloody but unbowed" is infinitely stronger and more cheerful than that they should be quitting—all the fine talk, the death of their friends and countrymen in vain. All right, they were suckers, but they were always that in one sense and if it was despicable what was the use of telling their story?

The public will feel this—they feel what they can't express—otherwise we'd change our conception of Chinese palaces and French scientists to fit the conception of hill-billies who've never seen palaces or scientists. The public will be vaguely confused by the confusion in our mind—they'll know that the beginning and end don't fit together and when one is confused one rebels by kicking the thing

[1] Producers at M-G-M.
[2] Joseph Mankiewicz.

altogether out of mind. Certainly this step of putting in
the "new life" thought will not please or fool anyone—it
simply loses us the press and takes out of the picture the
real rhythm of the ending which is:

*The march of four people, living and dead, heroic and
inconquerable, side by side back into the fight.*

Very sincerely yours,

[F. Scott Fitzgerald]

TO MRS. EDWIN JARRETT [1]

[Metro-Goldwyn-Mayer Corporation]
[Culver City, California]
February 17, 1938

Dear Mrs. Jarrett:

The play pleases me immensely. So faithful has been
your following of my intentions that my only fear is that
you have been *too* loyal. I hope you haven't—I hope that
a measure of the novel's intention *can* be crammed into
the two hours of the play. My thanks, hopes and wishes
are entirely with you—it pleases me in a manner that the
acting version of *The Great Gatsby* did not. And I want
especially to congratulate you and Miss Oglebay on the
multiple feats of ingenuity with which you've handled the
difficult geography and chronology so that it has a unity
which, God help me, I wasn't able to give it.

My first intention was to go through it and "criticize"
it, but I see I'm not capable of doing that—too many obstacles in my own mind prevent me from getting a clear
vision. I had some notes—that Rosemary wouldn't express her distaste for the battlefield trip—she had a *good*
time and it belittles Dick's power of making things fun.
Also a note that Dick's curiosity and interest in people was
real—he didn't stare at them—he glanced at them and *felt*
them. I don't know what point of the play I was referring
to. Also I'm afraid some of his long Shavian speeches won't
play—and no one's sorrier than I am—his comment on

[1] Mrs. Jarrett had written a stage adaptation of *Tender Is the Night.*

the battle of the Somme for instance. Also Tommy seemed to me less integrated than he should be. He was Tommy Hitchcock in a way whose whole life is a challenge—who is only interested in realities, his kind—in going into him you've brought him into the boudoir a little—I should be careful of what he says and does unless you can feel the strong fresh-air current in him. I realize you've had to use some of the lesser characters for plot transitions and convenience, but when any of them go out of character I necessarily feel it, so I am a poor critic. I know the important thing is to put over Dick in his relation to Nicole and Rosemary and, if you can, Bob Montgomery and others here would love to play the part. But it must get by Broadway first.

If it has to be cut, the children will probably come out. On the stage they will seem to press, too much for taste, against distasteful events. As if Dick had let them in for it —he is after all a sort of superman, an approximation of the *hero* seen in overcivilized terms—taste is no substitute for vitality but in the book it has to do duty for it. It is one of the points on which he must never show weakness as Siegfried could never show physical fear. I did not manage, I think in retrospect, to give Dick the cohesion I aimed at, but in your dramatic interpretation I beg you to guard me from the exposal of this. I wonder what the hell the first actor who played Hamlet thought of the part? I can hear him say, "The guy's a nut, isn't he?" (We can always find great consolation in Shakespeare.)

Also to return to the criticism I was not going to make —I find in writing for a particular screen character here that it's convenient to suggest the way it's played, especially the timing—i.e., at the top of page 25 it would probably be more effective—

Rosemary didn't grow up. (pause) It's better that way. (pause) Etc.

But I'd better return to my thesis. You've done a fine dramatization and my gratitude to you is part of the old emotion I put into the book, part of my life.

Most sincerely,

F. Scott Fitzgerald

TO ROGER GARIS[1]

[*Metro-Goldwyn-Mayer Corporation*]
[*Culver City, California*]
February 22, 1938

Dear Mr. Garis:

In several ways, I am familiar with the melancholia you describe. Myself, I had what amounted to a nervous breakdown which never, however, approached psychosis. My wife, on the contrary, has been a mental patient off and on for seven years and will never be entirely well again, so I have a very detached point of view on the subject.

As I look at my own approach toward a practical inability to function and my gradual recession from it, it appears to me as being a matter of adjustment. The things that were the matter with me were so apparent, however, that I did not even need a psychoanalyst to tell me that I was being stubborn about this (giving up drink) or stupid about that (trying to do too many things); and so, to say that all such times of depression are merely "a moment of adjustment" is pretty easy.

I know this: that it is impossible to write without hope, and especially it is impossible to write cheerfully the sort of things in demand by the magazines when one is hospitalized physically or mentally and trying to draw sustenance from a dark-appearing world or from the childish optimism of nurses.

There was a period in my time of depression where I had T.B. and another where I had a broken back. (I lump the whole time together as covering about three and a half years.) I had to look far, far back into my life to write anything at all except about children and hospitals. My own life seemed too dismal to write about.

I think a great deal of your problem will depend on whether you have a sympathetic wife who will realize calmly and coolly, rather than emotionally, that a talent like yours is worth saving, will help you figure out how much strain, how many hours a day of strain you can stand and how many hours must be gven to a rigorous if not vigorous physical regime. In this your attention must

___
[1] A dejected magazine writer who had written Fitzgerald for advice.

be bent figuratively on such nonessentials as the "birds and flowers," the weight, the number of hours' sleep, the utterly non-toxic diet—even though this means a much smaller amount of production and a temporary reduction in your scale of living or if debt enters into it. If you get sicker, there is no question but that you must retire to some absolutely quiet place and be prepared to sacrifice three or four months of your life to build up your nervous system. This can be done by yourself with the help of a good friend, at a certain stage. If you let it go too far, you will need a sanitarium. I got myself in hand just before the latter and more unpleasant alternative would have become necessary.

In three old *Esquire* magazines of 1936, you will find three articles called "Crack-Up," "Paste Together" and "Handle with Care," which show the mood I was in at the time and doubtless you will find it quite parallel to yours. The writing of the articles helped me personally but rather hurt me professionally. They do not tell you how I gradually climbed out of the morass though there are hints in it of what course it finally took.

The question of will in these cases is very doubtful. Let us say that in my case the disease wore itself out. Let us hope that in yours it will also. But I assure you that if at the moment when I first became aware that my nervous system was out of hand, that there were unnecessary rages, glooms, nervous tensity, times of coma-like inertia, if I had, instead of trying quick remedies like a couple of days in the hospital or a one-week trip, taken off several months, I would have saved at least a year of my life.

One of the best psychiatrists near you is Dr. James Rennie, consultant at the Phipps Clinic, Johns Hopkins Hospital, Baltimore. He was in charge of my wife and was a kindly friend to me during my own struggle. The men around New York all seem a little bit overnervous themselves, to me. The most helpful man in my wife's case was Dr. Robert S. Carroll of Highland Hospital, Asheville, North Carolina. However, he is less a consultant than a practicing clinician. His strong point is that toxic conditions of the blood from diet, etc., play a tremendous part in nervous disturbances. But if it ever came to the point where you thought you ought to lay up under medical care, his is the sanitarium which I should choose, and I have had my wife in a half dozen in this country. And it is quite reasonable in price.

Phipps Clinic in Baltimore is really a sanitarium for diagnosis. It is rather unfortunately situated, to my mind, in the middle of a big city.

I find that living alone in a very small town did more to restore my nervous strength than any other one thing, though I must say the months there were not highly productive.

I hope you will get something out of this letter that will be of value to you, and if there is any point on which you would like me to go further, please write me again.

With hope that by the time this reaches you, you will be seeing some point of light in your trouble, I am

Sincerely yours,

F. Scott Fitzgerald

TO MRS. MARY LEONARD PRITCHETT

Metro-Goldwyn-Mayer Corporation
Culver City, California

March 4, 1938

Dear Mrs. Pritchett:

Sorry I could not get word to you before you sailed.

I am out of touch with the stage in New York, but have talked to Sidney Howard and several other playwrights here regarding your suggestions for the casting of *Tender Is the Night*. Invariably, Margaret Rawlings has seemed a very good choice for Nicole to those who have read the book, and, equally unanimously, they have been against Beulah Bondi.

Nicole should have not merely glamor but a practically irresistible glamor. In fact, my ideal casting would be Katharine Hepburn or Margaret Sullavan, with the beauty of Loretta Young.

Oddly enough, the character of Tommy, or rather some of the mannerisms of Tommy, were taken from Mario Braggiotti, the brother of Stiano. It would be a delightful coincidence if Stiano played the part.

Thank you for your interest in the casting. They have really done an awfully good job and, in the reading, all the parts seemed very fat and tempting. Bob Montgomery out here is one of several actors who keep recurring to the playing of Dick Diver.

With very best wishes,

Sincerely yours,

F. Scott Fitzgerald

TO DAYTON KOHLER

Metro-Goldwyn-Mayer Corporation
Culver City, California

March 4, 1938

Dear Mr. Kohler:

Your project of a survey of contemporary literature sounds interesting. I should think that whether it should be a success or not would depend rather on its unity than its variety. If you follow what has been said about the names you mention, you could very well produce a book which would be a mere recapitulation and summary and would be outclassed by a later manifestation of literary vitality —much as Carl Van Doren's two books on the American novel, published in 1920, have become obsolete, as well as the studies of Henry S. Canby and Stuart P. Sherman. Mencken's book, *Prefaces,* on the contrary, is still very much alive.

I should think you would approach the Houghton Mifflin people with something more than the outline which you have sent me. Some of the names I find in it are meaningless. Elinor Wylie as a novelist, for example, is entirely imitative of Max Beerbohm and others. Elsie Singmaster I never heard of. _____ _____ is not even as faintly important as, say, Harry Leon Wilson. And who are _____ _____ and H. L. Davis? Why Wilbur Daniel Steele, who left no mark whatsoever, invented nothing, created nothing except a habit of being an innocuous part of the O'Brien anthology? Dorothy Canfield as a novelist is certainly of no possible significance. Cora Jarrett was a realer person.

Canfield simply got hold of child education as an early monopoly and what she has to say is less important than Willa Cather's "Paul's Case."

Does Maxwell Anderson deserve a special section? Have you read Edmund Wilson in *The New Republic* upon his blank verse? *Winterset* seemed to me a complete fake. James Ahearn is certainly a much more important figure of the past than Augustus Thomas.

In fact, your list includes so much of the mediocre, so many men who are already covered with dust, that I cannot find a line through it. If you'd confine yourself to twelve contemporaries, instead of fifty, you would find, I think, that they swept up everything worth saying. Perhaps I am wrong. Some people seem to look on our time as a sort of swollen Elizabethan age, simply crawling with geniuses. The necessity of the artist in every generation has been to give his work permanence in every way by a safe shaping and a constant pruning, lest he be confused with the journalistic material that has attracted lesser men.

Perhaps I misunderstand your intention. If so, I apologize and await an answer.

Sincerely,

F. Scott Fitzgerald

TO MATTHEW JOSEPHSON

The Garden of Allah Hotel
Hollywood, California
March 11, 1938

Dear Matty:

Glad you enjoyed Hollywood. Something you said makes me fear you carried away one false impression. In the old days, when movies were a stringing together of the high points in the imagination of half a dozen drunken ex-newspapermen, it was true that the whole thing was the director. He coordinated and gave life to the material— he carried the story in his head. There is a great deal of carry-over from those days, but the situation of *Three Comrades,* where Frank Borzage had little more to do than be a sort of glorified cameraman, is more typical of today. A Bob Sherwood picture, for instance, or a Johnny Mahin script, could be shot by an assistant director or a script girl, and where in the old days an author would have jumped at the chance of becoming a director, there are now many, like Ben Hecht and the aforesaid Mahin, who hate the eternal waiting and monotony of the modern job. This is a necessary evolution that the talkies brought about, and I should say that in seven out of ten cases, your feeling that the director or producer was the great co-ordinator no longer applies.

It was great meeting you. Anything I can ever do for you here let me know. Best wishes.

Scott Fitz

Sid [1] and I had lunch and he spoke so affectionately of you and of your wife.

TO MR. AND MRS. EBEN FINNEY

The Garden of Allah Hotel
Hollywood, California

March 16, 1938

Dear Pete and Margaret:

I waited an unpardonably long time to write you, but I wanted to see if I could manage to give Miss (or Mrs.?) Hoffman[2] a decent hearing here. What I have arranged, I will come to presently, but first I want to tell you what I did. I went first to Metro-Goldwyn-Mayer and twice missed the head man and got no encouragement—nothing but a blank statement that they were not interested in listening to music by amateurs or even professionals. The acute cause of their attitude I soon found was that they have five law suits on their hands because they have done that, and at this moment Cole Porter is being sued for a great sum by a woman who played him her pieces and

---

[1] S. J. Perelman.
[2] A friend of the Finneys who had written some songs which they sent Fitzgerald.

then accused him of stealing melodies from them. I then went to 20th Century-Fox and Warner Brothers and met the same situation. Next I concluded that I had better hear the tunes myself. I had them played over by a musician but didn't think his opinion was honest—then who should occur to me but our old friend ____ ____, who had written me a month before that he was in Hollywood and would like to see me. I went to call, with the music. It was rather depressing to see ____, who was so sprightly at Princeton, turned into a down-at-the-heels, very discouraged-looking pansy. He told me a little of his story— that he had been out here ten years, had written two thousand tunes (they were all scored and piled on his piano), had had half a dozen auditions and no luck at all except some incidental music that he had written for a Nelson Eddy radio broadcast and the two or three pieces that he had in the New York show, *New Faces*. He played over some of his own tunes—easily the best were the ones that he and I wrote together for the Triangle—finally, without its seeming to be the object of the visit, I brought out Miss Hoffman's pieces. They seemed to me so far ahead of ____, there was no comparison. Especially I liked "Beautiful Things," which has a real swing and a good lyric and, I should think, just that quality that catches on.

A friend then took, or promised to take, the songs to Paramount, but nothing came of that and, as time was passing, I thought I'd make another onslaught on M-G-M. This time, I got an introduction from my producer to the top man in the music department, Mr. Finston. He seemed more practical than anyone I had talked to and I asked him what would happen if young authors got no hearing on the ground that perhaps they might bring suit for plagiarism. I told him the number of people who had turned down my own stuff when I was young, but that never had anyone refused to read it, and tried to make him see it from the point of view of the incipient young musical talent who actually had something to offer. Nothing doing. He wouldn't have them played over. However, he did say that he would definitely get her an audition in New York, where for some reason they haven't got the overwhelming fear of law suits which hangs over the moving pictures. He promised me (and I am waiting for the carbon copy of his letter to Miss Hoffman—and I will check

on it) that he would see positively that her stuff got an
audition in New York from the people with whom they
deal there, perhaps a musical subsidiary of the M-G-M
office.

This seems little to have accomplished after this long
wait. Perhaps there is some secret trick to breaking in
that I don't know, but there was the experience of _____
_____, an accomplished musician, after ten years which
was far from encouraging. It seems to be a very crowded
profession. Certainly my advice to her is to follow exactly
what Finston says in his letter because, though he was
not especially encouraging, he seemed an utterly honest
man and was trying to do the best he could as a favor to
the producer who introduced me. He said also that he was
returning the music to her in your care.

I will now answer letters (which I do all in great gobs
every two months). The party that Peaches and Scottie
gave seems a long way off now but I am glad it was a success and that the ticket matter straightened itself out.
Peggy's account of the other festivities of Christmas fill
me with a vague melancholy which is not even nostalgia,
that is, I would never want to go through the time of life
again Peaches and Scottie are in, but I am sorry for anyone who believes as much as they must believe. There is
something very special to be written about the psychology
of pretty girls. Lately I have run into two who were great
belles of my time and who are now ravaged with dope. The
reason is that life promises so very much to a pretty girl
between the ages of sixteen and twenty-five that she never
quite recovers from it. By pretty girl I mean what used to
be called the belle type, the type with "it." Ernest Hemingway once said that you could never go back emotionally,
or, with more accuracy, sensationally; having had a sensation in the emotional sense, one would not be inclined to be
content with a lesser sensation, so a belle nowadays, unless
sobered by a flock of children, is liable to go on seeking the
intensity of that game of playing with men. None of our
colleges have succeeded in inventing anything to compete
with the kind of love that doesn't have to be paid for with
responsibility.

I think Scottie at fourteen was in a fair way to a dis-
proportionate youth. Lacking Peaches' calm temperament,
she had projected herself into the world of sixteen and,

of course, was taking it all much more hysterically than a girl of sixteen would. The convent-like attitude of Miss Walker's was just right for her. I think she caught up on her precocity by a full year and I not afraid for her now in the same way that I was then. These are the days, I should think, when the next star on the horizon is the chance, remote but always possible, of an unfortunate early marriage or an equally unfortunate early love affair. I found that Scottie, with the one man she could invite to school this year—for the senior tea—had chosen a Princeton boy now in his last year at Yale Law School. I suppose it was nothing but sheer bravado. There she, when the other girls were writing to prep school and college boys, would dazzle them by producing an actual man of the world. I put my foot down immediately, because a boy of that age, if he happened to be loose in principle, could twist a sixteen-year-old girl around his finger. The boy happened to be a nice boy, but the idea was absolutely bogus and phoney. Every once in a while, such delusions of grandeur overtake my daughter—is the same true of Peaches?

I wouldn't tell Scottie this but I am really not very concerned about whether she remains a virgin after the age of twenty, but I think it is of the greatest importance that the girl doesn't throw herself away for any trivial or inessential reason, and every year makes such a difference. I still believe in the strictest chaperonage, formal or secret (by which I mean a pretty close check upon a girl's movements), because my theory follows Pope's statement that Evil (I am using the word in its old-fashioned sense), first looked upon as terrible, longer looked upon as tolerable, finally becomes attractive. He said it much better, with a beautiful rhyme. Also, I am hot against a child of Scottie's background ever having any traffic with liquor, and don't like cigarettes either, simply because it takes up so much unnecessary energy and is such a comfort to the idler and the loafer. Moreover, if she ever takes up a sedentary profession like mine, it will be awful for her. I smoked myself right into T.B. Did you notice the recent pronunciamento about cigarettes in *Time?* So you see, in general I am still the old-fashioned parent.

To go back to Miss Hoffman—I took one song to a party where I knew Rodgers and Hart were going to be, and had it played over. Rodgers thought it was very good, but all he could advise me to do was to try to get it played over in some studio. I didn't know him well enough to ask him to do anything about it. So you see that this appears to be the wrong door to knock at. There is something about Hollywood, everybody very highly paid and camping on the job, which makes it harder to approach from here than if one is in New York with the magic of distance giving desirability. Not only has no one been willing to give the stuff a break but no one has been able to tell me—and that includes Irving Berlin, with whom I talked about six months ago, before I got this music—just what gets a song-writer a start. Somehow, they get involved with a manager, a lyric writer, a playwright, and a show is staged and a show clicks. They are part of the line-up and it seems to miraculously make them professionals. They don't seem to cross that line alone in the way writers do. I remember at Princeton, Cam Clark and others used to come down and pick the best of the hundred or so compositions composed on the campus. There seems to be nothing like that in the professional world, at least out here, and it is terrible to think how many good songs go unpublished when old hacks, such as Romberg has become, continue to grind out repetitions of themselves for operettas. It simply can't be bucked from here.

With affection to you both, and regrets that this is such a pessimistic report,

Ever yours,

[Scott]

P.S. Been doing a picture for Joan Crawford. About one-third through. Is an original and quite a different job from the dramatization of *Three Comrades*. However, this time I have the best producer in Hollywood, a fine showman who keeps me from any amateur errors, and I hope to finish the picture alone. Do you remember Ted Paramore of Hill? He was my collaborator on *Three Comrades*.

TO MISS MARTHA FEUERHERM [1]

[1] Miss Feuerherm, who said she was making a study of Fitzgerald's life and works, had asked him for a reading list.

Hollywood, California
March 16, 1938

My dear Miss Feuerham:

In regard to your letter about F. Scott Fitzgerald, we refer you to the following:

F. Scott Fitzgerald: His Youth and Parentage—C. B. Ansbrucher, Berlin. Privately Printed.

F. Scott Fitzgerald: The Image and the Man—Irene Kammer Thurston. Brentano's, 1937.

Fitzgerald As I Knew Him—J. B. Carstairs. Scribners, 1928.

F. Scott Fitzgerald and the Rise of Islam. Harcourt, Brace and Howe, 1922.

The Women Who Knew F. Scott Fitzgerald—Marie, Comtesse de Segours. Editions Galantiere, Paris.

I hope that these books will serve your purpose.

Sincerely yours,

J. P. Carms
Secretary

TO FRANCES TURNBULL[1]

[*5521 Amestoy Avenue*]
[*Encino, California*]
November 9, 1938

Dear Frances:

I've read the story carefully and, Frances, I'm afraid the price for doing professional work is a good deal higher than you are prepared to pay at present. You've got to sell your heart, your strongest reactions, not the little

---

[1] Frances Turnbull, a sophomore at Radcliffe, had sent Fitzgerald one of her "Sketches by a Debutante."

minor things that only touch you lightly, the little experiences that you might tell at dinner. This is especially true when you *begin* to write, when you have not yet developed the tricks of interesting people on paper, when you have none of the technique which it takes time to learn. When, in short, you have *only* your emotions to sell.

This is the experience of all writers. It was necessary for Dickens to put into *Oliver Twist* the child's passionate resentment at being abused and starved that had haunted his whole childhood. Ernest Hemingway's first stories, *In Our Time*, went right down to the bottom of all that he had ever felt and known. In *This Side of Paradise* I wrote about a love affair that was still bleeding as fresh as the skin wound on a haemophile.

The amateur, seeing how the professional, having learned all that he'll ever learn about writing, can take a trivial thing such as the most superficial reactions of three uncharacterized girls and make it witty and charming—the amateur thinks he or she can do the same. But the amateur can only realize his ability to transfer his emotions to another person by some such desperate and radical expedient as tearing your first tragic love story out of your heart and putting it on pages for people to see.

That, anyhow, is the price of admission. Whether you are prepared to pay it, or whether it coincides or conflicts with your attitude on what is "nice" is something for you to decide. But literature, even light literature, will accept nothing less from the neophyte. It is one of those professions that want the "works." You wouldn't be interested in a soldier who was only a *little* brave.

In the light of this, it doesn't seem worthwhile to analyze why this story isn't salable but I am too fond of you to kid you along about it, as one tends to do at my age. If you ever decide to tell *your* stories, no one would be more interested than

Your old friend,

F. Scott Fitzgerald

P.S. I might say that the writing is smooth and agreeable and some of the pages very apt and charming. You have talent—which is the equivalent of a soldier having the right physical qualifications for entering West Point.

TO BUDD SCHULBERG

5521 Amestoy Avenue
Encino, California
February 28, 1939

Dear Budd:

I didn't send my Dartmouth impressions[1] because I know that when one is once separated from a picture any advice is rather gratuitous—seems to come from a long and uninformed distance. However, if Walter[2] still wants to use the Indian school for a prologue it would be very funny if the Indian students were being solemnly addressed by Ebenezer when you cut outside and pick up young squaws approaching on snow shoes, bursting into the school and dancing around with the young braves. From there you could dissolve to the station and the arrival of the girls.

Also your introduction of some character at the station might be a student smashing baggage, followed by a newly arrived girl. And his turning suddenly, mutual recognition: the pay-off is his finding that he has picked up the baggage of his own girl.

On that same working-your-way-through basis, I got a kick from the student waiters going out of character and talking to the guests—like the man who hired himself out to do that sort of thing.

The picture seems temporarily very far away, and I am engrossed in work of my own. But I wish you well, and I won't forget the real pleasure of knowing you, and your patience as I got more and more out of hand under the strain. In retrospect, going East under those circumstances seems one of the silliest mistakes I ever made.

Always your friend,

[Scott]

---

[1] Schulberg and Fitzgerald had collaborated on the script of a movie whose setting was the Dartmouth Winter Carnival.
[2] Producer Walter Wanger.

TO JUDGE JOHN BIGGS, JR.[1]

[*5521 Amestoy Avenue*]
[*Encino, California*]

[*Spring, 1939*]

Dear John:

Your letter with its family chronicle fascinated me. It was nice to catch up a little. I remember Baba as a wild fascinating little witch with a vague touch of *Wuthering Heights* about her as she wrestle   vith her brothers. One girl in a family of boys has her dangers—like one boy in a family of girls who inevitably has a touch of the milksop —anyhow I'm glad Baba has temperament and sorry you've had to send her to reform school so young . . . .

As to sons—that's another question. I'd feel on a big spot if I were you. Tho you're not a worrier. With daughter I can feel sure she's about like me—very little of her mother save the good looks—like me with less positive artistic talent and much more natural social talent. She hasn't the *loneliness* of the artist—though one can't be sure that means anything. Ernest wasn't lonely superficially —what I mean is that in spite of the fact that Scottie edited her school paper and wrote the school play she doesn't *care*—doesn't care deeply and passionately so that she feels the necessity to say. And it's just as well. Nothing is more fatuous than the American habit of labeling one of their four children as the artist on a sort of family tap day as if the percentage of artists who made any kind of go of the lousy business was one to four. It's much closer to 1 to 400,000. You've got to have the egotism of a maniac with the clear triple-thinking of a Flaubert. The amount of initial talent or let us say skill and facility is a very small element in the long struggle whose most happy [end] can only be a mercifully swift exhaustion. Who'd want to live on like Kipling with a name one no longer owned—the empty shell of a gift long since accepted and consumed?

To go back. I won't discuss boys. They are incalculable. But I would like to sit around with you for hours discussing men, in particular J.B., Jr. and F.S.F. I would make you

---

[1] Fitzgerald's friendship with Biggs began at Princeton where they had roomed together the fall of 1917 and co-edited the *Tiger* and the *Lit.* Biggs was to be Fitzgerald's legal executor.

read some of the stuff that's stirred me lately, and append this list, culled from two years.

a. *Julius Caesar* by James Anthony Froude. Don't be appalled—it's as modern as Strachey and I find from Max that Scribner never lets it go out of print.

b. *Flaubert and Madame Bovary*. Absolute tops.

c. *The Culture of Cities* which you must have read.

d. *The Trial*—fantastic novel by the Czech Franz Kafka which you may have to wait for but it is worth it—it's an influence among the young comparable only to Joyce in 1920–25.

e. As for Americans there's only one—Jerome Weidman, whose two books have been withdrawn as too perspicacious about the faults of his own race. He's a grand writer tho—only 25 and worth fifty of this Steinbeck, who is a cheap, blatant imitation of D. H. Lawrence. A bookclub return of the public to its own vomit.

f. (I am now writing this letter for my files as well as to you.) The best *individual* novel of the last five years is still Malraux's *Man's Fate*. I fought against reading it—liking neither the scene nor what I thought was going to be the attitude—but *Jesiss*, once I'd gotten into it—it's as absorbing as the *Farewell to Arms*. On the other hand *Man's Hope* is hasty journalism—about as good as Ernest's Spanish stuff. (He agrees with me about Steinbeck by the way—thinks he's a phoney, like Farrell.) You know how generous I feel toward new men if they have something, and I hope you won't read under this a jealousy of which I think I'm incapable. I keep waiting for Odets to produce somethng fine.

For God's sake, order these right away and for good jazz I append Guedalla's *Wellington*, and Burne's *Lee, Grant and Sherman*—they'll kill a night of insomnia. Hayes' book on Lincoln neither brings us closer nor further away —ends by being a bore because he seems to have been conspicuously non-communicative about what we have now decided were the great moments. I guess Lincoln was just too busy to throw him his little crust of attention and he was out whoring somewhere.

I hope you'll be a better judge than I've been a man of letters. I've worked here on the best jobs—*Madame Curie, Three Comrades, Gone with the Wind,* etc.—but it's an uphill business and the only great satisfaction I've had has been paying off my debts—which amounted to *about $40,000* at the end of 1936. At that point, despite Becky Sharp's dictum that you can live on your debts for awhile, people begin to distrust you—and someday in Dostoevskian manner I'm going to write about the great difference between how you high-heartedly helped me over a hurdle and the heartburnings and humiliations I went thru in the process of approaching you. (That sentence is as full of "h's" as a passage in the later Swinburne.)

Anyhow we have always been great good friends to each other and that is a satisfaction as Gertrude Stein would say. I am glad for Bobby as only an old lunger can be glad (was she ever one). I only play ping-pong but if she ever condescends to that let her have a table ready at the point where our paths next cross.

Scott

TO MRS. FRANK CASE

*5521 Amestoy Avenue
Encino, California
May 3, 1939*

I seem to be inadvertently writing you from a sick-bed, but not a very serious one—though I think without your prompt action a week ago it might very well have been. I love New York in a very special way, but somehow the Doctors Hospital couldn't quite compete with the balmy spring California and I took up my bed and walked, so to speak—at least as far as the airport.

Sheilah came out to see me yesterday and told me of another great kindness of yours which I hope life will someday enable me to repay—that you had telephoned her from New York telling her you thought I was in trouble and that perhaps she was the person to help me. The situation goes back several months further than the break between Sheilah and me, however.

Very much against my will, I was persuaded to take a job to which I felt spiritually inadequate because I needed a rest from pictures and because my health was going steadily worse. I was going to sleep every night with a gradually increasing dose of chloral—three teaspoonfuls— and two pills of nembutol every night and 48 drops of Digitalin to keep the heart working to the next day. Eventually one begins to feel like a character out of *The Wizard of Oz*. Work becomes meaningless and effort a matter of the medicine closet. To the last job, I brought a great deal of individual enthusiasm, but by the end of the last week I was doing it on gin and to a person of my constitution the end of that is fairly plain.

I am sorry though it was so very plain. I am sorry that I ended up by putting up such a poor showing in front of you who have treated me always with—well, "kindness" is a very inadequate word.

I found Flora flourishing and glad to see me back. She is a very nice heritage. It seems honestly awful to have caused either of you distress—I am a little dim on the last few hours in the hotel,[1] and I don't think Dr. Graham wanted to be very explicit about it, but if there was any damage take care of it either directly with me or with Harold Ober with whom I have a running account and whom I am afraid, after twenty years, will not be very much shocked by any of my enormities.

With deep respect and affection,

[Scott]

TO S. J. PERELMAN

[*5521 Amestoy Avenue*]
[*Encino, California*]
June 7, 1939

Dear Sidney:

Seeing your apparently dead but only sleeping pan in the magazine, I was reminded to address you on several things. One is that while you once inherited a baby nurse from me I have now evened matters up by owning your

[1] Frank Case ran the Algonquin hotel where Fitzgerald had been staying.

1937 Ford which gives excellent service. But the real purpose is this—that Laura's brother (Nathaniel West) sent
me his book[1] and a very nice letter with it which has totally
disappeared since a trip I made to Cuba, and I don't know
where to reach him to answer it.

The book, though it puts Gogol's *The Lower Depth* in
the class with *The Tale of Benjamin Bunny,* certainly has
scenes of extraordinary power—if that phrase is still in
use. Especially I was impressed by the pathological crowd
at the premiere, the character and handling of the aspirant
actress, and the uncanny almost medieval feeling of some
of his Hollywood background, set off by those vividly
drawn grotesques. The book bears an odd lopsided resemblance to Victor Hugo's *Notre Dame de Paris,* except
that the anonymous builders of the Middle Ages did a
better job with their flying buttresses than Mannix, Katz
and Company with their theory of the buttocks in place.

Anyway, all good wishes to you. I'll be out of pictures
at least till late fall, working on a novel. Best to Laura.

Ever your friend,

[Scott]

TO TOM F. CAREY, JR.

[*5521 Amestoy Avenue*]
[*Encino, California*]
June 9, 1939

Dear Mr. Carey:

My friend and landlord, Edward Everett Horton, handed
your letter over to me thinking that as a Princetonian
and a professional writer I could answer your questions
to your satisfaction. He told me he was very fond of
your father and asked me to speak to you as frankly and
helpfully as possible.

In the first place, there have been in the past (and in
what pictures considered better times) attempts to hire in-
experienced writers—what they call "junior writers"—and

[1] *The Day of the Locust.*

groom them to be useful. The particular attempt about which I know the method and its eventual outcome was made at Metro about three years ago when Eddie Knopf (then Scenario head) brought in a dozen young men who had written for the college magazines at the University of California, Stanford, etc., paid them what is here considered a living wage for a writer and hoped that genius would turn up among them. The outcome was that one boy has made something of a record—he did a solo job on *Shopworn Angel*—I can't remember his name at the moment—and the others were "let out" to the last man with every wave of the recession in 1937–38.

This Metro experiment did not necessarily prove anything—certain ones I know were only there through pull, but I *do* know that it convinced Metro—the largest, richest and in some ways most experimental studio here—that the idea was not good. I had a young protégé in the East whom I brought out here, who—though he had written over one hundred stories for the pulp magazines—was never able to sell himself to Metro with whom I was then under contract—*unless* he came equipped with an idea *and* access to the powers-that-were. He had the access but he did not seem to have the idea or to be able to get it on paper so he has returned to the somewhat desperate business of pulp-writing in the East.

If a young man, however, has "made the slick paper magazines" it is an entirely different story. Two or three stories in the slicks, especially a minor triumph such as Richard Sherman's "To Mary with Love" in the *Post* several years ago, can set a man for a whole Hollywood career. I know a young Dartmouth man, a recent graduate, who has every access to the heads of companies but who has just chosen to go East and continue some work he has in mind for *Colliers*—there's no secret about it—it's young Budd Schulberg—thus seriously curtailing his income, but he leaves with the conviction that these people are more impressed with what comes out with the imprimatur of an important magazine in the East than with almost anything done here.

This resume of the situation applies to the present time —there was a period when the eastern writer was suspect —he was "high hat," he did not know the medium, and wouldn't take the trouble to learn it—and in those days people entered scenario-writing through the oddest channels—but I believe that time is gone.

Hardly a man here is in the big money who has not a best seller or some striking stories or a successful play to his credit. (A few exceptions to this are John Lee Mahin and Robert Riskin, who are among the half dozen best picture-writers in the business.) But the rule still stands.

And all this is subject to the vagueness that surrounds this industry. There is none of it that I could swear to. I have been out here almost two years though with my eyes open and this is what I would tell my daughter if her literary ambitions were far enough developed to make her yearn toward the flesh pots of Hollywood.

With very best wishes to you,

Sincerely,

F. Scott Fitzgerald '17

P.S. Edward Everett Horton gave me *carte blanche* in answering this letter but to your questions I must respond even more vaguely. I am sure that if you had professional material in your portfolio and were on the spot Mr. Horton would be only too glad to give you letters to the heads of any Scenario department but he could not guarantee, any more than I could, their mood toward your work or their studio's attitude toward untried authors. I broke into the literary world by selling stories to the now defunct *Smart Set* at $35.00 a shot (some of them had been in the *Nassau Lit*) and then kept cracking at *The Saturday Evening Post,* but every man's literary beginnings are different. However, I do know that 80% of what is classified here as "talent" has made its reputation in the East.

TO KENNETH LITTAUER[1]

[*5521 Amestoy Avenue*]
[*Encino, California*]
July 18, 1939

Dear Kenneth:

I was of course delighted to finish off the Civil War

[1] Editor of *Colliers.*

story[1] to your satisfaction at last—I may say to my satisfaction also, because the last version *felt* right. And after twenty months of moving pictures it was fun to be back at prose-writing again. That has been the one bright spot in a situation you may have heard from Harold Ober: that I have been laid up and writing in bed since the first of May, and I am only just up and dressed.

As I told your Mr. Wilkinson[2] when he telephoned, the first thing I did when I had to quit pictures for awhile was to block out my novel (a short one the size of *Gatsby*) and made the plan on a basis of 2500 word units. The block-out is to be sure that I can take it up or put it down in as much time as is allowed between picture work and short stories. I will never again sign a long picture contract, no matter *what* the inducement: most of the profit when one overworks goes to doctors and nurses.

Meanwhile I am finishing a 4500-word piece designed for your pages. It should go off to you airmail Saturday night because I am going back to the studios for a short repair job Monday.

I would like to send the story *directly to you,* which amounts to a virtual split with Ober. This is regrettable after twenty years of association but it had better be asked under the anonymity of "one of those things." Harold is a fine man and has been a fine agent and the fault is mine. Through one illness he backed me with a substantial amount of money (all paid back to him now with Hollywood gold), but he is not prepared to do that again with growing boys to educate—and, failing this, I would rather act for a while as my own agent in the short story just as I always have with Scribners. But I much prefer, both for his sake and mine, that my sending you the story direct should be a matter *between you and me.* For the fact to reach him through your office might lead to an unpleasant cleavage of an old relationship. I am writing him *later in the week* making the formal break on terms that will be understood between us, and I have no doubt that in some ways he will probably welcome it. Relationships have an unfortunate way of wearing out, like most things in this world.

[1] *"The End of Hate," Colliers,* June 22, 1940.
[2] An editor at *Colliers.*

Would you be prepared, in return for an agreement or contract for first look at the novel [1] and at a specified number of short stories in a certain time, to advance me $750.00, by wire on receipt of this letter—which will be even before the story reaches you Monday? This is a principal factor in the matter at the moment as these three months of illness have got me into a mess with income tax and insurance problems. When you get this, will you wire me yes or no, because if you can't I can probably start studio work Friday. This may be against your general principles—from my angle I am offering you rather a lot for no great sum.

                              Ever yours with best wishes,

                              [Scott]

P.S. If this meets your favorable consideration the money should be wired to the Bank of America, Culver City. If not would you wire me anyhow because my determination to handle my magazine relationship myself is quite final.

P.S. (2) The novel will run just short of 50,000 words.

TO KENNETH LITTAUER

                              [5521 Amestoy Avenue]
                              [Encino, California]

                              [Probably late July, 1939]
Dear Kenneth:

Here's another Hollywood story. It is absolutely true to Hollywood as I see it. Asking you to read it I want to get two things clear. First, that it isn't particularly likely that I'll write a great many more stories about young love. I was tagged with that by my first writings up to 1925. Since then I have written stories about young love. They have been done with increasing difficulty and increasing insincerity. I would either be a miracle man or a hack if I could go on turning out an identical product for three decades.

[1] The Last Tycoon.

I know that is what's expected of me, but in that direction the well is pretty dry and I think I am much wiser in not trying to strain for it but rather to open up a new well, a new vein. You see, I not only announced the birth of my young illusions in *This Side of Paradise* but pretty much the death of them in some of my last *Post* stories like "Babylon Revisited." Lorimer seemed to understand this in a way. Nevertheless, an overwhelming number of editors continue to associate me with an absorbing interest in young girls—an interest that at my age would probably land me behind the bars.

I have a daughter. She is very smart; she is very pretty; she is very popular. Her problems seem to me to be utterly dull and her point of view completely uninteresting. In other words, she is exactly what I was once accused of being—callow. Moreover she belongs to a very overstimulated and not really adventurous generation—a generation that has been told the price of everything as well as its value. I once tried to write about her. I couldn't.

So you see I've made a sort of turn. My hope is that, like Tarkington, if I can no longer write *M. Beaucaire* and the *Gentleman from Indiana,* I can make people laugh instead as he did in *Seventeen* which is completely objective and unromantic.

The second thing is my relation to Ober. It is completely vague. I've very seldom taken his advice on stories. I have regarded him as a mixture of friend, bill collector and for a couple of sick years as backer. So far as any editorial or financial dealing, I would much rather, as things are now, deal directly with an editor. For instance, if this sort of story is worth less to you than a story of young love, I would be perfectly willing to accept less. I would not want any agent to stand in my way in that regard. I think all the agents still act as if we were back in the 1920s in a steadily rising market.

So can I again ask you to deal telegraphically with me? I hope this story amuses you.

Ever yours,

[Scott]

TO MRS. LAURA FELEY [1]

[5521 Amestoy Avenue]
[Encino, California]
July 20, 1939

Dear Mrs. Feley:

I don't know whether those articles of mine in *Esquire*—that "Crack-Up" series—represented a real nervous breakdown. In retrospect it seems more of a spiritual "change of life"—and a most unwilling one—it was a protest against a new set of conditions which I would have to face and a protest of my mind at having to make the psychological adjustments which would suit this new set of circumstances. Being an essentially stable type I managed to cling on until there was a mixture of the patient's adjustment to the situation and the situation's adjustment to the patient.

And that, in such a case, is about all there is to do. The sensitive cannot make themselves overnight into specimens of the "tough-minded"—the great ally is time, though I know that is a pretty old saw. Time was my rescuer and there was a friend concerned too, though I rather despised her intellectually and drew more nourishment from what she didn't say than from what she did.

To come closer to your case: the word nervous breakdown covers a multiplicity of conditions, as your doctor has probably told you. It may mean anything from a collapse of the central nervous system, a case of schizophrenia that the family doesn't want to acknowledge or a little mood of Irish melancholy. A girl having lost a man is liable to suddenly build him up into the only man in the world when, had things run smoothly, it is doubtful if he would have long interested her. You must know cases of this. I knew a high-strung girl who had an unfortunate "trial marriage" with a man, which went badly—after which she went to Europe, turning down a series of good matches—returned to the scene of her early disaster to find the lost love, took one look at him and thought, "My God, how did I ever happen to go for *that!*"

---

[1] Mrs. Feley had suffered a nervous breakdown and had written Fitzgerald for advice.

From what you tell me in your letter (and at such long range it is impossible for me to speak in anything but the broadest generalities) I can only say this: that if you are in any mess caused by conflict between old idealisms, religious or social, and the demands of the immediate present, you will probably have to make a decision between them. That is all too frequently a problem of these times—I hope the generation now growing up will shake free of it.

The doctor is probably your best friend, certainly much better than anyone you will find in your family—and if you have reason to think he is *not* your best friend, your very first move should be to find another. I don't mean a *series* of doctors, but another doctor whom you have good reason to think is equipped to deal with a case requiring intelligent handling.

With best wishes,

Sincerely,

[F. Scott Fitzgerald]

TO MISS HELENE RICHARDS[1]

*5521 Amestoy Avenue
Encino, California*

July 27, 1939

Dear Miss Richards:

Attached is some biographical data. Sorry I have no picture but I may say that out here I am known as the old "oomph man." So any haberdasher's advertisement will do as a portrait.

Will you tell that so-called Mr. Gingrich that I am accustomed, in my haughty way, to some word of approbation if not ecstasy about my contributions. Bland and chaste as your check was, it somehow lacked emotion. However, we are accepting it.

Sincerely,

F. Scott Fitzgerald

[1] Miss Richards, Arnold Gingrich's secretary, had asked Fitzgerald for some personalia to accompany a story in *Esquire*.

TO MORTON KROLL[1]

[5521 Amestoy Avenue]
[Encino, California]
August 3, 1939

Dear Morton:

Because your story was so perfect technically and so absolutely sincere I am going to take the risk of making an unasked-for suggestion. Someone once said—and I am quoting most inexactly—"A writer who manages to look a little more deeply into his own soul or the soul of others, finding there, through his gift, things that no other man has ever seen or dared to say, has increased the range of human life."

That is why a young writer (and I shrink at the word as much as you do) is tempted, when he comes to the crossroads of what to say and not to say as regards character and feeling, to be guided by the known, the admired and the currently accepted as he hears a voice whisper within himself, "Nobody would be interested in this feeling I have, this unimportant action—therefore it must be peculiar to me, it must not be universal nor generally interesting nor even right." But if the man's gift is deep or luck is with him, as one may choose to look at it, some other voice in that crossroads makes him write down those apparently exceptional and unimportant things and that and nothing else is his style, his personality—eventually his whole self as an artist. What he has thought to throw away or, only too often, what he *has* thrown away, was the saving grace vouchsafed him. Gertrude Stein was trying to express a similar thought when—speaking of life rather than letters—she said that we struggle against most of our exceptional qualities until we're about forty and then, too late, find out that they compose the real *us*. They were the most intimate self which we should have cherished and nourished.

Again, the above is inexact and all that I have said might lead you astray in the sense that it has led Saroyan astray and the late Tom Wolfe in imagining that writing should be a cultivation of every stray weed found in the garden. That is where talent comes in to distinguish between the standard blooms which everyone knows and are not particularly exciting, the riotous and deceitful weeds, and that tiny faint often imperceptible flower hidden in a corner which, cultivated à la Burbank, is all it will ever pay us to cultivate whether it stays small or grows to the size of an oak.

This is all too professorial. I felt you were trying to characterize with your fat boy. You failed to get a strong effect because (a) it was too facile a characteristic which you merely repeated from time to time to give him visibility and stability (b) anyone who could write that story so well and with so much observation must certainly be able to see deeply enough into himself and others and to dredge forth a more vivid person than a mere clumsy gawk about whom "it was just too bad." And let me say that I think if you had done so the story, because of its honesty so far as it went, and because of its economical and dramatic straight line, might very well have been salable.

Your friend by proxy,

[F. Scott Fitzgerald]

TO MORTON KROLL

5521 Amestoy Avenue
Encino, California

August 9, 1939

Dear Morton:

I claim the last word. You're entirely right that one's first influences are largely literary but the point where the personal note emerges *can* come very young (*vidé* Keats). I'll go further than that. I believe that with the natural prose-writer it might very well come long before twenty, depending on the amount of awareness with which it is looked for—and, referring directly to the classics, my mother did me the disservice of throwing away all but two of my very young efforts—way back at twelve and thirteen, and later I found that the surviving fragments had more quality than some of the stuff written in the tightened-up days of seven or eight years later.

A last word supplementary to my somewhat ponderous letter: if you were learning tennis you would form yourself not upon an eccentric like Tilden, for example, but upon players with classic styles like Cochet or La Coste (my references are of the dim past). You cannot imitate a mannerism with profit; a man might labor over Tilden's tennis style for six years, finding at the end that it simply couldn't be done without Tilden's 6'6" in height.

The Hemingway of *Farewell to Arms*, the Joyce of *Dubliners*, the Keats of "The Eve of St. Agnes" [and] "The Grecian Urn," the Mark Twain of the great central parts of *Huckleberry Finn*, the *Daisy Miller* of Henry James, the Kipling of *The Drums of Fore and Aft* are great English classics in a sense that such grands things as *Shropshire Lad* are not. Oscar Wilde for all his occasionally penetrating guesses was as Whistler said, a provincial at bottom—he tried imitating *The Shropshire Lad* in the "Ballad of Reading Gaol," and with the borrowed and, hence, phoney mood produced something only a few steps up from Robert Service.

(One last great parenthesis. It just happens that the most *classical* classics are in French while the most eccentric classics seem to be in English. If you had French, for example, I would recommend you the "Maison Tellier" of Maupassant rather than that Kipling piece as a completely classical short story.)

Don't answer this. I am keeping your letter and will sell it for a great profit later on.

Yours,

[F. Scott Fitzgerald]

TO DR. JOHN G. VOIGT [1]

[*5521 Amestoy Avenue*]
Encino, California
August 11, 1939

Dear Dr. Voigt:

I'm terribly sorry but I haven't had a picture taken for

[1] Dr. Voigt, a Fitzgerald fan, had asked him for a photograph.

about twelve years. This is no stall. I think now that I shall
wait until it's time for a death mask because I am in that
unattractive middle-aged phase that doesn't seem safe to
record for prosperity. (This is not a misprint.)

Thank you for your very kind letter. Hope someday
we may meet.

Sincerely,

[F. Scott Fitzgerald]

TO EDGAR POE [1]

5521 Amestoy Avenue
Encino, California
September 18, 1939

Dear Ed:

You have an early Chaldean handwriting but an excellent heart. And our tastes must be similar because the dressing gown is a beautiful piece of lechery. Thank you. I
have named it Celalume[2] and shall think in its depths.

Best to Babe—sorry I didn't see her. I've been on the
run between Universal and United Artists (where Niven
is and isn't going to finish his picture) and on the point
of suing R.K.O. for keeping me awake on their lot across
the street. I am so tired of being old and sick—would
much rather be a scared young man peering out over a
hunk of concrete or mud toward something I hated than
be doing this here stuff.

Ever yours,

[Scott]

---

[1] Fitzgerald's lawyer in Baltimore.
[2] A play on "Ulalume" by Edgar Allan Poe. Mr. Poe was descended from
the poet.

TO MISS KENT

5521 Amestoy Avenue
Encino, California
November 6, 1939

Dear Miss Kent:

I'm sorry that I could not conscientiously recommend this in its present form. You have an idea—but scarcely a story, do you think? I thought at first there was going to be an element of *Ramona* about it—that someone in the tribe was going to engage our interest. But no. We get a slowly mounting feud between two opposing forces—something that should be crammed into the first part of a story, and not have to sustain it dramatically throughout. I don't think there's enough here to hold the reader's attention. If there was some sort of relation between the widow of an American colonel and the prince of an Indian tribe, or vice versa between the Indian princess and a captain of the U.S. troops, the story might gain some poise and balance.

This is not suggested as a way to make it a success. Some better way will probably occur to you. It is only said to tell you what I feel is lacking in your outline: a point of real interest, a true climax rather than a succession of incidents which do not build to an instant of real excitement. That's what people buy.

Sorry I cannot be more helpful. Please feel quite free to send me anything else you may write.

Sincerely,

F. Scott Fitzgerald

TO JEAN OLIVIER

[5521 Amestoy Avenue]
Encino, California
January 29, 1940

Dear Miss Olivier:

Thanks for your letter about "The Lost Decade" and

many apologies for not answering before. I am afraid Mr. Trimble was drunk during those ten years, which is easier than one would think if one has the money.

You write in such a good English style that I am going to take the liberty of asking you *never* to sign yourself "Miss" Jean Olivier. You wouldn't like to get a letter from your namesake signed "Mister" Laurence Olivier, would you?

Sincerely,

F. Scott Fitzgerald

TO EDWIN KNOPF [1]

5521 Amestoy Avenue
Encino, California
February 1, 1940

Dear Eddie:

An hour after I called you a letter came asking if Mc-Bride could use my sketch, "The Night Before Chancellorsville," in an anthology. Armed with this coincidence I'll enlarge a little on my idea.

You may remember that the battles of Fredericksburg and Chancellorsville were fought respectively late in 1862 and early in 1863 and very nearly upon the same Virginia battlefield. I would begin my story with two girls who come South from Concord seeking the body of their brother who has been killed at Fredericksburg. They are sheltered, puritanical girls, used to the life of a small New England town. On the train going down they run into some ladies of the type pictured in my story. Moreover they encounter a charming Union cavalry captain with whom the gayer of the two Concord girls falls in love.

As in the story, the train rides right into Jackson's surprise attack at Chancellorsville—the Union retreat and the Confederate advance. The girls are separated and their first task is to find each other. One of them meets a Con-

[1] Story editor at M-G-M.

federate private from Alabama who at first she dreads and dislikes. In a Union counterattack the Confederate private is captured. He is identified as a Mosby guerilla by a man who bears him a grudge and hung up by his thumbs. (This actually happened to a cousin of my father's in the Civil War and I have embodied the incident in another story called "When This Cruel War" [1] which *Colliers* bought last spring but has not yet published.) The northern girl cuts down the Confederate soldier and helps him to escape. The girl has begun by being impatient of her sister's gayety. During their time behind the Confederate lines she has conscientiously continued her search for her brother's grave. Now, after helping her enemy escape, and at the moment of a love scene between them, she finds that they are only a few yards from her brother's grave. Entwined with the story of the two girls I would like to carry along the semi-comic character of one of those tarts, using her somewhat as Dudley Nichols used the tart in *Stagecoach*.

There are two Civil Wars and there are two kinds of Civil War novels. So far, pictures have been made only from one of them—the romantic, chivalric, Sir Walter Scott story like *Gone with the Wind, The Birth of a Nation*, the books of Thomas Nelson Page and Mary Johnson. But there is also the realistic type modeled primarily on Stendhal's great picture of Waterloo in *La Chartreuse de Parme*, Stephen Crane's *The Red Badge of Courage*, and the stories of Ambrose Bierce. This way of looking at war gives great scope for comedy without bringing in Stepin Fetchit and Hattie McDaniel as faithful negro slaves, because it shows how small the individual is in the face of great events, how comparatively little he *sees*, and how little he can do even to save himself. The Great War has been successfully treated like this—*Journey's End* and *All Quiet*—the Civil War never.

We can all see ourselves as waving swords or nursing the sick but it gets monotonous. A picture like this would have its great force from seeing ourselves as human beings who go on eating and loving and displaying our small vanities and follies in the midst of any catastrophe.

[1] Published as "The End of Hate," *Colliers*, June 22, 1940.

I would like to write this story, with any encouragement. What do you think?

Ever your friend,

F. Scott Fitzgerald

TO DR. CLARENCE NELSON

*5521 Amestoy Avenue
Encino, California*
February 7, 1940

Dear Dr. Nelson:

Just to tell you I have not forgotten you nor what I owe you. Physically the situation is really miraculously improved. Financially it is still as bad as ever but I just don't see how it can go on being this bad. I have had no fever now for well over six weeks, feel no fatigue beyond what is normal, cough only a very little bit in the mornings and usually that is all for the whole day. In other words, as far as I can determine the disease is absolutely quiescent and, if anything, I have been more active than at any time since I took to bed last March.

I suppose that my absolutely dry regime has something to do with it but not everything. Oddly enough the little aches around the elbows and shoulders return from time to time whenever I have had a great orgy of Coca-Colas and coffee.

With very best wishes and hopes that soon I may be able to do something substantial about your bill.

Sincerely and gratefully,

F. Scott Fitzgerald

TO ARNOLD GINGRICH

*5521 Amestoy Avenue
Encino, California*
February 7, 1940

Dear Arnold:

What would you think of this? You remember that about

a week ago I wrote asking you about the publication of "Between Planes." [1] You said that you hadn't intended to publish it until after the Pat Hobby stories. Why don't you publish it under a pseudonym—say, John Darcy? I'm awfully tired of being Scott Fitzgerald anyhow, as there doesn't seem to be so much money in it, and I'd like to find out if people read me just because I am Scott Fitzgerald or, what is more likely, don't read me for the same reason. In other words it would fascinate me to have one of my stories stand on its own merits completely and see if there is a response. I think it would be a shame to let that story stand over for such a long time now.

What do you think of this? While the story is not unlike me it is not particularly earmarked by my style as far as I know. At least I don't think so. If the idea interests you I might invent a fictitious personality for Mr. Darcy. My ambition would be to get a fan letter from my own daughter.

Ever your friend,

[Scott]

TO MR. AND MRS. S. J. PERELMAN

5521 Amestoy Avenue
Encino, California
phone: STate 4-0578

May 13, 1940

Dear Sid and Laura:

This is a love missive so do not be alarmed. I am not giving a tea for either the Princess Razzarascal or Two-ticker Forsite. *But* I am leaving this Elysian haunt in two weeks (the 29th to be exact) and sometime before that nonce I wish you two would dine or lunch. I know Sunday isn't a good day for you because of the dwarfs and Saturday next I'm going to Maurice Evans' and Sunday I'm engaged (now you know, girls, isn't it *wonderful?*)

—but any other day between now and the 28th would

[1] "Three Hours Between Planes," *Esquire*, July, 1941.

be fine. I *want* to see you and very specifically you, and for the most general and non-specific reasons. The days being at their longest it is no chore to find this place up to 7:30, and perhaps the best idea is dinner. We could either dine *à quatre* or add the Wests and some other couple— say the Mannerheims or Browders—and afterwards play with my model parachute troops. At any event, side arms will not be *de rigueur*.* Sheilah will be with me, just as merry as can be, to greet you on the porch with a julep. I have just reread *Crime and Punishment* and the chapters on gang labor in *Capitalist Production* and am meek as a liberal bourgeois lamb.

Call me up on the party line or drop me a note. The only acceptable excuse is that you're going on vacation or have impetigo because I want to see you.

> With spontaneous affection,

> [Scott]

* Outer boom or gaff on an old New England square-riggered ship.

TO MRS. HART FESSENDEN [1]

> *c/o Phil Berg Agency*
> *Beverly Hills, California*
> *May 29, 1940*

Dear K:

Seeing that Hester's first born was the last man tapped for Bones reminded me of you both. Doesn't that make about the fourth tie in a line and, as you two formed my first ideas of "Vassar Gals," I wonder if you knew that my daughter has been one now for some two years, so I must have been suitably impressed. She wanted to go to Bryn Mawr (to be near Baltimore where she came out last year) but I put my foot down—it was Vassar or nothing.

In these times speaking of oneself seems old-fashioned, but in the last three years I've known every extreme of

[1] The former Katharine Tighe who had grown up with Fitzgerald in St. Paul.

sickness and health, riches and poorness, success and failure, and only in the last few months has life begun to level out again in any sensible way. The movies went to my head and I tried to lick the set up single-handed and came out a sadder and wiser man. For a long time they will remain nothing more nor less than an industry to manufacture children's wet goods.

Tell me some news about you and yours if you ever get time.

[Scott]

TO LESTER COWAN [1]

> [1403 North Laurel Avenue]
> [Hollywood, California]
> *June 26, 1940*

Dear Lester:

Thinking over what we discussed yesterday I've listed many flaws in construction. The introduction of the little girl's voice at the beginning of Sequence B is confusing, and I agree about the insufficiency of the last sequence, which leaves the little girl out of the picture for so long. From the middle of the Ritz Hotel stock-market scene, the script must be not only revised but invigorated with a new note—in which Honoria will participate dramatically.

I agree with you also that we must build a scene on the dock around the parting of Honoria and her father— a scene which will clearly show the spark already established between them. I like the new scene we outlined which shows Honoria at the beach at Brittany learning to dive and writing to her father's trained nurse about it.

The changes in the story of Charles Wales' business dealing, etc., can wait—I want to make clear his real reasons for going to Europe, to make stronger his reasons for signing away the guardianship of the child, his affection for the nurse, his motivation for going back into the market and whether he wins or loses there—and finally what

----

[1] The independent producer who had commissioned Fitzgerald to write a script of "Babylon Revisited."

he learns from the whole experience—but this all goes with the big revision.

Now about the other matter. Originally the child was to have been eight or nine years old. If she is to be slightly older, say at the very end and apex of childhood, the period of "Goodbye to dolls," she would of course be more aware and articulate about what is going on. *Not at every moment*, because a little girl of eleven lives halfway between a child's world and that of an adult. But if she's been well brought up she is beginning to realize her social responsibilities (in that regard I was very impressed with the Temple kid—no trace of coyness or cuteness, yet a real dignity and gentleness).

On the other hand this is a real child and I don't think that I would want to put into Honoria's mouth anything approaching the dying speech of Little Eva or the less credible children of Dickens. They ring false upon the modern ear, and, though they make certain sections of the audience weep, they revolt and alienate the intelligent section of the audience, including especially young people between eighteen and twenty-five, and create an atmosphere of disbelief in what happens thereafter.

Therefore, though no one is more responsive than I am to true sentiment and emotion, I still hold out against any sentimentality. This is not the old story about "Daddy's little helper"—it is a mature dramatic piece and whatever child you find for it must have an emotional range larger than the First Reader. I want what happens in this picture to be felt in the stomach first, felt out of great conviction about the tragedy of father and child—and *not* felt in the throat to make a fat woman's holiday between chocolate creams.

Going back to young Shirley Temple: if the personality that she has in private life could be carried *almost without heightening* over into the picture, I believe she would be perfect. She has reached a point pictorially and by reason of natural charm where any attempt to strain and stress her prophetic conduct would seem a vulgarization. She is a perfect thing now in her way, and I would like to see that exquisite glow and tranquility carried intact through a sustained dramatic action. Whoever you get for the part would have to forget such old dodges as talking with tears in her voice, something that a well brought-up child wouldn't.[1]

[Scott]

TO ALICE RICHARDSON

Santa Barbara, California
July 29, 1940

Dear Alicia:

Your letter and Scottie's reached me here the same day —here where with a producer I am working on a story for little Miss Temple. Santa Barbara is supposed to have some escape magic like Palm Springs, but no matter how hard you look it's still California.

Daughter speaks of you with great admiration, says you have grown a full cubit since Baltimore, put your hair up, and stand like a modern Pallas Athene in mid-career. How well I remember Philippe's castle drawn by a friend of yours and Gertrude Stein's passage through Baltimore. It was a solemn winter but there were worse to come and in retrospect those months have an air of early April.

I am sincerely sorry not to have seen you—not only from curiosity but because you were always so determined things would be right that I'm glad they've turned out right. And turned out as you hoped and intended.

Your old friend,

Scott

P.S. Isn't Hollywood a dump—in the human sense of the word? A hideous town, pointed up by the insulting gardens of its rich, full of the human spirit at a new low of debasement.

---

[1] The letter was apparently unfinished, for it wasn't characteristic of Fitzgerald to conclude as abruptly as this.

TO MRS. NEUVILLE [1]

1403 North Laurel Avenue
Hollywood, California
July 29, 1940

Dear Mrs. Neuville:

I thought the other day that a large rat had managed to insert itself into the plaster above my bedroom and workroom. I was, however, surprised that it apparently slept at night and worked in the day, causing its greatest din around high noon.

However yesterday, much to my surprise, I deduced from the sounds it emitted that it was a dog, or rather several dogs, and evidently training for a race, for they ran round and round the tin roof. Now I don't know how these greyhounds climbed up the wall but I know dog-racing is against the law of California—so I thought you'd like to know. Beneath the arena where these races occur an old and harassed literary man is gradually going mad.

Sincerely,

[F. Scott Fitzgerald]

TO MRS. NEUVILLE

1403 North Laurel Avenue
Hollywood, California
August 12, 1940

My dear Mrs. Neuville:

The woman across the hall takes her dog on that bare and resounding roof every morning. It is impossible to work or sleep while the riot is in progress. Today we had some words about it and she informed me of her intention to continue—though if I took to rapping on her roof she would doubtless consider it an outrage.

I believe that the roof was locked when I took this apartment and I request that it be locked again. As a respecter

---

[1] Fitzgerald's landlady.

of the rights of others I know she has no legal or moral right to perpetuate this nuisance.

Sincerely,

[F. Scott Fitzgerald]

TO BENNETT CERF

[*1403 North Laurel Avenue*]
[*Hollywood, California*]
December 13, 1940

Dear Bennett Cerf:

I told Budd [Schulberg] I was going to write you a word about his novel [1] with permission to quote if you wanted. I read it through in one night. It is a grand book, utterly fearless and with a great deal of beauty side by side with the most bitter satire. Such things *are* in Hollywood— and Budd reports them with fine detachment. Except for its freshness and the inevitable challenge of a new and strong personality, it doesn't read like a first novel at all.

It is full of excellent little vignettes—the "extra girl" or whatever she is, and her attitude on love, and the diverse yet identical attitude of the two principal women on Sammy. Especially toward the end it gets the feeling of Hollywood with extraordinary vividness. Altogether I congratulate you on publishing this fine book and I hope it has all the success it deserves.

Sincerely,

F. Scott Fitzgerald

TO RALPH CHURCH [2]

1403 North Laurel Avenue
Hollywood, California
December 17, 1940

Dear Mr. Church:

I hope the appearance of this pamphlet about the clubs

---

[1] *What Makes Sammy Run?*
[2] Business manager of Princeton's yearbook, *The Bric-a-Brac*.

means what I think it does—that the pictures and membership lists will be eliminated from *The Bric-a-Brac* proper. I've often wondered what the non-club men thought when they brought *The Bric-a-Brac* home with all that emphasis on Prospect Avenue.

For a dozen years Princeton has sunk steadily behind Yale and Harvard in their attitude toward this monkey business. *The Bric-a-Brac* could do a magnificent job by leaving out the clubs or else print in addition pictures of all the clubs who eat at tables in Commons.

Sincerely,

F. Scott Fitzgerald

Index

Katherine Anne Porter

long recognized as one of America's great literary talents, and author of the brilliant novel SHIP OF FOOLS

THE LEANING TOWER AND OTHER STORIES

a collection of nine of her subtle and penetrating short stories

Varying in setting from the Deep South to New York City to Berlin in the 30s, all have in common the author's remarkable insight and storytelling skill.

A LAUREL EDITION   *now only 50c*

LAUREL EDITIONS
BY EVELYN WAUGH

THE LOVED ONES
A macabre report on high living and low morals in Hollywood, executed "with loving horror."—Saturday Review 50c

A HANDFUL OF DUST and DECLINE AND FALL
The moral decay of the British upper classes laid bare in two masterpieces of satire. 75c

BRIDESHEAD REVISITED
This ferocious commentary on the half-degenerate Oxford College playboy is one of Waugh's most mature and penetrating novels. 75c

VILE BODIES and BLACK MISCHIEF
Two superb short novels: the first, an outrageous look at pre-war London high society; the second, a zany portrayal of colonialism on the run in Africa. 75c

SCOOP and PUT OUT MORE FLAGS
The newspaperbusiness and military life are pungently satirized in these two delightful novels. 75c

MEN AT ARMS and OFFICERS AND GENTLEMEN
Two acid novels about Guy Crouchback, middle-aged bachelor, and his grotesque and disillusioning experiences in the British Army during World War II. 75c

helpful letter about *The Great Gatsby*. It is about the only
criticism that the book has had which has been intelligible,
save a letter from Mrs. Wharton. I shall duly ponder, or
rather I have pondered, what you say about accuracy—
I'm afraid I haven't quite reached the ruthless artistry
which would let me cut out an exquisite bit that had no
place in the context. I can cut out the almost exquisite, the
adequate, even the brilliant—but a true accuracy is, as you
say, still in the offing. Also you are right about Gatsby being blurred and patchy. I never at any one time saw him
clear myself—for he started as one man I knew and then
changed into myself—the amalgam was never complete in
my mind.

Your novel sounds fascinating and I'm crazy to see it. I
am beginning a new novel next month on the Riviera. I
understand that MacLeish is there, among other people (at
Antibes where we are going). Paris has been a mad-house
this spring and, as you can imagine, we were in the thick
of it. I don't know when we're coming back—maybe never.
We'll be here till January (except for a month in Antibes),
and then we go Nice for the spring, with Oxford for next
summer. Love to Margaret and many thanks for the kind
letter.

Scott

[Paris, France]

[Probably September, 1925]

Dear Sir:

The enclosed explains itself. Meanwhile I went to Antibes and liked Archie MacLeish enormously. Also his
poem, though it seems strange to like anything so out-
rageously derivative. *T. S. of P.* was an original in comparison.

I'm crazy to see your novel. I'm starting a new one myself. There was no one at Antibes this summer except me,
Zelda, the Valentinos, the Murphys, Mistinguet, Rex In-
gram, Dos Passos, Alice Terry, the MacLeishes, Charlie
Bracket, Maude Kahn, Esther Murphy, Marguerite Na-

mara, E. Phillips Oppenheim, Mannes the violinist, Floyd
Dell, Max and Crystal Eastman, ex-Premier Orlando,
Etienne de Beaumont—just a real place to rough it, an escape from all the world. But we had a great time. I don't
know when we're coming home—

The Hemingways are coming to dinner so I close with
best wishes.

Scott

c/o Guaranty Trust
[*Paris, France*]

[*Winter, 1929*]

Dear John:

My depression over the badness of the novel[1] as novel
had just about sunk me, when I began the novelette[2]—
John, it's like two different men writing. The novelette is
one of the best war things I've ever read—right up with
the very best of Crane and Bierce—intelligent, beautifully
organized and written—oh, it moved me and delighted
me—the Charles Town country, the night in town, the old
lady—but most of all, in the position I was in at 4 this
afternoon when I was in agony about the novel, the really
fine dramatic handling of the old-lady-and-silver episode
and the butchery scene. The preparation for the latter was
adroit and delicate and just enough.

Now, to be practical—*Scribner's Magazine* will, I'm
sure, publish the novelette, if you wish, and pay you from
$250–$400 therefor. This price is a guess but probably
accurate. I'd be glad to act as your amateur agent in the
case. It is *almost impossible* without a big popular name to
sell a two-part story to any higher-priced magazine than
that, as I know from my experience with "Diamond Big as
Ritz," "Rich Boy," etc. Advise me as to whether I may
go ahead—of course authority confined only to American
serial rights.

---

[1] An unpublished novel by Bishop.
[2] "The Cellar," a short story by Bishop, published in his collection, *Many Thousands Gone.*